A World Passed By

GREAT CITIES IN JEWISH
DIASPORA HISTORY

KAMIONKA STRUMILOWA. SYNAGOGUE MURAL SHOWING VIEW OF JERUSALEM

A World Passed By

BY

MARVIN LOWENTHAL

GREAT CITIES IN JEWISH

DIASPORA HISTORY

Joseph Simon / *Pangloss Press*

A WORLD PASSED BY
Original edition, 1933, Harper & Brothers
Third printing, 1938, Behrman's Jewish Book House
Copyright 1961 by Marvin Lowenthal

This redesigned edition by Joseph Simon, 1990

[*No estate of Marvin Lowenthal could be located, but the genuine claims of any
heirs will be honored if and when they come forward*]

Library of Congress Cataloging-in-Publication Data

Lowenthal, Marvin, 1890–1969.
 A world passed by : great cities in Jewish diaspora history / by Marvin Lowenthal.
  p.   cm.
 Reprint. Originally published: New York : Harper & Brothers, 1933.
 Includes bibliographical references.
 ISBN 0–934710–19–8 : $34.50
 1. Jews—Europe—History.   2. Jews—Europe—Civilization.   3. Europe—
Description and travel—1919–1944.   4. Europe—Ethnic relations.   I. Title.
DS135.E8L68   1990
940'.04924—dc20   90–30824
                                                                  CIP

CONTENTS

	Publisher's Preface to this Edition	vii
	Foreword by Marvin Lowenthal	ix
	Introduction: The Trail of the Wandering Jew	xiii
I.	Ancient Israel in the Louvre	1
II.	Tale-telling Stones from Palestine	22
III.	Paris—"That Great City"	45
IV.	The Newer Paris	58
V.	Crowns and Mantles in Cluny	70
VI.	From Champagne to Brittany	85
VII.	The Southlands of France	101
VIII.	Andalusian Courts and Gates	119
IX.	The Golden Age in Toledo	147
X.	Through Northern Spain and Portugal	163
XI.	Havens in the Low Lands	188
XII.	Survivals in England	210
XIII.	Rome and the Eternal People	230
XIV.	Italy—"Land of the Dew"	244
XV.	A Thousand Years along the Rhine	271
XVI.	The "Gassen" of South Germany	295
XVII.	Prussia and the North	311
XVIII.	Bohemia and its Borders	330
XIX.	Cities of the Danube	346
XX.	The Four Lands of Poland	356
XXI.	The Balkans to the Sea	379
XXII.	Under Islam in Africa	389
	Appendices	434
	Illustrations, between pages	446–447
	Bibliography	447
	Glossary	463
	Index	467

PUBLISHER'S PREFACE TO THIS EDITION

While browsing through an antiquarian bookshop I came upon an out-of-print book by Marvin Lowenthal titled "A World Passed By," published in 1933. I couldn't put it down until I had read it through. It was a panoramic study as well as travelog of the places that were the great Jewish centers of diaspora history in Europe and North Africa. It described cities where Jews comprised large and important segments of the population. The book gave details about all the places where they had lived as honored and respected contributors in the arts, sciences, and government.

In my reading of Lowenthal's book I learned how, in each city and period of time, as acceptance was replaced by repression, Jews were, again and again, expelled or forced to flee. In clear and beautiful description he painted a picture of the tragic changes of fortune that have become Jewish diaspora history over two millenia—never totally destroying the Jewish culture and people, although sometimes reduced to a fragment of past glory.

I strongly felt that such a great work should be brought back into print, as I had done earlier when I discovered a lone tattered copy of a 1907 edition of a twelfth-century Jewish classic, "The Itinerary of Benjamin of Tudela—Travels in the Middle Ages."

Republishing "A World Passed By" represented an additional important contribution since many of the historic buildings, artifacts, and scenes described in this book have been obliterated by the Hitlerian madness. Many priceless Jewish objects were stolen, many melted down, and can never be seen again. Only a soul-wrenching few were preserved by the Nazis as a planned future museum of *A Vanished People*—a ghoulish remembrance of a proud people and their culture. This systematic destruction of a thousand years of Jewish presence in Europe was intended to be *the final solution*.

Therefore, this book represents a remaining remembrance of those events and places. As you did with Benjamin of Tudela, you can now travel through each Jewish place and experience. You may no longer "see" the presence of Jews in "A Thousand Years Along the Rhine;" or "Fame-Crowned" Prague, as the Jews called it; or Jewish life along the Danube, where Jews arrived with the Romans; or in the "Four Lands of Poland"—down from the lower Volga (Khazaria) in the eighth century, and Kiev by the ninth century; and up from Germany in the twelfth and thirteenth centuries—invited in by Polish kings to become the middle class of a Poland with only nobility and rulers on top and a mass of illiterate peasants below.

As Lowenthal describes the Jews of early Cracow: "Red Jews, black Jews, yellow Jews; Jews of every dimension vertical and horizontal; Jews in every and no degree of health and prosperity . . . their character, in the planes and shadows of their faces, in their speaking eyes, in their cunning, sorrow, wisdom, patience, fire, and impenitent despair. . . . Rembrandt would have done better in Cracow than bland Amsterdam."

FOREWORD

This book is meant for both pleasure and use.

As for its use, I planned it to be a comprehensive guide—the first in any language—to old and often little-known seats of Jewish civilization in Europe and North Africa. And I have tried to communicate something of the delight I found in wandering among these neglected scenes which, though they lie on the beaten highways, offer a new world for travellers. I have hoped, as well, to serve lovers and creators of art and architecture who may be in search of Jewish forms and symbols.

However, I soon discovered that in describing the art, monuments, and survivals of the Jew, the men who fashioned them and the legends they evoke, I was retelling Jewish history. So the pleasure of the book, if any, will lie in reading it and watching the epic of Israel unfold itself in the shards and stones left from the drift of forty centuries.

Some explanation may be desired as to my distribution of space. The large number of pages apparently devoted to Paris is an illusion. I have made the oriental collections of the Louvre tell the story of ancient Israel and thus serve as a prelude to the adventures of the mediæval Jew, which embrace most of the book. The Louvre is likewise used to introduce the round of ancient Jewish symbols which reappear throughout the subsequent centuries, and at the same time to furnish an interpretation of similar collections in the British and Berlin Museums.

And I have used the Jewish Room of Cluny, again in Paris, as an occasion to describe, once and for all, in detail, the ritual art which will be met in London, Frankfort, Berlin, Breslau, Prague, Vienna, Warsaw, Odessa, and other cities containing Jewish collections. Americans will find an excellent preparation for this art in a visit to the museum of the Jewish Theological Seminary in New York, or (when opened) the museum of the Hebrew Union College at Cincinnati.

Western Europe has received the major share of attention, thereby meeting the traveller's convenience and the dictates of history; and so far as the latter permits, cities and towns have been ordered with a certain respect for railways. I have tried to keep an eye on Baedeker as well as on the Jews.

The chapters on France, Holland, and England are fairly complete, and Italy hardly less so, since in these lands monuments are comparatively few and visitors many. Spain, though less frequented, is presented at length for the beauty of its remains and for the capital influence of Spain and the Jew upon each other. Much has been left unsaid of Germany where the relics are legion; but the gaps are partly filled in an appendix touching on localities omitted in the text. Poland, though frequented not at all, is treated with enough detail, I hope, to persuade the reader to see for himself its many treasures, easily the most original creations of Jewish art. Here, too, the text is pieced out with an appendix listing over one hundred Polish and Russian towns and villages, the names of which—as an old English antiquarian once complained of Hebrew—"make but indifferent Musick," but lead to a wealth of beauty.

Although the relics of the Holy Land found in European museums have been given their proper emphasis, Palestine itself is omitted for obvious reasons—it alone, to say nothing of Asia, needs a book apart. Moreover, the book has been written time and again.

No one is more sensible than I of the many oversights committed in an attempt to cover nearly thirty lands, six hundred towns, and four thousand years. Some, I confess, are deliberate. I cannot imagine anyone interested in learning that a ring inscribed in Hebrew has been dug up at Deza; that a Jew worked, together with a Fleming and a Spaniard, on the *sillería* of Astorga's cathedral; that Rashi refers to a sculpture of David and Goliath still to be seen (on Goliath-strasse) in Regensburg; that a stray Marano community lingers along in Gex; or that the synagogue of Buchau-am-Federsee possesses, contrary to all usage, a belfry and a bell. After the mediæval tombstones I have lavished on the reader, who will want to know that there are thirteen more of them in Znaim?

Other omissions may be laid to my skepticism. I do not believe that the so-called *Tanzhaus* in Rothenburg was a Jewish marriage-hall. The bishop of Lemberg made, I'll warrant, no untoward advances to Golden Rose. Moreover, every book must come to an end.

Even so, there doubtless remain numerous and important omissions due to nothing less than ignorance.

Ignorance, too, and carelessness must account for many of my errors. But not all of them. I once related to a friend the story told me by the beadle of Worms (see p. 279) regarding the miraculous rescue of the woman who, I claimed, was the mother of Judah the Pious. "Not so," said my friend, "I too was in Worms; and the woman, I might tell you, was the mother of Rashi." "You were listening," I replied, "to another beadle."

Yet enough inexcusably remain. Although I have visited the lands I describe and pored over more documents, local histories, tombstones, and synagogue inscriptions than I care to admit, mistakes are inevitable and we are all apt to listen to the wrong beadle. And since the value of this book depends on the accuracy and choice of detail, I shall welcome every correction of fact and added store of information.

To avoid confusion I might note that Biblical references relate to the translation entitled *The Holy Scriptures* published by the Jewish Publication Society of America; the quotations are likewise taken from this work, except when for literary reasons I have chosen the Authorized Version.

The bibliography is not intended to be complete, but rather to serve the general reader and traveller.

My obligations overwhelm me. First of all, to the many travelling friends and friends of friends who used to troop to my door and ask me what there was to see of Jewish interest in Portugal or Lithuania; then to Elisha K. Friedman who proposed that I relieve myself of these inquiries by writing the present book; to Lillian Laser Strauss, Julius S. Weyl, and Morris K. Wolf of Philadelphia, and Ralph Wolf of New York, without whose substantial encouragement the book would never have been done; to Professor Alexander Marx, librarian of the Jewish Theological Seminary of America, and Dr. Adolph S. Oko, librarian of Hebrew Union College, for the facilities they extended me for illustrative material and research, not to speak of their wise advice; and, finally, to the curators of museums and synagogue beadles, the lovers of the past in France, Germany, and Poland engaged in the discovery and preservation of Jewish antiquities, and the Jewish artists still devoted to recreating the old traditions—all too numerous to mention—who have helped me on every side.

MARVIN LOWENTHAL

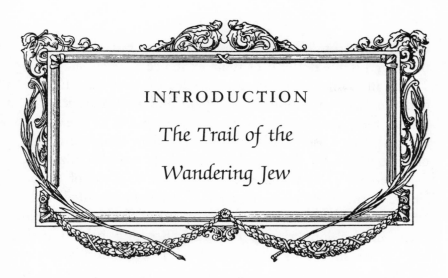

INTRODUCTION

The Trail of the

Wandering Jew

IN EVERY corner of Europe and North Africa the wandering Jew has left the blazings of his trail.

His camping sites, usually called ghettos, where he has
halted generations on end, still keep his memories and something of his fugitive possessions: time-worn synagogues
steeped in legend and rich with beauty; broken walls and
gates guarding perhaps a vestige of traditional life against
the siege of modernity; moss-bound cemeteries where sleep
the dead of ten centuries—unchronicled humanity as well as
heroes, martyrs, philosophers, and saints; catacombs in the
South and graveyards in the East carrying a burden of strange
symbolism and art; subterranean baths the work of bold and
skillful engineers; old romantic houses with secret doors and
storied cellars; street-corner inscriptions signalling to the
passerby a forgotten tragedy; and museum collections of
abandoned treasures, the heirlooms of the race.

The synagogues, as in Segovia, Cordova, or Lemberg, often
stand within a stone's throw (and many were the stones
thrown) of a famed cathedral. The cemeteries, as in Pisa,
often lie literally and figuratively in the shadow of a renowned historic pile. The ghettos, as in Avignon, wait around

the corner from a tourist postcard shop. But the average traveller knows nothing of their existence.

Yet, like the cathedrals and castles of Christian Europe and the Moslem antiquities of Spain and North Africa, the Jewish monuments embody and perpetuate one of the oldest cultural forces of the Western World. They, too, are a part of Europe's past and the heritage of our common civilization.

Moreover, every stone, every beam, every morsel of tooled silver, hammered brass, figured embroidery, painted wall, fretted stucco, and illumined parchment evokes its own moment in the long drama of Israel. Looking behind each morsel, we shall find a man; and with little effort we may see the drama re-enacted. Our ears properly attuned, we shall hear history repeating itself.

The first two thousand years are told—or seen—in the collections of the Louvre and the British Museums. We follow, in seals and stones, the trail of Abraham from Ur into Canaan. We share the gusto—and even behold the swords—of centuries of conquest, and the piteousness and glory of centuries of defeat. We watch, through these trials, the soul of the Jew take temper and form. Then, with the decline and fall of the Jewish state, we see the trail multiply and Israel adrift on the roads of the world.

The earliest dispersions were in the East—Babylonia and Persia; in Egypt—Elephantine far up the Nile and Leontopolis and Alexandria down the delta; on the shores and isles of Greece—Priene, Miletus, Delos, Athens, and Byzantium; and, finally, in Rome, in her midland empire along the Rhône, Rhine, and Danube, and in her Mediterranean provinces of Gaul, Spain, Mauretania, Carthage, and Libya.

The last records of the classic age and the first of the mediæval dawn show the Jew possessed of his own quarters in every important town. *Vici Judaeorum*—Jewries—they were

called in dying Latin, and the name was repeated and man-
gled in the first stammerings of modern tongues.

So, despite the lack of Baedeker maps bearing the legend,
"Here is the site of the former Jewry," the traveller will have
little trouble in identifying its remains. Towns in England
still preserve a *Jewry Street* or *Jewry Lane*, even as London
has its *Old Jewry*, which, we will soon discover why, adjoined the great market of the Cheape, or Cheapside. In
France hardly a city or town lacks a street named—we shall
not say in loving memory, but at least named—for its Jews;
there is nearly always a *Rue des Juifs, Rue aux Juifs,* or *Rue
de la Juiverie* designating the former ghetto. Even the villages of Germany boast, if that is the word, their *Judengasse,
Judenstrasse, Judenhof,* or similar tag. In Belgium it reads
Jodenstraat and in Italy *Via dei Giudei* or *Giudecca*, but the
meaning is the same.

This easy method of identification breaks down in Spain.
But, fortunately for the traveller, as fast as the Spaniards of
the fifteenth century expelled the inhabitants of a Jewry, they
renamed it *Barrionuevo* or New Quarter. And today we have
only to seek a street or square of this name to discover in it
the old quarter of the Jews.

The location of these ghettos tells us, more than any records, of the character and role of the Jew in early mediæval
society. The Jewries are generally to be found along the walls
and near one of the main gates of the city (or the boulevard
and square that now mark the wall and gate)—that is to
say, in the spot where the Jews as the chief importing and
exporting merchants of the town would naturally settle for
sound business reasons.

When the Jewry lies elsewhere, it is safe to look for it
adjacent to the local cathedral, town hall, or castle, and therefore near one of the central markets. So we find it in Segovia,
Cologne, and Chambéry. And, in such cases, we are reminded

of how often the mediæval Jew was owned by the church and civil authorities, who kept him close at hand for ready protection—and extortion.

The occupation of the Jew with goods and money, particularly as a dealer in exports and imports, came largely from the character of his dispersion. Nothing resembling the latter exists today, and it was unique in the Middle Ages.

World Jewry, like Islam, was what Christendom meant to be but failed—a community bound together by custom and faith rather than by politics and power. Like Islam, too, Jewry spoke a common language, read a common literature, and escaped the Christian error of compelling unity through a centralized hierarchy. But there the likeness ends. Jewry was alone in its flexible government—in which exilarchs in Babylonia, tribal sheiks in Yemen and North Africa, synods along the Rhine and chief justices in Spain could reign side by side, or melt and pass without destroying the discipline of communal life. It was alone in its absolute divorce from military ambition, its comparative unity of blood, and the range of its dispersal. Christians and Moslems spread in separate worlds, and the Jews spread in both.

The need of discipline for the maintenance of the faith, for the free play of Judaism as a social cult, and for mutual aid against a hostile world made the ghetto inevitable even before it was compulsory. And segregation was rendered natural by the general mediæval custom of consigning a city quarter to each craft and trade.

Then in an age when foreign commerce was difficult, when warfare rent counties and cities, when Normandy was more remote from Provence in speech, ways, and politics than France from Malabar today, the pacific body of Jewries, one in blood, tongue, and faith, even if separated by mountains and seas, became the obvious channels of intercourse. And as economic need (and taxes) drove the Jewries in ever wider search of markets and wares, the dispersion grew link by link until, knitting together the myriad states of Europe and the larger worlds of Christendom and Islam, it caught in its net the very ports of Malabar.

Rabbis and scholars as well as traders—often all three were one—passed freely from one Jewry lane to another. They none too frequently died in the land where they were born. But they seldom felt themselves as alien. When Asher ben Yehiel took his Talmudic baggage from Worms to Toledo, or Rabbi Hushiel found himself and his store of Mishna transported from Bari to Kairuwan, we are too apt to think of the uprooting odyssey of a modern Russian Jew from Minsk to Minneapolis. Whereas Asher or Hushiel was no more put out by his new surroundings than a Russian Jew who moves from Minsk to Pinsk.

In addition to commerce, the ghettos resounded with the bustle of every permissible craft and trade.[1] Medicine, science, and philosophy were cultivated. Law-learning and theology, Jewish fashion, were not only a calling but a sport. The news of far places, brought by merchants and students, echoed in the synagogue and market. A palace revolution in Byzantium, the price of pearls in Danzig, and a Talmudic sally in Regensburg were the talk of Cordova. *Was diese kleine Gasse doch für ein Reich an sich war*, said an old inhabitant of a typical ghetto—"Our little lane, what a kingdom it was!"

The heroes of this kingdom, as we cross their tracks in a dozen lands, bear neither sword nor sceptre. They do not clank. Jewry, it is true, knew something of statesmen and financiers. But the men whom the ghetto praised and cherished were rabbis, martyrs, scholars, and poets. The complaint is often made that mediæval Jewish history is hardly

[1] See p. 331.

more than literary criticism spiced with massacre. Yet little else can be expected from the chronicles of a civilized society.

Something, however, was done besides writing books. There are the monuments and relics of a dozen arts.

Foremost are the synagogues. Like all architecture, they gave form to the institution they served. And so far as the institution was peculiar to Jewry and expressive of its needs, the stones and their form were original.

Even in its beginnings, the synagogue was not the shrine or dwelling of a deity, nor was it a theatre of sacred rites. It arose while the Temple in Jerusalem was still the house of God, the sacred edifice, and the scene of sacrifice for the nation.

Instead, the synagogue was a place of prayer—to a deity in no way symbolized or held to be present in that place more than another. Next, it was a place of teaching. And, finally, it was a seat of local government.

Its early names in Hebrew meant House of Prayer, House of the People, and House of Assembly—the latter was translated as *synagogue* in Greek, and recalls the *Meeting House* familiar to New Englanders and Quakers, who were nourished on the Jewish tradition. As a place for teaching the Law of Moses, it early received the name, in Latin, of school; it is still called *scuola* among Italian Jews, *Sjoel* among the Dutch, and *Schul* among German and East European Jews.

And as a place of government, it was at once the court house, social centre, and legislative hall of the community.

When we come to look, then, at the oldest European synagogue, or rather its ruins, on the island of Delos,[1] it will not be surprising to find it in appearance a secular edifice. Like the earliest synagogues surviving in Palestine and dating

[1] See p. 387.

from the second or third century B.C., it is a basilica—the favourite form of public building in antiquity.

The earliest Christian churches were likewise basilicas, as they would be, for most of the first Christians were Jews. Indeed, it is sometimes hard to distinguish an antique synagogue from a primitive church. But the difference becomes striking when we turn to another early ruin: the synagogue of Naro[1] near Carthage, dating from about the fourth century C.E. Churches by then had definitely taken the form of a shrine and a theatre of mystic rites. The synagogue of Naro, however, resembles in plan nothing so much as a modern social centre, with rooms for schools, assemblies, and, for all we can tell, gymnastics.

In mediæval Spain the secular form survives in Cordova[2] and in Samuel Halevi's state synagogue of Toledo.[3] Beginning with the two-aisled structure in Worms[4] (built in 1034) the form persisted in Central Europe—as we may see in Prague and Cracow—until the Renaissance. And the wooden synagogues of Poland, derived from the plan of a manor house, carried on the tradition, in Eastern Europe, to the nineteenth century.

By and large, only the synagogues built under the influence of the Renaissance and, more particularly, the Counter Reformation (Italy, Holland, France, and the stone structures of Poland) abandon the tradition.

Even these synagogues, as do all until modern times, reveal in their interior arrangement the emphasis on teaching and prayer. Once inside an old synagogue—past the days of antiquity—one cannot mistake it for a church, as one might easily mistake a modern temple. Every device is used to render prominent the platform (*bima*) from which the

[1] See p. 409.
[2] See p. 128.
[3] See p. 154.
[4] See p. 277.

prayers are chanted and the Law is taught. It is mounted either in the centre of the hall or, as in Italy, given equal rank with the ark which contains the scrolls of the Law. And in Poland, this central platform, rising in stone from floor to ceiling, has given birth to one of the few inventions of the Jew in architecture.[1]

The decoration of the synagogue, as of the church, changed according to the tides of fashion and varied from land to land: arabesque stuccos in Spain, stained glass in Cologne, murals and painted ceilings in Germany and Poland, gildings and marble inlays in Italy, and everywhere carved wood and stone. The most original touches will be found in the wrought-iron grills and wood-carvings for the ark and *bima* in Poland, the "music" panels of Posen, and the murals in the wooden synagogues of Eastern Europe and South Germany.

The purely Jewish element of this decoration lies in its symbols, which are repeated not only in the embellishment of architecture, but in textiles, potteries, metals, manuscripts, and in the shape and adornment of ritual objects (see chap. V.).

The spirit as well as the experience of the race are given form in the pine-cone and palm representing the tree of life; the citron, willow, pomegranate, vine, grape-cluster, and ram's horn, treasured from the ancient life on the soil of Palestine and from its rural festivals; the lion of Judah and the crests of the other eleven tribes, reminiscent of a vanished polity remembered again in the three crowns of the kingdom, priesthood, and law; the two trees for the written and oral law, the mountain for their source on Sinai, and the fence around the mountain for the protective barrier of the Talmud; the zodiacal signs with their hint of the Babylonian science and worship of the stars; the seven-branched candle-

[1] See p. 366.

stick (menorah), the two columns of Jachin and Boaz, the
urn, altar, shew-bread table, and other vestiges of the glories
of the Temple; the magic six-pointed star (shield of David),
the funerary infolding ribbon and rising lily, the peacock for
immortality, the dove for the human soul, the fish for the
resurrection of the dead, signs picked up from obscure sources
and carried down the ages; the four creatures—lion, leopard,
stag, and eagle—taken from the Talmud to typify devotion
to the will of God; and the sacrificial goat, Israel's mate to
the Christian lamb. The arts in which these symbols are
woven become, like all art, an epitome of history.

The use of animal and sometimes human forms in the
murals of a synagogue, the carvings of a tombstone, and the
embroideries and metal-work of ritual art may surprise the
reader who believes that the Jews remained uncompromis-
ingly true to the letter of the Second Commandment. But the
injunction against making "a likeness of anything" that is in
heaven, earth, or sea, received diverse interpretation.

Some rabbinical authorities permitted sculpture in relief
but not in the round. Profiat Duran, a fourteenth-century
liberal, held that "looking on beautiful shapes and pleasing
sculpture and pictures" in a synagogue "enlarges the heart,
enlivens it, and increases the power of the mind." Rabbi
Ephraim of Regensburg, an eminent authority of the twelfth
century, saw nothing objectionable in the birds and fish
woven in a pulpit cloth, for "pictures of these creatures, no
matter how realistically done, are not worshipped by the
Gentiles."

On the other hand, Rabbi Eliachim of twelfth-century
Cologne ordered the removal of a stained glass window in the
local synagogue, because it dared to portray the likeness of
serpents and lions. And the great Rabbi Meir of Rothenburg,
the pride of Worms, forbade the use of birds and beasts in the
illumination of a prayer book.

In the ebb and flow of opinion, human figures were painted on the walls of Polish synagogues and then erased. Adam and Eve were hammered in their nudity on metal platters for the synagogue service and then blunted almost beyond recognition. Entire Biblical scenes were graven on the tombs of Ouderkerk, and only a furtive manikin and human hand smuggled on the slabs of Frankfort. And the pictures in a prayer book of Worms itself are counted among the masterpieces of Jewish illumination.

Not all of the original offices of the diaspora synagogue were of necessity sheltered beneath the same roof. Many Jewries gave themselves the luxury of a town hall, in which the communal affairs were administered. The most famous survivor is to be found in Prague.[1] Old schools and study halls still abound, although it is worth remarking that the college (*yeshibah*), which, in general, corresponds to the Moslem medersa, never glowed like the latter with stucco and alabaster *pilpul*. Perhaps the masters feared the distraction of their pupils; perhaps, to paraphrase the *Sayings of the Fathers*, they believed that the pupil who "breaks off his study and says, 'How fine is that curlicue, how fine is that carving,' him the Scripture regards as if he had forfeited his life."

Nothing authentic remains of another frequent dependency of a well-equipped ghetto—the wedding hall, or *Tanzhaus* as it was called in Germany and *Lazina* in the south of France. Except, if you will, a bit of iron grill-work in Worms.

But the womenfolk have left an architectural imprint in other ways. The mediæval synagogue, and perhaps the ancient, was adjoined by a women's annex. Many examples survive—the most pretentious again in Worms—but, on the whole, they were modest structures. Galleries for the women,

[1] See p. 341.

built into the synagogue proper, may have existed in antiquity; their first European appearance, apart from mediæval Spain, dates from the Renaissance. Far more impressive, at least along the Rhine, are the ritual baths—great Romanesque and Gothic halls, circular in shape, and sunk in the earth to the depth of three to five stories.[1] Fortunately, there was no need for sunlight, as the baths were used, in accordance with the Law, only after nightfall.

The cemeteries speak not only of the dead. Their Hebrew title, "House of Life," contains more truth than euphemism. As long as their stones keep head above ground, they house a living history. "And when they shall pass through the land and any seeth a man's bones, then shall he set up a sign by it . . ." (Ez. 39:15). The Jews have passed through many lands since Ezekiel's day, and by their signs—since become a common Hebrew word for tombstone—they are known.

The burial place, even in the patriarchal age, was, for one thing, the sign of permanent settlement. It was a pledge that if the wanderer depart, he would return. Abraham was a "stranger and sojourner" until he bought the cave of Machpelah.

Against all hazard and cost, the Jews have clung to their graveyards. If the visible stones are older than their Christian fellows, and in any given locality they usually are, it is largely due to the tenacity of the race in remembering the dead and to a horror of neglecting their signs. There is, however, another reason for the great age of the Jewish cemeteries—some of which, along the Rhine, date back a thousand years. Christians, as a rule, buried only the nobodies in the churchyard. The somebodies, local nobility and gentry, were given shelter and honour in the church itself. As a consequence, the nobodies, left to themselves, were forgotten from one

[1] See p. 281.

century to another. But since Jewish law forbids interment
in a synagogue, the somebodies of Jewry, men of wealth,
learning and sanctity, had to run the chance of common
burial under the open sky. Even a choice of plot was denied
them. Each man, ghetto clown or prince, was laid in the
ranks as it came his turn to die. Occasionally, it is true, a
disciple won the right to sleep by his master. Children were
often placed in a section by themselves—and, in Morocco,
prostitutes. Still, the general democracy of a Jewish graveyard
afforded an additional claim for cherishing it; the plain man
reaped the remembrance and reward of the saint.

Even when the Jewish cemeteries of mediæval Europe no
longer survive, their absence is eloquent of history. As we
shall too often discover, the wrath of Edom fell not only on
the living; but the sack and slaughter of a ghetto was followed by the destruction of the memorials of the dead.[1] The
mediæval Christian did not spend, no more than does the
modern Hitlerite, valuable time over Ezekiel—"they shall set
up a sign . . . that the land be clean."

Perhaps he was a Bible purist and wished to re-establish
the original tradition, among Israel, of an unmarked grave.
Inscriptions are unknown in Palestine until within a century
or so of the Christian era. The sign mentioned by Ezekiel and
the "pillar of Rachel's grave" were meant not as a memorial,
but to mark the bones of the dead against possible contamination of the living. The rock-hewn tombs of Talmudic times
were marked for this purpose with chalk, and the chalking
was renewed at proper intervals. "Funerary inscriptions," says
the Talmud, "are not used for the righteous." Hence a mention of the dead on their tombs would have been a left-hand
compliment. This is possibly the reason for uninscribed tombs
prevalent in many Sephardic communities, particularly in
Morocco.

[1] See p. 297.

The later ossuaries of Palestine and the Jewish catacombs of antiquity—ranging from Palmyra to Rome and Carthage —were decorated with numerous carved and painted symbols.[1] The tradition was renewed in the Renaissance, and the cemeteries of Central and Eastern Europe are filled with the fantasies of the sculptor, who played in rebuses and symbols on the name, memory, and profession of the dead. As art, these fantasies reached their height in the carved and painted slabs of Poland.[2]

How many of these artists, architects, and craftsmen were Jews? The answer is neither simple nor sure.

Masons and builders were small and closed corporations in the Middle Ages, and it is not conceivable that many Jews designed or built the synagogues they paid for. In Poland of the Renaissance and eighteenth century, however, Jews plied most of the arts and crafts, and the names of a few builders have survived: Simcha ben Solomon Weiss, who built the seventeenth-century wooden synagogue of Nasielsk, an admitted masterwork dismantled in the last century; his father, Solomon Weiss of Luck; Judah Leb, who built the synagogues of Przedborz and Pinczow; Hillel Benjamin of Lask, whose work may be seen in Kurnik and Lutomiersk. And Judah de Herz, we know, restored the Pincas and Meisel synagogues of Prague in the seventeenth century.

We may be surer of our Jewish workmen when it came to the embellishment of the synagogue. Solomon Ibn Verga, writing in the early sixteenth century, speaks of Jews "in Persia and Media who can work the windows of the king so finely in wood and stone, it is as though they were made of gold and silver." Of such workers in wood, we have a record again in Poland: Ber ben Israel in Jewart and Uzlany, Samuel Goldbaum in Kempen, and Samuel Goldmanaz in Zabludow.

[1] See p. 234.
[2] See p. 375.

Among the mural painters we know of Eliezer Sussman, who worked in South Germany; Hayim ben Isaac of Sluck, in Mohilev; Mordecai Lisnitzki, in Chodorow and Gwozdziec (seventeenth century); Moses ben Jair of Rottsweiler, in Chodorow (eighteenth century); and Isaac ben Judah Leb, in Gwozdziec (eighteenth century).

Jews have been metal workers since the days of Bezalel—or Tubal Cain. We can follow their craft from a bronze platter of antiquity, in the Louvre, through elaborate wrought-iron grills and hammered copper plaques of the seventeenth and eighteenth centuries, in Poland, to the figured brasses of North Africa and the Orient today. Goldsmithing prevailed among Jews in all times and places. The filigree of Granada was a Jewish product. The Renaissance wedding rings now gathered in the Jewish collections of Europe were largely made in Venice, and presumably by Jewish hands. Chaucer, in describing a coat of mail (*Sir Thopas*, 2053-54), praises it as

"a fyn hauberk
. . . al y-wroght of Jewes werk."

Weaving, dyeing, embroidering, and engraving in metal and stone have likewise been cultivated by the Jews throughout the centuries. Still, it may be difficult, when faced with any one object of ritual art worked in these crafts, to say that the artisan was a Jew. In many cases we know from the marks of the silversmith and engraver that he was not.

Glass-making and the kindred art of mosaics, as it was understood in antiquity, were Jewish specialties in both Egypt and Asia Minor. The story has come down to us of a Jewish glass-maker in Byzance who every time he blew a bottle found, to his dismay, a cross blown in its base. He naturally smashed the bottles as fast as he blew them; but as breaking bottles was expensive, he was finally driven to saving his material and his sensibilities by becoming a Christian.

Jewish illuminators have occasionally left us their names. But in the case of an unsigned Hebrew manuscript, even if invariably written by a Jew, it is hard to judge whether the miniatures and marginal decoration came from a Jewish brush. Among the known limners are Joseph bar Ephraim who "copied" the Haggadah (Cod. Hebr. 200) of the Munich Staatsbibliotek; Solomon Halevi bar Buya, responsible for the miniatures of a Pentateuch (MS. II, 17) of the Leningrad Public Library; Joseph Ibn Hayyim of Corunna, who illumined a Bible now in the Bodleian Library (Cod. 2.322, Kennicott No. 1); Joshua ben Abraham Ibn Gaon of Soria (Bodleian, Cod. 2.323, Kenn. No. 2); Shemtob ben Abraham Ibn Gaon likewise of Soria, who painted a Bible now in the Sassoon collection (London); Elisha Cresques who worked on the Farchi Bible (also in the Sassoon collection); Jaffuda Cresques, who may have painted the figures on his *Atlas catalan* (Bibliothèque Nationale, Paris, Spanish MS. No. 30); Abraham Vidal, remembered for his *Privileges of Majorca* (Palma, archives of town hall); and Abraham ben Judah Ibn Hayyim of Loulé, Portugal, who presumably practiced the art of illumination, for he wrote a work on it (in Portuguese with Hebrew characters) in 1262.

Altogether, five hundred or more architects, artists, and craftsmen are known by name.[1] But, like all statistics, this may mean what you please. It is enough to know that Jewish art, whatever it lacks, did not lack for men.

The history of the Jew is a Gulf Stream through Europe, wet and salt like the surrounding waters, taking hues from the same sun, ruffled by the same storms, inhabited by the

[1] For the list, see *Mitteilungen zur jüdischen Volkskunde* (Hamburg), III Jahr. I Heft, pp. 113-117.

same creatures, but always with a different temperature and an individual direction. From his first appearance in Palestine, the Jew has absorbed the culture of his neighbour and yet maintained his own. And not content with being an ancestor, he has persisted as a contemporary. He has everywhere been a native—with a foreign past and the chance of a foreign future.

This experience, renewed in each generation, has given the Jew a perspective. He has become the natural, if unofficial and often unwelcome, critic of the Western World. In the Joban sense he is the Adversary of the nations. And his history can be used as the touchstone or coördinates of civilization.

Seen through his eyes—or through his monuments—the past takes unwonted shape. Customary history is turned inside out.

Crusaders, we discover, were cut-throats. The Church was a perplexed conqueror, contemptuous and fearful of her victims. Saints wore halos of blood. Easter was a season of the year when a man walked in terror of his life. Christian art was Jewish shame. Godfrey of Bouillon, Richard of the Lion Heart, St. Louis of France, Ferdinand and Isabella are hissed, and Pedro the Cruel and the heretical Emperor Frederick are applauded. Renascence took place in the Dark Ages and the darkest age began with the Renaissance. The Moor at the gate brings glad tidings, and the march of Christian soldiers is the signal for despair. Not princes and warriors change the face of the world, but grubby translators, ink-stained astronomers, and calculating merchants. Patriotism is an appeal to slaughter. The secret of survival lies not in the sword or purse, but in the school. Cities proud of their past are damned as "cities of blood," and others, unaware of their virtue, are hailed as "righteous places." The victories of civilization are not recorded on battle monuments, but in a few casual words of English, French, or German, cut on an alien's tomb.

The statues of the Church Triumphant and the Synagogue Defeated which greet us at cathedral doors, the patient explanation of the New Faith and the Old repeated on the stained glass within, are mere signs and tags of the long-drawn struggle between Rome and Jerusalem. The battle resounded at every ghetto gate, it raised its smoke at every Inquisitional pyre, the cry of it rang through a thousand laws. When the Jew, every morning for centuries on end, drew on his cloak with the little "Badge of Shame" stitched to its sleeve, he donned it as a uniform in the army of his God. When the Christian, obsessed by the mystery of the Passion, time and again accused the Jew of stabbing a Host or killing a child, he too was fighting for the honour of his Lord.

Looking back, today, on the energy spent on the one side in fire, bloodshed, and engines of physical and moral torture, and on the other in resistance, courage, and ruse, and on both sides in hate, we feel the tragedy of it all. But worse than tragedy, it was waste—the waste of precious human effort in the defence of fiction. That a battle should wage for two thousand years over an Only-begotten Son and a Chosen People, shadows and legends, is beyond scorn or lament. One can only hope that there are no gods to mock at men.

"Thou tellest my wanderings . . . are they not in thy book?"—we have set as the sign of our tale. But a phrase, you will note, has been dropped from the verse. If you turn to the source, you will find the omitted words. "Put my tears," they read, "in thy bottle."

It is well said. We have bottled up the ever-welling tears, and we have chosen to laugh in order not to weep.

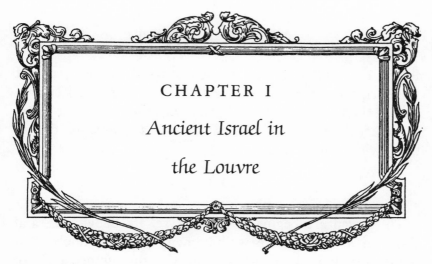

CHAPTER I

Ancient Israel in

the Louvre

ALTHOUGH Jews have lived in Paris after their fashion, that is, off and on following the winds of tolerance, since Roman times, the city has never become famous in Jewish annals or legends. No light of glory has descended on it as upon Cordova or Toledo, and no halo of martyrdom as upon Worms or Troyes. Great men in Israel were not born there, great books were not written there, and spirited deeds usually managed to happen elsewhere.

Yet the unsuspecting traveller will be happily mistaken if he imagines that, having heard little of Paris in Jewish history, he will find little there to recall its long adventurous course.

Probably no city is richer in Jewish relics, except for architectural monuments, and certainly no city possesses memorials evoking a longer span of this singular history. Benjamin of Tudela, who had travelled far and seen much, spoke wiser than he knew when he called Paris, as that older traveller Jonah once called Nineveh, *ha-ir hagedolah*—Paris "that great city"!

The present traveller, if possessed with a little patience and curiosity, may relive the Jewish experience from the beginning to the day before yesterday; from its legendary sources in Ur of the Chaldees, through the rise and fall of the kingdoms of

Israel and Judah, the subsequent two thousand years of wandering in exile, the reëntry of the Jew to normal citizenship in the French Revolution, and with the rustling of leaves in the gardens of the Tuileries, to dreams of a restoration of the Jewish homeland.

꒰ᐢᐢ꒱

The adventure begins at the Louvre. Its Babylonian and Assyrian antiquities are well known; yet it is doubtful if many curious souls who have gaped at the winged bulls of Khorsabad or glanced at the delicate art of the Babylonian seals have realized that all about them the stones are retelling the ancient history of Israel. Not the history alone, but the manners, rites, laws, myths, cult, clothing, and kitchenware of the old Hebrews, graven in enduring rock by their contemporaries, await our prying, imaginative eye. Like the trophy Joshua set up by the ford of Jordan, "these stones shall be for a memorial unto the children of Israel for ever."

The Jews themselves have left hints and tokens of their ancient life in the pottery, sculpture, inscriptions, tombs, and jewellery gathered in the Jewish Room,[1] where an eccentric visitor occasionally strays, but immediately loses himself for lack of catalogue, labels, or knowing guide. Yet a little friendly information, and ever the prying, patient eye, will bring him closer there to old Judea than the usual Palestinian tour.

We enter the Asiatic Department (Musée des Antiquités Asiatiques) under the great colonnade at the rear of the Louvre. The collection is distributed among two rooms on the ground floor, the stairway behind them, and three rooms on the first floor. Since neither chronological order, nor classification by subject matter, is observed, nor the history of Jewish culture dreamed of in its arrangement, we must disregard the

[1] See Chap. II.

visitor's comfort in grouping together the principal strands in Israel's story.[1]

We pass directly through the main gallery. According to the sign on the wall, we are now in Salle de Susiane II; but judging from our surroundings we are in the sacred East four to five thousand years ago.

A polished black column dominates the centre of the room. Its peculiar shape, a rude cone, recalls the "abominable" device which the misguided Israelites "built on every high hill" (I Kings 14:23) and which the English Bible translates as an innocent "pillar." It is obviously a sacred object. Its lengthy inscription, however, suggests that it is not a *mazzebah* or "pillar," but a "stone of testimony" such as Joshua set up under the great oak of Shechem, such as, he said, "has heard all the words of the Lord, and shall therefore be a witness against ye, lest ye deny your God" (Josh. 24:26-27). Above the inscription we see, in fact, the carved figure of a deity resplendent on his throne. His shoulders send forth beams of light. The confused mass above his head lours like a thundercloud. Before him stands a reverent mortal fearfully receiving "all the words" of the flame- and storm-clad god. The scene is terribly familiar, and we are tempted to identify it with the magic name of Sinai.

But this is centuries before Sinai; this is Hammurabi, king of Babylon (c.2100 B.C.) receiving his famous Code of Laws at the hands of the sun-god, Shamash. Yet the resemblances are not altogether deceitful. Many of the laws of Hammurabi's code, which are set forth in the main body of the inscription, find an echo in the Torah of Israel. The statutes dealing with circumstances common to life in Babylon and Canaan, provisions touching on agriculture and the relations between man and wife, master and slave, sometimes betray a similar-

[1] See p. 414 for a summary of the chief objects of Jewish interest, classified room by room.

ity of language that makes it hard to doubt that the lightnings of Sinai are not reflecting the sun-rays of Shamash. For the rest, the broad resemblance of tone and intent is generally credited to a common origin in the legal traditions of the Semitic peoples.

A debate over precedence is fruitless. Whether not only Moses but the later legislators of Leviticus and Deuteronomy repeat, if they do not copy, something of the spirit of their remote Babylonian predecessor, in no way modifies the fate of the two codes. The tablets of the Law have become a corner-stone of our civilization; at the least they have been written on the blackboard of our Sunday-schools and ofttimes on the hearthstone of our homes, while the stele of Hammurabi ends its days as a museum piece.

A humbler reminiscence of Moses will be found in the rear of the Mastaba Room (Nouvelle Salle de Susiane, south wing of the Louvre). A fragment of a stone monument stands in the bay of the second window to the left. The lower band of sculpture on the fragment represents marching soldiers. At their head, a king is distinguished by his beard, and by an inscription projecting from the end of his nose. This is Sargon the Great, king of Akkad and Sumer "and the four quarters of the world" towards 3000 B.C. At least fifteen centuries before Moses, Sargon tells us (in a tablet now in the British Museum)[1] that he too was born in secret, placed by his mother in an ark of bullrushes daubed with pitch, set adrift on the river, and drawn from the water by "Akki the irrigator." So legend, like legislation, repeats itself.

Michelangelo has accustomed us to the puzzling image of Moses as a venerable figure with two horns sprouting from his brow. A meagre knowledge of Hebrew enables one to trace these strange, and apparently misplaced, growths to their literary source ("When Moses came down from the

[1] See p. 426.

mount, the skin of his face sent forth horns." Exod. 34:29), which leaves, however, their presence still unexplained. To our confusion, the Western World has associated horns with frivolous fauns and certain less frivolous creatures of Christian mythology. And popular wit has added unhappy domestic complications. Yet a casual glance at Chaldean art will resolve the dilemma of the horns. As attributes of majesty and strength, they adorn the heads of cherubim (Grande Gallerie, Nos. 12 and 13), angels (Nos. 1 and 2), and gods (Room VI, third case to left, No. 145). The two-horned Moses and the two-horned Alexander doubtless owe their common peculiarity to this Babylonian convention. The cornuted husband alone remains a mystery.

Moses is not the only ancient Hebrew whose fate is associated with Hammurabi. According to the usual interpretation of the fourteenth chapter of Genesis, Hammurabi appears there under the name of "Amraphel, king of Shinar," who with three other monarchs suffered a rear guard attack at the hands of the patriarch, Abraham.

We know little enough about Abraham, whether he be a tribe, a myth, or a man; we know, however, just a little more about his times and his background. The records of his "age," recovered from the sand-hills of Mesopotamia, are among the treasures of the collection.

In the first room on the second floor (Salle de Suse VI), at the first window to the right, stands a case filled with clay tablets. They are covered with fine wedge writing. Temple inventories and commercial book-keeping from the dynasty of Ur of the Chaldees! Since they date many centuries (2700 B.C.) before Abraham left his homeland, we may be fairly certain that Jewish history, so far as it begins with the great patriarch, dawns in no savage desert, but in the heart of a highly organized culture. A people who keep books (as well as herds and flocks) may be credited with many other trappings of civilization, including an original conception of God.[1]

The chief deity of Ur, whose temple lists are before us, was the moon-god Sin. In case 2, Room VIII (Petite Salle de Suse VIII), a little farther along the same floor, lies a seal cylinder representing a sacrifice to this god. He is readily identified by the crescent moon above his head. We see a man, hardly to be distinguished from Abraham's father, Terah, accompanied by his wife, approach the god with his offering, while behind them a servant prepares the sacrificial feast. The whole scene, familiar enough to Abraham if not to us, breathes a quiet dignity. Back again in Room VI, in the second detached case to the left, a magnificent seal depicts Dunghi, king of Ur (2700 B.C.) bringing an offering to the same deity.

The god Sin bears other curious relations to Abraham. Eupolemos, a Jewish writer of the second century C.E., designates the birthplace of Abraham as Kamariné, which is derived from "Kamar," the Arabic word for moon. The name of Abraham's wife, Sarah, means "princess," the common title of Ningal, the moon-goddess. His brother's wife bore the name of Milcah, or "queen," another title bestowed on that goddess. His nephew was called Laban, or "moon." The name Abraham itself can well mean "the father who has risen." The number of Abraham's "trained men," 318, strangely corresponds with the number of days the satellite is visible during the year. And finally, Abraham's second home, Harran, was likewise a center of moon-worship, where traces of the cult, in the form of Sabaism, survived until the Middle Ages. These coincidences go far towards confirming the Biblical association of Abraham with Ur and Harran, and the religious character of the wanderings of his family. Any further conclusion that the God of the Hebrews derived from the lunar deity of the Babylonians is, of course, gratuitous.

[1] See p. 226 (British Museum).

⌒ᴧᴧᶺᵔᓇ

Obeying the divine call, Abraham left his country, his kindred, and his father's house, and with his departure the saga
of Israel begins. His son, Isaac, and his grandson, Jacob, take
up the burden of his wanderings in search of the land of
promise—a quest pursued, even when blindly, by their children to this day. The migrations of the patriarchs were, it
will be remembered, directed at critical moments by consul-
tations with their divine guide. Such colloquies were not
strange to Abraham's world, and we need not feel astonished
that the Biblical narrative betrays no surprise at their fre-
quency or intimacy. Numerous seal cylinders (Rooms VI and
VII, detached cases) depict interviews of this nature. Men and
gods, in those days, conversed freely.

On such occasions the deity, as might be expected, is sometimes seated on a throne. The "Throne of God" has indeed
entered so profoundly into our religious imagery that we accept the Babylonian convention without question. But what of
that related image, God's footstool? Repeatedly the Psalmist
sings, "Let us worship at His footstool." Our conception of
this article of divine furniture, borrowed from the picture of
a Western monarch seated on a throne, his feet propped by a
stool, is quite mistaken. Look once more (Room VI, second
case to the left and Room VII, first case to the right) at the
seals depicting these "holy conversations." The footstool usually appears when the god is represented standing erect. One
foot is slightly raised and poised upon the stool; the long garment of the deity is drawn back and upward so we may more
readily see the foot-rest. "The earth is my footstool," proclaims
Jehovah through the mouth of Isaiah (Is. 66:1); and we may
be persuaded that in the mind of the prophet, Jehovah is seen
not seated, but standing in the skies—His garment, the man-

tle of heaven, slightly raised, and one foot poised on the underlying world.

Two minor but charming details of the patriarchal saga find, by chance, their illustration in the Oriental monuments. Rebecca's journey from her father's house in Harran to the waiting Isaac is a charming idyll. "Rebecca arose, and her damsels, and they rode upon camels." A rare Syrian terra-cotta (Room VIII, first case to left) permits us to see damsels very much like them, mounted two by two on a big, comfortable saddle, their faces, as in the Biblical story, unveiled. We know from the later adventures of Rachel (Gen. 31:19-35) that the saddle was big—big enough to hide the stolen teraphim. And we know, too, from a rather delicate detail, that it was comfortable. Seated on its soft bulk, hidden in her tent, Rachel slyly pleads, "Let not my lord be angry that I cannot rise up before thee." Teraphim, little household gods such as Rachel stole and Laban sought in vain, are found distributed among the wall cases of Room VI; the best-known example figures as No. 212 in the case opposite the fourth window (Grande Gallerie I) on the ground floor.

⁂

Besides these domestic godlets, the patriarchal tribes carried to Palestine a rich booty of myth and legend. Perhaps the adventure of Rachel and the teraphim hints at the part the women-folk played in the transmission of that imaginative treasure which later generations refined and bequeathed to humanity in the Biblical stories of Creation, the tree of life, and the Flood.[1]

Glimpses of the Babylonian treatment of this folklore abound in the stones and seals of the Louvre. A favourite theme in the seal cylinders (Room VI, third detached case to

[1] See p. 226 for Creation and Flood tablets in the British Museum.

left and right; Room VII, first case to left and right) turns on the primeval combat between the god Marduk and the dragon Tiamat. With the slaughter of Tiamat, who personifies the waters of original chaos, the work of creation, in the Babylonian Genesis, is well under way. Marduk cuts the pierced and slain dragon in two parts, one of which he moulds into the firmament of heaven. Scholars agree that Tiamat corresponds to the Biblical "deep" (Hebrew *Tehom*), whose face, "in the beginning", was covered with darkness. The old sea-dragon, however strange to the spirit of the Bible, is never altogether vanquished; it intrudes its monstrous head in Job, the Psalms, and most unmistakably, in Isaiah. "Awake," exclaims the prophet,[1] "O arm of the Lord, awake as in the days of old; art thou not it that pierced the dragon, that dried up the waters of the great deep?" As the seals testify, the Babylonians, too, never forgot the epic battle with the "slant serpent."

Eden, a purely Hebrew invention, is apparently unknown to Babylonian mythology. Nevertheless, two objects familiar to the Garden find their counterpart in Babylonian and Assyrian art. A sacred plant, guarded by an angel or deity (No. 2 in Room I, and No. 24 in Room II, ground floor—both on a colossal scale), its fruit, on occasion, about to be plucked by god or mortal (Room VII, first case to right, second floor), appears to be of kindred species to the "tree of life" planted "in the midst of the garden," and later transmuted by the Jews into their favourite symbol for the Torah, "a tree of life to them that lay hold of her." The cherubim who, after the Fall, were placed at the east of the Garden, to keep the way to the tree, are recognized, at least by scholars, in the great winged bulls with bearded human heads, which, as we see them today, flanking the entrance to the main hall, guard nothing more paradisiacal than a museum.

[1] Is. 51:9-10; also see Is. 27:1; 30:7; Ps. 89:10f.; 74:12-19; Job 26:12f.; 9:13.

In the same hall, Nimrod, the "mighty hunter before the Lord," glares upon us in the guise of Gilgamesh (Grande Gallerie I, Nos. 16 and 17), the mythical hero of a Babylonian epic, crushing a lion to his breast. The wild ox, with whom Job is taunted—"will he abide by thy crib?" and whom the Psalmist fears—"save me from the lion's mouth, yea, from the horns of the wild oxen"—still stalks in proud majesty (colossus in Room VIII). Guardian angels (Grande Gallerie, Nos. 4, 21, 23) keep their watch against the walls; though far from an ignoble effort to render with hammer and chisel something akin to the apocalyptic figures haunting the visions of Daniel and Revelations, they confirm at best the instinct of the Hebrews to keep their sacred imagery free from the bonds of plastic art. Gods and angels, myths and legends, even heroes, teraphim, and camels, immortal in the life-giving word, lose somewhat of their genius when they seek the grosser habitation of a stone.

⁓⋏⋏⋍

With the conquest of Canaan by the twelve tribes, the history of Israel emerges from the shadows of myth and legend. The migration of the patriarchs, the sojourn in Egypt, the escape from slavery, and the adventures in the wilderness which preceded the conquest, all have an undoubted basis in facts. But the difficulty lies in determining the nature of these facts. We have seen to what extent the Babylonian monuments reproduce the atmosphere of the early stories. The Egyptian monuments, in turn, render a similar service and bequeath to us reminiscences of the Ark, the golden calf, and the bitterness of bondage. Once their inscriptions[1] mention the presence of Israel, not, it is true, in Egypt, but in Canaan. The Egyptian Department of the Louvre (Antiquités Egyp-

[1] See p. 412 (Cairo).

tiennes, Room III, second floor) contains a lively and, we may well believe, a faithful portrait-bust of the pharaoh Akhenaton or Amenhotep IV, whose lone and valiant protest against the polytheism habitual to all of Israel's neighbours should endear him to the worshippers of the One God. Akhenaton, it should be recalled, figures in the Tell-el-Amarna letters, and with these letters appears the first probable mention of the Hebrews in secular history.

The clay tablets found at Tell-el-Amarna in Egypt contain, among other correspondence, letters written in the fourteenth century B.C. by the petty rulers of Palestine to their overlord, the pharaoh of Egypt. A number of them are from the hand of Abd-Khiba, governor of Jerusalem. Abd-Khiba complains of an invasion of desert tribes whom he calls Habiru and whom most scholars identify with the Hebrews. The majority of these invaluable tablets are now in the Berlin and the British Museums.[1] But a half-dozen of them are to be found in the Asiatic Department of the Louvre (Room VI, case before second window to right); and though we may be unable to read their crabbed dots and strokes, we know that between the lines, cutting deeper than the frightened scribe, flashes the sword of Joshua.

Bronze weapons such as the Israelites used in storming the walled towns of Canaan (Room VIII, first case to left) and bits of pottery[2] spun by the newly settled invaders are all that remains of those heroic days.

The newcomers were engaged in a greater destiny than moulding pots or carving stone. Despite occasional reluctance and flight, they remained servants to an ineffable vision. In the travail of the prophets, the labour of the priests, and the brooding of the scribes the vision gained power and form,

[1] See pp. 325, 425 (Berlin, London).
[2] See p. 27.

and a God of righteousness and mercy was bequeathed to the hearts of men. Although the legends of Israel, her secular life, and even her outward cult, share with her Semitic neighbours a common tradition, the vision is hers alone. In its nature, no traces of it linger in the monuments of the age. The vision was and remains stubborn to art. Even the words that sought to express it are rude and imperfect symbols. Nevertheless, since this expression is human and has its date in history, it too has its associations with the times that gave it birth.

Both the popular and prophetic imagination clothed the vision in the garments of a storm. Jehovah gives his laws amid lightning and thunder. "The Lord thundered in the heavens, and the Most High gave forth His voice . . . in the whirlwind and in the storm is His way." (Ps. 18:14; Nahum 1:3). The ruder imagination of Israel's neighbours has left us graven images of the storm-power. Teshub, god of the Hittites, known to the Syrians as Hadad (Room II, left rear wall), still strides across a stony sky, brandishing his lightning bolts and thunder ax. The Syrian god, Reshef (Room VII, first case to left), whose name in Hebrew means the lightning flash—"before Him goeth forth the pestilence and fiery bolts go forth at His feet" (Hab. 3:5)—still darts and dances before our eyes. Curiously, his name, in the bilingual inscriptions, is translated "Apollo," likewise a god of flame and plague.

The Hebrew struggle against the all-too-human cult of physical instincts and natural forces has burned for ever in our memories the names of Astarte and Baal, and a hate for their names. They are the villains of the Bible epic. Yet the images of Astarte seem innocent enough (Room VI, first wall case to left; high case near second window to left, Nos. 194-203; and third case to right, Nos. 191-209: Room VII, sixth window case to right). Astarte receiving the homage of a dancing faun and Astarte poised on the horns of young goats, Astarte slim and delicate as a dream of modern girlhood, Astarte the great mother and eternal woman, as we see her through the eyes of these ancient artists, still casts her spell on us and renews our wonder at the stern renunciation of the Hebrew. Never does he seem more "peculiar" among the sons of the mothers of men.

Baal is different. As a grotesque, somewhat amusing fellow (Room VII, numerous examples in case between windows at left) he arouses neither sympathy nor wrath. But the sly mouth and cruel eyes of the enthroned Baal of Hamon (same case, No. 190) arouse sinister suspicions. They are sadly confirmed by a nondescript clay jar (duly labelled) on the lower shelf of the same case. When discovered in the ruins of a temple at Carthage, this plain vase, with its deceptive air of a big ginger-pot, was filled with the bones of newborn babies. Infant sacrifice has damned the name of Baal, and his later transformation into a sort of Greek sun-god (stele from Byblos, corner of stairway, behind Room II) cannot restore his reputation.

The early cult of Israel, so far as it turned on animal sacrifice, rural altars, and small hill temples, differed little from the prevailing Semitic practice. Sacrificial scenes, typical of this cult, are still preserved in seal cylinders (Room VII, case in bay of second window to left) and elaborately chased metal (Nouvelle Salle de Susiane, bronze plate). The Assyrian altar, at the very entrance to the Asiatic collection (No. 58), is of course an urban, sophisticated type. But the terra-cotta models of Phœnician temples (Room VI, first wall case to left) may well represent the sanctuaries of Canaan; and the miniature idols staring from their portals are not irrelevant reminiscences of "the golden calves that were in Beth-el and in Dan."

❧

The secular glories of Israel, such as they were, have vanished almost without trace. A single seal (Room VII, third
case to left, No. 122) recalls one of those "servants of the
king" who, we may be sure, were at ease in Zion. A signet,
it bears the inscription "Of Shobaniyo, servant of Uzziyo,"
flanked by two winged disks. On the reverse side, a dignitary
clothed in a long mantle, his hair caught in a mass behind his
head, bears a sceptre pointed with a crescent or flower. Neither Shobaniyo ("Jehovah has brought me back") nor his
master are known to history, but doubtless he belonged to
those upper classes whose life is painted for us by the caustic,
discontented hand of the prophets. Amos, in particular, re-
sented their habit of sleeping in ivory beds; and this unfortunate article of luxury has come to symbolize the insolence
and vanity of wealth. "Ye that lie upon beds of ivory and
stretch themselves upon their couches, that drink wine in
bowls, but are not grieved for the affliction of Joseph, the
revelry of them that stretched themselves shall pass away"
(Amos 6:4-7). The revelry has passed, but through the malice
of chance an ivory bed has remained.

It belonged to Hazael, "servant" of Ben-Hadad, king of
Aram and arch foe of Ahab and Jehu (ninth century B.C.).
Although no Israelite, he began his reign with the sanction,
however reluctant, of Elisha. "The Lord hath shown me that
thou shalt be king over Aram." And true enough, after the
dramatic interview (II Kings 8:7-15) with the prophet in
Damascus, he slipped into the palace bedroom, and while his
master slept, "took the coverlet and dipped it in water, and
spread it over his face, so that he died." Thus Hazael succeeded to the royal ivory bed.

If the beauty of carved ivory helps a bed to do its work,

Hazael slept well. The dozen surviving plaques (Room VIII, second case to left) reveal the cunning of a master artist who, we may suspect, learned his craft in Babylon or Egypt. He rules fantasy and nature with a sure hand. His winged genii, guarding a child-god (Horus?) poised on a lotus stalk, rival the happiest inventions of the Nile. As for his contented cows offering udders and caresses to their young—let Amos growl as he will over the kine of Bashan—they may quietly challenge the sculpture of any land or age.

Amos, however, with his memories of ravished Gilead, will not suffer Hazael to sleep in peace. "So I will send a fire into the house of Hazael, and it shall devour the palaces of Ben-Hadad, and the people of Aram shall go into captivity unto Kir" (Amos 1:4-5). To all appearances, Hazael died unmolested in his usurped bed; but the descendants of Amos will doubtless derive satisfaction from the monument to Za-kir, king of Hama (hallway to Jewish Room, close to window), chanting his triumph over Hazael's son.

ᐸᐅᐳ

Only the neighbours of Israel and Judah have left us their monuments, and since it is their business to retail victories, the Louvre collection assumes the air of a perverse hall of fame, where enemies are honoured. The Grande Gallerie is a sorrowful memorial to the destruction of Israel and the last days of Judah.[1] Its friezes are eloquent with "the noise of the whip and the rattling of the wheels, of prancing horses and bounding chariots, the horsemen charging, and the flashing sword and the glittering spear, and a multitude of slain" (Nahum 3:2-3). Mounted on his war-chariot, shaded by his royal umbrella, his fly-chasers swishing at either side (No. 62), we behold "even the king of Assyria and all his glory" (Is. 8:7).

[1] See pp. 226, 424 for material in British Museum.

As early as the ninth century B.C., the shadow of Asshur fell upon the little hill-state of Israel. A copy of a precious stele (between Nos. 62 and 70; original in British Museum) pictures the "servants" of Jehu bringing tribute to Shalmaneser, the Assyrian king. A file of Israelites (second band of reliefs, from top) laden with bowls, trays, baskets, bales, and sacks of unwilling gifts, trudge behind their ambassador who licks the dust at the feet of the conqueror. Shielded from the visibly piercing sun by his inevitable umbrella, Shalmaneser receives them with cool indifference. Next to the ivory and apes offered by a neighbouring set of victims (third band of reliefs), the Israelites probably made a poor showing.

A century later the Assyrians destroyed Samaria, and Sargon (portrait—No. 28) transported thousands of the conquered Israelites beyond the Euphrates. But a few years more, and the hosts of Sennecharib threatened the gates of Jerusalem. Two royal captains (No. 31) may well pass for the chief butler and chief eunuch who stood before the gates "and cried in a loud voice in the Jews' language" such magnificent vulgarities (II Kings 18:27) that they quite terrified the contemporaries of Isaiah huddled on the walls.

Although the fall of Nineveh delayed, it did not avert the doom of Judah. The Babylonians soon carried out the threats of their predecessors, and Judah joined Israel in exile (587 B.C.).

In friezes which once adorned the palace of Nineveh (Nos. 65 and 72) we can follow, as in a strange petrified cinema, the weary march to captivity. Although the victims are not Israelites, their fate is similar. The male captives, "princes, craftsmen, and smiths," plod in chains, burdened by water-skins and packs. The women-folk, with children in arms, ride in bullock carts stacked high with furniture and goods. Cattle for food, and if they endure, for ultimate sale, lumber along the trail. Exhausted or luckless wights who lag behind are quickened with blows. The guards appear alert and vigorous, and doubtless enjoyed first pull at the water-skins and the biggest helping to the boiled grain.

We come upon the captives camping en route (Room II, No. 72). Cooking is under way. Prisoners or soldiers eat lustily from a common bowl. A thirsty child drinks from a water-skin held aloft by its mother, while another thirsty gamin plucks impatiently at her skirt. The old men rest upon their packs. A horse is tethered near the fire. Friends offer weary comrades food, drink, and encouraging, gesticulative talk. Then the forced journey is resumed.

At last the wanderers reach the "great river" Euphrates, and we follow their march along its banks (Room I, No. 70). We gather from the sight of abundant fish darting in its waters that the diet, if not ·the misery, of the caravan enjoys a change. With a final blow from the guards, the exiles disappear from view.

As for their Jewish fellow-victims, we vainly listen for further sign of them before the muted harp (Room VI, to right) that comes down to us from the waters of Babylon. How shall they sing the Lord's song in a strange land?

⟨⟩

The epilogue to the Babylonian captivity is written in rude Hebrew characters scrawled in spirals on the inner surface of clumsy terra-cotta bowls, and breathing a spirit far removed from the Lord's song. Rare as they are curious, these inscribed bowls are to be found only in the Louvre (Room VI, case before first window to left; Room VII, case before window No. 6), the British Museum[1] and the museum of the Hôtel de Ville of Cannes. Dug up in the quarter of the city generally assigned to the Jewish exiles, they date (about fifth

[1] See p. 426.

century c.e.) from the days when the Talmud schools laboured in Babylonia—for despite certain impressions derived
from the prophets, Babylon continued to flourish a thousand
years after its capture by the Persians, and its Jewish community lingered on till the end.

Their contents, however, tell nothing of the pure and universal Judaism usually credited to the influence of the Captivity, and nothing of the enduring form given this faith by
the mighty architects of the Talmud. They reveal quite another and almost forgotten cult, wherein the Babylonians ex-
celled—the cult of magic.

First, the formula as we still see it was written in the bowl.
Then water, a prime magical element, was added to absorb
the virtues of the spell. The patient downed the brew and
thereby fortified himself against ·the demons besieging him
with disease, disaster, blues, or other manifestations of bad
luck.[1]

The formula provided a rather universal prophylactic. Bar
Hisdai, a Jew who lived on Housia Street, is assured protection against "all evil sorceries, all wizardry, spells, maledic-
tions, and curses of men or women, far or near, day or night,
from this day forth and for ever." Good angels are enlisted
to this end. In addition, "the great star who rules all other
stars from on high, who rides upon the heavens, to whom
belongs salvation, and who teaches magic to the magicians"
and the mystic "jujube tree" are both invoked for Bar Hisdai.
Another bowl begging protection for Amtar, the daughter of
Solomon, takes care to call the beneficent angels by name—
Rashiel, Bassuriel, Baruiel, Rayiel, Raphael, Bazuriel, Bada-
tumiel, Barakiel, and Badanuel.

The translation of a blanket formula for an entire household in the "locality of Bahran" will serve as a typical sample

---

[1] It is possible the bowls were placed, without water, in the foundations of
houses and served as traps to catch the demons.

of this debased Judaism. The original inscription, with its vague grammar, is in the popular Aramaic tongue:

"Here is an act of divorce against the demons Satan, Niriek, Zariah, Abturtura, Dan, and Lilith. May they disappear from the locality of Bahran . . . from the house altogether. Beneficent Lord, shatter thou the king of dreams and demons, the great power of Lilith. I conjure you, Lilith, grandchild of the beautiful Lilith, male or female, I conjure you . . . May your heart turn aside at the sceptre of the mighty man who has dominion over the demons, over Lilith, that daughter in the darkness. Ah, ah, I drive you away, from the house in Bahran, and from its surroundings. As demons write divorces and present them to their wives and their wives go away for good, so take your divorce, receive your written divorce, and hurry, fly, and quit the house in Bahran, in the name of the Lord God . . . go to darkness before the mighty arm, sealed with his ring so that one may know they are no longer there. For the good of his family. Amen, amen, amen. Selah." Lilith, you may know, can be met with in Isaiah (Is. 34:14), where she is usually disguised, in the English translation, as a "screech-owl" or "night monster."

A large seal cylinder (Room VI, third case to left, No. 122) permits us to witness the administration of one of these magical prescriptions. The witch doctor, "the mighty man who has dominion over the demons," stands before the patient, who tosses frantically on his sick-bed, a prey to the demons or the painful brew. Friends, relatives, or perhaps the demons themselves, hover about anxiously. Although the size and beauty of the seal makes it evident we are watching at the bedside of a rich native, we should have seen much the same performance at the cot of a Jewish labourer in the Babylonian ghetto. "Behold," reads one of our Jewish bowls, cunningly citing the Bible (Song of Songs 3:7; Num. 6:24; Is. 44:25), "Behold, it is the bed of Solomon, threescore mighty men are

about it, of the mighty men of Israel. Heaven send salvation
for life on the threshold of Ashir, in the name of the Holy
One, the Eternal, the great God of Israel, whose word no
sooner given is fulfilled. The Lord bless thee and keep thee,
etc. I frustrate the tokens of imposters and diviners."

This inquietude over demons and trust in exorcisms appears
remote and fantastic enough. Yet the smaller bowl in Cannes
contained a brew that flavours strangely of home. The inscription, even if you can read it, says little. Nana, daughter
of Khatima, wishes relief from the obsessions of a demon.
It is the crude sketch, painted in the centre of the bowl, which
betrays the nature of the obsession and reveals the demon to
be, in both senses, a familiar spirit. The magician was no artist, but he likely knew what he was about when he portrayed the evil one as an unclothed female, *visis genitalibus*
and with long claws and thin, streaming hair. Today Nana
would seek relief not so much in an exorcism as a *transfer-
ence*; and a set of these bowls, taking them all in all, would
make an admirable Freudian dinner-service.

Although the Talmud continued the Biblical warfare
against witchcraft and demonology, the Jewish masses in so-
called backward ages or lands seldom ceased to borrow the
superstitions of their neighbours or cling to their own. Charms
and spells still prevail among the Jews of North Africa and
the Orient. The East European Jew can still be found who
pins an amulet against Lilith on the cradle of his newborn
babe. Chassidism, for all its poetry, and Cabbalism, for all its
philosophy, are penetrated with magic. Traces of the old
hydromancy survive, a half hidden Babylonian water-mark,
even in the pages of the current Prayer Book. "And you shall
take you, on the first day, the fruit of the tree Adar, branches
of palm trees, a bough of the tree Aboth, and willows of the
brook; while I wave them, may streams of blessings flow in

upon me" reads the familiar meditation over the Lulab.[1] In the Succoth booth, we "bid the stream of life flow in on thy servant," a formula taken directly from the Cabbalists. Again in the Tashlich meditation, "recited on the banks of a river or of any other piece of water," pious Jews, naturally innocent of any magical intent, pray that the Lord will "cast all their sins into the depths of the sea."

The genius of Israel lies in this transmutation of magical scribblings into religious prayers inspired, as Israel Abrahams well said, "with a deep mystical fervor." We have seen this Jewish alchemy at work on rude gods and primitive myths. Like the Greeks, the Jews were lusty borrowers, and like all original peoples lead is turned to gold at their hands. Scattered about the world, they are still borrowing from all sides. And in Palestine, where we will turn to finger the relics of the past, they have set up a new alembic for the future.

[1] See p. 31 (Jewish Room).

LOUVRE. JEWISH MAGIC BOWL
See page 17

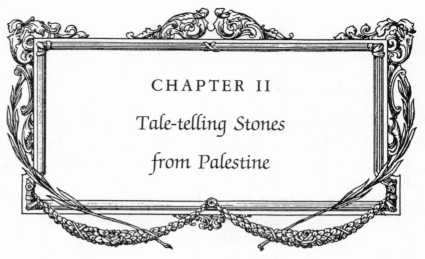

CHAPTER II

Tale-telling Stones

from Palestine

A CHINESE mandarin touring the Louvre and stumbling on the Jewish Room (Salle Judaïque) might wonder why a great museum treasured the debris of casual housewreckers. After the glories of the Babylonian or Greek collections, the odd scraps of stone and clay garnered from Palestine and its neighbourhood appear pitifully in need of explanation. And the mandarin would be doubly astonished to learn that these scraps were prized not only for their rarity, but for their profound and poignant interest.

The history of Jewish art attempts to explain the rarity of its relics. The ancient Hebrews, we are told, had little use and perhaps no talent for art. Just why, it is hard to say. The Biblical commandment "not to make a graven image nor any manner of likeness" can scarcely be held responsible, for it was never obeyed to the letter. If we are to believe the records, temple and court—the two sources of fine arts—were adorned with all manner of sculptured and perhaps painted imagery. Moreover, judging not from the records, but the remains, Israel's neighbours appear almost as poor in art as the Hebrews themselves. Nor, in the case of the Hebrews, can this absence of a characteristic art be due to sheer lack of a sense of beauty. Hebrew literature in its sensitivity and response to the beauty of nature and life knows no rival, save

Greek, among the ancient nations; and it is difficult to believe that a people who wrote the Psalms could barely fashion a vase or chisel a stone.

But any judgment on early Jewish art is rash. Too little remains. The chariots and ploughs of countless conquerors have obliterated trace and record of Israel's ancient cities. It is the history of Palestine, and not theories of religious prohibitions or racial incompetence, which best accounts for the poverty of our museum collections. While Babylon and Nineveh had the good fortune to be neglected, forgotten, and finally buried in a kindly sand, and while Egypt and Greece were for the most part spared by admiring conquerors and their peoples never uprooted from the land, Jerusalem—between its original capture by David and ultimate destruction under Hadrian—suffered no less than twenty-three sieges which thrice ended in complete devastation. The smaller cities of Palestine—Jericho, Samaria, Bethel, Hebron—vanished in a similar ruin. And instead of a saving oblivion, the fall of Rome led to successive waves of reconquest and resettlement —Byzantine, Persian, Arab, Frank, and Turk. "I will wipe Jerusalem as a man wipeth a dish, wiping it and turning it upside down." With such treatment, it is not to be expected that many art crumbs will survive.

And because they are few, and because of the fate that made them few, every relic dug from the wreck of centuries presents a riddle and evokes an epic.

卍

The large bas-relief of a Moabite warrior (No. 1, first window) carries us back to the march of the Israelites on Canaan.[1] It was found east of the Dead Sea, near Aroer "on the lip of the valley of Arnon," where Israel first entered into battle for

[1] See p. 10.

her heritage. If expert opinion is correct in dating it before the twelfth century B.C. it preserves for us something of the defiant image of the men of Balak who sought to bar the way to Moses and his desert horde. The short breeches suggests Egyptian tailoring and the plumed casque is Hittite, a mixture of styles much as we should expect in a border nation. And in his posture of armed pride our warrior seems waiting for the pen of Jeremiah (Jer. 48:19): "O inhabitant of Aroer, stand by the way and watch; ask him that fleeth and her that escapeth, 'what has been done?' "

"We have heard of the pride of Moab," says Isaiah; and thanks to a lucky find, we may read Moab's own testimony to his haughtiness and assumption of heart. The stele of Mesha, king of Moab (No. 2, facing entrance) recovered in the ancient capital of Dibon, sings Moab's victories over his traditional enemy, Israel. The monument was engraved shortly after 842 B.C. upon the dedication of a sanctuary to the national god, Chemosh—"the abomination of Moab," as the Hebrew prophets liked to style him. Its lengthy inscription is the oldest known document in the Hebrew (or very nearly the Hebrew) language, and Renan hardly exaggerates in calling it "the most important discovery ever made in the field of Oriental epigraphy."

The critical lover of the Bible, reading the denunciations of the prophets, has doubtless wondered what their victims had to say for themselves. And turning to the historical narratives, he has perhaps wondered how far a modern mind can trust the ancient Hebrew scribes, swayed as they were by religious passion, copying and likely colouring sources long lost to us. To such a reader the Mesha stele speaks with an authentic voice across twenty-eight intervening centuries. The enemy has "written a book"; his words are graven in the rock with an iron pen and lead.

"Now Mesha, king of Moab, was a sheep-master," begins

the Biblical account (II Kings, 3) and for years Moab, it appears, had suffered the dominion of Israel and the house of Omri. Then, on the death of Ahab, Mesha rebelled. Ahab's son, Joram, and Jehoshaphat, king of Judah, marched against the rebels. There were miracles by Elisha, towns were destroyed, the battle went against Mesha, and in desperation he sacrificed his eldest son as a burnt-offering to Chemosh, on the wall of Kir-hareseth. There the Biblical records, which are more concerned with Elisha than Mesha, break off; but later on (II Kings 10:23; 13:20) we casually learn that the Moabites must in the end have been victorious.

The Mesha stele relates the same story, merely gliding over the defeats which would be creditable to Jehovah and underlining the victories which naturally are due to the might of Chemosh. In the following translation a few of the building exploits of the Moabite king are omitted.

I am Mesha [Moses], son of Chemoshgad, king of Moab, the Dibonite. My father reigned thirty years over Moab, and I became king after my father. I built this high place for Chemosh of Kerichoch, high place of deliverance, because he has delivered me from every aggressor, and because he has made me see my desire upon all my enemies.

Omri was king of Israel and long oppressed Moab, because Chemosh was angry with his land. His son succeeded him, and he too said, "I will oppress Moab." In my days he said this, but I saw my desire upon him and his house, and Israel has been humbled for ever.

Omri had seized the land of Medeba, and [Israel] occupied it during his days and part of the days of his sons, forty years. But in my days, Chemosh has dwelt there.

The men of Gad had long occupied the land of Ataroth, and the king of Israel had built up Ataroth for himself. I attacked the city and took it, and I slew all the people of the city to rejoice Chemosh and Moab. I bore off from there the altar of Dodoh and dragged it before the face of Chemosh in Kerioth, where I made to dwell the man of Sharon and him of Maharoth.

And Chemosh said unto me, "Go, take Nebo against Israel." I went by night, and I attacked it from the break of day until noon. I took it and I slew everyone, seven thousand men and boys and women and girls and concubines, because I had devoted them to Ashtar-Chemosh. I took from there the vessels of Jehovah and I dragged them before the face of Chemosh.

The king of Israel had fortified Jahaz and occupied it during his campaign against me. And Chemosh drove him out before me. I took two hundred men of Moab, all their chief men, and I attacked Jahaz, and took it and joined it to Dibon.

I built Kerichoch, the park wall and the wall of the hill-fortress. I built its gates and its towers. I dug the moat about Kerichoch with the captives of Israel.

I built Aroer and the road of Arnon. I built Beth-Bamot, for it was destroyed. I built Bezer, for it was in ruins. . . . And Chemosh said unto me, "Go down and fight against Horonaim." I went and fought against the city and took it, and Chemosh dwelt there during my reign. It was I who . . .

The two accounts, the "White Book" of Israel and the "Black Book" of Moab, though both remain fragments, dovetail as happily as any war *communiqués* issued by enemy nations. And although Moab never dreamed of rendering a service to his oppressors, his stele more than any single monument confirms the general accuracy of Biblical history.

Again it is Israel's enemy who has left us a trophy of the religious wars which bloodied the slopes of Carmel. The contest of Elijah with the prophets of Baal, though clouded by legend, cannot altogether be dismissed as fiction so long as there remains, a stumbling-block to sceptics, the shattered slab (No. 115 second centre case) found near the so-called Grotto of Elijah. Its Phœnician inscription is still legible: ". . . the son of Abd [usir, son of . . .], son of [A]bdelim, son of Aris . . . the scribe and Baal . . ." The date is uncertain and Ben Abdusir is of course unknown; but it is none the less ironic to discover on Carmel, the "mountain of God" and the scene of Elijah's triumph, neither sign nor scrap of Israel but a stone sealed with the name of Baal.

The earliest Hebrew inscription of purely Jewish origin has no religious significance. It celebrates the completion of "Hezekiah's" tunnel (about 700 B.C.) which brought the waters of Shiloah within the walls of Jerusalem. The Louvre copy (No. 7, first window) was taken, while the original, which is now in Constantinople,[1] still stood where the workmen left it in the tunnel shaft. Although only a fragment, it reveals a curious interest in the technique of the undertaking rather than in the glory of the king whose name is associated with it. "This is the manner," says the inscription, "of the boring. When . . . the picks, one against the other. And when there were only three cubits more to be cut through, the men were heard calling to one another, because there was a . . . in the rock on the right and on the left. On the day of the piercing the diggers struck each to meet the other, pick against pick. Then the waters ran from the spring to the pool, twelve hundred cubits; and one hundred cubits was the thickness of the rock above the heads of the diggers."

The tunnel, it should be understood, was more than an ambitious piece of engineering. Jerusalem then, as today, was a city without springs or running streams within its walls; and always exposed to siege, it might well commemorate every incident of a work, even to the ring of the picks and the cry of the diggers, which assured it literal waters of salvation. The Book of Kings (II, 20:20) and Chronicles (II, 32: 30) both glorify the exploit, which was still remembered in the days of Ben Sira. He is happy to recall that "some did that which was pleasing to God . . . Hezekiah fortified his city and brought in water into the midst thereof; he digged the hard rock with iron." (Ecclus. 48:16-17.) And Isaiah uses "the waters of Shiloah that go softly" as the symbol of Israel's divine government.

꒰ᴥ꒱

The minor arts in the early centuries of Jewish history are represented mainly by pottery. A series of rude vases (Nos.

[1] See p. 384.

156, 166, 170) is characteristic of Canaanite ware. With its elaborate geometric patterns, the so-called "Jerusalem Vase" (No. 175) recalls Cyprian models of the eight and seventh centuries B.C. The numerous terra-cotta lamps in the centre cases which date from the Canaanite (Nos. 197, 198) to the early Christian (Nos. 208, 209) period show a singular persistance in form and but few variations in the decoration; we may be sure that lamps very much like them lighted to bed the successive generations of Israel.

A small and charming glass vase (No. 123, case beyond first window), possibly of Phœnician manufacture, furnishes an excellent introduction to early Jewish symbols. The pomegranate, citron, and grape-cluster which are spun into the body of the vase appear in the first Jewish coins of the Maccabean period and no doubt originate in remote tradition. Pomegranates, it need hardly be recalled, were embroidered on the robes of Aaron the High Priest (Ex. 28:33), and served as ornament, "two hundred in rows round about each capital" for Jachin and Boaz, the brass pillars of Solomon's Temple (I Kings 7:18). The citron, or *etrog*, is the "fruit of the goodly tree" which, together with branches of willow, palm, and myrtle, are borne by the Jews "to rejoice before the Lord" during the harvest festival (Lev. 23:40). In legend the citron is identified with the forbidden fruit of Eden, and in history Alexander Jannæus discovered that it made an excellent missile in the hands of his outraged subjects. Perhaps from its association with Joshua (Num. 13:23) and with the fruitfulness of the Promised Land, the grape-cluster, or *eschol*, became a popular national symbol. Aristobulus presented Pompey with a golden vine, and a similar trophy to the goldsmith's art hung over the porch in Herod's temple, "its branches drooping," says Josephus, "from a great height, the largeness and fine workmanship of which was a surprising sight."

A large bas-relief from a first- or second-century synagogue in Gadara (No. 117 left wall) presents three further symbols current in Jewish art. The seven-branched candlestick or menorah, which rises in the centre of the relief, is included among the furniture of the tabernacle in the wilderness and the Temple of Solomon. But since neither the Book of Kings (II, 25:13-17) mentions it with the spoils carried off by Nebuchadnezzar, nor Ezekiel in his description of the ideal temple, the earlier references are suspect. Scholars prefer to trace its origins to the Babylonian captivity. The opinion of Josephus that the seven lamps signify the seven planets, and their rabbinical interpretation as the seven days of creation seem to echo Babylonian star worship. In any case, the first undisputed description of a menorah comes from Zechariah, who writes shortly after the return from Babylon. "I have seen a candlestick all of gold," he relates of one of his mystic visions (Zech. 4:2), "with a bowl on top of it, and its seven lamps thereon; there are seven pipes, yea seven, to the lamp." The Second Temple, built after the return, possessed a menorah with at least more than one "pipe"; *Maccabees* (I, 1:22; 4:50) tells of its destruction by Antiochus Epiphanes and restoration by Judas. Josephus, in turn, mentions its presence in Herod's Temple.

Modern artists concerned with making a faithful copy of this old emblem will do well to scrutinize the base of the Louvre specimen. They will not find the polygonal prop familiar to us from the Arch of Titus nor the simple inverted cup of most contemporary models. In common with many ancient examples from tombs, friezes, and mosaics, and agreeing with the Talmudic account, the menorah from Gadara rests upon a tripod. But then, according to the rabbis, Moses himself had great difficulty with its construction. Three times he forgot the specifications which God gave him; he was unable to copy the model which God at length made for

him; and finally when God drew a design of it on the palm
of his hand, he could not execute it. So our artists may be
forgiven.

Though copies were forbidden to be made of the holy
archetype in the Temple, it was freely represented in the
decoration of terra-cotta lamps and sculptural designs; and
after the final destruction of Jerusalem, it became the most
cherished symbol of Judaism. During the first centuries of the
common era, in Galilee, Greece, and Africa, the menorah
appears in the sculpture of the synagogues that housed the
living faith of the vanished Temple. And throughout the
Roman Empire it stamps the catacombs, tombstones, and
sarcophagi of the Jewish dead (Nos. 103, 118, 127), who slept
beneath its sign with the trust of Christians beneath the cross.
It burns in the pages of rabbinic legend with the light of the
Shekinah; while its lamps glow the power of the nations of
the world will be held in check; and the Lord commands its
candles to be lit "that I might see you and give you yet
another chance to do a good deed, for which, if done, I will
reward you in the future world by letting a great light shine
before you."

The candlestick, as in the present bas-relief (No. 117) is
often flanked by the ram's horn and the *lulab*. One of the
earliest musical devices of mankind, the primitive ram's horn
or *shofar* is the ritual horn of Israel. It was the voice of the
shofar "exceeding loud" which rang from the thick cloud
upon Sinai when Moses "brought forth the people to meet
God." The walls of Jericho fell at its sound. It echoed through
the hill country of Ephraim the day Ehud slew the thousands
of Moab. At En-harod the *shofar* joined its blast in the night
with the crash of pitchers and the battle-cry of the valiant
hundred, "The sword for the Lord and for Gideon!" Throughout Biblical times it resounded on the festival of the New
Moon and on the First Day of Tishri, called "the memorial

of blowing," as well as on other solemn occasions. It gave the alarm in case of siege, flood, or pressing danger, and figured, perhaps magically, in rain-making ceremonies. The Romans, it is easy to understand, were bewildered by its frequent blowing and suspected its treasonable intent in a land of rebels. Later, other rebels, in the bitter moment of excommunication, trembled at its note.

Although the Jews, as befitted a race of music-lovers, made no scruples in adapting and modifying their other instruments, they clung stubbornly to the primitive *shofar*. To this day it keeps its ancient form and use; and the traditional notes, the deep *tekiah* and the shrill *teruah* usher in the New Year and dismiss Israel after the repentant hours of Atonement. Unlike the cornucopia of the Gentiles brimming with earthly fruits, the *shofar* is big with the dooms of the future. A day shall come when, as on Sinai, it will throb again beneath an awful breath. "The Lord God will blow the *shofar* and will go with the whirlwinds of the south" (Zech. 9:14). On that day promised of the prophets and become the hope of Zion, "a great *shofar* shall be blown, and they shall come that have been lost in the land of Assyria and dispersed in the land of Egypt, and they shall worship the Lord in the holy mountain of Jerusalem" (Is. 27:13).

The *lulab*, or "palm branch," placed to the left of the candlestick (still No. 117) is a ceremonial sheaf. Its use recalls primitive fertility rites. A palm shoot, two willow branches, and three sprigs of myrtle are entwined in the sheaf, which, together with the citron, comprise the "four species" sacred to the Feast of Tabernacles or Ingathering, the harvest feast of Israel. Echoes of this ancient festival—"after thou hast gathered in from thy threshing floor and thy winepress" (Deut. 16:13)—hark back to the days when the maidens danced in the vineyards of Shiloh and the young men of Benjamin, reminiscent, too, of the fertility motive, gathered in their wives (Jud. 9:27). It naturally surpassed in importance all other holy days. Rain, crops, and the life of the land hung on the success of its rites. And the calendar was coolly shifted to avoid suspension of the rites on a Sabbath.

When our bas-relief was fashioned and set in the synagogue across the lake of Galilee, men were perhaps still alive who remembered or who heard their fathers tell how, the Feast of Tabernacles come, the multitudes swarmed to Jerusalem. In the Temple, the altar of the court was decked with willows. Near it pressed the throngs of worshippers bearing the citron and the sacred sheaves. Each day for seven days the priests intoned the Hallel or Psalms of Praise (Ps. 113-118). And each time the line rang forth, "Give thanks to the Lord for He is good," the crowds waved their sheaves in ritual cadence —east, south, west, and north, up and down, and to and fro.

When should one begin to mention the Power of Rain? asks the Talmud. At the time one begins to wave the *lulab*. As the four species, Rabbi Eliezer explains, cannot exist without water, the world cannot exist without rain. So with boughs beating for the Power of the rain and the Luck of the year, the last psalm of the Hallel brought the rite to its climax. "I pray, oh Lord, save now!" cried the throng, "I pray, oh Lord, success now!" And when the psalm concluded with the signal, "Order the festival procession with boughs, even unto the horns of the altar," the multitude wound closely around the willow-draped block, and there rose the cryptic invocation, "I and He—save now!"—the familiar and magic cry of Hosanna.

Embroidering on Zechariah, the Talmud says that at the Feast of Tabernacles the world is judged as to whether it shall have rain. The judgment was no doubt invoked the wild second night of the feast. The Women's Court of the Temple flared with huge lamps. Spectators packed its galleries and worshippers thronged its pavement. Ranged on the steps of the Inner Court, the Levites chanted the Songs of Ascents (Ps. 120-124) to the sound of harps and flutes. Throughout the night, in anticipation of the "Drawing of the Water," the assembled multitude, merchants from the *souks* and peasants from the countryside, amid the clash of cymbals danced with lighted torches. If Plutarch had seen this night, he would not have made the mistake of comparing the *lulab* to the thyrsus and the Ingathering Feast to the Bacchanalia. But he might have recalled the old Cretan hymn to Zeus: "Leap for full jars, leap for fleecy flocks, and leap for fields of fruit."

The synagogues of Galilee turned the *lulab* and the *etrog* into stone. Today, it is true, the citron and the festive sheaf, meagre relics of the old mimetic rites, the drawing of the water and the sacred dance, are still paraded and waved at the harvest feast. The cry of Hosanna still rises in token of the power of the Lord—or is it the power of Man and the Lord? *I and He* ran the call—over the treasures of nature and over the "success" of the year. But the magic in a literal sense is gone; it was already long gone before the Temple fell; the spells and the wands alone remain.

A Gentile would have witnessed the Temple rites at considerable risks. If he read Greek or Latin he would likely— unless he were a mad Burton—decline to run them. Curt warnings in these tongues, affixed to the several gates leading from the profane outer court to the inner sanctums, were calculated to dampen undue curiosity. One of them, hailing from Herod's Temple, may still be read. The Louvre copy (No. 8, facing second window) was made at the time of its discovery; the original is now in Constantinople.[1] "No foreigner," runs the notice, "may pass beyond the barrier and wall which surround the sanctuary. Anyone caught inside must blame only himself for his punishment with death."

Almost needless to say, the purpose of the prohibition was

[1] See p. 384.

not to insure privacy or conceal the mysteries of the cult. Its intention, rather, was to keep the sacred area ritually clean. We meet today with scruples and bans impelled by a similar motive in orthodox mosques, in the care taken of a consecrated Host, and in certain taboos concerned with national banners.

Vast as it was, no vestige of the Temple's paraphernalia has come to light. Yet something must surely survive of a plant which in its heyday comprised an arsenal, granary, treasury, bakery, slaughter-house, court of justice, school, and sanctuary of a cult which in its elaborate pomp would have given a Catholic cathedral the rustic air of a Methodist crossroad church. But so long as the Temple area, now embraced by the Moslem Haram esh-Sherif, keeps its ancient sanctity and remains closed to the spade of the excavator, we are reduced to symbols and suppositions. Perhaps a hint of its innumerable utensils lurks in the two small bronze shovels (Nos. 19, 85) which, despite their classic design and resemblance to numerous Syrian specimens, might have served to tend the incense-offering or the sacrificial fires.

The imagination enjoys scant play with the stone pinnings (No. 10, first centre case) which once joined the masonry of Herod's Temple. Enough if it yields a light thrill. The Romans, when it came to destruction, did their work so well we are lucky—unless we go to Jerusalem—to be spared as much. And even in Jerusalem we may be tempted to ask once more with Sanballat (Neh. 3:34): "What do these feeble Jews? Will they make the old stones live again?"

かん

Fragments of palaces and tombs tease us with their furtive invocation of manners in the last centuries before Jerusalem fell. The rise of the Ptolemies in Egypt and the Seleucids in

Syria (third century B.C.) rapidly flooded Palestine with the trappings of Hellenism—social fashions, art, sports, luxurious brigandry, all the showy side of Greek life calculated to turn the head of Levantine barbarians. Fed on the new fare, Jeshurun waxed fat and kicked. The shattered base of a sculptured column, a bit of its fluted shaft, and a finely worked Ionic capital (Nos. 65, 66, 67), once we know they are associated with the name of Tobiah ben Joseph ben Tobiah, tell us the whole story as best a dumb stone can.

Tobiah was the great-grandson of Simon the Zaddik; and he could not have chosen a more pious ancestor and fervid champion of Judaism than the author of the deathless maxim: "The world rests on three things—Torah, Temple service, and deeds of loving kindness." Yet the descent begins rapidly. Tobiah's great-uncle was Onias the High Priest, "a little soul and a great lover of money." Tobiah's father, Joseph, became a mighty court Jew in Egypt, amassed great wealth through his redoubtable system of tax-collecting—a system based on another and simpler maxim, "Taxes or your life!"—and in enjoying the proceeds showed himself a rare and wild old man. Tobiah adopted the Greek name Hyrcanus and his father's ideas on what the world was based, murdered a couple of his jealous brothers, and set himself up (about 180 B.C.) as a robber baron across the Jordan. Like his remote successors in Renaissance Italy, he paid tribute to Greece through his love of beauty. Josephus eloquently describes his palace "built of white stone to the very roof," with its vast fortifications "lest it should be besieged by his brethren," its gardens, banquet-halls, fountains, courts, and friezes—"animals of prodigious size were engraven upon it." Altogether an Oriental's dream of the new civilization. If we go to Arak El-Amir in Transjordania, we may still see traces of the frieze of prodigious lions. Meanwhile here (No. 69, left wall), prodigious enough, is a lion's paw.

Bits of mosaic and the turn of a classic cornice (Nos. 61, 62, 63) provoke at least a mention of the Hasmoneans (143-37 B.C.) who led the first revolt against the new spirit of the West and then, as soon as bold Judas and Simon were dead, yielded promptly to its charms. Our fragments come from the tragic fortress of Masada, built by the Maccabees and the last to fall at the hands of the Romans. Further morsels of mosaic (No. 60) from the palace of Herodium, just south of Jerusalem, and a colossal female head (No. 114) found in the ruins of Sebaste recall the Herodian dynasty (37 B.C.-70 C.E.) which followed on the heels and in the footsteps of the Hasmoneans. The head is generally assumed to be a portrait of a member of Herod's family; if so, permitting themselves a sculptured likeness "in the round" was the least of their transgressions.

But the new culture has left its deepest mark on the tombs. Casts of the ornate pediments which crowned the entrance to the "Tombs of the Kings" (Nos. 25, 44, 45), the "Tombs of the Judges" (Nos. 48, 49) and other rock-tombs in the neighbourhood of Jerusalem (Nos. 52, 54, 55) reflect a florid Hellenism. A native touch, however, is caught in the grape-cluster and the rather Syrian rosettes in an otherwise Doric frieze from the Valley of Hinnom (No. 54, second window).

At first glance, the ossuaries found in the Jewish tombs (Nos. 15-18 along left wall, also Nos. 43, 51, 93) seem remote enough from classic influence. In fact, their decoration comes as near to being native as any relic of ancient Palestine. The border design of a ribbon folding upon itself, the single palm leaf, and the rosettes of six or multiples of six petals, common to almost every known specimen, are probably traditional funerary symbols. In addition, the engraving often includes the well-known cup, urn, and rising lily.

Yet in their own way these small caskets retell the familiar story of "assimilation." Not their decoration, but their form and very being betray the *drang nach Westen*. Wealthy Greeks and Romans, it is well known, often burnt their dead and consigned the ashes to a coffer or urn. The Jews, on the contrary, buried their dead. However slavishly they imitated Greek life, not only habit but religious law kept them, "even," as Sir Thomas Browne says, "in times of subjection and hottest use," from following Greek fashions after death. And more perhaps than law, they were restrained by hope—the hope of resurrection. Yet the lure of the neat coffer and genteel urn was not to be denied. So they hit upon the device of depositing the bones of the dead in these little ossuaries. Fragments of large stone vases (Nos. 14, 56), which reveal their use by the border of folded ribbon, show that these ancient assimilationists went from casket to urn. Safe from the forbidden fire, they still enjoyed a Greek dress. And if our modern Jews choose to think of their English Prayer Books, synagogue organs, and high silk hats on high holy days, they may smile, but they cannot mock at this old trick.

The Louvre ossuaries come, as we might expect, from the tombs of the rich. Most of them, however, dating from the first century B.C., still employ Hebrew for their inscriptions. "Joazar," reads the name on one of them (No. 16); and through another Hebrew inscription found in the same tomb (No. 53, second window) we learn that Joazar descends from the priestly family of the Beni Hezir mentioned in the Bible (I Chron. 24:15) and warrant that even the old stock went in for the show of a Greek grave. Another ossuary (No. 93, third window) found in Lydda, the ancient Diospolis, nearer to the sea and things Hellenic, and likely later in date, has abandoned Hebrew for Greek, although the deceased chooses to recall the name given him upon his circumcision: "Pyrinun or likewise Malthakes, grandson of Alkios Simon Gobar." From Tyre, Jaffa, and Lower Egypt numerous epitaphs (Nos. 103, 104, 119, 128-133) witness the spread of Greek among the Jews. But the inscription on the coffret of Joazar bids us

"*Shalom,*" and peace shall it be to him and to all who seek a new birth and even, if they will, a new burial.

⤝⤜

In after centuries the reliquaries of Christian saints took the general form of the Jewish ossuaries. But we need not wait that long to learn that the Jews were lenders as well as borrowers. Busy as they were following after the strange gauds of the Greeks, they were no less busy inducing strangers to seek the true faith. Throughout the Eastern World proselytes waited at the gates of the synagogue. Lovers of Horace and Juvenal will remember that Jewish bywords and tricks of speech were as current in the best circles of Rome as they are in New York. The Gentiles found in Judaism a refuge from the very worldliness and wealth admired of their Jewish imitators. Behind the religious appeal it is easy to discern, even from the jibes of the satirists, that they sought the Sabbath's rest and a life of discipline and renunciation. They were glad to share the rabbis' resentment against the vulgar money-grubbing of Rome. Gladly would they echo the Jewish denunciation of "this monster that devours the fat of nations, that forgives all for the sake of money." And if they cherished national grievances or political ambitions against the Empire, they drifted naturally towards the Jews who, for all the apery of their upper classes, smouldered with rebellion and at any moment threatened to set the Near East ablaze.

One of the most illustrious of these converts was Queen Helena of Adiabene. Her kingdom lay between Armenia and Parthia, two troublesome enemies of Rome. Jewish missionaries, worthy contemporaries of Saint Paul, won over not only the queen, but her husband and the two sons who in turn succeeded to the throne. She made frequent pilgrimages to Jerusalem, sent her grandsons there for a proper education, erected a palace in the Lower Quarter of the city, played Lady Bountiful to its citizens in seasons of famine, and lavished gifts on the Temple. One of these gifts, as the Talmud remembers it, reflects perhaps something of her puritan character or betrays the touch of a personal drama—a gold plate engraved with the passage of the Pentateuch (Num. 5, 19:22) which the High Priest read when a wife suspected of infidelity was haled before him.

Queen Helena was buried in the magnificent "Tombs of the Kings" built by the princes of Adiabene near the walls of Jerusalem. An interior door of the vaults (No. 34, left wall) imitating the woodwork of the day, two entire sarcophagi (Nos. 28, 30, second window) and three lids (Nos. 26, 27, 31) still tell their departed glory. For beauty we may well admire the rich lid (No. 26) garlanded with the native fruits and flowers of Palestine. But our interest lingers on the severe puritanic coffin of Helena (No. 28). Her Greek name, like her pagan past, is forgotten. "Zaddah the Queen," reads the inscription. At the moment of its discovery, the sarcophagus was still sealed. The skeleton was preserved intact, the head resting on a little cushion, the hands crossed above the thighs. After a moment's exposure, all save a few fragments crumbled to dust. Of Helena Ha'malka, the "righteous proselyte," there remains her good name and her jawbone (No. 29, first centre case) with its gleaming teeth.

Her grandsons fought beside the Jews in the Roman assault on Jerusalem. It is therefore hardly strange that Jewish coins (No. 37, first centre case) dating from the agony should be found in their tombs. Two of the coins, decorated with the sacred urn, were minted the very year Jerusalem fell (70 c.e.).

When pillage, massacre, and destruction had run their course, the Tenth Legion, whom the Jews had so bitterly discomfited on the Mount of Olives, were set to guard the smoking ruins. A length of the west wall was left standing to shelter them. And their ensign, a wild pig, rose triumphant over the desecrated city. But we need not trust Josephus or a length of wall to know that the Tenth Legion Fretensis were there. A battered brick (No. 20, second centre case) found near the spot is still legible: "L[egionis] decimæ F[re-tensis]." Nor need we wonder what these legionaries thought on, watching over desolation and the fallen Temple of Jeho-vah. They congratulated themselves that, unlike the unlucky Twelfth who had once yielded to the Jews, they had not been sent to the far Euphrates.

The fortress of Masada, over by the Dead Sea, held out two years longer. Josephus has left an appalling picture of its heroic and hopeless defence. In the end, the desperate patriots "embraced their wives and took their children in their arms, and gave the longest parting kisses to them"; and slew one another rather than fall in Roman hands. Eleazar, the last survivor, "set fire to the fortress" and then turned his sword on himself. When the Romans entered they found nothing "but terrible solitude and fire on every side."

A silly lump of scorified metal and stone, melted together by a fearful heat, it lies in a silly green cardboard box (No. 64, case facing second window). But it comes from Masada.

What fate brought this colossal eagle's head (No. 99, beyond second window, cast) to Arsuf, the Apollonia of the ancients and now ten miles north of Tel-Aviv? Roman eagles were plentiful in Palestine, and their presence in the Temple had led to bloody protest. Later, we know, the Jews grew recon-ciled or accustomed to them; and, plucked no doubt of their Imperial significance, placed them on the frieze of their syna-gogues. But this eagle, of all the Roman brood, deserves kindly consideration. A stone medallion hanging from its stony neck bears the Greek monogram of the Emperor Julian. Julian the Apostate the Christians call him. But Julian the Restorer the Jews would call him, had he persisted in his efforts to rebuild the Temple (361 c.e.). We shall never know the secret of the mysterious fire which halted the work and banished forever the new Jerusalem as an object of practical politics.

ᘒᕮᕮᕲ

Meanwhile, with the Temple gone, the Jews had turned their energies and hopes to the synagogue. The institution itself dates from the Babylonian captivity, if not earlier; and it supported the Jews in their wide dispersion both before and after the fall of the Jewish state. Traces of these houses of prayer—a fragment, an inscription, or a contemporary record —have been found as far east as Babylonia and perhaps China, and west in Morocco and Spain. Before the end of the sixth century they are known to have existed in at least 144 cities merely within the bounds of the Roman Empire.

The best preserved ruins of the ancient synagogue survive in Galilee. Within their walls the Talmudic doctors hammered forth the code of laws which still governs orthodox Jewry, and spun about the legal texts their precious web of parable, history, and legend. The lintel from the synagogue of Kefir Berim (No. 116, third window) is typical of the classic style prevalent in the second century c.e. And palæographists are grateful to Joseph Ha-Levi ben Levi, the donor of the lintel, for his long inscription taking credit for the gift and affording future generations an early example of the "square" Hebrew alphabet. The menorah from the synagogue of Gadara has already been discussed.

Something of a puzzle is furnished by the large fragment of a chased bronze platter (No. 97, second centre case), in itself the most notable work of art in the collection. Graven in the design is the familiar menorah assuring us we are dealing with Jewish handiwork—the delicate craft is carried on by Jews to this day in the Orient and North Africa. Near the

candlestick we find the representation of an edicule surmounted by a pediment and faced with double (?) doors.
If the artist intended it for an Ark of the Law or *Aron Ha-
kodesh*, as found in every synagogue, it is one of the earliest
known images of this sacred furniture. But perhaps it is meant
to be the frontispiece of a rock-tomb, or the Hekal of the
Temple, or the Ark of the Covenant such as we find it on a
frieze in Capernaum, or a synagogue itself.

A simple stone capital (No. 95, third window), found like
the platter near Ramleh, propounds a subtler riddle. Its early
Byzantine shape dates it from the fifth or sixth century. One
decorated face displays a wreath in high-relief, and within
the wreath a solemn invocation, *Heis Theos* (One God)! An
older Ionic capital, discovered near at hand, bears the same
Greek formula accompanied by a Hebrew text. It is therefore
possible that the present fragment comes from a synagogue.
But more likely it adorned a Monophysite church which in
its uncompromising monotheism and hatred of images harked
back at once to primitive Christianity and the spirit of the
Talmud. The old battle-cry, *Heis Theos,* which it sounded
through the south, echoes the *Adonai Ehad* of the Jews and
tunes the ear of Asia to the call of the future, *La ilah ill' Allah!*
In this trivial bit of rock we catch, we almost hear, the fer-
ment of the prophets at work leavening a new world.

But the old world was still unconquered, even in Palestine
itself. An ankle carved in stone (No. 9, case before second
window) and bearing the Greek inscription, "Pompeia Lucilia
has offered," is taken to be the foot of a god, perhaps Serapis,
which had been consecrated on his altar. Traces of the Jewish
fight against this form of worship linger in the Talmud. And
again, from Ashkelon, we find a gross relief (No. 80, beyond
first window) of the perennial Astarte flourishing as ever in
the third century as, in varied disguise, she flourishes today.

The three female figures likely represent the goddess in her three planetary phases. Yet if you choose to be physiological rather than astronomical in your interpretation, the sculptor has given you free play. But do not be betrayed by his clumsiness. Astarte, like Venus, was meant to be gentle and fair; and in Ashkelon, as we may see from a gracious plaque (No. 81, second centre case), her favourite symbol was a dove.

As the ancient history of Palestine draws to a close, the Jews tend to disappear in dim confusion. The Louvre commentary on their life, if we have followed it with any sense of its tune, dies away *pianissimo*. The son of Menahem in Haifa becomes a local but an "illustrious" count and functionary in the new Byzantine Empire. "The resting-place of Namosas, son of Menahem, legate and count *clarissimus*," we read on the lintel of his tomb (No. 119, third window); a man of wealth and taste can we judge by the prettily carved fragments of an ivory jewel-box (No. 120, case facing second window) found in his sepulchre and gay with Bacchic rout.

And one Joseph of Sidon, hovering near the homeland, took upon himself, beside the burden of the Law, a time-worn Jewish craft. He has left us his trade-mark (No. 126, case beyond first window) graven in raised Greek letters on a little bronze roller: "Joseph's—*Couturier*." The handle is still attached to the roller wherewith he stamped his snappy Tyrian mantles of impeccable cut and the very latest shades of purple; you may see a line of his models in the neighbouring Phœnician Room. *Shalom* Joseph, father of the Jewish cloak and suit trade!

The Moabite warrior who stood by the way and watched could tell us of fresh hordes up from the desert, bearing again the word of God on the point of their lance. And an Arab milestone (No. 113, third window) brings our story to its term. Caliph Abd al-Malik, who laid the foundations of the

Mosque of Omar on the site of the Temple (691 C.E.), placed it by the new road he built to Jaffa. "From here—eight [Arab] miles to Aelia." Aelia—the Jerusalem that was.

As they enter the gorge by Bab al-Wadi, Jewish taxi-drivers from Tel-Aviv daily pass the spot where it stood.

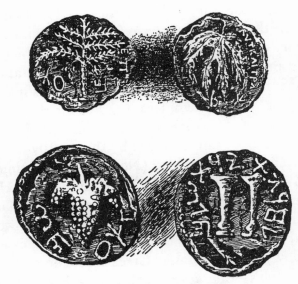

JEWISH COINS OF THE REVOLT UNDER
BAR-COCHBA (132-135 C.E.)
See page 84

CHAPTER III

Paris—

"That Great City"

KING CHILPERIC was in Laon, packing up his baggage to return to Paris. He was in a contented mood, proper to a "do-nothing" king who had recently strangled his wife to marry his mistress, arranged the assassination of his brother, and driven his son to suicide. He was almost in a philosophic mood.

"When I called to bid him good-bye," writes the good Bishop Gregory of Tours, "there came to him a certain Jew named Priscus, a commission agent who supplied him with luxuries. The king took the Jew gently by the hair and said to me, 'Come, priest of God, place your hands on him.' But the Jew resisted. 'Pig-head,' exclaimed the king, 'oh, unbelieving generation that will not acknowledge the Son of God promised by the voice of the prophets.' Whereat the Jew replied, 'God has no need to marry or enrich himself with children, and He suffers no one to share His reign.' " The old debate was on—it had now nearly rounded its sixth century. Bishop Gregory joined in with a bombardment of Biblical citations, some, alas! not to be found in any known edition of the Scriptures. "But despite these arguments, the wretch would not be convinced. The king, seeing him take refuge in stubborn silence, turned to me for a blessing, and left."

Priscus is the first Parisian Jew known to history. Jews were plentiful in Gaul during Roman days, and they probably found their way to Paris long before the Franks. But we do not hear of them until the barbarian invaders, with their fresh Christian zeal, bring them to our attention; King Childebert (554) forbade their appearance in public at Eastertide. In any case, the stiff-necked Priscus, purveyor to his majesty the king, worthily introduces us to his people and their manners in the Merovingian age—and after.

We next meet Priscus and the king in Paris itself. "King Chilperic," continues Bishop Gregory, "had this year [582] baptized many Jews, some of whom he held over the font with his own hands. Most of them, however, were purified in body but not in heart; they lied to God, returned to their old perfidy, and kept the Sabbath while pretending to honour the Lord's Day. Yet Priscus refused at all costs to accept the true faith."

The king wrathfully flung Priscus into prison, "that he be forced against his will." There he "falsely" promised to submit, but bribed the king to release him and delay his baptism until after his daughter's marriage. Meanwhile he quarrelled with a certain Phatir, one of the court Jews whom the king had succeeded in holding over the font. Phatir waylaid Priscus on a Sabbath while he was off unarmed to a secret destination, "no doubt to fulfil the law of Moses," and as a last argument slew him forthwith. After the murder, Phatir and his servants, "who were waiting in the adjoining square, took refuge in the Church of St.-Julien-le-Pauvre." Phatir managed to slip away, while his servants remained inside, stricken with the certainty that the king would promptly execute them. In desperation they permitted one of their number to slay the rest. Sword still in hand, the survivor made a dash from the church, only to be massacred by the mob outside.

Visitors in Paris usually visit the scene of this morsel of Jewish history. They may not know what happened there, but their guide-book has starred St.-Julien as the oldest church in the city. The ancient "refuge" is much remodelled but still charming, and its "adjoining square" gives an excellent view of Notre Dame. Phatir, by the way, paid for his crime. "A few days later he was killed by the relatives of Priscus."

During the next five hundred years, when things went well with the Jews, little is heard of them and less can be seen. Israel, we know, found favour in the sight of Charlemagne and his sons. The great Charles dispatched one Isaac the Jew along with an embassy to Harun-al-Rashid, who, by way of appreciation, returned him with an unicorn's horn. Charlemagne, Harun, and Isaac have become legends, while the horn of the unicorn, which never existed, is still to be seen in the Cluny Museum (Room XXIV).

Towards the end of the eleventh century, the century of William the Conqueror and Rashi of Troyes,[1] the Jews emerge dimly in the light of antiquarian lore, living a little north of the Louvre, obscurely and therefore no doubt happily. The name of their district, Champeaux, has long disappeared, together with its "tall, poorly built tenements and narrow, dark, and crooked lanes, barred by gates at every end."

Disappeared as well are most of the other districts inhabited by the mediæval Jews: the dædal of lanes around the Halle au Blé, or wheat-market, their richer homes in the present Rue de la Cité on the island heart of Paris, where later stood the *Pomme de Pin* of Villon and Rabelais; the *Juiveries* west of Rue St.-Martin, again east of the Châtelet—in the Street of the Devil's Poop (Rue Pet-au-Diable), now up the slope of Mont Ste.-Geneviève, and along the Rue de la Harpe and Rue Galande. The Rue Galande, it is true, preserves an arched wooden cornice or two which might have dribbled mediæval rain on Jewish heads. And the Rue de la Harpe, which was the main street of the Left Bank ghetto, takes its name from

[1] See p. 87.

a twelfth-century house-sign depicting King David playing on his favourite instrument.

Old tax lists supply us with the names of a few of the more prosperous inhabitants of the thirteenth-century Jewries. But no one, least of all the taxpayers and collectors themselves, is longer interested in the pitiful returns of Bernart the Runt, Ancron the Lanky, Jacon the jeweler, Joie the flour-dealer, Mosse the physician, Chiere the butcher, Cressin the hooder, or Haquin the barber.

But if living, our mediæval Jews moved almost traceless through the centuries; once dead, they at least left tombstones behind them. Fastened to the walls of the Thermes adjoining Cluny Museum are a series of these thirteenth-century slabs. They cling to the bricking of the old Roman baths like strange lichens, one dead world rooted to another.

"This is the tombstone," reads the oldest of them (No. 1), "of Solomon, son of the scholar Rabbi Judah, who departed for the Garden of Eden the year 901 [1230 C.E.]; may his soul be bound in the bundle of life." Floria, daughter of our master Rabbi Benjamin (No. 2), Rabbi Jacob ben Hayim (No. 3), Sarah, daughter of Rabbi Joseph Ha-Cohen (No. 4), Precieuse, daughter of Rabbi Eleazar (No. 5), Dame Floria, daughter of Rabbi Isaac (No. 6), our master Rabbi Solomon, son of our master Rabbi Judah (No. 7)—these forgotten souls, anonymous despite their names, departed for Eden at various dates terminating in 1281. The second Judah's slender claim to a place in history turns on the chance that we know of no earlier rabbi, although there may have been dozens, bearing the title *morenu*, "our master."

To stand beneath the massive brick vaults of Roman handiwork where Julian the Christian Apostate and Jewish Restorer slept on his hard pallet and, struggling to drive out the winter's damp, nearly stifled to death from the fumes of his brazier; to stare at the fresh, clean-cut Hebrew characters; to glance with a corner of the eye at the mossy and worn relics, church lintels, madonnas, and gargoyles, strewing the garden just beyond the grilled doorway—puts time out of countenance. But cross the highway beyond the garden (the Boul' Mich' with its street cars, says your waking self) and you enter the shade of the Jewish burial-ground whence came these stones, and fifty like them buried again in the storeroom of the museum. It's the Rue Pierre-Sarazin and the publishing house of Hachette? Nonsense! Before you, towards the Seine, lies the Jewish quarter in the Rue de la Harpe and Rue Galande; there is the Jewish mill across the river from St.-Julien-le-Pauvre, and just behind the church is the Rue du Fouarre, the Street of the Straw, where the schools are gathered and scholars of twenty "nations" sit on their straw beds in the cold halls and talk of how Nicholas Donin, shrewd apostate, will refute the old Jew magician, Yehiel, or King Louis will know the reason why. Dante, too, remembers that Vico degli Strami, and the straw that is none too clean.

Today there is nothing left that Donin or Dante could recall but the little church, these brick vaults, the name of Rue de la Harpe—and perhaps the tale of how Yehiel entertained King Louis.

Yehiel ben Joseph, called the "Sire Vives," presided over three hundred Talmud students, among others none less than Isaac of Corbeil, Meir of Rothenburg and Isaac ben Hayim— you can see part of Isaac's cabbalistic commentary on the Pentateuch in the Bodleian at Oxford and the tombstone of the wife of a Rabbi Yehiel, whether it be the same or no, in the courtyard of the Carnavalet museum here in Paris.[1]

Yehiel passed for a master of magic in his day, and among other magic he made a lamp which would burn without oil. Now King Louis IX, as a pious king should, hated the Jews, for, as he maintained, they were a poison to the realm. He

[1] See p. 84.

was not at all pleased with the precarious disputes between scholastic doctors and Talmudic scholars which figured among the popular sports of the time. The best argument against a Jew was a sword, "thrust," as he says in his quaint way, "into his belly as far as it will go." But his curiosity over magic lamps got the better of his piety, and he paid Yehiel ben Joseph a visit.

The knocker on Yehiel's door possessed the power of rooting to the spot whoever touched it, and King Louis found himself motionless on the rabbi's threshold. When Yehiel learned the identity of his visitor he courteously released him, and he explained the virtue of his lamp "which in place of oil was fed by a substance unknown at that time." Overcome by the demonstration, the king loaded Yehiel with honours, and was about to depart peacefully when his courtiers pointed out that Yehiel, for all his politeness, refused to drink a cup of wine which the king had touched. Whereupon the king ordered wine to be brought and Yehiel to drink it. Yehiel replied, "It is indeed forbidden me to drink of the wine which you or any Gentile has touched, but let the king order a basin of water to be brought and let him wash his hands in it." The king did so, and Yehiel instantly drank the water. "It is not your touch I fear," he said; "it is the Law."

Later on King Louis burned all the Talmuds in Paris and became a saint, and Yehiel went to Palestine and died.

On our way to the site of the older ghetto north of the river we may profitably linger before the façade of Notre Dame. A mediæval cathedral was a story-book for the people. Its sculpture and glass retell the lessons and dogmas of the faith. At the portals of Notre Dame we are greeted, for example, by the Last Judgment, the death of the Virgin, the symbols of the four gospels, and an array of saints and apostles. And here, as occasionally elsewhere, we are likewise met, on either side of the centre portal, by two large female figures representing the Church Triumphant and the Synagogue Defeated.

The Synagogue is quickly identified by every attribute the mediæval mind could devise for a fallen power. A snake coils about her brow, blindfolds her eyes, and leers with open fangs above her drooping head. In her left hand she holds a broken lance, its dulled and useless point falling behind her shoulders. Five tablets, the five books of Moses, are slipping upside down from the nerveless fingers of her right hand, seeking their place at the crown tumbled at her feet. The merest hind could grasp the contrast between this dejected creature and her neighbour, the Victorious Church, with the crown firm on her young self-assured brow, a flower on her breast, a potent sceptre in one hand and a chalice in the other, a full purse hanging from her belt, and behind her head not the point of a broken lance, but a halo.

Mediæval theologians and their artists were not accustomed to treat the Old Testament, likewise a Jewish product, in this mordant fashion. The four major prophets which are usually set as a pendant to the four gospels, the twelve patriarchs which stand by the twelve apostles, the sacrifice of Isaac which was felt to prefigure the agony of Jesus, all the favourite characters and scenes from the old Jewish sources are repeatedly portrayed in stone and glass, with sympathetic admiration. But the Church could well afford to be reverent towards these Jewish heroes—they were all long and safely dead. Not so the Synagogue.

In the early days when the Church was less conscious of her power, perhaps because her power was hardly questioned, her artists were altogether gallant in their portrayal of the defeated rival. In ninth- and tenth-century Carolingian ivories (at the South Kensington Museum in London and the Bibliothèque Nationale in Paris) representing the Crucifixion, the

Synagogue draped in a royal mantle may be seen seated on her throne and brandishing unbroken her banner and sword.

But much has happened between the carving of these ivories and the cutting of our statues on the front of Notre Dame. The Crusades had given Christian knights their first full taste of Jewish blood. Christian commerce, stimulated by these same Crusades, took notice of the purse hanging from the girdle of the Synagogue and grew eager to transfer it to a girdle closer home. Growing tastes for luxury and the refinements of civilization increased both the opportunities and the odium of Jewish usury. In the thirteenth, that "greatest of centuries," a wave of heresy, obscurely and perhaps not altogether wrongfully attributed to the influence of Judaism, brought the Inquisition into being, Innocent III denounced Christian protection of Jews, and the Lateran Council decreed they must wear the "wheel" as a badge of shame. The popular arts were quick to exploit this new attitude. Hymnals and mystery plays pictured the Jews and their synagogue in an infamous light.

The imagists of Notre Dame were not alone in following the new fashion.[1] In the south portal of the cathedral of Strasbourg, the Synagogue, vastly superior as sculpture to the restored work of Notre Dame, is again represented blindfolded, but this time shorn even of her mantle. In the north portal of the cathedral of Bamberg she stands on a column, to which are attached a Jew in his characteristic pointed hat and for his companion a devil. Notre Dame of Trèves, St.-Seurin of Bordeaux, and Notre Dame of Rheims are likewise furnished with Defeated Synagogues. At Amiens, before the main portal of the cathedral, the symbol for the enemy is more subtle—a withered tree with an ax laid to the trunk. And anyone who chooses to climb the tower of Notre Dame at Paris will find, among the chimeræ and grotesque beasts and devils, a hectic Jew capped by a pointed bonnet.

[1] See pp. 95, 315 (Bourges, Wittenberg).

Up in that mighty belfry, far from the passions of the street, one cannot be unsympathetic towards these imagists or their masters. The Synagogue *was* the enemy. It was worse—an embarrassment. The Church could not afford to destroy the Jew as any common heretic or unbeliever, for even as Innocent III was compelled to admit, they were "the living witnesses of the true religion." Yet what unruly and dangerous witnesses! "As long as there remained a member of the Old Faith who denied the New," writes Darmesteter in a memorable passage, "the Church felt ill at ease in its heritage. More than one Christian, entering a sordid ghetto house to raise a loan or have his horoscope read, and loitering in the twilight to speak of deep and holy things, left for home a troubled soul and fit for burning. The Jew was skilled at laying bare the weak spots in the Church. To this end he had not only a profound knowledge of Scriptures, but a wit sharpened by oppression. He was the master of incredulity, the mentor of rebellion. He is to be found at work in the immense blasphemy plants of a Kaiser Frederick or the princes of Swabia and Aragon. It was he who forged the weapons of reason and irony which the sceptics of the Renaissance and the Free-Thinkers of the seventeenth century were to wield with deadly effect. A sarcasm of Voltaire is nothing but the last resounding echo of a quip whispered six centuries before in the dark alleys of the ghetto."

We shall never understand the survival of Israel if we imagine the mediæval Jew weak at soul and hunted in spirit. He felt himself to be a power, however fallen, and the warfare unremittingly waged upon his person proved him as such. The Lateran Council (1215), among other restrictions, again forbade him showing his face in public from Good Friday to Easter. It would be a mistake, based on subsequent unhappy history, to suppose this decree a measure taken for his own safety. You do not know the mediæval Jew. "We hear that some of them," reads the decree, "do not hesitate on such days to dress themselves in their best finery and mock the Christians who in memory of the Passion go clothed in solemn mourning." That terrible Jew flanked with devils on the tower of Notre Dame is a fit symbol of the fear of the Church.

Directly north of the Rue de Rivoli, between the Tour St.-Jacques and the Hôtel de Ville, lies a network of narrow streets still recalling the "dark alleys" of the mediæval ghetto. A mere slit running from the Rue St.-Martin to the Rue Beaubourg, the Rue de Venise "is one of the oldest and narrowest streets in Paris." It was once called the Ruelle des Usuriers (Usurers' Lane)—Jewish enough—and Baedeker waxes almost dramatic in declaring "it still retains its cut-throat aspect of the fourteenth century." "Cut-throat" it undoubtedly was, if we think of the fate of its Jews. Near at hand are the equally ancient Rue des Lombards, by its name another street of money-lenders, and the Rue Quincampoix, which must have been singularly attractive to the Jews, for in the eighteenth century, nearly four hundred years after their banishment from its charms, they sought it out once more. The whole district has been condemned to destruction, and you must hurry if through nostalgia or curiosity you desire a breath of air from the good old days.

A few blocks east (No. 24 Rue des Archives) stands an eighteenth-century church, now devoted to the Protestant cult. It is a landmark in the Jewish history of Paris. Here, in the year 1290, lived a Jew named Jonathas. A Christian woman pawned her best clothes with Jonathas, and when it came Easter and time to wear them, she lacked the money to redeem them. So instead of a cash payment she agreed to bring Jonathas a wafer of the Host. Jonathas took it and attempted to cut it to pieces with a knife. Blood began to flow from it. In terror he threw it into the hearth, but it danced in the flames like a bird of fire and refused to be consumed. Desperately he plunged it next into a cauldron of boiling water, and the water became crimson but the wafer remained whole. He tried to seize it, but now it flew about the room out of his grasp. Despite all his efforts, he could not destroy it. Meanwhile, his little son, standing at the door of the house and noticing passers-by on their way to Easter services, called out to them, "It is no use going to pray to your God—my father has killed him."

So the people of the neighbourhood, learning of the scandal, dragged Jonathas to Simon Matiffart, Bishop of Paris, who exhorted him to renounce his false notions of religion. And when he refused, he was promptly ordered to be burnt alive. As he approached the pyre he exclaimed, "Ah, if only I had by me a certain book which lies in my house, the fire could not harm me." The bishop was a reasonable man, ever seeking the truth where he could find it, and he ordered the book to be brought and given to Jonathas. As a manifest proof, however, that his punishment was agreeable to Heaven, the Jew was consumed forthwith, book and all.

The house "where God was boiled," as Queen Clemence called it, was shortly after rebuilt into a chapel, and then, out of the proceeds of the property of Jonathas and his Jewish neighbours, a monastery was added to the chapel. Later the monastery was abolished, and in 1754 the chapel was rebuilt by one Dominican, Brother Claude, who, as Dulaure remarks, "might have been a good monk but was certainly a bad architect." Until the Protestants took over the church (in 1812), it still preserved the knife which Jonathas plunged into the Host.[1]

A step farther east is the Rue des Rosiers, where the Jews must have lived before their expulsion, much as they do today. Two corners along this modern ghetto lies the Rue Duval, which at least as early as the fifteenth century was called the Rue des Juifs. It is a pity the name has been lost, for with due

[1] See pp. 169, 208 (Segovia, Brussels).

regard to royal edicts and the police *Inspecteur des Juifs*, Israel has clung tenaciously to this little street throughout the centuries. The *kosher* restaurants which flank it today are the lineal descendants of the "secret" Jewish inns of the eighteenth century, and so persistently have the Jews been associated with it, tradition points to a house which has harboured the race since mediæval times. If so, the traditional cookery has vanished, unless we suppose that in the reign of St.-Louis, the French Jews ate *gefüllte* fish.

Upon their "final" expulsion from Paris and France in 1394, the Jews, perforce, left several memorials to the city. Their last years in Lutetia were passed in suffering sack and extortion. The riots of 1380 drove them for shelter to the old prison of the Grand Châtelet, which occupied the present *place* of that name, and there the children of the refugees received enforced baptism. A year before the exile, seven Jews, accused of abducting an apostate, were condemned to be whipped of a Sabbath at the markets of Les Halles where modern tourists come to eat onion-soup in the small hours of the morning; on the next Sabbath the same seven were whipped in the ill-famed Place de Grève, opposite the present Hôtel de Ville; and on the third Sabbath in the Place Maubert —where today the statue of Étienne Dolet stands as a monument to Christian kindness. Finally, our seven were fined 10,-000 livres to have a new bridge built from "la porte de Petit Pont jusques à la porte de derrière de l'Hôtel Dieu." And the spoil derived from the banishment of the Jews was used, in part, to repair the Pont Neuf and build the chapel in the Château of Vincennes. One may still admire the two bridges and the chapel.

The departure of the Jews is related, in a rather obscure fashion, to the curious figure of Nicolas Flamel, alchemist, necromancer, and philanthropist. Flamel appears to have been a scribe and was certainly a poor and unimportant person towards the end of the fourteenth century. Suddenly he became enormously wealthy, and since stock-markets were unknown, his wealth was attributed to magic. According to one account, which was picked up as far away as Turkey and as late as 1704, Flamel learned, from the papers of a Jew which were confided to him on the eve of expulsion, the secret of making gold. Leaving legend aside, one may imagine that Flamel, as a friend and confidant of the Jews, enriched himself in handling their affairs preparatory to their departure. In any case, Flamel threw his money about piously. He helped build the Church of St.-Jacques-de-la-Boucherie (the tower, a later structure, still stands), and among his charities is a hospice not too far away, at 51 Rue de Montmorency, and now converted into a restaurant.

It is reputed the oldest dated house in Paris (1407), its stone façade is handsomely carved, and since the food is excellent and there are more than three centuries to wait until the return of the Jews, one may go there to lunch.

EARLIEST KNOWN PORTRAIT OF A MEDIEVAL
JEW (ENGLAND 1227)

CHAPTER IV

The Newer Paris

RUE SUGER is a narrow street, one block long, leading west from the Place St.-André-des-Arts. Near at hand the Place St.-Michel resounds with modern traffic. At a large window above St.-André the ghosts of Little Billee and Taffy look down at you from the Laird's studio. But we are concerned with Bohemians of an older age. In the eighteenth century Rue Suger was called Rue du Cimitière-St.-André-des-Arts, and in it centered the life of the Portuguese or Sephardic Jewry, one of the three Jewish communities then reëstablished in Paris.

After three centuries of enforced absence the return of the Jews to Paris in the reign of Louis XV was one of the signs of the times. The Age of Reason was at dawn, and men remembered the word of Montaigne, "After all, 'tis setting one's conjectures at a very high price, to cause a man to be roasted alive upon them." So, although despised, the Jews began no longer to be banished or burnt. France was turning from Charles IX to Voltaire. And, equally favourable to the Jews, France was turning in a giddy rage to John Law, *systèmes,* Mississippi Bubbles, Casanovan lotteries, and the gods of the casino. The thirst for gambling, whether on the Bourse or over the green table, and with it the need for cash, loans, and pawns brought the Jews a precarious but hearty welcome. They returned to Paris under the safe-conduct of Tolerance and Speculation.

Ashkenazic Jews drifted in from Alsace-Lorraine, Germany, and Poland. Artisans, copper-engravers, diamond-cutters, tradesmen, fortune-hunters, army purveyors, and bankers, they settled in the former haunts of their race, along the Rue St.-Martin, north of the river. The Jews from the Four Communities of the Comtat Venaissin,[1] who had never left France, congregated in the little streets, long disappeared, around the church of St.-Germain-des-Prés and the Café des Deux Magots. And the Sephardic Jews, from Bordeaux and Bayonne in the south and from Holland in the north, occupied St.-André and the Rue Suger.

They lived, akin to bootleggers, accepted but harried and without rights. Their synagogues, remarks a Jewish traveller of the time, "exist only by a miracle." The "miracle," although our traveller, whom we shall meet again, would never have acknowledged it, was the work of that miracle-hater, Voltaire. The tragedy of their situation, prolonged through the ages, is compassed in the words of the Sire de Heusse des Cotes: "Jews are not a people one need handle with regard; they deserve no consideration; they are not citizens of the state." *They are not citizens,* here lay the source of Jewish woes since the days of Theodosius II, and here was to lay the spring and master-word of the Jewish program for the future. But the Rights of Man and the Sanhedrin of Napoleon are still nearly a century away.

Like the district east of Rue St.-Martin, which we have already visited, the Rue Suger, though it has lost its old name, still preserves its old character. Big-bellied houses sinking backward on their beams for age, gracious Louis XV doorways, hand-wrought grillings, gas-lamps that almost recall the old *lanternes*, little has changed since our traveller, Rabbi

[1] See chap. VII.

Haim David Azulai, come from Hebron to collect funds for his theological seminary, paced its pavement in amazement. We can readily imagine him, in turban and robe, Oriental fashion, entering the house now labelled No. 3. For from 1770 to 1826 this house sheltered the synagogue of the Sephardim. It is, however, useless to follow on his heels; the synagogue occupied no more than a room or two—perhaps the abandoned chapel of the Collège de Boissy, on the second floor—and has vanished long ago, and with it Saul Cremieux, who furnished the oil for a year, Isaac Oliviera, Abraham Salvador, Moyse Spire, Aaron Serur, David Cavaillon, Moyse Carcassone, and all their tribe.

Rabbi Azulai, as he explains himself, had cause to be amazed. The streets of Paris—he visited them in 1777—"are wide enough for two coaches to pass at ease." The city itself "is of great beauty, and everything is to be found in it, but all at a very high price, except prostitution, which is very cheap." He gaped at the Pont Neuf, "a great bridge, long and wide," where, it is said, "never in the twenty-four hours is there an instant without a white horse, a monk, or a trull passing by." He was puzzled beyond words at the Christian lords and ladies who took him up, a mere Jew, and begged from him morsels of Cabbala and a blessing. He had not read, of course, Anatole France's *At the Sign of the Queen Pedauque*.

But more than all, he was confounded at the new spirit manifest among the younger Jews. One young Portuguese, Jacob Lopez Laguna, no doubt often to be met with on the Rue Suger, dared dispute his authority. "I was much pained and afterwards made inquiries about him. I was told extraordinary things; my informants said definitely, they had had it from himself, from his own mouth, that he had studied the books of Voltaire." This was not all. "What is more, a man of standing told me that here in Paris, at the table of the master of the house, he did not drink wine prepared by Gentiles, but that he would go forthwith and drink with him in a Christian inn." Surely nights, around the corner on the Place St.-Michel, our rabbi must have heard these young Voltairians carousing, hot-headed Moyse Astruc, Salomon Ravel, and Israel Dalpuget, flashing their swords, Jews though they were, and rowing with the police. They grow impatient, these firebrands, to have it said *they are not citizens.*

We may visit the Sephardim in their last resting-place, the old Jewish burial-ground at 44 Rue de Flandre, beyond the Rue Faubourg St.-Martin, in La Villette.

The quiet garden dotted with tombstones lies, surrounded by walls, at the end of a courtyard. The earliest burials date from 1720, but despite its present air of tranquillity, the peace the Jews found there was, for many years, as illicit and troubled as the prayers in their synagogue.

Towards the end of the eighteenth century the house facing the street was an inn, the Auberge d'Etoile, and the innkeeper, one Matard, eked out his revenues by burying Jews in his garden, fifty livres for an adult, twenty or thirty for a child. Then Matard was discovered skinning his horses and cattle in the garden "and mixing the flesh and bones of these animals with the relics of the dead." So in 1780, after protracted negotiations with the authorities on the part of that paradoxical figure, Liefmann Calmer, "opulent" Baron of Picquigny, aided no doubt by the increasing inroads of tolerance, the Jewish nation, *la nation juive,* secured legal possession of a burial-ground in Paris, for the first time since the Middle Ages.

The oldest existing stone commemorates Salomon Perpignan, who was, the inscription tells us, "one of the Founders of the Royal Free School of Design, established in 1767, under the glorious reign of Louis XV, in the city of Paris, for the improvement of the Arts, and appointed by Mons. Lenoir, Lieutenant Governor General of Paris, to the office of Syndic of the Avignon Jews." He died February 22, 1781.

The next grave of interest testifies to the most decisive turn in Jewish history since the fall of Jerusalem. The tombstone of one Patto of Bayonne speaks no longer of the glorious reign of Louis XV or any other Louis. "The Most High God," it says, "has called me in my twenty-third year. I prefer my present lot to that of slavery. Oh immortal soul, seek to live free, or follow me, like a good republican! Here is the resting-place of the blessed Samuel Fernandes Patto de Bayonne, died the 28th of Prairial of the Year II of the French Republic, One and Indivisible." There are more than echoes of the National Assembly's oratory in these few lines; for the Jew, there is the *fact* of an Abbé Grégoire, and together with young Patto is buried forever the reproach, *they are not citizens*.

The stones echo the typical names of the southland: a Nonez and Silveyra of Bayonne, Rebecca Henriques of Bordeaux, the "lovely" Rebecca Cappadoce Pereira of Amsterdam, the "generous, honoured, and intelligent" Elie Ravel and his "chaste and much respected" wife, Rebecca Iturah, and many others who still live in the diary of Rabbi Azulai. And here is a Dal-puget—one Mordecai—whose brothers or cousins played the dandy in the arcades of the Palais Royal. One wonders what happened to their mock titles (Aron Dalpuget used to call himself M. d'Aroniche and Israel Dalpuget no less than M. le Marquis d'Albuche) when it came to ordering their tombs in the garden of Innkeeper Matard.

It will surprise no one who has read Zangwill's *The King of Schnorrers* or who has followed the tragi-comedy of Jewish snobbery, to learn that the despised Askenazic or "German" Jews of the period must sleep apart from their Sephardic brethren. Their burial-ground lies at the other side of Paris, south of the Porte d'Orléans, between Nos. 94 and 96 Grande

Rue, Montrouge. The entry is through a small gate (key at the offices of the Paris Consistoire, 44 Rue de la Victoire).

Cerf Berr, who was to play an active part in securing the "emancipation" of the Jews, likewise secured this resting-place "for all Jews, of either sex, and of German, Polish, Dutch, or any other nationality." It is a phrase; no Sephardim are there.

The German, Polish, and Dutch Jews rattled no swords and shrank from assumed titles and other evidences of "assimilation," so it is not surprising to find their epitaphs, unlike the Sephardim, written with one exception in Hebrew. The names, too, carry us to another world, one where, according to modern romantic notions of the ghetto, we find "real" Jewish life. Beila, Scheinka, Rechela, Klercha, Yentela, Edel, Milka, Blümela, Fratcha, Reizela and ("the chaste, young, pious, and fair") Goutrat for the women; Wolf, Asher, Zevi, Juspa, Yeisl, Jekel, and Josel for the men.

The oldest of the eighty-six surviving stones dates from 1788. Burials ceased in 1809.

Most of the epitaphs breathe a pious rhetoric, in obvious contrast to the simplicity of the mediæval Jews and the worldliness of the Sephardim. "Here lies a generous man," says one of the older stones, "who followed the ways of righteousness. He lived by the work of his hands all his years on earth, and his trust was in God. He fed the hungry, far and near. His name was known with esteem: Solomon Zalman Levi of Hassfurth. He died, was buried, and departed for Paradise Tuesday, the 8th of Adar, in the year 5558 [1798]." A baker, Aaron Moses son of Berl of Berlin, "of a righteous family," has noted on his tomb that he "conducted his bakery with uprightness." A young scholar earns the following praise: "Here lies a just and honourable man, a prince of the Law, a fountain of wisdom. His name befitted him and he was worthy of it; scarcely thirty-seven years old he was a light [Ur] in the study of Talmud, Joseph Uri Schraga, called Feiss, son of the departed Zevi of Eydtkuhen and son-in-law of the most pious Gaon and divine cabbalist, the departed Wolf Berl." The women fare equally well: "Here lies a woman of valour," reads a typical tribute, "whose husband loved her as the apple of his eye and set her above all his gold and fortune; all her life she taught her sons the way of righteousness; just, up-right, and reputed, under the name of Eve Leah Gütele, wife of Zechariah Mendele Pozna, she died enjoying a good name, on the good day [Saturday] and was buried Sunday, the 10th day of the month of consolations [Ab] with great honours, in the year 5569 [1809]."

One grave may hold us for a moment, for the occupant lives elsewhere than in his epitaph. "Here," it reads, "lies the Parnas and Manhig and administrator of the community of Paris, the pious Jekel, son of the holy Aaron Segal Gold-schmidt of Amsterdam." We may meet Parnas Jacob Gold-schmidt in the pages of Rabbi Azulai. "Then I went," he writes, "with David Naquet, to Jacob Goldschmidt, a rich and eminent Ashkenazi. It was a miserable day; the snow was fall-ing, the distance was great, and we could not find a coach. When we got there he behaved as all Ashkenazim do, full of doubts and arguments; the end of it was he gave us twelve francs."

A street name, Rue de l'Abbé Grégoire (just beyond the Bon Marché), is all that commemorates the bestowal of citizen-ship on the Jews, one of the minor but significant works of the Revolution. The service of Henri Grégoire, a member of the cloth, in emancipating the Jews and enabling France to set an example to Europe as the United States had previously set an example to France, is perhaps too well known for repe-tition. "Fifty thousand Frenchmen arose this morning slaves; it depends on you whether they shall go to bed freemen"— these words of the Abbé Grégoire, uttered before the National Assembly (October 1, 1789), deserve in a city of inscriptions at least a granite slab.

The work of emancipation was consolidated, with a typical gesture, by Napoleon. He summoned from its two thousand years of sleep the Sanhedrin, and seventy-one rabbis and laymen out of the four corners of Europe met, February 9, 1807, in the Hôtel de Ville of Paris (the present Hôtel de Ville is an approximate replica of the old building, burnt under the Commune), and gave Napoleon and the world satisfaction on elementary points of Jewish law. For himself, Napoleon was doubtless more anxious to gain Jewish support in his campaigns against Germany (and he got it) than in learning whether Judaism forbade polygamy. Still at work, the Sanhedrin was suddenly dissolved a month later. A certain Count Chaptal gives a curious reason. "I was dining one day," he writes, "with the Emperor. Suddenly the Cardinal Fesch entered with a troubled look. The Emperor remarked it and asked, 'What is the matter?' 'Matter enough,' said Fesch. 'Do you want to bring the world to an end?' 'What do you mean?' asked the Emperor. 'Don't you know,' Fesch replied, 'the Scriptures say that the world will come to an end when the Jews are reunited as a nation?' Everyone laughed. But the Emperor changed his tone, appeared troubled, arose, and went to his study with the cardinal, and did not reappear until an hour later. And the next day the Sanhedrin was dissolved."

Crossing the battlefield of Marengo a score of years later, the young Heine takes occasion to say, "What is the greatest task of our times? Emancipation. Not merely the emancipation of Irishmen, Greeks, Frankfurter Jews, West Indian blacks, and similarly oppressed peoples, but the emancipation of the whole world that has now found tongue and breaks the iron reins of Privilege." But it has proved a task which in its very success has often turned its beneficiaries into victims. An older Heine learned this to his cost. "The later history of the Jews," he learned to say, "is tragic, and yet to write of it would only provoke laughter—this is the most tragic of all." He was to learn even bitterer things.

Lovers of Heine may rightfully wish to visit the Paris, or what remains of it, where he spent almost half his life. Some will seek in it the haunts of the sweetest of German lyric poets, others the camping-grounds of the soldier in "the liberation war of humanity," and others again the pleasure-grounds of the happy Hellene, "the great Pagan No. 2." And lastly, there may be those who, not without piety, wish to follow the "shuffling steps" of the century's exemplar of *Judenschmerz*.

The Passage des Panoramas (leading from the Boulevard Montmartre) is inseparable from the memories of Heine the Pagan; there he sought his adorable French teachers, whom he repaid with immortality in his *Neue Gedichte*, and now, when the electric lights and the living Dianes and Clarisses desert the old place of nights, his ghost perhaps returns "to see," as he once confessed to Boerne, "if none of the girls I know has a new dress." He was obsessed with the dainties of this arcade. Even Heine the Jew, who treasured his manuscript copy of Judah Halevi, remembers to compare its binding with the colored bonbon boxes "of Marquis in the Passage Panoramas." Marquis still sells his bonbons there.

Heine the revolutionary frequented the arcades and cafés of the Palais Royal, where "Louis Philippe reigns upstairs, and downstairs M. Chevet sells his sausages"; more than once he visits Rothschild, 15 Rue Lafitte, and with something more than mockery calls him "the greatest revolutionary of our day"; at 50 Rue St.-Sauveur he dines with Balzac and Eugène Sue and disputes against the monarchism of the one and the socialism of the other; and with Boerne we see him walking in the gardens of the Tuileries where "the chestnut trees, with their thousand green tongues, softly sing the Marseillaise."

He met his incomparable Mathilde in the Passage de Choiseul, off the Rue St.-Augustin (1834?), where he took her from selling gloves to poet-keeping; and he married her in the Church of St.-Sulpice (1841). In 1834 he was living at No. 3 Cité Bergère (behind the present Palace Music Hall) where Grillparzer found him in two small rooms, with a library of borrowed books; the house and the whole charming little lane remain unchanged. Later, his apartment on the fifth floor of 41 Rue du Faubourg Poissonière received, among its distinguished visitors, two not unknown Jewish "champions of the Holy Spirit"—Ferdinand Lassalle and Karl Marx. And still later (1848), when misfortune and disease brought on the final attack of *Judenschmerz*, he spread his famous "mattress-grave," strewn with tears and wit, in the third-floor-back of 50 Rue d'Amsterdam. Here he wrote his Hebrew Melodies, *Prinzessin Sabbath, Jehuda Halevy,* and *Disputation,* and here he wrote his last judgment on Emancipation: "I am no longer 'the freest German after Goethe,' no longer the Great Pagan No. 2, no longer the life-loving, hale and hearty Hellene; I am now only a poor Jew sick unto death, a picture of misery, an unhappy man."

After six years of suffering, he was moved to the fifth floor of 3 Avenue Matignon, and from its balcony caught between his fallen lids a glint of the Champs Elysées sun; and there he died (February 19, 1856).

> No mass will be sung,
>   No *kaddosh* will be said,
> Nothing said and nothing sung
>   Around my dying bed.

It is (imperfectly rendered) the opening words of the little poem to Mathilde, bidding her visit him in the cemetery of Montmartre.

The grave is easily found (to the left on Avenue de la Cloche). The portrait bust by Hasselriis, and the gold harp on the shaft are unmistakable. A flower-pot at the base of the shaft spills with visiting-cards from Germans the world over; the inscription notes that the monument was erected by the Free-Thinkers of Vienna; behind it rises a neighbouring shaft marked with the name "Paradise," provocative of Heine's neatest wit; and though neither mass nor *kaddosh* was said, a few pebbles will often be found laid tenderly on the tomb, the traditional homage of the Jew at the grave of a martyr or a saint.

The ways of emancipation have been peculiar and many. Not every Jew found in the new freedom a bed of pain. Yet, in the fitful light we have been pursuing up and down the back streets and alleys of the centuries, with Yehiel's words ringing in our ears, "It is not your touch I fear; it is the Law," and with the image before our eyes of the Synagogue standing obdurate if defeated at the central door of Notre Dame, there is a placid irony in contemplating the graves of even the more fortunate of these freedmen: Fromental Halévy—he sleeps near Heine—who bore the same name as the authors of the *Ode to Zion* and the *Lecha Dodi* and who from his bed of roses left to the world *La Juive*; Jacques Offenbach the son of a *hazan* and creator of burlesque opera; Ludwig Boerne, sleeping in Père Lachaise amid, as Heine maliciously notes, "generals of the Empire and actresses of the Comédie française—dead eagles and dead parrots"; and, likewise in Père Lachaise, Baron Achille Fould, who provided a blessed example of the equality now enjoyed by the Jews, that is to say, again according to Heine, "the ability to attain, just like a Christian, the highest political office without any merit except money." But it is wiser not to go to Père Lachaise. Instead we may linger in Montmartre by the grave of Renan, or place a wreath, without thorn for him or for us, on the tomb of Solomon Munk—a free scholar in Israel.

Two notes, the echoes of not unfamiliar music, close for us the century.

The one, a bugle-call on the parade-ground of the military prison in the Rue Cherche-Midi: Captain Dreyfus, emancipated Jew, is being freed from his uniform and degraded with full military dishonours.

The other, a sound of wind through the trees. Back again in the gardens of the Tuileries, the year 1895, a handsome bearded Jew is pacing, and drinking in the greenery, the sedative precision of the lawns and walks. If his mind is seeking its customary historic parallels, it is conjuring up the figures of those two Jews, journalists like himself, two foreigners writing feuilletons for the German press, two dreamers and knights of the Holy Spirit who likewise found this ground sacred and these chestnuts "trees of freedom." Then the bearded Jew, the song of the trees in his ears, hurries again to his near-by room in the Hôtel de Castille, Rue Cambon, just behind the Ritz bar. And we see Theodor Herzl sitting on the edge of his bed and writing another chapter of *The Jewish State*.

SHOFAR, OR RAM'S HORN
See page 30

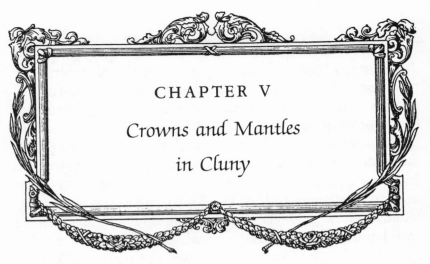

CHAPTER V

Crowns and Mantles
in Cluny

THE wonder-working Rabbi Judah Löw of Prague lived,
says the legend, in an old house presenting a dismal sordid appearance to the outer world. But behind its humble
door, by a miracle, stretched sumptuous apartments radiant
with wealth and beauty.

Although, in stern fact, the ghettos concealed no such hidden treasures, by miracle or otherwise the Jews strove as well
as they could to adorn the life behind their wretched walls.[1]
And like other peoples they spent their best efforts on their
dearest passion, the worship of God. But their religious art,
born of the furtive circumstances of the ghetto, was of necessity random and transient. It was likewise imitative. Lacking
a permanent folk-life to inspire their own creative powers,
Western Jews like better men before them borrowed the
beauty of their neighbours.

Yet the objects upon which they spent their borrowed beauty
were native to their faith, and to that extent distinctive. The
Torah and its trappings have no likeness in the Christian or
Moslem cult. Again, Jewish ceremonies, more often than
Christian, belonged to the home; and Passover dishes, Purim
plates, Hanuka candelabra, and Sabbath cup and spice-box
tell in art the intimate and peculiar life of the people. Our

[1] See p. 296 (Regensburg).

introduction has already discussed how far this art was the work of Jewish craftsmen.

The same circumstances that stunted the originality of Western Jewish art brought about its rapid destruction. Mobs, sack, and flight made short work of religious furniture. Little survives earlier than the sixteenth century. Books the Jews clung to, or Christian collectors prized and rescued, but a Sabbath cup of the thirteenth century is indeed a find.

* * *

The excellency of the Cluny collection (Cluny museum, room XVIII) lies in both the age and rare quality of its objects. Frankfort, Berlin, Prague, and the Jewish Theological Seminary of New York can boast of larger collections and sometimes items of greater historic interest, but Cluny more than elsewhere gives a rounded view, seen through exquisite specimens, of the art that enriched the synagogue and home across the ghetto centuries.

Moreover it permits us to follow the Jew step by step through the major experiences of his life. From the eighth day of his birth to the hour he breathed away his soul, he lived by the rule of his faith, and its every turn and tool received an impress of beauty. To call this beauty religious art is misleading, unless we understand that for the Jew there was no other, because life itself was religion.

Eight days old the Jewish boy enters the covenant of Abraham. His mother usually embroiders or has embroidered for the occasion a long swaddling-cloth, which she later presents to the synagogue and which is destined to wrap together the scrolls of the Law. It is a happy gesture, binding the badge of the covenant about the Law, at once pledging the youth of Israel to its defence and invoking on them its instruction. The name of the new son and his date of birth are woven in gay colours on the band, together with appropriate sentiments expressed in a wish that the child grow up to know the Law, to stand beneath the wedding canopy, and to give himself to good works—a wish that is the program of Jewish life. What mother patiently stitched the Cluny bands (cases 2, 3 and 4)[1] in satin and linen, and whether their unknown sons lived to stand beneath the wedding canopy we never shall know; but in any event the sixteenth-century bands from Italy (case 3) are much prized for their age and the seventeenth- and eighteenth-century bands (cases 4 and 2) for their delicate workmanship and beauty.[2]

Implements pertaining to the rite of circumcision may be seen in case 3. Two of the four knives dating from the seventeenth and eighteenth centuries are distinguished for their finely graven handles: one in steel with the figure of a seventeenth-century *mohel* or officiant holding a cup and knife in his hands; the other engraved in crystal with the scene of the sacrifice of Isaac. This case likewise contains an eighteenth-century silver plaque, bearing in repoussé the same scene, with the Hebrew inscription, "And he bound Isaac his son and laid him on the altar" (Gen. 22:9). Near it stands a small sixteenth-century silver-and-gold cup of German origin; it is the same that we have seen the *mohel* bearing in his hand. It was destined to hold a bit of sand and ultimately the severed foreskin; its interior shows in relief Abraham making Isaac a son of the covenant, and around the outer border runs a Hebrew legend, "And Abraham circumcised his son Isaac when he was eight days old" (Gen. 21:4).

[1] For the guidance of the visitor, we have labelled No. 1 the wall-case by the mantelpiece, No. 2 the corner wall-case, No. 3 the flat case by its side, and No. 4 the flat case opposite the mantelpiece.

[2] See p. 280 for a remarkable collection of Torah bands at Worms. The many specimens in the museum of the Jewish Theological Seminary of New York are delightful for their folk quality and elaborate embroidered symbols.

འ᠊ᡣ᠊ᢌ

To "grow up to know the Law," the first wish of the Jewish mother, takes the lifetime of her son for its fulfilment. Daily he sets aside a fixed time for its study. At least thrice a week he hears it read in the synagogue. His joys and griefs, holidays and holy days, as well as his working hours, fall beneath its sway. It is not, therefore, surprising that every form in which it was written and every implement that surrounded its public or private use were honoured by his art.

The rich and massive Ark of the Law (*Aron ha-ḳodesh*) which stands in a corner of the Cluny room introduces us at once to this art and to the most sacred feature of the synagogue. It served to hold the scrolls of the Law, the Torah, which, as we have seen, dominates Jewish life. Usually the ark is built into a niche or recess of the east wall of the synagogue, but detached arks are not uncommon; they are so represented on gilt-glass dishes dating from the Roman Empire and in mediæval manuscript illuminations. A splendid modern example of the detached ark may be found in Temple Emanu-El of San Francisco.

The Cluny ark, in heavy walnut, comes from Modena, and, dated 1472, bears the marks of its dying Gothic and newborn classic age. The oval escutcheon near the top contains the Hebrew inscription, "Consecrated to the Lord," and the apposite familiar words from Isaiah, "For out of Zion shall go forth the Law." The upper border reads, "The Law of the Lord is perfect, restoring the soul; the testimony of the Lord is sure, making wise the simple; the precepts of the Lord are just, rejoicing the heart; a glorious throne set on high from the beginning is the place of our sanctuary" (Ps. 19:8-9; Jer. 17:12). The lower border gives the date in the following chronogram, "This shrine was wrought in honour of the

Most High and Mighty, in the fifth millennium, the year 'Bless the Lord, oh my soul.' "

The pulpit standing next to the ark likewise hails from Modena. Its pure Gothic panels, in rosace design, probably indicates its greater age. Indeed it is considered the oldest known example of the *ammud*, or table from which the scrolls of the Law are read. A leopard worked into two of the front panels symbolizes the power of faith, perhaps suggested by the verse from the *Sayings of the Fathers*, "Be strong as a leopard to do the will of thy Father who is in heaven."[1]

In the synagogue itself, a curtain or veil (*parochet*) usually hangs before the ark. Cluny possesses two specimens, one in red Genoese velvet embroidered with the Ten Commandments, the other of mouse-grey material and altogether an ingenious piece of work. Its rich designs and elaborate inscriptions are embroidered in metal spangles, the whole betraying an Oriental, perhaps Persian, origin. The first line of the inscriptions, in abbreviated form, recalls the symbol of the Temple veil: "This is the gate of the Lord, the righteous shall enter it" (Ps. 118:20). Below it, in full, is the verse, 'I have always set the Lord before me," etc. (Ps. 16:8). Then, in two lines, the verse, "Be glad in the Lord and rejoice," etc. (Ps. 32:11). And, finally, the whole of Psalm 67 is worked out in the form of a menorah. A palm, representing the tree of life, rises and spreads fanlike from a basket in each of the lower corners.

Over the pulpit hangs another curtain, very small, in red velvet, and embroidered with the Hebrew initials for the words "Crown of the Law." It was originally made for a portable Torah-case.

The veil of the ancient Temple concealed, we are told, nothing. The invisible presence of God hovered behind it. But the veil of the synagogue, hanging before the ark, con-

[1] See p. 371.

ceals the written word of the Lord. The Torah, or scroll of the Law, bearing this word in the five books of Moses is, it may well be imagined, the holiest object of the Jewish cult. Its parchment must be specially prepared and ritually clean. Infinite pains go into the writing of the letter-perfect text, and a prayer is uttered by the scribe each time the name of the Lord is penned. In contrast with the wealth of adornment lavished on the trappings of the scroll and the shrine that houses it, not the slightest decorative flourish is allowed in the writing or margins. Once completed and installed in a synagogue, the scroll is guarded from every conceivable profanation. Time and again Jews have gladly given their lives in its defence.

Cluny possesses only small portable scrolls intended for household use, and our interest lies chiefly in their rich casings. Two handsome specimens stand on a table near the grey ark curtain, the hammered brass dating from the seventeenth and the carved wooden case from the eighteenth century. Another, in repoussé metal-work studded with semiprecious stones and dated 1707, comes from Vienna (case 1), and a fourth, in delicately beaten silver likewise goes back to the eighteenth century (case 2).

The two wooden rollers of a large synagogal scroll are generally mounted with precious metal caps, known as pomegranates, or *rimonim*, and often hung with tiny bells. A pair of silver *rimonim* set with such bells (case 1), a solitary *rimon* from the seventeenth century (case 2), and two mere mites (case 4), all of them of charming workmanship, reëcho, however faintly, the golden bells and pomegranates upon the skirts of Aaron the High Priest (Ex. 39:25).

The scroll is usually surmounted, as well, by a massive crown, symbolizing in gold and silver the Crown of the Law, which, together with the Crown of the Priesthood and the Crown of the Kingdom, are the peculiar attributes of Israel. Cluny offers a noble eighteenth- and a smaller seventeenth-century example of these headpieces meant for no mortal brow (case 2).

Furthermore, the scroll is clothed in a silk or velvet mantle (*mappa*), of which Cluny furnishes no striking specimen. Over the mantle is suspended a breastplate (*tass*) in precious metal. Cluny's most exquisite example (case 4), of seventeenth-century Dutch workmanship, is one glowing mass of filigree set with lions, angels, and cherubs. Woven into the filigree are the three traditional crowns surmounting a delicately wrought model of an unwound scroll; inserted between the open scroll, a removable metal plaque bears the inscription "Pesach" and indicates that the Torah it once adorned was used on the Passover festival. The whole is hung with bells. Three smaller breastplates of the same period and origin, and a German example likewise of the seventeenth century (case 4) were destined for the services of the New Year and the Sabbath.

A metal pointer (*yad*—Hebrew for "hand") hanging down the front of the scroll completes its visible adornments. Seven chased silver examples (case 4) show the beauty and pains lavished on this humble tool, merely meant to keep the reader of the Law from losing his place. The tips are, as customary, shaped like a hand with forefinger outstretched. One seventeenth-century specimen is mounted with a pomegranate, rampant lions, and a crown. Another "hand," slim and elegant, dating from the eighteenth century, holds a midget pointer in its grasp and gleams with a jeweled ring on its finger and bracelet on its wrist. All of them bear the names of their donors.

A Hanuka candelabrum, commemorating the Feast of the Maccabees, ordinarily stands at the right of the ark in a traditionally equipped synagogue. The Cluny example (on the pulpit) with its nine branches, eight for the candles and one for the lighter, is a splendid piece of seventeenth-century metal-work. Two huge wooden candlesticks of Italian origin face the Cluny ark.

The chief functions of the synagogue were instruction furnished by the readings from the Torah, and prayer directed by the ritual. A magnificent thirteenth-century (?) quarto (case 2), written in Ashkenazic script by one Rabbi Eliezer Manuel and containing the services for the entire year, with incidentally the famous *Alenu* prayer[1] in its full uncensored form; an illuminated octavo (case 3) "finished the fifth of Adar, 5272 [1512], at Ferrara by the humble hand of Moses ben Hayim Achrish, one of the exiles from Jerusalem who lived in Portugal" and bound in red velours; and a quarto (case 3) printed in Amsterdam, 1765, and caught with silver clasps, all tell of the care limners, scribes, and binders took to provide a wealthy Jew with worthy means for his devotions.

On high festivals, above all the New Year and Day of Atonement, the officiating rabbi clothes himself in rich white robes, of which Cluny offers (case 2) a heavily embroidered eighteenth-century ephod and bonnet. On the same Day of Atonement, when the congregation fasts for twenty-four hours, the women-folk are wont to ease their hunger with the smell of spices and perfumes. Seven tiny silver boxes (case 4) of Dutch origin and cunning workmanship were fashionable for this use in the seventeenth century. A few are shaped like flowers, and their silver petals are contrived to open out and then yield their odour. One of them bears on its petals the pleasant labels, Rosemary, Lemon, Muscat, and Lily—altogether a toy to delight the heart of Bezalel.

Women, too, often affected the miniature scrolls, cased in silver filigree and containing the *Book of Esther* (four in case 3), for as women they were especially bidden to attend the deeds of Shushan's queen, when they were read forth on the Feast of Purim. One of these tiny scrolls fashioned like a

[1] See p. 98.

locket, with a gold enamel face, is a pure delight. The somewhat larger scrolls (three in case 3) were used by the men-
folk, and the four magnificent examples framed and hanging
on the walls were intended for public reading. It has long been
the custom to illustrate these *Books of Esther* with illuminations, miniatures, or prints, wherein special *brio* is given to
"the rich blue of Mordecai" and the hanging of Haman and
his ten sons.

Significant embroideries were displayed in the synagogue
on certain festivals. Such are the white oval pieces on Cluny's
wall; one for the New Year bearing an embroidered *shofar*;
another for the first day of Passover, stitched with the likeness
of a sheaf of green grain recalling "the first fruit of thy
labour" and a Hebrew inscription, "Herb yielding seed,
thresh! thresh!"; and a third for the last day of the Feast of
Booths when the community prayed for rain. The emblem
stitched on the latter is a rain-cloud surrounded by the Hebrew invocation: "The thing in its due season, here below, as
the dew of light is thy dew! To Passover and beyond, the rain
of beneficence! Lift up Thy voice from the eighth day of
Booths and beyond! The Lord of Hosts be with us, He is the
creator, He maketh and bringeth rain for us in its due season,
the former and the latter rains!"

The wedding canopy, which covered the second wish of
every Jewish mother for her son, was in olden days almost
as accessible, one might even say inevitable, as the Law. Celi-
bacy was not only something of a social stain, but treason to
the race, diminution of the hope for the Messiah, and diso-
bedience to the command of God. Marriages were accordingly celebrated with the utmost pomp and cheer. Glints of
the joy of spindle feasts and wedding banquets still gleam in

the magnificent array of sixteenth- and seventeenth-century betrothal and marriage rings, the gems of the Cluny collection (eighteen in case 4). Many of them double and treble hooped, some worked with miniscule floral conceits, others mounted with tiny filigree temples, and a few set with stones, they one and all bear the phrase "*Mazel tov* (good luck!)," or its initials, either embossed on their outer or engraved on their inner surface. In the marriage service, the groom places the ring on the forefinger of the bride while uttering the formula, "Behold, thou art consecrated to me by this ring, according to the law of Moses and Israel." But as the generous size of the ring testifies, the bride never undertook to wear it. Most of the Jewish wedding rings of this period were made in Venice.

And one may be sure that the parents swelled with pride, the young couple—for they were usually very young—with hope, and the guests with critical admiration at the marriage contract (*ketubah*), its rich illuminations and its precise substantial terms. As the text explicitly said, "This is not to be treated as an illusory contract." Indeed, it provided a liberal and solid protection for the wife. In Cluny's two examples (above pulpit) we need no longer concern ourselves with the scudi and zuzai dowered on Nathan Molcho and his bride Grazia Halevi in the city of Modena, 1756 (?), or on Moses David ben Obadiah and his Donna Simcha, daughter of Gedalia of Sinigaglia, October 6, 1775, in Ancona "by the sea." But we may well admire the illuminated border of Molcho's contract, gay with the signs of the zodiac and scenes taken from the typical occupations of the seasons. Marriage contracts, worded in their essentials much the same as our present specimens, have been found among the fifth-century B.C. Jewish papyri of Assouan (now in the Cairo museum and the Bodleian Library of Oxford); and illuminated examples are known to go back to the eleventh century C.E.

Another durable token of the bridal feast was the wedding ode, such as the illuminated Hebrew sonnet (on wall, left of case 3) addressed to Messer Israel ben Jacob Hayim and Donna Miriam, daughter of Shem ben Samuel Menahem, on their marriage in Italy two centuries ago.

Installed in their new home, we may be certain that the married pair first of all nailed a *mezzuza* by their door, a small parchment inserted in a case or tube (three in case 3) and inscribed with passages from Deut. 6:4-9 and 11:13-21. The name of God, *Shaddai,* appears through an opening in the case, and a pious Jew, passing through the doorway, touches the sacred word with his finger and then presses it to his lips. Its use is a fulfilment of the Law, "Thou shalt write these words upon the doorposts of thy house," and in the popular mind a shield against the spirits of evil.

The joys of home life are again reflected for us in the gold and silver *kiddush* (sanctification) cups. Cluny's sixteenth-century German specimen (case 3), like its seventeenth-century Dutch and eighteenth-century Palestinian mates (both case 2), and like all of their kind, were filled with wine for the blessing upon the advent of the Sabbath, a blessing likewise given over bread and light. A small silver cruet, dated 1567 and of German workmanship (case 4), may have served to pour the wine into the *kiddush* cup.

The departure of the Sabbath is also sped with blessings, this time over wine, light, and the sweet scent of spices, each intended to mark the separation (*habdalah*) of the day of rest from the approaching week of toil. Cluny possesses a remarkable assortment of the spice-boxes used in this ceremony. In general they are the most ornate objects in the home ritual, as we may see in the sixteenth- to eighteenth-century examples (four each in cases 1 and 2, two in case 4) chiefly of Dutch and German origin. The favourite turret model probably derives its shape from the mediæval Christian reliquary and monstrance (examples in rooms XVI and XXV), just as the Church had previously borrowed its chalice from the *kiddush* cup. The use of spices to mark the close of the Sabbath may well symbolize the delights of the passing day, but Rashi tells us otherwise; spices, he said, should be smelt on this occasion because after its day of interrupted labours, hell begins to exhale a bad odour.

The Feast of Maccabees is celebrated by kindling lights, one on the first day and one more progressively for each of the seven succeeding days of the festival. The Hanuka candelabra used on this holiday take, as we can judge, a wide variety of form and decoration (cases 1 and 2). The most remarkable examples are the fourteenth-century (?) French triangular wall-lamp (case 4) dating from before the expulsion of the French Jews in 1394, then the two sixteenth-century Italian wall-lamps enlivened with centaurs, lions and cherubs, and the upright candelabrum, likewise of Italian origin, surmounted by a figure of Perseus (all in case 1). The oil-burning lamps are not necessarily older than the candlesticks; the use of oil long persisted out of deference to the Talmudic story of the Temple lamp which with one day's supply of oil burnt miraculously for eight, on the triumph of the Maccabees.

A single Strasbourg plate of the eighteenth century (case 2) tells of Purim, another joyous festival when, as the inscription reminds us, Jews were bidden to "send portions to one another and gifts to the poor" (Esther 9:22). The frolics of the feast are recalled in the picture of a villainous Haman leading in triumph a magnificently mounted and smiling Mordecai across the bowl of the dish.

The eighteenth-century bronze statuettes of Moses and Aaron, as well as the small sixteenth-century Moses carved in stone (top of case 1), were probably household ornaments, if indeed they were ever used by Jews. And the Spanish translation of the Pentateuch, printed in Amsterdam by the famous

Manasseh ben Israel (case 2),[1] like its innumerable fellows in Hebrew and every other tongue known to Jews, is a household necessity. So, too, the eighteenth-century silver-embroidered bag (case 2) destined to hold the praying-shawl or *talith*.

Seal-rings, medals, and seventeenth- and eighteenth-century coin-shaped amulets (case 4) nearly complete our home furnishings. One amulet, in gold alloy, with a pentagon inscribed on its visible face, may detain the curious visitor; its formulas are half Jewish and half Christian in sentiment, and probably of Marano origin. Another amulet, or rather amulet case, shaped like a swollen medallion, was intended to be suspended from the neck of a sick person and contained the spell proper to the ailment. The shekel, near by, is not genuine. Readers of Ludwig Lewisohn's *The Last Days of Shylock*, as well as lovers of Jewish history, may stop to stare at the bronze medal bearing the portrait of young Gracia Nasi, the cousin of Joseph, Duke of Naxos.

❧❦❧

The third wish of the hopeful mother, that her son give himself to good works, usually and unfortunately translated as charity, has every facility offered for its fulfilment. Every Jewish home contained an alms-box (the use is vanished with checkbooks) which rang with the coins of family and friends on all possible occasions—in moments of joy, God be thanked, and in times of sorrow, God forbid and God reward us for our merits. Of the Cluny specimens, the eighteenth-century silver cup (case 2) comes from the East. The Spanish terracotta cup or box (case 2), dated 1319 (?) and of the utmost rarity, presents an inscription defying interpretation. But the seventeenth-century silver box from Nurnberg (case 4) tells in a few plain words the spirit and intent of old-fashioned

[1] See p. 198.

Jewish alms. "A gift in secret," it reads—and we wonder what our federated charities would think of it—"tameth anger" (Prov. 21:14).

༄་ᢏᢣᡃᢌᢣᢃ

Leaving the Jewish room, we may pause for a moment to examine an exquisite enamel plaque from the twelfth-century Rhinelands (room XVI, first case left, by window) depicting a Crucifixion, with the traditional Synagogue to the right of the Cross.[1] If you care for such things, you may puzzle yourself as to why the very early representations of this scene—as, for example, on gilt-glass dishes found in the Roman Christian catacombs—placed Mary and John on either side of the Cross; or if you find this natural in view of the Gospel account, you may wonder why Mary and John later gave way to the figures of the Church and the Synagogue—as in the present plaque; and finally why at a still later period—there are examples in the same case—Church and Synagogue again give way to Mary and John. Or you may wish to view the unicorn's horn (room XXIV) brought to Charlemagne by the Jew Isaac, along with the elephant whose name was Abulabaz, both gifts of Harun-al-Rashid. The Hebrew tombstones in the *thermes* have already been described.[2]

And leaving Cluny, we may spend an agreeable hour in the exhibition rooms of the Bibliothèque Nationale, studying its collection of ancient Jewish coins. The library possesses over 400, and a score are on show (cases 12 and 17). They date from Simon Maccabee (No. 1812) through the reigns of Herod the Great (No. 1784—portrait) and Herod Agrippa symbolized by his royal umbrella (No. 1823) down to the defence and fall of Jerusalem (Nos. 1828, 1830) and the last revolt un-

[1] See p. 95 (Bourges).
[2] See p. 48.

der Bar Kochba (Nos. 1837-1839). The library treasures, as well, some 1,400 Hebrew manuscripts, in number and importance second only to the Bodleian at Oxford. Many of them are illuminated, and illustrated with miniatures.[1] Among the general manuscripts, it might be worth your trouble to ask for a glimpse of the *Liber Continens* of Rhazes (Lat. 6192). It is a thirteenth-century translation into Latin of an Arabic medical work, made by the Jew Farrachius of Sicily at the order of Charles of Anjou. It contains a portrait of the translator—the first authentic likeness of a Jew that has come down to us from the Middle Ages. Or perhaps you would like to look at the *Atlas catalan de Charles V* (Spanish MS. No. 30), made by the Jew Cresques of Palma in Majorca in 1375—an amazing example of the accuracy and detail of Arab-Jewish cartography.

The library of the Alliance Israélite (at the Ecole Normale Israélite Orientale, 59 Rue d'Auteuil) likewise contains a number of illuminated Hebrew manuscripts.

The Carnavalet museum, dedicated to the antiquities of Paris and located in the heart of the modern ghetto, contains three Hebrew tombstones (in courtyard) dating from the thirteenth century.

In the chapel of the great archæological museum of St. Germain-en-Laye (south wall) is a seventh- or eighth-century stone found in Auch, decorated with *lulab* and menorah and inscribed in Latin of doubtful interpretation; likewise a small thirteenth-century Hebrew tombstone found in Limay, near Mantes, commemorating a lady named Belnia; and finally a copy of the famous Latin inscription of the tombstone in Narbonne, the oldest Jewish inscription known in France.

[1] Among the Hebrew MSS. containing miniatures are Nos. 7, 15, 123, 311, 359, 418, 423, 584, 586, 592, 593, 617, 640, 643, 644, 646, 1146, 1333, 1388, 6912.

CHAPTER VI

From Champagne

to Brittany

FOR travelling purposes the history of the Jews in northern France can be reduced to a small compass.

As commissaries and traders, the Jews probably followed the dust of the Roman legions into northern Gaul. Later, during the barbarian invasions, they followed, no doubt, the wake of the Frankish armies from over the Rhine. At an early date they emerge from the records owning vineyards and estates and engaged in crafts and trades, in local and foreign commerce, and in rudimentary banking.

Throughout the Middle Ages the character of this Jewry differed little, in interests, customs, ritual, and literature, from that of the Rhinelands. Indeed, the Jewish culture of northern Europe first blossomed in the region between Mayence and Paris. From beginning to end its tone was coloured by the practical exclusion of the northern Jew from public life and contemporary intellectual currents. Thrown back upon itself, it largely found voice in impassioned synagogal poetry, sage commentaries and supercommentaries on Scripture and Talmud, in the development of Jewish law and the strengthening of communal organization. Its work may today seem remote and recondite, but it was far from sterile; the discipline of life which preserved the Jewries of central and eastern Europe through bitter centuries and which formed the orthodox Jew-

ish spirit, the Jewish soul, so far as it now survives, owes a profound debt to Gershom, Rashi, and Tam, to the Jew of
northern France and the Rhinelands.

Memorable dates come few and far between. The Crusades
(eleventh and twelfth centuries) marked the first great turning-point in the fate of all French Jewry. Hitherto they had
shared, despite the varying humours of the Church, the general fortunes of the Gentile world. Thereafter, intolerance
bred by these religious excursions, the ever-widening warfare
of the Church against heresies and infidelities, and the rise
of Christian commerce partly born of renewed contact with
the East, fell hard on the Jews. Persecutions in the thirteenth
and recurrent expulsions in the fourteenth century culmi-
nated in the second great turning-point—in 1394 the Jews
were driven from France. Aside from temporary and local
exceptions, the expulsion held good for every corner of the
land. The Jewries of the Comtat Venaissin, alone to escape,
will be treated in the following chapter.

The long absence of the Jews from the land, together with
the turbulence of French history in the fifteenth and sixteenth
centuries, a period of foreign invasions and civil warfare,
probably accounts for the scarcity and poverty of their surviving relics. If rarity determines value, the few stones and
ghostly street names which we meet scattered through the
provinces are above price. With difficulty they tell us of the
rich and creative life they once witnessed, but their rarity, in
any case, leaves us clear as to the tragedy that overwhelmed it.

In seeking out these relics, our itinerary will take us, with
a certain respect for railroad connections, first through north-
eastern France, from Champagne and Burgundy to Savoy and
the Franche-Comté, and then, beginning with the Ile-de-
France, gradually westward through Norman lands to the
farthest coast of Brittany.

ᑫᐳᐱᐸᑫᐳ

Old Troyes with its timber houses and mediæval streets interlaced and embraced by the winding, branching Seine, sets a perfect frame for an antique synagogue, *beth ha-midrash,* or graveyard, for a relic recalling the Jewish glories of its past. The frame is there, the glories are not wanting, but no sign of a relic remains. Yet, in any Jewish itinerary, Troyes cannot be overlooked. Its name is too great.

Rue St.-Frobert, in the borders of the Gallo-Roman site of the city, recalls the likelihood that the ghetto stood in the parish of St.-Frobert; and there is an equal likelihood that the present Church of St. Pantaléon, just beyond a nest of old lanes, was originally a synagogue. Two other street names, however, bring us closer to the city's Jewish fame. The present synagogue stands in the Rue de la Petite Tannerie, which is paralleled by the Rue de la Grande Tannerie. These streets of the Little and Big Tanneries remind us that in the eleventh and twelfth centuries tanning was a major industry of the town. The parchments of Troyes gained so much renown that scholars naturally flocked to this source of raw materials. And Rashi, who was born in Troyes (1040), after studying in the Rhinelands, returned there to write his immortal works and found his immortal school.

Once we leave the Bible lands, two names are known to every Jew—Rashi and Maimonides. Rashi's place in the Jewish world cannot be fixed merely by calling him what he was, a commentator of the Bible and Talmud, or even the greatest commentator. Until modern times, Jews lived by the Bible and Talmud. Their faith, law, literature, and thought were fed, and the breath and motion of their daily life turned on a Biblical or Talmudic word. And Rashi of Troyes made his rendering of that word authoritative and universal. To this day his dicta frame the pages of every ordinary edition of the Talmud and many orthodox editions of the Bible. The Jews came to know the law that ruled their being through the eyes of Rashi. Except that he was nothing of the sort, he might be compared to the compilers of the Napoleonic code and Locke, Kant, and Wellhausen rolled into one; nothing of the sort, because these modern codifiers, political thinkers, philosophers, and Bible critics never touched the masses of the Western World as Rashi touched Jewry. For nearly a thousand years every Jewish schoolboy, willy or nilly, knew Rashi, and every adult Jew, a dozen times a day, bent his life to the master's word. "Thanks to him," said a scholar of his age, "the Law has come to life again." And thanks to him, the Jew of the Atlas and the Carpathians, the Italian piazza and the English lane, together shared that life.

Rashi spent the better part of his days in Troyes. He earned his living, as do so many still in the land of Champagne, by cultivating the vine. In the vintage season, we know, he had to cut short his flow of commentaries. "All the Jews," he writes, excusing the brevity of his letter, "are now busy in the vineyards." In another letter he describes the wine-presses of Troyes and notes an improvement in their machinery. Doubtless he would have welcomed the discovery, centuries later, of the bubble.

Due to the prestige of his school and to the fairs for which his city was famed, Troyes became a seat of the first Jewish synods in Europe. Their significance, too, is hard to appraise in modern terms. The Jews lived by the Talmud, but they survived by the force of communal discipline. The rabbinical synods of Troyes (in the lifetime of Rashi and again in 1150 and 1160), like those of Mayence, set the mould for this discipline. Beset as the Jews were by enemies and by changing conditions beyond their control, only a free surrender to voluntarily accepted authority kept alive the tiny dispersed communities, forever menaced by oppression, extortion, bribe, and treason. Much as Rashi defined the content of these Jewish worlds, the synods provided their defence. And content and defence are both stamped with the name of Troyes.

Rashi lived to see the menace rise. The First Crusade (1096) swept east through Troyes, leaving it undamaged but troubled, and wreaking its wrath on the Rhine.

Godfrey of Bouillon, the story goes, consulted Rashi before he set out on the great adventure. With his knights at his heels, he entered the school at Troyes. He found it empty, for although the rabbi awaited him, he had taken the precaution to render himself invisible. After proper assurance Rashi took visible form and told Godfrey he would reign three days over Jerusalem, be overcome by the Moslems on the fourth, and return to Troyes with only three horses. "If I return with one horse more," said Godfrey, "I shall throw your body to the dogs and exterminate the Jews of France." Godfrey returned, the story concludes, accompanied by three knights—in all, four horses. He naturally sought out Troyes to carry through his threat. But as his little cavalcade passed beneath the gate of the city, a large stone loosened and fell, killing a knight and his mount. In astonishment and contrition Godfrey hastened to the house of the master. But Rashi, meanwhile, had passed away. The sole doubt that can be thrown on the story arises from the fact that Godfrey never returned from Palestine, but died in Jerusalem five years before Rashi.

A note in an old manuscript from the school of Troyes tells us that "as the owner of a fig tree knows when it is time to cull the figs, so God knew the appointed time of Rashi, and plucked him in his hour." The time was July 13, 1105.

The "wrath of Edom" eventually fell upon the Jewry of Troyes and bequeathed it a crown of martyrdom. In 1228 the local office of the Inquisition, on a charge of ritual murder, burnt alive thirteen Jews. Their fate was sung in contemporary

Hebrew elegies and, not unworthily for the home of the troubadour Chrestien, in a touching French plaint. In the simple verses we can still see, as the French Jewish poet saw him, Rab Isaac of Chatlain

> mounted to the pyre,
> His God he goes to greet across the leaping fire.

Nor are we too far away to no longer hear his wife, who followed him

> and raised her voice on high,
> "Oh, my man's death is mine and my man's death I'll die,"
> And near she was with child and far they heard her cry.

Rab Isaac's two young sons are mounted next:

> The child he grew afraid, the smoke upon his eyes.
> "I burn," he called, "I burn"; the elder stopped his cries,
> "Oh, brother mine, I swear, you go to Paradise."

The wife of the elder, he still a lad and she a girl, knew how to die with contempt.

> The young wife was so fair, they sought to preach her free,
> "But say the word, fair dame, a squire we'll give to thee":
> "I give you this," she said, and spat for all to see.

So died the thirteen in a fierce joy which echoes in the Wilde-like beat of the verse and tells somewhat of the secret of Israel.

> In carol high and clear their voices loud resound,
> Like dancers gaily out to dance a village round;
> But gay they could not dance with hands so tightly bound,
> Yet dance they did to shake the dust upon the ground.

Up the side wall of the cathedral of Troyes a gargoyle embodies the spirit of this Christian love, a gargoyle in the form of a grotesque Jew with pointed hat and buttoned jerkin, a fat purse slung from his belt, one hand pressed behind his neck, the other thrusting forth his beard; and when it rained,

the gargoyle-Jew, in retaliation and no less love, spewed heart-
ily on Christian heads below.

.⤲⤳.

Provins, west of Troyes and one of the most picturesque
towns within a day's journey of Paris, still keeps in its old
frame a lane called Rue aux Juifs (Street of the Jews), bordering the tiny creek north of the main thoroughfare. The Jewry
of Provins also had its noted schools a century after Troyes,
which may seem as strange and far away today as the fact
that in the thirteenth century the town itself boasted 80,000
inhabitants.

A street name, too, remains of the Jewry of Sens, south of
Provins and likewise charming in its old houses, mediæval
walls, and cobbled lanes. Its Rue de la Grande Juiverie—its
Big Jewry Street—opens south from the Grande Rue, close to
the Yonne bridge and the former gate of the town. Behind it
lies a narrow alley, doubtless the Rue de la Petite Juiverie.
And this is all that tells of a Jewry which dated from the sixth
century, which marshalled its roll of scholars, including the
bold and witty Joseph ben Nathan Official, and left a name
in innumerable parchments—unless, and it is unlikely, the Rue
Sinson, at the west end of the town, echoes the name of Rabbi
Simson, the "prince of Sens."

In Dijon, whence rabbis went up to Troyes for the synod
of 1160, we can come a trifle closer to our vanished Jews. We
can finger fragments of thirty-seven of their tombstones, dating from the twelfth and thirteenth centuries (the majority
in the Musée Archéologique of the Hôtel de Ville); the inscriptions are badly mutilated. These shattered stones are the
sole survivors of a Jewry whose beginnings are lost in history
and whose history itself is for most purposes equally lost.

Travellers in Dijon usually visit the Chartreuse of Champmol to view the Well of Moses, a famous sculptural group, the work of the fourteenth-century Dutch artist, Claus Sluter, and his school. The figure of Moses is imposing in its cloven beard and horned majesty, a splendid forerunner of the still more famous work of Michelangelo. Together with Moses, five other prophets, David, Zechariah, Isaiah, Jeremiah, and Daniel, guard the well in dramatic posture. The figures were not chosen by chance, nor do their scrolls bear haphazard legends, nor do the angels above them weep from mere artistic fantasy. The whole group, it happens, illustrates a contemporary mystery-play called "The Judgment of Jesus," in which Mary pleads before the prophets that her son be spared the agony of the Passion. Originally, in carrying out the theme of the play, the Well was surmounted by a crucified Jesus. The angels, as we see them in the sculpture, are weeping at the verdict of the prophets. For they, in turn, are rendering judgment in the words taken from the play and now inscribed on their scrolls, Moses saying (Ex. 12:6), "And the whole assembly of Israel shall kill the lamb at evening," David saying (Ps. 22:16), "They have pierced my hands and my feet," and Zechariah (Zech. 11:12), "So they weighed for my hire thirty pieces of silver." Unwittingly, the artists have erected a monument to another drama, The Tragedy of Israel, played before no pasteboard scenes but on the wide stage of the world; and it is fitting they have made the angels weep. The robes of the prophets, incidentally, are play costumes, differing from the hitherto-prevailing mediæval Jewish garb and setting a new fashion long observed in both Christian art and its Jewish imitations.

Burgundy, for the rest, offers a Rue de Juifs in Beaune, almost directly behind the cathedral; in Chalon-sur-Saône a collection of Merovingian coins (Musée Denon) to remind us that among the sixth-century mint-masters of the city were two Jews, Jacote and Priscus (555)—perhaps the same Priscus we met in Paris; and in Mâcon (Hôtel de Ville) seven tomb-stones dating from 1260 to 1310, discovered north of the city near the brook Rigolletes, where stands a country-house still called "Sabbat" and claimed to be the site of the mediæval synagogue—adjoining it is a great well, perhaps the ancient *mikveh.*

Southeast of Burgundy, the mountains of Savoy gave refuge to the Jews on their expulsion from France. Chambéry, the capital of the ancient county, still perpetuates their memory in a Rue de la Juiverie. Its location at the foot of the thirteenth-century fortified *château* affords a clue to the relations sub-sisting between the refugees and the ruling powers: the counts of Savoy kept their Jews within easy reach.

At Vesoul, in the Franche-Comté, the present Chapel of La Charité stands on the site of the mediæval synagogue which, on the expulsion of the Jews, naturally fell into Christian possession. In our wanderings we shall often meet with this rather subtle fashion of commemorating what the Church called the "Old Faith."

And then, before we return to the neighbourhood of Paris, we might take a spurt into Lorraine and note in Lunéville (Place des Carmes) the statue of its native son, the Abbé Grégoire.[1] Contemplating his effigy and his work with grati-tude, we may pardon the good abbé his strange opinion that "since Josephus" it has taken the Jewish people "seventeen centuries to produce a Mendelssohn—for the lack of anyone better they make boast of Akiba, Maimonides, Kimchi and Gerson."

꒰ᐢ᎒ᐢ꒱

The towns in and surrounding the Ile-de-France comprised a single world in the Middle Ages, and their rabbis, it is not

[1] See p. 64.

surprising to learn, moved in close and frequent contact. In the village church (for example) of Limay, near Mantes, and not far from Paris, a large Hebrew tombstone embedded in the wall above the baptismal font commemorates "Rabbi Meier, son of Rabbi Elijah—died the 3rd day of the portion Tazria, the year 5003 [March 17, 1243]." Of course it is only the stone and not the rabbi that has received, as it were, Christian burial. Now this Rabbi Meier was likely the father of Rabbi Jacob of Provins, who, together with other Ile-de-France authorities, engaged in that astonishing discussion, at the home of Menahem Vardimas in Paris, as to whether the knots in the phylacteries must be retied daily, a discussion at the least astonishing because it was also shared by Rabbi Elijah ben Judah of Paris, the father of our Meier and already dead for some years, by Rabbi Tam, the grandson and successor of Rashi and also long dead, by the prophets Samuel and Moses, and by the mystic Metatron, and surely astonishing because in the course of the debate the spirit of Rabbi Tam managed to outargue Moses on a point of Mosaic law.

In Mantes itself are three tombstones dating from the late thirteenth century, and in the near-by hamlet of Sennerville, at the bottom of a millrace, beneath the wheel of the mill, two other Hebrew tombstones.

Chartres still preserves along the river, below the central market, its Rue aux Juifs; and like St.-Denis, its cathedral possesses a magnificent window (sixth on north aisle) telling in glass the philosophy of the Old and New Covenant, the Christian version of the relation between Judaism and Christianity. We shall explain the symbolism of these windows when we come to Bourges. Meanwhile, en route, we may note in Orléans another Rue des Juifs behind the cathedral and not far from the site of the old city wall.

Bourges, too, has its Rue des Juifs immediately behind its cathedral. Although the presence of Jews has been detected in this city since the sixth century (when the usual efforts were made to convert them), and although the records of lawsuits survive to testify to their continued presence for seven hundred years thereafter, no Jewish scholar is known to have risen in Bourges, a rare case in the local literary annals that make up the bulk of Jewish history. But Bourges provides an excellent occasion to pursue a subject which plays at least as great a part in Jewish history as any catalogue of scholars—the relation, that is to say, of the Church and Synagogue.

The sculptured Synagogue on the façade of Notre Dame in Paris[1] illustrated the mediæval Christian attitude toward Jewry and its central institution; the window of Bourges cathedral (Chapel of Notre Dame de Lourdes in the apse) usually called the New Alliance, illustrates the theory and justification for this attitude. The Old Testament, runs the theory, merely prefigured the New; and a half-dozen Biblical scenes, glowing in the glass, depict the argument: Moses strikes water from the rock (which is the Roman guard piercing Jesus with his lance), Moses sets up the brazen serpent (foretelling Jesus on the cross), the widow of Zarephath brings Elijah the two sticks of wood (again the cross), Abraham sacrifices Isaac (the crucifixion), Jonah escapes from the whale (Jesus arising from the dead), etc.

The New Faith, so prefigured, comes to supplant the Old. This is subtly rendered in the uppermost medallion, where Jacob is blessing Manasseh and Ephraim; the patriarch crisscrosses his arms so that his right hand falls on the head of the younger grandson, Ephraim (the Church). And it is rendered unmistakably in the central (small) medallion, where Church and Synagogue stand in the guise of two female figures, one on either side of the crucified Jesus; the Church catches his blood in her cup, while the Synagogue, blindfolded, her staff broken and her crown tumbled down, bows

[1] See p. 51.

her head in dismay. Above her head dimly shines a moon in eclipse, whereas above the head of the Church a sun bursts into glory. Jeremiah, according to the theory, foretold this eclipse and gave the mediæval artists their theme. "Woe unto us," says Lamentations (5:16-17), "for we have sinned, the crown is fallen from our head, for this our heart is faint, for these things our eyes are dim." And the lowest medallion in our window (a half-circle) shows Judas in pointed, mediæval Jewish bonnet, receiving the price of betrayal.

The central medallion which, as we have seen, sums up the whole theory, is repeated in the cathedral of St.-Denis (near Paris) with even bolder imagery; here the dying Jesus crowns the Church with one hand, and with the other strips from the Synagogue her veil. The symbol of the veil, a favourite in these pictures of the Synagogue, finds its epitome in the mediæval verse, *"Quod Moyse velat Christi doctrina revelat"* ("What Moses hides, Christ's teaching reveals"), and its source in the words of Paul, "When Moses is read, the vail is upon their heart; nevertheless when it shall turn to the Lord, the vail shall be taken away" (2 Cor. 3:15-16).

With variations, the same theme recurs in the glass of Chartres, Mans, Rouen, Tours, Lyons, and Poitiers. There was, it appears, no lack of schools to teach the doctrine which, however we may judge its truth, darkened in deed and fact the light of the Synagogue and plunged it into a night without respite and almost without end.

The night that engulfed the mediæval Jew receives curious illumination, though no ray of light, in the scratchings of its victims on the walls of the donjon-keep of Issoudun. The little town of Issoudun lies southwest of Bourges, and its Tour Blanche (in the gardens of the Hôtel de Ville), built by Philip Augustus at the end of the twelfth century and named after Blanche, mother of St.-Louis, furnishes its chief attraction for the traveller. Unless he is prepared by now for such surprises, it may seem an unlikely place to stumble on our Jews and catch the very signatures of their agony.

The tower is magnificent in its gloom; an architect, we sense at once, can surpass sculptor and painter when it comes to contriving night. Even on the second floor, it takes us all the daylight penetrating the narrow splayed windows to discern the casual inscriptions of its mediæval prisoners. Let us turn to the left of the south window and read the largest and clearest of them. "Two brothers," says the loose Hebrew script, "are prisoners, Isaac and Hayim, may they live! God be their aid, to draw them from darkness to light, from bondage to freedom! Amen, amen, selah!" A little lower to the left comes the date: "They entered the 3rd day of the portion Vay-hi, the year 64 [December 17, 1303]." The lines, in all, rhyme, and were begun over again, perhaps out of black boredom.

On the same wall, farther south, are two more Hebrew lines (cut through by the sketch of a knight): "I am condemned . . . imprisoned since . . ." We can read no more. Still farther south we can decipher the name "Abraham ben Natanel" and below it a pathetic confusion, "prisoners of the tower . . . Jerusalem . . . arise thou . . . Israel," and again the refrain, "God draw us from darkness to light."

Among the total half-score Hebrew names we meet "the daughter of Menahem" (west wall, left of window), a young *fiancée* imprisoned with we no longer know whom.

Although, indeed, we know precious little of any of them, we can guess why they came to this dark tower. A local historian tells us that "Philip the Fair, clever contriver, locked the Jews in cells in order to extract from them, by torture and terror, whatever they could be made to yield." But Philip is not alone to blame. One of the victims, Joseph ben Yakar ha-Cohen, scratches above his petition—"The Lord preserve us and send us his promised blessings"—the five coats of arms

of his oppressors, local lords of the time. And Joseph, awaiting the promised blessings, may have gazed from the window
of the tower on the little brook below and mused ironically
on its name—Arnon—the same that flows to the Promised
Land.

More illumination in Blois, from the heart of the *château*
country and the banks of the Loire. On March 26, 1171, at the
lowest count, thirty-one Jews, among them sixteen women
and a newborn babe, were burnt alive. They were accused of
ritual murder, the first charge of the kind in France, and
they died chanting the *Alenu* prayer, "It is for us to praise the
Lord." The churchmen, we are told, "who heard it from afar
wondered at the melodious strains"; later they looked into
their meaning, and because the prayer alludes to "bowing
down to vanity and gods that cannot help," it too became a
martyr and suffered the mutilations of the censor. The an-
niversary of the burning of Blois became a fast day for European Jews; dirges in its memory entered the synagogal service; Blois took its unsavoury place in Jewish geography as an
Ir ha-dam, a City of Blood; and no Jewish traveller who
passes the tiny Rue des Juifs (close by the Loire bridge), with
its old houses exhaling the past upon him, can fail to catch the
smell of smoke. But let him not rake up the ashes of extinct
tragedies to illumine new hates. Jews never perpetrated ritual
murder, and Christians never, as a Jewish dirge accuses them,
carved gods out of stone; the errors expiated in the old fires
were mutual and, it is hoped, forever consumed. *Alenu,* "it is
for us" who remember the victims to cease, in our own worlds,
from playing the oppressors.

The *château* country contains but few other fugitive reminiscences. The Jewry of Tours lay in the present Rue des
Maures (between the cathedral and river), well within the
old Gallo-Roman boundaries. Jews, in fact, were there early
enough, for in 580 a Jewish tax-collector was thrown into a

well and killed. The appearance of this Jewry, when its inhabitants paid the king at Easter thirty sous and a half-pound
of pepper, and at Christmas two loaves of bread, a pitcher of
wine, and another half-pound of pepper, may be guessed from
the numerous thirteenth- and fourteenth-century houses
(Rues Briconnet, du Murier, des Cerisiers, du Poirier, etc.)
now the pride of the city. Southward, in Niort, a Rue de la
Juiverie survives near the market, and in Angoulême, a Rue
des Juifs (now Rue du Grand Font) close to the railroad station and just off the main highway to Limoges.

ᴄⱌⰕ

Turning again to the north, we may follow a new trail out
of Rheims. A Synagogue Defeated appears twice on the walls
of Rheims Cathedral, above the left portal on the west front,
and again near the rosace above the portal of the south front.
In Amiens the Synagogue appears once more (by the main
portal) in the shape of a withered tree, an ax laid to its trunk.
In Rouen, the Rue aux Juifs has risen in the world and is now
the address of the famous fifteenth-century Palais de Justice;
the synagogue of the modern community (No. 71 of the
charming Rue des Bons-Enfants) occupies the former church
of Ste.-Marie-la-Petite and, despite too willing guides, is not
an ancient Jewish structure. The New Alliance window of
the cathedral stands in the farthest right bay of the apse. Caen
still retains its Rue aux Juifs at the foot of its old *château.*
For further sign of Jews we must desert Normandy, where
they flourished in the heroic days of the Conqueror, and penetrate the farthest reach of Brittany. Nantes, we know, fur-
tively welcomed the Jews, who passed themselves off as New
Christians—another and different New Alliance—on their
first creeping back to northern France in the seventeenth century; but what have we to do by the far headland of Finis-

terre? In Landerneau, the last important railroad station before Brest, stands an old men's home under the care of the
Sisters of St. Joseph. In its chapel lies a tombstone with a
Hebrew and Portuguese inscription. "The tomb," it says, "of
the honourable Isaac Malogrado di Leon, who was killed in
the French war, on the 6th of Ab, the year 5454 [July 27,
1694]. His resting-place shall be glorious!" We must go to
Amsterdam or Bayonne for analogous inscriptions. The mystery is perhaps lightened if we remember that a Dutch-Eng-
lish fleet assaulted Brest in June of that year. Otherwise, Isaac
di Leon, like so many of his race, remains an unknown soldier.

BRIDAL PAIR UNDER WEDDING CANOPY.
FROM AN EMBROIDERED TORAH BAND
See page 72

CHAPTER VII

The Southlands of France

THE Palace of the Popes crowns a high hill in Avignon, before it spreads a sunny square, and west of the square the city falls swiftly to its walls and the Rhône. Clambering down a lane named appropriately La Pente Rapide, which drops from the square, or mounting upward from the river front and walls, through the Porte de Rhône, either way you will find yourself in a network of alleys pressed about by huge formless masses of masonry, more like giant boulders than human dwellings, and twice spanned by a bridging house. There are no gutters underfoot; instead, a steady stream of refuse pours at random, most anywhere. Overhead the blue sky has shrunk to a patch caught in the jagged eaves; the sun, even the sun of the Midi, has fled.

While the vile streams wet your feet, draining off the heeltaps of mediævalism, note if you will the street signs, for these crevices are streets: Rue de Vieille Juiverie, Rue Reille Juiverie, Rue de la Petite Reille. You are in the ancient ghetto. Despite very occasional repairs, its lanes and passages are much as they were before the days of Gersonides, and the houses, in truth, are old, worn, huddled, and depressing enough to pass for a faithful sample of a thirteenth-century Jewry, whence naught but the Jews have fled.

On the (northeast) corner of the Rue Vieille Juiverie and the tiny Reille Juiverie stands a low battered hulk, older, if anything, than its neighbours, or at least more desolate. The natives will tell you it was once a Jewish "convent," by which they mean a synagogue. The interior discloses a single vaulted chamber, the south window still keeping its round Romanesque arch. Not more than a handful of worshippers could have been seated in this venerable cell, but in the eleventh and twelfth century the need was no greater and later it may have served for a *beth ha-midrash*. Altogether, it is plausible that we have here the original synagogue and perhaps the nucleus of a later and larger one. Gersonides, who lived in the new ghetto in the centre of town, were he to return today, would hardly feel that the old place had changed; at least he could still complain of the difficulty of finding a Talmud.

As for the new ghetto (established in 1226), it has disappeared save for the street names, Place Jerusalem, Rue Jacob, and Rue Abraham, and for a few old houses in the Rue Abraham recalling in their extreme height and the tumble down penthouses on their roofs the congestion prevalent in most Jewries. The modern synagogue on the Place Jerusalem stands on the site of its mediæval predecessor.

Accordingly, it is more profitable to linger in the older quarters, a forgotten world, and evoke, if we can, something of its perished life. The synagogue we have before us; we may elect what buildings we choose to house the social hall *(Lazina)*, school, matzoth bakery, *kosher* slaughter-house, ritual bath *(mikveh)* and administration offices *(Lazara)*. The latter would have repaid a visit, for this little world was a self-governed state, electing its own authorities and assemblies, making its own statutes, and levying its own taxes (with due heed to the Papacy). Its laws were benign, its care for the poor and weak was sure, and its discipline, enforced by fine, imprisonment and excommunication, was both foolproof and just. Even so, its punishments were tempered with Jewish charity; prisoners for debt, we may observe, were allowed to go home every night and take Saturdays and Sundays off from jail—and this in the full tide of the Middle Ages. A reminiscence of this communal care is caught in the inscription (now in Musée Calvet, Salle du Moyen-Age) of a much later date. "This house," it reads in part, "was founded at the expense of the community, through the efforts of four men . . . who made personal sacrifices for the people in building it . . . 1st day of Elul, the year 5502 [Aug. 30, 1742]." The "house" was probably a free hospice for needy travellers *(hachnasat orchim)* or a public study-hall *(beth ha-midrash)*, two frequent dependencies of a synagogue.

These few dripping alleys and their little republic, or something very like it, must have been all the ghettos of the Midi. And the Midi, together with Spain, from which it is hardly to be distinguished, nourished the most fruitful epoch in the two thousand years of Jewish exile.

Jewish communities existed in these southern lands—continuously—longer than in Palestine. Jews likely landed at Nice and Marseilles even before the days of Cæsar, and during Roman rule they spread along the Mediterranean shore to Gibraltar and beyond. Inland, traders among them mounted the Rhône, past Avignon, to Lyons, and the Garonne to Toulouse. When Mohammed captured the East, these southern Jews became the natural link between Christendom and Islam; Jewish merchants bound together the two worlds, and Jewish vessels, under Jewish captains, sailed the Mediterranean seas.

The creative life of these communities was only comparable to that of Spain, and again to ancient Palestine. And the impress of this life upon European history, however little recognition has been given it, is but little less than that of the Bible. On both sides of the Pyrenees, Jews, unlike their northern brethren, entered more or less freely into public life; they frequented the courts of caliph, king, and count, and shared the general learning of the world about them, in their day and partly due to their efforts, the most cultivated world of Europe. Medicine, astronomy, optics, mathematics, physics, poetry, and philosophy passed in Jewish hands over the bridge of the Midi, the Pont d'Avignon, from the Arab to the Christian world. In Provence, Languedoc, and the Comtat Venaissin, as in Spain, the Jews for the only time in their European career were in their own name a roundly civilized people, possessed and productive of spiritual goods, both sacred and profane, bearing their own trade-mark.

Yet who of the ten thousand English visitors that pour monthly through this southern world thrills at the name of David Kimchi, whose commentaries on the Bible profoundly influenced every page of the Authorized Version? Of the ten thousand monthly American visitors, is anyone found stricken before the synagogue in the Place Jerusalem, overcome with the realization that Gersonides must have lived near by while he was devising his quadrant, the so-called "Staff of Jacob" which took Columbus safely to the new world? What Jews of these and other ten thousands give a thought to the Ibn Tibbons? Who among them enjoys a memory of the mathematical, astronomical, musical, ethical, and philosophic works of Abraham ben Hiya? Does anyone prowl in the moonlight of Provence, unable to sleep in the excitement of visiting the boyhood haunts of Jacob Anatoli, the first translator of Averroës? Who indeed loses sleep over Averroës?

Instead, we thrill at the sight of the Papal Palace, although it is questionable if benefit to the human mind was ever derived from a single man (save the visitor Petrarch) who trod its pompous halls. We wait for moonlight to admire the Arena at Nîmes, as precious a work in the spiritual history of mankind as the Yankee Stadium. We readily succumb before the portal of St.-Trophîme at Arles, oblivious either to our ignorance of its meaning or, if we are not ignorant, to our derision of its import. We are enchanted by fortifications and waterworks—the walls of Carcassonne and the Pont du Gard.

The reason is not far to seek. Jewish civilization in the Midi was religious and intellectual; Roman and Christian civilization was, in addition, æsthetic. Things of the mind and heart are, in their nature, ephemeral; only beauty (sometimes) endures. Beauty endures because its appeal is basically to the senses, to the physical man; and the body is more constant, less fickle, than mind and soul, which vary with the winds of invention, chance, and interests.

The Roman aqueduct over the Gard no longer holds water, and neither does Jewish philosophy. The Maison Carré at Nîmes is without worshippers, like Jewish liturgy. The Palace of the Popes is an empty ruin, like Jewish mysticism. But the aqueduct, temple, and palace are incorporate; and their sensual appeal, because it is sensuous, is comparatively immortal. The Jewish civilization of the Midi has vanished almost without trace because it catered almost solely to the gusty, impermanent whims of the mind and soul.

No one more than the Jews lived to regret the departure of the Popes from Avignon (1377). For with their going came a business depression, and with the business depression the only too familiar and modern (*vide* Germany, Rumania, Austria, Hungary, Poland) outburst against the Jews. To the visitor of today the economic system of Avignon in the days of the Popes is as apparent as though the ledgers were spread before his eyes. Walls and towers stand on both sides of the Rhône, the central transportation system of fourteenth-century France, and by means of the walls and towers the citizens of Avignon taxed the traffic of an empire. Behind the walls and towers was the ghetto, old and new, and partly through their commerce and partly by means of usury, which is known today as banking, the Jews taxed the citizens. Above the ghetto rose the Papal Palace, and by means of moral suasion the Pope in his palace taxed the Jews. And finally, in turn, by reason of the death of an obscure Jew in Palestine, the Pope protected the walls and towers. When he departed again for Rome, the chain of mutual protection and taxation was snapped, and the Jews, being the weakest link, were crushed in the ensuing crash.

A half-century before, Philip IV had ruined the remainder of the French Jews. The aftermath of the Albigensian Crusade had even before that impoverished the Jews of Languedoc, who doubtless derived small satisfaction from observing that the Albigensian heretics had preferred, in a certain sense, Judaism to Catholicism, once they realized that they had lost forever their offices as bailiffs to rich counties.

Mysticism can endure poverty, indeed it feeds on human misery. But science, like philosophy, art, and liberty, flies from the window when the wolf is at the door; and it hardly needed the final expulsion, at the end of the fourteenth century, to destroy, save for a vague tradition of occultism, the Jewish civilization of the Midi.

Only in the Comtat Venaissin, the little territory surrounding Avignon, the Jews lingered on under Papal protection; and in Carpentras and Cavaillon, long after Jewish philosophy and science had fled, in the twilight of their decadence, by a strange paradox, synagogues were built and still stand, which are truly things of beauty.

༄༄

One hour by auto-bus brings us to Carpentras, nestled in the flanks of Mount Ventoux, and a few minutes more to the town-hall. In the northeast corner of the town square (Place de la Mairie) lies the entrance to one of the two most precious synagogues of France, and now a national monument.

The exterior, you need not be surprised to observe, is a nondescript blank. More than hiding a certain wealth within, this mask reveals the furtive soul and fears of the worshippers who dared expose themselves as little to the sun of the Midi as to the leaden skies of London, Berlin, or Lemberg. The Synagogue, we have already learned, goes blindfolded.

Once penetrating the mask, we enter into the sumptuous age of Louis XIV. Wainscot, pilasters, and capitals catch in their rich carving a faint light projected from high dusty panes and filtered and broken through a maze of hanging lamps. As a French scholar truly said, the building breathes a soul; no tracked tragic spirit haunting the laden atmosphere, but a tough, doughty soul that wrestles in every stick and stone and speaks bold in every peculiarity of the old pile.

The original structure (dating from 1367) has largely disappeared under its many trials and transformations. The cellar, no longer visible, housed the women's synagogue at a time when the Papal authorities permitted no additions aboveground. The present roof, during the eighteenth century, provoked years of contention with these same authorities, years of official measurements and counter-measurements, years of now being hoisted upward and again being thrust downward, in an effort to allay both the fears of the Christians lest the synagogue overtop the town church, and the pride and push of the Jews. The windows were pierced in the teeth of enormous lawsuits. During the enlargements of 1741-43 the east wall was advanced perilously near the adjoining church of the White Penitents, who feared the clamour of Hebrew prayers; and in the varying winds of legal judgments, its round window, above the ark, was repeatedly broken through and sealed anew. The west gallery was originally a separate room, used perhaps as a study-hall; merely removing the partition and throwing it open to the synagogue proper cost a world of legal pains—and cash. Small wonder if the architect went nearly mad. Peace, and the synagogue itself, were not finally restored until 1784 (date on tablet of the Law, beside ark).[1]

This west gallery was not, as most synagogal galleries are, destined for the women. In the foreground sat the *parnas,* *gabbai,* and other authorities. The graceful Louis XV canopy surmounting, as it were, the "royal box" in the centre of the gallery, indicates the *bima* or platform from which the officiant chanted the services and from which the Law was read, an arrangement apparently peculiar to the Comtat Venaissin. The wrought-iron balustrade and massive menorahs decorating the gallery deserve for their beauty this place of honour. And the women were given the narrow balconies on either side of the ark and along the north wall.

The east wall, of course, shelters the Ark of the Law *(Aron ha-kodesh)* framed in sober panels of carved stucco, and set off again by iron railings. To the right of the ark, a small niche supports a tiny, richly upholstered Louis XVI chair, altogether a piece of doll's furniture. Its use is embroidered into the upholstered back. "This," reads the embroidered Hebrew words, "is the chair of Elijah." Although it may seem too small for the purpose, the chair served to accommodate the prophet, who always appears on the occasion of a circumcision. But there is just a possibility that these southern synagogues, like those of Alexandria and Cairo, kept the tradition

[1] The synagogue was again restored in 1930.

of being accorded a special visit by Elijah; if so, and if we can judge by the size of the chair, the hope of his return was not very great.

Certain dependencies of the synagogue still survive. A low vaulted cellar, entered from the courtyard south of the main structure and lighted dimly by its doorway, houses two complete matzoth bakeries, both equipped with ovens pierced deep in the walls, long-handled wooden shovels still resting on their racks overhead, pronged markers to stamp a design in the cakes, and huge stone kneading-blocks. The bakeries existed as early as 1625, and perhaps long before. One of the kneading-blocks, naturally, bears the name of its donor: "Gad of Digne—a gift—1652." (And up in Digne itself, southwest of the cathedral lies a Rue de la Juiverie, in memory of Gad and his tribe.) The courtyard provides a well, near at hand so no time should be lost and leavening set in before the cakes were done. The bakeries have long been out of use; and decay, neglect, and that ineluctable quality which permeates a human tool, be it book, palace, or matzoth shovel, once it is discarded and for generations undisturbed, lend their touching appeal. In a thousand towns of Europe similar bakeries have rotted into nothingness, leaving of the shouting bustle, the meticulous ritual, and the mingled fear and joy that once marked their use, no trace save Egyptian darkness. Fear? Of whom—Pharaoh? Man has been doomed to eat his bread in the sweat of his face, but the Jews alone, chosen people, to bake it in the trembling of their lips.

Still another stairway descends into a subcellar hewn out of the living rock. The stairs are broken off and leave the visitor staring, with the aid of a match, into the ancient *mikveh*. A stone trough conducted the water from somewhere overhead to the pool below. A romantic Frenchman has written of this sightless hole: "Under the synagogue, a bath, where on the eve of their wedding bathed the young brides. The shade of the Shulamite haunts this retreat, and the perfume of the Queen of Sheba." It is a pity the portly matrons of old Carpentras could not have heard his flattery. Today the shade of the Shulamite is indistinguishable in the inane blackness, blacker far than her tents of Kedar, and there is need of perfume.

The *Carrière*, as Jewries were called in these southern lands, has disappeared. A street name, Rue de la Vieille Juiverie, survives of the older quarter, leading from the Cour des Platanes (site of the town walls) and spreading through the tortuous Rue de la Fournaque. Not even a name remains of the later Jewry, pressed about the synagogue, fifteen hundred human beings cramped in towering tenements rising like a horrid Mount of Purgatory in the heart of the town (and still visible in the old prints, in the town museum). Life in this mount, however, need not be thought one round of exaction and expiation. Poetry wrought in the soft Judeo-Provençal dialect of the *Carrières* echoed in the panelled walls of the synagogue. Never were Purim plays written with more fancy or acted with more feeling. Thanks to Armand Lunel's delicate and merry novel, *Nicolo Peccavi,* and his translation of a typical Purim play, *Esther de Carpentras,* the traveller may revisit this vanished Jewry in the hands of a sure guide.

The old stones in the Jewish graveyard (northeast of city, in the La Fontrouse quarter, near aqueduct), which likely dates from 1343, have nothing to tell, for the reason that the Papal authorities forbade inscriptions—as indeed they forbade dirges and candles on the road to burial. Most of the stones from a still earlier cemetery were seized and built into the town walls: a stray few have found refuge in the town museum (Boulevard de Musée).

Cavaillon, third of the famous Four Communities of the Comtat, lies an hour south of Carpentras. Nothing need detain us in L'Isle-sur-Sorgue, the fourth of these communities, which we pass on the way, eager as we should be to glance at the most exquisite synagogue surviving in western Europe.

Half-suspended in air, it spans the Rue Hebraïque, formerly the heart of the ghetto (leading from the Rue Fabrice); and unlike Carpentras and most anywhere else in its day, its exterior makes a show of beauty. The delicately wrought railings of the balcony which leads to the main entrance on the second floor, the finely panelled doors and well-proportioned windows, the whole airy and gay, breathe the best traditions of the eighteenth century. The secret of this unwonted beauty turns, of course, on its location; the façade faces a courtyard hidden from the street and safe from notice, envy, and the itch to smash something.

Its interior (restored in 1774 and 1930) provokes even keener surprise. Louis XV to the last festoon of its carved wainscot, to the last flourish of gilt on canopy, crown, and ark, at once elegant and courtly, it is more like a boudoir than a house of prayer, altogether the sort of synagogue Pompadour would have ordered had she been the mistress of a Jewish banking lord.

The general disposition of gallery, *bima,* and ark resembles Carpentras, save that the women-folk prayed in a room apart, on the ground floor, and the Elijah chair is perched on a bracket high up the corner of the east wall. But what a change of temper! The gallery, coquette in its sinuous balustrade and dainty panelling, was surely built for M. le Marquis, his powdered lady and their powdered silken-breeched witty *libertins* —what *parnas* could ponder here how best to turn the bishop's wrath or what *gabbai* brood over new and crushing taxes? And the canopy, garlanded and wreathed in grace, surely it was meant to catch and toss again the strains, not of the *ma'ariv* chant, but of Mozart. And the portal of the ark, fenced in joyous iron and crowned with gilded fruits, opened —to the sound of the maestro's fairest trio—on a banquet not

dreamed of by the sages when they made of the Law a
shulchan aruk, a "spread table." Yet, however surprising, this
happy *decor* was not inappropriate to a people who welcomed
the Sabbath as a bride and, shaking the ghetto slime from
their heels, became in this mansion of their God once again,
not a marquis, but a prince.

༼ᑎᎪᏙ༽

The Midi begins at Lyons, where fumes of the south mount
from the vine-clad valley of the Rhône, where onions give
way to garlic, butter to oil, and where *gefüllte* fish is baptized
quenelles de brochet, and *quenelle* is itself but a Gallicized
knoedel. But between Lyons and the Comtat Venaissin we
have missed little more exciting than two street names—Rue
Juiverie in Lyons itself, behind the church of St.-Paul, framed
with old houses, and in Vienne another Rue Juiverie south of
the cathedral; then in Saint-Paul-Trois-Châteaux (one of
those abandoned, forgotten, mediæval walled towns unknown
to the tourist and the delight of the true traveller) a room of
the presbytery wrongly reputed to have been a synagogue, because a stone embedded in its wall and doubtless taken from
the vanished synagogue of olden days, bears the Hebrew
words for "The Law of the Lord is perfect, it is pure" which
are dotted to date the year 5205 [1445]; and in Malaucène,
north of Carpentras and outside the boundaries of the Comtat,
the remains of a ghetto gate.

Taking our way south from Avignon and then swinging
west across the foot of the Pyrenees to Bordeaux and the Atlantic shore, we shall meet with numerous but elusive re-
minders of an extinguished Jewish world.

In Tarascon a Rue des Juifs, close to King René's imposing
fourteenth-century *château*, and, if you can evoke it, the memory of Joseph ben Abba Mari ben Joseph ben Jacob Caspi. In

Arles another Rue des Juifs (now Rue D. Fanton) one block north of the Place du Forum, and a tombstone (Musée de Ville) keeping green as a tombstone can the memory of "our master Meier of Marni" who flourished anytime between the seventh and thirteenth centuries—and this is all for Arles, where, tradition has it, Vespasian on the fall of Jerusalem sent a shipload of captives, where from that day for fourteen hundred years Jewish captives, or, as you may prefer to call them, Jewish outcasts, plied their trade in the Place du Forum; in the twelfth century they dealt chiefly in kermes, which, as you know, concerns neither usury nor old clothes. In Aix, still another Rue des Juifs (now Rue Venel) north of the Hôtel de Ville and near the central markets, where time was the Jews traded in "silks, spices, and wax." So much for Provence.

Languedoc, for us, begins with stately Nîmes, where a covered archway on the Boulevard Victor Hugo reminds us of the ancient portal leading to the ghetto in the Rue de l'Etoile and Rue Fresque lying behind; where in the Rue des Greffes the inscription of a tombstone, now upside down and serving as the lintel of a gateway, reminds us of "the wise and venerable Rabbi Isaac"; and where a statue of Bernard Lazare (in the public gardens) reminds his liberty-loving townsmen of another Jewish "warrior of the Holy Spirit." In Mende, far in the hills north of Nîmes, beyond the gorge of the Tarn (who but an incorrigible traveller will go to Mende?), are the lost fragments of a synagogue—a pointed arch and a Romanesque portal facing a courtyard, corner of the Rue Notre Dame and Rue Leopold-Monestier; the synagogue was converted into a convent in 1306 and almost completely remodelled in 1789; the Rue Notre Dame itself was formerly the *Juytaria*, or Jewry; and the Fountain of the Black Virgin, near the synagogue, once was known as the Fontaine des Juifs. Moneylenders, toll-keepers, horse-dealers, and traders, the Jews have left their mark, or was it Judaizing heretics? on the gazetteer of the entire countryside: Montjezieu (Jews Hill), Salmon, Gimel, Mont-David, Jordane, Obed, Booz (Boaz), and Reilles (Ruth), all place-names in western Lozère.

Lunel (south of Nîmes), "formerly famous," says Baedeker, "for its muscat grapes" and perhaps a little for its former sages, also presents the vestiges of a synagogue (in Hôtel de Bernis, Rue Ménard); it presents, too, a statue—may its shadow never grow less—of Charles Ménard, whoever he may have been, but no sign of the Ibn Tibbons, Gerundi, Don Astruc or the other "sages of Lunel."

Montpellier conserves the traces perhaps of a *mikveh* (in cellar of No. 1 Rue de la Barallerie), little enough for the "Mother of Israel," the "Holy Mountain," as Jews loved to call the city their commerce had enriched, their medical science had helped render famous throughout the mediæval world (Hebrew and Arabic were the languages of instruction, till the twelfth century, in its great medical schools), and their battling over Maimonides, the ancient battle between science and faith, had immortalized in Jewish geography. But Phocæan Greeks, Romans, and Saracens, who also battled here in their own way, have nothing more to show in Montpellier.

Beziers does better—in its Musée Lapidaire the longest and finest Hebrew inscription in France. Decorated with a border of vine leaves and tendrils, the stone commemorates the inauguration of a synagogue in the middle of the twelfth century (1144 or 1174) "as a memorial for the children of Israel that our generations may know what God has wrought for us . . . the exiles of our people, inhabitants of this city." The Jews, relates the inscription, had been expelled from the city and their synagogue devastated; "its bricks had fallen" and now, upon their return, they "have rebuilt it in hewn stone." Rabbi Halafta, "one of the great and leading men of our city," furnished the ground and paid the costs—"count it to him for good." The inscription concludes, inevitably, with the hope of a speedy redemption, return to Jerusalem, and "re-building of the Temple." If the earlier date is correct (1144), we are sharing our admiration for the inscription and for Rabbi Halafta with those great mediæval travellers Abraham Ibn Ezra and Benjamin of Tudela.

Narbonne (Musée de Ville), by way of rivalry, offers the oldest known Jewish inscription in France. A tombstone, dated 668 c.e., marked with a menorah, and inscribed in Latin, save for the Hebrew words for "Peace upon Israel," it reads: "Here rest in peace the three children, of blessed mem-ory, of master (*dominus*) Paragorus, son of the late master Sapaudus, to wit, Justus, Matrona, and Dulciorella, who lived, Justus thirty years, Matrona twenty years, Dulciorella nine years. *Shalom al Yisroel*. They died in the second year of our lord, King Egicanus." In their foreign dress we are not likely to recognize in Paragorus (Greek: consoler) the Hebrew Menahem, in Justus the Hebrew Zaddik or perhaps Joseph, and in Dulciorella no other than Naomi. Narbonne, too, has a dedicatory inscription (museum catalogue, No. 205) from a synagogue, saying in part: "The synagogue, Holy Ark, and east wall were finished in the month of Tebet, the year 5000 [1239 or 1240] . . . we also hope to see the Temple rebuilt when God shall have turned our captivity." And finally, two mediæval tombstones, one (No. 206) exceedingly enigmatic, and the other (No. 207) much mutilated. But of Narbonne's "Jewish kings" and Narbonne's scholars, its "eminent men of learning" as Benjamin of Tudela called them, "and great notables," no further word.

In Toulouse, the Musée Raymond, famous for its collection of coins and medals, contains a rare and yet very human item of Jewish magic. A small flat grey stone, shaped obviously for an amulet, it bears in Hebrew the words, "accident of sleep." The intention of the amulet is clarified by an additional in-scription citing the first line of Genesis 49:24; and without resorting to cabbalism, we can refer the reader to Montaigne's cure for a troubled friend, in his chapter "On the Power of the Imagination." The same museum (Salle Egyptienne) contains another rare and, here in Toulouse, remote inscription; it is graven on a block of Parian marble and hails from Berenice on the coast of Cyrenaica (Africa)—a vote of thanks passed by the Berenicean Jews, in the days of Cæsar Augustus, to ex-Governor Marcus Tittius for the justice and benevolence he accorded them during his term of office, a resolution to crown him with an olive wreath and sing his praises every new moon and to set up this tablet of Parian marble in the best place in the town amphitheatre. And the Musée des Beaux Arts (north gallery of cloister) possesses the fourteenth-century tombstone of the "venerable Don Vidals Solomon Nathan." And at the door of the cathedral of St.-Stephen, for four hundred years or more, a Jew had his ear boxed every Good Friday morning. And the Shepherds (Pastoureaux) massacres of 1321 put an end to the Jewish community of Toulouse and left for us a memory in Carcassonne, where the Jews took refuge behind the battlements we so admire today, and there, betrayed by their guard, fell to a man.

From Toulouse we might mount the Garonne to St.-Bertrand-de-Comminges, where the river breaks through the hills, in search among its Roman ruins of a trace of Herod Antipas and his wife Herodias, father and mother of Salomé, who were exiled here by Pompey (72 B.C.); or descending toward Bordeaux, we might visit the *château* of Montaigne (near Lamothe-Montravel) even for better reasons than his mother's Jewish blood.

One of the main streets of Bordeaux, the Rue Judaïque, recalls the mediæval Jewry which lay outside the walls of the city, beyond the Porte Dijeaux or Jews Gate (Place Gambetta), and which, like Arles, claimed its origin in a boatload of Vespasian's victims. The statue of the Synagogue Defeated on the Church of St.-Seurin (left of south portal) may be compared with the similar representation on Notre Dame of Paris.[1] Here the Synagogue still keeps her purse, for the Jews of Bordeaux were no mean force in the commerce of the port, not only in the thirteenth century when this monument was set up in their dishonour, but long after, when a new community made its appearance.

It was a curious community, affecting a strange appearance. On the heels of the Jewish expulsion from Spain and Portugal (1492 and thereafter) bands of wealthy Spanish and Portuguese Christians, or rather New Christians, or in truth disguised Jews, descended on Bordeaux, Bayonne, and their surrounding towns. For two hundred years they kept their disguise, baptized, married, and died in the Church, multiplied to some thousands strong, and achieved such social position and commercial power that the authorities of Bordeaux rose to their defence when Louis XIV presumed to question their presence in his Jew-free realm. Then, at the turn of the eighteenth century, after time enough to have become actually the Christians they seemed, bit by bit they dropped the mask— and in one street alone (Rue Bouhaut) the police reported three of their seven synagogues. By 1776 they had secured royal consent to practise their new-old faith, and upon the outbreak of the Revolution they were the first to receive citizenship among the Jews of France.

Three of their old cemeteries survive. In Bayonne (beyond the suburb of St.-Esprit) the earliest tombstone extant dates from 1690; on the older graves the inscriptions are in Hebrew and Portuguese, curiously running from the four sides to the centre of the stones. The second graveyard, at Bidache (east of Bayonne), lying before the entry to the town, preserves inscriptions from 1669 to 1767. And the third, at Peyrehorade (north of Bidache), on the highway leading back to Bayonne,

[1] See p. 51.

really three cemeteries in one, preserves dates from 1637 to 1826.

We can gather from these dates that the mask dropped earlier in these little towns than in Bordeaux itself. But, as elsewhere, the stones tell little we would know. That Haim Isaac Lopés Colaço "desired to take wings to the eternal dwelling-place," that "the delightful singer of the songs of Israel" Raphael Moses Souza "desired to go to heaven better to serve God" (both from Peyrehorade), that Leah Rachel Mendes d'Acosta Brabo "has gone down to draw with joy the waters of salvation" (in Bayonne), tells us nothing of the drama, daily renewed, of their double lives. Only their names resound like trumpets from beyond the Pyrenees—Pereyra, Cardozo, Lopez, Abrabanel—trumpets announcing the *paseo de la cuadrillo* when the gates swing open in the bull-ring.

SABBATH LIGHTS—18TH CENTURY

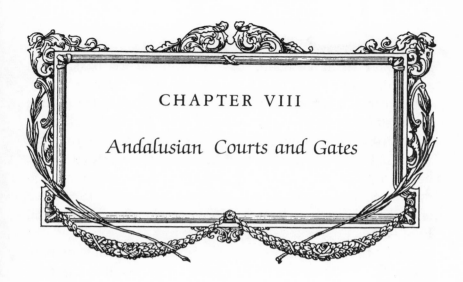

CHAPTER VIII

Andalusian Courts and Gates

TO THE Arabs of the desert Andalus is a name, says Doughty, "which ever sounds in their ears as the name of a mistress." And to the Jews it is the name of a lost romance. The fifteen centuries of adventure and achievement in Iberian lands remain romantic even to the illusions that grace their memory.

In the alleys of Salonica, behind pushcarts in Amsterdam, and peddling bananas in Seattle, the descendants of Spanish Jews remember themselves as viziers to the caliphs and treasurers to the kings. Scions of old Portuguese and Spanish families, now bankers in London or merchants in New York, praise, though they perhaps no longer read, the Hebrew lyrics of Ibn Gabirol and Judah Halevi—for there were poets in Andalus as not since David's day.

And Jews the world over, whose forefathers were never known to set foot south of the Pyrenees, start with pride at the mention of Spain: pride at the recollection of a land where, almost alone in Europe, Jews shared the common occupations of the people, tilling the soil and plying the prevailing run of arts, crafts, and trades; where, as seldom afterwards, they rose to historic station as financiers and statesmen;

and where, as never again, they made in science, philosophy, and literature a Jewish mark on Western civilization.

But quite in keeping with the Quixotic character of this pride, the thrill and tug of memory stop short at the thought of a return. Although Spain has opened her gates for fifty years, not more than a handful of Jews have resettled in the home of their remembered glory. They have not forgotten that when last seen those Eden gates flamed with the sword of a banishing angel—the sword of the Inquisition and Expulsion.

Their first settlements are lost in Roman and perhaps Phœnician antiquity. With true Castillian swagger, the Jews of Toledo and other venerable cities were wont to date their "exile" from the days of Titus, Nebuchadnezzar, and even King Solomon. It may not have been an idle claim. The Semitic ring to many Spanish place-names—Malaga (Phœnician *Malaca* from *malach* "to salt"), Cartagena (New Carthage), Carteya (Phœnician *Carta* "city"), Tharsis (Biblical *Tarshish*), Cadiz (Phœnician *Gadir* "fortress"), Adra (Phœnician *Abdera*), Cordoba (from Phœnician *corteb* "oil-press")— not only recall the Phœnician trading-posts beyond the "great waters," but perhaps the presence there, as well, of the "children of Judah" whom Tyre and Sidon "sold far from their border" (Joel 4:6).

Their Spanish career was doubtless well under way in Roman days. Jewish coins found in Tarragona (Museo Arqueológico) tell as much. Paul implied no less when he wrote his intention of visiting Spain; the first Christians were habitually recruited in Jewish communities. The gravestone of a Jewish girl, Annia Salomonula, recovered in Adra and now vanished, fixes at least one community in the third century c.e. Anti-Jewish church legislation in the next century carries the contemporary records from Roman into Visigothic rule.

Whoever chooses to pick up the Jewish trail at its first visible emergence will go to Elche—Elche of the palms—Helike of the Phœnicians—north of Cartagena by the sea. The ruins of the ancient city lie near the neighbouring port of Santa Pola. On a hillock, as the Talmud prescribes, and close to the site of the *thermes*, a bit of mosaic pavement and the stumps of long-fallen walls tell what they can of a sixth-century synagogue.

The niche, or apse, for the Ark of the Law is plainly discernible protruding from the east wall. Framed in geometric mosaic designs, in themselves prophetic of the arabesques that were later to flower in the Alhambra and El Tránsito, the Greek inscriptions mention archons and presbyters, the officials and elders of the Jewish community. The use of the Greek tongue among Jews in sixth-century Spain testifies to the old attraction of Hellenism for Israel,[1] as well as to the power and spread of Byzantine arms. Belisarius, we are reminded, was this century sweeping North Africa, the Balearic Isles, and the southern coasts of Spain; Count Julian of Byzance was still to rule in Ceuta when the Arabs came.

It is, therefore, not surprising to discover in Tortosa (museum of Santo Domingo convent) that the sixth-century gravestone of "Meliosa daughter of Judah of blessed memory" is inscribed in Greek as well as Hebrew and Latin. As for Latin, it was almost inevitable among a people long living in the Roman world. So we naturally find it on a seventh-century stone in Tarragona (cathedral cloister) commemorating "Isidora daughter of Jonathas and Axia." Though the stone is adorned with menorah and *lulab*, even the time-honoured formula, "Peace on all Israel," is rendered in the language of Titus. Merida and Sagunto likewise preserve Latin Jewish stones of the Visigothic age.

Up to the end of the sixth century the Visigoths, partly be-

[1] See p. 35.

cause they were Arians and not imbued with the right doctrine, behaved tolerably well toward their Jewish subjects. But from the year King Reccared I (589) embraced the faith of Rome, the official treatment of the Jews went from bad to worse. Thousands were driven to unwilling baptism. By the close of the succeeding century the remainder were reduced to slavery, their property declared confiscate, and had the Christian power endured, the romance of the Spanish Jews would have ended before it ever began.

The decree of slavery was passed in 694—not altogether an irrational measure, for the Jews were suspected, in their extremity, of conspiring with their brethren in Africa against the Visigothic state. And, no doubt, the Visigothic kings had their ears to the ground—and heard the oncoming tread of Moslem hosts.

In 711 Tarik landed at Gibraltar. As town after town fell into Arab hands, they were placed in the guard of the local Jews, leaving the invaders free to move northward. Among the conquerors there are rumours of Berber-Jewish chieftains: Kaulan al-Yahudi who overran Catalonia; Tarif, "a Jew of the tribe of Simon," who was first to set foot on Spanish soil and who has left his name not merely in the city of Tarifa, but in nearly every governmental budget of the world; and the two sons of Queen Cahena, the African Deborah, who led against the Cross some twelve thousand Berber lances. In four years the conquest was all over but for the shouting.

And if Charles Martel had not stopped the advance between Poitiers and Tours (732), Paris instead of Cordova might have been the first civilized city reborn in western Europe. Happily for the traveller, it was Cordova. The conservative Spaniard is slow to change the face of his towns, and the Jewry of the old Moorish metropolis still stands, in its essentials, as it did when the boy Moses ben Maimon pattered down the street that now bears his name.

⌘

"The treasury of science, the minaret of piety, and the abode of magnificence"—so an Arab writer chanted the glories of Cordova when ten miles could not bound its gardens, streets, and squares, when twenty public libraries flourished within its walls, and thousands of writers toiled so fast to fill their shelves that they wrote themselves out of parchment. Somewhat yet remains of the Arab boast: the white interlacing "Oriental" lanes, the hot sky above, and for monuments, the gates, the ruined Alcázar, the bridge across the Guadalquivir, the incredible mosque, and, not least, the outlying palace-city of Medinat az-Zahra.

The Alcázar, stripped and gutted, is not altogether empty of memories for the Jews—revisitant ghosts or prying tourists —who may recall the dependence of the Juderia on its battlements for protection in good days and refuge in bad. The mosque, too, has a word. Its "acre of low roof laid on a grove of marble columns" gives countenance, and perhaps a note of resemblance, to the vanished synagogue of Alexandria, the largest in antiquity, which was so vast, says the Talmud, that the cantor's voice could not reach its confines.

But you must go to az-Zahra, beneath the hills four miles west of the city, for a true token of Cordova's "magnificence" and some understanding of the Jewish share in it. Now reduced to sundry broken columns, excavated walls, and a small collection of mosaics, chapiters, and pottery, Medinat az-Zahra gave the tenth century the proud show of a palace one-half mile wide and nearly a full mile from the front door to the back. Four thousand columns upheld its roofs. It was built by Abderrahman III, rightly surnamed the Great (912-961), who brought Cordova to her peak of splendour and whom Hasdai Ibn Shaprut, physician and Jew, served by way of beloved counsellor, wily diplomat, and unofficial vizir.

Hasdai was the first court Jew of historic magnitude since the two Josephs of Egypt and the head of a notable line of successors in Moslem and Christian Spain. As physician to Abderrahman and, later, Hakim II, he ministered to his masters' bodily ills and, as superintendent of customs, to their financial wants. As diplomat, in the pillared chambers of az-Zahra he subtly manipulated the ambassadors from the Holy Roman Empire and distant Byzantium. As scholar, he sweated with a Latin-speaking Greek beneath these same pillars and wrought an Arab translation of a medical work of Dioscorides, thus inaugurating the intellectual commerce in which Jews were to become adept.

Turning to his own people, Hasdai patronized Hebrew grammarians who squabbled their way into history, and Hebrew poets whose early "chirping" in new-fangled rhymes and meters awakened fresh beauty in the ancient tongue. After many failures, he managed to dispatch a messenger, one Isaac ben Eliezer of Germany, to the almost fabulous and altogether remote Jewish king of the Chazars, whose capital lay a continent away, on the banks of the Volga. "Daily," he wrote the Chazar monarch, "I must hear the Gentiles say: every people has its country save the Jews. If I knew there was a spot where Israel was free, I would give up my office, leave my family, and wander over land and sea until I could kneel before my own king." But when he learned from the warm reply of Joseph, the Chazar ruler, that such a spot existed and he had only to come in order to be given "direction of the kingdom," Hasdai remained where he was, in the cool courts of az-Zahra.

Returning to the city, we halt before a massive crenellated gate, the Almodóvar, which pierces the western wall with a high pointed arch. Its slight horseshoe spring betrays its Moorish origin, and its location accounts for its ancient name, Bab al-Yahud (Jew's Gate), for it leads directly to the former Jewry.

In the days of Hasdai, the parched fields lying before the Almodóvar gate were, we may be sure, dotted with booths and tents where throngs of Moors and Jews trafficked with the wares of an empire. The refinements of life, it need hardly be recalled, were introduced to Europe by Saracens and Jews. The list runs into "some thousand objects" the names of which, in the various European languages, can be traced to Oriental sources; multitudinous luxuries that have now become necessities in the way of fabrics, household furnishings, fruits, flowers, vegetables, gems, medicines, and musical instruments. Offhand we have merely to think of cotton, velvet, satin, cashmere, muslin, gingham, serge, sash, shawl, chemise, carpet, tapestry, divan, alcove, carafe, jar, valise, peach, lime, artichoke, asparagus, spinach, tulip, lute, tambourine, ruby, turquoise, jasper, jade, nitre, soda, laudanum, alum, and alcohol.

Jewish traders, whose continental trade routes have been described for us by a ninth-century postmaster-general of Bagdad, can be made fairly responsible for the introduction of "oranges and apricots, sugar and rice, senna and borax, bdellium and asafœtida, sandal wood and aloes, cinnamon, mace, and camphor, candy and julep, cubebs and tamarinds, slippers and tambours, mattress, sofa, and calabash, musk and jujube, jasmine and lilac" as well as the limousin, or royal, breed of French horses. To the gates of Cordova the Jews fetched, above all, silks and spices from India and China, and barbarian slaves from the southern plains of Russia.

Among the booths and tents, mark across the ages the figure of Jacob Ibn Jau, silk merchant and flag manufacturer, an imposing figure "accompanied by a guard of eighteen men clad in silk" befitting the prince and chief-justice of a chain of

Jewish communities stretching from the Duero in Castille to Segelmessa in the Sahara. Mark as well the captive Babylonian, Moses ben Enoch, snatched at sea by an admiral of the caliphate and now redeemed by the Jews. Moses in rags brings a vile price, and the Cordovan Jews are no less amazed than the admiral—who later tried to boost the ransom—when they discover that beneath his tatters he conceals a veritable mastery of the Talmud. Such mastery, perfected in the schools of Sura, was unknown to Spain; and Moses, raised to spiritual leadership of the caliphate Jewries, may be said to have brought, with the help of the admiral, the saving discipline of the Talmud to the far west of Europe. There, as in Champagne and the Rhinelands, it burgeoned into new life at the very moment it was dying in the East. Hasdai, too, had his share in this momentous transfer. He spent large sums importing accurate copies of the Talmud from the waning schools of Sura and Pumbeditha on the theory, which pleased the caliph, that it was cheaper to bring the books to Cordova than to be sending students, endowments, and fees to Babylonia.

But if gazing across the centuries proves too great a strain, you may buy a ticket to Morocco, only a few hours away. There, at the entry to most any town, you will see a gate much like the Almodóvar, and the field before it swarming with Moors and Jews as they swarmed in Cordova a thousand years ago. Moses ben Enoch, Ibn Jau, and Hasdai will still be there, though under other names, and dwindled in stature like the Moorish empire itself. The articles of Jewish commerce alone have radically changed: no longer silks and slaves, but German hardware, English cottons, and American five-and-ten-cent luxuries.

Cordova's Jewry, which opens behind the Almodóvar gate, follows the city wall to the little Plaza de las Bulas, hard by the Alcázar, and then veers east to the Orange Court of the cathedral-mosque. Its main street, a long narrow lane, is called Calle Maimonides, lest we forget that here was born the prince of Jewish philosophy. By a curious trick of fate or climate, Cordova, we may add, has given birth to Seneca, no unknown thinker among the Romans, and Averroës, the glory of Moslem metaphysics. Averroës has left his name to an alley in the old Jewish quarter, Seneca has left his to an apocryphal house near at hand, and all three philosophers remain in this way remembered and unread.

Yet in their day Averroës and Maimonides dowered Europe with goods more esteemed than sofas, peaches, or borax. They gave to mediæval man a universe. Averroës (1126-98) made Aristotle available and intelligible to the Arabic-reading world, and later, through the medium of Hebrew translations, to the Latin west. That Averroës was shortly damned for this service—so you will see him in the famous paintings of the Spanish Chapel of Santa Maria Novella at Florence and in Santa Catarina at Pisa—takes nothing from its worth. Maimonides (Rabbi Moses ben Maimon, or Rambam, 1135-1204) in turn made the heretic universe of Aristotle acceptable to believers of the Bible, and thus forged a reconciliation between reason and faith which, adopted by St. Thomas, has endured, as far as Catholics are concerned, to the present hour. But he need detain us no longer, for a mere boy he was driven out of Cordova by unphilosophic Moslem monotheists from the Sahara, and we shall cross his tracks again in Fez and Old Cairo.

The low whitewashed houses of the Calle Maimonides, largely dating from the fifteenth century, must differ little from the Jewish dwellings of the "golden age." In contrast to its mean exterior, itself a blind against optimistic looters and tax-collectors, each reveals behind its solid doors a typical Moorish patio, bright with flowers and flanked by slender columns supporting horseshoe arches, which in turn support balconies set off by carved wooden balustrades. We have merely to summon a half-dozen Jewish families from a similar house and patio in any Jewish quarter of present-day Morocco, plant them in this Cordovan home—perhaps it was the very dwelling of these families five hundred years ago— and our domestic picture of Spanish Jewry is complete. In such a house and patio Judah Halevi and Moses Ibn Ezra, "the fathers of song whose sun rose in the west," read to their bearded and turbaned admirers the new splendours of Hebrew poetry, and Abraham Ibn Ezra dropped his sly philosophic doubts as he was to drop them in the houses of a dozen lands.

Halfway down the street (No. 16) stands the one authentic monument of Cordovan Jewry. The synagogue built by Hasdai's father withstood the anti-Jewish riots heralding the fall of the caliphate (1012) but was swept away in the similar riots that marked the triumph of the Almohades (1148). The new synagogue built by Christian consent when Ferdinand III captured the city (1236) fell prey to Christian violence in the year of wrath 1391. But a second synagogue, likewise erected under Christian grace in 1315, survives. It is one of the few left in all Spain.

A side garden leads to the single doorway, and the doorway to a single almost cubical chamber (6.95 x 6.37 x 6.16 metres), poorly lit by a window in the south wall and another small aperture added later to the east. Despite centuries of use for other purposes, the building still maintains its traditional Jewish features. A niche in the east wall shows the former abode of the Ark of the Law. A balcony, upheld by a column and a projecting pier, spans the south wall; and here the women-folk were curtained from view by a partition mounting to the ceiling and pierced by three arched casements. The west wall is broken by a magnificent cusped arch, now closed but perhaps originally a second portal; the house behind it, done in the same style as the synagogue, is suspected to have served as a study-hall or administrative office for the congregation. Indeed, the synagogue has suffered only one radical change; its present Gothic vaulting is an eighteenth century substitute for the original *artesonado* ceiling.

Nothing but time and neglect have altered the beauty of the arabesque panels and frieze which bind the four walls together in bands of glory. Like the stuccos of El Tránsito[1] they are notable examples, among the few that remain, of Jewish *mudéjar* art. Woven into the flowing geometric harmonies are the familiar shield-of-David, palm leaf, and tree of life.

In the panel above the arch of the west wall, a pair of traditional symbols assume unwonted form. The citron, or *etrog* —or possibly the pomegranate—is represented in cross-section as though the fruit were cut in half. To find it similarly treated, you must go back a dozen centuries and beyond the seas to Rome (Museo Borgiano), where a gilt-glass dish from the Jewish catacombs shows the same sliced fruit.[2] What stray illuminated manuscript or itinerant copyist brought the model to Cordova is a minor mystery for the historian of art. Above the citron in our west panel, the *lulab* waves in nodding branches. Altogether, it is sad to think how many architects, racking their heads for decorative detail in modern synagogues, have overlooked this simple but exquisite *motif*.

Even in Palestinian days the Jews rendered their synagogues eloquent with inscriptions.[3] The fashion passed to Spain, where it was doubtless encouraged by a similar Moslem custom, and leaving but few traces in central Europe, flourishes again in seventeenth- and eighteenth-century Poland. Hebrew lettering, as the visitor in Cordova may judge, yields only to Arabic for decorative use. The Biblical quotations, chiefly from the Psalms, which speed and rise and dip from

[1] See p. 155.
[2] See p. 237.
[3] See p. 41.

corner to corner across the arabesque panels render almost literal the prophecy of Habbakuk, "For a stone shall cry out of the wall." The Cufic inscription near the west arch, "The kingdom is the Lord's" (Ps. 22:29), is a seal and imprint of the Moorish culture on the Jews. The Hebrew lines are aptly chosen. Over the lintel we read, "This is the gate of the Lord into which the righteous shall enter" (Ps. 118:20). And the two verses over the east niche, for the Ark of the Law, turn the mind as well as the eye toward Jerusalem: "I will worship toward thy holy temple . . . one thing I have desired of the Lord, to behold the beauty of the Lord and to enquire in his temple" (Ps. 138:2; 27:4).

To the right of this niche, the charming dedication gives the date of the synagogue and the name of its founder: "A little sanctuary and house of testimony, built by Isaac Mehab son of the illustrious Ephraim; erected in the year 75 [1315] as a building for an hour.[1] Arise, oh Lord, and hasten to rebuild Jerusalem!"

The "building for an hour" has now stood its six centuries, serving, after the expulsion of the Jews, as a "little sanctuary" for hydrophobiacs under the invocation of Santa Quitería, and after 1588 as a "house of testimony" for a shoemakers' guild, and since the discovery of its original purpose, in 1884, as a national monument.

Calle Maimonides ends in the Plaza de las Bulas, once, no doubt, the market place where Jewish housewives bought their fish and vegetables. To the east lies the Calle de la Judería, formerly part of the ghetto, but now modernized beyond the hope of recapturing old memories. Yet a pair of fifteenth-century houses, fairly opposite the main portal of the cathedral, were witnesses and in a sense participants in a dramatic episode.

The episode harks back to the year 1391. In this year the

[1] Literally "Son of an hour."

streets we have been traversing, as so many other Jewish streets in Spain, ran red with the blood of massacre. Hundreds of victims fell in the Calle Maimonides. Other hundreds fled the city. But hundreds more remained, embraced Christianity, and became known as New Christians—a title to distinguish them from the pure-blooded old-line Spanish Christians.

Three generations now pass, time enough, one might think, to abolish whatever distinctions existed between Old and New Christians. But not so. In 1473, the terminal date of our episode, the Bishop of Cordova created a brotherhood *de la caridad*—such as you may see parading of an Easter Sunday in Cordova today—to which, by a familiar-sounding regulation, no New Christian could belong.

The brotherhood, with their long robes, high-pointed hoods, and masks, held their inaugural procession March 14th. As they marched down the little street toward the Calle de la Judería, the paraders no doubt remarked that no tapestries were hung from its windows and no bunting whipped in the breeze, for this street was now a part of the New Christian quarter, and New Christians were not celebrating a brotherhood from which they were barred.

As the parade passed one of those fifteenth-century houses already noted, a New Christian girl on the top floor was unfortunately busy fulfilling her usual mediæval morning task of throwing the slops from the window. And, unfortunately and accidentally, the slops, in falling, splashed on a statue of the Virgin carried in the procession.

An outcry went up at once. In a few moments the whole quarter was put to sack, and some hundreds of New Christians met their death in these little streets.

The New Christian poet, Antonio de Montoro—a fifteenth-century preincarnation of Heinrich Heine—describes these events, of which he was almost victim, in sad satiric verse. What, he asks, was the use of our becoming New Christians in order to be killed in 1473, when by remaining Jews we could have been killed in 1391, and thus have enjoyed eighty years more of peace?

The poet exaggerates, of course. Not all the Jews were killed in 1391. A number stayed on in Cordova long enough to be banished—for good—in this same year 1473.

During his siestas, the leisurely traveller might do worse than ponder on Montoro, a typical prey to *Judenschmerz*. Born a Jew in Cordova (1404), he adopted Christianity for reasons better guessed than known. After picaresque adventures abroad—including a tour of Italy as an astrologer, capture by Moorish pirates, and marriage, despite his Christian wife at home, to a Moslem girl in Fez—he returned to Spain. Here he haunted the court of Queen Isabella, in company with a band of New Christian poets whose hearts, like his own, burned with self-hate. Belonging to a guild of Old Clothes Dealers, he liked to plague himself, although well-to-do, with the epithet *El Ropero*—Ol' Clothes Man. But most of all, these renegades liked to plague one another for their Christian masks. Commendador Roman, of this bitter crew, taunts Montoro for limping with the stoop and shuffle of a junkman and a Jew. Montoro retorts, "As for you, if you went back to your home town, everyone would call you by your real circumcised name, and on Sabbath eve you'd gorge yourself with *adafina* and stuffed goose-neck." Adafina? It is the *schalet* of Heine.

Pages of this pitiful raillery survive, perhaps worth reading for the one magnificent rebuke stung from Montoro's shame-ridden soul. "We belong to the same race," he cried to a fellow mud-slinger, "and the insults you receive are mine, and the wrongs I suffer are yours."

On another occasion, a noble don hesitated to give him a suckling pig, uncertain as to whether he continued to be a Jew in his tastes. "Dear man," exclaimed the poet, " 'tis to

eat piglets I became a Christian." We think of Heine and the
silver spoons.

At seventy, Montoro complains to his queen that he cannot
efface his original stain, that despite his years in the Church,
he is still called "the old contemptible Jew."

> O Ropero amargo, triste
> quo no sientes tu dolor . . .
> por do mi culpa se escombre
> no pude perder al nombre
> de viejo puto y judío.

There is nothing to add to this plaint but the words, again, of
Heine: *Ich bin jetzt nur ein armer Jude, ein unglücklicher
Mensch.*

Jesters like Montoro, lashing their own folly and burning
for punishment, had only a few years to wait, when in the
Plaza de la Corredera, to the applause of the best people, they
burnt in earnest. The first *auto-de-fé* flamed in this square before the close of the fifteenth century. It became a semiannual
performance, with "small time" acts—*autillos*—thrown in
every month. The triple balconies overlooking the plaza were
built (1683) to give the nobility and Church dignitaries, who
came from miles around, a better view of the show. Everything, in fact, was done for the comfort of these distinguished
spectators, who on one occasion—while three victims were
burnt alive and fifty-five others condemned to prison "in per-
petuity"—consumed 4 calves, 8 hams, 30 pounds of lamb and
truffles, 186 chickens, to say nothing of wine *ad lib.* and huge
baskets of cherries, biscuits, and jellies, all at the expense of
the community. For this single performance, the cost of provisions, not including firewood, came to 392,616 maravedies.
But it was worth it. A contemporary report, detailing the
death agony of a young man, one Antonio Gabriel de Torres,
who at the last moment prayed "piteously" for God's mercy
and refused to let the executioner bind his legs, says that his

sufferings furnished *gran consuelo y edificación por todo el público*—"great joy and instruction to all present."

It was another and final contribution of Cordovan Jews to Spanish civilization.

⟨ᡒᢣᡪᢌ⟩

Seville has little unspoiled to show for its five hundred years of the Moor. The boasted Giralda is sadly transformed for anyone who has seen its mates in Rabat and Marrakesh. The several Moorish "chapels" which have survived the conversion of mosques into churches bear all the mutilated and equivocal marks of a Morisco. Yet the Moor can be sensed, latent, in every twist of the streets, in every shadow cast across the tiling of a patio, in the café songs and dances, even in the *saetas* poured full-throated to the Virgin on Holy Week. Hearing their tremulous notes, you hear, if you have ears, the muezzin singing from his minaret—and the *hazan* from his *bima*. Nevertheless, the words are most holy, Roman, and Catholic. Altogether, to discover the Moor—and the Jew—you must penetrate the language of Seville, her lanes and courts, and seek to catch its hidden tune.

Nothing, hidden or otherwise, remains of the Jew under Moorish rule. Yet, for a century, it had been a brilliant show. When Cordova's caliphate fell, the Jews fled, as we shall learn, to Granada, where certain signs and stones recall their high station. And when Granada, in turn, succumbed to dynastic wars, in which the Jews took the wrong side, fortune smiled on them in Seville. But today there are only historical allusions to prove the services of Jewish courtiers, physicians, astronomers, and vizirs to the Abbadite and Almovaride kings (1042-1147). And the next century, which saw the rise of the Almohades and the building of the Giralda, saw Israel driven to forced conversion, servitude, and general eclipse.

For once the march of Christian soldiers augured well for the Jews. When Ferdinand III captured Seville (1248) it was no flattery that brought them, Torah in arms, to welcome him at the gate. It was no empty gesture to tender him a key to the city (now in the treasury of the cathedral), whereon one may still read the Hebrew inscription: "The King of Kings will open, the king of earth will enter." And there was more than lip service in the Hebrew epitaph they devised for his tomb (in the Capilla Real of the cathedral).

"Here is the sepulchre," it tells us, "of the great king Don Fernando, lord of Castille, Toledo, León, Galicia, Seville, Cordova, Murcia and Jaen. His soul rests in the Garden of Eden— he who conquered all Spain, upright, just, powerful, valiant, pious, and modest, who feared God, who served Him every day, who vanquished and destroyed all his enemies. He lifted up and honoured all his friends. He captured the city of Seville, which is the head of all Sefarad [Iberia]. And there he died, the night of the sixth day [Friday], the 22nd of Sivan, the year 5012 of Creation [1252]."

"He lifted up and honoured all his friends"—translated from eulogy to the language of fact, this meant, for the Jews, that Ferdinand and his son Alphonse the Wise gave them an extensive and handsome quarter in the city, threw in the mosques for use as synagogues, and protected the whole with walls and gates.

This opulent Jewry now goes by the name of El Barrio de Santa Cruz, much prized by guide-books and tourists as "one of the oldest parts of Seville." You may pace off its former boundaries, passing northwest from the Alcázar, along the site of the city walls to the Puerta de Carmona, thence south to the church of San Nicolás, which faced one of the ghetto portals, and to the Calle de Méson del Moro, where rose an iron gate, and so back eastward to the Alcázar and its gardens. The third and main gate, leading as in Cordova to fields beyond the walls, is reduced to a street crossing called the Puerta de la Carne. But in its time it was known as the Bab al-Chuar in honour or memory of a certain Min Joar, Jewish real-estate magnate.

A labyrinth of cool mediæval lanes, the Barrio readily evokes its past. It is not hard to people its multitude of ancient white-washed houses with the thirty thousand Jews who flourished in its patios, prayed in its twenty-three synagogues, traded in drugs, spices, jewellery, silverware, silks, and money on the broad market place before the chief synagogue (now Plaza de Santa María la Blanca), set their workshops and smithies near the many smaller squares, and steamed themselves in the great baths off the Calle Cruces—a noisome slit of a street which up to the last century affrighted the Christian populace with retributive demons and ghosts.

Of the chief synagogue, which was converted into the Church of Santa María la Blanca (Our Lady of the Snows) following the massacres provoked by Fernando Martínez in 1391, a side portal, facing the Calle Archeros, still survives; its horseshoe arch may even go back to Moorish days.

The nest of streets north of the synagogue, though down at the heels, conceal a store of gracious patios dating from the Judería. Nos. 2 Calle Archeros and 19 Calle Verde are calculated to spur the imaginative traveller to further search. Beyond the Calle Verde rises the Church of San Bartolomé on the site of the last synagogue to fall into Christian hands. To the east lies the Calle de los Levíes, named from forgotten members of the Levite tribe and one of the few streets to house a remnant of Israel after Don Fernando Martínez had worked his will. The suite of patios in No. 4 still show signs of their Jewish *mudéjar* origin and may easily arouse whatever visions you wish of "arched casements and lolling Jewesses in broad-sleeved crimson tunics"—the sort of Jewesses that Don Juan, who lived in No. 23, missed a sight of by two centuries.

West of the Calle de los Levíes, the ancient ghetto wall paralleled the Calle Conde de Ibarro (noteworthy patios in Nos. 18, 20, 22) to its gate opposite San Nicolás. Across from the church is the convent of Madre de Dios, now a medical school and once a synagogue. A few steps eastward will bring you again to Santa María la Blanca and the old Jewish market.

Instead, you may choose to wander through the southern half of the Jewry, past the Calle de las Doncellas, where No. 17 should startle you with its pure African lines, the Callejón del Reinoso, for all the world a bit of a Moroccan mellah, the smiling square of Santa Cruz, likewise the site of a synagogue (and later the burial-place of Murillo), and finally into the restored and beautified portion of the Barrio.

Roses, geraniums, and over-roofing vines colour and shade the Callejón del Muro as (we hope) they did in the days of Judah Abrabanel. The leafy canopy, stitched with blossoms, arching across the Calle de la Pimiento keeps green the legend of the Jewish spicer who gave the lane—more a bower than a thoroughfare—its name. Our spice-dealer found himself without goods or money, and in desperation, Jew though he was, prayed to the Virgin for one or the other. The next morning found flourishing before his doorway a huge pepper tree, and nothing remained for him but to pluck the berries, sell them, and buy himself a new cloak for baptism.

The near-by Calle Vida, pressed against the gardens of the Alcázar, which sends its verdure spraying over the wall, was haunted nights—so runs the tale—by the amorous King Pedro in quest of romantically-minded Jewesses. Over the wall, incidentally, is the patio where Pedro daytimes held open court and won his title Pedro the Cruel, or according to others, who evidently won their cases, Pedro the Judge. We shall meet Pedro again in Toledo, together with his treasurer, Samuel Halevi, at the house of El Greco.[1]

The Calle Susona (lying between Pimienta and Vida) commemorates at once romance, legend, and history. The Susons or Shushans were a prominent Jewish clan, again to be met in Toledo. The Seville branch had embraced Christianity after the grim days of 1391. Two generations later, a band of New Christians, including Don Diego Suson, conspired reasonably enough against the threatened establishment of the Inquisition. Suson's own daughter, the "fermosa fembra," revealed the plot to her Old Christian lover, and her father found himself among the first to be burnt in Seville. La Susona thereupon retired to a convent. On her deathbed, stricken with remorse, she willed that her corpse be hung before the house she had sprung from and betrayed. For years, it is said, her skull cast its shadow across the little street that took the name of Muerte, *Death,* and now bears her own—Susona.

The single tombstone of Rabbi Solomon ben Abraham Yaish (in the Provincial Archæological Museum, No. 294) must serve as a memorial for the long line of notables and scholars, royal treasurers, tax-collectors, and astronomers who once walked the lanes of the Barrio and graced the courts of Alphonse the Wise and his heirs. As for Rabbi Solomon, his inscription informs us that he was a "reader of omens in the stars, a tree of knowledge, a skilful physician hiding within him the book of medicine" and that he died in 1345.

On the eve of a *corrida,* throngs of local gentry, specialists in the finesse of death, hasten to the meadows of La Tablada, beyond the Paseo de las Delicias, and there appraise and pity the bulls marked for imminent agony. There is a lure, a *gran*

[1] The landmarks of Seville pertaining to Samuel Halevi and his master, Pedro the Cruel, are mentioned in the next chapter, pp. 152, 153.

consuelo, and substantial food for the soul of man, ever hungry for tragedy, in the contemplation of a living creature doomed to painful extinction. Moreover, the visit to these fields is an old Seville custom. For three centuries, beginning with the extinction of Don Diego Suson and his friends in 1481, the local gentry trooped to La Tablada meadows to feed this self-same hunger—at the fireside of the *autos-de-fé.*

But not every New Christian or ex-Jew altogether vanished in smoke. The traveller is urged to search the second-hand bookstores of Seville for a copy of *El Tizón de la Nobleza Española* by the Cardinal Don Francisco Mendoza y Bovadilla (born 1508), who takes no small glee in digging up the Jewish roots of scores of the noblest family trees in Spain. And when, as a docile tourist, you are led through the splendid palaces of the Ponce de Leóns, the Dukes of Alba, and the Medina Sidonias, you will do well, though likely in vain, to look among the ancestral portraits for that prolific old Jew and royal treasurer, Ruy Capón, who obviously belied his name, or for Inés Hernandez Estevez, the equally prolific daughter of a converted shoemaker. But no vanity excels family pride, of which the Jews themselves are in every sense the most incurable victims.

The last service which the Jews in Spain rendered their country, and incidentally themselves, finds its monument in Seville. The elaborate tomb of Columbus (in the cathedral) marks, though it naturally does not mention, the persuasive arguments and still more persuasive loans made to Queen Isabella, in favour of the Atlantic venture, by Luis de Santangel —who marched as a relapsed Jew in an *auto-de-fé* of 1491. It likewise marks the five Jews who sailed in the unforgettable fleet—among them Luis de Torres, converted before he boarded ship at Palos and the first man to step ashore in the Americas. It marks Joseph Vecinho, a Portuguese Jew, who headed the Lisbon committee of scientists that voted down the mad project, but who nevertheless kept the respect of Columbus for his excellent navigation tables. It marks, more remotely, the quadrant of Gersonides and Jacob Machir, the "staff of Jacob," that guided the *Santa Maria* across the waters. And it hints at the suspicion that Columbus himself was a Jew—hence the veil he threw about his birthplace and ancestry. But this latter point may be left to the gentle dispute of historians, while we merely note that the year the Jews were expelled from Spain saw the discovery of a new world—for all men, and not least for them.

Except for Granada, the remainder of the southlands, dotted with historic towns, has forgotten Israel. New Street, or Calle Nueva, a name commonly given to the old quarter of the Jews after their expulsion, lingers near the site of the city wall (Calle del Muro) in Jerez, behind the alcázar in Rondo, and close to the ancient town square (Pl. de la Constitucion) in Malaga, the birthplace of Ibn Gabirol. In Murcia, the Jewry lay by the gate of Orihuela, beyond the walls. The Church of San Blas in Carmona stands where stood the synagogue. And in Lucena, famed for its Talmudic schools—where Judah Halevi sat at the feet of the venerable Al-Fasi (b. 1013— d. 1103)—the inhabitants will tell you there might have been a street called Nueva, or even Judería, but if so, it was a long while ago. There is nothing to be done but to agree with them.

꒰ᔓᔓ꒱

Granada, by name and origin, is linked inextricably with the Jews. When Arab writers first mention this locality, they speak of Elvira, the Iliberis of the Romans, and bordering it a hillside town which they call Gharnatha al-Yehud (Gharnatha-of-the-Jews). They take care to explain that Gharnatha should be pronounced Granata, meaning pomegranate. Then the Jews complicated matters by calling the town Rimon (Hebrew for pomegranate), thereby leading to the supposition of an ancient Phœnician shrine in these parts, dedicated to the Biblical god of "the house of Rimmon." Finally, they lent a certain confusion to the whole question by claiming that Gharnatha-of-the-Jews was first settled by Tubal, the son of Japhet, and named after Grana, a daughter of Noah.

Anyway, Gharnatha, which Arab chroniclers tell us was "compact with Jews" at the time of the Moorish conquest, stretched down the hill from the Tower of Bermejas to the bend of the Darro River, or in more modern terms, from the Alhambra-Palace Hotel to the Cervantes Theatre. The Jewry clung to this slope throughout its history. One of its gates, the Puerta del Sol (Bib Maurur) lay a little northeast of the picturesque Casa de los Tiros. Local tradition holds that the chief synagogue stood on the site of the present church of Santo Domingo, where a granite dog, symbol of the Dominicans, keeps watch above the portal against any threat of relapse. To this day the natives of the quarter are nicknamed *los peludos* (the hairy folk), reminiscent of the long-departed earlocks and beards.

By wandering through the lanes and courtyards of the Albaicín, the old Moorish hill section of the town, you may gain a picture of how those beards and earlocks lived. The great and wealthy Jews, *naggidim* and *nesiim*, swanked about, we may be sure, in such colonnaded carved-stucco courts as you will find in the Casa del Chapiz (14 Cuesta del Chapiz). And the common folk had small cause to complain in the less pretentious but charming patios to be met most anywhere on this swarming hill (for example, Nos. 12, 29 Calle de San Luis; 21, 28, 37, 39 Calle del Agua de Talavera; 3, 19 Calle de la Mina; 2 Calle Yanguas; 5 Calle de Bravo; 14 Calle Horno del Oro; 5 Calle de la Victoria). The present swarthy population, gadding and crying in the streets, needs no genealogical

research to prove its Moorish blood. Indeed, throughout Andalusia, as well as in most of northern Spain, Moor and Jew rise
like a deep blush beneath the skin of the "purest" Don.

A hint, too, may be had of where and how the Jew worked,
in the touch that is left of the ancient *souks*. Fifth Avenue has
nothing to rival the fragment of the Alcaicería, or silk-market
(near the cathedral), its pillars slim and elegant as the ladies
that used to flash between them, its tooled and graven arches
curving like the pomegranate. Close at hand, the jewellery
souk enticed the same fair customers. Goldsmithing in Moslem Spain, as in North Africa today, was almost exclusively
a Jewish craft; the Moors contemned it as they did usury. The
delicate filigree and inlaid enamel work of Granada, its pride
and specialty, still gleams, though with less cunning, over
Jewish furnaces in the *souks* of Morocco.

"Whoso did not see the splendour of the Jews in Granada,
their good fortune and their glory, never saw true glory—for
they were great through wisdom and piety." Thus wrote the
chronicler, Solomon Ibn Verga. To Western ears this is a
strange definition of glory—to be "great through wisdom and
piety"—nothing comparable, it appears, to *la gloire* of the
French. Since wisdom and piety are not apt to throw up Arcs
de Triomphe or lay out Siegesalleen, it may be difficult for us
to catch sight of this Jewish "splendour" at this late date.

Yet while wandering over the Albaicín, we may have stum-
bled on sundry remains of the eleventh century: a shattered
span of the Kadi bridge across the Darro, the ruined baths in
the Carrera del Darro (No. 37), the Puerta de los Estandartos
or Gate of Banners cut into the old Moorish walls of the city,
a worn stretch of the walls themselves, and behind them the
Casa de la Lona on the square of San Miguel. These are the
sole relics of the Zirite kings. The Casa de la Lona, a spraw-
ling abandoned hulk, is known to readers of Moorish history,
Baedeker, and Washington Irving as the storied Casa del

Gallo; and it marks, most inadequately, the palace of the great Habbus and the cruel wine-soaked Badis. In the annals of Jewish glory, it marks the court where Samuel the Nagid (Prince) and his son Joseph guided the destinies of the Zirite state and lifted Granada to the summit of her power.

Born in Cordova (993), Samuel was a trained Talmudist, grammarian, mathematician, philosopher, and master of seven languages. After the sack of his native city he fled to Malaga, where he ran a small spice-shop at the foot of the Alcázar. Here he eked out his profits on peppers by writing business notes and love-letters for the servants of the palace. His fine penmanship presently brought him to the notice of the governor, who took him to the royal court in Granada. And Samuel, in the end, became vizir of the realm.

When King Habbus died (1038), the usual Berber strife broke loose over the succession to the throne. Samuel backed Badis, who proved the victor, and thereby kept his office as vizir. In battlefield and council-chamber, as well as in tournaments of Talmudic learning and even at the task of compiling a Bible dictionary, Samuel showed himself the *nagid*, and a prince crowned with the four diadems of Israel: the crown of Torah, the crown of priesthood, the crown of kingdom, and, "excelling them all," the crown of a good name.

What is more, the wisdom and justice of his rule won him a tribute from the Moors. A contemporary poet, Monfatil, praised him in verses which later Moslem writers quoted with scandal and horror: "Oh, thou who unitest in thee every virtue and who art above other men as gold is above copper—if men could distinguish true from false, they would pattern their words on thy mouth, and if they sought to please God, instead of kissing the Black Stone of Mecca, they would kiss thy hands whence their many blessings flow." Samuel, too, was something of a poet; more than enough to inspire the critical simile, "cold as the snows of Hermon or the poems of Samuel the Nagid."

But there were poets without him. In the Casa del Gallo we could have heard Solomon Ibn Gabirol, "the pious nightingale singing out of the mediæval night love-songs to the rose —the nightingale whose rose was God." Hebrew and (thanks to Zangwill) English literature knows Ibn Gabirol as a poet. But Latin scholasticism and the doctors of the mediæval night knew him as a philosopher and Arab. The *Fons Vitæ*, or *Fountain of Life*, by Avicebron, was "widely read in Latin Europe for centuries," and it contributed no little to the spread of Neo-Platonism in the Middle Ages and the Renaissance. You may have somehow neglected the *Fountain of Life*, in which case you differ from Roger Bacon, Dante, and Giordano Bruno. But then, not until the nineteenth century was it discovered that Avicebron and Ibn Gabirol were one.

We could likewise have met the poet Moses Ibn Ezra before he left Granada, a baffled and broken-hearted lover. And grammarians and translators, when grammar and translation were honoured arts, on the hill of Albaicín.

The glory came to a sudden end. Joseph, the son of the Nagid, succeeded his father as vizir. And, like his father, he too inspired Moorish poets. But their verses rang with a different and more accustomed sound.

"I have come to Granada," sang Abu Ishak Ibn Said, "and I see that it is ruled by the Jews. They have divided between them the capital and provinces. They wax fat on taxes, sit at laden tables, and clothe themselves with finery, while Moslem fare is poor and Moslem cloaks are ragged. The head of this monkey band [our Joseph, son of the Nagid] has lined his palace with marble, kept us suppliant at his gate, and mocked our holy religion. Out with our swords—he is a sheep fat for the killing—nor spare his flock of friends and kin gorged on our spoil!"

Never had poet more gratifying response from his public. The Jews were hunted through one short Sabbath (December 30, 1066), and four thousand of them fell victims to Joseph's "glory." Joseph himself hid in the cellar of his marble palace and blackened his face with charcoal in the hope of passing for a Moor. But he was quickly discovered, killed, and hung to a cross before his own gate.

Thereafter, for four centuries, the Jews of Granada confined their attention to filigree, enamel-inlaying, and other crafts free from splendour and slaughter.

And is there to be no word of the Alhambra? Built in the autumn of Moorish rule, its magic halls knew nothing of the Jews. But there came a day, March 30, 1492, when Ferdinand and Isabella, newly installed as conquerors, convened a solemn assembly in the world-renowned Hall of the Ambassadors. It is to be feared that their majesties gave little heed to the beauty about them, the sevenscore patterns pressed in its red and blue walls, and none whatever to the unintelligible Arabic inscriptions forever repeating, "God alone is conqueror."

Instead, they were occupied with a state paper, which after due consideration they signed. The paper decreed the expulsion of the Jews from Spain.

A short while later, the Alhambra witnessed another scene. Don Abraham Senior, leaving his escort of thirty mounted mules at the gate, crossed its courts, and together with Don Isaac Abrabanel received audience from the king and queen. Abrabanel stood high in their favour and Senior, the official head of all the Jewish communities in Spain, stood higher still, for it was he who had brought about the royal match. And now they came to plead the cause of their people. Ferdinand and Isabella listened unmoved. Finally Abrabanel added to his plea the offer of substantial "gifts and donations." At this Ferdinand began to waver. Then, the story goes, Torquemada, the Grand Inquisitor, flung a crucifix before the royal pair and cried, "Judas sold his Master for thirty pieces of silver—your majesties wish to sell Him for 300,000 ducats of gold—here He lies—take Him and sell!"[1] Whereat Isabella turned to the Jews and answered them in the words of Solomon, "The king's heart is in the hand of the Lord." And she added her private gloss. "You believe your woes come from us? The Lord has prompted the heart of the king."

There was little left to be done. Don Isaac took boat for Naples. Don Abraham took to the water of the baptismal font. Torquemada returned content to his quarters—you may still visit them in the Cuarto Real del Santo Domingo (behind the Isabel la Católica Theatre). The Jewish masses, in untold misery, hundreds of them dying by the way, left the land they loved and served—the last shipload, it is said, passed a little squadron setting out from Palos for parts unknown. And Ferdinand and Isabella found themselves glorious tombs in the royal chapel of the cathedral of Granada.

Standing before their pompous sculpture, or better yet before the simple lead coffins in the vault below, you may seek to understand the terrible decision—cruel in its day and stupid in retrospect. Torquemada and all he stood for had a part. But more than this, seven centuries of ceaseless struggle to drive the Moor from Spain and create a unified state had given birth, in its triumph, to a new overriding national soul. The Moor had gone—and now the Jew. It was not the proverb of Solomon that moved the royal heart, but the battle-cry of the Cid, *Santiago cierra España*—"Saint James and close your ranks, oh Spain!" Inquisitive Sancho Panza once asked, "Pray is Spain open, that it wants to be closed up?" Ferdinand and Isabella have answered. And history has added its own gloss: that a nation which substitutes battle-cries for vision, and cruelty at home and robbery abroad for wisdom, shall indeed be closed up.

[1] For a modern painting of this scene, see p. 164.

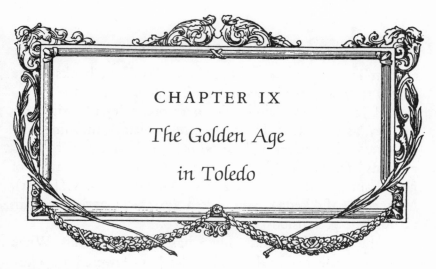

THE little Church of El Cristo de la Luz tells the story of Toledo. Its Visigothic columns are relics of three centuries of occupation by northern barbarians. The building as a whole is a ninth-century mosque of the southern invaders. After the Cid cantered down to its door, it received its final transformation as a mediæval Spanish shrine. And its name and legend are bound up with the Jews. Goth, Moor, Spanish Christian, and Jew together wrought the wondrous city.

The legend, incidentally, relates that in the days of Athanagild, Visigothic king of Toledo (554-67), wicked Jews secretly daubed poison on the feet of a crucifix which hung in the church. But at the first move of a pious old lady to kiss its toes, the feet promptly withdrew from her lips. A statue of this character was naturally not allowed to fall into the hands of the Moors, and upon their capture of the city (712) it was bricked into the church wall, together with a lighted lamp. Nearly four hundred years later (1085), when the Cid rode triumphant through the streets, his good horse Babieca halted before the church, sank to its knees, and refused to stir. At once the wall was broken open and the statue discovered. The lamp was still burning. Hence the name, El Cristo *of the Light.*

The Jews themselves have legends which prove their presence in Toledo long before the Goths. From the banks of the Tagus they wrote Pilate a letter of protest against the execution of Jesus. They claimed, furthermore, a Jewish origin for the city, as witness its Hebrew name, Toletala, meaning "exile" (*taltel*), "wandering" (*tiltulim*), or, if you prefer, "generations" (*toledot*). The Palestinian echoes in the names of neighbouring localities—Escalana (Askelon), Jopes (Joppa), Maqueda (Makkeda), and Aceca (Aseka)—gave a certain air to their pretensions.

Of the Moorish period, only a half-legend remains. When one-eyed Tarik besieged the city, the Jews lowered a spokesman from the walls, who agreed to open the gates provided liberty be granted their race. Once within the gates, the Moors gave an undying impress to the city. Centuries after their political power had vanished, Arab speech and Arab science ruled Toledo. The voice of the Christian may have spoken from cathedral and alcázar, but it was the hand of the Moor which built towers, palaces, and chapels, and guided the pen across Hebrew and Latin parchment.

Besides medicine, astrology, courtly etiquette, and swordmaking, the Toledan Christians learned tolerance from the Arab, and it was the liberty cultivated by the new conquerors, with Alphonse VI and the Cid at their head, that makes Toledo for the Jews what Cordova is for the Moors, a city of precious monuments and abiding memories.

Their broad quarters spread above the mighty gorge of the Tagus, from the Puerta del Cambrón (built by Alphonse VI in 1105) to the Paseo San Cristóbal. A smaller Jewry called the Alcána (Hebrew *kanah* "to buy") adjoined the cathedral and served as a general market for silk-merchants, jewellers, and spicers. It was in this same Alcána that Cervantes tells us he bought the immortal manuscript of Cid Hamet Benengeli, and where, as late as the end of the sixteenth century, he said he would have no trouble in finding a Toledan who could still understand Hebrew.

At least a dozen synagogues—"beautiful like none elsewhere" said the poet Al-Harizi—rose in this new Jerusalem. So it was called for its learning, piety, and splendour, and so it can still be called, though every Jew is fled, for its hills capped with Oriental streets and its rude encircling cañons. The rocks and flame of Zion speak in the voice of the prophets, and without setting foot in either place we can sense that similar rock and fire have found a strangely kindred issue in the brush of El Greco.

Two synagogues remain to prove Al-Harizi's boast. Even today they are like none elsewhere. To begin with, they are unavoidable, for every gamin in Toledo spends his daylight hours begging the privilege (with tip) of conducting the traveller to their doors.

The larger synagogue, sometime known as the Church of Santa María la Blanca, stands in a tranquil garden, once the heart of the ghetto, back from the lip of the gorge. No one knows when it was built. A wooden beam found in the near-by church of San Juan de los Reyes and now in the Provincial Museum (gallery) bears the following inscription in Hebrew: ". . . erected on its ruins in the year 940 [1180]. . . ." If this fragment, like others discovered in San Juan, comes from our synagogue, the date does not belie the general character of the structure; and its founder may well be Joseph Ibn Shoshan who was known to have endowed a house of prayer towards the end of the twelfth century, and whose family led the affairs of Jewry and shared with Fermosa—the much-dramatized "Jewess of Toledo"—the favor of Alphonse VIII. Of the Shoshan synagogue, it was said, "What is this that God hath wrought for Moses and for Israel!" If, however, Santa María la Blanca was not built by Shoshan, the exclamation still holds good, but opinion prefers to place the work in the thirteenth century.

The plain façade—though formerly enlivened by twelve broken-arched windows—and the bare face of the walls have all the indifference of a mosque to outward show. They betray, as well, a proper respect for blinding sunlight, and, it may be supposed, a Jewish reluctance to attract overmuch attention. In any case, the exterior ill prepares the visitor for the sight within.

Once past the portal—the doors are newly installed but of *mudéjar* origin—the sensitive lover of architecture is lost in a fugue of curves, of rolling lines and forms, without beginning or end, growth or decline, accent or logic, like the divinity they seek to evoke. The massive octagonal piers and interlocking horseshoe arches spring abruptly from the west wall, order the hall into nave and four aisles in their spacious march, and break in full career against the east, as though they were a detachment, rendered apparent by the builder's magic, of a ceaseless invisible host—a hundred-foot slice of infinity.[1]

The piers are crowned with capitals that have no kin in this world—an interplay of filets, pine cones, and floral growths unknown to botany—each a shade different from its fellow. Bands of stucco carved in geometric design and sown with almost indiscernible conches, "shields of David" and stylized lilies, surmount the colonnade of the nave, dropping rich medallions in the spandrels; they are presumed to date from the thirteenth century. Above the bands, pillared casements face the interior of the nave, column and arch moving in a continuous arcade. Behind them lay, no doubt, the women's galleries.

Each morning the worshippers in these aisles proclaimed, at the outset of their prayers, "the unending Unity that hath neither bodily form nor substance." No builder, to be sure,

[1] Literally, 81′ x 63′; the nave is 60′ and the aisles 40′ and 50′ high.

could make a blue-print on this basis. But to those who find in pure geometric abstraction the true idiom of faith, who take ecstasy in the swell and lift of the naked line rather than in the grosser vesture of imitative art, who, in short, prefer synagogues and mosques to temples and churches, Santa María la Blanca comes as close as brick, mud, and plaster can to meeting their desires. The Jews liked it so well they had their synagogue in Segovia built after the same pattern.[1]

Since those days, the building has served many desires unforeseen by the architect. In 1405 the Christian authorities, aroused by the anti-Jewish preaching of St. Vincent Ferrer, converted it into the church of its present name. Because of the massacre which (in 1391) preceded this seizure and somehow followed most of the activities of the pious preacher, later and more Christian men have intimated that the new church should not have been called St. Mary of Snow, but San Vincente de la Sangre—St. Vincent of Blood. Red, we know, are the handsome tiles fitted, shortly after the transfer, to the base of the piers. But this, of course, does not reflect the popular view at Toledo, where in the pulpit of Santiago del Arrabal you may still see a wax statue of Vincent, the wax arm outstretched in oratorical wrath against the Jews, as the original arm was stretched when the saint inaugurated his crusade in that very church five hundred years ago. The Ark of the Law will never be reinstalled in Santa María la Blanca, the portals in the north and south walls, now dwindled to a vestige, will never be reopened, the pillar-shaped alms-box in the corner—once a Moslem or Hebrew tombstone—will not ring with *zedakah*, but it is something that St. Vincent and his terror are reduced to wax-works.

In the sixteenth century the building became a refuge for penitent magdalens, and in the eighteenth century a barracks,

[1] See p. 169.

next a warehouse, and then a dance-hall. Today it is a national monument.

The second synagogue—"like none elsewhere"—is tied to the fortunes of the house of El Greco. The Casa del Greco, which lies at the end of the ghetto lane passing behind Santa María la Blanca, takes its name from the supposition that Spain's greatest painter lived somewhere on the premises. But two centuries before El Greco moved in with his easels, it was the palace and home of Samuel ben Meir Halevi Abulafia, treasurer and minister to King Pedro the Cruel. And its imposing façade and mighty portal mark one of the few historic mansions of the Jew left in Europe.

Samuel Halevi (1320-60?) rose to power partly through his own genius for finance and partly through the king's genius for marital entanglement. Samuel handled the royal revenues to the satisfaction of Pedro and the enrichment of himself, but more than that he enabled the young monarch to keep at his side the beautiful María da Padilla in the face and fury of his wife, Queen Blanche de Bourbon, of her French friends and their French armies, and of his stepbrother Henry, who used the intrigue to further his own designs on the throne. At Seville you may still see the apartments in the Alcázar which Pedro built for María from the revenues provided by Samuel's excellent management, the garden bath she splashed in while her courtiers drank its waters, and in the royal chapel of the cathedral, lying side by side, the tombs of the king and his beloved.

The career of Samuel betokened the peak of Jewish political influence in Spain. Lesser Samuels, living in lesser mansions, thronged the court. A Jewish poet, Santob de Carrión, did his best to improve Pedro with a rhymed volume of proverbs, and Abraham Ibn Zarzal took charge of his horoscope. In the civil war which followed upon Pedro's passion for María and Henry's ambition for Pedro's place—a war which brought the

Black Prince from England and Du Guesclin with his Grandes Compagnies from France—the Jews sided with Pedro and suffered all the horrors of his cause.

At length, when Pedro found himself imprisoned in the castle of Montiel and his stepbrother waiting to murder him —as he shortly did—in the next room, he turned for the last time to the astrologer Zarzal. "You told me the stars promised I should reign the greatest king in Castille, that I should vanquish the Moors and conquer Jerusalem; why, then, has it all turned out otherwise?" Zarzal replied with another question. "Will a man," he asked, "sweat mightily if he takes a hot bath in January?" "Surely," answered the king. "Yet," said Zarzal, "sweating is contrary to all the rules of January weather. So your sins and wicked government have plunged you into a mortal sweat contrary to all the rules of your horoscope."

If Zarzal likewise read the stars of his people, he must have seen, upon the death of Pedro (1369), the clouds blacken, restrictions tighten, and exactions increase. The storm broke in the massacres of 1391—the turn of their history, when the Jews without aid of horoscope looked upon the road leading to the Expulsion. Unfortunately, Israel could do nothing to avert its fate as victims to a trust in princes and court favourites.

Meanwhile, Samuel, who had once written a treatise on astronomy, may have examined his own stars and decided, happily for the art of Spain, not to wait until he was an old man—as so many of his kind—to found a house of prayer and leave a name to posterity. When he was merely thirty-five or thereabouts he ordered built next to his mansion the exquisite synagogue of El Tránsito. Happily, we say, for within a year or two Pedro turned against his treasurer, locked him up in the Golden Tower (*Torre del Oro*) at Seville, and had him tortured to death for his wealth.

We may descend into the cellars of Samuel's house in Toledo, as did the royal officers, though we shall find nothing to show for the 70,000 doubloons of gold, 4,000 marks of silver, or 20 chests of jewels and costly garments which, together with 80 Moorish slaves, fell as booty to the king. Empty, the cellars are still impressive—tiers of ancient vaulted caverns fit to fill the popular imagination, as they did in the days of a later owner, with breath-taking rumours of black magic. Their full extent is unknown; some claim they lead to the synagogue, to King Pedro's palace, to the devil himself. But to at least one explorer, who poked about as well as he could, these cellars never held anything blacker than charcoal bins or more breath-taking than onions, and their only magic brew, magic enough, was casked and sealed Amontillado.

Halevi's synagogue is princely like the man himself. Every stone of it reveals, as seldom in a church and almost never in a synagogue, the presence and personality of the donor. Samuel, true to his character, built for divine worship not a sanctuary, but a state salon. We can fairly see him choosing, with fine care and discrimination, the shade of rose marble for the colonnettes, the six—no, 'tis better seven—cusps for the arches, the precise intricacy for the lattice windows, and the flora for the frieze. As to the latter, no banal imitation of the Moor in Granada, enough of that in Pedro's Alcázar, no servitude either to Gothic naturalism, but a happy balance, as Jewry is balanced between Islam and Christendom—entwined, then, in the arabesques are palm leaves, vines, pine cones and citrons for Israel and, a neat stroke, lilies for Queen Blanche of Bourbon. Lions, of course, and Castillian turrets for Pedro. The ceiling no less than cedar of Lebanon—a job it was getting the orders filled *via* Malaga, Old Cairo, and Syrian Tripoli, and once delivered, thumbing designs for their *artesonado* coat of many colours.

The hall, when Samuel had finished his task, was of noble proportions (70' x 53' x 40'). Its lines are kept pure by the reticence and low relief of the decoration. Not a capital is permitted to project and break the even sweep of the walls. It would have been a word spoken out of turn in a court assembly. The women's gallery is discreetly withdrawn behind the south wall, and its occupants, the wives and daughters of the bluest blood of the *aljama*, could only be detected by an arm occasionally flashing beyond the carved casements. The ark stood visible but retired in an alcove screened by a triple-arched portal.

The decoration is the perfection of Jewish *mudéjar* art. Almost the entire east wall is covered with patterned stucco, like Oriental tapestries, catching and turning the light in pale green and pink. High under the rafters an arcade of fifty-four double columns, interspersed with blind casements and lattice windows, moves across the remaining walls. Beneath the arcade stretches a broad frieze, alike in richness but differing in design from the stuccos to the east. And below the frieze, coloured murals stained the present bare plaster.

Taken as a whole, or fondled in detail, El Tránsito is a triumph of wealth tamed by taste, of grandeur unblemished by overdisplay, and of beauty so delicate it may well be the beauty of holiness.

Did Samuel himself, or a committee of rabbis, select the magnificent Hebrew inscriptions which, as in Cordova, play an integral part in the decoration? They were admirably, even dramatically, chosen. "How lovely are thy tabernacles . . ."—the 84th Psalm spells itself in luminous letters across the extreme top of the east wall, then the north and west wall, ending halfway along the south. The remaining space resounds with the 100th Psalm of thanksgiving, "Shout unto the Lord, all the earth. . . ."

The same note of gratitude is repeated in the second row of inscriptions (beneath arcade) which begins on the north wall with Psalm 105:1-15, "O, give thanks unto the Lord.

. . ." And the "shout" of praise is reëchoed in the succeeding lines of Psalm 96:1-12, "Sing to the Lord, all the earth. . . ."

The third row likewise begins on the north wall (under frieze) with psalms that respond one to the other in an ordered chorus: Psalm 99, "The Lord reigneth, let the peoples tremble . . . ," then Psalm 61, singing up and down the window frames of the west wall, "Hear my cry, O my God, attend unto my prayer . . . ," then beneath the women's gallery two psalms of Ascents, the 133rd, "Bless ye, bless ye the Lord . . . ," and the 121st, "I will lift up mine eyes unto the hills. . . ."

The east wall is a resonant anthology of praise and petition. Facing it in their daily prayers, the worshippers read the plea of their own hearts. Three parallel bands of psalms mount upward from the lower border of the frieze, pass across the top of the triple archway before the ark, and descend again to the left of the arch. The outermost band, which rises near the angle of the wall, contains Psalm 111 in full, "Hallelujah. I will give thanks unto the Lord. . . ." With it the congregation opened, as it were, their high negotiation. The next band, close to the ark, speaks for their mingled humility and hope, by reciting five verses, each of which begins, "But as for me": "But as for me, in the abundance of Thy lovingkindness will I come into Thy house [5:8], . . . let my prayer come unto Thee in an acceptable time [69:14], . . . I am like a leafy olive-tree in the house of God [52:10], . . . the nearness of my God is my good [73:28], . . . unto Thee, O Lord, do I cry, in the morning does my prayer come to meet Thee [88:14]." And the innermost band, almost touching on the shrine, cries with reiterated "Hear": "Hear the right, O Lord, attend unto my cry . . . [17:1], Hear the voice of my supplications when I lift up my hands to Thy holy sanctuary . . . [28:2], O Thou that hearest prayer, unto Thee doth all flesh come . . . [65:3], Give ear, O Lord, unto my prayer . . .

[86:6], O Lord, hear my prayer and let my cry come unto Thee . . . [102:2]."

The women's gallery is eloquent with similar but badly mutilated verses, of which we may note the aptness, over the portal, of the Song of Miriam (Ex. 15:20-21).

As for the Arabic legends, distributed throughout the frieze and on the capitals of the arcade, they remain countless and uninterpreted. Their presence, however, is significant. When Latin ceased to be a living tongue and became the language of the church, the Jews abandoned it in their religious inscriptions. And throughout the Middle Ages they refused to substitute another vernacular—save Arabic. Yet when El Tránsito was built, presumably in 1357, Arabic had dropped from spoken use among Toledan Jews for nearly a century. But it was still treasured, as we see, and Moorish freedom not forgotten. Indeed, the use of a vernacular in Jewish inscriptions is a sure test of the humane culture of an age. Disregarding contemporary boasts, you may read in Jewish graveyards and synagogues if a people or period were genuinely civilized. Holland and France saw their first vernacular inscriptions among the Jews in the seventeenth century—strangely and pathetically enough in Portuguese. Germany saw its first in the nineteenth century. Spanish inscriptions, like Portuguese, appear in far-off lands (Turkey, America) where exiled Jews enjoyed a light denied at home, but never once appear within the borders of Spain.

The long dedication below the east frieze, on both sides of the ark, puzzled eighteenth-century Spanish scholars. The beginning (in the escutcheon) is easy: "Behold the sanctuary dedicated to Israel and the house that Samuel built." The end, too, is obvious, expressing, as all mediæval dedications, the hope for a restoration of Zion. However, in the course of it, the Spanish scholars deciphered mention of an imaginary architect, one Meir Abdeli, who has since prospered in guides and travel-books.

Yet even read correctly, the dedication is a puzzle—not in linguistics, but in human nature. After a brief salaam to the Creator and King Pedro, it is one interminable panegyric to Samuel Halevi. We are not, however, perplexed that he is called a "stronghold, tower, peer among the best of the world, great heavenly chariot, column of uprightness, veil of authority, saviour of Israel" and a score of similar Oriental compliments. It meant no more than any eulogy. Nor are we baffled at its unblushing publication while the man was still alive. Other days, other ways. But we are puzzled to know what the Toledan Jews thought when they first read these *alabanzas* to the "saviour of Israel" who "pursues the welfare of his people," knowing that only two years before, some thousand of their folk had been slaughtered in Toledo streets because of popular hatred against Samuel. We fear the inscription is less eulogy than whitewash, and we wonder if the mutilations which have broken away letters and whole words were really due to Christian neglect and not to Jewish wrath.

The date of the synagogue is somewhat uncertain. It was built, according to the best reading of the dedication, in the year "Good for the Jews," which as a chronogram works out to be 1357. Other authorities, nevertheless, put it at 1362. This much we know: the year it was finished had been designated, a century before, by Abraham ben Hiya, the astronomer, and Nahmani, the cabbalist, as the year of redemption for Israel.

The beauty of the synagogue—"eyes have never seen its like," says the dedication, "ears have never heard tell of it"— may well blind us to the Christian and Jewish tombstones which, strewn near the ark, together tell its fate. Upon the expulsion of the Jews (1492), the synagogue was given to the Knights of Calatrava, who transformed it into the Church of San Benito—whence, here and there, its Renaissance details.

Their tombs still rest before the vanished altar. Later, the church was consecrated to the Death (*El Tránsito*) of the Virgin. And in 1888 it became a national monument. As such, the Jewish stones have found in it a last abode. Lady Dona, daughter of Solomon Albalgel and wife of Abraham ben Moses ben Shoshan (large stone split lengthwise), "one may say of her that she has been sought out" and that "she died in 1349," and nothing more. Of Hayim ben Moses (extreme left) and Rabbi Moses Halevi ben Abi Shab . . . (cylindrical stone) still less. And Rabbi Menahem ben Zerah (centre), who died in 1385, surely never dreamed his memorial should one day lie before the Ark of the Law in "the house that Samuel built."

Joseph Al-Nequah had no such luck, with his tombstone plastered next to the bakeshop in the wall of the Corral de Don Diego, nor the nameless Levite whose stone lies upside down above the doorway of 9 Calle de la Plata. Sir Thomas Browne would have turned a fine phrase on the vanity of Moses ben Joseph ben Abi Zardil (d. 1353) and Jacob Aben El Sarcasan, a fellow-physician (d. 1349), who, together with a third notable of the fourteenth century, ordered themselves tombs of such vastitude that for fear of cracking the pavement they are denied place in the synagogue, and are left to cool in the hallway of the Provincial Museum.

The Museum likewise contains cabbalistic medals, fragments of painted stucco from El Tránsito (gallery), and a curious Spanish translation of several of the mural inscriptions from this synagogue, made by Don Juan Josef Heidek, "son of Rabbi Jonathan Levi, chief rabbi of London, and teacher among the Jews until God enlightened him with the truth and he was baptized at Colonia in 1783."

But gaping at tombstones and museum trinkets will tell you little of the inner spirit of Toledan Jewry. Its finest achievements were wrought behind closed doors in the dark ghetto lanes.

Slipping beneath vaulted *cobertizos* and down sombre alleys, hidden from the sun and the populace, we can easily fancy ourselves engaged in the same quest as bold Christian scholars of eight centuries ago. When Toledo fell under Christian rule, they came from distant lands, Italy, France, and Britain, in search of precious booty—the famed science of the Moors. And they found it in Jewish hands. Patiently and secretively—for science smelled of the black arts and the faggot—in the towering houses of the ghetto, clerks with their Latin and rabbis with their Hebrew and Arabic worked a magic transfusion of knowledge.

We need not be too curious to identify the very tenement where Gerard of Cremona got the *Almagest* of Ptolemy. Or where Judah ben Moses Cohen turned the astronomical lore of the Moor into Spanish. But it is a pity that a plaque cannot be nailed to the house where Avendeath (c. 1090-c. 1165) first wrote Arabic numerals into a Latin manuscript. His translation of a Persian work on calculation introduced our present system of numbers to the Western World and marked the beginning of the whole of modern mathematics.

These little streets are poor memorials of the rich creative life which flourished at the side of "mere" translation. Here were born Judah Halevi and Abraham Ibn Ezra—"count it for good." Here the martyr Abraham Ibn Daud (c. 1110-c. 1180) wrote his chronicles and his philosophy—he was an Aristotelian before Maimonides and pretty much anyone else in western Europe. And here the cantor in a local synagogue, Isaac ben Sid, scanning the stars from the heights above the Tagus, helped prepare the lists of planetary movements for Alphonse the Wise—the so-called Alphonsine Tables which laid the foundations of modern astronomy. Galileo and Kepler knew the work of the Toledan *hazan*.

There are other ghosts to be met in these dim byways. What synagogue was this—perhaps the very one where Isaac sang between the stars—that has left its vague trace in 15 Calle del Angel? You may do what you can to reconstruct a sanctuary, college (*Yeshibah*), or study-hall from the horseshoe arches, Visigothic capitals, and niche in its half-sunken basement and its neighbouring basements, not a hundred feet from Santa María la Blanca. In the Calle de Pozo Amargo (Street of the Foul Well) you may remember the romance of Rachel, the daughter of Levi—or any urchin will repeat it to you. Her father made away with her Christian lover, and losing her mind she fancied she saw the face of her beloved peering at her from the bottom of a well. Plunging to its depths, she joined him in an illusory and fatal kiss. Or, not far off, before the ruins of King Pedro's palace, you might hear belated echoes of that disputation in *"der Aula zu Toledo"* rendered famous by Heine, were it not for the regrettable fact that it never took place. Still, there is something for Heine, and maybe for you, in the sole (Arabic) inscription that remains, "Lasting glory and perpetual prosperity to the master of this house!"

The cathedral cloisters are a meet place for final meditation on Israel in Toledo. They are said, for one thing, to stand on the site of a synagogue of the Alcána. For another, their walls literally illustrate the doom that overtook the Jews. We saw that the first memory of them, among the Christian populace, lives in the perverse legend of El Cristo de la Luz. And now we may see the last memory painted in the legend of the Lost Child of La Guardia, an equally perverse tale which has given its name, Niño Perdido, to one of the cathedral portals and which Bayeu has fixed with his brush among the frescoes of our cloister. The charge of murdering a child for ritual purposes, in the northern town of La Guardia, was levelled against the Jews towards the close of the fifteenth century, and more than any one other rhyme or reason made their expulsion inevitable.

Trumping up charges in order to exterminate an unpopular minority smacks of tactics too familiar, even in our day, to waste on it a moment's meditation. The question these cloisters invite us to ponder, and which they alone might answer, turns on the reason for the unpopularity of the Jews. Odd, is it not? that with the many tales that can be told of poets, statesmen, philosophers, and scientists who laboured in the Judería to the glory of the city, Toledo remembers only the Jew smearing poison on a crucifix, hoarding doubloons in a cellar, destroying a Christian suitor, and murdering a Christian child. Odd that the Jews stuck to their unpopular posts, that seldom "faint of heart and weak by nature"—to quote a fifteenth-century Jewish phrase—"they crossed over the bridge." What bridge?—the Alcántara spanning the Tagus with its promiseful meadows on the other side? Odd, too, that those who did cross over insisted on returning *via* the ruined Roman amphitheatre, beyond the walls, where were played the largest number of *autos-de-fé* in Spain.

We await the answer from the cloisters.

JEWISH WEDDING RINGS
See page 79

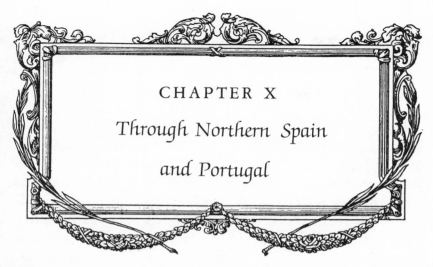

CHAPTER X

Through Northern Spain
and Portugal

FOR three hundred and fifty years the Moor ruled the lower half of northern Spain. His frontier, far into the eleventh century, ran from the mouth of the Miño River (now the northern bound of Portugal) east to the Pyrenees behind Huesca, and then cut southward to Tarragona. This meant that, in general, the upper half of northern Spain stood fast by the Cross. But the character of its loyalty differed. Catalonia on the east coast had tasted Moorish civilization, and moreover lay continuously exposed to the refinement of Provence and the magic of the south winds blowing from Valencia. Galicia, on the west coast, also knew the Moor; but Galicians were not the folk to profit greatly by this knowledge. Whereas Asturias and much of Old Castille—true virgin Spain—exposed to nothing but the ocean on one side and a battle line on the other, remained rude, pure, and uncompromising in their Christian virtues.

These four disparate regions—the southern zone where the learned Moor had reigned for centuries, versatile Catalonia to the east, slow-witted Galicia to the west, and the obdurate doughty marches to the north—wielded, as we shall see, a corresponding influence on the Jew. His genius was as quick to blossom in the sun of Barcelona as to droop in the salty mists of Finisterre.

,᠁

To get almost anywhere else in these parts, the traveller must begin at Madrid. A country town until long after the Expulsion, it has nothing of its own to show for the Jews. Only the most incorrigible antiquarian would be interested to know that its Jewry (facing San Lorenzo church) now bears the ambiguous name of Calle de la Fé (Street of the Faith). And what can one make of the fact that in 1480 Jews and Moors were compelled to enliven Corpus Christi day by exhibiting their national dances?

But as a city of museums and libraries, Madrid does somewhat better for the country as a whole. The Museo Arqueológico Nacional (south wing) preserves a capital from the "new synagogue" of Toledo (Santa María la Blanca?), inscribed in Arabic and Hebrew. The Arabic reads, "Blessing, faithfulness, prosperity, and security"; the Hebrew says, "Blessed shalt thou be when thou comest in and when thou goest out" (Deut. 28:6). It is obviously the fragment of a portal. The museum likewise offers casts of several Hebrew inscriptions, and for those who wish concrete evidence of Moorish science, a pair of Arab astrolabes, one of the eleventh century, wrought with astonishing precision. The Museo de Arte Moderno (in the Palacio de la Biblioteca y Museos Nacionales) contains a romantic painting, by E. Sala, depicting Torquemada's plea for the expulsion of the Jews,[1] and the Biblioteca Nacional (same building) a number of Hebrew manuscripts.

The most eloquent manuscript in Spain is the "Bible of Olivares" in the palace of the Duke of Alba. In 1422 Don Luis de Guzman, grand master of the Order of Calatrava in Toledo, interrupted his hunting, novel-reading, and chess-play-

[1] See p. 145.

ing long enough to ask Rabbi Moses Arragel, of the near-by town of Maqueda, to prepare a vernacular translation of the Scriptures with a running commentary. The request speaks for the finer side of life in Spain; it would have been impossible, in the year 1422, in almost any other land of western Europe. The execution of the work speaks no less for the breadth and freedom of Jewish learning. Rabbi Moses ranges, in his notes, from classic authorities—Aristotle, Euclid, Pliny —to church doctors and Talmudic sages; and he does not hesitate to differ from either accepted Christian or Jewish interpretation.

The 334 miniatures which adorn the Bible portray, as freely, the two traditions. The illustration of a synagogue interior and, on the frontispiece, the portrait of Rabbi Moses presenting his completed work to Don Luis, are invaluable items in the album of Jewish social history. Miniature-painting, it need hardly be recalled, was the photography of the mediæval world—a mirror of life. A limner may have hoped for beauty, but if he failed in exactitude he was not worth his salt. The "Bible of Olivares," apart from art, is therefore a volume of snapshots, and gracious ones, of a vanished world.

Something of the same exactitude breathes from two paintings in the Prado, which would have pleased Don Luis and Rabbi Moses as little, we feel, as ourselves. We cannot say how they would have judged, as works of art, Juan de Borgoña's "Auto-de-fé" (ground floor, first of the Salas de Alfonso XII) or the same subject by Francisco Rizzi (storeroom, inquire of guardian). But taking them as works of exactitude Rabbi Moses would have shuddered, and Don Luis, moved and troubled, would have sighed for the decencies of chess.

Both pictures are contemporary records. Juan de Borgoña painted, about 1500, the first known representation of the *quemadero*, or Inquisitional pyre. He is photographic to the point of showing you, while the victims burn, an inquisitor

frankly gone to sleep. Boredom, no doubt, for the whole spectacle is simple and matter-of-fact. However, they ordered it
much better in the following century. Francisco Rizzi (1608-
85) covered a vast canvas with the imposing Madrid *auto* of
June 30, 1680. We see among those present King Charles II,
his wife and mother, and in pomp beneath the royal box, In-
quisitor-General Don Diego Sarmiento de Valladares. Over
seven hundred notables throng the grandstands. We may be
sure that no one slept. Madame Villars, the wife of the French
ambassador, in fact tells us as much. "Everyone," she writes,
"was compelled to be present who did not have a physician's
certificate to serious illness, unless he wished to run the risk
of being thought a heretic." The artist is not altogether apt
in distinguishing between the eighty-odd living victims and
those already dead—some thirty-two wretches who passed
away in prison, but who are nevertheless present for condemnation in effigy—life-size puppets bearing in their puppet
hands little boxes containing, as it were, their own bones.

From our present historical—and safe—perspective, we can
see that Spain was merely carrying on the tradition of Rome.
In the old Colosseum were reënacted the legends of by-gone
days, the agony of Prometheus and the amours of Jupiter,
with realistic details. And in the Plaza Mayor of Madrid they
preënacted, also with realistic detail, that legend of the future
known as the Last Judgment.

The Plaza Mayor itself has been restored, so at least you
may know how the back-drop looked on June 30, 1680. The
burnings for this and similar *autos* took place in the square
of the Glorietta de San Bernardo, now consecrated by a monument to martyrs of a different liberty, who fell, fighting the
French, on May 2, 1808.

But it is high time to set forth for the varied regions of
northern Spain. Our first journey will take us through Old

Castille, León, Galicia, and then, in a wide swing east, Navarre.

꒰ᐛ꒱

Segovia, the goal of every tourist, lies beyond the Sierra de Guadarrama—mountains which send an icy blast on Madrid and, more than the Pyrenees, divide two cultural worlds. The famous Roman aqueduct and walls of the city are fortuitous survivals; their like might have lingered anywhere in Spain. The traces of the Moor—in the Casa de Galicia and the name of the town square—are common to three-quarters of the land. But the dozen Romanesque churches could never have been seen south of the Guadarrama ridge. They speak the language not of a *diwan*, but a *chanson de geste*. Before the capitals of San Millán we are back again in Caen or Vézèlay.

The ghetto of Segovia—where we will find the same spirit—has lost nothing but its Jews and an occasional brick or tile. Joseph Ibn Shemtob or any one of its former inhabitants could pick his way as surely among the old lanes as your Segovian of today.

The Old Jewry—for there are two—cuts between the cathedral and the city ramparts (Calles de la Judería Vieja, de Barrionuevo, and Santa Ana) and drops to the market place inside the Socorro gate, plainly indicating the dependence of its folk on the church for protection and on commerce for a livelihood. The New Jewry (Calles de la Judería Nueva, and Almuzara) mounts, between towering houses, back to the centre of the town. Its main street shows, here and there, an upper window sealed in with brick or stone, a memorial of the last years of the Jews in Segovia when every avenue of intercourse with the Christians was closed, even the innocent view from an upper casement.

In both Jewries, the numerous half-timber houses with overhanging storys (especially in Barrionuevo, Santa Ana, and Judería Nueva) tell as much of the northern soul as the most pretentious Romanesque fane. There are no patios—that tells something, too. And the studded oak doors (cf. 3 Barrionuevo, 4 & 8 Santa Ana) set in great stone jambs and ponderous lintels or framed in a heavy round arch—the very doors where knocked our Shemtobs and Benvenistes—are forbidding as a Church edict.

But the Moor had been in Segovia, and all was not as dour as it looks. The Jews, in their day, carried on the weaving bequeathed to the city by the Arab, and still a specialty of the town. Scholars, too, thrived in this borderland between science and faith. For a hundred days of the year 1455 Joseph Ibn Shemtob kept within his studded oak door to complete undisturbed his master work on Aristotelian ethics; once he emerged there was no mistaking his conclusion, although today it has an equivocal ring, "The laws of Aristotle make men, the laws of Moses make Jews." Jacob ben Jacob Ha-Cohen, the cabbalist, stayed behind another oak door to extract both laws from the shape and significance of the Hebrew alphabet. And Alphonse the Wise, patron of learning, walked in the gardens of the Alcázar at least long enough to bring a thunderstorm from the skies with his scandalous conceit, *a consultarme el Creador otra sería la armoniá del universo*—"had the Creator consulted me, we'd have had a better world." Finally, the Juderías furnished their quota of court physicians and royal advisers. Abraham Senior[1] was born in Segovia, and Meir Alguadés died there—on the block.

One synagogue remains, after a fashion. It was destroyed by fire in 1899, but it has been rebuilt in nearly its pristine form and style. Again, it has been, these last five centuries, a church under the name of Corpus Christi. Yet even in its restored

[1] See p. 145.

state and despite, or perhaps because of, its service as a church, it epitomizes the story of the Jew in Segovia.

The outer entrance is through a narrow Gothic archway on the Calle de Juan Bravo (south side). A long courtyard leads to the main portal, Moorish in design. The interior resembles the Toledan synagogue of Santa María la Blanca,[1] although smaller in size and lacking its loveliness of detail and grace of age. The nave is flanked with two aisles, each with seven bays. The upper arcade of casements, in the nave, were originally blind, and it is therefore supposed that the women-folk were seated in the east aisle. The arching and capitals fairly duplicate Toledo. First built in the thirteenth century (?), or at least long after the Moors had fallen from power, the whole structure is a lingering testimony to the sympathy of the Jew for Arab culture. Almost at the heels of the cathedral, the synagogue, too, looked over the valley of the Clamores for all the world to know that the One God of the desert had come to Segovia.

The first bay, which serves as a vestibule, at once confronts the visitor with drama.

A modern plaque presents, in low relief, the figure of a furtive sacristan passing a Host to a richly-clad Jew and receiving, in return, a heavy bag of gold. Beneath the transaction appears the following account, in Spanish: "In 1410 the sacristan of San Facundo sold a consecrated Host to a Jew. Joyfully the latter convoked those of his sect in the synagogue, where they gave themselves over to horrible blasphemies and sacrileges. The crime was miraculously discovered, the guilty punished by being drawn and quartered, and the synagogue was confiscated and consecrated to the Christian cult under the invocation of Corpus Christi. In thanksgiving thereof a festival is celebrated yearly in each parish, and because there were four-

[1] See p. 149.

teen (*catorce*) parishes existing at the time, the celebration is called the *Catorcena*."

The inscription does not tell the whole story. The miracle which disclosed the crime was nothing less than a Heaven-sent earthquake which, according to a seventeenth-century writer, "split the arches and the piers and so they have remained to this day." For proof, you have a modern painting on the vestibule wall, that plainly shows the synagogue cleft with the awful shock, the Jews fleeing in terror, and the wafer of the Host rising unscathed from a fire in which, it appears, the villains had hurled it. Any further doubt may be removed by inspecting the wall behind the altar; it is still, despite the reconstruction, torn with a jagged fissure.

The earthquake, in fact, has rumbled along in learned periodicals to the present time. Spanish zealots have demonstrated, with plans and specifications, that the state of the south wall, behind the altar, bears every evidence of the disaster. On the other hand, Spanish liberals and Jews have shown, with other plans and blue-prints, that the Ark of the Law stood before the north wall, where is now the vestibule, that the fissure is therefore at the wrong end of the nave, that the wall which harbours it is of later date and never belonged to the original structure, that the confiscated synagogue was first called Iglesia Nueva, a name devoid of any association with the story of the Host or Body of Christ (Corpus Christi), and, finally, that careful inspection after the fire of 1899 revealed the piers and arches had never been disturbed. Oddly enough, no word in the whole debate is devoted to the problem of how a crack in a building seven hundred years old would prove an earthquake, or how an earthquake would prove that Don Meir Alguadés purchased a Host from the sacristan of San Facundo.

Don Meir, we know, was physician to Henry III and got himself executed on the charge of poisoning his master. He is also known to have received the famous letter of Profiat Duran, with its satirical refrain, "Be not like your fathers," and its plea to disregard logic and science in favour of the mysteries of the Trinity and Eucharist—altogether the sort of letter, without need of earthquakes, to bring a man to grief.

A pleasanter tale is painted among the frescoes of the cathedral cloisters (northwest corner). María del Salto, a Jewess, and of course beautiful, was accused of committing adultery with a Christian, and condemned, as the custom was, to be thrown from the mighty Peña Grajera (Crow's Cliff) beyond the walls. As she stood on the brink of the cliff, with her arms bound, she called upon the Virgin to save her "as you would a Christian." And when she went hurtling through the air, a dove suddenly appeared, sustained her in her fall, and she alighted unharmed. She became a Christian, died in 1237, and left a monument beneath the fresco. Besides the fresco, you have as evidence the Church of the Virgin of Fuencisla, built at the foot of Peña Grajera in memory of the miracle, and the cliff itself.

There are other cliffs to visit, and it is a pity they do not commemorate merely a legend. Across the valley from the Jewries runs a rock-cut road, the Cuesta de Los Hoyos, which, besides giving a panoramic view of the city—one of the unforgettable sights of Spain—leads, as the name of the road and slope indicate (*hoyos*—pits), to a series of small grottos. The steep flank of Los Hoyos was once the Jewish burial-ground. The gaunt drop on one side, the wall-encircled and city-crowned hill on the other, and the dry bed of the Clamores falling in terraces between, inevitably recall Jerusalem seen from the Mount of Olives. It is hardly surprising to find the Jewish tombs, so far exposed along the roadway, to be hewn in the rock like the ancient arched shelf-graves (arcosolia) of Palestine. Beyond the tombs, small caverns

begin to appear, above and below the road, the caverns of
a story that is no legend.

When, in 1492, the time limit set by the decree of Expulsion had expired, the Jews of Segovia fled in despair to the
home of their dead and the grottos of Los Hoyos. There
they sent back a final and vain plea to the city authorities.
And there, in the little caverns, some submitted to baptism
and the remainder were slain. For years after, the slope was
known as the Prado Santo—the Holy Field. No doubt because of the baptisms.

꒜ㅅ᠀

Avila, shut from the world by its ring of ramparts and
towers, was long the centre of religious mysticism. The Christians had St. Theresa and the Jews a school of cabbalists.
There remain numerous memorials of the saint, there is even
the tomb of that exemplar of piety, Thomas de Torquemada,
but nothing of Abraham, the thirteenth-century messiah.
And the Judería (now Calle de Esteban Domingo) has altogether lost its mediæval character.

Moving roughly northwest to the sea, we encounter city
after city which has sheltered in its time large Jewish communities. While here and there a tombstone, a street name,
or the vestige of a synagogue survive, the farther we go the
less we see and hear of anything approaching an intellectual
life.

The ghetto of Salamanca, which lay along the walls (by
La Vera Cruz) gave birth to a few Talmudists and the
famous astronomer and geographer, Abraham Zacuto, who
played an important part in the Portuguese discoveries of the
fifteenth century. The neighbouring town of Bejar preserves
a thirteenth (?) century stone (in the Ducal Palace) inscribed in Hebrew, "Doña Parvena—resplendent is the daugh-

ter of the king in her household"; it is possibly the fragment of a synagogue dedication. Zamorra boasts the ruins of the palace of Doña Uracca who lives in the romance of the Cid, and whose *almojarife*, or chief tax-collector, was the incredible Ruy Capón, Jewish forebear to a score of Spain's noblest families.[1] Nothing in Valladolid tells of Abraham Benveniste, who administered the finances of Castille under Juan II (1406-54), but there is still the church of San Pablo where the Cortes passed their anti-Jewish decrees of the fifteenth century. Palencia has a Calle Nueva commemorating the ghetto (southeast of cathedral), and a rare old tombstone (Museo Arqueológico Provincial) of Samuel ben Shealtiel the Nasi, whose house, we learn from the inscription, fell down on him in 1097.

León, city and province, extended many privileges to its Jews, from time to time placing them on the same civic level as the Christians. But we are now in the region that never altogether yielded to Islam, and although its Jewries prospered, they have left no names in history. However, Mar Yahia ben Joseph ben Aziz, the goldsmith of León who died November 18, 1100, Mar Abraham of Puente Castro, or Castro-of-the-Jews, who was killed two years later, Mar Judah ben Abraham ben Cotna, dying in 1094, and Abishai ben Judah in 1135 (all four stones at provincial museum in convent of San Marcos) were doubtless honoured in their day when they walked the Judería (now Calle Nueva) adjoining the cathedral square.

The synagogue of Bembibre (sixty miles west of León), built towards the end of the fifteenth century, proved too attractive to be left in Jewish hands; it was converted into a church before the Expulsion, and still stands under the vocable of San Pedro.

Galicia keeps a Rua Nueva by the walls of Lugo, and

[1] See p. 139.

another Rua Nueva south of the cathedral in Santiago de Compostella. Corunna, a remote port in the mediæval world, was known as every port; here are traces of a sanctuary at No. 4 Calle de la Sinagoga in the suburb of La Palloza, a cistern near by for the *mikveh*, and emptying in the sea, a little brook called the Arroyo de los Judíos, near the site of the cemetery which yielded three fragmentary stones. Remoter still, the village of Ares on the little peninsula between Puentedéume and El Ferrol was once settled by Jews, whose houses can be identified by their exterior stairways, and a touch of whose synagogue remains in the horseshoe arches of the present parish church (Santa Eulalia).

History (and the railroads) compels us to retrace a great part of our way in order to reach Burgos, for the immediately intervening territory of Asturias and Old Castille knew nothing of the Moor and, perhaps for this reason, hardly more of the Jew. Burgos throngs with memories—of Joseph Pichon, the *almojarife* of Henry II, who was executed as a "slanderer" at the command of the chief rabbi; of the learned Solomon Halevi who after the persecutions of 1391 became a Christian under the name of Paul de Burgos and ended primate of Spain and bitter enemy of his race; of a peculiarly sacred Torah which drew pilgrims from far and wide; of scholars, merchant princes, and poets—and it is a pity there remains nothing to be seen but an iron-bound coffer (Corpus Christi Chapel of the cathedral) which that magnificent rascal, the Cid, once filled with sand and left with Raquel and Vidas, two singularly unsuspecting Jews, as pledge for the loan of good honest gold.

Navarre has blown hot and cold on the Jews. King Sancho el Mayor (1034) invited them to repopulate the cities vacated by the retreating Moor, and for two centuries they flourished. But when the kingdom passed into the hands of Louis IX of

France, Israel felt in Pampeluna no less than in Paris the hard rule of a saint. The populace evidently learned to like the manners if not the rule of their new masters, for in 1328 they celebrated the downfall of the French dynasty by a general massacre of the Jews. The survivors lingered under familiar disabilities—too poverty-stricken to be annoyed during the nation-wide attack of 1391—until their ultimate expulsion at the close of the fifteenth century.

Pampeluna, the capital of Navarre, saw its older ghetto (in the Navarreria, close to the cathedral) fairly obliterated by French troops in 1276; and the newer one (near the Magdalena bridge) has succumbed to time. The visitor of today had, therefore, better occupy himself with the bull-ring and local fiestas than in searching for sign of the bazaars where silks, jewellery, and shoes (it sounds like Morocco and so it must have looked) were bought from the Jews, or for word of Samuel Alfaqui (fl. 1390), physician to Queen Leonora, whose two sons grew up to be jugglers esteemed in these same fiestas, or of that astonishing rabbi, Hayim Galipapa (c. 1310-c. 1380), who anticipated modern scholarship by discovering that the Book of Daniel deals with the reign not of Nebuchadnezzar, but Antiochus Epiphanes, and who anticipated Reform Judaism at least to the extent of permitting hair to be combed on the Sabbath and little children to accept a slice of cheese from well-meaning Christians. The town of Estella, on the other hand, preserves its old Judería, so valiantly defended in 1328 against the combined onslaught of burgher and peasant. As for Tudela, the oldest and most important seat of the Jew in Navarre, its name cannot go unmentioned in a book of travel, for here was born Benjamin ben Jonah, better known as Benjamin of Tudela—"his repose be in Paradise"—who wrote of his far journeys through the East to China (1160-73), a century before Marco Polo.

⟨༽⊁⊀༼⟩

Setting out from Madrid for the eastern provinces of Aragon, Catalonia, and Valencia, our traveller will likely make his first stop at Saragossa. Yet the intervening towns offer certain names and ghosts. Alcalá de Henares, birthplace of Cervantes, had its Jewry, and a famous one, too, in the Calle Mayor and Calle de la Xinoga (Sinagoga); its scholars, duly converted, worked on the great polyglot Bible (*Biblia Complutensis*) of Cardinal Ximénez; and it may be guessed what troubled ghosts haunt the thousands of Inquisitional files in the Archivo General Central. Guadalajara marks its ghetto with a Calle de Barrionuevo Alto and Barrionuevo Bajo—"Barrionuevo" or New Quarter, it may be recalled, was the common designation given, after the expulsion of its inhabitants, to the old quarter of the Jew—both running along the north wall, from the Madrid to the Saragossa gate. Calatayud, over the border of Aragon, owes its name either to Ayub, a Moor who built his castle (Kalat-Ayub) near at hand, or to the Jews who settled there (Calatal-Yehud—Castillo de los Judíos) at least as early as the reign of Abderrahman III of Cordova. The Jewry extended from the church of Santa María de la Peña to the Mocha tower. One Samuel ben Solomon, who died in 919, managed to leave us his marble tombstone. And centuries of rabbis and preachers have been indebted for their sermons to the philosopher, theologian, and pulpiteer, Isaac ben Arama (d. 1493), himself but one of the long roll of scholars who dignified these rude adobe tenements.

Saragossa, capital of Aragon, housed its Jewry, perhaps 5,000 families, in a great arc along the city wall (now Coso boulevard) from the church of San Gil to Santa María Magdalena. The chief synagogue, which resembled the Corpus Christi of Segovia, occupied the site of the present Jesuit Church of

San Carlos. In appearance, the quarter remains the oldest in the city, a network of time-forgotten lanes; but nevertheless it will take sharp eyes to see on the Calle de Barrionuevo (or Veronica, by San Gil) footstep or phantom of Hasdai ben Joseph, vizir of Al-Muktadir (1047-81) when the Moor ruled Saragossa, or Sheshet Benveniste, adviser to Alphonse II in the next century, or Isaac ben Sheshet (1326-1408),[1] the Talmudist whose *responsa* throw a living light on the manners and events of his age, or Don Hasdai Crescas (1340-1410), the last of the great mediæval philosophers. Even the street names no longer recall, as they once did, the varied craftsmen of this rich and, until the end, light-hearted ghetto—weavers, dyers, goldsmiths, cutlers, tanners, saddlers, and shoemakers, each craft grouped, like the Christians, in a *cofradia*, or guild.

Of money-lenders no word. But in the Aljaferia (the alcázar, beyond the walls) it is amusing to remember that during the fourteenth century the Jews of Saragossa monopolized the craft—or art—of lion-taming. The court of Aragon maintained a troop of lions in the old fortress, much as bears are now kept in Basel and wolves in Rome; and the den was placed in charge of the race of Daniel.

The Aljaferia may likewise remind you that the Jews of the succeeding century enjoyed a fair monopoly on martyrdom. Its guardians delight in showing sample cells of the Inquisition prison formerly installed in this same fortress. They can hardly be restrained from leading you to the dungeon of Verdi's famous "Trovatore," and that in itself will keep you from forgetting that converted Jews were not the sole victims. Moriscos, Protestants, sundry heretics, alert and questioning minds and unlucky wights of every breed, contributed to the bonfires of faith. But sympathy for Jews or Judaism was the typical crime, and freedom from this sympathy the test of Christian virtue. "I firmly believe," says Sancho Panza, giv-

[1] See p. 408.

ing himself a clean bill, "whatever our Holy Roman Catholic Church believes, and I hate the Jews mortally."

Instead of wasting time over an operatic hero, if you have a mind for thrills you will do better to pause at the tomb and statue of Pedro Arbués, buried beneath a florid baldachino with imposing spiral columns in his own chapel (last on south aisle) of the town cathedral. Pedro, "the darling of Torquemada," inaugurated the *autos-de-fé* of Saragossa (1484), and after a few performances he was slain, while attending mass, by two Maranos. One of them, Juan de la Abadia, was rather excusably incited to the act by the execution of his sister and condemnation of his father at the hands of Pedro's tribunal. The other, Juan Esperandeu, on general principles did not like the Inquisition. Once dead, Arbués was given the grace to accomplish what he had never done alive: he saved the skin of a "New Christian" Jewess, who escaped from the clutches of the Holy Office by claiming that out of Catholic zeal she had dipped her handkerchief in his streaming blood. Then, somewhat tardily—1867 in fact—Arbués became a saint. Saint Pedro Arbués, centre foreground in heaven, Francis of Assisi to right, Joan of Arc to left; there is a "Holy Conversation" as yet unrecorded by a painter's brush.

꧁ ༄ ꧂

Catalonia, the focus of a civilization comparable to Andalusia or Toledo, is more generous in the matter of relics. Manresa has a lane called Grau dels Jueus (Jews' Street), and beyond the walls a field known as La Fossana dels Jueus, formerly the Jewish burial-ground. Vich has a similar field, Tarrega the trace of a synagogue, and Figueras a Calle Nueva marking the former ghetto. The little town of Castellón de Ampurias (near Figueras)—its name recalling the "emporium" of its Greek founders—preserves almost unchanged a thirteenth-century Jewry in the Calles de la Llona, Muralla, Calabró, and Jueus.

Barcelona cannot forget the tribe so long as the great hill of Montjuich (Jew's Mount) holds watch over the city. It takes its name from the Jewish graveyard which lay on the east flank at least as early as the tenth century. A dozen tombstones from Montjuich (now in the Museo Arqueológico Provincial) do what they can to tell of a "community of wise men and princes" and keep alive the memory of Samuel ben Hilat (d. 1044); Doña Bonacept (d. 1270); Solomon ben Sidkia "united with his people" in 1304; Simon ben Mordecai (d. 1307); Enoch ben Shealtiel Sasporta (d. 1312); Joseph ben Baruch Abarbalia (d. 1322); Sidkia ben Solomon, who claims, if we may believe his epitaph, "light surrounded me since I reached my term, the day I was called on high" in 1371; Abraham ben David; Hanania, daughter of Moses the Jerusalemite; Reuben Somebody; the "young" Somebody-else son of Samuel Sharka (all undated); and Solomon Gracian ben Moses ben Shealtiel ben Zerachia, of whom the inscription says, "Solomon seated himself on his throne [died] in the year 1307." Mutilated stones cry out in unintelligible phrases from the wall of the convent Church of Santa Clara (left of porch).

The streets where lived our "wise men and princes," immediately west of the cathedral, keep much of their ancient appearance. The Calle del Call (Hebrew *kahal*, meaning "community"?) identifies itself, for *Call* in Catalonian towns, like *Carrière* in Provence, designates the Jewry. No. 5 of the Call, a Romanesque-Gothic house, preserves a fragment of the old ghetto wall. The Calle Santo Domingo del Call was originally "Calle de la Sinagoga Mayor," and an archway at the northwest corner of the Plaza de la Constitucion is claimed to be a portal of the vanished house of prayer. Several façades in this lane (Nos. 3, 5, 6, 8, 17) were likely familiar to the last Jews who lived in the quarter. The corner house of the neighbouring Calles Marlet and Arco San Ramon del Call shows the tombstone of "the martyr Rabbi Samuel of Sard" plastered next to the doorway; and the house itself, by a strange chance, purports to have been the home of the saint Domingo de Guzman,[1] who did so much to make it possible for Rabbi Samuel to earn his title of martyr. Finally, the Calle de Baños Nuevos (Street of the New Baths), at the western extremity of the ghetto, may remind us that these baths, disappeared a century ago, were built in 1160 by the Jew Abraham Bonastruc in partnership with Count Ramon Berenguer IV; similar establishments can still be seen in Gerona and Palma.

You will note that no tombstone is dated later than the fourteenth century. Jews ceased to die in Barcelona after 1391, for the good reason that the massacres of that year put an end to living there. Hasdai Crescas, whom we "met" in Saragossa and who was born in Barcelona, has left us a pathetic account of the disaster which, as he says, "wiped out" his native community. Many of the victims killed themselves by leaping from the housetops, and others "sanctified the name of God" in the general slaughter down the little streets we have just visited. "Among the many," writes Don Hasdai, "who sanctified the Name was my only son, a young bridegroom, whom I brought, a lamb without blemish, as an offering on the altar." It was with neither rhetoric nor a scholarly weakness for quotation that he signs his account, "I am the man who has seen affliction by the rod of His wrath—Hasdai ben Abraham ben Hasdai ben Judah Crescas."

An echo of the effort to recall the survivors lingers in the Calle de la Trinidad, leading from the Calle Aviño to the Church of San Jaime, two steps south of the Street of the Baths. The church was first built, in 1395, under the invocation of the Trinity, as a lure for converted Jews. The response was scant, the church was dismantled, and in the seventeenth

---

[1] See p. 165 (the saint presided at the *auto* painted by Borgoña).

century San Jaime took its place, leaving only the street name of Trinidad as a souvenir of a stiff-necked preference for Unity.

History, as pretty much everything else, has gone to sleep in Gerona. Within its walls, the white and yellow houses stretch their balconies and doze over the slow river. Roof-tops banked up the hillside and, above them, towers and spires dream against a mediæval sky. A mere glance at the town and you will rightly surmise that, together with Roman, Goth, Moor, Catalan count, and Aragonian prince, Israel, too, must be sleeping among its stones and memories.

Gerona, like Barcelona, has its Montjuich, or Jew's Mount, once a burial-ground, and its Call, which, it happens, has barely changed by as much as a coat of paint. The tortuous Calle del Call Judaic (now Calle Forsa) winds along the slope, paralleling the right bank of the river Oñar; its high and lordly houses drip with ivy and, save for a noonday spell, shut out all touch of sun, heat, or the living world. Two passages, more stairways than streets, climb to the Calle Escolapia, the upper bound of the ghetto. The northernmost and steeper passage, known as the Call Juhich, opened halfway up its flight into a small court which served as the Jewish "plaza." The south passage, which rises diagonally to Escolapia, had no other name than "the Calle-which-goes-to-the-synagogue." The synagogue itself may be found, radically remodelled into a private dwelling, at the foot of this passage; part of its dedicatory inscription lies in the Provincial Museum. The Jewish town hall[1] stood on the site of the present Chapel of San Mateo (north end of Calle Forsa) belonging to the Order of the Escolapians. Altogether a snug, stout little Jewry fit, as went the mediæval world, to render its inhabitants secure and happy.

The Provincial Museum (cloisters of San Pedro de Galli-

[1] See p. 341 (Prague).

gáns, gallery B) likewise contains tombstones from Montjuich, commemorating among these inhabitants David ben Joseph, Joshua ben Sheshet and wife, the "charming and delightful child" Joseph ben David, Solomon ben Judah of the Mercadel (d. 1288) and, finally, the "noble Estelina, wife of the excellent Bonastruc Joseph." The "noble Estelina" lives in history to the extent that her husband, although a leader of the community, was not chosen to go debating with the Christians at the great disputation at Tortosa (1413), and we fancy both she and he were quite content.

Somnolent Gerona has given birth to more scholars, taking the Call block by block, than any Jewry of Spain—indeed, to such numbers that the surname "Gerondi" was practically a title of learning. At least six of the name are known to letters. The greatest of them, Moses ben Nahman Gerondi (Nahmanides) practised medicine, wrote monumental works on the Bible, Talmud, and philosophy, and after dramatically leading the Jewish phalanx in the unhappy disputation before the royal court at Barcelona (1238), died, an exile, in Palestine, and found his grave in Haifa by the side of Yehiel of Paris.[1]

But his fame should not allow us to neglect his cousin, Jonah ben Abraham Gerondi the Saint (*he-Hasid*). Jonah led the opposition to the liberal thought of Maimonides, which was instrumental in having the public authorities burn a cartload of the philosopher's works in the Place de Grève at Paris (1233). Thereafter, Jonah fell victim to remorse. He vowed to go to the Holy Land and, by the shore of Galilee, beg forgiveness at the grave of the master.[2] He set forth to fulfil his vow, but, all too human, found himself detained year after year by an excellent position as Talmudic master in Toledo. Then he died suddenly of a strange illness (1263), and everyone said it was a penalty for delaying his journey of re-

[1] See p. 49.
[2] The tomb of Maimonides still stands in Tiberias.

pentance. Poor Jonah—you a *chassid*—a saint—and conscience-stricken at the burning of a book? As good, you say, kill a man as kill a good book? Real saints were made of sterner stuff. St. Pedro Arbués, who tossed men and women to the flames, St. Juan de Capistrano with a name writ over Silesia in blood, St. Vincent Ferrer, whose words awoke slaughter in a dozen ghettos of Spain, they would laugh at you for a chicken-hearted Jew.

Behind the cathedral and just above the ghetto, the blasted tower of Geronella, built like a small citadel, was in its heyday a reassuring sight. But in the storm of 1391, those who escaped death in the Call and fled to its thick walls for refuge found that even the Geronella failed them. And when, a few years later, the tower collapsed (1404), the Jews somehow received the blame, as they did for the subsequent plagues and earthquakes which ravished the town—perhaps as additional penalty for the weakness of its Jewish saint.

The Balearic Islands, now an excursion resort, were once a centre of commerce between Spain, France, the Barbary states, and Italy. Jews flourished in this mart as far back as Moorish days, and in Palma we find them cultivating the sciences of geography and navigation as naturally as they turned to philosophy in Andalusia and astronomy in Castille. The Moors had been notable cartographers (at a time when Christian maps looked like kindergarten scrawls), and when Aragon brought about their downfall in the thirteenth century, the Jews carried on. Jaffuda Cresques, "the map-Jew," who made the first map of the world to include the explorations of Marco Polo,[1] Moses Rimon "the parchment-maker," and Abraham Vidal the limner of the remarkable Privileges of Majorca (dated 1334, now in archives of the town hall of Palma) were typical of these schools.

It is useless to look for cartographers or Jews in Palma

[1] See p. 84.

today. They were driven, forever, from their quarters in the Calles de Sol and Montesión as early as 1435; and it purports little to know that the present churches of Montesión and Santa Fé stand in the place of the old synagogues. But you will find in the sacristy of the cathedral the only pair of Spanish-Jewish *rimonim* (ornaments for rollers of the Scroll of the Law) still extant. They likely date from the fourteenth century, their Moorish "architectural" design is charming, and there is drama in presuming they were given to the Cathedral, a century or two later, by some wretch of a Marano too frightened to keep them hidden in his home. Indeed, the story of the secret Jews, or "Chuetas," of Palma is a book in itself. Discreet questions addressed to the silversmiths of the Calle de la Plateria, where tourists go to buy the dainty purses and other silverwork specialties of the town, may reward you with a surprising tale.

The road to Valencia passes Tarragona, where you may find on the façade of No. 6 Calle de Escribanias Viejas (next to cathedral) two inscriptions from the graves of Hayim ben Isaac (d. 1300) and Hanan ben Simon Arlabi (d. 1302) which, together with the stone and coins previously mentioned,[1] are all that indicate that this was once called "the city of the Jews." The trilingual stone of near-by Tortosa has already been described.[2] Sagunto comes next. The entrance to its Jewry lay through a plain arch of hewn stone between Nos. 24 and 26 Calle del Castillo (on the way to the great Roman ruins); and behind the arch, the main street of the ghetto (now Calle de la Sangre Vieja) preserves in houses Nos. 7 and 11 four Gothic arches belonging to the synagogue. The children of the Sangre Vieja (Old Blood) used to prove their title by claiming possession of the tombstone of "Adoniram, servant of king Solomon," who died in Sagunto while

[1] See p. 120.
[2] See p. 121.

collecting tribute for his glorious master. Nothing remains in Valencia itself save, if you will, the house where Vincent Ferrer was born (117 Calle del Mar), on the border of the ghetto. Valencia likewise has the distinction of celebrating, August 1, 1826, the last *auto-de-fé* in Spain, the victim a most belated *relapso* into Judaism.

Portugal differs little from Spain in its Jewish history. The first settlements were a bit later, the natives a shade kindlier, and the final expulsion (1497) decreed more reluctantly, but executed with, if possible, greater cruelty.

In Lisbon the earthquake of 1755 destroyed practically all mediæval landmarks. There are left in the shattered church of the Carmo—fragments within ruins—three tombstones and one synagogue inscription. The sixth century double stone of Abba Mariah and Isaac ha-Cohen ben Yakhal and the similarly ancient stone of Rabbi Mosh [nuna?] come from Espiche, near the port of Lagos beyond the Pillars of Hercules. Then we jump over a thousand years to the inscription of the "young Judah Benrimoj," who died in 1814 and whose grave lay in the English cemetery (Rua da Estrella), where the oldest Jewish tomb, commemorating Joseph Amzalak, dates from 1804. The exiles, as you may see, have hesitated less over returning to Portugal than to Spain. The dedicatory stone, likely fourteenth century, hails from the synagogue of Oporto, and mentions the court minister, Don Judah Ibn Maner, and one Joseph Ibn Aryeh, "supervisor and master of the work." There are likewise casts of the tombstone of Joseph da Tomar (d. 1315) from the cemetery of Faro, and the dedication of a Lisbon synagogue built by "the wealthy Judah ben Gedaliah" in 1307 on the Judiaria Velha (now Rua dos Fanqueiros). The original is, by some chance, in Evora.

The long agony of the Maranos who, despite rack and fire, clung for centuries to their native land and their ancient faith, has naturally put no mark on modern Lisbon. We cannot expect to see the placard found nailed to the door of the cathedral one February morning of 1539. "The Messiah has not yet come," it boldly read; "Jesus was not the true Messiah." Nor the placard which next morning read, "I, the author, am neither a Spaniard or Portuguese, but an Englishman—not if you offer twice your reward will you find me." Nevertheless, the author was found, and had his hands cut off and the rest of him burnt.

Marano or Crypto-Jewish families still linger in and about the bleak mountain town of Belmonte (near Guarda in the province of Beira-Baixa). The story of their recent discovery and vestigial Jewish rites reads like invention. They have practised what they could remember of Judaism so long in hiding that today they have come to feel the efficacy of their prayers and ritual depends, like magic, on secrecy itself.

A visit to Belmonte may include, en route, a glimpse in Evora of the many Hebrew manuscripts in its public library, a tombstone and dedicatory inscription in the museum (next to cathedral), and the tribunal hall and cells of its Palace of the Inquisition (now private property, west of the Roman temple). Sound orthodox Christian sentiments may be deciphered beneath the whitewash of the cells. The municipal museum of Castello Branco contains the dedicatory inscription from the synagogue of Belmonte, dated 1297.

Tomar will serve as the last stop. On the Rua Nova (once the Jewry) you will find a small structure, the gothic vaulting of which is upheld by four central columns. Dark, musty, and impregnated with a *bouquet* of port and madeira—it was a storehouse for wine until day before yesterday—the poor cell is the one surviving mediæval synagogue of Portugal.

For later sign of the race to whom it is a monument you

must turn to many scattered lands—westward to Jamaica, Pernambuco, and Peter Stuyvesant's colony on Manhattan— the Barbary states to the south—the republic of Venice, the kingdom of Naples, the Mediterranean isles, and the old Turkish Empire to the east—and above all north to Holland.

And leaving the Spanish Peninsula, it is well to leave behind you the natural impulse to judge its peoples by their stupidity, fanaticism, and brutality. Virgin Spain was indeed one of the Foolish Virgins. We may go further and say she was a Wicked Virgin; her lamp has been found not only empty of oil, but filled with blood. But, "Sire," said the Marquis de Pombal, after the Lisbon earthquake, when King Joseph asked him what was to be done—"Sire, bury the dead and take care of the living."

TOLEDO. FROM DEDICATORY INSCRIPTION OF EL TRANSITO SYNAGOGUE
See page 157

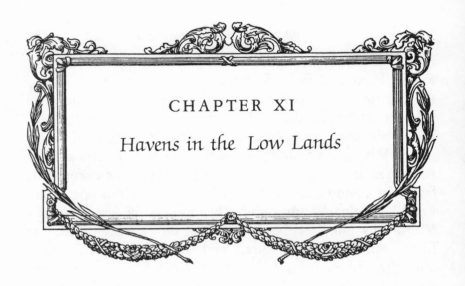

CHAPTER XI

Havens in the Low Lands

IN THE year 1593 two storm-tossed boats docked at Emden, and the passengers, a band of Portuguese accompanied by their women-folk, children, money, and jewels, repaired to a near-by inn and ordered roast goose.

They had come a long adventurous way. Setting out from Portugal for Holland, they had been seized by an English man-of-war. Its spacious Elizabethan captain fell in love with one of the catch, the fair Maria Nuñez, and brought them all to London. For a week-end Maria became the toast of the town, the Virgin Queen rode in a coach by her side, and when the fuss had subsided they took ship once more for the Netherlands. Again they missed their destination and, driven from their course, found themselves in the free port of Emden. Stumbling through the streets, they had remarked a house sign writ in strange characters. They stopped and stared in hopeful bewilderment, and as they stared they saw a lad deliver an exceedingly fat goose to the door of the house. And now, taking their ease in their inn, they bade the host prepare them a similar fowl.

The host, knowing well where to find the fattest geese, sought out the house with the strange sign, discovered the bird still lying on the table, and managed to buy it. His guests were delighted, never had they tasted its like—and indeed they had not since their great-grandmothers' day—and they asked whence it came. He answered, from a Jew. At once the Portuguese pricked up their ears and inquired where the Jew lived. The host told them, "in the house where hangs a sign in Hebrew letters."

Bright next day two of the strangers hastened to the house and spoke with its master, Rabbi Moses Uri Levi. But their knowledge of Plattdeutsch was not equal to the burden of their tale. The rabbi summoned his son, who had passed some time in Italy learning the art of printing, and who managed to catch the drift of what they said. They urged retiring to a back room. And there they confessed that, though Christians for generations, they too were of Jewish blood, that they had fled from Portugal to enjoy the religious freedom with which Holland had consecrated her new independence, and they begged the rabbi to take them, all ten families, into the covenant of Abraham.

Tongues would wag in Emden, the rabbi said; it were better done in Amsterdam. Spreading before them a map of that port, he pointed out the Montalsbaan tower near the shore of the Y (where it still stands), and counselled their leader to hire a house in the neighbouring Jonker Straat. "Bind a scarlet thread," he advised, as Joshua once advised Rahab, "to the window of your house for a sign, and in three weeks we will come to you, circumcise your males, teach you the law and way of God, and lead you in your prayers."

So it was done, and using a room in the house of Simon Palache, consul for the Sultan of Morocco, the first synagogue was inaugurated in Amsterdam. To be sure, there were difficulties. The police burst in one Day of Atonement, and the terror-stricken Portuguese felt they were back home again. Unable to clear themselves in Dutch, it hardly eased matters when, to their astonishment, they heard the officers, stout Protestants, roar at them to bring out "your crucifixes, monstrances, images, and other abominations." The comedy of religious errors ended before the magistrate, to whom the *parnas*, Jacob Tirado, explained in fluent Latin that they had come two thousand miles in order *not* to be Catholics; and permission was given them to build a public synagogue. In a short while the original ten families grew to four hundred.

Like everyone else, the Jews found Holland clean. Not merely window-panes and front stoops, but the hands and souls of the people. Whoever has lived about Europe since the World War will recognize this trait for rare. Perhaps we can better appreciate its rarity if we remember that Holland stood at the close of the sixteenth century where the nations of Eastern Europe and the Balkans stand today—in the first flush of a newly won freedom. This in itself should have been enough to loose a flood of intolerance, that is, if Holland had been guided by our contemporary fashions which dictate that the wisest way to use one's own liberty is to deprive somebody else of his.

Holland's provocation to hatred and violence did not end there. Our modern exemplars of freedom like to excuse their behaviour on the grounds of recent enslavement, economic difficulties, and patriotic exuberance. Yet dismembered Poland and gallant Serbia never felt an oppressor as ruthless as the Duke of Alva. Rumania, bursting with natural resources, knows nothing like the distress which triumph brought to a land of mudflats half in ruin and half under water. The nationalism of a Lithuanian is a pallid flame compared with the volcanic religious passions which seethed in the Low Countries. In fact, it lacked only the refinements of the twentieth century and the culture of a Pole to have made the rise of the Dutch Republic a signal for the fall of decency, as we see it now fallen almost anywhere east of the Rhine. But the Hollander of old, like the Czech—the shining exception of today —was clean.

How and why are hard to say. Certainly the Dutch did not borrow their cleanliness from the neighbours. England had just finished obliterating her Catholics and was preparing to do as much for the Puritans. France was fêting the Huguenots with the night of St. Bartholomew. John Calvin was being predestined by God to burn Servetus in Geneva, Germany was brewing her Thirty Years War, Portugal shipping victims for the Inquisition from Brazil and garrotting others in India, and the Spanish, because of a shortage of Jews and Moors, were in Flanders, behaving like Spaniards.

It was, therefore, an original idea of the Dutchman, independence once declared (1579), to plug up his dikes and, acting on the belief that a free man honours freedom, invite the oppressed of all nations to share his herring and cheese. The idea was, of course, not realized at once, or without occasional stains and delinquencies. Nations are neither heroes nor villains. But by and large the Dutch kept windows washed, front steps scoured, and a welcome sign over the door.

History is not always cynical, and the reward was great. A score of sects proved that religious tolerance could exist without damage to the land, among them Huguenots, Socinians, Arminians, Jansenists, Calvinists, Mennonites, Collegiants, Brownists, and an obscure body of left-wing English Puritans to be heard from under the name of Pilgrims. Merchants, craftsmen, and artists streamed from Flanders. Maranos resumed their Jewish faith, brought the diamond trade from Antwerp, and helped the Dutch wrench an empire from the Portuguese in the West and East Indies. Descartes and Bayle came from France and founded even a greater empire. The presses of Amsterdam became the open forum of the world—

and it is a calloused hand that can pick up today a Blaeuw or Elzivir without a tremor.

In less than two generations herring and cheese gave way to crystal beakers, lickerish fruits, plump oysters, and monumental roasts which set our palates tingling, even on undigestible canvas. The Dutch masters to whom we owe the record of these feasts sought a mastery of life—the good life here and now; they abandoned martyrdoms of saints and palavers in heaven for clothmakers bathed in golden light, a word over walnuts and wine, and the fertile mist across the fields of Haarlem. In less than two generations there were Grotius, Rembrandt, and Spinoza. It is a beautiful word, said the Greeks, *Isonomia*—"one law for all"—worthy, said the Dutch, to be spoken over the best walnuts and wine.

༺༒༻

When it suits you, then, to visit in Amsterdam the great synagogue of the Portuguese, built (1675) at the peak of their affluence, the pride of the city and perhaps the most impressive in Europe, you may look on it not only as a house of Jewish prayer, but a monument to Dutch virtue and human liberty.

It stands open and frank on the edge of the Jewish quarter —surrounded by a courtyard and low outlying buildings which throw the main bulk into stark relief. An archway (on Muider Straat) pierces the outer structures, once the seat of the renowned Etz Haim Seminary and now housing vestry-rooms, beadle's apartment, school, and *mikveh*, and leads directly to the Tuscan portal of the synagogue proper.

Within, a majestic barrel-vaulted nave flanked by slightly lower and similarly vaulted aisles, the whole supported by twelve mammoth Ionic columns and lit by huge round-arched windows, is the last word in classic dignity and strength. Gen-

erous proportions,[1] airiness and light measure the distance
which separates these free Jews of Amsterdam from the Middle Ages of Spain.

The Dutch architect, Elias Bouman, met the requirements
of Jewish worship in a masterly fashion. The Ark of the Law,
magnificent cabinetwork in Brazilian rosewood, marshals
across the east wall its Renaissance portico with five doors,
three pediments, and a dozen glossy pillars. The pediments
are surmounted with crowns—one each for the Law, Priesthood, and Kingdom; and the middle pediment, rising above
the others, frames the tablets of the Ten Commandments.
Along the architrave stream the names of the twelve tribes.
Without resorting, as in Italy,[2] to an imitation of baroque
Catholic altars—for its decoration is confined to an occasional
wreath and acanthus—the sheer mass and polish of the ark
give it dominance. The *bima*, likewise of rosewood brought
from Brazil, stands back from the centre of the nave, thus al-
lowing an impressive scope for the procession of the scrolls
when they are marched from the ark to the reading-desk. The
pews, be it noted, run lengthwise on either side of and facing
the *bima*, a traditional arrangement which tells at a glance
the emphasis given to the reading of the Law, to the synagogue
as a house of instruction. Resting on twenty-four Ionic pillars,
the balconies, one in either aisle and across the west wall, permit the women-folk full and clear access to the service. And
never moves a service in nobler beauty than at eventide when
the lustres hanging between and leaping from the great columns mingle the glow of their 613 tapers—one for each of
the Mosaic Commandments—with the scores of twinkling
candles among the pews; when polished balustrades, panels,
and pillars below and long lines of cornice and moulding

---

[1] Approximately 125' x 95'; centre aisle 45' wide; main columns 45' high,
their base 6' square; seating capacity nearly 2,000; foundations rest on 3,000
piles. There are 72 windows, corresponding to the 72 names of God.
[2] See pp. 252, 263 (Ancona, Padua).

above break into dancing flame; and the voice of the cantor, as though inspired by the illumination, intones a summons to eye and tongue, "Arouse thyself, for thy light is come; awake, awake, give forth a song, for the glory of the Lord is revealed upon thee."

Indeed, the architect succeeded so well that his work became a model for western Europe and colonial America; and we can follow his influence in London (1702), Berlin (1712), Rotterdam (1725), Newport, R. I. (1763), Charleston, S. C. (1794, since destroyed), and with modifications down to this day. But even more than at his influence he would be astonished to learn that his wedding of Jewish ritual to classic forms—the older generation who remembered Portugal and Spain corruscating with plateresque must have scorned its severity—resembles, save for its vaster scale, the earliest known synagogues of antiquity now scattered in ruins along the Sea of Galilee.

Still, his clients were mightily pleased. Thanks to a memorial drawn up on the occasion, we can see the inaugural ceremonies (August 2, 1675) in their full pomp: the burgomaster and other city and state officials shared in the glory while cantor Michael Judah Leon intoned a *shehecheyanu*, Moses Curiel opened the door of the ark, the Haham Isaac Aboab da Fonseca drew forth a scroll, David Immanuel held it, Isaac de Pinto unbound it, Moses Abraham Naar unrolled it, the Senhors Caminha, Ximenes, Azevedo, Ozorio, da Vega, Sasportas, and the Haham read from it, the latter being privileged to repeat the Ten Commandments, and Moses Pereira pronounced a *kaddish*; after which there were speeches without end and a garland of odes in Hebrew, Latin, Dutch, Spanish, Portuguese, and French. A few lines of the French, destined the next century to be the very tongue of liberty, tell in bad verse but noble sentiment the spirit that moved in every heart:

Chef d'œuvre de touts lieux sacrés,
Du premier temple la memoire,
De l'Amstle et son Senat la gloire . . .
Jouissez de la liberté,
Priez, prêchez, chantez sans craindre.

The sermon was delivered by Solomon de Oliveira.

Innumerable gifts testify to the continued delight of the faithful. Sixty-seven Torah scrolls, one among them brought from Spain and many hung with gold-threaded mantles; gilded and silver *rimonim*; elaborate crowns and filigree breastplates; precious spice-boxes—one inscribed in Portuguese with the names of the five senses and thanks to God for their use; two settees upholstered in Gobelin tapestry to serve the Bridegrooms of the Law; scrolls of the Book of Esther; bronze menorahs and silver *kiddush* cups; embroidered desk covers and Torah bands—form a veritable museum. By all means (*i.e.,* a tip) prevail on the beadle to permit a sight of the gilded pitchers and bowls used in washing the hands before giving the priestly benediction. A Nereid bearing aloft a silver conch and Jacob blessing Joseph are the disparate themes of two of the finest pitchers; Venus awarded the golden apple and Solomon receiving the Queen of Sheba (the latter a masterpiece of Adam van Vianen, dated 1694) wrought in repoussé across the hollow of the bowls, tell again the worldliness of these elegant Sephardim; there flashes in the golden apple the last glint of Cordova.

The connoisseur of synagogues and ghettos may begin to feel uneasy, if not disappointed, at finding himself in a community that has nothing to offer by way of persecution. If so, he may be directed to a tablet inserted at the right of the ark, which bears the names of the *parnassim* of the community when our synagogue was dedicated. Among them he will find mention of one Abraham Jesurun Espinoza—a kinsman of the philosopher, and a reminder that the only intolerance worthy to be recorded in Amsterdam was the intolerance of the Jews.

Apologists like to claim that the imprisonment, stripes, and ostracism bestowed on Uriel da Costa (c. 1585-1647) for believing in a creedless God—*jouissez de la liberté*—and the ban pronounced (in 1656) against Spinoza for holding that angels are imaginary, the soul mortal, and that God embraces matter as well as spirit, must be attributed to the Catholic background and discipline still lurking in this ex-Marano community. "One pays dearly," says such an apologist, "for crossing the threshold, even unwillingly, of the Church." Other whitewashers throw the burden on Jewish fear of public scandal—What will the Gentiles say if young Baruch continues to talk as he does! But in plain fact the Jews, being members of the human race, needed no one from whom to borrow bigotry or on whom to cast its blame. Excommunication was an old and well-tried Jewish device; and the Samaritans, Karaites, and champions of Maimonides could have something to say as victims of Jewish fanaticism. The idiosyncrasy of the Jews is shown, rather, in their curious refusal to torture, hang, or burn a man for his beliefs.

Behind the Portuguese synagogue, across the Jonas Daniel Meijer Plein—a square popularly known as the Mikveh Plein —lie three time-mellowed synagogues of the Ashkenazim. The Ashkenazic Jews came from Germany, and later Poland, shortly after the Portuguese. Long despised by the grandees from Spain and Portugal for their poverty, lack of worldly culture, and a little for their strange pronunciation of Hebrew, they were slow to reach the influence of their neighbours over the Plein. If anyone is impertinent enough to ask how they managed in 1671 to build the splendid Groote—or great— synagogue (entrance on Nieuwe Amstel Straat), inferior only in size to the Portuguese, we may whisper the word "mort-

gage" familiar to modern synagogue-builders. Daniel Stalpaert, the architect, achieved a minor masterpiece which, however, later restorations (the last in 1823) have robbed of much
of its fineness. The *bima* rises fairly in the centre of the nave,
as customary among the Ashkenazim. Worthy of inspection
are the embroideries and plate.

Behind the Groote and facing the square, stands the Nieuwe
synagogue, a less pretentious structure built in 1721; and upstairs next to the Groote on the Nieuwe Amstel Straat, will
be found the Derde Sjoel (Third Synagogue), likewise dating
from the eighteenth century. Near at hand, another charming
temple (built 1766), among the half-score that dot the neighbourhood, dreams of other days over the tranquil waters of
the Uilenburgwal. And no lover of ultra-modern Dutch architecture will want to miss the work of Harry Elte, whose new
synagogue is as remote, if you will, from tradition as the
present Jewish scene.

The Joden Bree Straat leads from the Portuguese synagogue
through the core of the Jewry—Amsterdam never knew a
compulsory ghetto—which still harbours the race who fled
there four hundred years ago, and whose poets hailed these
little canals and brick lanes as the New Jerusalem. No. 13
Waterloo Plein and the house next to the Church of St. An-
thony of Padua preserve their Hebrew inscriptions, no doubt
much like the one that attracted the first Maranos in Emden.
Save for a decline in fortunes—and poets—little has changed.
Dramas, to be sure, are no longer written in Hebrew—the first
since the Book of Job was composed in Amsterdam (c. 1642)
by Moses Zacuto, the fellow student of Spinoza; da Costas
are not striking a blow for liberty; and you will not find
Manasseh ben Israel in his home at 19 Joden Bree Straat. And
just beyond the rich de Pintos are gone, and their palace too,
on the Zwanenburgwal. The diamond-cutting trade has fal-

len into the hands of the German Jews, and down by the Nieuwe Markt, the remnant of Spanish glory deals

> Auf der Gracht mit sauern Gurken
> Und mit abgelebten Hosen.

Nevertheless, the spare frames, piercing eyes, and tenuous hands of the old hidalgos and the ripe allure of the women-folk—an exotic sight among the Dutch—have lost nothing of their *grandezza*.

Rembrandt knew what he was about when he settled in the Joden Bree Straat; he had merely to beckon from the window for one of those models which make his rabbis, philosophers, and beggars a gallery of seventeenth-century Jewish life, and his Old Testament figures, in their poignancy and strength, the manifest soul of Israel. Mocking nationalist theories, Rembrandt the Dutchman has, above all painters, caught the secret of the Jew, even as Theotokopulos the Greek has revealed the Spaniard.[1]

His house (No. 2 Joden Bree), now a museum of his art, will bring you nearer to the old Amsterdam Jewry than wandering through the streets. Here you will find the portrait of his friend and neighbour, Manasseh ben Israel (cat. No. 269), who persuaded Cromwell to reopen the doors of England to the Jews,[2] trafficked with all the Latin-sounding Dutch scholars of the time, wrote voluminously himself—Rembrandt, you will note, has illustrated his *Piedra Gloriosa* (36-b)—and established the first Hebrew printing-press in Holland. Here too is an etched portrait (278) of the physician Ephraim Bueno—the oil is in the Jan Six collection (208 Amstel Straat) —another close friend of the master, who likewise had a hand in that first Hebrew press. And then there are the etchings of "The Synagogue" (126) and "The Jew with the High Bonnet" (133); and in "Nebuchadnezzar's Dream," "Jacob's Lad-

[1] See p. 229 (Rembrandt in London).
[2] See p. 221.

der," and "The Pharisees in the Temple" we meet in Biblical dress the full tide of Joden Bree Straat. The apocalyptic works of the master, like Manasseh's writings on the imminent re-demption of Israel, reflect the Messianic hope common to Rembrandt and his Jewish friends, a hope which Sabbatai Zevi was to inflame and betray.

The so-called "Jewish Bride" in the National Museum ('s Rijks Museum) is now recognized to be Rembrandt's daugh-ter-in-law; and our present interest in this gallery is confined to Josef Israels' "Reading Rabbi" and "Jewish Wedding" (modern wing, room III). The near-by city museum (Stede-lijk Museum) contains another work of Israel "A Son of the Old Stock" (room III) which with "The Jewish Quarter" of Breitner brings the painted record of the Amsterdam Jew down to recent times. For the book-lover there are the 8,000 volumes of the Rosenthal collection (University library) and the Montezinos collection of 25,000 books and manuscripts in the Etz Hayim Seminary.

⌒⋏⋏⋏⌒

Perhaps the most fascinating relic of the Portuguese is their cemetery. It lies in the village of Ouderkerk (5 miles south of Amsterdam), along the banks of the Amstel. Founded in 1614, as the second burial-ground of the community, it has re-mained, unlike many of its kind, undisturbed to this day; and more eloquently than history, its stones speak the minds and manners of the dead. For the average Westerner, its sculp-ture, moreover, is one of the curiosities of Jewish art.

The watchman's house (foot of Dorp Straat) is as old as the acres it guards. A second structure, the chapel of the Rodeamentos (Port. *circuits* or *processions*), where the cere-monies for the male dead were held, contains a tablet dated 1705, with one David Espinoza Catela named as director of the graveyard. The path from the Rodeamentos to the river leads to a gate, its inscription dated 1616—when the grounds were formally opened—and bearing the promise from Ezekiel (Ez. 37:12), "Behold, O my people, I will open your graves and cause you to come up out of your graves, and bring you into the land of Israel."

Meanwhile there is time enough for contemplating a few of the six thousand venerable stones. In accordance with Sephardic usage, they mostly lie flat and somewhat raised from the ground, as you will find them in North Africa, the Balkans, and off Chatham Square in New York.

The tomb of the first occupant, David Senior, who died an infant in arms (April 11, 1614) still betrays in its plain inscription the mediæval tradition, soon to be broken, of a simple unadorned stone. It is regrettable no trace is left of the first adult; Manuel Pimentel, known to his Jewish comrades as Isaac Abenacar (d. 1614) deserves a memorial if only because he was the favourite card partner of Henri IV of France. As it is, we must be content that Henri dubbed him "the king of players."

Two years later, the stone of Don Samuel Palache, whom we met as a representative of the Sultan of Morocco to the States-General of Holland—that, too, was a merry game which the Dutch privateers and Moroccan pirates played with Spanish shipping—shows a new fashion. A lion and crown appear amid the inscriptions.

Decoration grew lavish by the middle of the century, in the form of floral designs, of mortal symbols such as skulls, scythes, hour-glasses, extinguished torches, axes laid to tree trunks, and weeping cherubs, and of heraldic crests perpetuating family pride. Dr. Jacob Morenu (d. 1667) boasts a vizor, acanthus, and crest embodying the wild oak (tree of life?). The brilliant young physician, Joseph Morenu Bueno (d. 1669 at the age of twenty) recalls his profession in the image of an open book, his fate in a skull and hour-glass, and his hope in laurels and roses. The Haham Isaac Aboab da Fonseca (d. 1690) who, as customary, shares a single broad slab with his wife, leaves us easy riddles in the scrolls surmounted by a crown, the double lamp, and "yet once more" the harsh and crude berries of the laurel. He won his laurels in many fields, as scholar, preacher, poet, and for more than fifty years head of the Amsterdam Jewry; nor will we begrudge him a sprig for being the first Jewish writer in America—when in an interlude as leader of the Pernambuco community he wrote an account of the Dutch-Portuguese struggle for Brazil (c. 1649). But his chief title to fame, for which there are no laurels, is the curse he pronounced "with the decree of the angels and the assent of God" on the body and soul of Baruch Spinoza.

Astonishing to anyone who believes that Jews have always refrained from a representation of the human form in their religious art, the adornment of these tombstones developed toward the end of the century into full-blown sculpture: entire Biblical scenes charged with a baroque love of dramatic and intimate detail. The episodes, sometimes running to nearly a dozen on a single stone, play upon the name, profession, pretensions, or destiny of the deceased. Altogether they make an exuberant volume of marble puns.

Mordecai Franco Mendes (d. 1688), who sleeps peacefully beside his wife, need not be suspected of marital difficulties for having included on his stone the transaction between Abraham and Abimelech; Abraham was no doubt merely one of Mordecai's given names. But Abraham Senior Teixeira (d. 1701), whom we judge a philanthropist in his day, illustrates himself in the guise of Abraham entertaining the angels; and when we recall that, according to traditional interpretation, these angels are the Divine Presence itself, we must confess that boldness of imagery can go no further. Samuel Senior

Teixeira (d. 1717) is hardly less intrepid with the scene of Samuel called of the Lord. His wife, Doña Rachel (d. 1716) tells her own fate in a representation of the passing away in childbirth of her Biblical namesake. Isaac Senior Teixeira (d. 1728) had two wives: the first, another Doña Rachel (d. 1694), met the same end as the wife of Samuel; the second, Doña Leah (d. 1724) bore him three children if we rightly interpret the three little trees carved at the foot of the stone; Isaac himself left six little trees—three doubtless attributable to the first marriage—and an appropriate motto, "And Isaac sowed in that land . . . and the Lord blessed him" (Gen. 26:12).

A musical prodigy, like so many Jewish lads in our own day, David da Rocha (d. 1708), is represented as the shepherd of Judea playing on his harp, with violin, 'cello, flute, pipes, and sheet music heaped at his feet, and again as the psalmist-king with verses streaming from his lips. His epitaph says that here below he was the glory of song, and up yonder he will be a song of glory. The cherubs wailing on the tomb of Abraham Roiz Mendes (d. 1708) as only baroque cherubs can wail, apparently have never stopped their tears to read the Spanish inscription, "Fear not, Abram, I am thy shield" (Gen. 15:1).

The masterpiece in this garden of sculpture, artist unknown, was the result of long planning on the part of the beneficiary, Moses van Mordecai Senior (d. 1730). No less than eleven Scriptural episodes adorn the broad roomy slab, the place of honour on the top being given to Moses receiving the tablets of the Law, and at the bottom to Mordecai led in triumph on a prancing charger. To the left, likewise at the bottom, appear the initials M. M. S. and to the right, since Mordecai was a merchant adventurer, a ship of Tarshish.

As we move eastward we shall learn in Hamburg, Prague,

and Poland, as well as in ancient Carthage and Rome, that religious sculpture and even religious painting are not altogether an anomaly in Israel.

The Askenazic community of Amsterdam, you may wish to know, have their early cemetery (purchased 1660) in Muiderberg on the now vanishing Zuyder Zee.

↷↝↜↶

The excommunication of Spinoza and, later, his expulsion from Amsterdam, rather missed fire as far as the victim was concerned. He had managed to withdraw from the synagogue before the ban was pronounced, and he had shaken the dust of the city from his feet—rhetorically, be it understood, for there is no dust in Amsterdam—before the authorities were moved by the Jewish community to eject him.

For a number of years (1656-60) he lived with his friends of the Collegiant sect, modified Mennonites, somewhere between Amsterdam and Ouderkerk. Then he moved to the headquarters of the Collegiants in the village of Rijnsburg, where, due to the loving efforts of his admirers, you can come as close to him as the intervening centuries permit.

The Noordwijk tram-line from Leyden will deposit you on the outskirts of Rijnsburg. Take the road (southwest) leading to the village, proceed in the same direction along Katwijk Straat, turn right on Lange Straat, and then left into Spinoza Laan. There beneath spreading ash trees lies the modest house where Spinoza passed his most fruitful years (1660-63) and which has now been converted into a semblance of how it might have looked in the days when he finished his criticism of the Bible and plea for free thought, the *Theologico-Political Treatise*, and his introductory work *On the Improvement of the Understanding*, and laid the foundations of the immortal *Ethics*; where he lived the first man free of any sect or creed—neither Jew, Christian, nor Moslem—since the fall of the ancient world.

Although little is known of the details of his life in Rijnsburg, because little seems to have happened outside philosophizing, enough has come down to us to furnish his house. We have the complete inventory of his personal effects and library, drawn up after his death with a view to settling his small debts (the barber who presented a bill of 1 florin for services to the "blessed" Mynheer Spinoza, the glover 13 pfennig, the notary 17 florins, the entertainment at the wake 19 florins, etc.); and in addition we know that he worked at lens-grinding, not so much to make money, for he had a pension from his friend, Simon de Vries, as to experiment in the science of optics recently given a boost by Leeuwenhoek, Drebbel, Zachary Jens, Huygens, and other Dutchmen.

So we have one room furnished with a seventeenth-century desk, armoire, chair, and bookcase. In the bookcase and armoire are gathered the library he was known to possess, the very editions to the year and format—some 150 volumes. Naturally, they embrace a large number of Hebrew tomes. The collection likewise includes the early editions of Spinoza's own works and the first writings for or against, mostly against, him.

On the desk, beside the pen, inkwell, and sand-pot lies a replica of Spinoza's şeal, a rose rising from its thorny stem and surrounded by the initials B. D. S. and the word *caute* (warefully). It is generally assumed that he meant to express by this word his attitude toward life, but more likely he meant it as a warning to his interpreters.

The room adjoining the study is fitted up as a workshop with an optician's lathe, a chimney with bellows, and a table laden with apparatus for performing the experiments he mentions in his correspondence. On the wall is affixed the famous admonition, *Bene agere et lætari*—"Do good and rejoice."

On the whole the effect is theatrical and perhaps a bit tricky; but, surrounded with the old furniture and books, and glancing from the workshop to the shady garden which smiles through the window, the visitor senses somewhat of the peace and nobility of the former tenant.

The reason for the work of this pious restoration is clear. Spinoza is the first philosopher since the Greeks who has an individual allure and piques a personal interest. He spoke with unsurpassed boldness and yet in the gentle voice of a sage; he wrote a radical ethics and yet lived what he wrote; he seems to say everything he had to say, and yet he is for ever hinting at something beyond all telling; he is both rationalist and mystic, atheist and God-intoxicated. Men come to his house as they came to the garden of Epicurus, in the hope of finding there a life.

As the vision of this life unfolds itself through patient study, as the accents in which it was revealed become a familiar voice, we are drawn closer to the man who sounded it; and the closer we are drawn the more elusive he becomes. His withdrawal fires our pursuit into a passion; as of Socrates or Jesus we ask, "What did he really mean?" We feel that his lips, if we could make him speak to the full, would breathe ultimate wisdom. We lend him, in the effort, our own insights, premonitions, and desires. In short, we make of him a Myth. And in the end the most trivial details of his life absorb us, his barber becomes cosmic, his smile an enigma. Baffled at resolving him, we yield to him as to a melody that needs no words.

Leaving the little house, we carry with us the spell of the verse inscribed over the doorway—lines of Camphuysen, the Socinian poet, who, unawares, has written the device of the *Ethics*:

Ach, waren alle Menschen wijs
En wilden daarbij wel,
De Aaard waar haar een Paradijs,
Nu is ze meest een Hel.

(Ah, were all men wise
And willed thereby well,
Earth would be a paradise
That now is mostly hell.)

A house is still shown in Voorburg (Kerk Straat), near The Hague, where the philosopher lived from 1663 to 1669.

In The Hague itself we may follow his footsteps to the end. He lived at 32 Veerkade, third story, during 1670 and 1671. And then he moved for the last time to the top floor front of 72-74 Paviljoens Gracht. Its high Dutch gable, which once sheltered the infinite attributes of God, and more recently the modalities of a brothel, now harbours the Domus Spinozana, a library, museum, and lecture centre dedicated to the study of the master. The doorway bears the one pregnant word *Vitæ*—"To life," we say in English—but Spinoza knew it best in the Hebrew *L'Hayim*!

A portrait-bust and seventeenth-century roses adorn a little garden in the rear. An inscription on the garden wall reminds us that "it is the part of a wise man to refresh himself with sweet scents and the beauty of green plants" (*Ethics,* iv, prop. 45).

The Nieuwe Kerk contains a tablet (to right of pulpit) marking his first grave, and the churchyard a stone commemorating the last resting-place—the exact spot unknown—with the inscription *Terra hic Benedicti de Spinoza in ecclesia nova olim sepulti ossa tegit.*

Between his dwellings in the Veerkade and Paviljoens Gracht stands a bronze statue of the philosopher, and it was at the foot of this statue that Renan pronounced final judgment on Baruch Spinoza: "C'est d'ici, peut-être, que Dieu a été vu de plus près."

〜✦〜

All else of import in the Netherlands is soon seen.

Among the paintings in The Hague, the Biblical subjects of Rembrandt, "Simon in the Temple," "David before Saul" (Mauritshuis, Nos. 145, 621) attest his mastery of Jewish character; the city museum (Gemeente Museum, No. 194) contains a probably authentic portrait of Spinoza; and two nineteenth-century canvases of J. Bosboom, "The Synagogue" and "Interior of a Synagogue" (Mesdag Museum, Nos. 40, 46), should give one pause not only for themselves, but for token of the persistent interest of Dutch artists in the Jewish scene—Bosboom carries on the tradition of Jacob van Ruysdael (1628-82) whose "Jewish Cemetery at Ouderkerk" ranks among the most notable works in the gallery of Dresden.

There remains the Portuguese synagogue of The Hague (Jan Evert Straat) built in 1726, resembling Bevis Marks in London;[1] and the Ashkenazic cemetery on the road to Scheveningen (Oude Scheveningsche Weg), a charming wooded spot with stones dating from the beginning of the eighteenth century.

Rotterdam built its Ashkenazic synagogue on the famous Boompjes quay in 1725; it was enlarged in 1791 and is now a sight of the town. Maastricht has a Joden Straat behind the town hall. And in Groningen (Ooster Singel Straat) to the far north of Holland, you may stumble again upon an old graveyard.

〜✦〜

Belgium has had time enough to accumulate a glut of antiquities. Jews were likely in the region on the tracks of

[1] See p. 222.

the Roman legions; their presence is mentioned in Tongres and Tournai before the close of the fourth century. And they prospered fairly well, even bearing arms among these warlike Gauls, until the rise of feudalism. Then the customary restrictions fell upon them, and in the fourteenth century a storm of persecution—Christian nerves being set on edge by the Black Death—swept them away. The massacres did their work so thoroughly there was no need for a formal decree of expulsion.

There survives, for the most part, nothing but reminiscent street names: a Joden Straat or Rue des Juifs in Antwerp (near Place de Meir formerly the chief canal), Ghent (near Place Laurent and edge of inner city), and among smaller towns, Cumptich, Tirlemont, Mons, Wasmes, Grosage, Bavai, Maroilles, Sains, Looz, Eupen, Spalbeck, and Wommerson. Louvain claims a lane called Chinstrée (Dog Street), presumed to have designated the Jewry. And we may have our suspicions as to Rue Neuve behind the cathedral in Bruges and Rue des Vieux Habits in Ypres.

Brussels has put architects, stained-glass-makers, painters, and weavers to work in order to commemorate fittingly the miraculous and bloody departure of the Jews. A commodious chapel added to the church of the patron saint, Ste.-Gudule, is dedicated to the purpose, under the name of the Chapelle du St.-Sacrament de Miracle. Windows, paintings, and tapestries tell the old story of a Jewish attack on a consecrated Host, its miraculous deliverance, and the punishment of the—victims. Unlike Paris and Segovia,[1] Brussels took the tale to heart and made a capital cult of its incidents and relics. Ste.-Gudule, the central shrine of the city, is practically become a monument to Jewish martyrdom.

According to the Christian account, Jonathas, a banker of Enghien, purchased in 1370 a Host from a sacristan. Shortly

[1] See pp. 54, 169.

after, Jonathas was found murdered in his garden. His wife and son fled with the Host to Brussels, where the wafer, by way of revenge, was taken to the synagogue and pierced with daggers. It bled miraculously, and the terrified perpetrators tried to rid themselves of it through the hands of a converted Jewess. She spread the tale, the leading Jews of the city were arrested, torture followed arrest, confession followed torture, and all concerned were cruelly slain and burnt. The Host survived astonishing trials during the uprising of the Calvinists two centuries later, worked many cures and miracles, and was last heard of when the French Revolution broke upon Brabant.

Four windows in the chapel give the story in sixteenth-century glass (by Bernard van Orley and Jan Haeck), and fifteen windows of the nineteenth century repeat it in the aisles. The tale is taken up again by twenty-six eighteenth-century paintings (from various hands) dispersed throughout the church. It is finally reiterated in six huge tapestries woven in the atelier of Jacques Vanderborght (during 1770-85) and now hung in the choir on high holy days and for the fête (first Sunday after July 13th) of the massacre.

There rests, for other proof, a field beyond the borders of Enghien called the Jardin de Jonathas, and in the heart of the town a venerable mansion, now a historic monument, known as the Maison de Jonathas.

In Brussels, however, nothing is left of the synagogue, which stood at the corner of the Rues des Sols, Terarken, and Douze Apôtres—near the steep Rue Montagne de la Cour—and if you do not hurry, these streets will have vanished in turn. But not so Godfrey of Bouillon, who surveys the scene from his pedestal on the Place Royale, his prophetic words done in bronze, *Dieu li vult*—"God wills it."

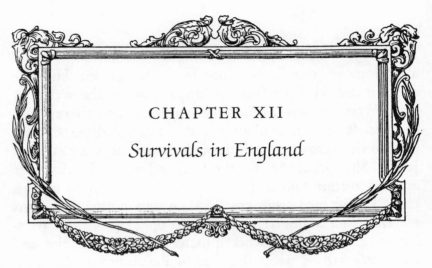

CHAPTER XII

Survivals in England

"THE island called the corner of the earth," as Abraham Ibn Ezra described England, has often claimed to be the home of the lost ten tribes. Only less fantastic is the sober existence of the little port near Penzance which ascribes its name Market Jew or Marazion (Mara Zion—"bitter Zion") to a colony of Jews who, together with the Phœnicians, traded for tin in Cornwall. But then, it is near Market Jew that Jack the Giant-killer killed the giant Cormoran, that King Arthur sailed away for ever on Dozmare Pool, and that belfries ring beneath the waves of the sunken land of Lyonnesse.

The Anglo-Saxons are more restrained than the Britons. Yet certain Angles, whether or not the very lads who won the handsome compliment in Rome, *non Angli sed angeli,* could have told something of Jewish slave-dealers who transported them to far lands and perhaps gave them the first notion of how big a world they could conquer.

Authentic history begins in 1070, when the Normans brought their Jews across the Channel. This first settlement ends with the expulsion of 1290. Then, for some 350 years Britain remained closed to Israel. From Chaucer to Shakespeare the Jew was only a legend and byword. But the bars were slowly lowered in the last half of the seventeenth century, and a new settlement, this time of Spanish-Portuguese from Holland and their German brethren, crept into being and paved the way for the present population.

The Angevin Jew and the Restoration Jew lived an age apart. Consequently, the fragments that remain, enough, despite the inroads of modernity, to give life to these disparate worlds, speak a widely different language. Antiquity becomes equivocal. The house of Aaron the Jew in Lincoln is mediæval to its drains; the synagogue of Bevis Marks is only as old as Queen Anne. It takes a timeless people to reconcile the two.

❧

Above the poets' corner in the triforium of Westminster Abbey you will find sundry chests, triple-barred and triple-locked. Technically they are called *archæ*—that is to say, arks. They can likewise be called arks of the law, but a different ark and another law from those we have hitherto been admiring. If you have the key, you may draw from these ancient coffers the whole adventure of the Jew in Angevin England—two centuries of wealth, learning, privileges, power, and tooth-pulling. They hold everything, like Pandora's box, except at the bottom there is no Hope.

The chests were used in the following fashion. When William the Conqueror brought over a colony of Jews from Rouen he had, like a Norman, shrewd business in mind. By loans and usury the Jews squeezed the people, and then the king squeezed the Jews. Since the Church forbade Christians to lend money at interest, the Jews—until the rise of Lombard and other Christian bootleggers winked at by the Church— had a monopoly on the traffic. And since Jews were barred by English guilds and feudal law from almost any other occupation, they had no choice but to pursue the monopoly. And since the Jews belonged to the king—their earnings, while they lived, and their property, when they died—he got the ultimate profits. And, finally, since the monopoly in itself, to say nothing of the greed of the king, made for enormous rates of interest, the whole commerce became an odious burden on the Church, the nobility, and indirectly the masses.

With true Norman genius for organization, the traffic was soon reduced to a system. The Exchequer at Westminster set up in various cities these chests, or *archæ*, now before your eyes. Every loan was negotiated in the presence of Christian and Jewish scribes and officials. The bonds, called *starrs* (Hebrew *shetaroth*), were written in duplicate, one part with the seal of the debtor to be held by the Jew, the other to be deposited in the chest. Often the bonds took the curious form of tallies, pieces of wood split asunder, bearing the name of the Jew in Hebrew or Latin, together with the amount of the debt, the latter sometimes indicated by notches. You may see a collection of these tallies in the Record Office museum (Chancery Lane—case H), and while you are about it you might note in the main archway a statue of Henry III (1216-72) who erected a Domus Conversorum, or Christian mission to the Jews, on the site of the present Record Office, well knowing that he was running thereby little danger of reducing the number of his royal usurers.

The starrs recorded in rolls at Westminster (whence the "Star Chamber"?) and now to be found in quantities at the Abbey and in the British Museum reveal a wide variety of debtors—castle-builders, crusaders, founders of abbeys and monasteries, as well as butcher, baker, and candlestick maker. Nine Cistercian abbeys built within a dozen years (1140-52) owed moneys to Aaron of Lincoln, who liked to boast that he had made a window at St. Albans and "given the saint a home when he was without one." The bulk of the debt, in fact, lay with the Church and nobility; and in the three-cornered fight between barons, prelates, and crown the Jews were drubbed on all sides.

The crown, meanwhile, profited enormously. A special office in the Exchequer counted off the notches, added up the starrs, and deducted the king's commission. When the total failed to meet the royal demands—crusading for Jesus abroad and fighting barons at home was expensive—interest rates were boosted and special levies laid on the Jews. In 1188, for example, the levy, or tallage, on the Jews came to £40,000, about two-thirds of Henry II's income. If the Jews proved recalcitrant, there was always the expedient of tooth-pulling. Abraham of Bristol (1210) lost 10,000 marks and seven molars to King John by this process.

When the Jews had the temerity to seek escape from their intolerable position as cat's-paws to the royal treasury, by asking the right to settle on the land, in other words to become normal British subjects, the Church authorities protested against the "impious insolence" of the proposal; and the crown naturally yielded to the Church, only too happy to combine, as the manner was, piety with business. And when in desperation the Jews sought leave to depart from the realm, they were curtly refused. Matthew Paris, likely present at the scene (1253), gives us a picture of Elyas, the head of English Jewry, begging the king's commissioners to "let my people go"—a picture which paints at a stroke the plight of mediæval Israel. "Elyas . . . taking counsel with his companions, answered for them all: 'O noble lords, we see undoubtedly that our Lord the King purposeth to destroy us from under Heaven. We intreat, for God's sake, that he would give us licence and safe-conduct of departing out of his kingdom, that we may seek and find a mansion in some other place under some Prince who bears some bowels of mercy and some stability of truth and faithfulness . . . How can he love and spare us, miserable Jews, who destroys his own natural English? . . . exacting from us those things we cannot give him, even though he would put out our eyes, or cut our throats when he had first pulled off our skins.' And speaking thus, with sighs and tears hindering his speech, he held his peace, falling almost into a swoon, ready to die. Which when it came to the knowledge of the Magistrates, they permitted them not to depart, saying, 'Whither will yet flee, O wretches? Behold, the King of France hateth and persecuteth you and hath condemned you to perpetual exile. Shunning Charybdis you desire to be drowned in Scylla.'" Altogether a shrewd and sorry business.

Lincoln shows us another side, if only the outside, of the business of being a Jew in mediæval England. Beneath its cream-yellow cathedral stand three twelfth-century houses, the oldest private stone dwellings in the land. The uppermost, on Steep Hill, belonged to Aaron the Jew. Its double-arched Norman casement on the second floor—the ground floor originally had no windows—and its stout ashlar walls, two and one-half feet thick, prove that the home of an English Jew, even if a prison, was his castle, and a sumptuous one in its day. A strong vaulted cellar doubtless served for the protection of both the owner and his wine.

It was no accident that this and the other Norman-Jewish houses in England should be the oldest and most luxurious examples of domestic architecture on the island. The need for a dwelling tough enough to withstand the assault of debtors and hence the slower attack of the centuries, is obvious. But, in addition, most of these early Jews hailed from Rouen, in the twelfth century the cultural centre of northern Europe; unlike the Anglo-Saxon populace, they knew quite as much about the amenities of life as the noblest families who came over with the Conqueror. Moreover, they were in constant touch with their brethren in Provence and Spain, where living was civilized, as it was not in England—indeed, so little that Richard of the Lion-heart showed his good taste by remaining, during his ten years' reign, just two months at home, only long enough, it would seem, to be crowned and prudently establish the Jewish department of his Exchequer. Hence the Jews led the way in England—as they and the Moors did in Spain—to the cultivation of refinement among the "middle classes." They inaugurated that sacred virtue—British comfort.

Besides his goodly mansion, Aaron had many grounds for content; he was the richest man in the country, the head of a wide chain of money-lending offices, and, added to the abbeys already mentioned, he helped build Peterborough and his own home-town cathedral. When hardly a step above Aaron's doorway, you admire the west portals and the three lower stories of the great west tower built with Aaron's money, you must remember that we speak of Aaron building Lincoln as one speaks of any banker building something; he advanced, that is, the cash, and in this case held the church plate and holy relics by way of collateral. Aaron's death (1186) must have been a true joy to Henry II—then expensively engaged at war with Philip of France—who naturally fell heir to the vast wealth of "his Jew," and who found himself put to the pleasant task of opening a special account in the royal treasury, known to research grubs as "Aaron's Exchequer." Not impertinently, Aaron's town house in London stood on part of the site of the present Bank of England.

Below his mansion in Lincoln, on the street called Strait, is another Jew's mansion, if anything roomier, displaying the same type of windows, a handsome Norman portal, and a great chimney opening from the main salon on the second floor. It is commonly presumed to have been the house of a Jewess named Bellaset or Belle-assez. Next door (to right) is a venerable building said to have been the synagogue. A small adjoining passage is still known as Jews' Court. And the house beyond, which contains a pit or well and belonged to a Jew

named Jopin, is reputed the spot where Little St. Hugh of
Lincoln met his fate.

> O yonge Hugh of Lincoln, sleyn also
> With cursed Jewes, as it is notable,
> For it nis but a litel whyle ago,
> Pray eek for us, we sinful folk unstable. . . .

So sang Chaucer at the end of his "Prioresse's Tale."

The story of the boy martyr, Hugh, allegedly murdered for
ritual purposes (1255), hardly needs repetition—the same tale
was told of a half-dozen localities in England, and we meet it
again in Troyes, Toledo, and the Tyrol[1]— and still less refu-
tation. The inquisitive may, however, be fascinated in following Joseph Jacobs' sleuth-work in reconstructing what probably happened in the houses of Bellaset and Jopin almost seven
hundred years ago (*Jewish Ideals,* pp. 192-224). Little St.
Hugh is buried in the south aisle of Lincoln cathedral, beyond
the transept, and, martyr or not, is forever blessed with the
soundless music of the Angel Choir.

Bury St. Edmunds boasts another Jew's house or possibly a
synagogue—a late-Norman structure called Moyse's Hall—the
long-vanished inhabitants of which grizzled the beard of
Abbot Samson. "Time and the Jews," if we are to believe
Carlyle, "will make a man's beard very grey." However, if
Abbot Samson was the man we take him for, it was not so
much his debts to the Jews which whitened his locks as sorrow for the slaughter of fifty-seven of them in 1190 by the
Abbey gate. Still, there are doubts. The good abbot, we note,
immediately thereafter expelled not the perpetrators, but the
survivors.

York, once the second city of the kingdom, has neither
house nor synagogue, nothing but a ruined tower to tell of
more monks and Jews in that year 1190, with a few crusaders
to boot. Clifford's Tower (in the castle) was the scene of the

[1] See pp. 89, 161, 351.

massacre familiar to readers of *Ivanhoe*. Romance aside, the trouble began in London upon the coronation of Richard. Certain leading Jews, who felt, no doubt, that they were paying for the show, had the poor judgment to attend the ceremony. Riot and death ensued. A wave of violence spread through the realm, taking in Bury St. Edmunds on the way, and reached its climax at York.

The entire Jewry took refuge in Clifford's Tower, where they were besieged by a mob of debtors, crusaders in need of practice, and rabble. Every morning a white-robed monk celebrated mass for the mob and exhorted them to their holy work. It is not at this date ascertainable, though it is a pity Carlyle gave the matter no investigation, whether or no his hair was also grizzled by the Jews. Certain it is, they one morning landed him on the pate with a stone. At this, the final assault began. Realizing they were doomed, the victims resolved, as once they resolved at Masada,[1] to kill themselves rather than tempt the mercy of their foes.

We will let the old chronicler, William of Newbury, tell us what followed: "Fire being set to the roof, they prepared for the sacrifice. Those whose courage was most steady took the lives of their wives, the famous Joce cutting first the throat of his dear wife Anna and then of his own sons. And when this had been similarly done by the other men, the leader cut Joce's throat" and killed himself. The remainder of the Jews, who were massed at the gate, "preferred to try Christian clemency." They announced to the besiegers, "We recognize Christian truth and desire its charity—receive us as brothers and let us live with you in the faith and peace of Christ." Speaking fair words in reply, the leaders of the mob induced them to open the gate, and then slew them to a man. The chronicler concludes with justice, "Their own blood baptized them, when defrauded of their plea."

[1] See p. 40.

The exquisite lancet windows known as the Five Sisters in York Minster are traditionally called the "Jewish windows"—possibly because the money spent on their execution came from Jewish pockets. Aaron of York, a son of the martyr Joce who escaped his father's knife, is known to have loaned money for church-building. If he had a hand in the Five Sisters he has left to York a happier memorial of his race than Clifford's bloody tower.

Most English Jewries—there were no enforced ghettos—lay near the market place, as in Lincoln. The sites of many of them are known, and remains are rumoured as in Norwich—where there is talk of vaulted cellars and a house called Music Hall, which may have been the Jewish marriage hall (the Jewry was located in the block between Hayhill, Little Orford, Saddlegate, and Back of Castle Streets). But the average traveller must be satisfied with two street names—Jewry Lane in Canterbury (off High Street) and Jewry Street in Winchester (between High Street and North Walls)—and the so-called Jewry Wall in Leicester (west end of St. Nicholas Church), a bit of Roman masonry which marks the quarter of the vanished servants of the ark.

Oxford had its Jewry along St. Aldate Street, from Carfax to the great gate of Christ Church. The synagogue lay opposite St. Aldate's Church, and the cemetery by Magdalen Tower and later on the site of the Botanic Gardens. Merton College, the oldest in Oxford, and the Guildhall were built on Jewish land. Several of the halls which formed the nucleus of the university were purchased from the Jews, notably Moyse's, Lombard's and Jacob's Halls. Indeed, it is presumed that it was the excellence of these accommodations—"Jewish comfort," it was likely called in the twelfth century—which attracted professors and students to the town. The Jews enjoyed a spiritual influence as well; several conversions to Judaism took place, and in 1222 an Oxford deacon became a proselyte and married a Jewess. The Church authorities burned him *pour encourager les autres*. Several years later, the Jewry was stormed by a mob and sacked; whereupon the king took the hint and limited the amount of interest the Jews could collect from the students, to 43 per cent.

But of all this, nothing pertinent remains to be seen. Instead, you may examine the so-called Bodleian Bowl in the reading-room of the Bodleian Library. Eleven pounds of bronze, 9¾″ high and 30″ around, it stands on three hoof-shaped feet and is served by two handles. Above the feet are graven a bird, a deer ("light as the eagle and fleet as the hart to do the will of thy Father who is in Heaven"?) and a floral design. It is of French make and bears the following inscription in Hebrew: "This is the gift of Joseph son of the holy Rabbi Yehiel . . . who answered and asked the congregation as he desired, in order to behold the face of Ariel [Jerusalem] as it is written in the law of Jekutiel [Moses]; And righteousness delivereth from death [Prov. 11:4]." Yehiel of Paris, as we have learned,[1] sought deliverance in flight to Palestine. He was accompanied by his son Joseph and three hundred disciples, including several English Jews. The bowl was probably intended for collecting alms to support either the schools or the persons of these bold men who had shaken from their feet the dust of Europe.

The Bodleian, it is perhaps needless to state, possesses, in addition to its magnificent library of printed Judaica, the largest collection of Hebrew MSS. (about 3,000) in the world. Here will be found the *Fox Fables* of Berechiah Ha-Nakdan, a twelfth-century fabulist, translator, and exegete supposed to have lived in Oxford and one of the few scholars among the early English Jews. Here too are the Elephantine papyri, the oldest known Aramaic MSS. (fifth century B.C.), retailing the life of a Jewish colony in Upper Egypt during the days of

[1] See p. 50.

Nehemiah; and many of the treasures from the old *genizah*, or synagogue storehouse, of Cairo. The University Library of Cambridge likewise possesses numerous *genizah* fragments, among them the Hebrew original of the book of Ecclesiasticus.[1]

Returning to London, we find that, so far as the first Jewish settlement is concerned, everything has been changed into something else. Old Jewry itself, off Cheapside, houses a police station and the offices of the British Debt; and since thirteenth-century methods in British finance no longer prevail, it is useless to look into either for our Jews. The one easily identifiable site of a synagogue is now St. Stephen's Church (Coleman Street); another, if you insist, faced the Church of St. Lawrence Jewry on Guildhall Yard. Jewin Street, once the cemetery, is visited, if ever, as a former residence of Milton. It is true, the name of Huggin Lane, leading from Wood Street, leads back to the Hagin family (French *Haquin*, Hebrew *Hayim*), who lived at No. 2 Wood Street seven centuries gone, and who were the most prolific literary family among the Angevin Jews.

But, all in all, it is better to await the Spanish-Portuguese from Amsterdam, who will meet a different England and bring with them a happier fate than the old bankers from Rouen.

ᘓᘏᘐᘎ

In the middle of the seventeenth century everything, including the lost ten tribes, conspired to bring about the return of the Jews. To begin with, a small group were already there in Marano masks, and winning the gratitude of Cromwell by the intelligence they gave him of the plans of the Spaniards in the New World and of exiled Charles and his plotters in

[1] See p. 227.

Holland. Then, the Bible-reading of the Roundheads provoked a certain interest in the people they read about, and the establishment of the republic (1649) helped to weaken a few of the old traditions and prejudices. Cromwell, moreover, had an eye on what the Jews of Holland had done in the way of expanding Dutch colonial commerce, and he saw no reason why they should not do as much for England. Finally, there was the matter of the ten tribes.

Inflamed by their Bible-reading and encouraged by the writings of such messianic-minded Jews as Manasseh ben Israel,[1] Christian millenarians became convinced that the restoration of Zion—as a prelude to the Kingdom of the Saints—was close at hand. The fulfilment of the prophecies only awaited the complete dispersion of Israel. Two of the twelve tribes were fairly accounted for; what of the others long lost? Manasseh ben Israel was able to satisfy himself and the English on that score. He had received intelligence, too, word from one Antonio de Montezinos, Jewish traveller in South America, that Reuben, Levi, and the other tribes had been met in Ecuador; had even, for proof, recited the *shema*. Clearly the dispersion was now complete—save for England.

Manasseh ben Israel, upon invitation, visited Cromwell, petitioned Parliament; and, as Carlyle says, "Law-learning, Scripture-prophecy and every source of light for the human mind" were contracted upon the question. In 1655 English law-learning pronounced there were no legal hindrances against the return of the Jews. The next year papers of denizenship were granted two Maranos already established in London. Then, due to the characteristic protests of the more conservative clergy and nobility, the matter was dropped. England never formally opened her doors. But a sort of precedent was set; and British before they landed, the Spanish-Portu-

[1] See p. 198.

guese Jews and a little later the Ashkenazim muddled their way in.

It was characteristic, as well, that the last disability was not removed from the English Jews (and Roman Catholics) until 1890; and that, meanwhile, these same Jews were seated in Parliament, received in the peerage, and elected Lord Mayor of London.

Midpoint between the long-abandoned mediæval ghetto and modern Whitechapel runs a short lane that houses the two historic synagogues of London. The upper stretch of the lane is Bevis Marks, where stands the Spanish-Portuguese, or Sephardic, synagogue, and beyond a jog where the lane is known as Duke Street lies the Great Synagogue of the Ashkenazim.

The Spanish-Portuguese is the older of the two, in fact the oldest extant in England—completed in 1702. It was built by Joseph Avis, a Quaker, who prosecuted none of the work on a Sabbath or Jewish holiday, and who donated the profits to the congregation. Queen Anne presented a beam from a royal ship, which was incorporated in the roof.

Like its neighbour, the entrance lies away from the street— up a court—hinting that its worshippers, despite John Locke's letters on Toleration, were taking no chances. The inscription on the drum over the doorway reads, in Hebrew, "Sanctified to the Lord, Holy Congregation of the *Gate of Heaven*, 1702." Although much smaller, the interior resembles the Portuguese synagogue of Amsterdam,[1] modified by late-Jacobean touches. A single hall, with balconies on three sides, the *bima* retired from the centre, and behind it a high-backed choir-stall, the ark divided into three bays and flanked by fluted Corinthian pilasters, the whole done in fine polished wood, is charming and impressive. The old candelabra—the large central chandelier was brought from Amsterdam—and the deep tones of

[1] See p. 192.

the worn benches cast a glow from the past, when the *Gate of Heaven* influenced the destinies of Jews not only in England, but in far-off Gibraltar, Jamaica, and colonial New York. And something in the archaic lines of the high-backed choir, the raised and canopied *banco* or wardens' pew against the wall, the little throne for the beadle, and the august panelling evoke memories of perukes, *ascamot,* and the high fantasies of Manasseh Bueno Barzillai Azevedo da Costa.[1]

Upstairs in the (modern) vestry-room may be seen a number of richly embroidered Torah mantles, a curious Elijah chair, a painting by Aaron de Chares (1674) representing Moses, Aaron, and the tablets of the Law, and portraits of sundry notables. Among the list of officials inscribed in the hallway are great names in their day: Sampson Gideon "patriot" at the bursting of the South Sea Bubble, Baron d'Aguilar of "Starve-crow Farm," Joseph Salvador "prince among merchants and philanthropists"; little but the names remain of these illustrious blue-bloods and brokers. England, however, has Disraeli who gave her an empire, and Samuel Elias who invented the "upper-cut," and she can be satisfied.

The Great Synagogue, built in 1722 and often restored, is architecturally as simple as Bevis Marks, but in size and lavishness far more pretentious. Crystal chandeliers and gilt paint proclaim the more recent but greater wealth of the Ashkenazim. The face of the three balconies, from end to end, is covered with the names of the (no doubt) original donors and the amount of their subscriptions. To the contemporary mind this may seem shameless advertising; but our modesty is chiefly custom. The French have as yet no such scruples; you can find on the walls of the basilica of Sacré Cœur a fair-sized directory of Paris. Still, the Great Synagogue had its moments, none greater than when the young Victoria paid it a visit and all eyes scanned the *parnas*, Lionel Mayer Roths-

[1] See p. 455 (Bibliography).

child, to see whether he would doff his silk hat in deference to the queen or keep it on in obedience to God—but these Ashkenazim had never been Maranos, and Rothschild kept untouched his hat and the honor of Israel.

The first burial-ground of the Sephardic Jews (253 Mile End Road—rear) is reached by traversing Whitechapel and the modern ghetto, a grey, dismal world with all the poverty and none of the colour, noise, and electric flare of the East Side of New York. However, to American ears there is something quaint in the blend of Yiddish and cockney accents, and Middlesex Street at market time on a Sunday morning throbs with that terrific energy bound to be loosed by any gathering of Israel.

Gone is the energy in the grassy acre dedicated to the departed and called, here as elsewhere, by a pathetic euphemism *The House of Life*. The first burial took place in 1657, and all of the stones date from the seventeenth and eighteenth centuries. They are for the most part unadorned, and inscribed in Spanish or Portuguese, with a stray marginal word in English. Nevertheless, the influence of Ouderkerk[1] shows in an occasional stone. In the northernmost row, a tomb (No. 12) bears a cartouche with a nude figure holding a sash. A little south, Aaron Francia (d. 1695—No. 45) displays his crest and a skull and cross-bones. In the eighth row, David Mendes (d. 1705— No. 65) offers the figure of a man touching a tree with his staff. Perhaps the only occupant to interest late-comers like ourselves is Antonio Fernandes Carvajal (d. 1659—northwest corner), the first Jew to receive denizenship from Cromwell. Coming as a Marano from Portugal to England (c. 1635), he was soon owning ships which traded from Brazil to India. In his early days he attended Mass at the Spanish ambassador's chapel in London; his increasing absence from services provoked an inquiry; the cat was out of the bag, but his fellow-

[1] See p. 199.

merchants squashed any semblance to an Inquisition on English soil. It was Carvajal's agents who kept an eye, for Cromwell, on Charles II and Spain.

The old Ashkenazic cemetery lies on Aldeney Road, farther east along Mile End.

Further trace of eighteenth-century Jews may be pursued in the synagogue at Exeter (St. Mary's Arches), built in 1763, and the Portsmouth synagogue (Prince Georges Street) of approximately the same age. Ramsgate deserves a word for its Montefiore Museum, its tomb of Judith Montefiore done in imitation of Rachel's Tomb near Bethlehem, and for a synagogue dated about 1800.

There will always be some one, we hope, who wishes to learn that Heine has a tablet on the house (32 Craven Street, Strand) where he lived while spending his uncle's letter-of-credit and writing the *English Letters*. Heine knew Ramsgate, too, and the pretty Irish girl who haunted its strand. Finally, there is the statue of that other Christian, Benjamin Disraeli, looking away from the Houses of Parliament.

❧

The British Museum is a storehouse and showroom for the history of many peoples, and not least the Jews. We can follow their career beginning with the days of Abraham or, if you prefer, the Flood and Creation itself. The reader has been led through a similar tour in the Louvre,[1] and it is hoped that, with the aid of a list of pertinent objects to be seen, he can readily make his own way in the present collection.[2]

Its Babylonian and Assyrian contributions to the panorama of early Jewish history are richer than in Paris. The hastiest traveller will want to view, even if he cannot decipher, the

[1] See Chaps. I and II.
[2] See Appendix B.

Babylonian stories of Creation and the Flood (Assyrian Room, table case A); the seal cylinders which picture without need of words a scene similar to the temptation in the Garden of Eden, the Babylonian Noah afloat on his ark, and Nimrod "the mighty hunter before the Lord" (Assyrian Room, cases B and E); inscriptions telling us of repairs made on the Tower of Babel and coloured bricks from a like tower (Second North. Gallery, Room III, case G); the almost incredible evidences of a high civilization in Ur of the Chaldees a thousand years before Abraham (Second North. Gallery, Room III), and a tablet giving us the inventory of cattle, sheep, and goats of a herdsman contemporary with and probably not unlike the patriarch (case H); sculptured reliefs portraying a "hanging garden" in Babylonia (Assyrian Saloon, No. 3), and the assault on Jerusalem and fate of the Jewish prisoners (Nineveh Gallery, Nos. 20-29); a series of Palestinian signets from the long-forgotten hands of Hebrew plutocrats and princes (Second North. Gallery, Room II, centre case); the stele of Shalmaneser III, showing Jehu bringing tribute from the kingdom of Israel (Nimrud Centre Saloon, No. 4); the Babylonians' and Persians' own account of the fall of Babylon (Second North. Gallery, Room III, cases E and G); and the flame-cracked and smoke-blackened reliefs from Nineveh (Kunyunjik Gallery) making visible for us the prophecy of Nahum (Nahum 3:13 and 15): "There shall the fire devour thee . . . the fire shall devour thy bars."

The Egyptian collection will in turn show us, as Ezekiel (Ez. 27:7) advertised them, "fine linen with broidered work from Egypt" (Room V, case G); models of storehouses such as Joseph filled (cases 183-187); and bricks made, it is true, *with* straw, but stamped with the name of Rameses II, likely the pharaoh of the oppression (cases 206-207).

There is nothing similar to the Palestinian relics of the Salle Judaïque in the Louvre, but by way of compensation the visitor may pursue the history of Israel long after the close of the Biblical account.

The Coin and Medal Room contains a series of moneys illustrating the Maccabean and Herodian dynasties, the destruction of Jerusalem at the hands of Titus, and the last revolt under Bar Kochba (case 8).

The Manuscript Saloon picks up the tale in the ninth century c.e. with the oldest known copy of a Hebrew Pentateuch (case G); and the adjoining King's Library carries it further with a display of finely illuminated and otherwise significant Hebrew manuscripts (case A), including portions of the original Hebrew text of Ecclesiasticus dated from the twelfth century c.e. and two legal questions submitted to Maimonides, with replies in his own hand.

Quite as beautiful and significant in their own way are the fourteen Renaissance betrothal and marriage rings (King Edward VII Gallery, case at far end). We may wonder if any sly humour lay in the band which shows, in coloured enamel, the temptation of Adam (No. 1331).

Finally, the library of the Museum contains some 2700 MSS. and over 19,000 printed volumes in Hebrew, and, no trifle, facilities for using them unrivalled on the Continent. Other collections of Hebraica and Judaica are to be found in the Jews' College (Queen Square) and the Mocatta library in University College (Gower Street).

The South Kensington or Victoria and Albert Museum illustrates the religious life of the late Renaissance and early modern period in a variety of ritual objects.[1] Unhappily, they are classified, as everything else in the museum, according to their materials, and are therefore widely dispersed. The rarest treasures of Jewish ritual art in London are to be found in the private collections of David Sassoon, Arthur Franklin, and M. S. Solomon.

---

[1] See Chapter V for character, use, and symbols of this ritual art.

The stairway of the textile department in the Kensington (Room 126) brings together in one large case an array of Jewish embroideries. Noteworthy are (1) a Torah mantle, eighteenth-century Amsterdam, adorned with brocade and silver filigree crowns, bells, and pomegranates, on the back a view of the Portuguese synagogue—its first home, and on the front various symbols, including altar, laver, flesh-hooks, fire-pans, Urim and Thummim, Aaron's rod, and David's harp; (2) a hanging for pulpit-desk, seventeenth-century Italian embroidered canvas, in centre the tablets of the Law, with Sinai in flames below and a thundercloud above, to right a wafer of unleavened bread, and to left the "four species," and beneath the whole two shofars; (3) a seventeenth-century Italian desk-hanging of velvet brocade trimmed with gold lace and fringes; (4) a seventeenth-century Italian Torah band of linen and silk stitched with Hebrew inscription; (5) a Dutch scroll of the Book of Esther, dated 1648, with silver filigree figures of Mordecai and Esther mounted on the rollers; (6) a seventeenth-century Italian amulet in engraved silver, set with garnets and corals; (7) an eighteenth-century Palestinian or North African linen cover for the Habdala service, gay with coloured wool embroidery representing the Temple, Wailing Wall, and pavilions dedicated to Rabbi Meir the Master of Miracles, Zechariah the prophet, and Absalom, son of David (!).

The metal-work department offers a large choice of sixteenth- and seventeenth-century marriage rings (Room 38, case Q8); an eighteenth-century Dutch brass lamp for the feast of Maccabees (case C473); a hanging Sabbath lamp of the same period and origin (case C473); a seventeenth-century and an eighteenth-century Augsburg silver spice-box, both of the usual turret design, and an amulet in silver repoussé (case C509); a seventeenth-century Dutch silver case for the scroll of Esther (between Rooms 38 and 39, case N6); and five nineteenth-century silver filigree spice-boxes from Aleppo, together with a nineteenth-century filigree case for the scroll of Esther from Salonica (Room 26, case C222), chiefly of interest to show the persistence of traditional designs in the Near East.

The neighbouring Natural History Museum contains a collection of plants and flowers prevalent in Palestine.

Rembrandt's profound understanding of Jewish character[1] may be followed in the National Gallery, which possesses the "Portrait of a Jewish Merchant" (Room XII, No. 51) with its shrewd yet kindly face, and "A Rabbi" (Room X, No. 190) unforgettable for its deep, anxious, and searching eyes. Rembrandt does not stand alone in this; indeed, he draws upon a sympathetic interest in the Jew already prevailing among Dutch artists, as we may see from the work of his predecessor, Hendrick Terbruggen (1581-1629), whose "Jacob and Laban" (Room IX, No. 4164) uses a Biblical theme merely as an excuse to paint the occupants and the interior of a Jewish home on Joden Bree Straat.

But Rembrandt's undisputed mastery may spur the amateur to a further study of his Jewish works in England (the list of owners is subject, in these troublous days, to change without notice): "The Rabbi in a White Turban" (Duke of Devonshire, Chatsworth), "Rabbi in a High Turban" (Earl of Derby, Derby House), "Rabbi in a Fur Cloak" (Buckingham Palace), "Rabbi with Flat Cap" (Royal Gallery, Hampton Court), "Head of a Jew with Brown Beard" (Earl of Ellesmere, Bridgewater House), and "Bust of a Bearded Jew" (Earl of Cowper, Panshanger).

In these flecks of oil and pigment are fixed the soul and summation of the Sephardic Jew whom we have followed from Elche of the Palms through four lands and eleven centuries.

[1] See p. 198.

CHAPTER XIII

Rome and the
Eternal People

WHEN in the year 160 B.C. Eupolemus son of Johanan, and Jason son of Eleazar, having come "a very great journey," walked up the steps of the Curia—still to be climbed below the Church of S. Adriano—and concluded an alliance with the Roman Senate on behalf of a barbarian chieftain named Judas Maccabæus, other countrymen of Judas were, it is presumed, already settled in Rome. Twenty years later, when further ambassadors from Simon Maccabæus brought a gold shield "of a thousand-pound weight" to the same Senate and exchanged it for a treaty recognizing the independence of their nation, a community of Judeans was assuredly established in the republic, for a decree of the same year ordered the expulsion of any Jew who had not taken out his naturalization papers. And for twenty-one centuries thereafter, that is until the present writing, the Jewish community of Rome has persisted without interruption. The story of an eternal people in an eternal city is bound to be long—indeed, it has already filled many volumes. Time, however, has been indulgent to the traveller and removed most of its tangible debris. Yet enough remains; and even confining himself to the more obvious survivals, he will find them, like signposts at odd corners, leading him down the maze of Roman Jewish history.

The district between the present Churches of S. Cecilia and S. Callisto, close by S. Maria in Travestere, on the right bank of the Tiber, was thick with Jews in the days when Horace taunted them for superstitious weaklings: "*Credat Judaeus Apella*—we enlightened minds don't believe that every thunderclap portends the wrath of God." One of their first synagogues stood near the site of S. Cecilia, almost within earshot of Cicero's oratory in the Forum Aurelium, while he thundered against "this multitude of Jews lobbying in our assemblies." The district, in fact, was not abandoned until, sixteen hundred years later, the Pope locked its inhabitants into the ghetto proper.

Meanwhile, other quarters sprang up in imperial Rome, densest in the Suburra (Via Cavour, below S. Pietro in Vincoli and Michelangelo's "Moses"), where the noise used to keep Martial awake nights, and beyond the Porta Capena along the Appian Way. Here, Juvenal tells us, the sacred grove of Numa had rented all its trees to Jewish beggars, and here swarmed pedlars with their baskets and fortune-telling Jewesses who would "sell you any sort of dream at cut prices."

Eleven synagogues, in all, are known to ancient Rome. Their appearance may be judged from a picture of one of them on the Capitoline Plan, a fifth-century mosaic map of Rome. The synagogue will be recognized by the curtains and lamp hanging between the two pillars of its doorway. But many more must be lost from the records, for the Jewish population is placed between 30,000 and 60,000.

Proselytizing flourished, winning such distinguished converts as the nephew of Domitian and the second wife of Nero. Apart from actual conversion, the observance of the dietary laws and the Sabbath became a fashion early enough for Horace to complain at the Jewish success in "pushing you" into their "crowd."[1] The Church of S. Pudenziana, reputed the oldest in the city, is built on the site and (in part) out of the materials of the house of Pudens, a wealthy Roman in Nero's day, who used to entertain a subsequently renowned missionary of one of the more obscure Jewish sects. You may see the marble columns which supported Pudens' porch, a fragment of the mosaic pavement which the missionary must have trodden, and under the altar in the left aisle a plank from the dining-table at which Simon Peter ate. This will tell you the respectable place occupied by the Jews in the early days before Jerusalem fell and the mass immigration set in from the East.

In the Conservatori Palace, next to the Capitoline Museum, a room (Sala degli Orti Lamiani) is devoted to the sculpture found in the Lamian Gardens. These were the gardens and this is the sculpture Gaius Cæsar, better known by his nickname, Caligula, fussed over while an Egyptian Jewish committee, headed by the philosopher Philo, sought to plead with him against his proposal to erect his own statue for public worship in the Temple at Jerusalem. Philo has left us a report of the mission to prevent this desecration, which makes as cynical reading as the annals of diplomacy afford.

Followed by a troop of gardeners, architects, and decorators, Caligula sped from hall to terrace, and at the heels of the gardeners sped the Jewish committee, vainly trying to edge in a word. Suddenly Caligula breaks off ordering a new-fangled window-pane and flings a question at Philo, "Why don't Jews eat pork?" Gravely the philosopher begins his reply, " 'Tis a custom; many peoples refrain from certain foods; there are some who do not eat veal. . . ." "Quite right," interrupts the emperor, "veal is terrible," and he dashes on to consider a bit of carving for a fountain. Again he halts. "And why," he turns on Philo, "do you Jews refuse to offer sacrifices to the em-

[1] See p. 38.

peror?" "A calumny," protests Philo. "We have offered heca-
tombs for your health." "Perhaps you have," says Caligula,
sprinting away, "but to another god. . . ." And he adds as he
runs, "So what good does that do *me*?" At the end of this rac-
ing interview, which covered most of the vast gardens, Caligula conceded, "After all, the Jews are not wicked in their
refusal to believe I am a god; they are simply foolish and
unfortunate."

The Lamian Gardens are once more bright with flowers
and sculpture (now Piazza Vittoria Emanuele), yet if he could
return to them, no one would be more astonished than Caligula to find not only the Roman Empire evaporated, its dregs
of ruins crumbling piecemeal in the sun or bottled up in
museums, but all around his beloved gardens the prosperous
shops of these unfortunate and foolish Jews. The only people
who could properly share his astonishment are the Jews of
Caligula's Rome, who, we may be sure, looked on Pudens as
just such an unfortunate fool for giving board and ears to an
eccentric immigrant like Simon Peter. Unless we include
Simon Peter, too, bluff and honest soul, and picture his bewilderment in trying to bring himself to sit in his present
chair.

⌔⌁⌕

Six Jewish catacombs have been discovered beyond the city
gates, and these galleries of the dead have yielded a precious
record of daily life during the Empire. Their 450 inscriptions,
their wall-paintings, sculpture, sarcophagi, lamps, trinkets,
glassware, and manifold symbols tell the names these Roman
Jews adopted, the languages they spoke, the synagogues they
built, the arts they cultivated, the different characters of their
communities, the progress of their assimilation, and in one
case how they looked.

Catacombs came natural to the Jews, enabling them to transfer their traditional methods of rock-burial in Palestine to the soft tufa of Rome. The oldest, on Monteverde, dates from the first century c.e.; and the early Christians, many of whom began life as Jews, borrowed the device from the mother faith. The greater preponderance of Greek inscriptions in the Monteverde catacombs, the occasional Hebrew epitaphs—few, it is true, but more numerous than elsewhere —and the restraint in the decoration, confined for the most part to the old ritual symbols, together describe an orthodox community clinging to traditional ways and speech. In contrast, a later catacomb, such as the Vigna Randanini with its comparatively large number of Latin epitaphs, the almost complete absence of Hebrew, the free use of carving and painting which did not draw the line at cupids, human figures, and even a winged Pegasus, belonged on the face of it to a Romanized liberal-minded congregation, who probably called their place of worship a "temple."

The Vigna Randanini, near the Church of S. Sebastiano (Via Pignatelli, off the Appian Way) is the only one of the six catacombs open to the public. If the light is sufficient (*i.e.* a tip), the paintings are worth examining for their symbolism. Traditional *motifs* will be identified at once: the menorah, *shofar, lulab,* altar, etc. But new forms of mixed origin likewise appear. Dolphin and other fish, despite their pagan looks, are Jewish, symbolizing the resurrection of the dead (Jonah and the whale?) and, it need hardly be said, they were adopted as such by the Christians. The peacock—all Randanini fowl are gorgeous—no doubt began its symbolic career as a pagan, but the Jews and Christians converted it to signify immortality, used it for this purpose throughout late antiquity, and then abandoned it.[1] Doves have had a strangely interrupted history. In the Monteverde catacombs they are

[1] See p. 409 (Naro).

graven on the epitaphs, sometimes in the act of plucking a leaf or picking at a grape, and their use makes it clear they represent the soul of the departed. Doubtless they served a similar purpose in the Randanini and other ancient burial-galleries. Then they vanish for over a thousand years and, how or why we cannot say, reappear with the same meaning in eighteenth-century Poland.[1] Curious, too, that the ram (a surrogate for Isaac and Israel?) should flash across the painted walls of Randanini and raise his horned head among its carvings, then disappear for fifteen hundred years, and finally become a favourite folk symbol again in Poland, and the sign and seal of Chagall. The ducks and chickens of these Roman Jewish paintings are either conventional decoration or forgotten pagan signs. The human figures representing Victory, Abundance, the Seasons, as well as sea-horses and winged Pegasus, are the measures of Jewish assimilation; they rank with modern synagogue pipe-organs and Sunday-morning services.

Most of the epitaphs and sculptured sarcophagi have been removed to museums. The largest collection will be found in the Lateran (Sala Giudaica). Noteworthy is the memorial (No. 29) of one Malka or Regina—surely she called herself Regina—which celebrates in Latin hexameters her good and pure life, her observance of the Law, and her trust in the resurrection. The use of secular verse and the piety of her sentiments together paint the portrait of a genteel, even fashionable, yet devout Roman lady "of the Jewish persuasion," whom we might have met a generation ago distributing her favourite charities in London or Paris. The same social class is reflected in the pagan-Jewish fantasies of a sarcophagus (next room) with a medallion bearing the menorah upheld by two Greek tutelary genii, and with a lively representation of the three Hebrew children in the fiery furnace; or still

[1] See p. 376.

more surprising, in a sarcophagus lid (Sala Giudaica) carved with the fully rounded figure of a reclining boy. The head is indubitably a portrait, Jewish to the curl of the lips and the turn of the nose; and the doting parents may be guessed in the pets they gave him while alive, a puppy and a pigeon, and now placed for the last time in his chubby stone hands.

The typical epitaph of Istasia and Priscilla (No. 101) shows a scroll, *shofar, lulab, etrog,* oil-jar, menorah, and snuffers. This recurrent use of the menorah and the presence of innumerable terra-cotta lamps sealed with the seven-branched candlestick, possibly take their significance for the dead from the Biblical verse (Prov. 20:27), "The spirit of man is the candle of the Lord." Among the untraditional symbols we find a bull (No. 10), spade, ivy leaf—used perhaps as a punctuation mark (Nos. 4, 11), and the doves (Nos. 73, 91).

Roman sculptors had their problems with the early Christians as well as the Jews. The Museo Cristiano in the Lateran is filled with sarcophagi from the Christian catacombs which witness the rise of new themes for classic art, and chisels that hitherto modelled the gods of Olympus are now trying their edge on Habbakuk, Jonah, Elijah, Abraham, and Moses.

Further Jewish inscriptions will be found in the cloisters of S. Paolo fuori le Mura, in the Kircher Museum (Room 50) and, together with sarcophagi, in the Thermes Museum. The Thermes collection (Wing IV, Room 3) provides another menorah (sarcophagus No. 373) flanked by winged genii and accompanied by a vintage scene; terra-cotta lamps stamped with the figure of Mother Eve and with the spies returning laden from Canaan; and among the epitaphs the familiar German Jewish name Sigimundus (Siegmund—Hebrew *Shalom*) commemorating the first German Jew known, or rather unknown to history.

The rarest objects found in the Christian and Jewish catacombs are round plaques of gilt glass (*fondi d'oro*) used for dishes, for the base of drinking vessels, or simply as wall decoration. They consist of a film of gold leaf and occasionally red and blue pigment tooled into a design and pressed between two layers of tinted glass, which are then fused into a solid whole—a forgotten or abandoned art that probably had its origin in Alexandria. Apart from the 150 specimens in the Vatican (Museo Cristiano, Floor I, Room 11) and a small but choice assortment in the Museo Borgiano (Collegio di Propaganda Fide) and the Biblioteca della Vallicella (adjoining the Chiesa Nuova), you may fairly ransack Europe for their like.

The Jewish examples in the Vatican are of capital interest. One of them, giving a view of the Temple in Jerusalem, is judged from its style and superior workmanship to be the oldest in the collection and made in Alexandria itself; if so, it may well date from the days when the Temple was still of this world. The Holy of Holies, its colonnaded court, and the city and symbolic palm trees beyond, are quaintly rendered; in the foreground stand ritual vessels, the *lulab* sheaf, and a lighted menorah burning red against a breeze; the Greek inscription invokes a blessing on the "House of Peace." Later specimens (in the Vatican and Borgiano) centre their design on the Ark of the Law, in itself enough to show that the synagogue has supplanted the fallen Temple. A Borgiano example gives, besides the customary symbols, a curious salad of borrowings and variants. The doors of the ark are open, showing nine scrolls of the Law, single instead of the now familiar double rolls; on either side of the ark a bird stands upon a globe, one bird possibly representing the soul standing in the world of the living and the other in the world to come; the citron, or *etrog*, is pictured in cross-section as though sliced in half;[1] and the menorah, beneath the ark, rests on an

[1] See p. 129 (Cordova).

omphalos—the navel of the earth. This navel, sacred to the Greeks, appears frequently in the Jewish specimens at the Vatican, sometimes tipped sidewise, looking much like a rubber nipple. On one plaque it is accompanied by the young god of Fortune, with the inscription "Gad" (Hebrew for "fortune") as much as to say, *Mazel-tov* (good luck)!" The usual inscriptions, with the name of the owner, run to pious ejaculations: "Rest in peace!" "Live in holiness!" "Drink and say the blessings!" They are written in a Greek-Latin jargon which assures one that the workmanship of the glass, its cunning and its beauty, are Jewish, and which speaks—like the mismated symbols—no less eloquently of an uprooted and already cosmopolitan people.

The monument to their deracination is, of course, the Arch of Titus, erected in celebration of the fall of Jerusalem (70 c.e.). Its marching conquerors, shew-bread table, trumpets, and menorah have become the commonplaces of illustrated Jewish Sunday-school books. Such is the nature of victories.

꒰ᴧᴧ꒱

The Ponte Fabricio, built in 62 b.c. by the consul Fabricius and reckoned the oldest in Rome, has been known time out of mind as the Jews' Bridge. It leads directly to the quarter where the Jews settled thickest in the Middle Ages and where, with incredible thickness—some 15,000 in a half-dozen tiny blocks—they were immured behind the ghetto gates of 1555. Italy was late in establishing compulsory ghettos; the institution, though not the name, existed, as we have seen, in France and Spain centuries before; but Rome made up for lost time by keeping its Jews under lock and key until only sixty years ago—a tribute to the conservative virtues of the Church.

Little of account remains—happily, for not alone was it the most overpacked ghetto on record, with all the filth and stench that inhuman herding aggravated by an annual mud bath from the Tiber floods imply, but its maintenance into the full tide of modernity besmirched the honour of Christendom with even a fouler stain. It was an evidence of temporal power for the destruction of which the Papacy may well thank the wicked Garibaldians.

For over a thousand years after the fall of the Empire the Jews of Papal Rome lived, for Jews, comparatively unmolested. There was, to be sure, the little matter of rendering homage to every newly elected Pope on Monte Giordano (present Palazzo Taverna or Gabrielli, Via de Coronari), or before the arch of Septimus Severus in the Forum, or, bitterer still, before the Arch of Titus; the chief rabbi presented a scroll of the Law to the pontiff, who returned it contemptuously over his left shoulder, with a few appropriate remarks on the stiff-neckedness of Israel and with a gift of alms, representing, it must be confessed, an inconsiderable rebate on the taxes which the Jews paid to the Church. There was the matter of censoring Hebrew books conducted in the Dominican cloister next to S. Maria sopra Minerva, and burning those beyond hope of censorship in the adjoining square. The Biblioteca Casanatense, which occupies the old Dominican quarters, still contains a number of confiscated manuscripts. Then there were the races of half-naked victims chosen for their fatness, along the Corso, during two hundred and two carnivals (1466-1668). But the Jews were permitted, so the inscription tells us, the use of drinking-water from the fountain of Acqua Paola by Paul V (1612).

Despite these inconveniences, life was on the whole better than in most Christian lands. Commerce and manufacture flourished; numerous cardinals and popes placed their business affairs in the care of the Jews; banking, however, did not become a Jewish monopoly, for the Lombards stood for no nonsense from canon law on the subject of usury. Traditional learning rose to new heights in Talmudic schools that dated from the otherwise Dark Ages; Nathan ben Yehiel compiled in 1101 a lexicographical study of Talmudic literature which ranks in its way with the exegetical achievements of Rashi[1] and which remained the only work of its kind until the nineteenth century. Poetry and philosophy were cultivated in a wide intercourse with Gentiles; historians are never tired of pointing to the friendship of Immanuel of Rome and Dante, and lovers of Hebrew have not ceased to relish the gaiety and humanism of Immanuel's verse or the wit of his contemporary, Kalonymus ben Kalonymus, Provençal by birth but Roman by the affection the city gave him.

The Renaissance brought new contacts, and again historians like to point to Elijah Levita, master of Hebrew and his pupil, Cardinal Egidio (1470-1532), who exchanged lessons in Greek for the key to the Cabbala, both, as Levita said, "taking sweet counsel together." Egidio's sympathy for Hebrew learning led him to defend Reuchlin and Reuchlin's battle for the Talmud in the bold words, "Fighting on your behalf, we defend not you but the law, not the Talmud but the Church." When David Reubeni came to Rome (1524), it was natural that the first man he turned to should be Cardinal Egidio, and symptomatic of the times that the Cardinal became the champion of Reubeni and his plans for the restoration of Zion. Indeed, no better picture can be had of the tide of daily living in Rome and the warmth of Christian and Jewish relations than Reubeni's diary. And, throughout, the Church could point with pride to the fact that Jews were never massacred in the capital of Christendom.

[1] See p. 87.

꙳

But the fair face of things was changed by the Counter Reformation. It became imperative that the contamination of the Christian world by Bible-readers must cease, and all avenues to its unorthodox interpretation be closed. The segregation of the Jews played, therefore, a natural, if minor, part in the warfare of the Church against Protestantism. And June 12, 1555, Paul IV in his bull *nimis absurdam* built the ghetto of Rome. It was merely accidental that its walls were raised by the arch and palace of Octavius, where, seated on ivory thrones, Titus and Vespasian reported to the assembled Senate that Jerusalem had fallen.

The principal gate opened from the present Piazza del Pianto, formerly Piazza Giudia and the market where thereafter Jews and Gentiles were to meet. It was only curiosity-hunters like Montaigne who crossed the threshold.

Today, all but a few unsavoury fragments have been swept away, though the Via del Portico d'Ottavia and the neighbouring Via Reginella may give you a sight and smell of what the old ghetto was like. Hucksters trundle their carts up and down the dusty pavement and eat their garlicky suppers on crowded doorsteps. Children sprawl, fleas swarm, donkeys bray, and goats and dogs occupy themselves as they are wont. Even for Italy there is a superfluity of life; humans, animals, and insects should for the sake of the simplest laws of physics agree on the occupancy of this limited space.

At the bend of the Via del Portico stands S. Angelo in Pescheria, the little baroque church where, from 1584 to 1847, the denizens of the ghetto were compelled to listen to Christian sermons. Every precaution was taken for the benefit of their souls. Ears were pried into, lest they be found stuffed with cotton; and a beadle paced the aisles, wand in hand, to see that no one feigned to sleep. Surely the walls of a church never held a more attentive audience. The desert God was little of a humourist, but it may be hoped He smiled, if wanly, and not the least of Israel's prophets drooped his head. The church is quite empty now.

The present synagogue, which has proudly supplanted the five famous predecessors lodged in one tenement, is a gaudy affair—indicating the sins the Jews could have committed in the way of baroque; but it deserves a visit for the manuscripts, photographs, paintings, and other memorials relating to the vanished Jewry and now collected in the vestry-room. A series of nineteenth-century paintings by Ettore Roesler Franz, reproducing the ghetto in faithful detail before its demolishment, may be found in the Museo Benito Mussolini (Palazzo Caffarelli). And the old ritual objects—crowns, mantles, and bells—from the Catalonian synagogue, one of the renowned five, are treasured in the little house of prayer, across the river, on Lungo Tevere Sanzio (No. 12).

The majority of the inscriptions in the vestibule of this modest synagogue commemorate charitable and educational foundations of the seventeenth and eighteenth centuries, when, as never under freedom, every Jew stood by his brother. One of them will tell you in a few words the whole story of the Papal ghetto. It relates the founding of a dispensary for medicines and drugs in the year 1635. What of it? The point it labours is that after nightfall, even in the case of mortal need—a need which in Jewish law, the law of the Pharisees, permitted one to break any and all of the 613 commandments—the legislation of the Church forbade an inhabitant of the Jewry to pass outside its closed gates.

In the Circus Maximus are gathered the mediæval dead. Many of the stones were brought, since the creation of the cemetery in 1775, from older burial-grounds. One will note a dearth of inscriptions earlier than the nineteenth century.

The reason is twofold: before 1625 the Church forbade in
Papal territory the use of epitaphs save for rabbis and other
distinguished men of learning; and from 1625 to 1775 it forbade inscriptions altogether. Wise regulations calculated to
spare the writer no little labour and the traveller valuable time
that can be spent, now that the journey through Jewish Rome
is done, in appreciating the grandeur of St. Peter's.

ROME, MUSEO BORGIANO. GILT-GLASS FROM
JEWISH CATACOMBS
See page 237

CHAPTER XIV

Italy—

"Land of the Dew"

TO ITALY, the centre of the ancient world, Jews flocked from all sides. They came from Greece, Egypt, and North Africa, and those who did not come from Palestine were brought. Long before the Empire fell they had settled by choice or force in Sicily, Sardinia, Calabria, Apulia, Malta, and the northern provinces. As time went on and slaves became slave-dealers, peasant louts rose to Talmudic masters, and provincial shopkeepers to world traders, they found their lot so pleasant that, turning a phrase from Genesis (27:39), they punned on the name of Italy and called it *I-tal-yah*— "land of the dew of the Lord."

Italian Jews have twice appeared on the stage of world history, as usual for Israel a little behind the scenes; during the flush of the Middle Ages when Frederick II, in the teeth of excommunication, brought philosophy and science back to southern Europe; and again at the dawn of the Renaissance when Jewish mysticism and the revival of Hebrew coloured the texture of the newborn age. In return, Italy has time and again proved a welcome haven to the Jews, refugees from France and Germany and, above all, exiles from Spain. And from the day that Niccolo Pisano finished carving his pulpit in Pisa until the day before yesterday, the Italy that moved

244

one hundred years ahead of the rest of the world moved its Jews, more sluggishly, it is true, along with the tide.

By chance, the surviving stones will enable us, journeying from the southlands to the Alps, to follow the story beginning with the twilight of the classic age at Capua and ending in eighteenth-century Venice. But our itinerary is in one respect deceptive. Milan and other northern cities had their Jewish communities as early as Naples or Venosa. We are trailing monuments—not migrations.

༄༅

Capua introduces us to the Latin Jews by way of a tombstone (Museo Campano) belonging to Alfius Juda, the president some sixteen hundred years ago of the local congregation. Similar stones may be seen in the National Museum of Naples (*raccolta epigrafica*) gathered in Pozzuoli—the ancient Puteoli—and Naples itself. Josephus tells us there were Jews in Puteoli directly after the death of Herod (4 B.C.). One of the earliest of these epitaphs recalls a less happy circumstance: Claudia Aster—peace on her soul—is styled the "captive daughter of Jerusalem." T. Claudius, who provided her grave, speaks of himself as the president of the synagogue and a freedman of Cæsar Augustus (31-14 B.C.) and thereby gives the first definite evidence of a synagogue on the continent of Europe. And Paul, we know, tarried a week among the "brethren" in Puteoli, and where Paul tarried there were Jews. The jargon spoken by this people living in the very shadow of Virgil cannot be described. An unfortunate captive bound to an alien tongue and dead at the age of seventeen is mourned as *Benus filia rebbetis Abundanti*, which may be taken to mean, "Venus, the daughter of Rabbi Abundantius."

But we dare not linger over tombs. The land abounds with

them, and while it provides a touching surprise to stumble on a lost waif in France or Spain, only the born antiquarian, your true rock-lizard, will want to poke into the countless stones of Italy.

The National Museum of Naples offers a pretty puzzle in the mural painting from Pompeii (entresol, Sala VIII) which is obviously a caricature on the Judgment of Solomon—and the first Bible picture in the world. The painter must have picked up the tale of the two mothers and the dead baby— barbaric, to be sure, but clever—from a Jewish or Christian slave, little suspecting that its source was to inspire literally miles of painted walls and canvas.

If we are to remain in Naples, we must jump an age. The Castel Capuano or La Vicaria looks much as it did when Frederick II, the *stupor mundis*, finished it for his palace (1231). However, the people who crowd its halls are changed. Today it is criminal lawyers and their motley clients; seven centuries back it was scholars, scribes, limners, and translators; and not least among the latter Jacob Anatoli of Marseilles, who had come to help Michael the Scot pour the science of the Greeks and the teachings of Arab and Hebrew philosophy, mathematics, and astronomy into Latin, for all of Europe to read. Together with Anatoli were a school of Jewish translators who had profited from Arab rule in the Sicilies and who disgorged their accumulated learning at the command of Frederick, as their brethren were disgorging under Alphonse the Wise in Toledo.[1] Perhaps it is worth remembering that at this very moment English kings were likewise inducing their Jews to part with certain accumulated treasures, and that the difference measures the poles of mediæval civilization.

On the waterfront, the imposing Castel Nuovo has also suffered little change. Charles I of Anjou, who succeeded the Hohenstauffens towards the close of the thirteenth century,

[1] See p. 160.

built it for his residence and kept it equally thronged with scholars. Charles, we are told, had Moses of Palermo especially trained to translate works of medicine, among them a classic on horse diseases. The largest and heaviest of all incunabula, when it came to be printed two centuries later, was Rhazes the Persian's medical encyclopædia, translated at the command of Charles by Faraj ben Selim (Farrachius or Farragut), a Jew of Girgenti. You may see the original translation in the Bibliothèque Nationale at Paris,[1] as Charles saw it when Faraj handed him the finished manuscript, and on the frontispiece you may see the gesture itself, and the figure and face of Faraj and Charles. The house of Anjou, in its castle on Naples Bay, pursued the patronage of learning as a family custom; in the fourteenth century Robert the Good put Kalonymus ben Kalonymus[2] to work compiling a treatise on mathematics and astrology, and translating the philosophic masterpiece (*Destruction of Destruction*) of Averroës.

Frederick spent little time in Naples. He was happier in Palermo stirring up trouble with the Church and getting himself, from his association with Arabs and Jews, the reputation of a free-thinker. So if you choose to transfer his factory of scholars to his palace in Palermo, history can offer no objections. Unfortunately, his town residence, the Palazzo Reale, has undergone so many changes that the Arabs who laid the foundations, the Normans who built it, and Frederick who added improvements of his own would recognize nothing of it save the *Joharia* or Brilliant Tower. And his country palace, La Favara, once the boast of Arab and Jewish travellers, is reduced to a chapel and a few broken arches, surrounded not as it was by gardens and a vast artificial lake, but dull tenements.

Still, a Phœnician-Punic-Arab-Jewish feel persists in Pa-

[1] See p. 84.
[2] See p. 240.

lermo; you catch it in the Sala Araba of the museum, in the unsuspected horseshoe arches of the Palatine Chapel and the Inquisition Palace (now Palazzo dei Tribunali), in street names, Cufic inscriptions, and bits of converted mosques, and in the votive tablets (Corte Grande of museum) to Baal Ammon, ancient rival of Jehovah. Frederick knew and loved that feel—he granted Arabs and Jews equal rights with Christians —and it is not surprising to learn that when his tomb (cathedral, right aisle) was opened in 1781, he was found buried in Arab dress.

Nothing but a passing rabbi's description remains of the synagogue or the once flourishing Jewish community (near church of S. Niccolo). "The synagogue," writes Obadiah da Bertinoro in 1487, "has not its equal in the whole world. The stone pillars in the outer courtyard are encircled by vines of a thickness I have never seen before . . . the vestibule has three sides and a porch where there are chairs and a splendid fountain. On the east end there is a stone structure shaped like a dome, the ark. It contains scrolls of the Law adorned with crowns and *rimonim* of silver and precious stones to the value of 4,000 gold pieces (according to the statement of the Jews who live there) and laid on a wooden shelf and not put in a chest, as with us . . . the synagogue is surrounded by numerous buildings, such as the hospital, the hospice for travellers without money, and a magnificent mansion where those who are elected sit in judgment and regulate the affairs of the community." Five years later the Jews were driven from this ·synagogue, as from all Sicily and other Spanish dominions. Memories of those who tarried behind may be invoked in the aforesaid Palace of the Inquisition and in the little Piazza Bologni, the showground for the *autos-de-fé*.

To the far west, Trapani has a Via Giudecca, or Street of the Jews, under the shadow of the mountain sacred to Melkart, god of Tyre. The wealth of its vanished inhabitants, belated rivals to their old Phœnician neighbours, may be judged even by the ruined splendour of its homes—a pair of twelfth-century houses with brilliant Norman-Arab mouldings over the arched portal and above the windows, as well as a fifteenth-century mansion (the Spedadello) capped with a protective tower.

In Syracuse we return to the ancient world. Here among the relics of Greeks and Carthaginians may be found catacombs of the Jews.[1] They lie north of the present mediæval town (which preserves a Via Giudecca in honour of the vanished Jewry) and east of the Greek necropolis. Inscriptions and terra-cotta lamps stamped with the menorah have been collected in the museum.

Leaving Syracuse, we may travel towards almost any point of the compass and unearth more of these catacombs. Immediately south, they have been discovered in Noto. A short sail in the same direction brings us to Malta, where at least five Jewish catacombs in the suburbs of Città Vecchia (Cemetery of S. Agata near Church of S. Paolo) have been identified by the menorah graven on the walls. Near at hand, a Roman villa on Museum Road contains a mosaic possibly representing Delilah shearing the locks of Samson. And while in Malta, one will do well to read of the Knights of St. John and their curious and profitable traffic in Jewish slaves—from 1530 to the close of the eighteenth century. Then we may move west to Carthage and more catacombs.[2] Or north-west to Sardinia, where Tiberius dumped 4,000 Jewish soldiers, ostensibly to fight brigands, actually in the hope of hearing the last of them, and where in Sant' Antioco their descendants dug subterranean burial-vaults for our inspection. Or we may go southeast to Cyrene and likewise see the work of our Jewish moles.

[1] See p. 233 (Rome).
[2] See p. 409.

Instead, however, we will proceed north to Venosa. Apulia, it happens, can take us from antiquity to the end of the Middle Ages. In Taranto (museum in cloisters of S. Pasquale) we may find a number of fourth- and fifth-century epitaphs in Latin and Hebrew, and in Brindisi an equally ancient stone. In Venosa itself the Jewish catacombs (north on road from railway station) are the most elaborate known. Their passages are nothing short of streets lined with sunless tenements and chapels. The epitaphs dating from the first centuries of our era run to Hebrew in surprising numbers, and for the rest are inscribed in Judeo-Greek, and in a Latin that would depress the ghost of Horace should he ever revisit his birthplace.

Seven Hebrew epitaphs (in the churches of S. Trinita Abbey, Venosa) bring us out of the wreck of classicism into the dim mediæval dawn. They date from the ninth century, and remind us that the earliest signs of European Hebrew learning arose in Oria, Otranto, Venosa, and other Apulian towns, conceivably in the wake of a now forgotten Byzantine Jewish culture. Ahimaaz ben Paltiel has left us a fresh and detailed chronicle of life in Oria, running from family trees to scholarly achievements and political affairs a thousand years ago, when the barren heel of Italy was a battleground for Byzantines, Latins, and Arabs, and the Jews were in the thick of flying spears.

Then the Normans laid the dust, and after them the Hohenstauffens put their mark on the land. Frederick rebuilt Lucera and manned the city and his castle with 20,000 Saracens; the castle is still there, and if you look closely at the townsfolk, the Saracens as well. His son Manfred founded the port of Manfredonia and got Abraham ben Hasdai to translate from Hebrew the pseudo-Aristotelian dialogue, *The Book of the Apple*.

Abraham's contemporaries have left in the neighbouring

port of Trani a synagogue (Via Sinagoga) built, according to the inscription, in 1247. Its fortified air, appropriate to the times, and the large double-arched Gothic casement, lend it a certain beauty. The interior is badly shattered, but enough remains to show that the synagogue proper occupied the second story, as it does in most of Italy, leaving the ground floor for vestry-rooms and communal affairs—an arrangement due either to a hope for safety or, more simply, to a desire for quiet. Trani, like Gerona in Spain, gave its name to lines of distinguished scholars.

In the sixteenth century Spain emptied Sicily and Calabria of its Jews, and persecution and emigration did for the rest of southern Italy, with the result that in four hundred years there was hardly seen a Jew from Naples south to Cape Passero.

꙳꙳꙳

The church of S. Gregorio Minore in Spoleto survives as a mediæval outpost north of Rome. It was a synagogue until the sixteenth century, when the adjacent market place (Mercato) and Spoleto saw the departure of the Jews. Improving on their ghetto policy, the Papal States rid themselves of the race altogether, save for financial reasons in Rome and Ancona.

Moving to Ancona, we find ourselves dropped into the late Renaissance. The Jewry lay in the Via di Bagno, and the sixteenth- to seventeenth-century synagogue bears all the characteristics of the period. With its large frank portal and its numerous regularly ordered windows which have become so accepted in even the humblest Main Street block today that we can barely appreciate they were once a novelty, the exterior, like that of most Renaissance synagogues, resembles any one of the more modest *palazzi* scattered throughout Italy. It houses the Italian rite belowstairs and the Levantine above. The Levantines—Jews of the Levant mixed with a strain of Spanish exiles—were richer; and their long, well-proportioned hall, beamed ceiling broken by barrel-vaulting, the ark against one wall and the *bima* against the other, is eloquent of the new style. The ark is purely classic in its lines, whereas the *bima* shows the outcropping of baroque. In the Italian, it is the ark which has gone Jesuit.

Ancona and the cities about it tell somewhat of the changes in the world since we left Trani with its fortified air and pointed casement. Pesaro, Fano, and Rimini saw the printing of Hebrew books by the famous Soncino presses in the first decades of the sixteenth century. Pesaro, which preserves a noble synagogue of the same century and a cemetery older still (on road to Villa Imperiale), became, like Ancona, a haven for Spanish exiles, and witnessed a temper not noticeable since the fall of Jerusalem.

When, in 1556, a year after the creation of the ghetto in Rome and as part of the general reaction of the Church, twenty-four Maranos were burnt in Ancona (Piazza Mostra), many of the survivors, Jews and Maranos together, fled beyond the border of the Papal States to Pesaro. There, by way of retaliation, they planned with their brethren in Turkey to divert the trade of Ancona, which spelt the life of the city, to the neighbouring port. The plan, however, collapsed, as many Jewish efforts do, through lack of coöperation; the Turkish Jews thought of their profits and the Ancona Jews of Papal vengeance. But the very scheme was a sign of a novel spirit. If you wish to see what underlay that spirit and not merely read about it, you will go to Florence and you will note that the Via Giudei, the old Street of the Jews before they were thrust into a ghetto, lies directly behind the house of Machiavelli.

Florence is the inevitable background for a discussion on

the Renaissance, and the Piazza Vittorio Emanuele invites any further talk on Renaissance and Jews, for it covers the site of the demolished ghetto, and it is well lined with café tables. Every traveller has been told that the revival of classic forms in the art of the fifteenth and sixteenth centuries betokened a new outlook on the world. The statement need not be questioned, although it might embarrass one to tell how the faith that built S. Lorenzo differed from the faith that built Or San Michele. Avoiding that puzzle, we shall consider, most hastily, the extent to which the Renaissance synagogue of Pesaro, and the score like it in north Italy, betray a different Jewry from the mediæval builders of Trani. The stones have changed— what of the spirit?

For answer, one may say that the spirit changed, but not so much as the stones. The invention of printing brought a wider distribution of books, and poems appeared in the early products of the Hebrew press extolling the art "which enables one man to write with many pens." Italian Jews and Spanish exiles threw themselves into secular literature: Samuel Usque, driven from Portugal, wrote dramatic poetry (1553); Leone di Sommi Portaleone (d. 1591) turned out poems and plays, directed a theatrical troupe in Mantua, and wrote the *Dialoghi sull' Arte Rappresentativa*, the first work ever devoted to stagecraft; Guglielmo de Pesaro, a member of Lorenzo de' Medici's charmed circle at Florence, produced the earliest modern book on dancing, the *Trattato dell' Arte del Ballo*; and the philosophic *Dialoghi di Amore* of Leo Hebræus (Judah Abrabanel, d. 1535) has become a world classic. Rabbis did not hesitate to draw on ancient mythology to illustrate their sermons, even referring to "quella santa Diana"—to that holy Diana! Elijah Delmedigo of Crete taught young Pico della Mirandola his Hebrew and his Aristotle and a touch of Cabbala; Lorenzo de' Medici drew, besides dancing masters, Hebrew scholars and physicians to his court, and physicians and scholars got as well as gave. Moses da Castellazzo (beginning of the sixteenth century) took a place among the painters of Venice, Joseph Levi of Verona worked in bronze, a Jacob da Carpi (b. 1685) combined historical painting with art-dealing. Jewish bankers and rabbis had their portraits ordered, quite like Medicis and cardinals.

Yet the Renaissance never penetrated the Jew so deeply as the Christian. For one thing, he had had his "renaissance" more than three centuries before, in Spain and Provence. He had learned science, philosophy, and the humanities together with the Moor; Hebrew had enjoyed its rebirth under Gabirol and Judah Halevi. Again, reading and writing were never, in mediæval Jewish life, a closed privilege of the clerics; education had been practically compulsory and universal. Indeed, Renan goes so far as to maintain that "France was slow" to profit by the Renaissance "because it was destitute of Jews."

But the major reason why the Jews stood aloof was because they were kept aloof, partly by their own and partly by their enemies' intolerance. As to their own intolerance, we might note that Maimonides had been beaten to earth and they had no wish to help him rise again; moreover, they saw in the fate of the Maranos a clear warning against assimilation. The ranks of regularly ordered windows on the Renaissance *palazzo* meant, if nothing else, new security, new personal freedom. The same windows lit the synagogues, but neither free nor safe Jews looked out of them. The golden moment passed; and the new birth for the Christian brought the old death to the Jew, bands of Renaissance saints, Bernardino of Feltre, Carlo of Borromeo, set their halos sparkling with human tears, and the Counter Reformation turned the synagogue, once again defeated, more closely than ever upon itself. In the end humanism gave way to mysticism, the illusions of art to the illusions of the Messiah, and science surrendered to a progressively hardening discipline in the Mosaic law.

⤙⤚

We may now return to our stones.

The ghetto of Siena is most satisfactory; architecturally it is intact as few or none elsewhere, and there are no Jews. "Intact" is a favourite word in Italy; travelled people will tell you in Florence that you must see Siena, for it is more "intact"— these many centuries doing nothing but piling up moss, rust, decay, and occasionally smell. Beauty, however, can be fungoid, and despite its origin is to be enjoyed like mushrooms, a little, for the flavour.

Except for coats and pants and sundry bicycles, Siena stands as it did in the fifteenth century and before. Narrow streets of the stone palaces of the nobles and narrower alleys of the brick and plaster tenements of the nobodies take you to where the nobodiest of this dawning Renaissance once lived. The two square blocks of the Jews, tumbling down the hill on which Siena is built, betray their status in every sunken line and dark hole, yet it should be noted, only a trifle darker and more sunken than the rest.

The archway which held the ghetto gate (Via di Scotte, opposite the Church of S. Martino) leads from the Loggia del Papa, a centre of communal life, to the Piazza del Mercato, the town market. Passing beneath the drip of washes hanging from the little arches which span the Via di Scotte, you quickly reach the synagogue. The building dates from the seventeenth century (?), although the interior was restored in 1786. The upper hall, which is devoted to the cult, has its women's balcony in the rear. There is the usual display of plate, crowns, and mantles, and the brass doors of the ark are wrought in elaborate design. One panel shows the marks of being split open with an ax, token of an unfriendly visit of the neighbours some centuries back, and a source of revenue to the beadle. In the Palazzo Municipale (fourth landing of main stairway) stands a statue of Moses, by Antonio Federighi (1420-90), which formerly adorned the ghetto well and which —a true Renaissance touch—never troubled the conscience of Siena rabbis until, in 1740, visiting Polish Jews cried scandal.

Life in this little ghetto is vividly, and with much unconscious humour, painted for us in the diary of a querulous gossip-loving huckster, whom the English translator likes to call "that dirty dog of Siena."[1] We see him, not the translator but the huckster, engaged in bloody riot over a piece of black damask, and a ban read over him in the synagogue, "the first time it was done." We hear him complaining when the Grand Duke—Galileo's Grand Duke—visits Siena, and the Jewish tax-collectors, enemies of long-standing, lay on him an intolerable levy—"from me they demanded a pair of sheets, a bed-canopy, a pillow and blanket, twice as much as imposed on anyone else." But we learn, withal, that he is willing to pay fifteen lire a year to master the art of reading.

Pisa, too, preserves its old synagogue (Via Palestro), built in the seventeenth and remodelled in the last century. But its cemetery speaks more to the point. One way of learning who and what a people were is to learn how they are buried. The Christians of Pisa were plainly artists, for they are buried in a picture-gallery. The walls of their Campo Santo carry above a quarter mile of masterpieces; lining the walls are enough Greek and Roman sculpture to furnish a museum. This Campo, as everyone knows, dates the Renaissance; here is the Roman sarcophagus that gave Pisano the hint for his pulpit, and here is the Greek urn from which he took the head of his High Priest, the hint and the head that were later to be Donatello and Michelangelo. In death, these Pisans fertilized their land with a new beauty.

The Campo Santo is built into a corner of the still-standing

[1] See p. 456 (Bibliography).

city walls. If you pass through a gate to the left, turning your back on the blinding marble of the cathedral, Baptistry, and Leaning Tower, you will find yourself in the old Jewish grave-yard. It lies beneath the dried brick walls, shut out from the glory. Thin cypresses, wild flowers glowing lightly in the tall grass, crumbling granite tombs lying flat as in Rome, the Hebrew melting away in the years, a few simple sculptural flour-ishes, graven acanthus and carved lamps—here is shade and peace, and that is all. The carved acanthus gives promise of the new art, but a tender growth, it never went further. The stone lamps never took fire. Yet in an age when every man was born an artist, what magic could have been wrought with the force that once pulsed this dust, energies that, turn-ing from art, bound Brazil and Hamburg, Stamboul and Tangier, Bagdad and Pisa in golden ties, and intellectual passions that codified the statutes of the universe. As it is, the two civilizations sleep side by side, with the wall between.

In Livorno, something came to flame. The Spanish Jews, whose spirit we have seen at Ouderkerk,[1] who gave Spinoza to Holland and Leo Hebræus to Italy, were at work. The synagogue (Via Reale) is one of the notable monuments of the city. Built in 1603 and restored in 1866—hence the de-pressing exterior—it is a library of symbolism. Fifty symbolic *motifs*, mingled with Hebrew inscriptions, are carved in stucco on the coffered ceiling. The women's balcony, shut in with lattice-work and resting on slender marble columns tipped with classic capitals, the *bima* and ark of motley marble, the ark doors richly tooled and inscribed within, and the gleam-ing parade of scrolls (dating from the fifteenth to the eight-eenth century), bells, and crowns, make a sumptuous, almost a Catholic, display. Livorno was what the old Jewish chron-icles would call a *mekom ha-zedek* (a righteous place), for it knew neither restrictions nor persecutions since the first

[1] See p. 199.

Maranos founded the community at the end of the sixteenth century. The present Hebrew press, which supplies the Near East and North Africa, dates, with interruptions, back to 1650. Opposite the synagogue is the house where Mose Montefiore was born (1784).

Bologna will detain us for two stones. The acanthus of Pisa is putting forth buds; and the tomb of Menahem F. di Abramo Daventura (Museo Civico), dated 1555, with its pair of columns surmounted by an arch—a favourite *motif* in manuscript illumination denoting the two pillars before Solomon's Temple—its floral designs and heraldic goat point the way to the funerary sculpture of Prague and Ouderkerk a century to come. The monument of Sabbatai Elchanan ben Isaac Eliacimo da Rieti (Scuola d'Antiquaria, vestibule) goes much farther in its almost free sculpture of female figures, and cherubs serving as caryatides. How far at least two of these renaissance Jews have gone may be judged by glancing at the plain mediæval stones likewise gathered in the Museo Civico (Sala XV). Of the Via Giudei, leading from the curious leaning towers in the Piazza di Porta Ravegnana, little characteristic survives but the name.

As long as the house of Este ruled Ferrara, it too was a "righteous place," and sheltered one of the largest and most prosperous Jewries of Italy. Under Ercole I, the community numbered 3000 souls, native Jews and Spanish-Portuguese *émigrés*. When we visit their synagogues we wonder, as we do before any monument of mediæval or Renaissance Europe, at the singular energies of its peoples. Three thousand Jews— and all Ferrara could have been lost in two wards of Newark, N. J.! That a pound or guilder once bought fifty times as much as now is not beyond explanation. But that one head and one pair of arms wrought and did for fifty today remains a disquieting puzzle. We boast of our machines; Ferrara,

Florence, Nuremberg can take the better part and boast of their men. Does the human spirit devaluate like money?

The Jewry—there was no compulsory ghetto until late into Papal rule (1664)—lay immediately off the Mercato and the cathedral square (present Via Mazzini and Vigna Tagliata). The synagogue of the Italian rite, in the Via Mazzini, glows, despite its restoration, with the mysticism of art and faith. The panelled walls and ceiling, which, like most of the structure, dates from the beginning of the sixteenth century, the ark done in intarsia, the gilded lamps and candelabra, the *bima* with its columns of precious wood, its embroideries in gold and deep colours hanging from pulpit and balustrade, combine in solemn harmonies. In the same building the Spanish synagogue, less altered by restoration, sounds even a richer note. White marbles play against black; the ark recedes behind a colonnade in a semicircular apse, its portals clad in silver repoussé alive with intricate designs; the *bima*, likewise in marbles, tosses the light from a dozen silver fixtures and from the "candles of the Lord" lining the walls in memory of the dead; Torah mantles and their gold and silver apparatus enhance the splendour. Near at hand, the Levantine synagogue rivals the Spanish in everything but size.

Before leaving Ferrara, we might remark the four prophets on the columns of the cathedral portal. They probably represent Moses, Isaiah, Jeremiah, and Daniel, and they are engaged in telling something of import to the figure of a twelfth-century Jew. We can readily imagine what, at least in the artist's mind, they have to say; and the group carries us back to the story of the Old Faith and the New as told in the window of Bourges.[1] Similar groups may be found on the columns of the cathedral portal at Verona, and in bas-reliefs at either side of the portal at Cremona.

Parma, on the way to Cremona, houses the famous de Rossi

[1] See p. 95.

collection (Biblioteca in Pilotta Palace), which includes over 1600 Hebrew manuscripts, many of them illuminated, as well as sixty-two different examples of the hundred or so known incunabula and thousands of later volumes. It possesses the only known copy of the first book printed in Hebrew, Rashi's commentary on the Pentateuch, dated February 5, 1475 and published in Reggio of Calabria. Most of the early Hebrew presses were established in the north. In Casal Maggiore, a few miles from Parma, the Soncinos set up their type in 1486.

Casale Monferrato, west of Cremona and well into the Piedmont, preserves an impressive synagogue, built in 1595 and enlarged in 1662. Its deeply groined arches and massive ribs, the oratorical flourish of the *bima* set like a theatre box in the side wall, the luxury of its mural inscriptions, do not deceive one as to the former importance of this lost and now altogether provincial community. Casale lay on the road to the Ligurian coast and France; and synagogues, like way stations, flourished in Moncalvo, Acqui, and Nice.

The Jewry of Mantua furnished an exuberant display of Renaissance versatility. Its printing-press was established in 1476; in the following century the community provided the ducal court with a standing troupe of actors; Solomon Rossi, composer, singer, instrumentalist, and rabbi, adorned the same court, together with his sister Europa, and his compositions adorned the synagogal liturgy. It is significant to note that among the ghetto regulations drawn up by the state in 1612, no Jew was permitted, without special license, to teach or practise in a Christian home the arts of "singing, playing, or dancing." But the old synagogue and houses of the Via P. Fortunato Calvi, where these regulations fell, have vanished; and the reconstructed Vecchia Scuola Grande (Old Great Synagogue) on the Via Gilberto Govi does not warrant tarrying, nor the piazza where Solomon Molcho paid for his delusions at the stake. Mantua has as many Jews today as Ferrara four hundred years ago; but both Jews and Christians have lost the magic touch.

The very location of the Jewry in Verona—next to the fourteenth-century Chamber of Commerce (Casa dei Mercanti) and adjoining the central Piazza delle Erbe, the site of the Roman forum—tells the essence of its history. The present synagogue on the old ghetto site (Via Portici) was completed in 1929, but the sixteenth-century *bima* of a vanished predecessor may be seen in the offices of the community. The Verona Jewry is distinguished for having rejoiced at the creation of its ghetto (1599) and annually celebrated the event with torchlight processions and psalms of praise. "It is good to give thanks to the Lord" for something.

Padua brings us close to the heart of the old Venetian Republic. Many of the vassal towns of this former sea queen trace their Jewish population back to Roman days. In Padua, a stroll around the borders of the Jewry will disclose its story. To the north, the ghetto lanes lead directly into the Piazza delle Erbe, the trading centre of the town throughout the centuries; although their business had its ups and downs following the tides of exclusion and restriction, in the year 1615 the Jews owned eighty-four out of the eighty-six general stores in the city. To the north-west, the ghetto opens on the Monte di Pietà, the public loan-office founded through the efforts of S. Bernardino of Feltre, and by intent and location, directed against the Jewish bankers—it might be added, in vain. The western portals of the ghetto (Via Daniel Manin, Via dei Soncini) face the cathedral and episcopal palace, whereby synagogue and church could keep a watchful eye on each other. Finally, the north-west corner of the ghetto flanks the university, with which the Jews had continuous relations, not only as money-lenders to the faculty and student body, but as teachers and students themselves.

Padua, in fact, was for long generations the sole European

university open to Jews. Even so, they were limited to the study of medicine and, in minute numbers, law. During the period when translation figured capitally in the intellectual life of the Continent, Padua had its Jew Bonacosa who turned Averroës' medical work into Latin; and in all probability it likewise saw the translation from the Hebrew of Avenzoar's *Aid to Health* and Maimonides' treatise *On Hygiene*. Among the Renaissance teachers—they were not ranked as professors—we find an Abraham de Balmes, a Judah Minz, and Elijah Delmedigo whom we first met in Florence, and who was apparently as much at home in medicine as philosophy, rabbinics, and Cabbala.

As elsewhere, the Jewish population of Padua was in part native and in part comprised of wanderers from far lands. This becomes apparent when we visit the synagogues, which rank among the most beautiful of Italy.

The synagogue of the Italian rite (Scuola Italiana, Via S. Martino e Solferino) is the oldest and noblest. It was built in 1548, radically remodelled in the first half of the seventeenth and restored in the mid-nineteenth century. No longer in use, it suffered a certain amount of house-wrecking at the hands of Rumanian students who abused the hospitality of Italy a few years ago.

Most significant is the disposition of ark and *bima*. The hall is oblong, and the ark is placed not, as one expects, at the far end of the hall, but midway against one of the long side walls. The *bima* faces it against the opposite side wall. As a result, no worshipper is seated more than half the length of the hall from the *bima* and ark where the law is read and the services conducted; whereas in a modern synagogue, half of the audience is, of necessity, removed from both rabbi and cantor by more than half the length of the auditorium; and in the usual traditional synagogue, where the *bima* stands in the center of the hall, the officiant must perforce turn his back on half of the congregation. Nothing better marks the anarchy of Jewish life than the fate of this Paduan invention; except for two or three Italian towns, it has been altogether neglected.

Every detail in the Italian *scuola* is wrought with dignity and beauty. The *bima* rises, a light and graceful throne, reached on either side by a flight of ten steps; its wooden canopy enters the barrel vaulting overhead, a vaulting which breaks the otherwise flat coffered ceiling in a flight from *bima* to ark, thus accentuating the two dominant features of the cult. The ark is splendid in marbles and repoussé, even if too obvious an imitation of a baroque Catholic altar. The vaulting above the ark is pierced by an oval light through which the women-folk, seated in a room above, attended the services.

The Spanish synagogue (Scuola Spagnuola, same street), founded in 1617 by Sephardim from Turkey, Holland, and Brabant, and likewise abandoned, looks considerably older than its date. The closely beamed ceiling and the heavy unclassical columns give it a Gothic touch. A small courtyard in the rear contains an exquisite Renaissance lavabo.

The third synagogue (Scuola Tedesca, Via delle Piazze), built in 1633 by the Ashkenazim, supplanted an earlier *scuola* of the Germans, who were long accustomed to flock to north Italy for refuge or for trade. Surpassing the other structures in size and show, it now serves the three congregations. Like the churches of baroque Italy, it is an Aladdin's cave of glittering lamps, kaleidoscopic grained and tinted marbles, flashing curves and flying masses. Yet its present brilliance is nothing to the days when Persian tapestries, Cordovan leathers, and rich majolicas added to the general riot. No visitor will fail to be impressed by the mighty ark capped with a baroque pediment, the two tiers of women's balconies, one above the other, set behind lattice-work in a side wall, the magnificent

Hanuka lamp a masterpiece of Renaissance metal-work, or the total effect—so difficult of achievement in modern life—of boundless wealth yet genuine religious emotion.

One of the first cemeteries, closed in 1509, lay beyond the bastion of La Rotonda, outside the city walls; from this grave-yard came the fragments of the monument to the illustrious Isaac Abrabanel[1] now in the Casa Forti (9 Via dell' Arco). Other fifteenth-century stones will be found in the Museo Civico (raccolta lapidaria). The sixteenth-seventeenth-century burial-ground (16 Via S. Giovanni di Verdara) contains over 200 well-preserved tombs, and the nearby seventeenth-eight-eenth-century graveyard (Via Zodio) as many more. The stones tell again of the scattered origin of the dead—a German Abraham Eilpron (d. 1593) or Samuel Judah Katzenellen-bogen (d. 1565) whose son, Saul Wahl, so runs the legend, was for a night king of Poland; a Spanish Nathan Benvenisti (d. 1787) or Benzion Ghirondi (d. 1815); and an Italian Solomon Marini (d. 1670) or Abraham Luzzatto (d. 1586).

෬ᢣᢏ

Many of the remaining Venetian possessions preserve their Renaissance synagogues, and tombs of an earlier date. For the traveller who may wander among these lovely and little-vis-ited towns, we may rapidly note what awaits him.

Este, south-west of Padua, contains a cemetery (Via Olmo, near Church of the Salute) with seventeenth-century stones, many boasting the family crest; Montagnana, west of Este, a sixteenth-eighteenth-century graveyard (Contra della Spina, close to the mediæval town walls); Rovigo, between Padua and Ferrara, a seventeenth-century synagogue, beneath it a beth ha-midrash of perhaps the preceding century, beyond the Porta Acqua a seventeenth-century burial-ground, and outside

[1] See p. 145.

the Porta S. Francesco (end of Via dei Tribunali) an eighteenth-century cemetery.

North of Venice, we will find in Treviso (Museo Comunale) fourteen mediæval tombs and fragments, mostly commemorating German traders, such as Jacob of Norimberga (d. 1386), Jacob Ebreo, son of Lupo di Battenberg (d. 1397) etc.; in Asolo (loggia of Palazzo Comunale) two stones of the Gentili family, dated 1528 and 1613; in Conegliano, an Ashkenazic synagogue (Contrado di Ruio) built in 1675 and a sixteenth-eighteenth-century cemetery on the Cabalan hill (Via del Ghetto to church of the Madonna del Carmine, then up slope to right); and in Vittorio, farther north, an eighteenth-century synagogue.

San Daniele del Friuli, north-east of Venice near Udine, contains a seventeenth-eighteenth-century cemetery; and Cividale, beyond Udine, preserves several fourteenth-seventeenth-century stones in its Museo Archeologico.

The traveller who insists on remote by-ways will find that the Jews have preceded him in the overseas empire of Venice. He may plume himself on visiting Spalato, but the Jews had a synagogue in its Diocletian palace soon after it fell to ruins, and they have left a first-century (C.E.) necropolis in the near-by town of Salona. Spanish Jews still keep their sixteenth-century synagogue in Corfu, and Greek Jews an older one. And in Crete, remote enough, you will discover the synagogue of Canea much as it was four hundred years ago; and while its mate in Candia has been substantially restored, the antique crown of the ark is preserved in the Museo Civico.

༒

The ghetto of Venice is easily the most renowned in Europe. It is the dean of the Italian ghettos and the godfather of the institution wherever it be found. Established in 1516, it took its name from a cannon-foundry (*geto* or *ghetto*) which had years before existed on the older island where the Jews were confined, and gave this name to its many imitations and by extension to the device itself. Its government in Venice, its schools, social and religious bodies, and daily round of work and play, to say nothing of the colourful personalities who flourished in its gates, have been so ably described that, as nowhere else, we can enter into the life of this most peculiar and portentous institution of the last millennium of Jewish history.

Although banned from residence in the city, Jewish traders from Germany and the Levant had long frequented the marts of Venice. They fringed the mainland with their settlements, set up warehouses on the island of the Giudecca (whence, perhaps, its name), traded in the *fondachi* and markets, and by 1515 they had ten shops on the Rialto bridge itself. Then, the Venetian state, alarmed in its piety yet anxious to profit by Jewish trade, decided to recognize the presence of the Jews but render them innocuous by segregation.

Spanish-Portuguese Jews and Maranos soon joined the earlier Italian, German, and Levantine settlement, and the four communities set up a little sub-state on two of the northern islets of the town. Travellers, merchants, scholars, and pilgrims to and from the Holy Land crossed its squares from the four corners of the world. One Elijah of Pesaro, who voyaged from Venice to Cyprus in 1563, has left a letter telling us how a Jewish traveller buys his ticket (at higher rates!), disposes of his luggage, selects his cabin, arranges for his *kosher* food, and leaving the ghetto before sundown, prudently boards his galley the night before it sails.

The canals washed the Renaissance to the ghetto quays. Academies of what we should now call "serious thinkers" cultivated polite literature and philosophy; singing, strumming, dancing, card-playing, art-appreciating, and other humane pastimes became the fashion; the beautiful Sarah Coppio Sullam (1590-1641) studied Latin, Greek, Spanish, and Hebrew, opened her *salon*, disputed wittily with learned and gallant priests, and wrote a sheaf of poems; Simone Luzzatto produced the first social study and modern apologia of the Jew; and the unlucky but immortal Leone da Modena—epitome of the Renaissance—plied in and out of Venice his twenty-six professions.

The brilliance of the scene suffers comparison with Cordova, Toledo, and Worms in only one respect. Like its Christians, the Jews of Venice never ventured far beyond a loyalty to business, piety, and the patronage of the arts. You will search their ghetto in vain for a Gerson, a Rambam, or a Meir of Rothenburg, for great names in science, philosophy, or rabbinics. But, then, you may vainly dredge the history of all Venice for a first-rate mind.

The rout is vanished now, poets, scholars, ladies, and the gold that brushed their bosoms; and for further word of them, their names at least, you must go to the old cemetery on the Lido, between the Church of S. Niccolo and the Adriatic shore. Sand and weeds have eaten many of the slabs, but there is still to be found the crested stones of Spanish and Portuguese wanderers come to rest, the grave of Elijah Levita, whom we last saw by the side of Cardinal Egidio in Rome,[1] of Sarah Coppio Sullam, Simone Luzzatto, Leone da Modena, and perhaps the ghost of Disraeli revisiting the tombs of his forefathers.

Outwardly, little has changed in the ghetto. Even the Jews remain, although, like the rest, a trifle down at the heels. And walking the narrow streets and little squares, you may easily relive their fortunes.

You disembark on the Rio di Cannaregio, beyond the Ponte delle Guglie. The main street, Il Ghetto Vecchio, meets you at the water's edge. Here you will see neither a Cà d'Oro nor a

[1] See p. 240.

Fondaco dei Turchi, yet this pinched sunless lane, compact with high tenements, housed a nobility whose family trees threw in the shade any *palazzo* on the Grand Canal, and whose sons held something, too, of the East in fee.

Passing the site of the old gates, you will remark a tablet (on wall to left) dated 1704, which announces that by orders of the city Executors on Blasphemy (*Esecutori alla Bestemmia*), an official Religious Security League, all converted Jews are forbidden intercourse with the inhabitants of the ghetto— a prudent measure.

On the first square (Campanello delle Scuole, to left) stands the Spanish synagogue, founded in 1584 and rebuilt in 1655, the only one of the six survivors to remain in use on the Sabbath. The plain exterior, resembling the tenements on either side, will never suggest that its architect was Baldassare Longhena, who built the great Church of S. Maria della Salute. But Longhena turned the interior into the most grandiloquent synagogue of Italy. The intricate masses of the ark, pediment on pediment set in the frame of a huge arch resting on the two traditional pillars; the encircling women's gallery swung high under the gilt-and-stucco encrusted ceiling; the marble Corinthian pilasters and draped Roman casements, the carved wainscoting, balustrades, and cornices, and the flamboyant chandeliers, it is all, if you will, rhetoric. But it is hardly fair to set up our modern impotence to wield effective rhetoric as a virtue and canon of taste. With half an eye we should be able to see the delight Longhena took, and the Maranos newly celebrating their Judaism received in this grandiose creation. A nineteenth-century restoration supplanted the old *bima* with an organ. Among the many treasures, some of which are kept in the vestry-rooms, may be remarked an ark curtain embroidered entirely in seed-pearls.

The Levantine synagogue faces the Spanish and was likewise built in the seventeenth century. Its *bima* is a masterpiece of wood-carving; and the hall as a whole, which has suffered little restoration, is to modern, if not to Venetian, taste the noblest in the ghetto. Beneath it is the Luzzatto scuola, founded as a private synagogue in the seventeenth century and built into its present site in the eighteenth century; it is used for mourner's prayers. The ghetto inn stood on the main street (to right), a few doors beyond; before securing bed and board, its guests were required to get a clean bill from the vigilant Executors on Blasphemy.

A span at the foot of the main thoroughfare leads to the small island of the Ghetto Nuovo which, despite its name, is the original and older Jewry. It consists of a broad square, the stretch of cobbles broken by three well-heads. An inscription and an old doorway immediately to the left are all that tells of the private synagogue of the Mesullamim, bankers, patrons of learning, and the most influential family when the ghetto was founding; some of its descendants today are still bankers and patrons in Hamburg, London, and New York. To the right, almost in the angle of the square, stands the seventeenth-century Italian synagogue where Leone da Modena exercised his eloquence before large audiences of Jews and Gentiles. The scuola Canton comes next, a private synagogue of unwonted magnificence, founded in 1532 and restored in the last century. Midway along the east side of the square lies the Ashkenazic or Great synagogue, the oldest in the ghetto. It dates from 1528, but has been restored and embellished many times since. Despite the frequent tinkering, it retains its ancient character, as witness the circular gallery for the women, the gold leaf on the ark, and the Hebrew inscriptions flowing around the cornice.

Before we leave the old square of the Ghetto Nuovo—the gondola will wait—it will repay us to conjure up, if we can, the fairest day the Jews of Venice, their ghetto, and this square ever looked upon. The Christian almanach reads July 10,

1797, and the Jewish *luach* says it is the eve of the 17th of Tammuz, and the day following the Jews will mourn the breach by the Babylonian armies in the walls of Jerusalem, 2383 years before. But the armies of the French Revolution are in Venice, and the calendar of young General Bonaparte tells the world it is the 22nd of Messidor in the first year of Italian freedom.

A vast throng of bluecoats, Venetian citizenry and priests, and Jews with hearts in their throats swarm the piazza, clamber on the wells, and hang from the windows. There is a noise of battering, rending, and dragging; the ghetto gates are hauled to the centre of the square; they are smashed with axes, and, before a Tree of Liberty reddening with the happy flame, are forever burnt to ashes. And in a new corner of Europe men are learning to stammer *Liberté—Egalité—Fraternité.*

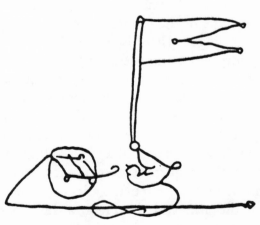

SIGNATURE OF SOLOMON MOLCHO
See page 260

CHAPTER XV

A Thousand Years

Along the Rhine

THE Jews floated down the Rhine behind the Romans, from Argentoratum to Colonia Agrippina. In Argentoratum, more recently known as Strasbourg, they left red baked-clay vessels stamped with the seven-branched candlestick and dating from the early settlements on this new frontier. In Colonia, which is now spelled Cologne, a document from the reign of Constantine (321) attests to their presence by denying them certain privileges.

The arrival of the Franks (c. 460), with their imperfect notions of Christian behaviour, prevented further interference with the Jews. Almost nothing is heard of them for five hundred years, a fair sign, and we find them in the tenth century, when their history properly begins, engaged in commerce, viticulture, and finance.

Their subsequent career was determined by two remote factors: the claim of the Roman Emperor Titus to the personal possession of the Jews after his conquest of Jerusalem, and the independent spirit of the Germanic tribes.

Titus' claim was renewed by the kaisers of the Holy Roman Empire and, as a result, the Jews eventually became imperial property, thereby gaining a freedom of movement unknown to the serf and average merchant; they spread through the Reich, and like mobile cells nourished the trade of the Rhine and Danube. Only the backward plains and the jealous Hanseatic ports in the north saw little of their tall pointed bonnets. Meanwhile, the old tribal love of freedom showed itself in what is called the "particularism" of Germany, in the refusal of its innumerable petty states to lose their identity in the Empire or even to unite on a common policy. Consequently, whenever the Jews were expelled from one barony, free city, or mark, they usually found refuge in another. Or whenever they left a state because of intolerable conditions, they were usually invited back. The failure of the Reich to achieve unity probably spared the German Jews from the general expulsion that befell them in England, France, and Spain.

Their outer history turns on a few unforgettable circumstances: the Crusades which were celebrated by atrocious massacres along the Rhine; the Black Death (fourteenth century) which led the populace not to a consideration of drains and plumbing, but again to the slaughter of the Jews; and the progressive rise of Christian commerce culminating in the power of the Fuggers (sixteenth century), which meant the progressive decline of Jewish trade; and the Thirty Years War (seventeenth century) which overwhelmed Germans and Jews alike.

If there were no other history, the tale would hardly be worth telling. But the recurrent Teutonic fury, a sorry weakness in an otherwise admirable people, and the recurrent Jewish martyrdom, a matter of perverse pride in its otherwise admirable victims, throw into stark contrast the inner life which is perhaps the truer picture. In the face of perpetual obstacles, or because of them, the Jews of mediæval Germany forged an intellectual and social discipline which, spreading eastward to Poland, Russia, and the Danubian states, has brought millions under its sway. And reaching southward, the German Jews time and again injected the iron of their civilization into the thinning blood of Spain.

But the mention of Spain gives the measure of their achievement. Barred from castles, courts, and the intellectual forums of Germany, its Jews had scant use for science, pure literature, or philosophy; and even if the bars had fallen, the German mediæval baron was not the man to inspire an interest in the humanities. We need not look for a Judah Halevi or Maimonides among the Jews, nor, by the same token, for an Abderrahman or Alphonse the Wise among the Germans. When, at length, the Renaissance awakened Germany, it found Jewish fortunes at low ebb, and except for a brief moment in Bohemia, left them untouched.

The awakening did not come to German Jewry until the late eighteenth century—but what an awakening! For a hundred years or more its energies not only wrought, for what it is worth, modern Judaism—and contemporary Jews, even the most detached among them, are too much its products to be its judge; but reaching beyond the Judengasse helped, in inordinate measure, to create modern Germany; and reaching farther still, has gone to transform modern society and thought. Moses Mendelssohn, Zunz, and Herzl are symbols for the Jews; Heine, Boerne, and Lassalle for the Germans; Karl Marx, Freud, and Einstein for the world.

⌒⋏⋏⌒

Cologne had its Jews, as we have seen, when the Roman arch, with the name of the town written on it, did not stand before the Church of St. Maria im Kapitole, for the reason that St. Maria was still unknown. When the city was rebuilt after its destruction by the Normans—seven hundred years later—the Jews were assigned a handsome location, between the Rathaus and the present Laurenzplatz. The short street before the Rathaus door was the Judengasse, and its inhabitants had only a step to go to meet their customers in the Alt-markt and Heumarkt. A tablet, dated 1266, now in the treasury (*Schatzkammer*) of the cathedral, tells us all we need to know of their economic circumstances; the inscription promises them, on the part of Archbishop Engelbert II, special protection, including a pledge that no Christian money-lenders will be tolerated. The Archbishop, it must be understood, rented the Jews from the Emperor, and had good reason to protect their lives and purse. However, this same year twelve of his *protégés* were martyred on the fantastic charge of furnishing arms to "Moors and Tartars."

Still, the thirteenth century was the happiest in the Judengasse. The preceding hundred years had brought the Crusaders twice to Cologne; the following brought the Black Death, as a result of which the Jews were saved from the plague by being burnt; and the fifteenth century brought the Dominicans. The latter came to exterminate the Hussites, and while they were about it took care to banish the Jews. Although Cologne saw no more of them until 1798, when the French Revolutionary armies taught the city new manners, they were never entirely absent from the minds of its burghers. For Cologne was the home of Hochstraaten and his obscurantists —better described in their native German as *Dünkelmänner* (men of darkness)—who could not sleep nights at the thought that Jews were allowed to read the Talmud, and whom Ulrich van Hutten lampooned into immortality.

When the Jews departed (1426), their synagogue was rebuilt into the present Ratskapelle, opposite the town hall; a broken column in the west gable survives from the old house of prayer. The cellar of the Plasmann House, next to the town hall, is presumed to be the ancient *mikveh*[1]—the dressing-room with niches for clothes-cupboards and benches recall the twelfth-century baths of Worms and Speyer. The Rheinisches Museum contains a few eighteenth-century Passover dishes

[1] See p. 109 (Carpentras).

and an ark curtain of the same period, from Deutz. Further fragmentary signs of the Jews may be seen in the recently discovered cemetery beyond the Severins Tor (54 Radebergerstrasse). The inscription on the gate claims that it was used from Roman days down to 1695; the latter date means that the Jews of Deutz, across the Rhine, and other neighbouring towns enjoyed the privilege of burial outside, long after they lost the right to live inside, the walls of Cologne. About fifty broken stones have been unearthed, among them the memorial of Eliakim ben Ephraim of Bonn, murdered in the streets in 1171, the son of Ephraim ben Jacob who has left us an account of the Second Crusaders, the heroic followers of Bernard of Clairveaux, seen through the eyes of their victims.

But only Heine can characterize Cologne with the proper inelegance.

> Dummheit und Bosheit buhlten hier
> Gleich Hunden auf freier Gasse,
> Die Enkelbrut erkennt man noch heut'
> An ihrem Judenhasse.

☙❧

Fairer scenes await us up the Rhine, past Düsseldorf, where Heine was born, past the Lorelei he sang, beyond the vineyards and the hills. Out of the wide valley mists steam visions of kobolds, tarn-helmeted warriors, charcoal-burners crouching in Grimm fairy-tale forests, minnesinging shoemakers, wanderlusting students, brown beer-mugs, rabbis with yellow rings on their sleeves, in fact of everything *"recht echtdeutsch romantisch verrückt."* Shaking the mist from its towers, the city of Worms invites us to its narrow streets, narrow underfoot, but narrower overhead where the gables brush one another's brows, and bids us welcome to the Middle Ages.

Worms was called Little Jerusalem longer than we care to

believe. Legend—another Rhine legend—claims that its Jews declined Nehemiah's invitation to return to Palestine because, so they said, they lived in a Jerusalem of their own. In any case, Speyer, Worms, and Mayence—often called by the single name *Shum*, taken from their initial letters—were centuries on end seats of learning and spiritual prestige. In far-off Russian Mohilev, a synagogue mural of the eighteenth century pictures a city of domes, palms, and towers which has every mark of Zion but which is labelled "Worms." Only in Prague can we come as close to touching the hem of the mediæval German Jew.

The Judengasse begins at the Mayence gate and curves snug against the city wall. A smaller gate, recently restored, is named after Rashi,[1] in token of his student days in Worms. Gate, wall, and many of the high gabled houses have outworn the centuries.

The synagogue is the oldest in use on the continent. The main structure, devoted to the men-folk, was first built in 1034, as witness the tablet (now immured next to the ark) giving the date and the name of the founder, Mar Jacob ben David, whose memory is blessed with a Sabbath prayer to this day. A later inscription (to right of outer doorway) again praises the good man and his wife Rachel. However, little remains of his work; the structure was radically rebuilt in the last quarter of the twelfth century and often restored.

The portal is pure romanesque, not unlike the entrance to the local cathedral. Half washed away by the years, a few names may be faintly discerned cut in the stone jambs, a signal honour for their owners.

The interior introduces us to the synagogues of central Europe, which appear to have maintained a common form until the Renaissance. The vaulting, we note at once, is upheld by

[1] See p. 87.

two central columns—in this case capped with romanesque chapiters. With the exception of modest buildings spanned by a single vaulting, the use of central columns prevailed from Worms to Chelm. Whether to distinguish the synagogue from a church or to emphasize its function as a "house" of study and as a communal "house" of the people rather than a shrine we cannot say, but as a result we have a chamber resembling the refectories, armouries, courts, and other secular halls of the Middle Ages.

Again, in Worms as elsewhere, the *bima* rises between the central columns, and the ark stands against or within the east wall. Furthermore, the pews formerly ran lengthwise (as they still do in Prague[1]), facing not the ark but the *bima*. Without waiting to hear a service, we learn at a mere glance that it consists of lessons read to the congregation from a central desk, and of community worship directed not to a shrine or sacred object, but to an omnipresent deity. The ark, however venerated, is out of sight and serves primarily as a bookcase for the texts. Needless to say the auditorium and stage of a modern synagogue, architecturally influenced by the Protestant cult, betray a different conception of the Jewish service, one in which the congregation is an audience, the rabbi and cantor with the aid of the choir are performers, and the ark, mounted in the middle background of the stage, dominates the spectacle.

Returning to Worms, we find the women's synagogue opening through a large arch to the left. A renewed inscription above its outer portal indicates that it was built in 1213 at the expense of Rabbi Meir ben Joel ha-Cohen and his wife Judith, "who ruled his house like a king's daughter." Supported by a single central column, and Gothic in vaulting, consoles, and windows, it is almost as large and quite as im-

[1] See p. 339.

pressive as its mate. The open archway uniting the two is a modern invention; originally the women's annex was walled apart, and small windows (as in Prague) provided the only access to the service.

Unfortunately for the sniffers-up of antiquities, the synagogue of Worms has always belonged to German Jews, with the result that it is eternally scrubbed, polished, swept, and painted, and therefore hardly looks its age. But if the traveller feels put out at its fresh appearance, he need only listen to the beadle weave the web of history and legend that has gone into its stones, and he will quickly forget the varnish and soap.

He will reverently touch the Torah written in prison by the very hand of Rabbi Meir of Rothenburg (even though he suspects it is by Meir of Eger), and still read from three times a year. He will look appreciatively on the wall lights at either side of the ark when he learns that they commemorate two strangers who, in some dim century, saved the community from death.

"It was near Passover"—we are not paraphrasing the present beadle, but his illustrious seventeenth-century predecessor, Juspa Shammes—"when a church procession passed down the Judengasse and water thrown from a window somehow drenched the crucifix. The Jewish community was ordered to produce the offender or else die to a man on the coming Passover. Since the offender, if there was one, could not be found, the Jews prepared to meet their end. Early on the morning of the first day of the fatal feast, as the beadle came to open the synagogue, he found two strangers waiting at the door. 'What do you want?' he cried, 'and whence do you come? Haven't you heard that every Jew found in Worms today will be killed? Flee while you can!' Whereat the strangers confessed it was they who had emptied the unlucky bucket, and begged leave to pray before they surrendered to the authorities. Despite the beadle's protest that he had never before laid eyes on them, that as total strangers they could not have committed the outrage, they persisted in their story; they entered and prayed, gave themselves over to the city judges, got themselves hanged, and saved the community." So the candles are affixed to the wall in their memory, "and to this day," concludes Juspa Shammes, "no one knows who they were, but many think they were angels sent from the Lord."

Or you may follow the beadle to the narrow lane which runs along the east of the synagogue, where he will point to a recess in the wall, that obviously serves no architectural purpose. A true and good woman, he will tell you, was walking down this lane when suddenly she saw a great cart drawn by two mad horses dashing down upon her and like to crush her to death. She called upon the prophet Elijah for aid, and in a twinkling the wall of the synagogue gave way, she stepped into the niche, and her life was saved. It happened she was with child at the time, and the baby, who was born some months later, grew up to be the great Rabbi Judah he-Hasid of Regensburg (d. 1217).[1]

But a greater man than Judah the Pious or even Meir of Rothenburg has left his name, and perhaps his chair, in the synagogue of Worms. Built against the west wall is a small Gothic chamber with a round apse, called the Rashi Chapel and popularly claimed to be the school where Rashi taught. A Gothic stone cathedra, set in the wall next to the apse, purports to be the seat of the master; around it stand the stone benches of his pupils. But the facts do not bear out the claim. Rashi studied but probably never taught in Worms. If he did teach there, it was in the *yeshibah* (college) which stood on the site of the present Jewish hospital. The chapel, despite its Gothic

[1] See p. 299.

air, was built, as the inscription over the doorway proves, in 1624 by David Oppenheimer. There remains only the chair, which likely came from the vanished *yeshibah*. The little room, however, contains a twelfth-century illuminated copy of Rashi's commentary, and a number of manuscript prayer-books, some with fourteenth-century miniatures. A tray suspended from the ceiling holds the unleavened bread (*erub*) which is distributed at the borders of the Judengasse to sanction the distance objects may be carried on a Sabbath without breaking the Law, and which in a larger sense signifies the unity of the congregation.

A museum in the women's synagogue preserves a number of notable relics. Belowstairs will be found tombstones, house lanterns, grillings, and fragments of the seventeenth-century stone *bima*. On the second floor is a collection of ark curtains, candelabra, Torah crowns, spiceboxes, and other ritual furniture, including two handsome Elijah chairs[1] of the seventeenth and eighteenth centuries. On the wall hangs a portrait of Michael Gernsheim (d. 1772), the last "Jews' bishop" of Worms, a title popularly given to the *parnas* of the community.

Among the manuscripts are the famous Worms *machzor* (prayer-book) of 1272, magnificently illuminated, another prayer-book of 1472, and a large assortment of Imperial privileges, letters of protection, and other official documents of the sixteenth-eighteenth centuries.

Most remarkable, however, is the vast store of Torah bands[2] (*Wimpeln*), over six hundred in all, which give the stitched names and birth dates of generations of Wormser Jews, reaching back to the year 1570. In these strips of needlework, with their quaint picturing of family devices often taken from the

[1] See p. 108 (Carpentras).
[2] See p. 71 (Cluny).

sign of the house where the child was born—a wheel, horse, hat, star, ball, powder-flask, horseshoe, and the like—one may follow not only three centuries of handicraft, but trace to their first embroidered flutter widespread clans of modern Jews.

In the garden behind the Rashi Chapel a stone hut half protrudes above the ground, and an ancient flight of steps drops to its dark portal. It is the entrance to the *mikveh*[1] (ritual bath for women), one of the most astonishing structures that have survived from the Middle Ages.

The ritual bath, it should be noted, requires a constant supply of living water. Rain water will not serve, nor water drawn from a well. In many localities along the Rhine, springs or river-fed pools are to be found only at great depths. Since it was against the ritual law to raise the water in buckets, and since modern piping was unknown, nothing remained but to drop the bath, its house and all, down to the level of the hidden spring. As a result, these Rhine baths may be likened to donjon towers, with their winding ramps and chambers, sunk by Merlin's magic into the profundities of the earth.

Judged by its style, as well as by an inscription fixed to the retaining wall of the synagogue courtyard, the bath was built about 1186, at the cost of a certain Joseph. It was excavated in 1895.

The barrel-vaulted stairway winds in a descending spiral around the walls of the well, pit, shaft, or whatever one chooses to call the main subterranean hall. Forty-one steps lead us to the bottom of the bath. Halfway down, the stairs open into a vaulted chamber, with small dressing-rooms on either side, where a balustrade and arch, powerful in their clean Romanesque lines, overlook the pool. A small aperture in the ceiling of the main shaft, the well-head if this were a

[1] See p. 109 (Carpentras).

well, drops a pillar of sunlight on the waters below, the only illumination save for the lamps which, in olden days, burned in the niches still to be seen in the walls of the stairway and dressing-rooms. A descent into this sunken castle, darker for the fitful flash of stifling wicks and the imprisoned column of the sun, and haunted by forgotten whispers, should have been cleansing enough, without the virtue of a ritual plunge.

The well-head is now covered with an iron grill, the sole relic of the ancient *Tanzhaus*, or marriage-hall, a familiar institution in the old life of the ghetto and the scene of weddings and public festivities.

Baths similar to Worms may be seen elsewhere along the Rhine; the most elaborate in Andernach, built in the latter half of the fourteenth century, and dropping over fifty feet; another fourteenth-century example in Offenburg i. Baden (Glaserstrasse), where the stairs lead downward in a straight line to the central shaft; and finally in Speyer and Friedberg.

Great names and stirring memories greet us in the cemetery of Worms (Andreasstrasse near the Andreas gate) which, dating from the eleventh century, is one of the oldest in Europe. The sagging battered stones, deployed in aimless ranks, are hard put in their battle with the centuries, but the fight goes on. The worst enemy is not moss, time, or weather, but the unpleasant custom of the German Christians to vent their wrath, as the occasion requires, not only on the living Jews, but the dead, a custom recently revived among other glories of the past by the romantic Nazis. The survival of the cemetery in Worms is a tribute to the unpatriotic tolerance of the city.

The form and design of the tombstones repeat, like a primer for students, the history of west-European architecture. Square tops and round-arched mouldings illustrate the Romanesque of the eleventh and twelfth centuries; pointed mouldings usher in the thirteenth-century Gothic; broken and ogee curves come a hundred years later; classic pediments bring in the Renaissance; and plump extravagant lines and touches of sculpture—crests, punning devices, and house signs—announce the age of baroque.

The history of the community is rendered no less visible and foreshortened. Broken slabs set in the wall of the graveyard commemorate twelve elders who, peculiarly enough, died the same year, 1096, the year that, it happens, dates the First Crusade. It is not a triumph of coincidence. When the Crusaders descended on Worms, the twelve elders went to the city council and begged protection for the Judengasse. Upon the rejection of their plea, they killed themselves. Eight hundred of their fellows who lacked the foresight of the leaders— bating the women-folk, who cast themselves in the Rhine— fell at the hands of the army of Godfrey of Bouillon—"may his bones," piously adds an old chronicler, "be crushed."

Two stones, standing side by side, bring us as close as time permits to the greatest rabbi of mediæval Germany, and to the drama of his life. Under the left stone lies the remains of Rabbi Meir of Rothenburg, better known as Maharam. He was born in Worms (c. 1215), studied under Yehiel of Paris,[1] lived a good part of his life in Rothenburg, and wielded preëminent power among the Jewries of central Europe by virtue of his learning, wisdom, and character. His decisions governed the financial and spiritual life of the Judengassen from the Rhine to the Vistula, and his copious legal and moral writings still hold a place in the literature of Israel. "Light of the Exile," he was called, a title shared only by Gershom of Mayence and Rashi of Troyes. The light which he received from Yehiel he passed to his pupil Asher, who carried it to Spain and Portugal—a torch kindled with neither the mystic

[1] See p. 49.

flame of an Eleazar of Worms nor Maimonides' cold light of reason, but a disciplinary fire that tempered the soul of the race.

In 1186 Meir crossed the Alps, perhaps on a journey to Palestine or possibly to escape the exactions of the Emperor Rudolph. He was seized in a mountain town of Lombardy, imprisoned in the Imperial castle of Ensisheim (Alsace), and held for a vast ransom. Forbidding the Jewish communities to raise the sum demanded for his release, he spent his remaining years in the castle keep, where he died in 1293, studying, teaching, and governing to the end. Death, however, did not free his body, which the government judged was worth as high a price as ever. Fourteen years later, Alexander ben Solomon of Frankfort managed to collect the huge ransom, and Rabbi Meir came to his last rest in the graveyard of Worms. Alexander asked but one reward—to be buried next to the master he redeemed. He had not long to wait. The next year (1303) he was placed by the side of Meir. And from the number of pebbles, tokens of veneration, heaped on both tombstones, it is hard to tell who, in our day, is honoured more.

Near at hand stands the stone, with renewed inscription, of Rabbi Baruch (d. 1281), the father of Meir. The shattered slab of Maharil (Jacob ben Moses Mölln, d. 1427), the Meir of his century, will be quickly recognized because, unlike the others and contrary to Jewish custom, it does not face the east. Isaac ben Eleazar Halevi, one of Rashi's teachers, and Eleazar of Worms (Eleazar ben Judah ben Kalonymus, d. 1238), who wrote the *Rokeach*, conversed with angels, and while reading, as he tells us, the portion *Vayesheb* in Genesis saw the Crusaders burst into his home and kill his wife and children before his eyes—these and generations of their kind are sown in the old burial-ground until its dust is compounded with learning and dreams. And, in parting, you may place a pebble on the tomb of that retailer of miracles and legends, Juspa Shammes (1604-78).

Against the south portal of the cathedral you will find the customary statues of the Church and Synagogue.[1] Blindfolded, her crown and tablets of the Law falling to the ground, the Synagogue is seen slaughtering a ram. While the theme is Biblical and the intention honest, it is a trifle anachronistic; slaughter in the thirteenth century was not the prerogative of the Synagogue.

⌒⋏⋏⌒

Speyer adds to the story a dilapidated wall of its fourteenth-century synagogue, in which may be distinguished the niche for the ark, a portal, and a window or two. Traces can likewise be seen of the east wall belonging to the women's annex. Both were destroyed during the sack of Speyer by the French in 1689. The Judenbadgasse where these remains are found, as well as the Judengasse itself, have otherwise lost their ancient character.

But in the garden behind the synagogue may be found the entrance to one of the great ritual baths (key at police station in Maximilianstrasse) of the Rhine country. The stairs lead first to an underground waiting-room, where the stone benches built into the walls now await their women-folk in vain; they then dip to a finely vaulted and balustraded balcony which opens into a tiring-room, and finally they wind down to the pool, seventy-two steps beneath the surface of the earth. The lovely Romanesque capitals in the balcony, the careful workmanship throughout, testify to either greater means or a better state of preservation than in Worms. The structure dates from the twelfth century.

[1] See p. 51 (Paris).

Two arched casements from the gable of the women's synagogue, as well as several tombstones, some dating from the twelfth century, are preserved in the Historical Museum (Real Gymnasium).

Mayence boasts a cemetery (85 Mombacherstrasse) containing the oldest tombs in central Europe. Mounting the wooded hillside where the stones take their ease in the shade, you clamber back through the centuries, each slab another milestone of time, until you break into a newly planted field. Here are gathered (and numbered) the stones which were dispersed as building-blocks, house signs, and trophies throughout the city after the destruction of the old graveyard and a temporary expulsion of the Jews in 1348. Of the two hundred that have been recovered, four hail from the eleventh century, and most of the remainder from the thirteenth century. Only a single stone (No. 159) has been found dated between the years 1089 and 1184—the century of the Crusades which fairly annihilated the community.

One of the early stones (No. 164), though the date has been battered away, marks an epoch in Jewish history. It commemorates Rabbi Gershom ben Judah (960-1028?), the "Light of the Exile," who, founding the first great school in the Rhinelands, is the father of Talmudic tradition in northern Europe. Another eleventh-century stone (No. 1) tells the origin of the tradition: the name it bears, Rabbi Meshullam ben Kalonymus, takes us back across the Alps to Lucca, Rome, Bari and Otranto,[1] where scholars brought the Talmudic discipline from the East—the same century that Moses ben Enoch, in rags, startled the Jewry of Cordova.[2] The neighbouring tombstone (No. 2) binds the last link; it is inscribed with the name of Rabbi Jacob ben Yakar (d. 1064), who was

[1] See p. 250 (Apulia).
[2] See p. 126.

the pupil of Gershom and the teacher of Rashi; behind Gershom lies Italy, Babylonia, and Palestine, while Rashi leads to France, Poland, and wherever the Talmud rules today—the "chain of tradition" is joined together in a rod of hallowed ground.

The museum in the community-house next to the new synagogue (42 Hindenburgerstrasse) preserves an excellent collection of ritual art and local antiquities. Among the latter, a few fragments of carved wood come from the vanished houses of the ghetto, which lay off Klarastrasse in the present Synagogen and Hochsynagogenstrassen. A parchment scroll of selections from the Prophets (*Haftorah*) deserves attention, though not for its age or beauty. One of Napoleon's *tambours de regiment*, ignorant of its character, used it for a drum-head and beat the Imperial armies into Mayence on the words of Isaiah. It is doubtful if the Jews, when they discovered the profanation, were much annoyed. They had reason to be tolerant. Only a few years before, the Judengasse, which remembered the hosts of Godfrey de Bouillon, saw a new and different army march in from France. On the 26th of Fructidor of the sixth year of the French Republic (September 12, 1798), the municipal council of Mayence ordered the ghetto gate destroyed *auf feierliche Weise*—"with suitable festivities."

But the decree came too late. On the preceding day the watchman at the gate, unaware that times had changed, sought to prevent honest Moses Cahn and his young wife from moving their household goods out of the ghetto into the free world on Klara Street. As they came to blows, a French officer happened by. Godfrey de Bouillon would have blushed for his words—*"vous avez parfaitement raison, je vais vous envoyer des secours, démolisez donc cette vieille baraque"*— "Good for you," he cried to the Jew. "I'll send you help, and away with that old contraption!" No sooner said than done;

and the next day the demolished gate was burned with suitable festivities.

⟨⌖⟩

Zu Frankfurt kam ich am Shabbes an
Und ass dort Schalet und Klösse;
Ihr habt die beste Religion,
Auch lieb' ich das Gänsegekröse.[1]

The religion and *Gänsegekröse* linger much as Heine found them, but gone from the famous Frankfort Judengasse are the old houses which, the poet said, "looked at me as though they wished to tell me troubled stories, stories that men know well, but no longer want to know and would gladly forget." One remains, the Rothschild house, and men are never tired of repeating its story.

The house stands midway along the Judengasse (now 26 Boernestrasse), and despite its restoration looks much as it did in 1780, when Mayer Amschel moved in with his wife Gütele and a considerable number of their eighteen children. Though it bears a red shield (*rot Schild*) over the left doorway, it was called "At the Green Shield," and the Rothschild family, which can be traced back to the middle of the sixteenth century, took their name from a vanished and far older sign. A family of Schiffs, as you may learn from the sign of the ship above the right-hand door, shared the house; the upper floors were rented to roomers, and in all sixty or seventy persons lived in the four stories and garret of a building not over thirty feet wide. An average ghetto home (built 1712), it had nothing of the splendour of the neighbouring Oppenheimer mansion, and it was a far cry from the palace of Sam-

[1] Translation at reader's risk:

To Frankfort I came on a Sabbath
And ate there Jewish tidbits;
Their religion is the finest
And so is their goose giblets.

uel Halevi in Toledo.[1] Still, it was enough to hold the wealth of a Rothschild.

A narrow hallway opens on one side to the kitchen, with its oven, pump—a modern improvement in Gütele's day—and separate cupboards for *milchig* and *fleischig* foods; and on the other side to a shop which occupied most of the ground floor. In the rear a small chamber, where Gütele died (1849), now serves as a family synagogue.

A snug stairway descends to a front cellar, while a secret panel in the hall gives access to a rear cellar, where, during the Napoleonic wars, Mayer Amschel hid the money of his best customer, the Landgrave of Hesse-Cassel, money which the Landgrave had earned selling his Hessians to help the British pacify their American colonies. Another secret stairs descends from the Schiff domain. The cellar itself is much older than the house, and on occasion it must have concealed not Hessian or other money-bags, but ghetto fugitives hiding for their lives.

Behind the little courtyard is the stone shed where Mayer Amschel set up business. His stool and table are still there, and the strong box where princes left and took their gold, a tricky box with a fake lock and secret spring calculated to fool the bank robbers of a simpler age.

The second floor back opens on a low roof where the Rothschilds and Schiffs took the air in summer, and in autumn celebrated the Feast of Booths—a small arbor or tabernacle awaits their return. In the front, a parlour with its old furniture more or less untouched overlooks the street; here is the armchair Gütele sat in, and with the aid of the "busybody" mirrors watched the world go by, except when Mayer Amschel sat in it and with the aid of the same mirrors detected whether the knock on the door below meant a customer or a bill-

[1] See p. 152.

collector. A chair for Browning and sitters made to his hand
—the last of the line of Hasdai and Aaron of Lincoln.

Boerne remembers *"der alte Rothschild"* as *"ein braver*
Mann, piety and greateartedness itself," and there is no
reason to doubt him, for rich men, like saints, seem to possess
a peculiar talent for goodness. On the memorable evening
when Boerne walked the street that now bears his name, arm
in arm with the young Heine, and Boerne's spirit burnt
brighter than the hundreds of Hanuka lamps set in the windows, and things were said to make the fortune of modern
wits, they stopped before the Rothschild home. "Look," said
Boerne, "in this little house lives the old Letitia who has borne
a brood of financial Bonapartes, the mother of all loans, who
despite the world-wide power of her sons refuses to leave her
ghetto castle; tonight, in honour of the Feast, she has hung
her windows with white curtains, her candles dance, yet when
the good woman looks at them tears come to her old eyes, and
she remembers with bitter joy the days when Mayer Amschel
stood at her side, and her little boys lit little candles on the
floor and leaped about them in boyish glee, as is the custom in
Israel."

When our two friends reached the end of the Judengasse
where lies the cemetery, Heine recalled that his father used to
speak of cattle pastured in the hallowed ground and their bel-
lowing which kept the neighbours from sleeping nights. And
Boerne, born in the ghetto, explained that Jewish cattle-deal-
ers for miles around—cattle-dealing was a major Jewish industry in south Germany of the eighteenth century—by way
of dedicating the first-born bulls to the Lord brought them to
the Frankfort graveyard, where they chewed the cud and bel-
lowed to a ripe old age. "But the old cattle are dead," said
Boerne, "and the new no longer hold to the true faith; their
first-born remain quietly at home, when they don't, that is, go
to the water—yes, the old cattle are dead."

Countless sons, true to the old stock and faith, are kept alive in this famous burial-ground, if leaving a good name on a moss-eaten stone be a manner of living. As in Worms, the form and decoration of the stones tell the century they were hewn. The oldest dates from 1272; the latest, 1829. Over seven thousand still hold up their red sandstone heads, and twenty thousand more are sunk beneath the ground.

The sculpture, mostly from the seventeenth-eighteenth centuries, plays on the name of the dead or on the sign of the house they once inhabited. Derived from house signs we have the names and carvings of a funnel (Trichter), tree (Grünebaum), ship (Schiff), ostrich (Strauss), castle (Schloss), fishnet (Reis—from the Frankfort dialect expression *Räuse*); and among the animal names and crests, a stag (Hirsch), hare (Haas), horse (Ross), lion (Loeb), bear (Baer), eagle (Adler), cock (Hahn), etc. As elsewhere, a pitcher signifies a Levi in recalling the Levitical privilege of washing the hands of the priest or *cohen*, the outstretched hands themselves commemorate a Cohen, the tablets of the Law a learned man, and grape-clusters otherwise undistinguishable sons of Israel.[1] Human figures occasionally appear: a representation of Job, several busts signifying the name Schwarzkopf, Weisskopf and the like, and three scenes of Adam and Eve in the garden of Eden.

The rabbis are grouped to the north. The most popular among them, if one may judge by the number of pebbles, candle-ends, and scribbled pleas and prayers scattered about his tomb, is Pincas Horowitz, usually known as "The Face of Salvation," who denounced Mendelssohn for daring to translate the Pentateuch into German and who sanctioned the burning of that scandalous work in Vilna, the year 1782. The date will illustrate how late the Renaissance came to Jewish

[1] See p. 336 (Prague).

life, and the candle-ends and scribbled pleas how, for many Jews, the Middle Ages have not ceased.[1]

The Jewish museum, installed in the early nineteenth-century bank of the Rothschilds at the far end of the Judengasse (146 Fahrgasse), is one of the most fascinating in Europe. In the first room are gathered household objects, sacred and profane. Here are old house signs from the ghetto—a wooden stork, drum, ring, and green hat; metal work from fan-lights —an ostrich and bears; the bannister and door from the birthplace of Boerne; and sundry eighteenth-century furniture. The religious relics include calendars, Sabbath lamps, *mezzuzot*, a brass dish for the speeding of the Sabbath tooled with the figures of Adam and Eve, Hanuka lamps such as Boerne and Heine saw gleaming in the windows—one a rare sixteenth-century glazed lamp painted with angels and three pairs of lovers under the inscription "Amor," a case filled with delightful spice-boxes—among them a seventeenth-century turret in silver filigree and another in eighteenth-century enamel, and finally numerous utensils for the Passover: eighteenth-century painted dishes and a richly-chased silver platter; rollers and prongs for making the unleavened bread; a case of Passover-eve prayer-books running from Mantua, 1560, to Würzburg, 1734, each appropriately illustrated.

The second room is devoted to synagogal objects: an eighteenth-century *bima*, ark, and bronze menorah; a selection of ark curtains, Torah mantles, bells, crowns, and shields; illuminated contracts, marriage rings, wedding-odes, and seventeenth-century silver girdles, all recalling long-forgotten matches—the betrothal girdles were given to the bride by the rabbi on behalf of the groom, and to the groom by the mother of the bride, on the Thursday before the wedding; and, in natural sequence, a collection of material pertaining to the circumcision—two Elijah chairs (Empire period),[2] knives, sand-

[1] See p. 400 (Morocco).
[2] See 108 (Carpentras).

cups, a treatise on the operation illustrated with miniatures, and several Torah bands (*Wimpeln*) bearing the name and birthplace of the new son of the covenant.[1]

The two remaining rooms were formerly the offices of the Rothschild brothers who remained at home. Here, among the old furnishings, are portraits of Mayer Amschel and Gütele, the brevets of nobility bestowed on their children—and a passport of one Ludwig Boerne.

The public library (*Stadtbibliotek*) keeps on exhibit a number of its Hebrew treasures: a thirteenth-century illuminated Bible from the south of France (No. 4); a north Italian *Mishneh Torah* of Maimonides with six miniatures dating from about 1400 (No. 6); a delicately adorned prayer-book of the Roman Jewish rite, done at the end of the fifteenth century (No. 8); a fifteenth-century Italian Passover service with exquisite pen drawings and coloured miniatures (No. 9); and other illuminated manuscripts.

Among the printed works on exhibit are a commentary of Gersonides (Mantua c. 1477—No. 189)[2]; a Soncino Talmud (Soncino 1483—No. 190)[3]; a Soncino Bible (Soncino 1488—No. 191); a *Tur Orach Hayim* (by Jacob ben Asher, Leiria 1495—No. 195), a unique copy, as the incunabula of Portugal are apt to be, thanks to the Inquisition; the first illustrated printed Haggadah (Prague 1526—No. 246); early Latin translations from the Jewish liturgy by Thomas Murner (Frankfort 1512—Nos. 248, 249, 250); and German astronomical works on Jacob's Staff (by Jacob Köbel, Frankfort 1531—Nos. 260, 261) which carry us back to the glories of Provence and Spain.[4] The library contains fifty-six Hebrew incunabula.

On the Bockenheimeranlage, one of the park boulevards of the city, stands a monument to Boerne (by Kaupert) repre-

[1] See p. 71 (Cluny).
[2] See p. 260 (Mantua).
[3] See p. 260 (Casal Maggiore).
[4] See pp. 104, 140.

senting Liberty enlightening Germany, and on the near-by
Friedbergeranlage (opp. No. 14) a monument to Heine (by
Kolbe) representing it is hard to say what. You may follow
the footsteps of these two writers to the suburb of Bornheim,
where the synagogue contains a twelfth-century bronze ewer,
and where, so at least Heine reports on the Sabbath he drank
coffee there with Boerne, "the Jewish girls are charming and
the whole place smells deliciously of *schalet*."

꒰ᐢ⸝⸝ᐢ꒱

Friedberg in Hessia, an hour from Frankfort, will reward
you with a thirteenth-century subterranean ritual bath, finished with even greater skill and beauty than the *mikveh* of
Speyer, and in the synagogue a small but precious collection
of sixteenth-seventeenth-century spice-boxes, seventeenth-
eighteenth-century Torah shields, and an eighteenth-century
Torah crown.

Strasbourg, which opened the story of the Rhine with its
red shards, may fittingly conclude it—even though of its long
and adventurous history the Judengasse keeps nothing but its
name (Rue des Juifs, behind cathedral). A rich exhibit of
local Jewish antiquities fills a room in the Alsatian Museum
(Palais Episcopal), and several thirteenth-fourteenth-century
tombstones will be found in the university (Collection
archéologique). The statues of the Church Triumphant and
the Synagogue Defeated on the south portal of the cathedral
are easily the most beautiful of their kind.[1]

Alsace is dotted with ancient Jewries, and though tangible
remains are few,[2] tradition holds sway as nowhere else in
France, the tradition and discipline of life which, sweetened
with *Simetkuchen*, *Crimselich*, and *Linzertorte*, carried the
Rhineland Jews through a thousand chequered years.

[1] See p. 51 (Paris).
[2] See Appendix C.

CHAPTER XVI

The "Gassen"

of South Germany

WHETHER you read its history or look at its map, the south of Germany presents at first glance a political and geographical tangle. Its rivers, however, bring order out of the chaos, and since we are concerned with a trading people we can do no better than follow these flowing highways. South Germany, as Baedeker understands the term, falls into three great river basins—the Danube southernmost, the Neckar in the west, and the Main to the north. The core of the whole region lies, as we shall see, in Regensburg.

⟨~⟩

The German Danube, on the map, curves like a great arch. Its keystone is Regensburg. In the days before railroads, the city was the chief gateway for commerce with Vienna, Constantinople, and all points east. Behind Regensburg, the valleys mount towards the Main basin at Nuremberg and again at Rothenburg, while in the west they lead to the Neckar basin at Hall, forming the obvious trade routes to the Rhine, Netherlands, England, and Scandinavia. Northeast, the Raab Valley leads past Floss to Bohemia and Poland; southward the Isar and Lech drop from the Alps and Italy. Regensburg was truly *Mittel-Europa.*

The Jews claim to have lived in the city when its Roman name was Regina and traffic ran by rafts to Vindobona and the Euxine Sea. It is undoubtedly the oldest Jewry in Bavaria, and enjoys the distinction of being the first German ghetto to receive official mention (1006-28). In the twelfth and thirteenth centuries its merchants were opening markets for German wares in Constantinople, and north in Kiev and Vilna. It was altogether natural that Petachia, the great mediæval traveller of Regensburg, should begin his journeys (1170-87) in Prague, and move along established grooves through Poland, Ukraine, Crimea, Tartary, and on to Persia.

It was natural, too, that in the days of Petachia and transcontinental commerce Regensburg should vie with the Rhine cities for preëminence in Jewish culture. Things went so far that a woman, Litta of Regensburg, paraphrased the book of Samuel in Nibelungen rhymes. A fifteenth-century Christian chronicler describes the wealth and refinement in which the head of the Jewish community, the *Hochmeister*, lived on or near Tändlergasse (Rag Alley), the ghetto street which evidently did not belie its name. "The house was a hideous pile, with closely barred windows, and seemed scarcely habitable. A passage led to a dark staircase, from which one had to grope one's way in the gloom to reach the entrance in the rear." But within, all was different. "A well-protected door opened into an apartment decorated with flowers and rich splendid furniture." And then the chronicler loses himself in a breathless catalogue of polished panels, many-coloured tapestries, costly carpets, cupboards filled with jewels, gold chains, bangles, and rare antiques, a couch of Oriental design, high-backed gilded chairs, cushions of shorn velvet, a private synagogue gleaming with precious stuffs, and "a superbly inlaid oak table garlanded with flowers and laden with dainty viands and a glittering wine-jug."

The end came in 1519. Regensburg had shown unwonted

patience through the Crusades, the Black Death in 1348-49 when massacres in Germany were as widespread as they were in Spain of 1391, and the epidemic of expulsions and ritual-murder charges in the fifteenth century. But at length the weight of taxes, aggravated by priestly fervour, charges of poisoning wells, and the ritual-murder case in Trent (1478) put patience to flight. The mention of taxes touches on a typical situation in Germany, somewhat resembling the state of affairs in England. The emperor owned the Jews of Regensburg, as elsewhere. That meant one tax. Then he pawned his Regensburg Jews to the dukes of Lower Bavaria, and that meant another tax. Then the dukes gave a concession on the Jews to the city council, and that meant a third tax. And with every tax went the right, naturally, to extract special levies. Meanwhile the Jews, contrary to fable, had no way of coining money out of the air. Every pfennig they paid had to be taken from their customers. As a result, prices and interest rates grew intolerable, and priestly sermons and tales of poisoned wells fell on willing ears.

The Jews were given two hours to strip their synagogue, and five days to leave the city.

Once they were gone, the mob demolished the synagogue, and there rose in its place a chapel, "Zur schönen Maria," which became the seat of miracles and the goal of pilgrimages, and which was afterwards rebuilt into the present Neupfarr church.

Famous throughout Germany for its beauty, the synagogue (built about 1237), a Gothic structure with three central columns and a later Renaissance façade, has been preserved for us in two etchings by Altdorfer, made either immediately before or after its destruction.

Next, the mob attacked the cemetery, and its four thousand stones were dispersed far and wide. Many were used for building purposes, and others plastered in the house fronts as trophies—a custom not unlike the Indian device of hanging enemy scalps over the home wigwams.

You may still see these trophies at No. C135 Emmerans Platz; at the entry to the Invalidenkasse on Neue Waaggasse (off Haid Platz); on the third story of Vor der Grieb at the corner of Waaggäschen (near Haid Platz); and most elaborate of all, in the courtyard of the house (B80 Untere Bachgasse) belonging to Burgomaster Amman who ordered the expulsion. The burgomaster was not content to plaster on his wall the tombstone of "Genele daughter of Rabbi Jekutiel, a woman of valor" who died two years before; but he took care to carve beneath it the following inscription: "Kaspar Amman—Anno Domini 1519, on the Monday evening of the Feast of St. Peter the Jews were expelled from the city of Regensburg and within a week were seen no more. Laus Deo."

Another stone was carted twenty miles up the Danube to Kehlheim, where the apothecary shop, as one enters the village, flaunts the memorial of "Orgia daughter of Rabbi Judah, who went to her rest in 1249." Next to it may be found a copy of the Wittenberg *Judensau*[1]—a capital in the cathedral of Regensburg features a similar sow standing before a Jew in a fourteenth-century pointed bonnet. And farther still, in Weltenberg, the garden wall of the Klösterl inn shows the stone of "Verona daughter of the *parnas* Moses" who died in 1220. Similar spoil may be seen in the villages of Straubing, Cham, Mintraching, Kleinprüfening, and Regenstauf, until one might imagine that the heavens rained Hebrew tombstones. But Baedeker recommends, for the environs of Regensburg, an excursion to Walhalla where we may admire the busts, portraits, and commemorative tablets of the heroes of Germany.

A score of slabs, dating from 1243 to 1489, are gathered in

[1] See p. 315 (Wittenberg).

the Historical Museum of Regensburg (St. Ulrich Church), where are likewise preserved a candlestick, bowl, and jar from a mediæval Jewish home, and (in same case) two skulls from the old cemetery. To complete the tally, there is the famous Judenstein (Jews' Stone) on the square of the same name (near Hl. Kreuz Church). It is popularly ascribed to the wonder-working Rabbi Judah he-Hasid (d. 1217); and although the good citizens, scandalized at its honourable location, once dragged it beyond the city walls, on the following night it flew back to its old place. This is more than curious, for the stone is dated 1347, and its inscription commemorates, not Judah the Pious, but one Moses ben Joseph.

Still, the very name of Judah was likely enough to work magic. We have already read—and seen—the extraordinary circumstances that preceded his birth.[1] He established a famous school in Regensburg, and counted among his pupils two men who have that great distinction in Jewish letters of being called not by their proper names, but after the best known of their books: Rokeach (Eleazar of Worms)[2] and Or Zarua (Isaac of Vienna)[3] Judah was a wayward youth, given to hunting, archery, and other worldly delights, unable even to repeat the Eighteen Benedictions. But after his change of heart he became a master of miracles; he restored fertility to married women; Elijah sat at his Passover meal; he knew the date of Israel's redemption; and he acted as official "seer" to the Duke of Regensburg. But of his written works little remains except his notes on Petachia's travels and his share in the *Sefer Chassidim*, a fertile source of Jewish mysticism.

Many of the Regensburger Jews—thanks to German "particularism"—settled in the near-by village of Sallern, where their presence is celebrated in a Latin inscription walled in the local parsonage (*Pfarrhaus*).

[1] See p. 279 (Worms).
[2] See p. 284.
[3] See p. 347.

The refugees perhaps consoled themselves with the news that the Christians of Regensburg now had to pay double taxes, as well as the sums which the Jews owed annually to the emperor and the bishop—sums which were paid until Napoleon cancelled the debt in 1803. The clergy and populace quarrelled over the new "miracle" chapel which supplanted the synagogue, and a plague smote six thousand in the city. But, on the other hand, the Christians could console themselves with the thought that the rising commerce of Nuremberg, and the Fuggers in Augsburg would have ruined the city, anyway.

The Jews returned piecemeal at the close of the seventeenth century; but they were not able to open a public synagogue until 1841.

The other great cities of the Danube basin, less tolerant than Regensburg, banished their Jews so long ago that few traces of their mediæval life remain; the towns and villages, especially north of the river, do a little better in the way of seventeenth- to eighteenth-century relics; and except for the synagogue of Bechhofen, which will be described shortly, the reader greedy for details is referred to our Appendix C.

The Main basin is dotted with historic names, first and foremost Nuremberg on the Pegnitz. Unfortunately for us, the city drove out its Jews (1499) at the dawn of its greatness, and the amusing jibes of Hans Sachs were expended against a vanished enemy. Though the Nuremberg fairs were frequented by Jewish traders in the seventeenth century—on payment of a high tax—the first of the race permitted to resettle there was a lottery agent, no doubt kin to the immortal Hyacinth Hirsch, a little more than a hundred years ago.

Accordingly, the tokens of the past are scant. The first

synagogue was supplanted by the present Church of Our Lady (Frauenkirche) in consequence of the Black Death and the massacre of 1349; its location on the market place identifies at once the importance and character of the old Jewry. The second Jewry took in a large area bounded by the present Heu, Inneren Laufer, Rotschmieds, and Tucher Gassen; its main street is still called Judengasse. The second synagogue, built about 1352, has left us a fifteenth-century stone pediment for the ark, carved in the prevalent flamboyant style and inscribed in Hebrew, "Crown of the Law"; it now rests in the vestibule of the modern synagogue, which fairly faces the birthplace of Hans Sachs. For many years the pediment adorned the doorway of No. 8 Wunderburggasse in the heart of the second Jewry; the house originally belonged to one Joel Mayer and after the expulsion fell into the possession of the sculptor, Veit Wirsperger; over the round portal and ancient iron-bound door runs a seventeenth-century rhymed inscription:

> Der Stein is nach den Juden blieben
> Da sie von Nürnberg wurden vertrieben,
> Von Hauskauff und Gassen, fürwahr,
> Im Tausend 499 Jahr,

> (This stone remains of the Jews
> When they were driven from Nuremberg,
> From houses and streets, forsooth,
> In the year one thousand four ninety-nine.)

The old church cloisters in the Germanic Museum (Germanisches Museum) contains fragments of mediæval tombstones, the galleries a few scattered relics of ritual art, notably an ark curtain and Passover plates, and the manuscript collection two magnificently illuminated Haggadahs.

Fürth, which lies only five miles away—at the junction of the Pegnitz and the Rednitz, which together form the Regnitz—takes up the tale where Nuremberg breaks off. It was another Little Jerusalem and, more than that, a "righteous place,"[1] although in truth it had hardly time to be otherwise. The first settlement does not date before the early years of the sixteenth century. Jews from Ansbach at the head of the Rednitz and from Bamberg at the mouth of the Regnitz congregated at this midway town after the downfall of the Nuremberg community. Thanks to the rivalry between the Margrave of Ansbach and the Prince Bishop of Bamberg, privileges were showered on the Jewry of Fürth—to the chagrin of Nuremberg; and before the end of the seventeenth century it was the most flourishing Judengasse in the land. Refugees streamed in from all sides, particularly from Vienna after the expulsion of 1670.[2] For a hundred years or more it shared in the prosperity which followed the revival of trade after the Thirty Years War—a revival in which the Jews played a considerable part—and became a thriving hive of rabbis, court Jews, and bankers.

Its synagogue (off Bergstrasse), built in 1617, was reproduced inside and out by eighteenth-century etchers illustrating scenes of Jewish life. The main structure, however, has been transformed by subsequent restorations, and its original state can best be judged by a much later example in Heidingsfeld. But the general layout of the synagogue and its appendages remains much as it was, characteristic of what may be called Jewish town-planning, to be seen again in dozens of German and Polish Jewries. The communal offices, schools, and official dwellings for the rabbi, beadle, schoolmaster, etc., face the street on four sides. Within lies a large courtyard, where were celebrated the blessing of the New Moon, the procession of the Rejoicing of the Law, and the other festivities portrayed in the old prints, as well as those weddings which Glückel of Hameln rightly called *magnifique*. The

[1] See p. 257 (Livorno).
[2] See p. 348.

principal synagogue rises in the centre of the courtyard, with a half-timber mate—the Kaal synagogue built in 1697—on the south. In the old days, a *kosher* slaughterhouse stood to the west, and somewhere on the premises a prison and hospital. The group as a whole tells you that the Jewry constituted a self-governing state, as indeed it did, with its own senate, a court of justice, school system, and sanitary police. The near-by cemetery (foot of Blumenstrasse) and its venerable stones complete the picture.

A chain of Jewries, stretching from Fürth to the eastern border, sprang up in the sixteenth to seventeenth centuries, linking Franconia with Bohemia and Poland, the Nuremberg fair with its rival in Lemberg. Fifteen miles east of Fürth is Schnaittach with a Jewry founded immediately after the expulsion from Nuremberg. Its synagogue, built in 1570 and remodelled in 1735, preserves many of the original features, which reveal the influence of the Pincas synagogue in Prague.[1] A Polish touch will be found in the Eternal Lamp built into the east wall. The women's annex is still a separate structure as in mediæval days; casements pierced in its north wall afford the only access to the service in the men's synagogue. The handsome railings in these apertures come from the old *bima*; ark and painted ceiling are typically neo-classic. Beyond Schnaittach comes Sulzbach, where a Hebrew press fed Germany and the east from 1669 to 1851. The synagogue is late (1826), but it conserves the old style of its neighbours beyond the Bohemian border.[2] An eighteenth-century marriage stone (*Chuppah-Stern*) survives on the outside of the north wall, a projecting boss shaped like a six-pointed star and peculiar to old German synagogues. Engraved on the stone are the Hebrew initials for *mazel tov*, ("Good luck!")—the customary wedding felicitation. Weddings, as we noted in Fürth,

[1] See p. 342.
[2] See p. 344.

commonly took place in the synagogue courtyard, and after the couple were joined the groom shattered a glass against the marriage stone. The meaning of the gesture is obvious; moreover, the six-pointed star, or seal of David, assures, we are told, protection against the devil, who naturally becomes active when a marriage is on foot. The synagogue in Floss, built in 1815, brings us almost within hailing distance of Tachau and the road to Pilsen and Prague.

Directly north of Fürth lies Baiersdorf, the home of the court Jews of Kulmbach-Bayreuth. The most famous of them, Samson Baiersdorf, whose daughter married a son of Glückel of Hameln, built the present synagogue in 1712, replete with fine embroideries and candelabra. "His enemies will humble themselves before the man who builds a house of worship," says the Talmud; and, if true, no man stood in greater need of building synagogues than Samson Baiersdorf. However, in remembering these court Jews, we are apt to think of them only as rich men, powerful schemers, and hazardous livers, as heroes fit for romantic novels. They were more than that. The turn of fortune which brought them to the service of the German states after the Thirty Years War, brought the Jews, almost for the first time in German history, in close contact with the learning and manners of the secular world. Samuel Oppenheimer at the court of Vienna, Jost Liebmann at the court of Berlin, Leffmann Behrens at Hanover, paved the way for Moses Mendelssohn, for the *salons* of Fanny Itzig, Rahel Varnhagen, Henrietta Herz, for the Jewish "renaissance."

The cemetery adjoining the Baiersdorf synagogue is strewn with ornamented stones resembling the baroque displays of Poland. Among the historic graves may be seen the tomb of Moses Hameln, who copied out his mother's memoirs—writings that take us back to this vanished world.

An unusual glimpse may be had of this world in the curious village of Tüchersfeld, lost in the hills of Franconian Switzerland (Fränkische Schweiz—train from Baiersdorf to Elbermannstadt, then nine miles east). It is curious not only for the jagged peaks on either side, but for the outcropping of roof-tops and houses among the crags on the left-hand ridge. The villagers call these houses the Judenhof (Jews' Court) and know nothing more about it. Climbing the slope, we find ourselves in an abandoned village, partly built in the court of a ruined castle and partly hewn into the natural rock; it is a settlement of seventeenth-century Polish Jews, refugees from the Chmielnicki massacres. The synagogues for men and women, communal bakery, and, down by the brook, the ritual bath, remain like an enchanted Judengasse, the sticks and stones as they were, the life dormant or fled, awaiting a wand that will never be waved—an image of Jewish tradition.

〜〜〜

Bamberg brings us to the Main itself, and one of the lesser known treasures of Jewish art—a synagogue lined with mural painting.

In addition, Bamberg possesses a thirteenth-century synagogue (Alt Judenstrasse, now a Turnverein hall), substantially altered after its conversion into a church following the Black Death massacres of 1349—slaughter so atrocious that the inhabitants of this little Judengasse set fire to their homes and cast themselves in the flames, thus fulfilling in a novel fashion the old German tag, *"Die Juden werden verbrannt."*[1] The choir, upper stories, and roof are later additions, and the low vaulting gives evidence that the floor originally lay below the street level, as in Prague and Lemberg. At the right of the central portal of the cathedral may be seen a finely executed

[1] See p. 313 (Erfurt).

statue of the Synagogue Defeated;[1] below is a mediæval Jew with his characteristic pointed bonnet, and perched on the bonnet a devil in the form of a winged monkey leering down at his victim—or comrade.

The painted synagogue deserves closer attention. Originally it was built into the ground floor of a half-timber house in the village of Horb—a rustic barrel-vaulted *Betstube*. In the beginning of the eighteenth century a Jewish artist, Eliezer Sussman ben Solomon, the son of a cantor either in Brod (Bohemia) or Brody (Galicia), set to work in the Franconian countryside, turning the little rural synagogues into gaily painted boxes. For his Galician origin we have the resemblance of his work to the painting in the synagogue of Jablonow on the Pruth, and the probability that his clients were Polish Jews driven to Germany as a result of the Chmielnicki uprising. On the other hand, most of the mural paintings in Poland, which can be traced at least as far back as the Isaac synagogue (Cracow, 1640), are of a ruder and, to modern eyes, more expressive character. Sussman finished his decorations at Horb in 1717; and in recent years the ceiling and walls have been transported to the Municipal Art Gallery of Bamberg (in Treppenhaus of gallery).

The painting covers every fleck of space from the baseboards to the uppermost plank in the barrel vault, a coloured riot of flowers and vines, enlivened by birds, beasts, walled cities, and ritual symbols. Renaissance accuracy is combined with a mediæval love for the grotesque; and something in the cramped scale and scrupulous detail of even the larger subjects recalls the art of the limner. Sussman worked more like a manuscript-illuminator than a mural-painter.

The ceiling contains heraldic lions, horses, unicorns, and an elephant-and-castle taken almost directly from the margin of old parchments. A recurrent *motif* among the profusion of

---

[1] See p. 51 (Paris).

flowers and tendrils is the symbolic pomegranate. Ducks, geese, cocks, hares, foxes, native and exotic woodbirds, dart across the verduous canopy. And a Hebrew inscription runs like a selvage mark around the lower border.

The drum above one of the end walls is dominated by two rampant lions sounding trumpets and supporting an inscribed medallion; at the right appears a bowl of harvest fruits topped with *lulab* branches; at the left a view of Jerusalem looking like Alt Nuremberg, and above it the green peak of Sinai planted with two trees symbolic of the written law (Torah) and oral law (Massorah); over the whole hangs another bowl of fruits, flanked on either side by a *shofar*. The east wall is surmounted by the representation of fringed curtains with more lions and, to one side, a pair of storks with intertwined necks—signifying piety.

Würzburg (Luitpold Museum) preserves another painted synagogue, practically intact. It hails from the near-by village of Kirchheim, where, as in Horb, it occupied the ground floor of a dwelling-house. Sussman executed the murals in 1739-40 and signed the work with his own hand. The synagogue is re-erected in the museum much as it stood in its native village, even to the benches, the wooden grillwork across the casements which opened into the women's annex, and the decorated panels of the *bima*; as a result, the murals lose little of their intended effect. Unlike Horb, the walls are symmetrically divided by floral designs framing lengthy (restored) inscriptions—more suggestive than ever of being papered with old illuminated manuscripts. On the west wall appear two views of Jerusalem; but birds and beasts no longer play among the leafage in the vault.

Back in the Danube basin, the village of Bechhofen (twelve miles south of Ansbach) preserves a timber synagogue, simple as a barn, which was probably built in 1681, and was painted by Sussman in 1733. Except for a freshening of the murals in 1914, little has been changed since the artist laid down his brush. Again we have the panelled spaces, as in Würzburg. A shewbread table is the centre of attention on the north wall, and a lighted menorah on the south. The ark is richly carved and the wall about it sown with inscriptions, foliage, and symbolic lions, trees, trumpets, and harvest fruits. The timbers of the barrel vault are alive with birds and beasts—unicorn, horse, lion, hare, fox, elephant, and squirrel—the 104th Psalm set to line and colour. Two trumpeting lions flanked by Jerusalem and again the harvest fruits, share the drum of the west wall; and beneath are panelled inscriptions, among them, appropriately near the doorway, the saying from the Talmud: "Since Jerusalem has fallen, closed are all the gates of heaven save one—the gate of tears."

A fourth painted synagogue, possibly the work of Sussman, will be found at Unterlimpurg, near Schwäbisch-Hall in the Neckar basin.

Würzburg, we should not fail to note, was the court where Süsskind of Trimberg, the only Jewish minnesinger known to history, sang his famous *Lieder*. How he ever launched on his career in the grim thirteenth century we cannot divine; but the reasons he gives for abandoning it will be echoed by Antonio de Montoro[1] two hundred years later, and again by the German Heine. Süsskind's farewell to his art may be roughly rendered as follows:

> I have gone on a fool's journey with my art,
> The great lords will give me nothing for my song;
> So I'll forsake their courts
> And let my beard grow long and gray,
> And in the good old Jewish manner I will live,
> Walking softly in my way;
> My cloak will cover me, from hood to shoes,
> Meekly I will go my way,
> And sing no more a courtly song
> For lords who scorn my lay.

[1] See p. 133 (Cordova).

In Würzburg there is no street called Judengasse; when the Jews were expelled in 1561 their quarter was appropriated for the present Julius Hospital, and a new settlement was not tolerated until 1798. Meanwhile, the neighbouring towns and villages, true to the German tradition of going their own way, welcomed, or at least admitted, the Jews. Höchberg, Veithöchstein, Allerstein, and Schweinfurth still possess the eighteenth-century synagogues built by the exiles from Würzburg.

More important is the synagogue of Heidingsfeld (six miles south of Würzburg). Although built as late as 1780, it keeps many of the old features rendered familiar in the etchings of Fürth. The women's annex, for example, is still a separate structure divided into an upper and lower gallery and pierced with heavily screened casements enabling the women-folk to hear but scarcely see the service. Several of the lamps date from the early eighteenth, and ark curtains and Torah mantles from the seventeenth, century. In the courtyard, the marriage stone bears the Hebrew initials for the words from Jeremiah (Jer. 7:34), "the voice of the bridegroom and the voice of the bride." The adjoining Talmud Torah (primary school) is a typical Main building of a century ago.

Rothenburg-on-the-Tauber, which gave its name to Rabbi Meir,[1] is, for all its antiquity, fairly stripped of Jewish relics. The reason is clear: January 8, 1520, the Jews departed from the city by invitation, and they were not readmitted until the nineteenth century. Some thirty mediæval tombstones have been gathered in the Lapidar museum, together with a Hebrew inscription commemorating the martyrs of 1295—"in the citadel outside the town," it reads in part, "they finished their work and killed and burnt our young and old." But one may still pace the Jüdengasse, literally, if not otherwise, in the footsteps of the great Rabbi Meir.

Modern bustling Offenbach—down the Main almost within

[1] See p. 283 (Worms).

sight of Frankfort—brings our survey to a curious close. We must, however, forget the bustle and modernity, and try to picture the town in its eighteenth-century quiet. The synagogue surviving from 1728, its neighbour the community house, built in 1770 and reached by a roofed-in overhead passage (Nos. 12-14 Grossemarktstrasse), the old courtyard and turreted staircase make it rather easy to turn back the clock. A list of pew-holders in 1706, the grandchildren of the first settlers during the Thirty Years War, enable us to people the simple prayer-house; it is with no familiarity that we call them by their given names, for they have left no others: Jacob the Elder, Leib the Physician, Meir the Tailor, Seckel the Teacher, Feibisch's son—what do they make of the great Sabbath candelabrum alive with human figures? The women's galleries, one above the other, must, for lack of names, remain untenanted.

And then, with the proper atmosphere, we will mount to the castle of the Count of Isenburg. A motley throng of Moravian and Polish Jews cool their heels in its yard, or if their purses are full, enter the reception-hall. The Baron of Offenbach is holding court. And who is he? None other than Jacob Frank, the last great champion of Sabbatai Zevi. Born, if you like, a Jew, but believing that the Messiah had come— not in the person of Jesus, but of Sabbatai; later a Christian but imprisoned thirteen years for obvious heresy; and all his life a persuasive scoundrel—or devout mystic. He died and was buried in Offenbach, 1791, and the city archives still possess his crown and seal.

To this had come the Judaism of Meir of Rothenburg and Eleazar of Worms, what with the aid of Chmielnicki massacres and inbred conservatism. For a different enlightenment—*Aufklärung,* the Berliners call it—we must turn to north Germany.

CHAPTER XVII

Prussia

and the North

FOR a thousand years after the Romans penetrated the Rhine, the vast northern plain which sweeps to the Polish border, and for that matter without a bump to the Ural Mountains, knew little or nothing of civilization. The great rivers which cut it in parallel lines, the Weser, Elbe, Oder, and Vistula, flowed past barbarian citadels and camps, less touched by culture than Siberian streams of today.

Then, beginning with the tenth century, walled towns gradually arose at the headwaters in the hills, from the Harz to the Carpathians, and ports sprang up where the rivers joined the sea, at Emden, Hamburg, Stettin, and Danzig. The plain, which offered little protection to town dwellers, remained open to wandering Germanic and Slavic tribes; to this day the majority of the population east of the Elbe is Slav.

Under these conditions, it is natural to look for the earliest Jewries along the coast or in the hills. The ports, however, closed their gates to the Jews until the late sixteenth century. The Hanseatic League brooked no tampering with their trade nor offence to their religious conscience.

As for the hill towns, they were moody beyond belief, and their Jewries can best be described as a succession of unsettlements.

⌒∧⌒

Hildesheim, rightly proud of its ancient houses painted motley like a German toy village, every beam smiling with sculpture, furnishes as good a reason as any why mediæval Jewish relics are rare in the north. Consider the record:

1347—Jews first mentioned—as paying taxes.

1349—the *Memorbücher* now mention Hildesheim as one of the "martyr cities." What this meant is apparent when we learn that in

1351—Jews settled in Hildesheim *again*.

1439—number of Jewish families are limited to twelve, not counting the *Sangmeister* and *Schulklopfer*.

1450—new Jews admitted to the city.

1457—all Jews, old and new, are banished.

1520—hopefuls are permitted to reënter city.

1542—banished again.

1585—readmitted to protection by the Elector of Cologne, whose physician, obviously a skilful one, was a Jew.

1595—driven out because Nathan Schay and Marcus married their dead wives' sisters.

1601—allowed to return.

1609—accused of causing a plague, thrown out, and readmitted.

1660—thrown out, with the exception of two families.

1662—returned in good standing.

1700—forty to sixty families allowed protection.

1842—paying for this protection finally comes to an end.

Although the Judenstrasse (off the Altstädter market) still possesses a few half-timber houses, we submit that for the conservation of antiquities there was too much moving.

Almost the earliest traces of the race will be seen in Erfurt, which lies between the headwaters of the Weser and the Elbe. A small thirteenth-century synagogue, long dismantled, stands in the rear of 22 Fischmarkt (near Rathaus). Sixteen Hebrew manuscripts are preserved in the library of the Evangelisches Ministerium, and over eighty tombstones, dating from the tenth to fifteenth centuries, in the city museum. No stones exist later than 1458, for in that year the Jews were driven from the city, not to return until the close of the eighteenth century.

Henricus of Erfurt has likewise left us certain rhymes, written in the years of the Black Death (1348-49) which further explain the absence of Jewish monuments.

> Die Pestilenz regierte geschwind,
> Nahm hier viel tausend Menschenkind.
> Die Erde ganz erhet zur Hand,
> Die Juden werden viel verbrannt.

> (The pestilence like fury broke,
> And took some thousands of our folk;
> The earth against us quite has turned,
> And so the Jews, they will be burned.)

Die Juden werden viel verbrannt runs like a *leit-motif* through their German experience. We catch a recent echo of it in the declaration of a Nazi leader in Cologne: "Should the French reoccupy German territory," Reichsdeputy Boerger is reported to have said in 1932, "we will kill all the Jews."

Nordhausen, on the southern slopes of the Harz, can tell us more of this experience. The building which housed the thirteenth-century synagogue (corner Hüterstrasse and Frauenbergerstiege) and its fourteenth-century successor (20 Jüdenstrasse) still stand; near the latter, the Tuvesche house, with a well in its cellar, sheltered the mediæval *mikveh*; and set in the walls of the so-called Judenturm (on the Rähmen) may be seen four tombstones—two are dated from the fifteenth century, and the others commemorate "Ephraim ben

Abraham and his three daughters," who died 1348, and "Solomon ben Isaac" who died 1349, victims no doubt of the plague. The remaining victims are commemorated in the famous record found in an old prayer-book of Worms. The Jews of Nordhausen, men and women, were led to a wooden platform, and fire was lighted beneath. As the flames crackled, the martyrs chanted and danced for joy. "I rejoice," sang Rabbi Jacob, their leader, "for now I shall enter the house of the Lord"; and the women and girls responded, "And our feet will stand in thy gates, O Jerusalem." When the fire broke through the platform and the smoke hid them from view, the rabbi was heard to sing, "Come, O house of Jacob, let us walk in the light of the Lord." All were consumed without a sound of alarm or pain. Rabbi Meir of Rothenburg, who knew whereof he spoke, remarks on this self-discipline. "Whenever a man," says Rabbi Meir, "resolves to die for the Holy Name, nothing can prevail against him; although no one can put his little finger to a lighted candle without a scream, no matter how hard he tries to control himself, we see that the martyrs to the Lord never utter a cry."

Hanover, the last city to detain us in the Weser basin, speaks of the dawn of brighter days. Except for an inscription in the vestry of the Marktkirche, commemorating an expulsion in 1350 on the charge of poisoning wells, all tokens of the mediæval Jewry have vanished; even the old Judengasse is now called Ballhofstrasse. But the cemetery repeats the history of the better times, following the Thirty Years War. Here is the tomb of the founder of the modern community, the good Joseph Hameln (d. 1677), whose praises his daughter-in-law Glückel never ceased to sing. And here beneath the oldest tomb (1654) lies Solomon Gans, who married Joseph's daughter, Yenta, and fought for years over his inheritance; but, as Glückel says, "twenty sheets of paper would not hold all that came of it." And here are the tombstones of Simon and Heimann Heine, ancestors of the poet.

South-west, in the hills of Hessia, a half-dozen towns and villages preserve the synagogues of this happier age, bright little temples telling something of Voltaire and Frederick the Great in their clean neo-classic lines.[1]

∽⋋⋌∾

The Middle Ages have left their mark in an old town on the Elbe. To the Christian, Wittenberg is unforgettable for the ninety-five theses nailed to the door of its church. For the Jew, the same church is memorable on another score. Outside, near the roof at the south-east angle of the choir, on the side, tactfully enough, away from the Jüdenstrasse, is the notorious fifteenth-century sculpture of the *Judensau*—a sow giving suck to a piglet and two young Jews. Behind the sow stands a rabbi holding up its tail and, as Luther of the ninety-five theses describes him, "looks into the—Talmud." Beneath are carved the rather meaningless words, "Rabini Shem Hamphorash" (in Hebrew, *Shem ha-Meforash* denotes the ineffable name of God). The piece of sculpture must have been ordered and given to the church, says Luther, "by a learned, worthy man who was an enemy to the eternal lies of the Jews." To this, in any case, had degenerated the noble figure of the Synagogue Defeated,[2] once Teutonic fury set itself to hewing stone.

The *Judensau* was repeated in wood-carvings and sculpture, on choir stalls and church pillars, throughout Germanic and Belgian towns; a few examples are noted in our Appendix C.

The free city of Hamburg, near the mouth of the Elbe, held no traffic with the Jews until, at the close of the sixteenth cen-

[1] See Appendix C.
[2] See p. 51 (Paris).

tury, Spanish-Portuguese Maranos brought themselves a be-grudged welcome by bringing a store of needed capital. They became subscribers to the first bank; they put out at low rates of interest the money of their brethren still in Portugal and anxious to ship their wealth out of that thankless homeland; they built up trade with Sweden, Poland, the Barbary States, and the Indies, and in a smaller way played the same part as the Sephardim of Amsterdam. As in Amsterdam, the German Jews followed on their heels, first slipping into the adjoining city of Altona (then under Danish rule) and eventually into Hamburg itself. Glückel of Hameln, born in Hamburg (1646), gives us in her memoirs a living picture of this early Jewry.

And the dead have left a gallery of pictures in the old cemetery of Altona (Königstrasse, near Blücherstrasse).

On the way we pass the Jewish Hospital (Israelitisches Krankenhaus-Thalstrasse) founded by Salomon Heine and turned to bitter account by his nephew Heinrich:

> Ein Hospital für arme kranke Juden . . .
> Behaftet mit den bösen drei Gebresten,
> Mit Armut, Korperschmerz und Judentume!
> Das schlimmste von den dreien ist das Letzte,
> Das tausendjahrige Familienübel,
> Die aus dem Niltal mitgeschleppte Plage . . .

> (A hospital for poor sick Jews
> Stricken with three woeful infirmities,
> Poverty, bodily ill, and Judaism;
> The worst of the three is the last,
> That thousands-of-years'-old hereditary disease
> Their ancestors dragged out of plague-stricken Egypt.)

"Not steam-baths, douches, medicines, nor all the surgeon's apparatus," concludes the poet, "will work a cure."

The Sephardim, at least, seem to have found artistic sur-cease in death. Their quarter of the cemetery, founded 1611, displays the exuberance of sculpture which met us at Ouder-

kerk.[1] Examining the bas-reliefs spread like a sculptured pave-
ment in every direction, we find the same baroque play on
names and dramatic Biblical episodes. Abraham ben Joseph
Fidanque (d. 1652) is commemorated by the sacrifice of
Isaac, with Abraham dressed like a Rembrandtian Turk;
Donna Rachel da Fonseca (d. 1692) appears as Rachel the
Shepherdess bringing her flocks to water; Daniel Hayim da
Fonseca (d. 1690) is naturally seen as Daniel in the lions'
den. Other themes are introduced by the stone of Gabriel
Daniel Lopez (d. 1727), where Death appears leading the
departed soul to Paradise while a hand is reaching him a
crown; by Rachel, daughter of Solomon Israel (d. 1711),
where wolves are besetting a lamb shielded by cherubs—an
obvious symbol for Israel; by Isaac Mahorro (d. 1730), who
we learn is a scholar from the figure of a man sunk deep in
his book, while at his side a phœnix bears the motto, "We
are born to die, and we die to live." Hour-glasses, family
crests, banners, scrolls, death-heads, flowers—sometimes
dropped tenderly by a hand overhead—shields of David, and
tree-trunks cut to the roots, repeat themselves among the
details.

The German Jews possess a ground adjoining the Sephardim. At the north end, the tomb of Jonathan Eybeschütz
(d. 1764), "master of all the children of the Exile," recalls a
controversy over the messianic pretensions of Sabbatai Zevi,
over amulets, and magic that raged in the Senate, Bourse,
synagogues, and even the graveyards of Hamburg, and resounded through the Jewries of Europe, without, more the
pity, coming to the ears of Voltaire. The house of Jonathan's
chief opponent, Jacob Emden, author of no less than forty
works, still stands at 155 Breitestrasse (Altona), with the Hebrew inscription on the gable, "When thou buildest a house

[1] See p. 199.

then shalt thou make a parapet for thy roof," etc. (Deut. 22:8).

The German Jews likewise possess an old graveyard in Ottensen (Bismarckstrasse—founded 1664) and in Hamburg itself (Grindelhof—founded 1711); in the latter may be found the monument to Gabriel Riesser (d. 1863), the champion of Jewish emancipation in Germany.

Farther down the Elbe, at Glückstadt, Portuguese and Germans share, for once, a common burial ground, preserving more than five hundred stones—Eve, daughter of Isaac Palache, resplendent with sculpture, lying by the side of plain unadorned Gütele Drobesch.

In Hamburg, the Kunst- und Gewerbemuseum (on Stein Tor Wall) contains a number of seventeenth- to eighteenth-century examples of Torah pointers and other ritual objects in metal; and the Jewish community maintains a collection (Museum für Jüd. Volkskunde) of embroideries, spice-boxes, crowns, shields, etc., and local prints and antiquities of absorbing interest.

Of the synagogues, the oldest lies in Altona; it dates from almost the founding of the German Jewish community, three hundred years ago, and although rebuilt after the fire of 1713, keeps much of its original character. In Hamburg proper, the oldest survivor is likewise the German synagogue, built 1788; its location in a courtyard (off Marcusstrasse) reminds us that the Jews of the free city did not regain their own freedom until 1848. A little north, on Poolstrasse, stands the Reform synagogue, offspring of one of the earliest Reform congregations (1818) and the first congregation in Israel, since the fall of Jerusalem, to call their place of worship a "temple."

When Heine visited this famous "temple" shortly after his baptism, he had the good fortune to hear Rabbi Salomon preach against converted Jews, and at that very Sabbath dinner his friend Cohn "heaped burning *kugel*" on his head.

He confesses, however, he would have remained a Jew "if there had been no law against stealing silver spoons." As it was, he felt himself a true Christian—"I begin to run around with the rich Jews."

Meanwhile, at the back door of the Hamburg Temple, on Bäckerbreitengang, lived one Moses Lump, familiarly known as Moses Lümpchen. Heine and his wit, the Herr Doktor Rabbiner Salomon and his elegant sermons, though within earshot of Moses Lümpchen, disturb neither his spirits nor appetite. After running about the whole week long, a pack on his back, to earn a few marks, he returns on Friday evening to his little one-room home on Bäckerbreitengang, finds the Sabbath candles lit and the table spread with a clean white cloth, seats himself with his homely wife and homelier daughter, eats with them fish cooked in a pleasant white garlic sauce, sings thereat the mighty songs of King David, rejoices at the departure of the Jews from Egypt, and rejoices as well that all of the villains who wronged them died in the end, that Pharaoh, Haman, Titus, and their like are dead, but that Moses Lümpchen is still alive, his wife and child by his side, eating fish with white garlic sauce—and if the candles were to sputter and there were no Gentile at hand to trim them, and were Rothschild the Great to enter the room with all his cashiers, clerks, agents, and brokers with which he conquered the world, and were he to say, "Moses Lump, tell me what you want—whatever you wish is yours," Moses Lump would quietly answer, "Trim me these candles," and Rothschild the Great would confess, "If I were not Rothschild, would that I were Moses Lümpchen."

But Moses Lump never existed on Bäckerbreitengang—he is Heine's own invention? Perhaps he never lived on Bäckerbreitengang—but he dwelt in every other Judengasse of Europe and in every year of Europe's history; if he had not, there would have been no synagogues, no bells and crowns,

no heroism on burning pyres, no Rashi, Rambam, and Rothschild, and no Heinrich Heine.

Hamburg, for all the unkind things he said of it, does well
to give Heine a monument (on Barkhof) and, together with
his publisher, Campe, a medallion (59 Schauenburgstrasse);
for despite the grandeur of its port, the power of its banks,
the thickness of its walls, and the beauty of its towers, only
a poet possesses a city.

<hr />

The most important event in the Jewish history of Berlin
happened seventy-five miles away, in Dessau. There, on the
site of No. 10 Askanischestrasse, was born Moses Mendelssohn, September 6, 1729. The synagogue which received his
swaddling-band stands a few doors below, at the corner of
Schulstrasse. A little farther south lies the old cemetery where
his father is buried. A Mendelssohn Institute is built where
Moses was born, a street bears his name, and his monument
rises before the railroad station. For the rest, Dessau was less
advanced than the philosopher could have wished—its Jews
were tolerated as *Schutz-Juden* (in need of special Letters of
Protection) until 1848; for years thereafter they were required, in legal matters, to use the blood-curdling oath *More
Judaico*; and they were restricted to the Judengasse until late
in the nineteenth century.

When young Mendelssohn entered the gate of Berlin
(1743), a poor dwarfed, emaciated Talmud *bochur*, he found
a Jewry much like any other, except that it was new and raw
—as was its mate in London. Not a century before, refugees
from Vienna had installed themselves on Jüdenstrasse and
Spandauerstrasse, built a handsome synagogue, and now at
the insistence of the great Frederick were branching out into
unwonted manufactures. Essentially, it was the old ghetto

life, stringent within—a risk to cut your beard or finger a German book; and subject to rebuff and contempt from without. Yet, within a few years, Mendelssohn's philosophic essays were read by all of cultivated Germany (as they have not been since), Frederick grew curious to meet "a young Jew who actually wrote in German," and the renaissance was launched. Before Mendelssohn died (1786), his translation of the Pentateuch into German had given the Jews, hitherto averse to that language, a key to secular literature; and the real ghetto gates—not the wooden contraptions that still hung on their iron hinges—were opened.

On Spandauerstrasse is the house where Mendelssohn *lebte* and *wirkte*. Near by stands the Nikolai Church, the oldest in Berlin, and its quiet garden where Lessing, who lived over the way, walked with Mendelssohn once they had finished their chess, and talked philosophy in the sun—as Jew and Gentile had not talked since Renaissance Italy and Moslem Spain.

However, around the corner, an elaborate eighteenth-century palace, just recovered from baroque and softened now into a certain beauty, reminds us that the credit for the revolution does not belong to philosophers alone. It is the Ephraimsche Haus (corner Poststrasse), built in 1761 by Veitel Ephraim, court jeweller and minter to Frederick the Great. It is easy to turn up one's nose at the sort of Jew who made his fortune (and Frederick's) by clipping coins for the Prussian state. But, as we have had occasion to remark, the tie between the courts—especially the intellectually alert court of Brandenburg—and the Judengassen established by these *Hof-Juden* made it possible for a Mendelssohn to gain the ear of both the Christian and the Jewish world. And as for clipping coins, it depends on who does the clipping. Today half the governments of Europe have clipped their coins. When the Reichsbank turned out its billion marks to the dollar, it was only clipping a little faster than the Banca d'Italia, the Banque de France, and the Polska Krajowa Kasapozyczkowa. The least of them would make poor Ephraim kick himself up and down his broad eighteenth-century stairs for a piker, a bungler, a respectable honest man.

At one end of the Spandauerstrasse is the Ephraimsche Haus; at the other end is the Bourse. In between, hidden from the street (Heidereutergasse) because when it was built in 1712 it was forbidden to face a public thoroughfare, is the old synagogue. Its tall narrow windows have a Gothic air, the women's galleries are banked in two tiers to the west; otherwise it shows the influence of the synagogues of Amsterdam.[1] The ark curtain was a gift of Frederick William I.

Next to the Sophienkirche lies the first Jewish burial-ground (26 Gross Hamburgerstrasse), with a bust of Mendelssohn by the entrance, and his grave (No. 751) near the south wall.

Not many years after he went to his rest, Rahel Varnhagen is writing her husband of a visit Heine paid her. "His shoes smelled of the shoemaker—when he left we shot open the windows." His pages, Frau Varnhagen, still smell of the printer's ink, but nothing, it is to be feared, can freshen again the air of your long-closed, almost forgotten *salons*.

Along the Dorotheenstrasse, and on the Schiffbauerdamm overlooking the Spree, there are still to be found a few dignified mansions of late eighteenth-century Berlin, German editions of Belgrave and Washington Square, recalling candlelight, Byronic romanticism, Platonic love, and Salonic wit, all irrevocably extinguished. There is something pathetic about good talk, like butterflies. And, if we are to credit the magic of names, what good talk these *salon* Jewesses evoked! William von Humboldt, the Schlegels, Schleiermacher, Jean Paul Richter, Fouqué, Schadow, Boerne, Heine—and if we go back to Father Mendelssohn's time, Mirabeau, Herder, Lessing,

[1] See p. 194.

Goethe. It was Henrietta Herz, Rahel Varnhagen, and in Vienna Fanny Itzig, who midwived modern German literature.

Meanwhile, mocking the *salon* Jewesses "who with great gold crosses at their throats press into Trinity Church to hear Schleiermacher preach," other Jews cultivated their own garden. A step from the old synagogue was the home of the banker David Friedländer (47 Neue Friedrichstrasse), a pupil of Mendelssohn. Here Heine lived for two years (1822-23) while he taught between *salons*, along with Leopold Zunz, in Friedländer's pet "Verein für Kultur und Wissenschaft der Juden"; among the students was Solomon Munk, to whom we paid respects in Paris.[1] Mendelssohn, Zunz, Munk, it is another "chain of tradition," one on which hangs the modern recreation of Jewish history and thought.

Relics and tags of these fertile days enrich the Gemeinde Museum (29 Oranienburgstrasse), one of the most fascinating Jewish collections in Europe. Its mantles, ark curtains, crowns, *rimonim,* spice-boxes, betrothal rings, illuminated scrolls of Esther and marriage contracts, are triumphs of craftsmanship. Among the curiosities are prints and portraits, souvenirs of Jacob Frank,[2] and by way of illustrating our remarks on Dessau, a seventeenth-century print of a Jew taking the oath *More Judaico.* The library, in the same building, contains over 450 manuscripts and 50,000 printed volumes. And not too far away, in Grenadierstrasse, lies the modern "ghetto," in its manner another antiquity where the spirit that created the beauties and treasures of the past lingers on.

The Kaiser Friedrich Museum offers gilt-glass from the Jewish catacombs of Rome, and a shattered sarcophagus showing a menorah between olive trees and the customary ritual symbols (Abteilung der Bildwerke Christlicher Epochen).[3]

[1] See p. 68.
[2] See p. 310.
[3] See p. 235 (Rome).

Here too may be seen a stone plaque from the Greek synagogue of Priene (fourth to fifth centuries c.e.); in the centre
a menorah, caught in its base two scrolls of the Law, to the
left an *etrog* and to the right a *shofar* and *lulab*. The collection of Moslem art (Islamische Kunst Abteilung) contains
the oldest known Spanish rug, fourteenth century, ordered
for a synagogue, as well as the famous Tier-Teppich—"animal rug"—of Persian make, which came from a synagogue in
Genoa. The Rembrandts (Room 61) include the "Portrait of
a Jew" (No. 828m), "Portrait of a Rabbi (828a), "Money
Changer" (828d), and his usual authentic types in "Jacob and
the Angels" (828), the "Capture of Samson" (812a), and
above all in "Samson Threatening His Father-in-law" (802)—
the old Philistine, leaping from bed in a red nightcap, comes
straight from the pages of *Glückel of Hameln*.

Next door, the Altes Museum contains in its glass collection (Glassammlung) a pitcher from Hellenistic Palestine
stamped with the earliest-known representation of the Temple gate, probably the Gate Beautiful and ultimately the pillars before Solomon's Temple—a *motif* which has come down
the ages in manuscript illuminations, synagogue arks, ark
curtains, frescoes, Hanuka candelabra, and tombstones. Although comparatively neglected today, it ranks with the
menorah and shield of David as a capital Jewish symbol.

The Neues Museum preserves in the Egyptian collection
(Rooms XI-XII) a relief from the tomb of Sheshonk III
(Shishak), showing Jewish or Israelite prisoners of the tenth
century b.c.; and likewise numerous papyri from the fifth-
century (b.c.) Jewish colony in Elephantine.[1] Here, too, will
be found a Greek inscription (No. 7733) telling you that
Queen Zenobia of Palmyra and her husband have granted
the right of asylum to a third-century (c.e.) synagogue in
Lower Egypt, and a Greek-Latin inscription confirming a

[1] See p. 219 (Oxford).

similar right given by King Ptolemy Euergetes in the second
or third century B.C. The famous Tell-el-Armana tablets, several of which come from the hand of Abd-Khiba, governor
of Jerusalem fourteen hundred years before Christ, are not as
yet on view.[1]

Dropping down the centuries, as only one can in following
the Jew, we find in the Royal Library (Königl. Bibliotek) the
copy of Soncino's Hebrew Bible (printed in Brescia 1494)[2]
which belonged to Luther. And something further of the
Italian scene in the sixteenth-century synagogal throne from
Siena (Schloss Museum).

◌━◌

The long arm of Silesia thrusts deep into Slavic lands.
Breslau is as far east of Prague as it is west of Cracow; and a
little above Breslau three rivers take their rise, leading to three
worlds—the German Oder, the Polish Vistula, and the March
which passes through Moravia to Danube lands. It is therefore easy to see why Jews were settled in Silesia from an early
date—by the twelfth century at the latest, when the province
was still a part of Poland.

Upon emerging from the railroad station in Breslau, the
first thing you will see of the city is a Jewish graveyard. And
you will learn an essential point in the history of the community when you are told that it was first opened upon the
readmittance of the Jews in the eighteenth century.

Their expulsion had been accompanied by drama. In 1453
St. Juan de Capistrano, come all the way from Spain, stood before a vast throng in the Salzring (now Blücherplatz) and
preached against the Jews in the prevalent Spanish manner,
accusing them of perfidy in general and in particular of dese-

---

[1] See p. 11 (Louvre).
[2] See p. 252 (Italy).

crating a Host and murdering a Christian child. And shortly
after, July 4, 1454 to be exact, forty-one Jews were burnt in
the same Salzring and a memorial cross set up in honour
of the event; you may see the cross in the Silesian Museum
(Schlesisches Museum für Kunstgewerbe und Altertümer).
And the surviving Jews were driven from the city.

The little graveyard opposite the railroad station contains
but a century of stones (1761-1850) and, such as it is, a century
of decorative symbols: now and again a broken rose-stem, a
fallen tree trunk, or a candle burnt in two. The tombstone of
Michael Schlessinger, merchant, who died in 1831, bears his
name in Hebrew and Roman letters, and thereby hangs a morsel of *Kulturgeschichte*. The Jewry of Breslau only permitted
the use of the scandalous Roman characters[1]—true print and
imprint of Capistrano and all his works—upon direct and
specific command of the Prussian king. Still—despite our modern romanticists of ghetto life—it was high time Abraham
Geiger came to Breslau.

Of the mediæval settlement, which occupied the present
Ursulinerstrasse, there remain twenty tombstones now gathered in the modern Lohestrasse cemetery, the earliest dated
1203 and commemorating the "sweet voice" of the cantor
David ben Sar Shalom, and a sweet name, too, "David son of
the Prince of Peace."

During the centuries of banishment, the Jews built up communities in the neighbouring Silesian towns.[2] Finally, under
many limitations, they reëntered the capital in 1710. A visit
to the old Pokoy Hof (off Antonienstrasse) will show you
who they were and whence they came. The Hof was one of
the four yards, all in the neighbourhood, where Jews, native
or from abroad, were allowed to lodge. Here they installed
inns, warehouses, markets, and synagogues—caravanserais in

[1] See p. 157 (for use of Latin).
[2] See Appendix C.

a Gentile desert. And here you will find the abandoned eight-eenth-century Landschul, a synagogue of the born Silesians. Here, too, was the Lithuanian-Volhynian synagogue founded by Polish merchants in 1744, but moved to the near-by Gol-dene Radegasse in the next century. In the latter Gasse stands the Sklowerschul, which takes its name from its founder, Rabbi Mordecai Sklov—likely a native of the Lithuanian town of Sklov—whose son presented in his memory the pres-ent ark curtain in 1780. Both this and the Landschul possess eighteenth-century candelabra, embroideries, and silver Torah ornaments.

The later edifices testify to the growth and freedom of the community; the Tempel synagogue founded in 1796 and pos-sessing seventeenth- and eighteenth-century works of ritual art; the Storch, more imposing still, built in 1829; and finally the famous Theological Seminary, a monument to the reform leader and philosopher, Abraham Geiger.

Breslau is well stocked with Jewish art. The Synagogen Gemeinde (community offices) and the Jüdisches Museum Verein (secretariat: 3 Striegauerstrasse) possess notable collec-tions of eighteenth-century embroideries, silver-work, can-delabra, and illuminated marriage contracts. In addition, the Verein preserves a variety of local documents dating from the fourteenth to the eighteenth century. The Silesian Museum offers two rarities: a fifteenth-century seal ring once pressed on the correspondence of a certain Abba ben Abba, and so-called "Korn" medals—seventeenth-century tokens struck off in protest against the high cost of living and bearing the cari-cature of a Jew with a sack of grain on his back. Aside from the German custom of blaming the Jew for everything from plagues to rainy weather, his appearance on the medals may be attributed to the fact that quantities of wheat were exported in the late seventeenth century and Jews were to be numbered among the grain-dealers.

The library of the seminary contains over 250 manuscripts, many of them illuminated, and about 25,000 printed volumes, including a number of incunabula. The Breslau library (Staats- und Universitätsbibliotek) likewise possesses illuminated Hebrew manuscripts.

To round out our museums, we must mention the collection at Danzig, with its 800 objects, including prints, scrolls, and books (synagogue, on Vorstädtischer Graben). Danzig had its Judengasse, where the name still survives, on the Speicher Island since at least the fifteenth century, thanks to the good will of its Polish sovereign, Casimir IV.

And then the dean of Jewish museums in Brunswick, founded by Alexander David (1687-1765), the father of snappers-up of unconsidered spice-boxes. The present community was established in 1707; David built the synagogue (rebuilt in the nineteenth century) and shortly before his death presented it with his collection of antiquities. It is significant of the times that, without waiting for Zunz's *Verein* for Jewish culture, David Oppenheimer was picking up Hebraica and Judaica in Prague—his library is now in the Bodleian at Oxford—and Alexander David was gathering candlesticks and Torah mantles for the pure delight of it. David's finds, with later additions, are now housed on the ground floor of the synagogue. The high spots are perhaps the two illuminated eighteenth-century prayer-books, unusually happy despite their late date, and a seventeenth-century illuminated scroll of Esther. The silver-embroidered ark curtain of the old synagogue has its story: David was court Jew to the Duke of Brunswick, and in the course of business made a loan on exceedingly low terms (5 per cent) to the Empress Christine in Vienna; the only reward he asked for his nominal rate of interest was a slash of silk from the throne-room of the Hofburg, which he promptly dedicated to his throne of worship at home, after taking the precaution to have it embroidered with his name and the date (1732).

Brunswick, in conclusion, may boast of the most curious synagogue in Europe—a synagogue inside a church. You may well wonder how it came to pass that a church was ever so hospitable as to shelter a synagogue or that a synagogue was ever tolerant enough to accept the hospitality. It so happens that an old Pauline convent church has been converted into the Vaterländisches Museum; and in 1925 there was installed in its nave one of the little timber synagogues we have found dotting the south German countryside.[1] The Brunswick example comes from Hornburg (near Halberstadt), where the last Jew died in 1923. It was built in 1766, a survival of baroque, and contains four ceiling paintings, representing the ark, tabernacle, menorah, and shewbread table—naïve but not without taste. The ark carved with fruits, flowers, crowns, and arabesques, the *bima* and its railings, the disordered baroque candelabra, all are reinstated in their place. Nothing lacks but the worshippers. A church turned into a museum, and synagogue into a museum piece—is this a warning, or is it already a symbol?

[1] See p. 306 (Bamberg).

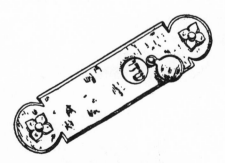

MEZZUZA, IN WROUGHT IRON
See page 80

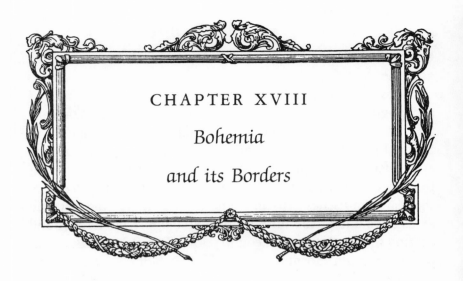

CHAPTER XVIII

Bohemia

and its Borders

"FAME-CROWNED" Prague, as the Jews called it, is a city of grandeur and beauty, if you keep away from anything built since 1800. The Hradčany, castle and cathedral set on a hill, furnishes the grandeur; and the baroque streets furnish the beauty, where every house dances with curlicues, and the scale is so small and the energy blends so happily with steep chimney-potted Gothic roofs that all one can think of are lanes of elaborate time-worn silverware.

Prague, too, is rich in Jewish monuments, stones cut by ancient hands, exfoliating legends and tales as bountiful as their fretted traceries, scroll-work, and volutes; and they, too, have their beauty.

The old Judenstadt, or Jews' Town—the Jewry was too extensive to go by the humble name of *Gasse*—which lay at the bend of the Moldau has largely been demolished; but one may gather the usual tale of a European Jewry; in the twelfth century a taste of Crusaders' swords not to be denied preliminary practice before engaging in the serious work of destroying Paynim; in the thirteenth century more Crusaders; in the fourteenth century a general imprisonment for the purpose of extorting gold, to say nothing of a general massacre in the Altneu synagogue; in the fifteenth century plunderings of the Judenstadt when the Hussites, whom the Jews befriended, were defeated; in the sixteenth century sporadic expulsions; in the seventeenth century devastation through fire; in the eighteenth century a total expulsion under the orders of Maria Theresa, who, we believe, always lived to regret she was not Isabella of Spain.

But a catalogue such as this—and it recurs perforce in our travels—falsifies the record. Jewish history is not a compendium of martyrdom, and Prague furnishes an excellent occasion to correct this common impression.

History finds the earliest reference to the Jews of Prague in 906—as victims of exaction, discrimination, or violence?—no, as traders in the local slave market, probably buying wares for export to Cordova.[1] In the Altneu synagogue a scarlet banner, embroidered with the shield of David, hangs over the *bima*; it was originally the gift of Charles IV (1357) in recognition of Jewish military valour. The prayer-shawl of Solomon Molcho is preserved in the Pincas synagogue, and there are Jewish families in Prague who can show you the ancestral swords worn by their Frankist forefathers when they planned to recapture Palestine by arms.

It is time we learned that Jews sometimes lived other than by usury. The inhabitants of the old Judenstadt, as we gather from their tombstones, were butchers, shoemakers, glovers, saddlers, tanners, dyers, threadmakers, upholsterers, satin-weavers, horse-dealers, wainwrights, wheelwrights, carters, porters, domestic servants, locksmiths, nailsmiths, hammer-smiths, blacksmiths, pewterers, glazers, potters, lamp-lighters, spicers, grocers, stone-cutters, engravers, lens-makers, salt-petre-burners, gunpowder-makers, barbers, apothecaries, physicians, midwives, scribes, printers, publishers, hatters, furriers, tailors, diamond-cutters, goldsmiths, silversmiths, sa-

[1] See p. 125.

loon-keepers, and musicians much in demand at Gentile festivities; and, if we are to believe their epitaphs, each one "plied
his trade with honesty and skill." And the Jewish fire department was the cynosure of the general eye.

We may learn all this and more in the famous Jewish
burial-ground (off 37 Josefovska Ulice), at the edge of the
old Judenstadt.

If there is any truth in the general belief that Jews like to
dwell in gregarious mass, the dead of Prague can consider
themselves happy. In not much more than an acre, twelve
thousand stones tread upon one another, and their number
falls far short of the sum total of the inhabitants. It is a ghetto
of the dead—literally so, for the space at their disposal was as
strictly limited by the public authorities as the little lanes
granted to the living. The congestion would be incredible if
it were not explained that the dead lie one beneath the other,
and the stones range themselves in ragged files, eight and ten
to the length of a burial-plot, like the forgotten dominoes of
a child out of the age of giants.

Despite the soft bending alders overhead and the quiet of
the neighbourhood, the effect is hardly one of peace. The
huddled stones stagger in torment; they are chipped, abraded,
and shattered in the noiseless struggle to maintain a footing;
and the dead seem trampled rather than buried—it is rush
hour all the way to eternity. Yet seen in another mood, when
the wind dies in the trees and the long grass is still, the stones
take ease and comfort in their friendly contact. The bosom of
Abraham is snug but warm. And the forefathers have com-
mingled their dust as intimately and selflessly as, alive, they
shared a common fate.

Abigdor Karo, Israel ben Salman Isaiah Horowitz, Judah
Goldschmied de Herz, Mordecai Zemach, Mordecai and
Frommet Meisel, David Gans, David Oppenheimer, Joseph
Solomon ben Elijah Delmedigo de Candia, Aaron Spira,

Hendel Bassevi von Treuenberg, Hayim ben Lissa, Judah ben Bezalel Löw: here lie their graves among the floundering and serried press of stones. Not a worthy of them lives, however dimly, in the highways or blind alleys of chronicled time by reason of martyrdom or pain; scarcely more than one is known to common fame, yet they and their kind are the stuff and fabric of Jewish history.

Karo (d. 1439), beloved elegist; Horowitz (d. 1572), a Levite of the Pincas family whose forefather founded and whose brother restored the present Pincas synagogue; Judah de Herz (d. 1625), the architect who rebuilt the Pincas and Meisel synagogues; Mordecai Zemach (d. 1591), printer and founder of the Gersonides press (none of us admits an ignorance of the Elzivirs, but who except a few eccentric librarians and scholars responds with the mildest twitch of recognition at the name of the Gersonides?); Mordecai Meisel (d. 1601), who established a synagogue still standing in his name, a poorhouse, *mikveh*, and public baths, who paved the streets of the Judenstadt and bestowed costly lamps on distant houses of worship in Poland and Jerusalem; and his wife Frommet, who, by the report of her epitaph, "made it her profession to decorate and furnish buildings devoted to sacred purposes" and who "never failed attendance at public worship, morning and evening, freely supported learned scholars and practised a gentle hospitality"; David Gans (d. 1613), chronologist, astronomer, mathematician, and geographer; Joseph Delmedigo of Candia (d. 1655), mathematician, metaphysician, theologian, philosopher, physician, and natural scientist, the pupil of Galileo, who disputed mathematics with Ali ben Rahmadan in Cairo, argued Cabbala with the mystics of Safed, corresponded learnedly with the Karaite Serach ben Nathan, practised medicine and clashed wits in the far erudite centres of Turkey, Russia, Poland, and Lithuania, wrote and studied in plague-stricken Hamburg, published in

Amsterdam under the wing of Manasseh ben Israel,[1] and in the seventy-five years of his life found, as he said, neither happiness nor home; Aaron Spira (d. 1679), ascetic, scholar, and cabbalist; David Oppenheimer (d. 1736), bibliophile and writer of stories, prayers, legal opinions, and cabbalistic rules, whose library is now a treasure of Oxford;[2] Hendel Bassevi von Treuenberg (d. 1628), "pious and kindly, generous not only to the poor of Prague but of all Bohemia, the open-handed patroness of scholars, schools, and synagogues"; Hayim ben Lissa (d. 1726), one of the three portrait-painters who have their tombs in Prague; and, finally, Rabbi Judah ben Bezalel Löw (d. 1609)—now encircled by the graves of his thirty-three disciples—who, quite apart from making the Golem, wrote a noble measure of philosophy, apologetics, sermons, moral essays, and Biblical and Talmudic commentary, who as mathematician and astronomer frequented the court of mad Rudolph II, together with Tycho Brahe and Kepler, and whom men delighted to call "the strong pillar upholding the house of Israel," "the pathfinder of the learned," "the wonder of his time," and "the glory of the Exile"—we add our pebble to the heap laid upon their tombs by generations of pilgrims.

⟨ᔑᐱᔓ⟩

The memory of Rabbi Judah Löw is clustered as thickly with legends as his grave with disciples. Everyone has heard of his Golem, which broke loose and nearly destroyed its creator and the whole ghetto as well, and which later served as a model for Frankenstein's monster; and the beadle of the Altneu synagogue will show you, up in the garret, the dust of its remains. Not so well known is the story concerning the

[1] See p. 198.
[2] See p. 219 (Bodleian).

children's hillock in the old cemetery, where, by the way, a special plot, the *Nefel Platz*, is set apart for still-born infants. A plague, so runs the tale, suddenly fell upon the children of the Judenstadt, carrying them off by the score. Undoubtedly the visitation was due to a sin committed by some one in the community, but what sin and which sinner no one could tell; and in despair the elders sought out the *Hoher* (tall) Rabbi Löw. He applied himself to prayer, and Elijah appeared to him in a dream and led him to the cemetery, and showed him that the graves of the newly-stricken children were empty—their little souls wandering disconsolately in the night. Next day Rabbi Löw summoned a disciple and bade him visit the graveyard at midnight, when the children left their graves, and snatch from one of them his winding-sheet. He did so and brought the sheet to Rabbi Löw. A few minutes later the child came begging for its garment. Before he would surrender it, the rabbi insisted that the child reveal the cause of the plague. It turned out that there were two evil-doers, Bella and Ella, who lived together in sin on a street called thereafter Belelesgasse. They were suitably punished, the plague ceased, and the souls of the children slept in peace.

However, one of the dead in this tranquil yard has never enjoyed his expected rest. He had been converted as a young man and served as a priest in St. Veit's Cathedral on the high hill. Upon his deathbed he asked to be returned to his own people, and he was buried next to the grave of a girl he had loved in his youth. But his soul has remained divided, and many a night he crosses the Moldau in a ghostly skiff, climbs the high hill, and plays penitential psalms on the great organ of St. Veit's.

The tomb of Rabbi Löw, built like a sarcophagus, marks a form common to Silesia, Bohemia, and Austria; and the rampant lion (Löw—lion) carved on its face fittingly introduces the varied symbolism of Prague's funerary reliefs. As we have

seen in Frankfort, the names and occupations of the dead
are represented in sculptural puns—a fiddle for a musician,
a pair of shears for a tailor, a hammer for a smith, and the
like. In addition to the insignia already remarked in Frankfort,[1] we find that a nondescript fish represents the name
Karp, Karpeles, Fisch, Fischl, or Fischeles; that the figure
of a woman means that a virgin sleeps in the grave beneath,
and if the figure holds a rose in its hand, the virgin was already betrothed. We might likewise note that the hands out-
spread in blessing, the token of a Cohen (priest), appear over
the family names of Katz (from *Kohen-zedek*—a righteous
priest), Cowan, Kuhn, and similar variations; and the ewer
for the Levite will mark the names not only of Levi and
Lewin, but Segal (from *Segen-leviah*—a vicar of Levitical
rank).

The earliest stone dates from 1389, although the cemetery
goes back to an unknown age. Sculpture first appears in the
sixteenth century, and in the next two hundred years reaches
a baroque florescence only to be surpassed in Galician Poland.

One might pause at the tomb of Maier Fischl (d. 1770),
not for the worn renaissance capitals, the delicately chiselled
wildflowers and graceful acanthus, but because there is drama
in it. In 1918, a mob of Czech patriots broke into the Altneu
synagogue and desecrated a Torah scroll by way of retaliation for an attack of German patriots on the Czechs in the
city of Eger, a hundred miles away. Then the problem arose
of where to bury the desecrated scroll. It was decided that
the most pious man buried in the cemetery during its six or
seven hundred years of existence should shelter the Torah
in his grave. In the old Jewish Town Hall and Burial Brotherhood, yellow records were searched and thumbed. And the
choice fell on Maier Fischl.

How, we may wonder, was piety measured. Who is more

[1] See p. 291 (Frankfort).

worthy to sleep everlastingly with the Torah, a wise man, a good man, a lover of one's soul, or a lover of one's people? What is a good man and what is wisdom? That none of the founders of synagogues and donors to the poor was chosen is to be understood; to build synagogues and give magnificently to the poor one must be rich, and no rich man, by any definition, can stand the test of piety. Joseph Delmedigo was obviously unfit; he had travelled much, and no traveller can remain pure. David Oppenheimer was a bibliophile, *ergo* a man of lust. Mordecai Zemach was a *publisher*. But what fleck stains Judah Löw, a touch of the politician or a spot of intellectual pride? And Abigdor Karo, beloved poet!

You might suppose that there was nothing in the records to learn of Maier Fischl, that to win the piety prize over six centuries of candidates he must have been a sheer nonentity, that indeed only such could never sin. However, this was not the case. Maier Fischl was chosen for the greatest honour in the power of the community simply because all his life he ran a school; in the world's eye no doubt an undistinguished occupation. But it carried on the "chain of tradition," and the choice of the Prague judges carries with it the secret of Jewish history.

❧❧

The Jewish Museum installed in the quarters of the Burial Brotherhood, next to the cemetery, harbours a rare display of old embroideries, illuminated scrolls of Esther, chased *kiddush* cups, filigree spice-boxes, candelabra, and wrought-iron railings from dismantled synagogues, silent bells and fallen crowns from the scrolls of the Law—unhappy *dibbukim*, things imprisoned between life and death, demanding either release into the grave, or back into the world where their beauty may be used again.

In the hallway may be seen a mediæval tombstone from Eger, one of the few survivors after the fourteenth-century destruction of the graveyard. Prints and photographs of the Prague Judenstadt, as it stood before its recent demolishment, hang on the walls. The most striking exhibit in the main room are the tooled brass columns which, together with a huge wrought-iron grill twisted and beaten into an intricate floral design, once flanked the *bima* of the now-vanished Zigainer synagogue; the so-called Swedes Hat worked into the design is the emblem of the Judenstadt, authorized by the emperor in reward for the valiant defence offered by the Jews against the Swedish invasion (1620). As we move eastward into Poland we shall find ever larger and more amazing stores of decorative ironwork, the manufacture of which is still a widespread Jewish craft—to be met with in North Africa and the United States of America.

Among the local curiosities are the eighteenth-century banner of the Jewish butchers' guild and its attendant emblem, a metal key three feet high, with the shield of David and the Swedes Hat projecting in filigree from its shank, and on top a lion grasping a meat-cleaver. It is a pity that modern trades and professions have left all the decorative joy of life to the barbers and pawnbrokers.

The offices of the Burial Brotherhood contain a quaint series of eighteenth-century paintings, depicting the various functions of the society, consoling the dying, tending the dead, etc. —excellent for a study of types and costumes.

❧❧❧

From without, the venerable Altneu synagogue (Rabínska Ulice) looks like a high-gabled Dutch dwelling, except that the windows are few, small, and barred. The main structure is surrounded on three sides by low plastered lean-to's—altogether, a building that would not attract a second glance unless one saw it on Fifth Avenue; and yet it is one of the few Jewish monuments in Europe to win that decoration beloved of caretakers, guards, and guides, a star in Baedeker.

Once within, you quickly discover why. You pass beneath the portal, with an exquisitely carved thirteenth-century grape vine, the symbol of Israel, springing from a mountain peak (Sinai?) in the drum overhead; you descend nine steps, and you find yourself plunged into the gloom of a distant century. Precisely which century is a nice question. The outbuildings date from the end of the fourteenth century on the south side, from the seventeenth century on the west—now a *beth hamidrash*; and end with the eighteenth century on the north, the last a women's annex. The central core, which is the synagogue proper, is early fourteenth century as it stands today, but how old it originally was defies conjecture.

Sunk beneath the level of the street, it is a cavern of prayer, with silver and brass lamps hanging from the ribs like stalactites. The *bima* rises between the two central columns and is surrounded by a high wrought-iron grill from which project a dozen more battered candelabra. The ark is reached by mounting five steps, flanked by curious lamps and huge candles set in Gothic stone holders; above the wooden columns of the ark rests a fourteenth-century stone pediment carved with five-petalled blossoms. Benches ranging around the walls and pressed close to the *bima*, their backs against the platform, recall in their shape the choir-stalls of a cathedral, and in their arrangement the old Jewish emphasis on the *bima* as the central feature of the synagogue.[1] Hebrew inscriptions are fading away on the grimy walls. And dimly, through mere holes in the north wall, can be seen a flicker of light from where the women sat apart and conducted their own prayers.

The walls remain unscrubbed, contrary to German custom,

[1] See p. 277 (Worms).

for two reasons: among their scratched *graffiti* appear, it is said, the name of God; and amid the grime may be seen, if you have willing eyes, the bloodstains of the martyrs who perished here on the terrible 18th of April, 1389. Abigdor Karo, beloved elegist, who described the horror of it has left us an heroic line, surpassing the understanding even more than do the passions which provoked the massacre: "So much torment," he writes, "has engulfed us—yet we have not forgotten the name of our God."

Legends, as well as grime, haunt these old walls. When the synagogue was projected, two rabbis from Tiberias visited the building committee and persuaded them to erect a house like the synagogue in Tiberias, which in turn was like the Temple of King Solomon; therefore its windows must be wider on the inside than the outside, for Solomon "made the windows broad within and narrow without" (I Kings 6:4); the vaulting must rest on two columns to recall Jachin and Boaz (I Kings 7:21); and the synagogue must stand below the surface of the ground that the officiant, when he prays, shall fulfil the words of the Psalmist, "Out of the depths have I cried" (Ps. 130:1). The two rabbis forgot to add, but the committee nevertheless saw to it, that the ribbing should divide the vaults into five parts, in order to avoid the appearance of a cross. Again, during the fire which ravaged the Judenstadt in 1558, two white doves hovered over the roof of the Altneu and protected it from the flames.

Finally, we are told how it came to be built. A poor man befriended a stray black cat, and as a reward found his wood-box filled with gold. Assured that it was a gift from God, he devoted it to erecting a synagogue, no other than the present Altneu. That is how it came to be built; and now we shall learn why. One day the cat reappeared, and the man sprang up to greet it. But it leaped into the Altneu synagogue and vanished down a large hole in the cellar. The man plunged

after it, the cat enticed him on and on, and at last he saw daylight ahead. When he emerged he found himself in a strange
city, and the people told him he was in Jerusalem. Whereupon
he died of joy.

Like every synagogue, the Altneu is built to cover a passage
to Zion.

Time was when this synagogue and the Jewish Town Hall
next door were the ganglia and fortress not only of the religious but the entire life of the Judenstadt. Although founded
at the end of the sixteenth century (by Mordecai Meisel), the
Town Hall was rebuilt after a fire in 1754, hence its Corinthian
façade and merry baroque tower. The clock dial set in the
mansard roof not only tells the hour with Hebrew numbers,
but the hands turn—for us—in the reverse direction; it is, we
suppose, fitting for the Jews that time runs backward. If we
wait long enough, the hour may strike when we shall see the
Jewish courts and senate once again at work jacking up the
fire department, settling the complicated divorce of Mordecai Zemach's daughter, dispatching Mordecai himself to
Rome in order to forfend a threatened expulsion, voting can-
non, redskins, maypole, triumphal-arch, and figures of Moses,
Aaron, and Gambrinus for the pageant in honour of Arch-
duke Leopold (1727), apportioning taxes, distributing sen-
tences of eight days' to four months' excommunication or
even a term behind the bars of the *katzel*—in short, adminis-
tering the affairs of the Judenstadt. Today, there is little to see
in the building but the old Hochschul synagogue; yet it
serves to remind us that similar Town Halls stood in the Jewries ranging from Frankfort to Avignon.[1]

The other surviving synagogues warrant a visit, if for noth-

[1] See p. 102.

ing more than their age and associations. The Pincas synagogue, which lies south of the cemetery, rivals the Altneu in years. It was probably founded by Rabbi Pincas Horowitz of Cracow in the beginning of the thirteenth century, and the ground plan still shows evidence of its mediæval origin. A descendant of the founder, Aaron Meshullam ben Isaiah Halevi Horowitz, ordered its restoration and enlargement, which was executed by Judah Goldschmied de Herz in 1535—a pious Jew, says Krautheimer, but a poor musician. Despite its nineteenth-century restorations, the two bulky tiers of women's galleries, the solemn round-arched windows, and the fragments of the old wrought-iron railing for the *bima* have their effect. Moreover, the synagogue preserves the relics of Solomon Molcho (d. 1532), the astonishing Marano who, inspired by David Reubeni, and by dint of prophesying a Tiber flood, almost persuaded the Pope to help restore Palestine to the Jews and quite persuaded himself that he was a precursor of the Messiah.[1] Here you will find his white linen caftan with its fancy silk border, and the red damask silk banner he bore when he visited Charles V at Regensburg—it is embroidered in yellow thread with the old acrostic battle-device of the Maccabees, "Who among the mighty is like unto God?" (The initial letters, in Hebrew, compose the word *Maccabee*.)

The adjoining Klaus synagogue, the largest of the old survivors, was founded by Rabbi Judah Löw himself at the close of the sixteenth century, rebuilt in 1694, and restored in the last century. Its barrel-vaulting, deeply splayed windows, and delicate floral stuccos on the ceiling all proclaim the Renaissance—Prague style. Little remains of the former splendour of the Meisel synagogue (entrance Joachimstrasse), as sung by David Gans. Mordecai Meisel, court Jew to Rudolph II, built it in 1591 after numerous and lengthy adventures; the *Hoher*

[1] See p. 260 (Mantua).

Rabbi Löw blessed him the day it was finished, and the good man was so modest that the saying survived, "Meisel had no seat in his own synagogue." It was rebuilt in 1691, and restored in 1894 on a smaller scale. The late Gothic windows and vaulting nevertheless speak for its age. Finally, the Wechsler synagogue (Josefska Ulice), founded by Rabbi Isaac Wechsler at the end of the sixteenth century, rebuilt after the fire of 1754, dulled and modernized since, looks nobler outside than within.

A third of the way across the famous Charles Bridge, which carries one over the Moldau to the Old Town, rises a gigantic crucifix bearing in huge gilded Hebrew letters the legend *Kadosh, kadosh, kadosh, Adonai Sabaoth*—"Holy, holy, holy, Lord of Hosts." The presence of the Hebrew sanctification is explained on a tablet at the base. In 1609 a Jew was accused of desecrating the crucifix, and the Jewish community was compelled to affix the Hebrew legend in letters of gold. The whole thing is a dismal jest, and one cannot blame the patron saint of Prague—as we see him a little farther along the bridge —for quietly submitting to be thrown into the river. The civilization of Europe, scratched anywhere in its monuments, is apt to reveal the savagery of its aboriginal tribes. Europeans are an unconscionably long time in leaving the caves of the Dordogne.

A hint of the *Hoher* Rabbi Löw lingers across the bridge on the Hradcany. Built in the walls of the castle moat are the huts of Rudolph's medicine-men. Rudolph II was an inquiring savage and gathered about him a band of alchemists. He built them a row of dwarf houses, abutting the great wall. Each cottage contains two rooms, a living-apartment and a furnace-room where the alchemist tried his art of turning lead into gold. We cannot say they were ever so used, but the back windows are admirably situated for bundling an inefficient alchemist into eternity. Defenestration was, as we know, a national sport in Prague. Anyway, it is easy to picture Rabbi Löw and Kepler walking down this lane, chatting at Rudolph's suggestion with the alchemist tribe. And of the two, Löw the sage and Kepler the savage, we should not be surprised if Löw listened more respectfully to the magic formulæ of the alchemists and scanned more attentively their astrological charts.

In conclusion, you may judge the height of the *Hoher* Rabbi Löw by looking at his mighty image in the Prague Rathaus. Whatever he may have been, he is now the only rabbi in the world to have a public statue raised in his honour.

⚘

Along the north-west frontier of Bohemia, numerous Jewish communities sprang into prominence during the seventeenth century, partly because the Jews were excluded from the larger cities, such as Brünn, Pilsen, Eger, etc., and partly because of the profits to be derived from a smuggling trade with Bavaria. More than a dozen rural synagogues are to be found in the neighbourhood of Marienbad, dating from the late eighteenth century, but showing earlier characteristics and wielding an effect on synagogal architecture across the German border. The trail from Prague to Tachau passed on to Schnaittach and Fürth, carrying ideas and blue-prints as well as smuggled merchandise. And some of the blue-prints came from farther east in Cracow and Lemberg.

The most accessible of these delightful little prayer-houses —which must likewise be conceived of as inns and trading-posts—lies in Kuttenplan, a few miles south-west of Marienbad. The present structure was built in 1756-59; partly, it should be said, at the expense of the local count, Sigismund von Haimhausen, for whom a prayer is said to this day. Here South German baroque—imported for the first time into the

Jewries of Bohemia and to be identified in most of the decorative details, meets the Polish renaissance—to be seen in the concentration of the vaulting over the *bima*, thereby emphasizing this reading-platform as the centre of the service, a characteristic of the Golden Rose synagogue in Lemberg.[1] (The *bima*, under the influence of the nineteenth-century Reform movement, has vanished.) The rabbi's house and a *beth ha-midrash* adjoin the synagogue; only the matzoth bakery and *mikveh* are lacking to make up the typical complex found repeatedly in these Bohemian villages. A list of further examples will be found in Appendix C.

Far to the east of Prague, Moravia saw the rise in the same seventeenth century of flourishing communities which linked Bohemia to Poland. Chief among them was Nikolsburg, near the March River,[2] a true "mother city" in Israel. The origins of its Jewry fade away in the Middle Ages. In the seventeenth century, the web of its great *yeshibah* (college) threw out threads to Fürth, Worms, and Metz in the west, Hamburg in the north, Pressburg and Vienna in the south, and Cracow, Lemberg, and even Vilna to the east. The web is shattered now, the Altschul synagogue, built in the seventeenth century, and the Neuschul before 1778, alone among the twelve older ones to survive, are neglected shells of their former glory; and the graveyard speaks eloquently but in vain of famous rabbis, no better remembered, we warrant, than Gerson Jokal, court jester to the prince of Nikolsburg—alas, poor Jokal!

[1] See p. 365.
[2] See p. 325.

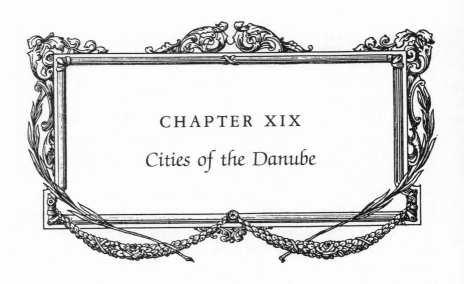

CHAPTER XIX

Cities of the Danube

JEWS are reputed to have trekked down the Danube Valley as early as the Romans; and in Vienna they have managed, with expulsive intervals, to outstay the very memory of the Eagles. If you will visit the Hoher Markt, a shaky rectangle in the heart of the city, given over to pushcarts and open markets, you may stare as long as you please without reminding yourself of Rome. Yet here was the *forum altum* of the colony of Vindobona, yonder Sina palace covers the site of the Roman prætorium, and here Marcus Aurelius died "much as if a prætor who has hired an actor dismisses him from the stage." (He may, however, have died at Mitrovitz, in Lower Pannonia, in which case the *Thought* we have taken the care to quote from him loses somewhat.) Ask anyone of the hucksters swarming the Markt after these things, and they will give you no word of them.

But step down any lane leading from the Markt to the river—the Judengasse, or even the Marc-Aureliusstrasse—and you are in the heart of Judea. And ask anyone in the market place, or where you will, concerning the Jews, and the words will come so hot, pro and con, you cannot doubt the Jews are a living entity in Vienna today.

A few doors west of the Hoher Markt lies the Judenplatz, where the earliest known Jewry built, in the thirteenth century, its synagogue at 7-8 Judenplatz, its slaughter-house across the way, its baths at 25 Wipplingerstrasse, its inn at 2 Stoss-im-Himmel, its public gardens in the Schulhof, its hospital at 9 Judenplatz; and where the city furnished stout gates, one at 3-5 Wipplinger, another at 20-21 Wipplinger, and a third at the top of Stoss-im-Himmel. But you need look up none of these addresses today, nor, for that matter, the home of Isaac of Vienna (Or Zarua).[1] The last of the old constructions, the hospital, came down fifty years ago.

The only memorial to remain is a tablet (2 Judenplatz) surmounted by a bas-relief representing Jesus baptized in the Jordan. The inscription on the tablet reads, in part: *Flumina Jordani terguntur labe malisque corpora: Cum cedit quod latet omne nefas. Sic flamma assurgens totam furibunda per urbem 1421, Hebraem purgat crimina saeva canum.* And the gist of it is—this beneath the figure of Jesus—that as the waters of the Jordan washes away sin, so fire has purged the city, in the year 1421, of its Jewish dogs.

It was not an accidental conflagration. Ninety-two men and one hundred and twenty women were carted in eighty-six wagons to the Prater and burnt alive. The ashes were hardly cold before the mob raked them over for bits of gold and jewels. *Schade um die Menschen,* said Strindberg, "it's a pity about the human race"—a phrase that might serve as the motto of history.

Another memorial of the mediæval Jews flames in the stained glass of St. Stephen's Cathedral—St. Stephen who in his day learned something about the human race; you may see the Jews in their pointed bonnets worshipping the serpent in the wilderness, although to take the curse from it you

[1] See p. 299 (Regensburg).

should remember that the serpent on a pole is in mediæval imagery symbolic and prophetic of the Messiah.

Thirty years after the holocaust, the Jews were back, this time across the Danube canal in the Leopoldstadt, where they remained in large numbers until the total expulsion of 1670. Thereafter they returned singly as "Tolerated Jews" by grace of individual letters of protection, with perhaps a few servants tucked under their wings. Two houses dating from before the banishment may still be seen (17 and 22 Tandlermarkt-gasse); the St. Leopold Church stands on the site of the chief synagogue. One of the boundary stones which marked the limits of this second ghetto, inscribed with a shield of David surmounted by a ball and cross and dated 1656, is preserved in the Historical Museum (Historisches Museum der Stadt Wien—Rathaus).

In the same museum you will find an etched portrait of a fascinating woman, born Vögelchen Itzig, banker's daughter, in Berlin 1757, and died Baroness Fanny von Arnstein in Vienna 1818. She was beautiful—"Madam," the old Emperor Joseph told her, "beauty is queen everywhere"—although her tricky Directoire curls and coquettish pearl ear-rings probably helped; but her eyes and mouth needed no help, and they tell you why she led the most brilliant *salon* in town, why during the Congress of Vienna, when Metternich was recarving Europe, the generals, diplomats, artists, princes, and poets, from the old Duke of Wellington to the young Franz Grillparzer, took their nights off drinking the champagne of her talk. And why poet Grillparzer, when he wrote his *Jüdin von Toledo*[1] was likely thinking of a Jewess of Vienna.

Needless to say, she did not live behind the boundary stones in the Leopoldstadt. The Jews of Vienna, from the late seventeenth to the early nineteenth century, were in fact divided into two classes: those who didn't—the rich and mighty; and

[1] See p. 149.

those who should have—the servants and petty traders under the protection of the rich, but who likewise didn't. The former numbered a handful—a Samuel Oppenheimer, Samson Wertheimer, the Arnsteins, a Baron d'Aguilar, imperial tobacconist who founded the Sephardic community and whose son we have met in London.[1] The latter numbered hardly more, and in the end they took up common residence behind the boundary stones of death.

The old cemetery (9 Seegasse), a confused mass of stones with here and there an attempt at the grandeur of a sarcophagus, brings together the settlers of the second Jewry and the magnificos of the return after 1670. The earliest tomb is dated 1450, the latest 1783. Set in the west wall are thirteenth- to fifteenth-century stones brought from near-by towns.

The decoration runs from a chaste renaissance to a lively baroque; but the symbolic representations of names and professions is rarer than in Prague. Once we leave the mediæval stones, the epitaphs grow in floridity like the cabbage leaves and volutes that surround them. The dead, we learn, crowned their heads with learning, led the community in justice and righteousness, and Judah Bacharach "was the first man to appear at synagogue every morning." The children were all that parents could wish for—little Gela Auerbach (d. 1620), "a rose of the valley, beautiful and carefree"; little Abraham Steinkopf, "a heap of nuts"; and young Samuel ben Israel Halevi ben Loeb Horowitz, although only a lad of six, "mastered the five books of Moses." The women are sped with gracious words: Sarah Gerson (d. 1639), "beautiful in figure, piety, and faith"; Libl Kaufmann, "a worthy woman like Hannah and Penina"; and Liba Beer Halevi, "lovely in her deeds like a tender rose." But all honour to Mordecai ben Zevi Mirls (d. 1654), who forbade any eulogy on his tomb.

Here, among the favoured who came to Vienna too late to

[1] See p. 223.

live behind the boundary stones, is Samuel Oppenheimer (d. 1713), the first Jew allowed residence after the expulsion, court banker to Leopold I, purveyor to His Majesty's armies on three battle fronts—with lions and scorpions on his family crest. And here is his nephew, Samson Wertheimer, who kept ten soldiers on guard before his palatial residence, who established a score of congregations in the Austrian Empire, who earned the sobriquet "Jewish Kaiser," and in whose epitaph are woven over three hundred and fifty quotations from the Bible and Talmud.

If you wish to pursue the tale, you will visit the second oldest cemetery (Währingerstrasse), used between 1783 and 1879, where lies the Baroness von Arnstein.

Relics of these Jewries, their inhabitants, and the art they fostered, are gathered in the five rooms of the Jewish Museum (28 Praterstrasse), not far from the Leopoldstadt ghetto and in the heart of its modern successor. The memorials range from mediæval tombstones to a completely furnished middle-class *stube* of the Biedermaier period. The embroideries, synagogal silverwork, illuminated scrolls, and ritual art of the home are as we have seen them in Frankfort, and sometimes worthy of Cluny.[1] Art is often an escape from life, but this Jewish art, if we view it aright, was a weapon in the fight for existence. The delicately graven pointer for reading the Law, tipped with a slender finger, was "their arm every morning," the embroideries were banners, and filigree *tassim* veritable shields bearing the date of battle.

It was not until 1811, despite the efforts of court bankers, tobacconists, and Jewish barons, that permission was granted to open a public synagogue. It was hastily thrown together and soon verged on collapse. Its successor, built in 1826, now the oldest in Vienna, stands on Seittenstettengasse, a step from the Hoher Markt where our story began. 1826—Beethoven

[1] See pp. 292, 70 (Frankfort, Cluny).

and Schubert were still alive, but more alive than either were the Holy Alliance and a post-war Europe which we have come to relive in 1926; no wonder the synagogue hid itself behind the mask of a nondescript business block, as it hid itself in London and Berlin a century before.[1]

This is gay Vienna, and when you stand by Herzl's grave (Döblinger cemetery), you will learn once more why, to understand a poet, you must seek the poet's land.

⟨⋋⋌⟩

Two great highways of Austria were in the Middle Ages strung with Jewish communities. One of them, the water route from Regensburg to Vienna—where, beginning with Passau on the German border, the Danube towns of Linz, Steyr, Enns, Ybbs, Spitz, Krems, Tulln, and Klosterneuburg all had their Jewries—has lost sign of these mediæval wayfarers. Indeed, little can be found in western Austria but a church inscription in the village of Rinn (near Hall and Innsbruck) recalling a ritual murder charge against the Jews in 1462; and farther west, almost by the shore of Lake Constance, a synagogue built in 1772 and a seventeenth-century cemetery in the town of Hohenems. No doubt due to an oversight, the Jewry of Hohenems enjoyed its own political government from 1849 to 1878. Finally, Lienz, in South Tyrol, shows a house (No. 164 of the main street) called "Samuel's," where it was charged that the Jews killed (1442) Ursula Böck, a child of four—for the usual imaginary ritual purpose. Only nine Jews lived there at the time, and none since. An inscription on Ursula's tomb, near the wall of the Johannes Church, keeps alive her memory and the pathetic nonsense of the charge.

The second highway followed the old Roman road from

[1] See pp. 222, 322.

Vienna to the southlands. Wiener-Neustadt, the first important town on the route, still preserves thirteenth- to fifteenth-
century tombstones (now gathered in the modern cemetery)
and a few fifteenth-century houses on the old Judengasse
(now Haggenmüllergasse). South-east of Wiener-Neustadt,
the village of Rechnitz offers an eighteenth-century synagogue with small landscape murals. Next comes Judenburg,
one of the oldest towns in Styria, settled, and from its name
possibly founded, by Jews in the tenth century. They were
expelled, as were all Styrian Jews, in 1469, but they left their
memorial on the city's coat-of-arms, which, besides an eagle,
bears the head of a Jew with pointed beard and tall bonnet, as
you may still see it in the town square. It is said that a Jew,
in his hurry to obey the decree of expulsion, managed to
strangle himself in a chain of the city gate, whence its name,
Judenthürl. Graz, farther south, preserves eight tombstones
of the fourteenth to fifteenth centuries, recovered from the
city walls and given asylum in the modern cemetery; the provincial museum (Landesmuseum) likewise contains a few
Sabbath lamps and silver shields and other ornaments for the
scrolls of the Law. Near by is a village called Judendorf.

Marburg—we are now in Jugoslavia, but mediæval history
and the ancient Roman road can hardly respect these recent
changes in the map—possesses several fifteenth-century tombstones in the city museum; and Laibach (now Lyubjana) an
old Hanuka lamp. Görz or Gorizia—for we are over the new
Italian frontier—brings us, with its seventeenth-century synagogue, almost in sight of the Adriatic, the end of the Roman-
Slovene-Teutonic-Italian-Jewish trail.

༄ᎪᎥᏗ

The water route from Vienna to Budapest takes us almost
immediately to Pressburg (Hungarian *Pozsony* and now

Czechslovakian *Bratislava*—a murrain on these new maps!).
Here or hereabouts the March River enters the Danube, opening the road to Moravia and by easy grades to the German
Oder and the Polish Vistula; and if you fail to take this road
to the north, you are barred by the Carpathians until you
reach the Pruth, a thousand miles east. Despite numerous
orders of expulsion, the Jews have clung to this gateway since
the twelfth century. Their Judengasse at the foot of the castle
(Schlossstrasse) preserves a seventeenth-century synagogue,
and the cemetery its ancient tombs. The Pressburgers or Bra-
tislavans or Pozsonyans are a conservative people; when the
new synagogue was built in 1892, the clergy raised objections
because of its proximity to the cathedral.

The land route brings us to Eisenstadt, the first town over
the Hungarian border. The Jewry, close to the Esterhazy
castle, occupied the crowded space between the castle square
(Schloss Platz), Klostergasse, Nonnengasse, and Hauptgasse.
The houses at the upper end of the Klostergasse (especially
No. 7, with picturesque courtyard) have lost little of their
antique character, with their Old World façades and their
vaulted ground floors, sunk like English basements, too far
underground for the health of the tenants and too near the
surface to be good for the wine. The synagogue occupied
rooms in No. 7 Klostergasse. Altogether you would hardly
suspect that in these few blocks existed a Jewry which maintained its own political administration, electing its own
mayor, up to twenty years ago, which reared in its time scholars and rabbis, and even one pseudo-Messiah. The cemetery,
with well over a thousand stones, runs the gamut of baroque,
from the first fillip to the final decadence.

Budapest, until within fifty years ago, comprised three
small cities—Ofen, Alt-Ofen, and Pest. Ofen (Buda), the old
Magyar stronghold, had as early as the twelfth century a
Jewry which clung to the southern base of the citadel; old

records show a Judengasse, a Jews' Gate, a Sabbath Gate, and a Sabbath Lane. The story that the Sigismund chapel, in the royal palace, was built on the site of the synagogue lacks proof but not plausibility.

The Turkish occupation (1541-1686) afforded the Jews an excellent lesson in putting faith in princes. Sultan Soliman, by way of releasing them from bondage, scattered them to the four quarters of his empire. And when in 1648 the Christians tried but failed to recapture the city, the Jews of Padua, a half-continent away, were stormed by a mob. The lesson was even neater. The Paduans, it seemed, attacked the Jewry by way of celebrating what they thought was a triumph of Christian arms in far-off Buda. Naturally, when Buda did fall, the scribe in the synagogue at Worms on the Rhine drew forth his pen and wrote in the old *Memor-Buch*, that sad calendar of Jewish events, the names of seventy-two more victims. Nor was the cemetery spared. Now, some centuries after the wrath is "overpast," an occasional tombstone comes to light in the most unlikely cellar wall, city bastion, or uprooted pavement.

In the eighteenth century a new settlement sprang up in Alt Ofen (Ó Buda), which lies near the old Roman medicinal springs; the Ludwigsgasse, down by the river, looks much the same as it did when the Countess Zichy gave the newcomers her protection. The rapid growth of the community may be judged by the "old" synagogue, built in 1821, a colonnaded Greco-Roman temple preserving more of the memory of Napoleon and the Madeleine than anything else.

The vast city of Pest, on the left bank of the Danube, easily the fairest city in Central Europe, was only a suburb in the days when Jews were not allowed to set foot in its streets. Even the mighty Samuel Oppenheimer, commissary for all the king's horses and men, must sleep nights across the river, in the humble little Ludwigsgasse. But towards the end of the eighteenth century the Jews were given quarters in three lanes of the Theresienstadt (Terezvaros), south of the present railroad station. Here you may visit a curious survival—the Orczy Mansion, which belonged to a baron of this name, and which the Jews took over as a warehouse, market, and synagogue—a vast hall with classic columns, balconies, and corridors, altogether a contrast to the caravanserai in Breslau.[1] The synagogue continues to function in one of the side rooms, and the grand *salon* of the baron is still heaped with bales and barrels.

Theodor Herzl was born, 1860, in the Tabakgasse (Dohány ut.), almost opposite the modern synagogue; he left the city, however, as a lad; no doubt, as it turned out, to the satisfaction of the present Budapest Jews—if there be any left, for the world has not heard of them these latter years.

Temesvar, while under Turkish rule, saw the growth of a Sephardic community (1552-1716), Jews from Constantinople, the Levant, and Portugal and Spain, who established a Jewry in the heart of the Old Town—a block bounded by the present Szerb, Varoshaz, Erzibet, and Jenö streets, a step from the modern synagogue. And they were happy enough until Prince Eugene freed the city. The modern synagogue, built in 1865, in that neo-Moorish style once so highly favoured by Reform temples and Turkish baths, is, together with its magnificent mate, the Sephardic synagogue of Vienna, the only one of the generation appropriate to the background of its builders. Stones dating from 1636 may be seen in the old cemetery.

Meanwhile, the thousand-mile ramparts of the Carpathians beckon, even while they forbid access, to another world.

[1] See p. 326.

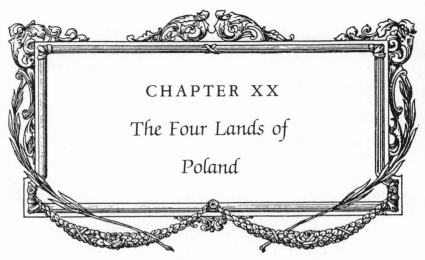

CHAPTER XX

The Four Lands of

Poland

JEWS have created an art of their own in Poland. Architecture, painting, sculpture, wood-carving, and hammered brass and copper take a form and character which, springing from the heart of the people, differs enough from the prevalent Christian mode to warrant, if ever, the title "Jewish art." Manuscript illumination, embroideries, and the smaller objects of ritual use which the Jews produced elsewhere are, after all, minor arts, and although their form is Jewish their temper usually is not. But in Poland the Jew seized, or was given, an occasion to express the soul of the race, its flame and force, in tangible beauty on a broad scale. This unwonted achievement is perhaps explicable by his compact mass—he lives in Poland as a folk occupying town and village in dense numbers; by the integrity of his life—for centuries he was under no temptation to yield to the flesh-pots of the Gentiles, who, unlike the Moslem in Spain or the Christian of Italy, were his cultural inferiors; and finally by the comparative tranquillity of his lot.

The common view of the Polish Jew is distorted by his present misfortunes. It is therefore salutary to recall that he was the last European Jew to leave his native soil. While English, French, Spanish, and German Jews were turned adrift, many of them, in fact, seeking refuge beyond the Vistula, the Polish

Jew remained in Poland, because for spiritual freedom and material welfare there was, bad as it might be, no place like home.

His misfortunes, too, are subject to the distortion of being contemporary. Yet seldom, not even recently, were they as dire as the suffering of other European Jews. The Crusaders, except for a late cut through Cracow, found Poland out of their route. The Black Death brought no such horrors as it did in Germany. Compulsory ghettos were few. The first extensive persecutions began only with the dawn of modern culture in Poland; and the Poles remained innocent barbarians long enough. Up to the World War the greatest calamities to overtake the Polish Jew—the Cossack massacres under Chmielnicki in 1648 and the Swedish invasions of the next decade—fell almost as heavily on his Christian neighbour. Today he is experiencing a mere taste of mediæval life as it was understood in the great cultural centres of Europe; and we find it abominable because we have forgotten what the Middle Ages meant for Israel.

Comparatively speaking—and it is a grim comparison that overlooks neither the exactions and humiliations inflicted incessantly on the Polish Jews nor the cruelty of which the Pole is master—Poland was a tolerable home from their first dim settlement to the decline of the kingdom in the late seventeenth century.

They probably drifted into the Polish plains from southern Russia, where they were established in the Crimea before the Christian Era, along the lower Volga (Khazaria) in the eighth century, and in Kiev by the ninth century. The first Jewish documents throw a light on their position—series of coins from the twelfth century and perhaps earlier. That Jews were mint masters means little in itself; so they were in Merovingian France[1] without suffering the less for it. But these

[1] See p. 92 (Chalon-sur-Saône).

coins of Poland are inscribed in Hebrew and bear such telltale mottoes as "Rejoice, Abraham, Isaac, and Jacob"; a land in which the native currency was Hebrew must have given the Jews a status in which they could rejoice.

But the bulk of Polish Jewry came from the west. In the twelfth and thirteenth centuries the kings of Poland took advantage of the mistreatment of the Jews in Germany, and invited them to fill a place in Polish society as traders and money-lenders. They built up a middle class, and spread even into the crafts. For long years the Poles themselves remained divided into a small group of landowners, nobility, and rulers on top, and a mass of peasants on the bottom. In between were the Jews. Every castle had its Jewish factor—superintendent and financial agent; and every village its Jewish trader, innkeeper, and often craftsmen.

The art born of these circumstances, which endured until the end of the eighteenth century, will be found in every town and hamlet of the land.[1] An adequate description of it surpasses the limits of a chapter, regrettable above all for its general neglect. The traveller in Poland likely to have an eye for it is usually an American Jew returning to visit his family, or an agent overseeing relief for the poor. If he were aware of it, he could discover treasures, literally untold, of more interest, we fancy, than relatives or poverty.

But he must hurry—poverty and oppression are rapidly leading to the disintegration and loss of all that is precious in this art.

❦

The railroad station of Cracow is a typical vestibule to Poland. It swarms with all the breeds of eastern Europe. Polish

---

[1] See Appendix C for a partial list of towns and villages where this art may be found.

students with white caps and thin noses; tall brown-bearded peasants from the High Carpathians wearing sugar-loaf fleeced hats, sheep hides trimmed with fleece, thonged belts hung with pistols and short knives—untamed, good-natured, lousy creatures; Russian gentry in sort of Prince Albert over-coats, surmounted by black beards which are in turn sur-mounted by black Astrakhan wool caps; officers in French uniforms; Polish peasants booted slickly up the thighs; Cra-cow merchants in misfit hand-me-downs; young beggars clad in flour-bags; officers' wives painting their lips and peasant wives nursing their children; and Jews—what Jews!

Red Jews, black Jews, yellow Jews (Chagall with his "Green Jew" is no doubt an unimaginative copyist); Jews of every di-mension vertical and horizontal; Jews in every and no degree of health and prosperity; they seem to sit on all the chairs, buy all the tickets, drink all the tea, and sleep on all the benches. Unlike the Gentiles about them, their diversity and interest lie not in their costume, but their character, in the planes and shadows of their faces, in their speaking eyes, in their cunning, sorrow, wisdom, patience, fire, and impeni-tent despair. Their gesticulations are the Book of Job, and their immobility the rock which brought Moses to his sin-ful grave.

Rembrandt would have done better in Cracow than bland Amsterdam.

It is this exuberance of personality, to be met wherever you enter Poland, and in no way diminished by contact with the mad Poles and the Carpathian winds, which marks the art of the Jews; subdued in the mediæval monuments, but blazing in his later works.

The Jewry of Cracow, built up in the fourteenth century, occupies the suburb of Kazimierz, south of the vanished city walls. Its synagogues, at least, are worthy of the ancient capital, the seat of Poland's earliest culture—largely of German and Italian importation—and the fairest of her cities.

In architecture the Polish Jews began where the German Jews left off. Significant of their plight, the latter practically ceased to build synagogues between the fourteenth and eighteenth centuries. The fourteenth century Alte synagogue of Cracow (foot of Ulice Josefska), like the old synagogue of far-off Chelm, carries on the tradition of central columns as we have seen it developed in Worms, Regensburg, and Prague, but with a sweep which makes it the largest mediæval synagogue in central Europe. It is built partly beneath the ground, as the Altneu in Prague. The original Gothic vaulting has been modified by sixteenth century restorations, which likewise account for the round-arched windows, the fortress-like exterior and its cornice-arcade. The *bima* introduces us to a superb example of Jewish craftsmanship: a vast wrought-iron sixteenth-century canopy which rises in an octagonal dome over the reader's platform. The worn almsbox, with some pretence at beauty, is dated 1407, probably the earliest art object we shall find in the East. Only the ark, a late baroque creation, while not out of keeping with Polish-Jewish temperament, grates upon the mellow dignity of the whole.

The second-oldest synagogue, called the Neue or Remuh, was built in 1553, either by Moses Isserles (known as Rema) or by his father. A transition structure, it is more interesting for its name than its character. Moses ben Israel Isserles (1520-72) is one of the men who cannot be slighted in the merest sketch of Polish Jewry. He and his contemporary, Solomon Luria (Maharshal) of Lublin, moulded the thought and soul of Jewry in the sixteenth century, as the Gaon of Vilna and the Baal Shemtob were to mould it anew two hundred years later. Unlike Luria the strict Talmudist, Isserles carried on the tradition of Maimonides—in Polish fashion, that is to say, he tried to reconcile Maimonides with Cabbala.

Still, he cultivated philosophy, reading "the wisdom of the uncircumcised Aristotle" even on the Sabbath, though, to be sure, only in Hebrew, occupied himself with astronomy and history, set himself against the growing extravagances of Talmudic dialectics, established with a masterful hand the religious customs of the people, and earned the title of a father of learning in Poland; a glance at his date will tell how late this learning developed. He was no less prominent in the early deliberations of the Council of the Four Lands, which became the governing body of Jewry in Great Poland (Posen), Little Poland, where we now find ourselves, Polish or Red Russia (Galicia and Podolia), and Volhynia, where we will shortly be.

Isserles' synagogue contains a Torah written by his own hand; but more to our delight a hammered copper vessel, on which are beaten the figures of Moses and Isaac. Hammered copper and brass, which we first met in the Palestinian collection of the Louvre,[1] and which can be bought in all the Jewish bazaars of the Near East and North Africa, is, like glass-making, an ancient craft of the race. In Poland it escapes the monotony of pure design and goes far on the way toward sculptured bas-reliefs; seventeenth- and eighteenth-century copper plaques used as mural ornaments may be found in the synagogues of Sandomir and Stepan.

The Isaac (Isaac Jacobowicz or plain Eizig Jekel) synagogue, built 1640, probably by the Italian architect Oliviero, brings us to the late Renaissance; four lofty barrel-vaults, a women's gallery screened by a stone arcade and balustrade, the whole as if poured in molten rock at one splash. The central columns, which are still to play a unique rôle in the synagogue, have vanished; but the *bima*—as in the Alte—remains domed by a magnificent wrought-iron canopy. And nothing in Jewish ironwork surpasses the grill and triumphal arch

[1] See p. 41.

which guards the approach to the ark, itself set above a flight
of steps. The Eternal Lamp (*Nir Tamid*) which in most
synagogues burns suspended before the ark, is here found in
a niche in the east wall, a peculiarity frequently encountered
in Poland. Finally, we meet in the Isaac synagogue the beginnings of mural painting—landscapes depicting Jerusalem,
Hebron, and Machpelah.

Landscapes have yielded to Biblical episodes in the murals
of the Wysoka (High) synagogue, built 1663, where Noah
floats on his ark, Moses receives the tablets of the Law, and
the exiles hang their harps by the waters of Babylon—unashamed human figures in a Jewish house of worship! Painting, judged by its many fragmentary survivals, was
widespread in the seventeenth- and eighteenth-century Poland; and if in need of explanation, must be laid to the irre-
pressible spirit of its people—they sit on all the chairs, they
talk with God and the angels as no Jews have dared since
Biblical days, and why should they not paint pictures? As in
Cracow, murals appear in sophisticated form, not to be distinguished from contemporary Christian work, on the walls
of the stone synagogues in Lemberg, Orla, Wyszogrod, and
Husiatyn. But in the little wooden synagogues of the same
period, lost in obscure villages, this decorative art takes, as we
shall find, a decidedly original turn.

The doors of the ark in the Wysoka synagogue are carved
with the familiar *lulab*, *etrog*, *shofar*, and by way of a new
symbol, the eagle. Wood-carving, like painting and metal-
work, grew to be a popular Jewish craft, reaching florid
heights in the arks at Zabludow and Selwa, where scrollwork,
foliage, birds, and beasts rise in a tangle from floor to ceiling.
More restrained but no less original are the so-called "music"
panels, late eighteenth-century carvings to be found in
Kempen, Kurnik, and other west-Polish towns, where drums,
trumpets, fifes, violins, and every conceivable instrument

sound a noiseless note on the doors of the ark. Three of these wood-carvers have left their names—Ber ben Israel, who executed the work at Jewart; Samuel Goldbaum at Kempen; and Samuel Goldmanaz at Zabludow.

Like the Alte synagogue, the exterior of the Wysoka is flanked by heavy buttresses, again hinting at a fortress; as we move eastward we shall trace these hints to their source.

The remaining synagogues of Cracow, the Kuppah, built 1647, and the Popper, built 1798, need not detain us. Of the numerous Chassidic study-halls and prayer-rooms lost in a maze of courts and alleys, where Jewish mysticism still beats its wings, the *stüblach* of Rabbi Nathan Shapiro, a seventeenth-century "saint" (*chassid*), is most worthy of note. His grave in the sixteenth-century Remuh cemetery, east of the Jewish quarter, shares the honours, when it comes to pebbles, candles, and written pleas, with Moses Isserles himself. An older cemetery, with partly excavated stones, lies off the Ulice Szeroka.

In the suburb of Lobzow we catch echo of a legend dear to the Four Lands. Here stand vague ruins of the castle of Casimir the Great (d. 1370) who, as every Polish Jew knows, fell captive to the charms of the fair Jewess Esterka, and sported with her in his Lubzow palace. Like the great Esther, she saved her people from untold perils and, outdoing Shushan's queen, founded three synagogues—one of which you may visit in Sandomir and another in Szydlow, both, it must be confessed, old enough to merit the distinction.

It is no legend that before Freedom shrieked and Kosciusko fell he visited the Alte synagogue (1794) and exhorted the Jews to join the battle for Polish liberty. You will note a street in Cracow and in Lemberg, both named Berka in memory of Baruch ben Joseph (Berek Joselowicz) who in answer to the appeal raised a Jewish regiment of light cavalry, killed almost to a man before the gates of Warsaw.

ᢒᢣᢣᡒ

The Jews were in Lemberg long before the Poles. In the early thirteenth century they were keeping shop along with the Ruthenians, Armenians, Tartars, and a mysterious people called "Saracens" who were Karaite Jews emigrated from Asia Minor and tinged with Chazar and Byzantine blood on the way. The Jews continued to do most of the shopkeeping even after the advent of the Poles, for in the sixteenth century they numbered 3200 out of a total of 3700 merchants.

The first persecution took place in 1592. If you recall the historical notes scattered through these pages, you will realize that this was a record. A century after the Spanish expulsion before a single Lemberg Jew is done to death! For light on this anomaly, you might observe that 1592 or thereabouts dates the earliest efforts of the Jesuits to civilize the Poles.

On the Ulice Blacharska, behind the Town Hall, stands the famous "Golden Rose" synagogue, a memorial of the coming of the Jesuits, and more than that, a monument to the stiff necks of the Jews. We have seen that the old synagogues of Prague and Cracow were built a bit underground, and we were given a legendary explanation in Prague, and we might assume a natural one for Cracow, that is, the gradual rise of the street level through the centuries. But neither holds for the Golden Rose, likewise dug into the earth. It is too recent a structure (founded by Isaac Nachmanowicz, 1582) to be clouded with legend or submerged by the accumulated dust of a city. When it was built, the Jews were forbidden to construct a building higher than the neighbouring cathedral. They were not content with the indifferent height of the latter, and determined to surpass it; they concluded that if they were forbidden to build up, nothing could stop them from building down. And down they built, sinking a quarter of the synagogue in the ground.

Whereupon the church authorities, with the aid of Jesuit talent, found a flaw in the title, confiscated the synagogue, and held it for a number of years (1606-11). Then—and now enters legend—Golden Rose, the daughter-in-law of the founder, pleaded in person before the archbishop, and like another Esther won her suit through her loveliness. The simile is not ours; the Lemberg Jews are well aware of it and celebrate their golden heroine in a special hymn on the Feast of Esther. The archbishop, too, deserves some honour for his sensitivity.

In any case, the synagogue was worth the struggle: a spacious Renaissance structure, the work of an Italian architect, Paolo Romano, and now seasoned by generations of devout prayer. The intersecting barrel-vaults, almost Gothic in effect, form a canopy over the *bima*, which is surrounded with an elaborate wrought-iron grill studded with rampant lions. The ark, freshly gilded and restored, together with the chandeliers, have all the dignity of the best Renaissance. On the east wall is a painted *mizrach*, and notable among the decorations are hammered metal reflectors for the wall lamps, one of them bearing a human figure in relief. The ritual treasures include a brass platter in which are worked a nude Adam and Eve standing before the Tree of Knowledge. As in Cracow, the Eternal Lamp burns in an unaccustomed place, this time in the vestibule, protected by a wooden shrine. To the right of the vestibule is an abandoned prison reminiscent of the day when Jewry policed its own affairs. As in all these synagogues, numerous side rooms serve for schools, vestry, and study-halls.

A few of the seventeenth-century mansions of the Jews likewise remain in this old quarter of the city. Solomon Frydmana (34 Ul. Boimov), Samuel Wieniowieckiego (32 Ul.

Boimov), and Simchy Menahem (19 Ul. Blacharska) would still find their armorial crests over the front doors.

Architecturally, the most important monument of Lemberg—and of Polish Jewry—is the Vorstädtische synagogue (31 Ul. Boznicza), built 1632 in the western suburb, then—and still—the centre of the Jewry. The Renaissance brought to Poland, where building committees and architects had the means to think about it, a logical repugnance to the awkward mediæval two-aisle hall, in which *bima* and ark are hidden from each other by the intervening central columns. The Italian and the Dutch Jews handled the problem by banishing the columns, but thereby robbing the *bima* of its emphasis. In the Vorstädtische synagogue, as early an example as is known, four piers were substituted for the annoying central supports. Rising from the corners of the *bima*, they join the flat girders overhead, and thus permit a free view of the ark while still emphasizing the reading-platform between their feet.

This device led to the one original contribution of the European Jew to architecture. If on your way from Cracow to Lemberg you take the pains to stop over at Rzeszow, you will find, first in the Alte and then in the Neue synagogue, the new arrangement of piers carried to an ultimate and magnificent conclusion. In the Alte (early seventeenth century), the four round piers have been completely merged into the stone *bima* below, and again in the vaulting overhead. However, the ceiling remains broken into a series of vaults like low domes; and the four columns could apparently be removed without damage to the self-sufficiency of the *bima* or ceiling. It is the Neue synagogue (late seventeenth century) which completes the invention. Here the four square piers rise into a stone canopy over the *bima* and merge into one central support for the ceiling by sending out four ribs which sweep to the four corners of the room. As a result, the hall is a single unit—the *bima* a rising jet and the walls descending sheets of stone. It is at once expressive of the Jewish cult in the days when communal prayer and the reading of the Law—rather than choir music and sermons—dominated the service, and unlike anything to be seen in mosque or church. Happy examples of this invention will be found in Przeworsk (near Rzeszow), Lancut, Lublin, and Luck.

Another novel feature of the Vorstädtische—we are again in Lemberg—is the stone choir built against the west wall and reached by a flight of stone steps pressed close to the wall. Here, too, at the right of the (west) doorway, will be found the Eternal Lamp enclosed in a stone shrine behind carved wood panels. The blind arcade running beneath the windows is common to many of the fortified synagogues such as we will meet in Zolkiew. A few traces remain of mural painting, for the most part destroyed in the pogrom of 1919, which devastated the quarter, not even sparing Berka Street, although one might have supposed that the name of Berek Joselowicz would have meant something to Polish patriots.

Many of the smaller synagogues deserve a visit for their treasures of ritual art, notably the Städische, with its eighteenth-century silver Torah crown in which are chased Jacob and the ladder of angels—in composition and feeling a world away from the conventional art of the silversmith. It is from this expressive metal-work, as well as from the wood-carvings of rural synagogues and the tombstone paintings of village cemeteries, that Chagall and his fellows drew their inspiration for modernist Jewish art.

The sculpture in the Lemberg cemetery, as in most others of Poland, would only lose by description. The art which we have been stalking eastward from Amsterdam reaches its culmination in the stones of Galicia. Its renaissance forms—columns, arches, and floral grotesques—are built up like architecture. Its baroque goes far beyond the vision of even a

Dresden or Prague master; Byzantine, Oriental, perhaps Armenian and Assyrian blood is mingled with the stones—it is well to recall the "Saracen" Jews who began their wanderings in Upper Mesopotamia and ended in East Galicia; and the camera fails as woefully as the pen in rendering the consequences. As well describe or photograph a Persian tapestry.

Tarnopol, Zolkiew, Brody, and mere villages such as Janow and Kamionka Strumilowa rival or surpass Lemberg. In contrast with Holland or Bohemia, the contemporary Christian art offers no model or clue; Polish tombstones are usually bare.

In Lemberg, the earliest stones date from the fourteenth century; decoration appears in the late sixteenth, and the finest work was done in the eighteenth century when western Europe lay under the pall of neo-classicism. The graves of the Karaites—"Saracens"—whom we suspect responsible for the textile and Assyrian *motifs*, although their own tombs are sober enough, lie close to the cemetery wall. Golden Rose (d. 1637) naturally bears away the palm for pebbles, pilgrims, and candles; regardless of legend, her epitaph is no doubt right in calling her "a valiant woman whom kings have looked upon and princes honoured."

꙰

The vicinity of Lemberg must not be neglected. In Zolkiew (twenty miles north), besides tombs of arabesque and baffling imagery, you will meet a typical example of the fortified synagogue. It needs, perhaps, a word of explanation. Many of the larger synagogues of eastern Galicia and along the frontiers of Podolia and Volhynia were built after the Cossack revolt of 1648, partly at the expense of the Polish overlords, to serve as a material as well as a spiritual refuge. Like early Romanesque churches in the south of France or St.-Michel in the north, they were both a house of prayer and a tower of strength. Based outwardly on the prevailing style of Polish town halls, they offer no originality as architecture, but decidedly a novel touch in the history of the synagogue. Crenellations for sharpshooters along the roof, massive buttresses calculated to stun a cannon-ball, and walls thick enough to discourage a siege again witness the protective interest of the Poles—now rather forgotten—in their Jewish subjects. German and Spanish Jews could have put to frequent use the synagogues of Zolkiew, Buczacz, Rzeszow, Husiatyn, Tarnopol, Luboml, Luck, Dubno, Kamenetz-Podolsk, and Zaragorod. The blind arcade above the cornice is characteristic of the exterior, and within are generally to be found another blind arcade, four central columns rising into the vaulting (of course quite foreign to the town halls), a great stone *bima*, and often traces of mural painting.

Chodorow (forty miles south-east of Lemberg) once hardly more than a village, brings to us the rarest that Polish Jewry offers—her timber synagogues. The Poles, like the East Prussians and Scandinavians, are masters of wood construction; they have fairly exhausted the delights of carpentry. And in every village the Jews hammered and sawed side by side with the Poles, building out of their own needs an original form. The rural synagogue is not an imitation of the neighbouring church. Both play the high fantastic, but each in a different key. The Jew required a structure that would house, besides the room for worship, a study-hall (*beth ha-midrash*), school, community office, and separate quarters for the women, and that in obedience to Talmudic law would tower above the Jewish settlement. Consequently, he turned to the manor house—as we found the mediæval Jew turning to a secular hall[1]—rather than the church as a starting-point. Out of its main hall and two ells he developed surely the most novel

[1] See p. 277 (Worms).

synagogue in his long history. Two of these humble but imaginative builders are known by name, Solomon Weiss of Luck and Hillel Benjamin of Lask, the latter responsible for the synagogues of Kurnik and Lutomiersk.

The typical form, as we see it in Chodorow, is a long hall, which is the synagogue proper. Two pavilions—there are often four—rise at the corners and provide for the community office, school, and study-hall. Often, as again in Chodorow, sheds are built against the side walls for additional accommodations. The two forward pavilions are usually united by a long low vestibule; a balcony or loggia (as in Chodorow) surmounts the vestibule, giving separate access to the women's gallery—sometimes the loggia is enclosed and serves itself as the women's annex. Finally, to attain the proper dominance, roof is added upon roof, each with its own broad eaves separated by bands of decorative inlay, three (again Chodorow), four, and even five successively over-topping roofs, the pavilions with their own multiple roofing, until the whole becomes a dazzling interplay of lines, planes, and shadows, a conglomerate of pagodas well worth a journey to Poland.

Chodorow, too, has preserved its mural painting. As we have remarked, the art arose among the Jews in the seventeenth century and spread to the smallest hamlet. Although the name of a painter has occasionally survived, the character of the work, to say nothing of its remote location, shows that it sprang from simple folk-artists intent on giving form to the naïve dreams of a Jewish village. Birds, beasts, fish, flowers, trees, vines, everything that lives, is painted in praise of the Lord. The subjects are much as we have found them in south Germany,[1] but wrought with less formalism and greater spirit. It is not for a moment great art; it is peasant art, in itself a rare note for the Jew—as though somewhere the brush

[1] See p. 306 (Bamberg).

had released the hidden long-forgotten soul of the Judean shepherds.

Symbolism, as in primitive Christian art—and this Jewish art mocks at the eighteenth century in its primitive fire—runs the gamut of the faith. A mountain peak planted with two trees is Sinai yielding the written and oral Law; hounds or foxes pursuing a hare is of course a fable for Israel; a pelican denotes love, a cock watchfulness, a parrot purity, a hawk alert senses, a rabbit domestic virtues, a zebra swiftness. Favourite among the symbols are the leopard, eagle, hart, and lion, recalling—may we repeat—the words of Judah ben Tema, "Be strong as a leopard, light as an eagle, fleet as a hart, and bold as a lion to do the will of Thy Father who is in heaven" (*Sayings of the Fathers,* V, 23). The zodiac recurs frequently —an old acquaintance which appears in the mosaic of a Palestinian synagogue of the first century, and which harks far beyond to the ancient Babylonian cult of the stars.

Painted synagogues will likewise be found in Zabludow, Kamionka-Strumilowa, Gwodzidz, and in Mohilev on the Dnieper (Russia). One of the best known, at Jablonow on the Pruth, has succumbed to fire.

The bond between this art and the mysticism rampant in the eighteenth century is more easily felt than proved. However, no traveller who reaches Chodorow will fail to proceed to Sadagora (over the Rumanian border) where the great wonder-working rabbis held their court; and no one who arrives at Sadagora will falter at going to Miedzyboz (over the Russian border) where stand the little *beth ha-midrash* and tomb of the Baal Shemtob (Israel ben Eliezer—c. 1700-1760), founder of modern Chassidism and last of the great Jewish "saints." And while on this tour of Jewish heterodoxies, there are of course the Karaites—who have never accepted the Talmud—with their ancient synagogues in Halicz and Tarnopol.

᠁

Lublin, perhaps more than any other Polish city, takes us back to the heart of old Jewry—houses, synagogues, caftans, earlocks, markets, beggars, and saints. To reach the Jewish quarter, which surrounds a castle-crowned hill beyond the Old Town, we must pass the Juden Tor (Jews' Gate, end of Ul. Grodska), and passing beneath this portal of the past, we discover that the old Hebrew clocks[1] work magic, that the past still ticks on. Except for the black caftans and brown fur turbans—a fourteenth-century Christian costume kept by the Jews out of pious romanticism—and sundry changes in the pronunciation of Yiddish, we might declare ourselves in any Jewry east of the Vosges mountains in any century from the thirteenth onward. This was Worms, Regensburg, and Prague.

The Krawiecka Street, first to our right, takes us as far as the eighteenth century, as typical a collection of Jewish houses as we will find in all Poland. Podzmancze, the next street, which abuts the castle hill, carries us to the sixteenth century with its Saul Wahl synagogue—a dull building but illuminated by the name of the Jewish king of Poland, king for a night in legend and court banker to Sigismund III in fact.[2] The Szeroka (Broad) Street, Broadway, in fact, of the ghetto, is crowded with memories and relics: the house (No. 19) where the Council of the Four Lands held its last *Judentag* in Lublin 1682; the family home (No. 28) of Horowitz "The Seer of Lublin," who loomed greater in the eyes of Polish Jewry than his contemporary, Napoleon; and then a nest of synagogues. But for the latter we will go beyond the castle hill to the little square facing Jateczna Street; here is the spacious

[1] See p. 341 (Prague).
[2] See p. 264.

Maharshal synagogue, built in the seventeenth century, with four columns and stone *bima* as in Rzeszow, boasting handsome candelabra and a brass platter wrought with a nude Adam and Eve, and named for the master Solomon Luria (Maharshal—1510-73), who together with Moses Isserles of Cracow shaped the thought of Polish Jewry; the Maharam synagogue next door, named for Rabbi Meir Lublin and magnificent in its grillwork; and then, at No. 8 Jateczna (Butcher) Street the kosher slaughter-house; and, finally, the old *beth ha-midrash* (No. 6), which guards on its shelves the treasures of the sixteenth- and seventeenth-century Hebrew presses of Lublin. The smaller synagogues tell us, even unvisited, somewhat of life in Lublin or any other Polish Jewry: the Kotlerschul belonging to the coppersmiths guild, the Mschorsimschul for the business clerks, the Parnasschul founded by a distinguished *parnas*, the Läuferschul (really the Saul Wahl) dedicated to the carters and porters, the Schneiderschul to the tailors, and the Klaus where the Seer of Lublin meditated away his days.

Proceeding the length of Jateczna Street, crossing a little bridge, and mounting a low hill, we reach the last abode of Lublin's *parnassim*, seers, and coppersmiths. The stones—the oldest is 1541—speak with the customary heraldic insignia and puns. There is nothing, however, but legend to speak of the neighbouring Franciscan cloister which sought for centuries to seize the cemetery, and its monks who were wont to clang their bells as noisily as they could when an interment took place, until finally the burial of a *zaddik* (saint) put an end to their nonsense; the *zaddik* rose from his coffin and uttered a prayer, whereat cloister, bells, monks, and all sank into the bowels of the earth.

Vilna, the Jerusalem of Poland, still pulsates. Traditional learning is receiving a new birth and garb in the work of the modern Yiddish Institute on history, literature, and thought. The spirit of Elijah the Gaon, though he might wince at its fruits, is not dead; and the old synagogues are more than shells for the fingering and delight of tourists.

Baedeker is irresistible on Vilna. "At the corner of the Theatre Square begins the Nemetska—or German—Street, which is inhabited exclusively by Jews and where may be found the Lutheran church." That is all. Yet in what other corner of the world can Baedeker or anyone else find a single courtyard housing twelve synagogues—these twelve out of a hundred and ten more in the city, to say nothing of minor prayer-rooms and Chassidic meeting-halls admittedly beyond the power of any guide-book.

Even we have only space for two: the Alte, probably built in the sixteenth century, with four central columns, heavy, almost Gothic, vaulting, and a *bima* girt with a wrought-iron grill; and the Great synagogue (in the Schulhof with eleven others), built about 1630, with a towering baroque *bima* set between four mighty columns. The façade of the latter may be noted for its double arcade set high in the gable. The point of this effort at outward beauty, common to many sixteenth- and seventeenth-century Polish synagogues, lies in its contrast with the smuggled air and cautious retirement of urban synagogues in other lands—save Holland—for over a hundred years thereafter. Venice, Berlin, or Vienna would not have dared an arcade.

The old burial-ground, by the River Wilja, gathers all the strands of decorative art from the ornate to the naïve, from baroque stones to the carved and brightly painted wooden slabs, of which more hereafter. Here is the tomb of Elijah the Gaon (Elijah ben Solomon, d. 1797), the glory of Polish Jewry. As the Baal Shemtob may be counted the last of the saints, the Gaon is the last of the undisputed masters of the rabbinic line which, as we saw, took its rise in Mayence nearly a thousand years before. The tomb of the Gaon is the final milestone in the road that begins with the shattered slab of Gershom, Light of the Exile.[1]

❦

Although Warsaw streams with life—above all on the throbbing mad Nalewki; and although for the past it has a notable museum (Bersohn Museum of Jewish Antiquities), lovers of beauty will seek, once again, the cemetery. For the Jewries of northern and eastern Poland have created a funerary art which in its sincerity and penetrating mysticism makes the fantasies of Galicia pale into decorative playthings, and shows the baroque of Altona and Amsterdam to be little more than pompous theatre. The stones of Warsaw—and the stones and wooden slabs of towns and villages of three-quarters of the land, to which Warsaw may serve as an introduction—hold no traffic with pagan cherubs, rhetorical skulls and hour-glasses, and seventeenth-century Bible characters in buskins and togas.

The early nineteenth century still echoes the prevailing Gentile style. Yet native Jewish imagery is seen in a view of the waters of Babylon, where the domed city rises behind a broken-masted ship; the ship is a purely Hebrew pun (*aniyah* meaning both *ship* and *lamentation*). Rebecca still comes to the well, but, in traditional repugnance to portraying the human form, only her hand is visible.

By the middle of the century all bonds are broken with contemporary European art. Probably the painted wooden slabs in the rural graveyards had never known the commonly accepted art forms; as they survive today they date from the

[1] See p. 286.

turn of the twentieth century, when, except for a few eccentric Frenchmen surely unheard of in Pruzany, European painting was at its worst; and their perishable material—village paint blistering on planks in deeply wooded cemeteries—accounts for the loss of earlier records.

The images now are drawn from the wells of Jewish mysticism, and their execution is free, naïve, and what modern jargon likes to call "expressionist." It is the work of sincere, untrammelled craftsmen, possessed more with their inward vision than the outer show of things. Chagall makes a confession when he paints the old graveyard at Vitebsk.

The familiar emblems for family names are dramatized: a stag (Zevi) is no longer a heraldic dummy, it has become a living animal pierced to the heart with an arrow. Other names are portrayed by delicate allusion—Miriam by cymbals, and Rebecca by sheep. A tree cut to the roots is no longer, as in Amsterdam, a copybook stump; it is now a fruit tree with its ripe burden falling to the ground. Homely contemporary objects are thrust unashamed into symbolic posture: a lamp (Gorodiczcze, 1898) is not a classic vessel raked from the dust-bin of convention, but such as the artist knew and used it, a common kerosene table-lamp; a headdress (used in Bialystok, 1913, for punning on a Russian surname meaning *hat*) is no Oriental cafiyeh, mediæval snood, Renaissance cap, or classic coif—it is a plain, serviceable derby.

And the bird, which we last saw on the gilt-glass and in the catacombs of Rome,[1] takes wing again in mystic and tender flight. For the living it supplants the human figure, and it clothes the soul of the dead. It cannot be presumed that the artisans of the Warsaw ghetto or the stonecutters and sign-painters of remote villages pilgrimaged to the Jewish

[1] See p. 234.

catacombs of Italy. They undoubtedly took the symbol from current mystic tradition; the Zohar tells that "the souls of the dead swing on the tree-tops and sing praise to God." But the Zohar, itself of venerable origin, may well have plucked from antiquity the Jewish-pagan symbol of the bird.

Two hands are blessing candles, and a bird swoops down and extinguishes the flame (Warsaw, 1866)—it is woman who has died on a Sabbath eve. A bird takes flight from the branch of a tree—it is Sarah Bratzlaw (Warsaw, 1881) abandoning the Tree of Life. This play of bird and tree appears in varied guise: the leaves of the branch often represent the number of children who survive; a branch without foliage means a life without offspring; in one poignant stroke (Warsaw, 1881) the bird is clinging to a blossom from a broken bough, while the bough falls with its berries—a youth has died, having enjoyed only the first bloom of life, its fruit beyond his reach. A branch bears six blossoms, the seventh falling, and a bird hovers by its side (Pruzany, 1905) —it is a woman who died in her seventh childbirth. Again (Warsaw, 1826), sheep wander disconsolate without a shepherd, their number that of the surviving children; a bird spreads its wings overhead—it is the departed mother still protecting her flock.

Most exquisite of all (Gorodiczcze, 1906), a table is set with bread and candlestick, awaiting the Friday-evening blessing of the housewife; at one side stands an empty chair, and on the other a bird holding a prayer-book; there are five sockets in the candlestick, only two of which are lit with candles—Sarah Treina, mother of five children, of whom two survive, has left a vacant chair, but her spirit still graces the blessing which ushers in the Sabbath.

As these carved stones and painted slabs tell the beloved place of the woman in the home, so they tell of the honour of the man: a bookcase (Warsaw) rises laden with tomes, next

to it a study table, and on the floor a crown; the table is bare
and the honour of the man, his crown of learning, is fallen.

The crown of sacred learning and the candle for a blessing
—these were, and in some lands still are, the guerdon of
Jewish men and women.

LUBLIN. MAHARSHAL SYNAGOGUE. DETAIL OF BIMA
RISING INTO CEILING
See page 373

CHAPTER XXI

The Balkans to the Sea

THE Jewries of Rumania are largely offshoots of Poland
—down the valley of the Seret into Bukowina, and down
the Pruth from Podolia into Moldavia.

In Bukowina, the cemeteries of Cernauti (Czernowitz)
and Sereth resemble Tarnopol and other Galician creations.
In Moldavia, the one notable monument is the old synagogue
of Jasi (Jassy)—a station on the historic highway from Poland
to Turkey. Built in the late seventeenth century and restored
in 1764, it affords the same play of painting, carving, and
metal-work that we found farther up the Pruth. Arches,
spandrels, and vaulting are covered by floral designs interspersed with lions, bears, and beasts unknown to zoölogy;
the *bima* is encircled by a wrought-iron grill; and the only
novel feature is a low-arched vestibule not unlike the narthex
of a church. Fifteenth-century stones survive in the Jasi
cemetery.

While the Jews of Rumania have done well by Rumanian
literature, their own cultural life, dominated by Chassidism,
has lain under the shadow of Polish Jewry; or, if you prefer
to listen to the Rumanian Jews, it is the other way around.
In any case, the country makes poor picking for antiquities.

In the South Balkan states we rejoin the Sephardim, who, except for brief intervals, vanished from sight after we left Italy.

When Ferdinand drove the Jews from Spain (1492), Bajazet, sultan of Turkey, is reported to have said, "What wise king is this who makes his own land poor and ours rich?" Welcomed by the sultan, Spanish and, later, Portuguese exiles enriched his land with commerce, the printing-press, and cannon-foundries, and settled in every nook of the rapidly expanding empire. The sixteenth century found Constantinople with the largest Jewry in Europe, its prestige and learning at their height, and for a sign, Joseph Nasi, Duke of Naxos, the brains of the Turkish court. But the enrichment of a land with Jews cannot save it, or them, from the price of misrule. The empire of the Turks was based on an unmitigated despoilment of its subject peoples. Within little more than a century the Jews were reduced to the level of the Balkans—as "backward" in the Jewish scale as a Bulgar or Croat in the common measure of Europe. Joseph Nasi, diplomat and duke, was succeeded in the popular eye by Sabbatai Zevi, charlatan or madman, who convinced half the Christian and most of the Jewish world that he was nothing less than the Messiah. A gross mysticism beset the people, meaning thereby a practical mysticism concerned with winning favours from the angels and the dead, and dispelling the contrarieties of fate by incantation. The Spanish Jew had risen like a luminous rocket in the Turkish Empire—and the stick is falling yet.

Sarajevo, known for a pistol-shot and a beautiful Haggadah, may serve as a model and type of these Spanish islets tossed in a Slavic-Turkish sea, for it has been largely spared from fire, the curse and sign of Turkish flimsiness and indolence.

The bazaar, in full Oriental cry and smell, makes mock of geography; one can hardly believe that Bosnia lies as far west as Silesia. However, the *souks* of coppersmiths and filigree-workers tell us that the Jews are at hand.

The Jewry lies a few steps to the north-west (between Ferhadija and Cemalusa Streets, beyond Predimaretom). The Turks call it the *Dshiffutané* (from Turkish *Dshiffut*, slang for Jew, and *han-hané*, quarter); the Jews call it the *Cortijo* in their Spanish speech and the *Chazar* (courtyard) in Hebrew; and the Croat-Serbs call it the *Velika avlija* (large court)—so, altogether, you should have no trouble in locating it.

You will find the older houses rickety wood-and-plaster nests set on vaulted stone basements protruding half above the ground; the nests may burn up as they please and leave the sturdy roots intact. Spanish, as we have hinted, is still spoken in these little courts and lanes, with the phrases and accents of a fifteenth-century Jewry in Toledo or Seville. Time, of course, has added a little more Hebrew to it, and worn off the grammatic edges.

The oldest synagogue, lost from view in a courtyard, was built in 1581, burned 1794, rebuilt 1821, and restored in the present century; its galaxy of hanging lamps is reminiscent of Spain and a foretaste of North Africa. If you can discover a Jew in his traditional costume, or beg the sight of one, you will have his history before your eyes. The striped silk under-garment with broad embroidered waistband is Moorish; the loose caftan is Oriental anywhere from Bagdad to ancient Cordova; the bodice for the women-folk is Slavonic; and their soft little fez, like Trim's Montero cap, only with a veil hanging behind and a coin or bit of embroidery over the brow, is Tunisian or more than we know. At least it is easy to see that the race trafficked in the great days between Barcelona and the East.

The prize of this traffic, and the pride of the city, is the late thirteenth-century illuminated Haggadah (in National Museum), which came from Catalonia *via* Italy. It is the most famous if not the fairest of its kind. However, unlike other examples—notably those of Nuremberg and Darmstadt[1]—Christian influence is obvious in the miniatures, and only the marginal decoration runs purely in the Hebrew tradition.

The strange cemetery on the hill to the south (Debelo Brdo) tells of the progressive inroad of the Orient. The earlier stones (seventeenth century), as in Spain, are more like boulders inscribed on a single trimmed surface than formal tombs. The later ones are half-cylinders of rubble and plaster, much as we can see them in Palestine or Morocco; but, unlike Morocco, a slab inserted in the front of the cylinder bears the epitaph. The five huge stones in the southernmost row mark the graves of the first *parnassim* of the community; the oldest dated stone is that of Samuel Baruch "the Righteous" of Salonica, died 1650. It is regrettable that nothing tells us of Nehemiah Hiyya ben Moses Hayyun, born this same year in Sarajevo, who turned Jewish heads with his wizardry and cabbala from Amsterdam to Jerusalem.

༺⋗ᐱᐱ⋖༻

The modern synagogue of Belgrade stands on the Jewrejska, site of the old Jewry, between the citadel and the river. Although Jews were likely here, as in all Danubian cities, long before the Turkish conquest, the present community dates from the privileges granted it through Joseph Nasi (sixteenth century).

Once in Belgrade, we may take two routes to the sea—through Bulgaria to Constantinople, and behind the Sephardic screen, to the ancient world; or down the Vardar Valley to

[1] See pp. 301, 431.

Salonica and the isles of Greece, another ancient Jewish playground.

Along the first route, Nikopol, a small town on the Danube, preserves the house where Joseph Caro (1488-1575) was brought as a boy by his father, fleeing from Spain or Portugal. Here he learned to set the table, Talmudically speaking, and trained himself for the authorship of the *Shulchan Aruch* (Prepared Table), the last great codification of Jewish law. Sofia, despite the Byzantine origin of its Jewry, offers nothing but a cemetery of uncertain age. Philippopolis, down the Marica Valley, does better with one of its four synagogues built in 1710 and its Jews at their traditional work-benches hammering brass and tin and cutting leather harness, as they hammer and cut throughout North Africa and the Orient; yet little enough for a community which counted the Jewess Theodora as its empress when the Turks captured the town (1360). The thirteen synagogues of Adrianople burned down in the fire of 1905, thereby saving themselves from destruction in the Balkan Wars; their names read like a gazetteer of European Jewries: Gregos for the original Byzantine Jews; Budun (Buda) for the Hungarian Jews; Ashkenazi for the fifteenth-century refugees from Germany; Italia and Apulia for Italian Jews; Toledo, Aragon, Catalonia, Majorca, Sicily for the Spanish; Portugal and Evora for the Portuguese exiles; and finally Gerush (Hebrew, "Exile") for all and sundry. The Jewish cemetery (east of city) makes one, and a large and old one, among the eighty-odd that ring the town; we do not know the Young Turk, but it will be surprising if wars, sieges, and Kemal Pasha have disturbed the sole occupation of the Old Turk, which, in cradle, bazaar, café, bed, and grave, was to sleep.

Every quarter of Constantinople has its Jewry, but the forty and more synagogues have risen and fallen like phœnixes in the century fires of the city. Only two, it appears, have survived to a decent age: the Achridah in the Balata quarter, built in the mid-sixteenth century; and the Cahal—so the Sephardim term a synagogue in the Levant—of the Señora, across the Golden Horn, in the Has Keuï quarter. The señora who founded the latter is no other than Gracia Mendesia (c. 1510-69), the forceful aunt and mother-in-law of Joseph Nasi, and the most distinguished Jewess of her century. For further token of the golden age in Constantinople, one must turn to the old cemetery, north of Has Keuï, on the road to Eaux Douces. And for the Byzantine age or earlier, we must go to Feodosia (Museum of Antiquities) or far north to Leningrad (Hermitage Museum) where are gathered the marble tombstones of Greek Jews who lived in the Crimea at the beginning of the Christian Era. But that would open up vistas without end: the Karaites and their fortress in Chufut-Kalé; the red-headed Krimchak Jews of Karasubazar (both in the Crimea); the Tartar-speaking mountaineer Jews of Kuba (Caucasia); and the Subbotniki, last relics of the Chazar-Jewish Empire, in Tiflis. Twelve tribes do not begin to account for the descendants of Jacob.

Instead, we may ponder the original inscriptions from Hezekiad's tunnel in Jerusalem, and the warning, in Greek, against setting foot in Herod's Temple (both Djinili Kiosk, National Museum, Constantinople).[1]

❧

The main railroad line from Belgrade to Salonica brings us near to Stobi (eighteen miles north-east of Gradsko). Stobi, or Isteb, or Stiplje, lying just north of the Iron Gate of Macedonia, preserves the traces of a synagogue, discovered within the last year, and as old as Europe can provide. It probably dates from the third century C.E., and though conversion into

[1] See pp. 26, 33 (Louvre).

a Byzantine church has modified its character, one of the pillars still bears the Greek inscription, "Tiberias Plychromos, head of the synagogue."

The synagogue of Stobi may help to make it clear why Paul, after the uproar in Ephesus, instead of heading straight for Athens, took an interminable detour "for to go into Macedonia" (Acts 20:1-2). And it may explain why Salonica was the first European city to hear the gospel preached, "ensample to all that believe in Achaia." True, the first explicit mention of Jews in Salonica is not until long after, when the gospel was preached anew (1096), at the point of the Crusader's lance. It is a curious mention—no word of massacres, but an exemption from taxes granted by Alexander Comnenus, emperor of Byzance, fearful lest the Salonican Jews side with the knights of the Cross!

When Sultan Amurath, by an inverted crusade, captured Salonica in 1430, the Jews received the glad tidings that they were to be placed on an equal footing with all non-Moslems, that is to say, the rabbis sat considerably below the salt, but no lower than the Greek bishops. Isaac Zarfati, settled in this paradise, cannot restrain himself from addressing a circular letter to the bedevilled Jews of Germany and Hungary: "Turkey is a land that lacks nothing. Is it not better to live under Moslems than Christians? Here you may wear what you please, whereas in Christendom you dare not dress your children in colours without the risk of their being flayed red and beaten blue."

His letter brought numbers of German Jews to Salonica, but the great Jewish influx began after the expulsion of the Jews from Spain. In the sixteenth century Salonica rivalled Constantinople for wealth and learning; in the next century Sabbatai Zevi outdid Paul by persuading the Salonican Jews that he was himself the Messiah—a remnant of these credulous Jews who assumed, as did Sabbatai, the guise of a Moslem, are still extant under the sobriquet of Dónmehs (apostates), and maintain their own mosque. And to this day Salonica is the metropolis, for culture, commerce, cabbala, and decay, of Spanish Jewry.

The Jews number nearly one-half the city's population, their Spanish tongue may be heard in the shadow of every Greek church and erstwhile mosque (it predominates in the Vardar, Ezi, and Charirion quarters), but their antiquities have for the most part fallen victim to fire. The oldest stone in their cemetery (east of the Roman triumphal arch) commemorates Isaac Bussalo, physician, died 1499.

And on clear days, Olympus, even as Epicurus said, regards with indifference the long comic-tragedy, from Paul instructing the Thessalonians, to Greek patriots attacking Spanish Jews out of appreciation for an American movie called "The King of Kings."

꙳ᔕᔓ

Arta has probably the oldest surviving community in Greece proper (west coast); the majority were wiped out by the Greek patriots fighting for the freedom of Hellas in 1821—you will hear nothing about it, however, in Byron or Shelley. Like Corfu,[1] Arta possesses a synagogue for the Greek Jewish rite, as well as a later one for the Sephardim. Zante, in the Ionian Sea, has a Jewry dating from the fifteenth century and a synagogue from the seventeenth century.

Corinth preserves a lintel (museum in Palea Korinthos) from its ancient synagogue, perhaps the very one where Paul "reasoned every Sabbath" (Acts 18:4). The Greek inscription on the lintel, "This is the synagogue of the Hebrews," which from its character has been dated as early as the first century c.e., shows in its crabbed execution the poverty and simplicity,

[1] See p. 265.

not of the generality of Greek Jews, but of the Hebrew-speaking immigrants, "tentmakers" like Aquila and Priscilla. It was in Corinth that the Pro-consul Gallio showed the philosophic temper of his brother Seneca and won immortality when a row ·broke out among our tentmakers as to the nature of the gods—"Gallio cared for none of those things."

Athens, Delphi, Mantineia, Patras, Ægina, Chalcis, Cos, and Delos have yielded either synagogal or funerary inscriptions telling us that the Jews had taken widespread advantage of the treaty which the Maccabees made with Hellas. A tombstone from Delos will be found in the Athens museum.

But Delos furnishes more than a mere inscription. The Jews set up a synagogue in this island of Apollo and treasury of the Athenian Empire, as early as the second century B.C. The present ruins date from its reconstruction in the fourth or fifth century of the Christian Era and are the most considerable survival of an antique synagogue on European soil. (Similar ruins exist in Miletus and Priene on the Asiatic shore of the Ægean.)

The synagogue is divided into two oblong halls, the larger for the men, the smaller for the women, with three portals between. Corinthian columns, now fallen, upheld the ceiling. The marble throne for the *parnas* is still in its place against the west wall; the legs are fashioned like the legs and paws of a lion, and between them, on the marble pavement, rests a stool of the same design. The community of Delos were no tentmakers squabbling over the nature of the Palestinian gods; their *élite* held, as we learn from an inscription, reserved seats in the Delian theatre; and, if we know our Jews, they subventioned heavily the latest music and drama, and among them ranked the brightest critics of Euripides who, we may be sure, had nothing more to say to the clever young men of the Hellenistic world.

Cos, off the Asiatic coast near Helicarnassus, spans the in-

terval between those bright young men and today. Its Jewish
colony, dating from the reign of Alexander, took charge of
investing the funds of the Greek temples; a sacrificial tablet
from the Temple of Adrastia and Nemesis, dated the first
century B.C., mentions these investments; Herod (he would)
contributed an annual prize to the local athletic games; a
Jew stole the mistress of Meleager, the leading wisecracker
of Cos; fourteen hundred years later the Knights of Rhodes
expelled the Jews; in 1747 Rabbi Eliezer Tarica built a synagogue which still stands; and in 1850 its Jews were accused of
ritual murder—the whole as mad and long a drama as any
played in a Greek theatre.

Rhodes, around the corner from Cos, preserves the most
imposing monuments of the Sephardic Jew in the Levant;
the Great synagogue built at the beginning of the sixteenth
century and the Shalom toward the end.

But we are encroaching upon the bounds of Asia.

LEMBERG. MEDALLION FROM SILVER
TORAH CROWN
See page 367

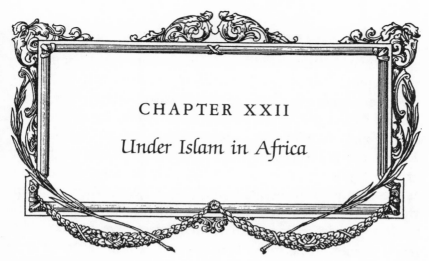

CHAPTER XXII

Under Islam in Africa

GIBRALTAR is more a point in time than in space. Once we desert its bars and their British sailors, the rock is eighteenth century. Moving northward brings us, every hour, nearer the modernity of Paris, whereas every hour southward takes us back along an ever-living and still trodden highway of the past—Tangier as Addison's father left it, Salé watching unwearied for its sixteenth-century pirate fleets, Marrakesh clamorous with the Middle Ages, until, behind the Atlas, stretches aboriginal and undated time.

Cordova, Avignon, and even Cracow demand something of the imagination to evoke life from their stones; but in Morocco, as in most of North Africa, we need use nothing but our eyes. The monuments of Europe, Jewish or otherwise, cast a certain shadow from the past, and darkly we can trace in it the shape and spirit of the men who reared them; but Africa, despite its sun, knows no such shadow—the men still walk who raised its towers, ply the trades that wrought its ancient handiworks, and live the faith that built its mosques and synagogues. If we would understand the Middle Ages, and much that lies behind them, which means, for us, to understand the stones, shards, parchments, and precious trinkets we have tracked across Europe from Lisbon to Lublin, we must turn from fumbling history or gaping at churches, synagogues, and castles, and go to Morocco.

Although historically youngest of North African lands, its natural wealth, teeming like California, and its long resistance to Europe, have kept its native culture green. Libya and Tripoli are mediæval, even primitive, enough to satisfy the greediest gourmand of the past, but they are poor and barren as their sands. And Egypt, Tunisia, or Algeria, while fat with wealth, are riddled with modern fashions.

Moreover, in setting forth from Morocco we can trace, in reverse order, to be sure, the course of Jewish settlement in Africa. The present population derives from three great drifts: Jews from Greco-Roman days, and perhaps Punic long before, whom the Arabs found as far west as the border of Morocco and who survive in patches among the cave-dwellers of Tripoli and mountaineers behind Fez; then a wave of Meso-potamian and Alexandrine Jews who followed the armies of Islam (eighth and ninth centuries) clean across the northern coasts and south into remote oases of the Sahara; and, finally, an influx of Spanish Jews, mere newcomers (fourteenth and fifteenth centuries) who have fairly swamped the earlier Jewries, at least in the west.

Nothing of the first settlements survives in the language of the ghettos; except for the younger generation who have taken on French, their inhabitants speak Judeo-Arabic or Judeo-Spanish. But the ethnologist has a mine to work in disentangling the Jewish folkways, beliefs, and magical prac-tices brought to Africa before the Talmud was begun or the Bible finished; and the student of folk-art another mine in the jewellery, tooled brass, and hammered copper, imme-morial crafts among Jewish workmen who brought their de-signs from—where? Persia, Assyria, Canaan? The Middle Ages which strike the eye in the mellahs are nothing but a recent frosting on the cake; within are hidden plums which come from an ancient tree such as grew in Shechem.

୧ᜰᜩ

Many travellers begin at Gibraltar. But its Jews are new-comers, compared, that is, with such venerable communities as New York. Sephardim from North Africa and the eastern Mediterranean, they settled on the Rock like homing pigeons, shortly after the English conquest in 1704. They speak Spanish, Judeo-Spanish, Arabic, and English, they maintain four synagogues (the most handsome on Line Wall Road) as well as continental trade-lines converging from alien worlds, from the Great Atlas and the Cotswolds, from the river Dra'a and the Rhine.

A large number of the merchants supplying local needs are likewise Jews. The number is, unfortunately, too large. Gibraltar is a free port, which means that it costs little to acquire a stock of goods and the merchants lack for nothing except—customers. Unhappy Ben Attar, unhappy Maimaran! What booted it, two centuries ago, when Mulay Ismail sat beneath the green umbrella, that you were Mulay Ismail's favourite Jews, that when Britain won the Rock you wrung from her free trade as part of the price of victory? What served it, Maimaran, that your father was trampled to death beneath the hoofs of a Sultanic horse, and that you had ridden to power and the vizir's saddle as part of the price of indemnity?

There is, as you may guess, romance behind the free trade of Gibraltar and its four little synagogues; but the thought of being able to buy cheap, with no one to sell to, is too distressing for further contemplation. "The merchants among the people," observes Ezekiel, "shall hiss at thee."

⌒᚛⌒

The true Moroccan, your man of Fez and peasant of the *bled*, calls Tangier a whore. And spits. This is the language, if not the gesture, of the prophets; and sitting at a café in the Little Socco, Tangier's centre of European trade, you may gain a new understanding of an ancient epithet.

Tangier commits harlotry in the eyes of the faithful not because she worships false gods, but because her sons sit on café chairs instead of woven mats, drink ginger ale instead of mint tea, eat brioches instead of flaked pastry, wear shoes (but not, praise Allah, socks) instead of babouches, and, when they can afford it, conduct their business in a shop in-stead of a booth. Like ancient Tyre (whose idolatry Ezekiel finds irrelevant), Tangier defiles its sanctuaries by the iniquity of its traffic.

"I have loved strangers and after them will I go," was Israel's pathetic plea, to which the prophets turned a deaf ear. Yet luckily for their descendants, Tangier went after the strangers she loved. As a result, her 15,000 Jews have seldom suffered ghetto insults and never known ghetto walls; and for generations many of them have been free and protected citizens of England, France, Italy, and other of her seducers. Moreover, they are enabled to preserve the fairer sides of their mediæval life: their courts, self-government, secular studies, and free philosophic mind.

You may visit the chief rabbi presiding in velvet cap and robe over the *Beth Din*, the House of Judgment (now lodged in the former German consulate, Chemin de la Montagne); his deep eyes are eloquent with texts and his long beard a majestic badge of office. Or if you call on the *parnas* of the community, you will find him, like another Ibn Tibbon, busy at an ancient Jewish trade; when last seen he was translating the *Lusiad* of Camoens from the Portuguese into Hebrew. And, with a little effort, you may pick up a young man in the Socco and while away an evening on Maimonides, talking homonyms, attributes, first causes, faculties, and the true tests of prophecy, until the electric-lighted shop fronts vanish, the Arabs stalk the road, masters again, and the moon throws the shadow of a minaret across the mediæval night.

The figure of a hand, with finger pointed upward, daubed beside a doorway, a six-pointed star worked into the grill, windows with a streak of blue in otherwise whitewashed lanes, quick-paced little men hung with black robes and capped in black, gaily kerchiefed women without veils, impudent children—there are no other signs, no walls and gates as elsewhere, to tell you the whereabouts of Tangier's Jewry. The synagogues, scattered like the Jewish lanes to the right and left of the main thoroughfare (Ez Zaguine), even the "big" Masaat Moshe, are modest structures, as they may well be when we come to consider their origin and number.

Altogether, the traveller will do wisely to set out across the *bled* on the straight enamelled roads, recently built for military purposes and the only token of change wrought in the land since the Berbers, whoever they were, first conquered the foothills of the Rif, whenever that might be. Mark Twain, like many better scholars before him—Antonio Malfante in the fifteenth century, Ibn Khordadbeh in the ninth, Procopius in the sixth, the Talmud in the fourth—has claimed the original conquerors of the land to be Canaanites who fled to Africa after their defeat at the hands of Joshua.

☙❧

Queen Isabella should be the patron, for at least she was the founder, of modern Tetuan. The original Phœnician or Berber city having long disappeared, it owes its present being

to the Moors and Jews who fled her royal Catholic piety at
the turn of the sixteenth century.

If the mellah, or ghetto, had not burned down a hundred
years ago, and if the Spaniards, since their recent occupation, had not added a new quarter to the city, Tetuan could
boast itself a perfect specimen of a mediæval Andalusian
town. Nevertheless, the new ghetto was built along traditional lines, and passing through the arch that once bore its
gate, at the north-east corner of the town square, you are free
to relive the golden age of Spanish-Jewish history. Though
we should warn you, all that is gold does not glitter.

Before we penetrate the gate we might glance at the plan
of a Moorish city, whether in Andalusia of the fifteenth century or Morocco today, a plan duplicated in most Moslem
cities of North Africa except for such dens of impurity as
Tangier or Alexandria.

A Moorish town is three towns, each confined by substantial walls, towers, and gates, and the whole bound together
by still more substantial fortifications. The most populous
of these inner towns is the medina, or Moslem quarter. The
most imposing is the kasba (the alcázar in old Spain), or governmental area, with palace, harem, and military barracks.
The third, and for us the most pertinent, is the mellah (the
old Spanish Judería), or ghetto, which generally adjoins the
kasba, so that the authorities can readily protect or oppress
its inhabitants. Its walls are apt to be as stout, even if its
gate is not so handsome, as those of the medina or kasba,
for the mellah is often shrewdly planted on the side of the
city most liable to foreign attack.

In recent years, a fourth town has frequently grown up
outside the interpenetrating maze of walls. This is the European settlement with its trust in machine-guns and airplanes
rather than bricks and stone.

Save for business and administrative intercourse—the

ubiquity of shoppers and tax-collectors—the four towns live
their own lives, the three races maintaining their own habits,
speech, and costume, no less apart than were their intervening walls the four seas. If some one were to ask us to tell the
history of the Jews in one word, we should answer that one
word is too many. For the history of all mankind can be told
in one word. Walls.

The houses behind the Jewish walls are to be distinguished
more for their internal arrangement than for the blue streak
around the windows. The door is wide open, and entry is
not only free, but welcome. Indeed, the open door is the sign
of the mellah. The Moslem door is always bolted, and even
if it were not shut, there would be nothing to see, for the
twisty passage behind it bars any view of the interior; whereas
the straight and gaping Jewish portal enforces the decorum
of living in a glass house or the equally unpleasant alternative
of washing the family linen in public. The Spaniard, we read,
ordered the Moors who stayed behind in Granada, after its
capture, to keep their doors ajar as a measure of prudence
against plot and rebellion. But the possibilities of rebellion
in the Jewish mellah must have always been remote. We suspect that its inhabitants, living in dense numbers like chickens
in a coop, would find the banging of doors intolerable and,
also like chickens, that they have found in social huddling a
vague security against the hawk.

The typical house consists of an interior court—the Spanish
patio—which opens on three sides into shallow living-rooms.
A balcony clings to three walls of the court and opens in
turn to three living-rooms on the upper floor. The six rooms
usually shelter six families. A common kitchen, storeroom,
and well are built into the fourth wall, which faces the street,
for such little cooking and washing that does not take place
in the court, where, indeed, most of the business of life is conducted, as it was in ancient Palestine. Here the women sift

semola for the eternal kus-kus, pound their grain for bread, nurse the babies, ply the needle, and retail the news of the world. As the sun shifts, they move from the doorway of Madam Dahan to that of Madam Azulai. When called within, they touch a finger to the gaily stitched woollen napkin which hides a *mezzuza* by each doorpost. And glancing at the ornamental crest painted near the portal on the occasion of every wedding—a mingling of flowers, mystic charms, and flourishes in bright blue, pink, and green—we may be sure that most of the talk in the courtyard concerns the present or future offspring of young Solika and Naphtali.

Tetuan is as fair a place as any to do the round of the synagogues, no less abundant than churches in a mediæval city. Its 6,000 Jews boast sixteen, besides six *yeshibot* (colleges) and uncounted study-halls. The Moroccan synagogue—it is called *sla* in the native tongue—is, like most of its kind in North Africa, little more than a remodelled dwelling. The interior court is roofed over and further enlarged by throwing into it the three lower living-rooms; the balcony serves as a women's gallery, and one or two of the upper rooms are converted into school or vestry. Sometimes they continue to be inhabited by the beadle or other favoured (or recalcitrant) families, and the odour of sanctity mingles with kus-kus, open plumbing, and laundry. And the cries of sleepless infants rise above the evening prayers.

Even the more elaborate synagogues, built expressly for their purpose, repeat the same features. The rude posts of the original balcony may be transformed into handsome pillars, the balconies themselves widened and adorned with carved railings, the upper rooms enlarged and lighted by windows, but the structure remains in outline a magnified dwelling.

In any search for the first architectural form of the synagogue, the oldest European examples are naturally valueless.

The still older Palestinian synagogues appear, from their ruins, to be Greco-Roman basilicas doctored up in Syrian taste. On the other hand, the Moroccan type gives every sign of being an indigenous growth, owing nothing to mosque or church. It is not unreasonable to suppose that the original synagogue of Ezra was anything more.

Apart from speculation, however, and disregarding the holes and dugouts of the primitive populations of Djerba or Abyssinia, we may look on the North African synagogue as the oldest purely Jewish model that survives. And its antiquity may redeem its undeniable ugliness and squalor. But they are no more than faults of proportion and taste. The groundwork remains for a beautiful and significant expression of Judaism in architecture. A house of prayer might well be, after all, not a temple, a bank, or a concert-hall, but a house.

The economy of these synagogues is likewise domestic, and accounts for their great number. They are practically all privately owned—by two or three families. This type of ownership dates from time out of mind. In the old days a rabbi of pronounced spiritual bent did not deign or dare to receive pay for his spiritual leadership; and if he were felt to be inordinately spiritual, a genuine *baraka* to his followers, he was presented a house which was thereupon converted into his synagogue. Traces of these privately owned synagogues will be found in eastern Europe as well as North Africa.

Generally the rabbi's son and perhaps his grandson succeeded to the rabbinate and inherited the synagogue. Marriage settlements, a dearth of male children, a bad religious season, or other circumstances might gradually divide the ownership among several families. Although a few communities have bought out the larger of these private concerns and thus created a communal institution, the price generally remains prohibitive. A good *baraka* is above the vicissitudes of the market.

The soul of a North African community burns in its synagogue lamps. Filled with vegetable oil which keeps the spluttering wick afloat, they hang like huge goblets, clamped in metal bands and suspended from the ceiling by long chains. Gold and silver inscriptions worked into the glass and thrown into relief by the flame commemorate the names of the dead. Besides its local gentry, the lamps of Tetuan glow with the memory of its favourite *zaddikim*, from the dim Talmudic heroes whose tombs lie scattered by Tiberias, down to its own native saint, Rabbi Ben Gualich, who died in 1870, at the age of ninety-three, and whose *baraka*, if you believe the Tetuan folk, is every whit as potent as that of Rabbi (or Prophet!) Elijah of Casablanca, Rabbi Chanania Ha-Cohen of Marrakesh, Rabbi David Buchidan of Meknes, Rabbi Eliezer Davila of Rabat, Rabbi Ephraim Maimaran of Salé, or even Rabbi Amram ben Diwan of Wazan.

Hanging in these huts of prayer, they tell us in letters of fire that the heart of these Jewries haunts Kinnereth rather than Zion, and more intimately—we do not say devoutly—communes with Rabbi Meir the Master of Miracles than with the too august Isaiah or Moses. Do not misunderstand. These little flares illumine more than a night of superstition. They throw their light upon blacker centuries of misery and death —in their feeble flame we may see the Jews of Tetuan dragged at horses' tails before the gate of the kasba, and, beyond, some faint ray of the Inquisition pyre.

⌒ᴝᴋ⌒

The worship of saints should take us to Wazan (Ouezzane, twenty-five miles east of Arbaoua, just over the border into French Morocco), where the hillside tomb of Rabbi Amram ben Diwan draws, twice a year, thousands of pilgrims from every mellah this side of the Atlas, bringing their sorrows, needs, and cares for his disposal. No common niche in his tomb could serve for the cases of candles flung into the propitiary bonfire. And no houses or khans would hold the vast throngs whose tents spread to the valley below. At night the camp fires gleam in long lines and the odour of roast mutton rises heady to the stars.

Yet it is not in human nature to suppose that every pilgrim who saddles his ass in the pass of Telouet or by the dunes of Agadir carries to Wazan a burden of misery. There are scandal, skylarks, and prune brandy all the way. A pity some young Moroccan Jew primed with modern tongues (we recommend a savoury English-French), his heart foolishly set on a clerkship in the National Bank of Fez, doesn't put aside his ledgers, catch the wind across the fields of crocus, and pick up again, gleefully returning to a still frequented mediæval road, the cunning pen of Dan Chaucer. The "Wyf of Sallee," mounted on the red saddle of her stoutest mule and riding forth to pray for strength to her good man—are ten children right reason for giving over his nights to the Zohar? —if no one will report her, she deserves to be invented.

However, you will likely visit Morocco at the wrong season for a sight of her—one always does. But an enthralling, if modest, substitute, for the Wazan pilgrimage awaits one every Saturday evening at the tomb of Rabbi (or Prophet!) Elijah at Casablanca.

On the way, from Tetuan, you may climb to the holy city of Sheshawan, lost in the western ramparts of the Rif, a city of tiles and towers like any town in the mountains of Andalusia; yet it had never suffered the profaning foot of a Christian—except for Charles de Foucault disguised as a Jerusalem rabbi and two other bold Europeans late in the nineteenth century—until the Spaniards permanently established them-

selves in 1926. Here, too, you will find a Jewry, perched like
an eagle's nest on the naked everlasting hills. Or you may
stop at Rabat-Salé, with its twin Jewries content, now that
piracy, slave-dealing, and commerce in ostrich plumes, gold
dust, and ivory have vanished, to cling to hammering pots
and pans and selling dry-goods, spices, and soap.

The tomb of Rabbi Elijah stands in a windowless dwelling
deep in the Casablanca mellah—directions are hopeless, but
then, you need only pronounce the magic name of El-i-ya-hu
(Hebrew for Elijah). At almost any hour the visitor will
find a pilgrim come to burn a candle at the semi-cylindrical
bulk built against a wall of the front room, and in the back
room, shut from light and air, the nearly invisible forms of
the sick, bundled on the mud floor. However, on the close of
the Sabbath the den becomes a frenzy of pilgrims; candles
flare by the hundred; groans, prayers, and the shrieks of the
women—a barbaric yell these Jewesses have plucked straight
from the lungs of Africa—proclaim, at least, a living faith.

If, by chance, a living faith displeases you, do not seek to
cast the blame for it on the Moslems. The Jews may have
borrowed their pirates from the Moors, but *zaddikim* and
geburim (saints and heroes) they have venerated since Biblical days. Pilgrimages to the tombs of Biblical, Talmudic,
and later-day saints have always had their vogue, no less
among European than Oriental Jews. It is certain that Yehiel
of Paris, Judah He-Hasid of Regensburg, and the Baal Shem
would be annoyed by any theory of Moslem origin. Even
the *baraka* exuded by the tombs is no Moorish invention.
"And it came to pass, as they were burying a man, behold,
they spied a band of Moabites, and they cast the man into the
tomb of Elisha, and as soon as the man touched the bones
of Elisha, he revived and stood upon his feet" (II Kings,
13:21).

༄༅

Marrakesh—twelve miles of battlements and gates capped with towers, palace roofs, and palms, and overhung by the Atlas snows—is the greatest Berber-Arab-Negro-Jewish show on earth, staged by half of Africa against a back-drop of red walls and white mountains. Its *souks* will offer you not only their wares and the delight of interminable bargain, but the living tide of mediæval commerce. Trades you read of in cold stone on the tombs of Prague[1] take heat and colour in the mellah of Marrakesh.

The jewellery *souk* before the mellah gate is no porphyry-columned Alcaicería as we saw the wreck of in Granada[2]—Marrakesh is poor in fine building-stone—it is nothing but a circular path roofed with rushes and flanked by booths of baked mud. Yet the sunlight straining through the leafy sieve flickers on metals and gems, on beards and turbans, no less golden than in the great age of Spain, and fuses with the tiny fire of the goldsmith's furnace. There are emeralds—we have seen them—the size and shape of a spark-plug.

The gate itself was built three centuries ago by Rabbi Mordecai ben Attar, who buried beneath the cornerstone a parchment inscribed with the names of the guardian angels; the mellah has never since been sacked, and Jewish women-folk kiss the arch as they pass. If we follow their white shawls and red kerchiefs we shall enter a world long lost to Granada —booth upon booth of flaming silks and cool cottons; crouching wood-turners, aged men who grasp their tools with their bare toes and spin the lathe with a cord; leather-workers inlaying ancient patterns, gold, blue, and cream, on trig handbags; tinsmiths, blacksmiths, and coppersmiths pounding in

---

[1] See p. 331.
[2] See p. 142.

strident chorus; a spavined nag revolving a millstone in a spider-webbed den half underground; olive-presses sluicing out a brown soup into greasy stone vats; braidmakers, children of five and six out in the street, holding in their little hands the long warp and crossing the thread, while their elders, snug in a shady booth, weave the varied woof; greybeards descending dark stairs from afternoon prayers, a slow parade of patriarchs, each weathered face catching a glory as it turns to the sun; beggars barefoot and maimed toasting greedily against a wall; spice merchants dozing among their sacks of saffron, their bundles of stick cinnamon and vanilla, their baskets of coloured peppers, ginger, allspice, and mustard, their jars and tins of cardoman, laurel, cloves, nutmeg, coriander, and cummin—dozing and dreaming aromatic dreams.

Such is mediæval Jewry at work. The beggars and patriarchs, too, do their share, the one to provide occasion for *gemiloth chasodim* (deeds of kindness), and the other to keep up *avodah* (the service of prayer).

Before the arrival of French competitors, the mellahs likewise controlled the banking and foreign commerce of the land. Through Jewish representatives in the port towns, the home offices in Marrakesh and Fez, and a network of dealers in the mellahs up the northern valleys of the Atlas and down the southern to oases in the Tafilalet and the Dra'a, reaching toward the heart of the Sahara, cotton goods, spices, sugar, tea, iron, and copper penetrated to the native *souks*; and grains, skins, rugs, leather wares, wool, and gums were shipped to the coast. In addition, the Jews still monopolize sundry crafts: goldsmithing, tinsmithing, brassworking, dressmaking, embroidering, and the manufacture of harness.

On the other hand, the Moslem produces the foodstuff of the country, the local weaving, the building material (the builders are both Moslems and Jews), and, until the French relieved them of the burden, furnished what government and justice could be found.

The Jew, in a word, depended on the Moslem for the native necessities of life, and the Moslem on the Jew for the imported necessities and many of the luxuries. On the printed page this interdependence sounds as dull as a consular report. But a half-hour's stroll through the medina and mellah makes it the most vivid characteristic of an interior North African town. And could we turn back the centuries, it is easy to imagine the same vivid impression from a stroll through mediæval Toledo, Frankfort, or Cracow. The ghetto of the Middle Ages was not merely a religious and racial warren, vaguely resembling the foreign quarters of our own cities, but an economic zone as essential to, but as distinct from, the rest of the city as our modern downtown section, factory district, or railway yards.

Acre on acre, the white flat and nameless tombs throw back the glare of the sun; in the distance, the city ramparts draw a red line against the Atlas snows; the *djeballa*, or waste-heap, of the mellah hides the sight of human habitation in its centuries of accumulated and calcified garbage. This is the Jewish cemetery of Marrakesh (east of the ghetto). There are tales, tales like history, of jewels and gold buried in the *djeballa* during the terror of pogroms.

The stones, mostly lying flat, are devoid of visible inscriptions. The tombs of the rabbis blessed with *baraka* as well as learning, of miracle-workers and saints, are to be distinguished by their raised semi-cylindrical form—in Meknes they take the size and shape of imposing cenotaphs—by the niches built into them for burning candles, by the bits of coloured thread tied to a pebble and laid on their curved tops, token of a prayer or petition, and by the pilgrims pressed around them. The sick are often brought from miles away and camped in tents at their flank. And beggars wait to trap sick, pilgrims, and mourners at the gate.

For all the mocking sun, no more dismal spot darkens the face of the earth. Shut off on the one side by the petrified rubbish of the past, blocked on the other by a mountain wall beyond which lies only the nothingness of the desert, and in between the white anonymity of death, the Jews touch their consummation and their term.

Fez is Arab, stone, and the Orient, as Marrakesh is Berber, baked mud, and Africa. But its Jews remain the same. After Marrakesh, the mellah of Fez is a twice, and not so well told, tale.

Facing the medersa of Bou Anania stands the house where Maimonides is said to have lived in the interval between his flight as a lad from Cordova and his ultimate career as physician in the suite of Saladin at Cairo. Its windows are thirteen, one for each of the principles with which he formulated the Jewish faith. On the façade of the medersa hang twelve silent chimes of the great clock built, according to the inscription, in 1357; we are told that Maimonides throttled their sound with a magic spell to insure quiet for his studies. But since the author of *The Strong Hand* died in 1204, the clock is evidently misdated.

Local balladists still sing the story of Sol Hachuel in the little cafés of the mellah. Sol—diminutive for Solika—was born in Tangier at the beginning of the nineteenth century. Fair as the sun, she was abducted by agents of the sultan and carried to his harem in Fez. Forestalling outcry, the authorities claimed she had been converted to Islam of her own free will and that her fate no longer concerned the Jews. When she denied her conversion, the Moslems, to save their face, had no other recourse than to try her for a relapsed convert. The penalty was death, and Sol found herself faced with the tragic choice of her Marano ancestors.

The choice was rendered harder by her youth, her beauty, and a dazzling career as the sultan's favourite. If she had turned to her European contemporaries for advice, her difficulty would no doubt have vanished. Heine would have written her three charming stanzas, something to the tune of *Mädchen mit dem roten Mündchen*, with a neat tag at the end explaining that he had undergone conversion for nothing more dazzling than a university diploma. Rahel Varnhagen would have added an encouraging note, without stanzas—what a chance, my *süsse* Solika, to serve the enlightenment of your people by opening a *salon* in the harem.

As it was, her family and friends did what they could to break her constancy. A group of converted Jews explained to her the nature and facility of lip service. But something stronger than youth and life, something of the spirit of the saints she was about to join and honour, held her to her faith. Eighteen hundred and thirty, the year Heine fled to Paris because they served no oysters in the prison of Spandau, Sol Hachuel's head fell, outside the palace wall, before the mellah gate. Her tomb in the cemetery of Fez burns, as you may believe, with perpetual candles.

In the ruins of the Roman city of Volubilis, twenty miles west of Fez, any *Kulturhistoriker* worth his salt could rebuild the ancient ghetto, its fifteen tinsmiths lodged against the outer wall, and add twelve cobblers and a rabbi, with nothing more to go on than the terra-cotta lamp stamped with a menorah and dug from its rubbish, not to mention the tombstone patently inscribed, "Mashrona, daughter of Rabbi Judah." The only difficulty in the whole operation turns on whether her name was not "Massarona."

And twenty miles south of Fez, in the first flanks of the Atlas, lies the little city of Sefrou, its mellah dating from shrouded centuries. Phœnician, Roman, Berber?—no one knows the origin or stock of these Atlas Jews. It appears too easy and incredible to assign them a Jewish origin. Who ever heard of anyone having a Jewish origin?

This much is conceded: before the Moslem era, the Ahel Sefrou, a Judaizing tribe of Berbers or a Berberizing tribe of Jews, were already settled in the jagged valley of the Wadi Haggai (take that late prophetic name for what it is worth), and along the torrents of the Wadi Yehudi, or Jew River. Not until the ninth century, when Fez was building, were a majority of these Judeo-Berbers converted to Islam. A stiff-necked minority hung on, and hang in their cragged valley yet. They were reinforced by Saharan refugees when Segelmessa, "city of great scholars and sages," fell (1145) and put an end to an empire of Jewish trade which stretched to Timbuctoo. And Spanish families, sixtenth-century *parvenus*, have of course lowered the tone of the ancient blood.

Three thousand Jews live in Sefrou, one-third of the total population. Their beauty, whether it be derived from Spain or directly from David's royal line, is remarkable.

If you reach this city the first day of the month of Adar, you may share in the annual picnic for the saints of the Mountain Cave—the Jews claim there are four, while the Berbers are content with one, but no less than the Prophet Daniel—and have your fill of Hebrew songs and dances, and crouched in the bowels of the earth, receive a blessing at the tomb of the four saints or one prophet. And on any day of the year you may see the women of the mellah, a throng of bobbing and multicoloured kerchiefs, doing the family wash in the river gorge cut through the heart of the town, a cheering sight—for the onlooker.

༤

If your appetite for Atlas Jews is unabated, there is Debdu, south of Taouirt, off the main highway to Algeria. Two-thirds of its 2000 inhabitants are Jews, mostly Spanish clans come from Murcia and Seville over four centuries ago, and now saddling their asses every Sunday for a week's trading among the villages which run in a chain down to Tafilalet and the vanished Segelmessa.

When you reach Oudjda, the border of Algeria, you will grow contemptuous of Daniel in Sefrou, for here is the tomb of Sidi Yahia ben Yunés, venerated by Moslem, Christian, and Jew, as John the Baptist who foretold the coming of the Messiah—although there is some difference of opinion among them as to the realization of the prophecy. And St. John becomes nothing if, leaving the main road at Lalla Maghnia, you descend a dozen miles to the coast, beyond Nedroma, and behold the last resting-place of Sidi Ucha, who is Joshua son of Nun. It does seem puzzling, however, that the Canaanites who lost and Joshua who won should both have fled to the Barbary Coast.

Tlemcen is one of the few accessible cities of Algeria with an old Jewish tradition. In the tenth century its rabbis were looked upon as authorities even by the schools of Babylonia. But in the thirteenth century, after its destruction by the Almohades, Abraham Ibn Ezra asked, as we do now, "What has become of the glory of Tlemcen?" All that we can find is the usual mellah (between the kasba and the town square), and the tomb of Rabbi Ephraim Encava, a Spanish refugee from the terrible year of 1391, who draws his thousands of pilgrims like Amram ben Diwan in the west.

The Jewry of Algiers is mostly Spanish, with a small strain of Italian added in the eighteenth century; and for travellers

A WORLD PASSED BY

fed on Daniel and Joshua, streets like the Rue de Chartres make a thin show. What with the inroads of modernity, nothing will soon remain worth seeing but the collection of ritual art objects in the museum (Musée d'Antiquités) and the mausoleum of Rabbi Isaac ben Sheshet in the cemetery. We left Isaac ben Sheshet a sober and learned Talmudist in Saragossa,[1] and now we find him the patron saint and guardian spirit, the miracle-worker and *Rab* of an African city.

Constantine—the Phœnician Cirta ("city") and once capital of the Numidian kings—has kept the ancient character of its Jewry more unspoiled than any other Algerian town. A third of its 30,000 "natives" are Jews, and hardly a Spanish interloper among them. The stock remains as it was when Justinian mentioned them in the sixth century, and probably no different from when the Roman built the monuments that bring tourist caravans to this mountain world. The hara (as the mellah is called east of Morocco) lies beyond the Place des Galettes, and its dens and cellars strangely resemble the once-inhabited dens on the Palatine Hill in Rome itself. The only noteworthy synagogue stands at the farther end of Rue Vieux, main thoroughfare of the hara.

Far to the south in Baghai, a Jewish necropolis, next to the Berber, Roman, and Byzantine ruins of the city, tells again of the old Saharan trade. This is the country of Cahena, the Jewish queen who fought the advance of the Arabs in the seventh century, and whose sons, reconciled to the Crescent, led Jewish-Berber lances against Spain.[2]

༈

On the slope of the Djebel Khaoui, overlooking the city and the sea, is the vast necropolis of the Jewish inhabitants of

[1] See p. 177.
[2] See p. 122.

Carthage, when it was rebuilt under Roman rule. The holes, caverns, and passages, half catacombs and half rock-tombs as in Palestine, are so numerous they have given a name to the hill (*Khaoui*—hollow) in which they are burrowed. The epitaphs, mostly in Latin, are painted or engraved; and the decorative *motifs* include the vine, menorah, winged genius, and flying horse much as in Rome.[1] The inscriptions, as well as lamps stamped with the menorah, Jewish amulets, and a sarcophagus sealed with the Hebrew name of Joab, have been gathered in the Lavigerie Museum of Carthage.

In the village of Hamman-Lif—Naro of the ancients—on the shore south of Carthage stand the remains of a fifth-century synagogue (near the Grand Fondouk), hardly more than the ground plan, but the most extensive to survive from antiquity. No less than fifteen rooms, including a women's annex and a summer synagogue, must have given it the air of a modern temple, community centre, and Y. M. H. A. rolled into one. We wonder if, when they were building it, our Jews ever glanced up the mountain behind them, a glance of scorn and pity for the fallen foe of Jehovah, the great Baal Karnaim, whose temple, long in ruins, crowned the summit crags.

The Bardo (or Alaoui) museum in Tunis shelters the pride of Naro's synagogue, the finest Jewish mosaic so far come to light—worked with birds, beasts, and flowers, sealed with the menorah, and inscribed in Latin by the donor: "Thy servant Juliana has set this mosaic at her own expense in the synagogue of Naro for her salvation." The central symbols bear out her intent: two palms for the tree of life, two woodbirds for the soul,[2] two peacocks for immortality, and two great fish for the resurrection. Another fragment of mosaic

[1] See p. 235.
[2] See p. 376 (Poland).

has left us the memory of "Asterius, son of the *parnas* Rusticus [and his wife?] Margarita, daughter of Riddeus." A third patch remembers "the *instruments* of Thy servant of Naro"—probably prayer-books, *kiddush* cups, or the like, given by a member of the community.

The vast hara of Tunis (north-east of the medina) reveals its ancestry in the names of the chief congregations—the Tunsi or original settlers when the synagogue at Carthage was probably still in use; the Grana, fifteenth-century refugees from Granada and other Spanish cities; and the Gorneyim, eighteenth-century arrivals from Leghorn. The Great synagogue of the Tunsi (in a courtyard, corner of Rue Sidi Mardoun and Rue Zarkoun) has pretensions to age and grandeur. You may see the Tunisian Jews at work in the jewellery *souk* (El Berka), and near by in the El Trouk *souk* given over to Jewish tailors who fashion all the rich native costumes of the city. And you may catch an unusual glimpse of their handiwork in the occasional Jewess who has not yet discarded her traditional silk blouse, tight brocaded trousers, sugar-loaf hat, pearl headband, and heavy gold bracelets.

Tripoli possesses a Big Jewry (Hara el-Kebira) and a Little Jewry (Hara el-Seghira). The main street of the former (Sciara Hara Kebira) is lined with the customary shops of jewellers and goldsmiths; and the El Mara *souk* for silks and the Attarine for spices are almost entirely in Jewish hands. The dying trade of cleaning ostrich feathers and polishing ivory, both carried on by women, can sometimes still be seen in the tortuous lanes of the Little Jewry. Three miles east of Tripoli lies the village of Amrus, inhabited exclusively by Jews, blacksmiths for the most part, wretched, poor, and half-blind. But for humanity run to earth, you must go sixty miles south (train and autobus) to the Jewish cave-dwellers of Gasr Garian.

CRAFTS

The site of Alexandria's ancient Jewry is known; it lay north of the present Fouad I Gate—the largest hara in antiquity and the home of Philo. There are a few inscriptions, too, in the Greco-Roman Museum of Antiquities. But what is Greek Jewry and Philo compared with the Elijah synagogue which, even if rebuilt recently, stands on the spot where the prophet walked during one of his frequent apparitions among men. If the present Alexandrians, instead of building anew, had appropriated the lovely old synagogue from Mahalla el-Kubra (north-east of Tanta), they would have had something to live up to the legend.

We are on surer ground in Cairo. Of the older monuments, the David ben Zimra synagogue was founded by a rabbi of this name who came from Spain in 1492. The Hayim Cafoussi synagogue commemorates a sixteenth-century *dayan* (judge) who was stricken blind, and when the community laid his affliction to his corrupt decisions, he prayed God to die if he were guilty, but, if not, that his sight be restored; and by the number of pilgrims who flock to his synagogue (or to his grave in the old cemetery south-east of the city), you may guess how the matter ended. The "Maimonides" synagogue has nothing, traditionally or otherwise, to do with the master. The three are to be found in the old Jewish quarter (Haret el-Yahud) north-east of the Muski; and all three, as well as the many lesser and newer ones, show by contrast to the wondrous mosques of the city how fleeting was the golden moment in Spain.

The Cairo where Maimonides lived was not Cairo at all, but Fostat, the first city founded by the Arabs upon their invasion of Egypt (640). It burnt down during Maimonides' lifetime, but he still continued to live near by, as he said in

his most famous letter, "a Sabbath day's journey from Cairo."
Excavations of Fostat may be visited, although the field of
scattered mud-bricks speak as little of Maimonides as the
Alexandria Customs House of Philo. The synagogue which
contained the treasure-laden *genizah*[1] has disappeared, but
the new one built on its site (near the Coptic church in Kasr
esh-Sham, once the Roman Cairo) keeps the old legends; the
spot is marked where stood the scroll of the Law written by
Ezra himself; a bibliophile bought it long ago, and it sank,
together with the bibliophile, in the sea near Alexandria.
Then there is the cave of Elijah where he made an appearance
some centuries back, and the wall where Jeremiah recited his
Lamentations. As for the spot where Moses prayed, piously
commemorated in Baedeker, we have it on the authority of
Meshullam ben Menahem of Volterra in 1481 that it lay in
a synagogue across the river next to the pyramids. But we are
not writing a vade-mecum for Moroccan pilgrims.

In the north portico of the Egyptian Museum you will find
a large black granite stele (No. 599) inscribed on both sides.
One side was used by Pharaoh Menephtah, son of Rameses II.
After a poetic account of his Libyan campaigns, he takes up
his conquests in Palestine and he says—in the sole mention
of the name that has come to light among Egyptian texts—
"Israel is crushed; it has no more seed." This was three thousand one hundred and fifty years ago.

After pondering the words of the pharaoh, you may take a
sleeper and go whistling through the Wady Tumilat or, as it
was once called, the Land of Goshen. You will pass a hill,
surmounted by ruins, called Tell el-Yahudiya, the Hill of the
Jews, where the young High Priest Onias IV obtained permission to build a sanctuary modelled after the Temple. You
will pass Bubastes, where the peasants manure the soil with
an inexhaustible supply of mummified cats, and where Joseph

[1] See p. 220 (Oxford).

was put in prison for the sake of an unpleasant cat. But you will see none of these things because of the Egyptian night.

And in the morning you will be in Jerusalem and in the land of Israel where our story, as we pieced together the threads in the Louvre, began; and where, despite Menephtah, seed is sprouting anew.

KAMIONKA STRUMILOWA. SYNAGOGUE MURAL SHOWING VIEW OF JERUSALEM
See page 371

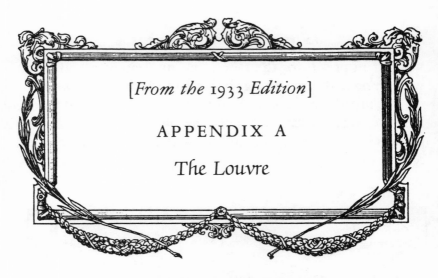

[*From the* 1933 *Edition*]

APPENDIX A

The Louvre

OBJECTS OF JEWISH INTEREST

I. MUSÉE DES ANTIQUITÉS ASIATIQUES:
GRANDE GALLERIE CHALDO-ASSYRIENNE **I**:

2. Angel before sacred tree.

4. Winged angel.

5, 6. Angels before sacred plant.

8. A chief eunuch (II Kings 18:17).

11. Assyrians besieging city—epoch of capture of Samaria
(722 B.C.).

12, 13, 14, 15. Winged bulls, or cherubim.

16, 17. Gilgamesh, or Nimrod.

18. Two-horned genius.

24. Deity and sacred tree.

28. Sargon II, conqueror of Samaria.

29, 30, 31. Officers of Sargon II.

43, 44. Assyrian kings, like Solomon, transport cedars of
Lebanon for construction of their palaces.

58. Assyrian state altar, with dedication of Sargon II.

62. Asshurbanipal, a "king of Assyria and all his glory."

65, 68, 69, 70. Transport of captives into exile.

83. Cast of "Black Stele" of Shalmaneser III (859-824

B.C.), showing tribute brought by Jehu from king of Israel.

106. Exorcising a bed-ridden patient.

212. Teraphim.

SALLE DE SUSIANE II:

72. Camp of captives.

8. Stele of Hammurabi.

6046. Hammurabi before the god Shamash.

Left of rear exit
    The god Teshub.

HALLWAY BEHIND SALLE DE SUSIANE II:

Before window
    Monument of Za-kir's victory over son of Hazael.

GRAND STAIRWAY:

First landing
    Baal as Sun-god.

Left wall
    Cast of throne of Xerxes, who was probably the Ahasu-
    eras of the Book of Esther.

SALLE DE SUSE VI:

Right of entry
    Stone relief of harpist and harp of eleven strings.

1st window to right
    Book-keeping and inventory accounts from Ur, 2500
    B.C.

2nd window to right
    Tell-el-Amarna tablets.

3rd table case to right
    Seal cylinders depicting Tree of Life, conflict of Marduk
    and dragon, combat with lions and wild oxen
    Terra-cotta Astartes (Nos. 191-209).

1st window to left
    Judeo-Chaldaic magic bowls

Terra-cotta incense-burner in form of Syrian temple.
2nd window to left
Collection of Astartes
Plaques illustrating animal sacrifice among Semites.
1st wall case to left
Terra-cotta incense-burners in form of Syrian temples.
2nd wall case to left
Urn from temple of Tanit, Carthage, containing bones
of sacrificed infants
Collection of Baalim, including Baal of Hamon (No.
190).
3rd wall case to left.
Collection of Astartes.
1st table case to left
Syrian Astartes from archaic to late Parthian period.
2nd table case to left
Large seal cylinder of Dunghi, king of Ur, 2700 B.C.,
sacrificing to Moon-god.
3rd table case to left
Large flat seal representing exorcism scene (No. 122)
Seal depicting two-horned god (No. 145)
Seal showing combat between Marduk and dragon.
GRANDE SALLE DE SUSE VII:
1st table case to left
Seal cylinders showing combat between Marduk and
dragon.
1st table case to right
Seal cylinders depicting angels and gods before sacred
tree and combat with dragon.
3rd table case to left
Palestinian jewelry
Hebrew seal of "Shobaniyo servant of Uzziyo"
Two-horned Babylonian god (No. 237).

6th window to right
Judeo-Chaldaic magic bowls
Astartes.

PETITE SALLE DE SUSE VIII:
Rear wall
Colossal relief of wild oxen.
1st table case to left
Reshef, Syrian god of lightning
Ivory plaque of Astarte, "The Great Mother," feeding goats
Bronze weapons of period of Joshua's conquest
Terra-cotta images of Syrian maidens mounted on camels.
2nd table case to left
Carved ivory plaques from the bed of Hazael.
Table case No. 2.
Seal cylinders showing sacrifices to Moon-god.

FIRST ROOM BEYOND SALLE DE SUSE VIII:
1st table case to left
Medal of Giovanni Boldu (No. 464), dated Venice, 1458, designed by himself; Hebrew inscription "Boldu of Venice," illustrating interest in Hebrew during early Renaissance.

SALLE JUDAIQUE (JEWISH ROOM):
(References are to black numbers on yellow background)
1. Type of "princes of Moab" such as Israelites encountered in their march on Palestine.
2. Stele of Mesa (Moses), king of Moab, retailing his victories over Ahab, king of Israel (ninth century B.C.). Oldest known document in a Hebraic tongue.
7. Cast of Hebrew inscription from tunnel of Shiloah (c. 700 B.C.).

8. Cast of inscription, in Greek, from Third Temple in Jerusalem, warning Gentiles from sacred precincts on pain of death.

9. Votive offering in form of human foot. The Talmud expressly forbade these votive reproductions.

10. Two stone pinnings from Temple in Jerusalem, probably dating from reconstruction by Herod.

15, 16, 17, 18. Jewish ossuaries, from first centuries before the Christian Era.

19. Bronze shovel for burning incense or tending sacred fire.

20. Brick stamped with mark of Tenth Legion "L[egionis] decimæ F[retensis]," which garrisoned Jerusalem after its capture by Titus.

21. Cast of Hebrew inscription, "Jonah and Sabbatiah, his wife, of Sicily [?]," dating sixth century C.E. and carved on column under the present Mosque of El-Aksa, Jerusalem.

25, 25 *bis*, 25 *ter*. Casts of frieze from Tombs of the Kings, Jerusalem, first century C.E.

26. Sarcophagus lid from Tombs of the Kings.

28. Sarcophagus of Queen Zaddah (Queen Helena of Adiabene), from Tombs of the Kings, which appears to have been built for her and her family, converts to Judaism.

29. Fragments of jaw-bone, teeth, and garments of Queen Zaddah.

30. Sarcophagus probably from Tombs of the Kings.

34. Stone door to sepulchral chamber in these Tombs.

37. Jewish coins from period of revolt against Rome and siege of Titus, found in Tombs of the Kings.

43. Jewish ossuary, found in one of interior chambers of above Tombs.

44, 45, 46, 47. Fragments of sculpture from these Tombs.

48. Cast of frontal from Tombs of the Judges, apparently burial-site of Jewish notables during Roman epoch. Typical specimen of Roman-Jewish art.

53. Cast of Hebrew inscription from so-called tomb of St. James in Valley of Jehoshaphat, probably burial-site, in Greco-Roman period (third to first centuries B.C.) of the Hezirs, priestly family mentioned in I. Chron. 24:13. Inscription reads, "This is the tomb and resting-place of Eleazar, Honiah, Joazar, Judah, Simeon, Johanan, the sons of Joseph, sons of . . . and for Joseph and Eleazar, the sons of Honiah . . . of the Beni Hezir."

54. Cast of Doric frieze from Jewish tomb in the valley of Hinnom.

57. Monolithic door from Jewish tomb in Sur Baher, on the road from Jerusalem to Bethlehem (first century C.E.).

58. Iron lock for above door.

61, 62. Fragments of mosaic from Masada, fortress built by the Maccabeans and the last to fall into the hands of the Romans (72 C.E.).

63. Fragment of cornice from Masada.

64. Melted metal and stone debris from Masada, relic perhaps of the fire which destroyed fortress (Josephus, *Wars,* VII, ix, 2).

65. Base of column from palace of Tyros built by Hyrcanus, about 180 B.C. in Transjordania (Jos. *Antiquities,* XII, iv, 11).

67. Fragment of capital from above palace.

80. Bas-relief of Astarte with attendants. Ashkelon (second to third centuries C.E.).

81. Plaque representing head of pigeon, found in Ashkelon. Doves were especially associated with Astarte in that city.

85. Incense or fire shovel.
93. Jewish ossuary from Lydda. Inscription in Greek, "Pyrinun or likewise Malthakes, grandson of Al-kios Simon Gobar."
95. Capital from church or synagogue (fifth century C.E.), found near Ramleh. Inscription in Greek, "One God."
97. Fragment of a chased metal platter, found near Ramleh. Worked in design are a menorah, and ark or small temple.
98. Metal weight in the form of a lion. Found at Ajalon.
99. Cast of fragment of a colossal eagle, representing the deified Emperor Julian, who proposed to rebuild the temple at Jerusalem.
103. Greek inscription, with menorah, from necropolis in Jaffa, "[Tomb] of Lazarus and Selaption, sons of Simon."
104. Similar inscription, "Hezekiah, son of Levi."
113. Arab milestone on road constructed by Abd al-Malik (685-705 C.E.), builder of the foundations of the Mosque of Omar. Inscription reads, "Abd al-Malik, the servant of Allah and commander of the Faithful—may the mercy of Allah be upon him—ordered this road to be built. From this stone to Jerusalem, eight miles."
114. Mutilated head of statue of a woman, probably portrait of member of Herod's family. Found in Sebaste (Samaria).
115. Fragment of Phœnician inscription, found on Mt. Carmel, near the so-called grotto of Elijah. ". . . the son of Abd[usir, son of . . .], son of [A]bdelim, son of Aris . . . the scribe, and Baal . . ."
116. Lintel from synagogue in Kefr-Birin, Galilee, second century C.E. Hebrew inscription, "May peace

be in this place and in all the places of Israel. Joseph Ha-Levi, son of Levi, erected this lintel. A blessing on his work."

117. Bas-relief of a menorah between *shofar* and *lulab*. Found in Gadara, across the Lake of Galilee.

118. Stone portal to Jewish tomb, with Jewish and Syrian sculptured *motifs*. Found near Acre.

119. Lintel bearing Greek inscription, "Place [of burial] of Namosas, son of Menahem, illustrious count and legate." Found in Haifa. Namosas was probably a Byzantine dignitary of Jewish origin.

120. Fragments of carved ivory coffer, belonging to the count.

121. Modern Jewish epitaph.

123. Small glass vase with typical Jewish *motifs*: pomegranate, citron, and cluster of grapes.

126. Bronze wheel for stamping trade-mark of Joseph the tailor. Greek inscription, "Joseph's—Couturier." Found in Sidon. (First Christian centuries).

127. Tombstone from Sidon, with menorah, *shofar* and *lulab*.

128. Jewish-Greek epitaph from Byblos. "This cave belongs to me, Joseph. If my son wishes to [be buried here], he may."

130. Jewish-Greek epitaph from the same cave. "All hail! The tomb of Joseph, son of the blessed Asterios."

131. Jewish-Greek epitaph from Leontopolis (or On—now Tell el-Yahudiya, Egypt), dated 20th of Mekhir of the 2nd year of Augustus (February 14, 28 B.C.), "The good Elazaros, dear to all."

132. Jewish-Greek epitaph from Leontopolis, 23 B.C. "Sabbataios, son of Somoelos, dead too soon, at the age of twenty-five."

133. Similar epitaph, without date. "O John, son of John, aged about twenty years, a young fiancé, beloved of all, good, without regrets, farewell!"
134. So-called vase of Cana. Probably modern.
156. Large two-handled vase, typical of pre-Israelite pottery prevalent in Canaan.
170. Type of pitcher found in Gezer (1800-1400 B.C.).
175. Elaborate Canaanite vase, 1800-1400 B.C. found in Jerusalem.
192. Large vase of type approaching Hebrew period in Canaan.
206. Lamp found in Nablus, Greco-Roman period. On reverse side a Samaritan variation of the menorah.

NOUVELLE SALLE DE SUSIANE:
Monument of Sargon I. (2800 B.C.)
Bronze plate, decorated with scenes and details of sacrifice as practised by Semites.

SALLES PHENICIENNES:
1st room
Examples, along right wall, of Tyrian fashions of dress, popular in Palestine.
2nd room
Vase from Amanthante, Cyprus, eight feet in diameter, with bulls carved between handles, suggestive of the "bath" in Solomon's Temple.

II. MUSÉE DES ANTIQUITÉS EGYPTIENNES:
SALLE III:
1st window to right
Portrait bust of Amenophis IV, the monotheistic pharaoh.

III. MAIN PICTURE GALLERY:
SALLE XXII:
2540. Rembrandt, "The Philosopher"
2546. Rembrandt, "Jew with Fur Cap."

[*From the* 1933 *Edition*]

APPENDIX B

The British Museum

OBJECTS OF JEWISH INTEREST[1]

ASSYRIAN TRANSEPT
   3. Sargon and officials (p. 16).
NIMRUD GALLERY
   2. Priest in divine headdress with horns (p. 5)
   28-29. Conflict between Bel and dragon Tiamat (p. 9)
   37-b. Angels and sacred tree (p. 9).
NIMRUD CENTRAL SALOON
   4. Black stele of Shalmaneser III—Jehu bringing tribute from Israel (p. 16).
ASSYRIAN SALOON
  In Gallery
   5. Capture of Lachish by Sennacherib on his way to the "fenced cities of Judah." Hezekiah surrenders the treasures of the Temple to Sennacherib at Lachish (II Kings 18:13-14).
  On Main Floor
   3. A "hanging garden" in Assyria
   10. Banquet of Assyrian king and his queen (cf. *Esther*)
   12. Inscription describing Sargon II's conquests in Judah.
Case at end of room: bands from the bronze gates of Shal-

[1] Page references are to more detailed descriptions in our chapters on the Louvre, Cluny, etc.

423

maneser III (cf. Is. 45:1-2). On band 5, ships of Tyre (Ez. 27:5-8). On band 12, a ship from Ararat.

NINEVEH (KUYUNJIK) GALLERY

Note the action of fire on the blackened sculpture (cf. Nahum, 3: 13 and 15)

20-26. Assyrians assault a city set on a domed hill, thought to be Jerusalem

27-29. Execution of prisoners with Jewish features

48-50. Torture of Elamite prisoners (cf. Is. 10: 4-5).

SECOND NORTHERN GALLERY—ROOM I

Phœnician and Hebrew Inscriptions

Case 3. Cast of inscription from tunnel of Hezekiah (p. 26).

Case 5. Cast of Moabite inscription (p. 24).

Case 8. Votive tablets from Carthage showing figure of a "hand" still a symbol of good luck among North African Jews

Case 9-13. Hebrew tombstones from Aden, fourteenth century C.E.

Case 13. Samaritan inscription (No. 556) quoting Deut. 6:7; 23:15; 28:6.

SECOND NORTHERN GALLERY—ROOM II

Centre case

Collection of Hebrew seals from Palestine

1032. Shahor ben Zephaniah

1034. Hananiah ben Gadiah

1041. Sa-el (God saves), with star and bull

1043. "For the remembrance of Hosea," with a gryphon

1049. Nehemiah ben Micaiah.

Shelf above seals

Glass vases from Beth Jebrin, near Hebron

Figures of Astarte (p. 12).

BABYLONIAN ROOM (SECOND NORTHERN GALLERY—ROOM III)

Centre black cases and wall cases 1-4, 39-43

Objects from Ur of the Chaldees, in 3000 B.C., a thousand years before Abraham. Among them, note (No. 121201), in mosaic, a fringed garment resembling Jewish prayer-shawl.

Table case H

Tablets from Ur, down to 1900 B.C., approximately the period of Abraham. No. 103406 is an inventory of the flocks of a herdsman (p. 5).

Wall cases 32-40

Bricks recording building of temple to Moon-god in Ur p. 5).

Wall cases 14-15

214. Sculptured tablet showing sun-worship. (cf. II Kings 23:11).

Wall cases 31-36

348-404. Series of bricks from Babylon mentioning Nebuchadnezzar II, the Nebuchadnezzar of the Bible.

Table case E

140. Babylonian tablet recording the fall of Babylon (cf. Is. 21:1-10).

Table case F

Tell-el-Amarna tablets (p. 11).

Table case G

17-19. Tablet telling of repairs on tower of Babylon (Babel), which, it says, was built in olden days and never finished.

Coloured brickwork from tower similar to the Tower of Babel.

80. Cylinder of Cyrus giving Persian account of fall of Babylon.

ASSYRIAN ROOM

Wall cases 1-2

1-5. Metal helmets and shield (cf. Nahum 2:3; Ezek. 23:24).

Wall cases 4-21 (upper and lower shelves)

37-52. Metal weights, shaped like lions, from Nimrud, and reckoned in manehs (Ezek. 45:12).

Wall case 35

1-11. Fragments of cylinder recording campaign of Sargon against Ashdod (Is. 20:1).

Wall cases 14-18

41. Inscription recording Ahaz king of Judah as tributary to Tiglath-pileser III.

Wall cases 20-22

Magic bowls, many with Hebrew text (p. 17).

Wall cases 25-26

135-157. Portions of crystal throne of Sennacherib.

Wall cases 38-45

Tablets containing astrological forecasts, and astrolabes. "Let now the astrologers, the star-gazers, the monthly prognosticators, stand up and save thee from these things that shall come upon thee" (Is. 47:13).

Wall cases 33-38 (5th shelf)

3. Sumerian hymn to Moon-god, whose word "createth right and ordaineth justice." (p. 6).

Table case A

Tablets giving Assyrian account of Creation and the Flood. Among them, No. 23 tells of Sargon and the bullrushes (p. 4).

Table cases B and E

11-12. Prism recording Sargon's conquest of Israel

20. Prism telling of Sennacherib's siege of Jerusalem

21. Prism giving details of the siege. "Hezekiah, himself, I shut up, like a caged bird, within Jerusalem, his royal city."

Table cases B and E (lower portion)
  Cylinder seals
    6. Seal of Darius (cf. Esther 8:8)
    7. Scene of man and woman standing with a tree be-
       tween them, in a garden (cf. Gen. 3)
    8. Seal with scene of the Babylonian Noah afloat on an
       ark
    11. Combat between Marduk and the dragon Tiamat
        (p. 9)
    41. Gilgamesh ("Nimrod the mighty hunter") slays a
        lion.

EGYPTIAN COLLECTION—ROOM V
  Table case G
    Exhibit of "fine linen with broidered work from Egypt"
    (Ezek. 27:7).
  Table case I
    Gnostic seals and amulets (second century C.E.), with in-
    scriptions using name of Jehovah and of the archangels.
    No. 24335 shows a menorah.
  Wall cases 183-187
    Models of granaries (cf. Gen. 41:56).
  Wall cases 206-207
    Bricks made with straw; some stamped with name of
    Rameses II, possibly the pharaoh of the oppression.
  Wall cases 235-236
    Images of Baal (p. 13).
  Wall cases 238-241
    Figures of the god Khnum, worshipped at Elephantine,
    where Jews had a colony and temple in the fifth cen-
    tury B.C. (p. 219).

EGYPTIAN COLLECTION—ROOM VI
  Wall cases 270-272
    Eye-paint boxes and other cosmetic devices (cf. Ezek.
    23:40; Jer. 4:30).

Manuscript Saloon

  Case G

    Or. 4445. Oldest known example of Hebrew Pentateuch
    —MS. of ninth century c.e.

King's Library

  Case A

    1. Samaritan liturgy, 1258 c.e.

    3. Hebrew lexicon of Menahem ben Saruk, 1091 c.e.
    Menahem flourished under Hasdai Ibn Shaprut
    (p. 124)

    Or. 5518. Portions of original Hebrew text of Ecclesiasti-
    cus, found in the genizah of the Cairo synagogue—
    probably twelfth century c.e. (p. 220)

    Or. 5519. MS. of two legal questions submitted to Mai-
    monides, with replies in his own hand (Arabic in
    Hebrew characters)

    Or. 5538. Two Hebrew letters, dated 997 and 1004, from
    the Cairo genizah

    Har. 5698. Richly illuminated Hebrew MS. of the *Mish-
    neh Torah* of Maimonides, Spanish work, 1472

    Add. 11639. Illuminated Hebrew MS. of Pentateuch and
    prayer-book, French work, about 1278. Visible minia-
    tures show Judith and Holophernes, Moses striking
    the rock, and the brazen serpent worshipped by the
    Israelites

    Add. 26968. Illuminated Hebrew prayer-book, Italian rite,
    1383. Visible miniature shows rabbi teaching school
    children.

Mediæval Collection—King Edward VII Gallery

  Case at far end of room

    1331-50. Collection of Hebrew betrothal and marriage
    rings (p. 79). Nos. 1331-32, coloured enamel, show the
    temptation of Adam, a menorah, and the blowing of
    the *shofar*.

Coin and Medal Room
   Table case 8
      Series of coins illustrating Biblical history, etc. The fol-
      lowing are noteworthy:
         1. Philistine coin, fourth century B.C., possibly men-
            tioning "Jahveh"
         2. Simon Maccabaeus, 136 B.C., showing *etrog, lulab,*
            palm tree
         3. Herod the Great, 37-4 B.C.
         6. Herod Philip II, 4 B.C.-34 C.E., showing a temple
        11. Herod Agrippa, 37-44 C.E., beneath royal umbrella
        12. Shekel of the First Revolt, 67-8 C.E., with cup and
            lily
        13. Sesterces of Vespasian, with legend "Judea Capta"
        14. Goldpiece of Titus, with similar legend
        17. Coin of Second Revolt, 132-35 C.E., showing *etrog,
            lulab,* and a tabernacle surmounted by a star,
            with inscription "Bar Cochba" (?).

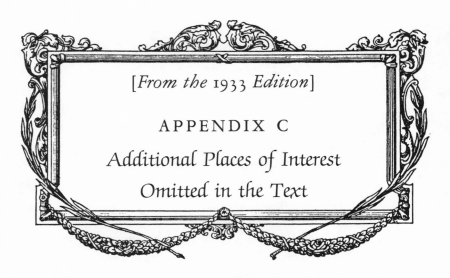

[*From the* 1933 *Edition*]

APPENDIX C

Additional Places of Interest Omitted in the Text

SWITZERLAND

Basel. Historical Museum: Thirteenth- to fourteenth-century tombstones. Veselianum Institute: 12 skulls from Jewish cemetery formerly on this site. Cathedral: choir-stall with carving of *Judensau*. Frey-Frynäum courtyard: thirteenth- and fifteenth-century tombstones.

Bern. Historical Museum: flag of Jewish shoemakers' guild, dated 1540.

Zurich. Eighteenth-century cemetery between near-by villages of Endigen and Lengnau; Jews of Switzerland restricted to these two villages from seventeenth to nineteenth century.

RHINELANDS

Bacharach. Ruined Church of St. Werner, dedicated to boy-saint whom Jews were accused of murdering (1286).

Bad Kreuznach. Synagogue, built 1735; restored.

Beilstein (on Moselle). Seventeenth-century synagogue, containing pewter ewer of Gothic period.

Camberg (Taunus). Eighteenth-century synagogue.

Coblentz. Museum (House of Syndics): Thirteenth- to fourteenth-century tombstones. Old houses in former Jewry on Burgstrasse.

Darmstadt. Landesbibliotek: famous Haggadah of fourteenth to fifteenth century (codex orient. 8), with 15 full-
page miniatures and 11 illuminated pages; also fourteenth-
century illuminated prayer-book (orient ms. 13).

Deutz. Cemetery dating from 1695; baroque stones.

Düsseldorf. 53 Bolkerstrasse, in court, house where Heine was
born (1799).

Falkenstein (Taunus). Half-timber synagogue.

Freudenburg (Rheinprovinz). Synagogue built about 1784,
with adjoining Talmud Torah (school). Old cemetery.

Limburg an der Lahn. Seventeenth-century synagogue, now
surmounted by church spire; half-timber apse for ark.

Oberwesel. Thirteenth-century church dedicated to St.
Werner (see Bacharach).

Ries am Rhein. Old cemetery.

Schwarzrheindorf (near Bonn). Seventeenth-century cemetery.

Trier. Museum: five fourteenth-century tombstones.

Waldesgrün (near Niederbreisig). Old cemetery.

Weisenau (near Mayence). Synagogue built in 1736, with
Gothic features.

ALSACE-LORRAINE

Colmar. Rue des Juifs, off Grand Rue; old houses Nos. 10, 15.
Unterlinden Museum: two fourteenth-century tombstones.

Epinal. Rue des Juifs next to modern Bourse.

Hagenau. Synagogue of 1819 contains dedicatory tablet of old
synagogue built in 1252. Cemetery with seventeenth- to
eighteenth-century stones.

Hagenheim. Cemetery with seventeenth- to eighteenth-century tombstones.

Jungholz. Seventeenth-century cemetery.

Metz. Rue des Juifs behind Hôtel de Ville.

Molsheim. Grand and Petit Rue des Juifs. In latter, building called "Klaus" with dedicatory tablet of mediæval synagogue.

Mulhouse. Historical Museum: Ritual art objects.

Mutzig. Eighteenth (?)-century synagogue.

Rouffach. Late Gothic synagogue, largely dating from fifteenth century, now in private hands; inscription on drum over door names donor, David ben Israel.

Schlestadt. Musée de Ville: ritual art objects. Cemetery with tombs from 1400. Fourteenth-century synagogue building now in private hands.

Sulz. Two eighteenth (?)-century synagogues.

Westhofen. Synagogue of eighteenth (?) century.

SOUTH GERMANY

Danube Basin

Amberg. Church of Our Lady (Frauenkirche) formerly a synagogue.

Augsburg. Judburg, the former Jewry, in centre of city. Maximilian Museum: thirteenth- to fourteenth-century tombstones. The Pulvergässchen (Powder Alley) so called from legendary Jew, named Tibsiles, who is claimed to have invented gunpowder.

Binswangen. Cemetery with baroque tombstones.

Deggendorf. Church of Holy Sepulchre (Hl. Grabeskirche) erected 1337 in gratitude for miraculous deliverance of a Host from desecration by the Jews; inscription on pillar describes the event and punishment of Jews. The scene is painted on city gate.

Friesing. Church with *Judensau* and inscription: "As easily as a mouse eats a cat, so a Jew becomes a true Christian."

Harburg (Ries). Synagogue built in 1754; the Landauer

house was previous synagogue. Cemetery dating from third quarter of seventeenth century.

Monheim (Swabia). Synagogue built 1705; converted into present Town Hall in 1741; ceiling still preserves Biblical scenes and characters carved in stucco (sacrifice of Isaac, Moses on Sinai, etc.).

Munich. National Museum (Room 72, cases 9, 10, 11): Ritual art objects, including especially fine Torah bands.

Pappenheim. Cemetery with tombs dating from fourteenth century. Synagogue (built 1811) uses Italian rite, introduced by Sephardic refugees coming to Germany by way of Italy.

Passau. St. Salvator Church stands on site of old synagogue. The Ilzstadt church (across the River Ilz) contains six stained-glass windows depicting story of desecration of Host by Jews (1477).

Thannhausen. Synagogue converted into chapel in 1718 (still called Judenkapelle), as result of Jews being charged with bewitching the local countess, thereby rendering her barren. At entry to chapel, old alms-box from synagogue, with appropriate sculpture.

Ulm. Judenhof behind cathedral. Museum contains numerous thirteenth- to fifteenth-century tombstones.

Main Basin

Altenkundstadt (Franconia). Synagogue with marriage stone dated 1756.

Georgenmünde. Synagogue built 1733, with adjoining Talmud Torah. Cemetery dating from fourteenth century.

Kissingen. Judenhof in corner of city walls (now Engegasse). In Town Hall, bearded figure with helmet commemorating Jew who, during siege of city by Swedes, cast bullets that never failed to hit their mark.

Miltenberg. Late thirteenth-century synagogue, now in possession of a brewery. The pediment of the mediæval ark is preserved in the modern synagogue.

Schwabach. Synagogue with marriage stone dated 1730.

Neckar Basin

Hechingen (south of Stuttgart). Synagogue in Goldschmieds-strasse (formerly Judengasse) built in late seventeenth century; restored 1852; possesses collection of seventeenth- to eighteenth-century embroideries and silver ornaments for Torah. Yeshibah built in 1796. Cemetery in use since seventeenth century.

Heilbronn. St.-Kilian's Church: sculpture of *Judensau* in choir.

NORTH GERMANY

Hesse

Borken. Synagogue built c. 1800.

Büdigen. Early nineteenth-century synagogue, with ark from predecessor, a late seventeenth-century half-timber structure now a warehouse, close to town wall.

Cassel. Museum: two sixteenth-century spice-boxes, Renaissance betrothal ring, eighteenth-century Torah crown, Biblical paintings by Rembrandt. Synagogue: magnificent ark curtain.

Gelnhausen. Massive baroque synagogue (near town wall) built 1656, rebuilt 1734; faces courtyard together with Talmud Torah and *mikveh*; marriage stone on wall of synagogue; two eighteenth-century Elijah chairs.

Münden. Synagogue and community house on courtyard, built c. 1800.

Rothenburg-am-Fulda. Early eighteenth-century half-timber

synagogue; ceiling upheld by four columns showing Polish influence; adjoining women's synagogue; and across inner courtyard old Talmud Torah.

Schlüchtern. Synagogue built c. 1700, now warehouse. In present synagogue an eighteenth-century Elijah chair.

Vollmerz (near Hecht). Eighteenth-century synagogue, with *mikveh*.

Witzenhausen. Synagogue built c. 1800; eighteenth-century alms-box.

Zwesten. Late eighteenth-century synagogue.

Silesia

Dyherrnfurth. Small, stout eighteenth-century synagogue now closed. Cemetery, in manor park, with stones dating 1689-1762, during period when Jews were not allowed to bury in Breslau; carvings of best baroque period—floral designs, and an occasional bird to be met again in Poland.

Glogau. Synagogue: early eighteenth-century *rimonim*, a Torah crown dated 1720, and shield 1727.

Langendorf. Synagogue: numerous art objects of eighteenth century.

Neustadt. Synagogue: many ritual art treasures, mostly from old community of Zülz (see Zülz); seventeenth-century silver alms-boxes, eighteenth-century spice-boxes, pointers, shields, crowns, *rimonim,* ewers, and basins.

Oels. Salvator Church formerly a thirteenth-century synagogue. Ground plan resembles Altneu synagogue of Prague. Small building to left likely housed sixteenth-century Hebrew press of Hayim Schwarz.

Striegau. St. Barbara Chapel formerly thirteenth-century synagogue; Romanesque arches and grape-vine *motif* in sculpture probably all that remains of Jewish period.

Zülz. A "righteous place"—from which Jews were never expelled. Synagogue, built 1774, now unused. Most of its treasures in Neustadt. Their richness due to Zülz serving as haven for Silesian Jews during seventeenth century, when they were allowed residence only here and in Glogau.

Elsewhere

Angermünde. Synagogue, Empire style, built c. 1800.

Burgsteinfurt (Westphalia). Synagogue built 1763; eighteenth-century Elijah chair.

Ellrich (near Nordhausen). Seventeenth-century half-timber synagogue; old Gothic panelled door.

Emden. Synagogue preserves ark dated 1701. Old *mikveh* in basement. On 2 Dahlerstrasse, stones inscribed in Hebrew, carved with crowns and dated 1629; on 8 Dahlerstrasse, another stone, dated 1716. Cemetery with seventeenth- to eighteenth-century tombstones.

Göttingen. Judengasse in centre of town. Ritual art objects in museum at 12 Ritterplan.

Halberstadt. Half-timber houses in Judenstrasse. Synagogue built in seventeenth century, renovated in 1879.

Heiligenstadt. Annenkapelle: choir stall with carving of *Judensau.*

Herford (Westphalia). Seventeenth- to eighteenth-century cemetery.

Leipzig. Jewish fur merchants still occupy old site on the Brühl, in fair grounds, which they did in seventeenth century.

Magdeburg. Cathedral: chapel under tower with sculpture of *Judensau.*

Meiningen (Saxony). Church of Mary Magdalene, near north gate, formerly a synagogue.

Münster. Jüdefelderstrasse (Jews Fields Street), near northwest site of walls; synagogue still occupies this street.

Wimpfen (Thuringia). Abbey church: *Judensau* carved on pillar in choir.

CZECHOSLOVAKIA

Northwest Bohemia

Chiesch (east of Marienbad). Eighteenth-century synagogue on highest spot near town wall.

Dürrmaul (south-east of Marienbad). Daughter community of Kuttenplan. Synagogue built 1803; double mansard roof, massive wooden *bima*; matzoth bakery, slaughterhouse, school, beadle's house and synagogue built in one complex.

Eger. Judenhof (off Judengasse), site of old Jewish Town Hall. Mordgässchen commemorates in its name a massacre of 1350. Four thirteenth- to fourteenth-century tombstones in old Eger Rathaus. Most of the stones were used for paving-blocks after destruction of cemetery by populace.

Klein-Schüttüber (north-west of Marienbad). Synagogue built 1808, rustic type. Single high-pitched roof, with tiny dormer windows. Matzoth bakery and dwelling adjoining synagogue.

Königsberg (north-west of Marienbad). Timber synagogue built 1802 on highest spot in village. Open vestibule for Feast of Booths. Resembles South German synagogues; mural paintings.

Königswart (west of Marienbad). Synagogue built 1764, restored 1848. Candelabrum with human figure waving thunderbolt.

Lichtenstadt (north-east of Marienbad). Synagogue of first decade nineteenth century; rabbi's house and bakery attached.

Luck (north-east of Marienbad). Early nineteenth-century synagogue with *beth ha-midrash* and bakery attached.

Neuzedlisch (south-west of Pilsen). Abandoned synagogue

built 1788; double galleries for women, and double mansard roof resembling wooden synagogues of Poland.

Pauten (north-east of Marienbad). Abandoned synagogue; lower story built of stone shelters dwelling, bakery, *mikveh*; upper story of timber; no separate gallery for women.

Petschau (north-east of Marienbad). Synagogue built c. 1765; date on wrought-iron railing of *bima*. Part of ironwork, showing Polish influence, dates from older synagogue in 1688. Ark curtain dated 1684. Building damaged by fire in 1904. Ark and wood-carvings notable, resembling Zolkiew in Poland. Building stands on edge of hill above town, partly supported by underlying buttresses.

Purschau (near Tachau). Massive synagogue, with rabbi's dwelling on ground floor; built on towering site.

Ronsperg (south-west of Pilsen). Synagogue built 1816. Oblong form, with ark against longer wall, as in Padua. Vaulted basement-like lower floor holds rabbi's study and *mikveh*; women's gallery shut off by heavy lattice-work. School and bakery to either side of vestibule.

Schoner (south of Marienbad). Rustic type of synagogue, of early nineteenth century.

Schönwald (near Tachau). Massive synagogue, with rabbi's dwelling on ground floor; towers over village; no annex or balcony for women.

Tachau (south-west of Marienbad). Late eighteenth-century synagogue. Town on old main road to Nuremberg.

Elsewhere

Jungbunzlau (45 miles north-east of Prague). Small collection of ritual art in synagogue; cemetery with seventeenth-century stones.

Krumau (Moravia). Formerly most important community after Nikolsburg. Seventeenth-century synagogue.

POLAND

Bialystok

Bialystok. Cemetery with painted tombstones.

Bielsk (30 miles south of Bialystok). Cemetery with painted tombstones.

Grodno. Seventeenth-century timber triple-roofed synagogue in suburb (Zaniemienskie).

Jedwabno (20 miles north-east of Lomza). Timber synagogue with triple roof.

Jeziory or Ozyory (12 miles east of Grodno). Seventeenth-century synagogue, with finely carved Elijah chair.

Orla (5 miles south of Bielsk). Stone synagogue with mural painting.

Sniadowo (18 miles east of Ostrolenka). Eighteenth-century five-roofed timber synagogue; loggia; pavilions with cupolas; delicate wooden traceries on windows.

Sopockinie (20 miles north-west of Grodno). Eighteenth-century timber synagogue with triple roof: two double-roofed pavilions.

Suchowola (20 miles north-west of Sokolka). Quadruple-roofed timber synagogue; two pavilions; excellent proportions.

Telaki (55 miles north-east of Warsaw). Triple-roofed timber synagogue; two pavilions; lean-to's; rich complex of lines and planes.

Wolpa. Triple-roofed timber synagogue; double-roofed pavilion; excellent proportions and design.

Zabludow (11 miles south-east of Bialystok). Double-roofed timber synagogue (built 1646, restored 1765); cupolas, lean-to's, frieze of inlay, paintings on walls and ceiling, altogether most characteristic of its type in Poland. Ark carved by Samuel Goldmanaz.

Zambrow (30 miles east of Ostrolenka). Seventeenth- to eighteenth-century synagogue.

Warszawa

Gabin (10 miles south of Plock). Excellent eighteenth-century timber synagogue.

Gora Kalwarja (20 miles south-east of Warsaw). Cemetery with painted tombstones.

Grojec (30 miles south of Warsaw). Cemetery on hill-top, with painted tombstones.

Rozany (40 miles north of Warsaw). Cemetery with painted tombstones.

Wyszogrod (40 miles north-west of Warsaw). Stone synagogue with mural painting; notable ark and a *bima* surmounted by a canopy.

Novogrodek

Baranowicze (on main railroad line, Warsaw-Moscow, near Polish border). Cemetery in grove, with painted tombstones.

Novogrodek. Cemetery with painted tombstones.

Selwa (20 miles west of Slonim). Synagogue with elaborately carved ark.

Slonim. Cemetery with painted tombstones.

Polesie

Brest-Litovsk. Cemetery with painted tombstones.

Kobrin (30 miles east of Brest-Litovsk). Synagogue with mural painting; note zodiac has birds instead of human figures for Twins and Virgin.

Kozangrodek (20 miles south of Lachwa). Eighteenth-century timber synagogue.

Lachwa (50 miles east of Pinsk). Eighteenth-century timber synagogue.

Pinsk. Baroque synagogue, with tower. Cemetery in grove, with painted tombstones.

Pruzany (40 miles north-east of Brest-Litovsk). Cemetery with painted tombstones.

Lublin

Chelm. Double-aisle gothic synagogue, resembling Cracow and Prague.

Gniewoszow (50 miles east of Lublin). Eighteenth-century timber synagogue, resembling Kurnik.

Kazmierz (30 miles west of Lublin). Cemetery with painted tombstones.

Parczew (35 miles north-east of Lublin). Seventeenth- to eighteenth-century synagogue.

Volhynia

Dubno. Sixteenth-century stone synagogue.

Leszniow (12 miles north of Brody). Seventeenth-century fortified synagogue.

Luboml (85 miles east of Lublin). Seventeenth-century fortified synagogue.

Luck. Fortified synagogue built 1626; four central piers rising from *bima* into vaulting. Eighteenth-century timber Karaite synagogue.

Olyka (12 miles east of Luck). Eighteenth-century timber synagogue.

Ostrog (25 miles south of Rovno). Seventeenth-century fortified synagogue; Renaissance barrel-vaulting; *bima* between four central piers; baroque ark.

Polonka (near Luck). Cemetery with painted tombstones.

Stepan (60 miles north of Rovno). Sixteenth-century synagogue, fortified in seventeenth century; hammered copper plaques as wall decoration. Cemetery dating from 1536.

Zdolbunowo (south of Rovno). Eighteenth-century timber synagogue.

Kielce

Begorja (35 miles west of Sandomir). Single-roofed timber synagogue, built in 1560.

Konskie (25 miles north-west of Kielce). Eighteenth-century timber synagogue; loggia.

Opatow (20 miles north-west of Sandomir). Old cemetery, with finely carved stones.

Opoczno (25 miles east of Piotrkow). Seventeenth-century synagogue.

Ostrowiec (30 miles north-west of Sandomir). Seventeenth- to eighteenth-century synagogue.

Pilica (40 miles north-west of Cracow). Single-roofed timber synagogue, with charming details; intricate corbels under eaves.

Pinczow (50 miles north-east of Cracow). Sixteenth-century stone synagogue; seventeenth- to eighteenth-century ritual art objects, including 27 ark curtains embroidered in gold and silver.

Przedborz (20 miles south-east of Piotrkow). Single-roofed timber synagogue.

Sandomir. Fourteenth-century stone synagogue, supposedly one of three built by Esterka, mistress of Casimir the Great; traces of murals; sixteenth- to eighteenth-century embroidered ark curtains; eighteenth-century candelabra; hammered copper plaque representing the spies returning from Canaan.

Szydlow (40 miles south-west of Sandomir). Fourteenth-century synagogue, popularly claimed to be founded by Esterka.

Wodzislow (40 miles north of Cracow). Fortress-like synagogue; double timber roof; heavy buttresses.

Lodz

Lutomierz (7 miles west of Lodz). Double-roofed timber synagogue; classic porch. Decorative inlay frieze. Built late eighteenth century by Hillel Benjamin.

Parzeczew (north-east of Lodz). Timber synagogue.

Posen (Poznan)

Kempen. Massive synagogue built 1815. Ark a masterpiece of wood-carving, using musical instruments in design—the work of Samuel Goldbaum. Wood-and-metal canopy over *bima*.

Kurnik (12 miles south-east of Posen). Triple-roofed wooden synagogue, built 1767, probably by Hillel Benjamin. Early eighteenth-century ark, with "music" panels as in Kempen. Eternal Lamp in shrine in north-west corner. Handsome Elijah chair. General character of building more classic than east and south Polish work.

Miloslow (30 miles south-east of Posen). Eighteenth-century synagogue; handsome canopy over *bima*.

Rakow (south-east of Kempen). Timber synagogue of same period and style as Kurnik.

Galicia

Brody. Seventeenth- to eighteenth-century fortified synagogue.

Buczacz (100 miles south-east of Lemberg). Seventeenth-century fortified synagogue.

Chodorow (40 miles south-east of Lemberg). Triple-roofed timber synagogue, built 1642; pavilions; mural paintings.

Chyrow (20 miles south of Przemysl). Eighteenth-century timber synagogue; classic influence.

Felztyn (6 miles east of Chyrow). Eighteenth-century timber synagogue in classic style.

Gwozdziec (east of Kolomea). Synagogue with mural painting.

Husiatyn (bordering Podolia, east of Lemberg). Seventeenth-century fortified synagogue; magnificent wrought-iron grill and triumphal arch leading to carved wooden ark; mural painting above.

Janow (near Trembowla, 20 miles south of Tarnopol). Seventeenth-century double-roofed timber synagogue; mural painting; seventeenth-century carved-wood ark; handsome Elijah chair. A score of stones in cemetery with highly original designs.

Kamionka Strumilowa (25 miles north-east of Lemberg). Seventeenth-century triple-roofed timber synagogue; elegant balcony; eighteenth-century mural painting. Cemetery with stones showing influence of textile designs.

Kosow (15 miles south of Kolomea). Eighteenth-century timber synagogue, resembling Kurnik.

Lancut (10 miles east of Rzeszow). Seventeenth-century fortified synagogue.

Mielec (30 miles north-east of Tarnow). Stone synagogue with two bastions; resembling Romanesque work.

Narol (near Jaroslau). Eighteenth-century timber synagogue.

Nowy Sacz (30 miles south-west of Tarnow). Seventeenth-century baroque stone synagogue.

Przeworsk (25 miles east of Rzeszow). Seventeenth-century stone synagogue similar to Rzeszow; handsome stone *bima*.

Rozdol. Eighteenth-century timber synagogue, resembling Kurnik.

Starasol (10 miles east of Chyrow). Eighteenth-century timber synagogue.

Tarnopol. Seventeenth-century fortified synagogue. Cemetery: magnificent Renaissance and baroque stones. Karaite synagogue.

Tarnow. Eighteenth-century timber synagogue.

Trembowla (20 miles south of Tarnopol). Seventeenth- to eighteenth-century fortified synagogue.

Zloczow (40 miles east of Lemberg). Eighteenth-century timber synagogue, presumably built by Hillel Benjamin.

RUSSIA

Podolia and Russian Volhynia, once within jurisdiction of the Council of the Four Lands

Jermolinsky or Jermolince (30 miles north-east of Husiatyn). Seventeenth-century synagogue.

Kamenez-Podolsk. Sixteenth-century fortified synagogue, built during Turkish occupation.

Lanckorona (18 miles north-west of Kamenez-Podolsk). Double-roofed timber synagogue.

Michalpol (15 miles north-east of Jermolinsky). Eighteenth-century timber synagogue.

Miedzyboz (35 miles east of Prosskurow). *Beth ha-midrash* and tomb of the Baal Shemtob.

Ostropol (18 miles south-east of Berdichev). Sixteenth- to seventeenth-century fortified synagogue; seventeenth-century triple-roofed timber synagogue, pavilions, loggia.

Pobrebyszcz (near Berdichev). Synagogue built 1688, restored 1730; magnificent eighteenth-century candelabrum, executed by Baruch, showing goat, cock, and wood-birds.

Zaragorod. Seventeenth-century fortified synagogue.

White Russia

Mohilev. Seventeenth-century synagogue with mural painting.

Narowla. Eighteenth-century timber synagogue.

Peski (north-east of Esthonia). Multiple-roofed wooden synagogue.

Uzlany. Eighteenth-century timber synagogue; ark in carved wood by Ber ben Israel.

LITHUANIA

Jurburg or Jurbork (between Kovno and Tilsit). Quadruple-roofed timber synagogue; two pavilions; loggia; elaborate pilasters.

Wylkowyszki (40 miles from Kovno near Polish border). Double-roofed timber synagogue; two pavilions; high gable over doorway.

THE "GREAT" SYNAGOGUE OF TOLEDO, THIRTEENTH CENTURY
See page 149

BRITISH MUSEUM. ISRAELITES (SECOND ROW OF SCULPTURE) BRING TRIBUTE TO SHALMANESER III

See page 16

LOUVRE. HAMMURABI RECEIVES THE LAW FROM THE GOD SHAMASH

See page 3

LOUVRE. ANCIENT GLASS VASE
FROM PALESTINE, SHOWING GRAPE
CLUSTER AND CITRON

See page 28

BERLIN. KAISER FRIEDRICH MUSEUM.
RELIEF FROM PRIENE SYNAGOGUE, ME-
NORAH FLANKED BY LULAB AND SHOFAR
AND BY ETROG

See pages 29 and 324

JERUSALEM. JEWISH OSSUARY
See page 37

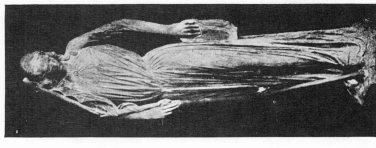

STRASBOURG. THIRTEENTH-
CENTURY SCULPTURE OF
SYNAGOGUE

See page 52

CLUNY. TWELFTH-CENTURY ENAMEL. JESUS BETWEEN CHURCH
AND SYNAGOGUE

See page 83

TROYES. A JEW PUT TO WORK AS A GARGOYLE

See page 90

PAINTED LINEN TORAH BAND, DATED 1816
See page 72

CLUNY. SAND CUP FOR CIRCUM-
CISION
See page 72

ELIJAH CHAIR FROM OSIORY (POLAND)
See page 108

NATIONAL   MUSEUM,
MUNICH.   CIRCUMCI-
SION KNIFE
See page 72

BELLS, MANTLES, AND CROWNS IN THE SYNAGOGUE OF LIVORNO
See page 257

CLUNY MUSEUM. SEVENTEENTH-CENTURY POINTER FOR TORAH
See page 76

OFFENBACH. SEVENTEENTH-CENTURY ARK CURTAIN
See page 74

AVIGNON. THIRTEENTH-CENTURY JEWRY
—ENTRY TO SUPPOSED SYNAGOGUE AT
RIGHT

See page 102

SYNAGOGUE OF CAVAILLON (FRANCE)
RESTORED IN THE EIGHTEENTH CENTURY

See page 111

AVIGNON. RHONE GATE LEADING TO
GHETTO

See page 101

CARPENTRAS. EIGHTEENTH-CEN-
TURY ELIJAH CHAIR PERCHED IN
NICHE NEXT TO ARK

See page 108

CORDOVA. FOURTEENTH-CENTURY SYNAGOGUE, WEST WALL

See page 128

CORDOVA. "JEW'S GATE"

See page 125

CORDOVA. MAIMONIDES STREET. GATE
TO FOURTEENTH-CENTURY SYNAGOGUE
IN BACKGROUND

See page 127

EL TRANSITO SYNAGOGUE. DETAIL OF NORTH
ARCADE
See page 155

TOLEDO. EL TRANSITO SYNAGOGUE, FOURTEENTH CENTURY
See page 154

TOLEDO. FOURTEENTH-CENTURY MANSION
OF SAMUEL HALEVI
See page 152

TOLEDO. TYPICAL LANE IN JEWRY
WHERE SCIENCE PASSED FROM MOOR-
ISH TO CHRISTIAN WORLD
See page 160

TOLEDO. CELLARS OF SAMUEL HALEVI'S MANSION
See page 156

SEVILLE. CALLE LEVIES. TYPICAL
FIFTEENTH-CENTURY PATIO
See page 136

SEGOVIA. THE JEWRY FLANKS THE
CATHEDRAL
See page 167

SEGOVIA. THIRTEENTH-CENTURY? SYNAGOGUE BEFORE RESTORATION
See page 168

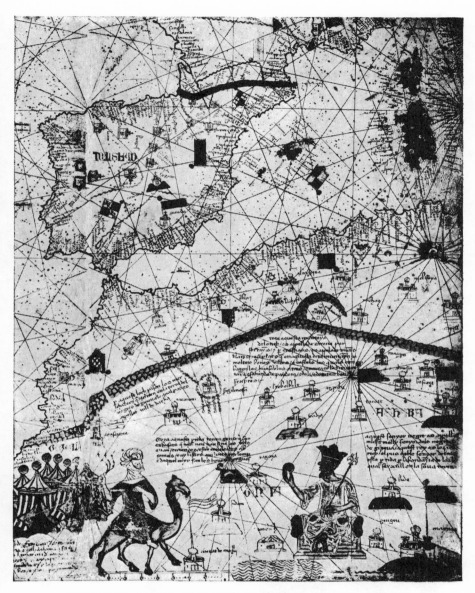

FOURTEENTH-CENTURY ATLAS MADE BY THE JEW CRESQUES OF PALMA

See page 183

CLUNY MUSEUM. SEVEN-
TEENTH-CENTURY SPICE-
BOX, GERMAN ORIGIN
See page 80

CLUNY MUSEUM. FOURTEENTH-CENTURY HANUKA
LAMP, FRENCH ORIGIN
See page 81

SILVER BREASTPLATE FOR TORAH
See page 76

PALMA. SPANISH RIMONIM NOW IN CATHE-
DRAL TREASURY
See page 184

LEMBERG. PLATTER IN "GOLDEN ROSE" SYNAGOGUE

See page 365

JANOW. EIGHTEENTH-CENTURY SILVER CROWN FOR TORAH

See page 367

LINCOLN. TWELFTH-CENTURY JEW'S HOUSE (OF BELLASET?)

See page 214

LONDON. SYNAGOGUE IN BEVIS MARKS (BUILT 1701)

See page 222

MANCHESTER. JOHN RYLANDS LIBRARY. THIRTEENTH-CENTURY HAGGADAH

See page 464

AMSTERDAM, THE PORTUGUESE SYNAGOGUE ON THE DAY OF ITS DEDICATION (AUGUST 2, 1675)
See page 194

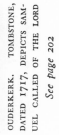

OUDERKERK, TOMBSTONE,
DATED 1717, DEPICTS SAM-
UEL CALLED OF THE LORD
See page 202

JANOW. EIGHTEENTH-CEN-
TURY TOMBSTONE
See page 368

OUDERKERK, TOMBSTONE,
DATED 1701, DEPICTS ABRA-
HAM ENTERTAINING THE
ANGELS
See page 202

ROME. JEWISH CATACOMB IN VIGNA RANDANINI
See page 234

VIGNA RANDANINI CATACOMB.
THE PEACOCK FOR IMMOR-
TALITY

See page 234

LATERAN MUSEUM. PORTRAIT OF A BOY FROM AN
ANCIENT JEWISH SARCOPHAGUS

See page 236

PADUA. THE BIMA IN THE SYNAGOGUE OF THE ITALIAN
RITE

See page 262

FERRARA. THE ARK OF THE LAW IN THE SYNAGOGUE OF THE SPANISH RITE

See page 257

WORMS. THE RASHI GATE
See page 276

FRANKFORT. ROTHSCHILD HOUSE
See page 288

WORMS. MEN'S SYNAGOGUE, TWELFTH
CENTURY
See page 276

WORMS. STAIRWAY IN TWELFTH-CEN-
TURY RITUAL BATH
See page 281

BAMBERG MUSEUM. CEILING AND EAST WALL OF HORB SYNAGOGUE

See page 306

PRAGUE. ALTNEU SYNAGOGUE AND JEWISH TOWN HALL
See pages 338 and 341

PRAGUE RATHAUS. RABBI JUDAH BEN
BEZALEL LÖW
See page 334

JOSEPH SOLOMON DELMEDIGO, "WHO
FOUND NEITHER HAPPINESS NOR HOME"
See page 333

PRAGUE. JEWISH CEMETERY

See page 332

PRAGUE. INTERIOR OF ALTNEU SYNAGOGUE

See page 339

LJUBOML. SEVENTEENTH-CENTURY FORTIFIED SYNAGOGUE

See page 368

CRACOW. WROUGHT-IRON BIMA IN ALTE
SYNAGOGUE

See page 360

ZOLKIEW. DETAIL OF IRON GRILL
BEFORE ARK

See page 368

SNIADOWO. SEVENTEENTH-CENTURY TIMBER SYNAGOGUE

See page 369

HUSIATYN. ARK OF THE LAW SURMOUNTED
BY MURALS

See page 371

SELWA. ARK IN CARVED WOOD, EIGHT-
EENTH CENTURY

See page 362

CEMETERY AT TARNAPOL (GALICIA) SEVENTEENTH- AND EIGHTEENTH-CENTURY
STONES
See page 367

PRUZANY. PAINTED TOMBSTONE, 1905
See page 377

GORODISCZCZE. PAINTED TOMBSTONE, 1906
See page 377

KAMIONKA STRUMILOWA. TOMB-
STONE (DATED 1770) SHOWING
ORIENTAL INFLUENCE
See page 368

GWOZDZIEC. BIMA IN CARVED WOOD

See page 444

CHODOROW. DETAIL OF MURAL PAINTING, SEVENTEENTH
CENTURY

See page 370

MEDIÆVAL SPICE SHOP IN MOROCCAN MELLAH
See page 402

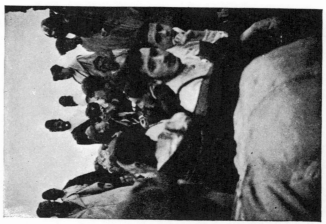

SEFROU, JEWS OF THE ATLAS MOUNTAINS
See page 406

HAMMAN-LIF. MOSAIC OF ANCIENT SYNAGOGUE (FIFTH CENTURY?)

See page 409

Bibliography

Abbreviations: J.E.—*The Jewish Encyclopedia.*
R.E.J.—*Revue des Etudes Juives.*
Fraub.—M. Frauberger in *Mitteilungen der Gesellschaft zur Erforschung jüd. Kunstdenkmäler,* Frankfort 1900 ff, vols. i-vi.
M.G. W. J.—*Monatsschrift für Geschichte und Wissenschaft des Judentums.*
Kraut.—Richard Krautheimer, *Mittelalterliche Synagogen.* Berlin 1927.
Cohn-Wiener—Ernst Cohn-Wiener, *Die Jüdische Kunst.* Berlin 1929.
Boletin—*Boletin de la Real Academia de la Historia.*

CHAPTER I.—ANCIENT ISRAEL IN THE LOUVRE

General: W. Lansdell Wardle, *Israel and Babylon,* New York, 1925, a summary of the conclusions of scholars, with bibliography. Alfred Jeremias, *The Old Testament in the Light of the Ancient East,* London, 1911. Friedrich Delitzsch, *Babel and Bible,* London, 1903 (both valuable chiefly for numerous illustrations).

Hammurabi: C.H. W. Johns, *The Oldest Code of Laws in the World,* Edinburgh, 1903.

Jewish Magic Bowls: Moïse Schwab, *Les Coupes Magiques et l'Hydromancie dans l'Antiquité Orientale,* in The Proceedings of the Society of Biblical Archæology, London, April 1890; idem, *Rapport sur les Inscriptions Hebraïques de la France,* in Les Nouvelles Archives des Missions scientifiques et littéraires, vol. xii, Paris, 1905.

CHAPTER II.—TALE-TELLING STONES FROM PALESTINE

General: René Dussaud, *Les Monuments Palestiniens et Judaïques: Musée du Louvre,* Paris, 1912. Cohn-Wiener. Adolf Reifenberg, *Architektur und Kunstgewerbe im Alten Israel,* Vienna-Leipzig, 1925 (all illustrated).

Moabite Stone: J.E., "Moabite Stone." *Cambridge Ancient History,* iii, pp. 372-373.

Symbols: J.E. under "Pomegranate," "Etrog," "Menorah," "Candlestick," "Shofar," "Lulab," "Tabernacles, Feast of," "Hosha'na Rabbah," "Hosanna." For Cretan hymn, Jane Ellen Harrison, *Themis,* Cambridge, 1912, p. 8. Plutarch's comparison is in *Moralia,* Table Talk, ch. v.

The Temple: J.E., "Temple." For account of its courts and ceremonies, Jack M. Myers, *The Story of the Jewish People,* London, 1909, vol. i, ch. viii.

Josephus and Hyrcanus: Josephus, *Antiquities,* vol. xii, bk. iv (in his best anecdotal mood).

Jewish Propaganda: Max Radin, *The Jews Among the Greeks and Romans,* Philadelphia, 1915, ch. xi, *passim.* On Adiabene, J.E., "Adiabene," "Helena of Adiabene."

The Tenth Legion: Josephus, *Wars,* vol. v, bk. ii, ch. 4; vol. vii, bk. i, ch. 3. For Masada, *Wars,* vol. vii, bk. viii-ix.

Julian and the Jews: Alice Gardner, *Julian Philosopher and Emperor,* New York, 1895, pp. 262 ff; Julian, *Letters,* xxv.

Synagogues: J.E., "Synagogue." Samuel Krauss, *Synagogale Altertümer,* Berlin-Vienna, 1922. Kraut., pp. 27-76. Heinrich Kohl and C. Watzinger, *Antike Synagogen in Galilaea,* Leipzig, 1916.

CHAPTER III.—PARIS "THAT GREAT CITY"

General: J.E., "Paris." Leon Kahn, *Les Juifs à Paris depuis le VI siècle,* Paris, 1889. J.A. Dulaure, *Histoire de Paris,* Paris, 1838.

Priscus: St. Gregory of Tours, *History of the Franks,* vol. vi, bk. v, ch. 17.

Tombstones: Schwab, *Inscriptions de la France.*

Tax List: R.E.J. 1, 61.

The "Synagogue" on Notre Dame: R.E.J. 65, 242 E. Viollet-le-Duc, *Dictionnaire Raisonné de l'Architecture Française*, Paris, 1875, under "Eglise." James Darmesteter, *Les Prophètes d'Israel*, Paris, 1895, pp. 185-186.

Nicolas Flamel: R.E.J., 18, 102.

Chapter IV.—The Newer Paris

General: J.E., "Paris."

Eighteenth century: Leon Kahn, *Les Juifs de Paris sous Louis XV; Les Juifs de Paris au Dix-Huitième Siècle*, Paris, 1894. For Rabbi Azulai's account of Paris, Elkan Nathan Adler, *Jewish Travellers*, New York, 1931.

Nineteenth century: J.E., "Sanhedrin." For Count Chaptal's anecdote, R.E.J., 26, 316. On Heine in Paris, William Sharp, *Life of Heinrich Heine*, London, 1888; Alexandre Weill, *Souvenirs Intimes de Henri Heine*, Paris, 1883; *Heinrich Heine—Gespräche*, ed. by Hugo Bieber, Berlin, 1926; *Heinrich Heine—Confessio Judaica*, ed. by Bieber, Berlin, 1925; Israel Zangwill, *Dreamers of the Ghetto*, ch. "The Mattress Grave." On Herzl, *Theodor Herzls Tagebücher*, Berlin, 1922, vol. i, p. 127.

Chapter V.—Crowns and Mantles in Cluny

General: Description of the type of objects found in Cluny, Fraub. iii; Cyrus Adler and M. Casanowicz, *Descriptive Catalogue of a Collection of Objects of Jewish Ceremonial*, Washington, 1901 (this collection is now in the Jewish Theological Seminary Museum of New York); J.E., under all objects mentioned.

Cluny: Georges Stenne, *Catalogue des objets d'art religieux de la collection Strauss de l'Exposition Universelle de 1878*, Paris. For MSS., R.E.J., 50, 136; 61, 294; for medals, 23, 136 and 317; for ark curtain, 63, 303; for Spanish alms-box, 25, 78. On marriage contracts, M. Gaster, *The Ketubah*, Berlin-London, 1923 (illustrated).

Tombstones at Carnavalet and St. Germain-en-Laye: Schwab, *Rapport*.

Bibliothèque Nationale: Portrait of Farrachius in *The Legacy of Israel*, Oxford, 1927, p. xxiii. The map of Cresques reproduced in colour in Charles de la Roncière, *La Découverte de l'Afrique au moyen âge,* Cairo, 1924, vol. i.

CHAPTER VI.—FROM CHAMPAGNE TO BRITTANY

General: J.E., under "France" and provinces, cities, and persons mentioned. Gross, *Gallia Judaica,* Paris, 1897. For inscriptions, Schwab, *Rapport.*

Troyes: Maurice Liber, *Rashi,* Philadelphia, 1906. Louis Finklestein, *Jewish Self-Government in the Middle Ages,* New York, 1924. For original French text of elegy on martyrs of Troyes, R.E.J., 2, 199.

Dijon: R.E.J., 6, 223. For "Well of Moses," Emile Male, *L'Art Religieux au Fin du Moyen Age en France,* Paris, 1922, pp. 70-71.

Mâcon: R.E.J., 4, 104.

Lunéville and Grégoire: R.E.J., 49, 153.

Window of Bourges and similar art: Male, *L'Art Religieux du XII siècle en France,* Paris, 1924, pp. 144 ff.; idem, *L'Art Religieux du XIII siècle en France,* Paris, 1925, pp. 133-203.

Issoudun: R.E.J., 20, 253.

Blois: German translation of dirge, Leopold Zunz, *Die Synagogale Poesie des Mittelalters,* Berlin, 1855, p. 24. History of *Alenu* prayer, Israel Abrahams, *A Companion to the Authorized Daily Prayer Book,* London, 1922, p. lxxxvi; J.E., "Alenu."

Nantes: R.E.J., 14, 80; 17, 125; 33, 88.

CHAPTER VII.—THE SOUTHLANDS OF FRANCE

General: J.E., under "France" and provinces, cities, and persons mentioned. For inscriptions, Schwab, *Rapport.* On influence of Jewish mediæval culture, *The Legacy of Israel,* Oxford, 1927, ch. "The Jewish Factor in Mediæval Thought" by Charles and Dorothea Waley Singer; Joseph Jacobs, *Jewish Contributions to Civilization,* Philadelphia, 1919, chs. iv, v; Louis Israel Newman, *Jewish Influence on Christian Reform Movements,* New York, 1925, book ii. Under various place names, consult index to first fifty vols. of R.E.J.; later articles of importance are cited below.

Carpentras: For recent restoration of synagogue, pamphlet *Les Synagogues du Comtat sont Sauveés,* published by Comité de

Sauvegarde des Synagogues Comtadines, Paris, 1930. For Hebreo-Provençal poetry, E. Sabatier, *Chansons Hebraico-Provençales de Juifs Comtadins,* Nimes, 1876; Don Pedro d'Alcantara (Emperor of Brazil), *Poésies Hebraico-Provençales du Rituel Israélite Comtadin,* Avignon, 1891; Armand Lunel, *Esther de Carpentras,* Paris, 1924.

Cavaillon: *L'Univers Israélite,* Paris, 1913, vol. 68, p. 606.

Languedoc: Saige, *Les Juifs du Languedoc,* Paris, 1881.

Mende: R.E.J., 73, 113; 74, 73.

Narbonne: *The Legacy of Israel,* p. 482; R.E.J., 55, 1; 58, 75 and 200; 59, 59; 61, 228; 62, 1 and 248; 63, 75.

Toulouse: German translation of tablet from Berenice, in Krauss, *Synagogale Altertümer,* p. 265; account of Cyrenaican Jews in Nahum Slouschz, *Travels in North Africa,* Philadelphia, 1927, chs. ix, x.

Bordeaux: Théophile Malvezin, *Histoire des Juifs de Bordeaux,* Bordeaux, 1875; idem, *Michel de Montaigne, son origine, sa famille,* Bordeaux, 1875, ch. ix.

Bayonne: Henry Léon, *Histoire des Juifs de Bayonne,* Paris, 1893.

Chapter VIII.—Andalusian Courts and Gates

General: J.E., under "Spain" and places and persons mentioned. For inscriptions, Moïse Schwab, *Rapport sur les Inscriptions Hebraïques de l'Espagne* in Nouvelles Archives des Missions scientifiques et littéraires, Paris, 1907, vol. xiv, fas. 3.

Cultural and economic life: On breadth of culture, see curriculum for youth, Israel Abrahams, *Jewish Life in the Middle Ages,* Philadelphia, 1896, pp. 365-367. For services of Spanish Jews to Western culture, *The Legacy of Israel,* ch. "The Jewish Factor in Mediæval Thought"; Jacobs, *Jewish Contributions to Civilization,* chs. iv, v. For a list of Jewish trades in Spain, Abrahams, *Jewish Life,* p. 247.

Elche: Boletin, vol. 29; *Bulletin Hispanique de Bordeaux,* Bordeaux, 1917.

Cordova: Ricardo Velazquez Bosco, *Medina Azzahra y Alamiriya,* Madrid, 1912 (illustrated). For correspondence of Hasdai and the Chazars, *Miscellany of Hebrew Literature,* London, 1872, vol. i, pp. 92-112; and for story of Moses ben Enoch, *Post-Biblical Hebrew Literature,* ed. and trans. by B. Halper, Philadelphia, 1921, vol. ii, pp. 123-126. On mediæval Jewish commerce, Jacobs, *Jewish Contributions,* pp. 193-205. For Halevi, *Selected Poems of Jehudah Halevi,* translated by Nina Salaman, Philadelphia, 1925. For short biography and study of Maimonides, David Yellin and Israel Abrahams, *Maimonides,* Philadelphia, 1903. Description of synagogue, Boletin v, pp. 361-399; R.E.J., 9, 157-158; 10, 244-247; Schwab, *Inscriptions,* pp. 364 ff. For episode of 1473 and story of Montoro, R.E.J., 43, 259. On *autos-de-fé,* R.E.J., 43, 126 ff.

Seville: José Torre Revello, *El Barrio de Santa Cruz,* Seville, 1929. Kyland C. Kirk, *The Secret of Columbus,* Washington, 1913.

Granada: Luis Seco de Lucena, *Historia de Granada,* Granada, 1916. Ernst Kühnel, *Granada,* Leipzig (n.d.). *Selected Religious Poems of Solomon Ibn Gabirol,* translated by Israel Zangwill, Philadelphia, 1923. For contemporary accounts of the expulsion from Spain, Höxter, *Quellenbuch,* ii, pp. 117-130.

Chapter IX.—The Golden Age in Toledo

General: J.E., under "Spain," "Toledo," and persons mentioned.

Ghettos: For larger Jewry, see Simancas (below). For Alcana, *Revista de Archivos, Bibliotecas y Museos,* Madrid, 1911, vol. 24, p. 48.

Santa María la Blanca: M. González Simancas, *Las Sinagogas de Toledo y el Baño Litúrgico Judío,* Madrid, 1929 (illustrated). R.E.J., 38, 251; 84, 5. Cohn-Wiener, pp. 137 ff. Inscription on beam, Boletin, 89, 318.

House of El Greco: Rafael Domenech, *La Casa del Greco,* Barcelona (n.d.).

El Transito: Simancas, R.E.J., 38, 351; Cohn-Wiener, 140 ff. For dedication and inscriptions (in part), Schwab, *Inscriptions.*

Funerary Inscriptions: Schwab, *Inscriptions;* for Corral de Don Diego, R.E.J., 65, 149; Calle de la Plata, Schwab, 266; Museum, Boletin 57, 209, and 67, 149, *Jewish Quarterly Review* (new series), 19, 145.

Intellectual Life: *The Legacy of Israel,* pp. 202-214. Jacobs, *Jewish Contributions,* ch. iv; J.E., under "Astronomy," "Mathematics."

CHAPTER X.—THROUGH NORTHERN SPAIN AND PORTUGAL

General: J.E., under places and persons mentioned. For inscriptions in Spain, Schwab, *Inscriptions Hebraïques de l'Espagne,* Paris, 1907.

Madrid: On the Bible of Olivares, J.E., "Arragel." For contemporary account of *auto-de-fé* of 1680, Höxter, *Quellenbuch,* ii, 115.

Segovia: R.E.J., 14, 254; Boletin, 9, 270-344-460. For account of controversy, R.E.J., 39, 209; I. Rodríguez y Fernández, *Segovia-Corpus,* Madrid, 1902. On María del Salto, Fidel Fita y Colomé, *Estudios Historicos,* Madrid, 1886, vol. vi, p. 65.

Navarre: José Yanguas y Miranda, *Diccionario de Antigüedades del Reino de Navarra,* Pampeluna, 1840.

Barcelona: F. Carreras y Candi, *Geografia General de Catalunya: La Ciutat de Barcelona,* Barcelona (n.d.). See index under "Call." I. Millàs i Vallicrosa, *Documents hebraics de jueus catalans,* Barcelona, 1927. Isidore Epstein, *The "Responsa" of Rabbi Solomon ben Adreth of Barcelona (1235-1310) as a source of the history of Spain,* London, 1925.

Gerona: Joaqim Botet y Siso, *Geografia General de Catalunya: Provincia de Gerona.* Barcelona (n.d.).

Palma: J.E., under "Chuetas."

Sagunto: Boletin, 57, 284.

Portugal: Samuel Schwarz, *Os Christãos-Novos em Portugal no Século XX,* Lisbon, 1925; *Inscrições Hebraicas em Portugal,* Lisbon, 1923; "The Crypto-Jews of Portugal" in *The Menorah Journal,* New York, 1926, vol. xii, pp. 138, 283.

CHAPTER XI.—HAVENS IN THE LOWLANDS

General: J.E., under places and persons mentioned.

Amsterdam: For first settlement, Höxter, *Quellenbuch,* iv, p. 21; Graetz, *Geschichte der Juden,* ix, 478. On Portuguese synagogue, Henriques de Castro, *De Synagoge der Portugeesch-Israelietische Gemeente te Amsterdam,* The Hague, 1875. For

French trans. of Uriel da Costa's autobiography, *Uriel da Costa, Une Vie Humaine,* trans. with introduction by A. B. Duff and Pierre Kahn, Paris, 1926; for German trans. Alfred Klaar, *Uriel Acosta,* Berlin, 1909; see likewise, Zangwill, *Dreamers of the Ghetto,* ch. "Uriel da Costa." On Rembrandt, William Bode, *The Complete Works of Rembrandt,* Paris, 1902 (illustrated).

Ouderkerk: Henriques de Castro, *Auswahl von Grabsteinen auf dem Niederl.-Portug.-Israel. Begräbnissplatze zu Ouderkerk,* Leyden, 1883 (illustrated).

Spinoza: *Chronicum Spinozanum,* The Hague, *passim.*

The Hague: For Portuguese synagogue, *Menorah,* Vienna, 1926, p. 426. On Ashkenazic cemetery, D. S. Van Zuiden *De Hoogduitsche Joden in 's Gravenhage,* The Hague, 1913 (illustrated).

Brussels: For story, monuments, etc., of the Chapel of the Sacrament, Henri Velge, *La Collégiale des Saints Michel et Gudule à Bruxelles,* Brussels, 1925 (illustrated).

Chapter XII.—Survivals in England

General: J.E., under "England" and places and persons mentioned. Albert M. Hyamson, *A History of the Jews of England,* London, 1928. Joseph Jacobs, *The Jews of Angevin England,* London, 1893.

Starrs and Archae: J.E., "Starrs," "Archa." M. D. Davies, *Shetaroth: Hebrew Deeds of English Jews Before 1290,* London, 1888. *Starrs and Jewish Charters Preserved in the British Museum,* Cambridge, 1930.

Lincoln: *Legacy of Israel,* Oxford, 1927, p. xxvii. Joseph Jacobs, *Jewish Ideals and Other Essays,* New York, 1896, ch. "Little St. Hugh of Lincoln."

Bury St Edmunds: Carlyle, *Past and Present,* chs. iv, xii.

York: On Clifford's Tower, *Legacy,* p. xix. For Five Sisters windows, C. A. Austen, *The Five Sisters,* York, 1923.

Oxford: On Bodleian bowl, *Legacy,* p. xviii. On Elephantine papyri, A. E. Cowley, *Aramaic Papyri of the Fifth Century B.C.,* Oxford, 1923. For library, J.E., "Bodleian"; also catalogues by Adolf Neubauer and A. E. Cowley.

London: Elkan N. Adler, *History of the Jews in London,* Philadelphia, 1930. Jacobs, *Jewish Ideals,* ch. "The London Jewry, 1290." On Bevis Marks synagogue, Moses Gaster, *History of the Ancient Synagogue of the Spanish and Portuguese Jews,* London, 1901. For complete architectural description, *Royal Commission on Historic Monuments,* London, 1929, vol. iv. On Manasseh Bueno Barzillai Azevedo da Costa, see Israel Zangwill, *The King of Schnorrers,* an immortal picture of eighteenth-century Jewish life in London.

British Museum: Books and MSS., J.E., "British Museum"; G. Margoliouth *Catalogue of the Hebrew and Samaritan MSS. in the British Museum,* London, 1899-1915. For Oriental collections, *British Museum: A Guide to the Babylonian and Assyrian Antiquities,* London, 1922. E. A. Wallis Budge (ed.), *Assyrian Sculptures in the British Museum* (illustrated). Rembrandts in England, Bode, *Complete Works of Rembrandt.*

CHAPTER XIII.—ROME AND THE ETERNAL PEOPLE

General: J.E., under "Rome," "Catacombs," and persons mentioned. Hermann Vogelstein and Paul Rieger, *Geschichte der Juden in Rom,* Berlin, 1895-96. A. Berliner, *Geschichte der Juden in Rom,* Frankfort, 1893. Jean Juster, *Les Juifs dans l'Empire romain,* Paris, 1914. Ermanno Loevinson, *Roma Israelitica,* Frankfort, 1927, guide-book to Jewish Rome.

Classical Writers and the Jews: Theodore Reinach, *Textes d'auteurs grecs et romains relatifs au judaïsme,* Paris, 1895.

Synagogues: Samuel Krauss, *Synagogale Altertümer,* Berlin-Vienna, 1922.

Philo: *Works* trans. C. D. Yonge, London, 1885, vol. iv, pp. 176 ff.

Catacombs: Nikolaus Müller, *Die jüd. Katakombe am Monteverde zu Rom,* Leipzig, 1912. Hermann W. Beyer and Hans Lietzmann, *Die jüd. Katakombe der Villa Torlonia in Rom,* Berlin-Leipzig, 1930. Raffaele Garucci, *Cimitero degli antichi ebreo . . . in Vigna Randanini,* Rome, 1862. Cohn-Wiener, pp. 118 ff.

Gilt Glass: Garucci, *Vetri ornati di figure in oro*, Rome, 1858 (illustrated).

Immanuel of Rome: English trans. of his poem, *Tophet and Eden*, by Herman Gollancz, London, 1921.

Kalonymus: For his typical satire on rich men, Höxter, *Quellenbuch* iii, 121; also J. Chotzner, *Hebrew Humour*, London, 1915, ch. x.

Friendships between Jews and Gentiles: Abrahams, *Jewish Life in the Middle Ages*, pp. 419-423.

CHAPTER XIV.—ITALY "LAND OF THE DEW"

General: J.E., under "Italy" and provinces, cities, and persons. On inscriptions, C. J. Ascoli, *Iscrizioni inedite o mal note Greche, Latine, Ebraiche di antichi sepolchri Giudaici del Napolitano*, Turin-Rome, 1880; Krauss, *Synagogale Altertümer*, pp. 244-260. For further inscriptions, mostly unnoted in our itinerary, consult G. Gabrieli, *Italia Judaica*, Rome, 1924. On printing, David W. Amram, *The Makers of Hebrew Books in Italy*, Philadelphia, 1909.

Palermo: Obadiah da Bertinoro's account, in Elkan N. Adler, *Jewish Travellers*, pp. 201 ff.

Malta: E. Becker, *Malta Sotteranea*, Strasbourg, 1913. Cecil Roth, *The Jews of Malta*, reprint from Transactions of Jewish Historical Society, London, vol. xii, pp. 187-252.

Apulia: Ahimaaz ben Paltiel, *The Chronicle of Ahimaaz*, trans. by Marcus Salzman, New York, 1924.

Trani: For synagogue, Fraub. i, 11; ii, 5.

Ancona: C. Ciavini, *Memoria storichi degli Israeliti in Ancona*, Ancona, 1898. For martyrdom of Maranos, Ludwig Lewisohn, *The Last Days of Shylock*, New York, 1930.

Florence: On Jews and the Renaissance, Israel Abrahams, *Jewish Life in the Middle Ages*, pp. 160, 340, 371, 420.

Siena: "The Memoirs of a Siennese Jew" trans. by Cecil Roth, in Hebrew Union College Annual, Cincinnati, 1928, vol. v, pp. 353 ff.

Livorno: Fraub. i, 22; ii, 14, 37.

Ferrara: On sculpture, Emile Male, *L'Art Religieux du XII siècle en France*, Paris, 1924, p. 145.

Parma: For library, MSS. *Codices Hebraici Biblioteca G. B. de Rossi*, Parma, 1803.

Mantua: Luigi Carnevali, *Il Ghetto di Mantova*, Mantua, 1884. On theatre, A. d'Ancona, "Il teatro Mantovano nel secolo XVI" in *Giornale Storico della litteratura italiano*, Turin, 1855, vol. v. For typical ghetto regulations in seventeenth century, Vasco Restori, *Mantova*, Mantua, 1925.

Padua: Antonio Ciscato, *Gli Ebrei in Padova*, Padua, 1901. On synagogues, Fraub. i, 12; ii, 24, 36. Cohn-Wiener, 173 ff.

Venetian Possessions: C. Morpurgo, *Inchiesta*. Cecil Roth, *Venice*, Philadelphia, 1930.

Venice: Cecil Roth, *Venice*. On synagogues, Morpurgo, *Inchiesta*. For voyage of Elijah of Pesaro, *Voyage Ethnographique de Venise à Chypres: Lettre d'Elie de Pesaro*, trans. by Moise Schwab, reprint from *Revue de Géographie*, Paris (September), 1879.

CHAPTER XV.—A THOUSAND YEARS ALONG THE RHINE

General: J.E., under "Germany" and places and persons mentioned. Adolph Kohut, *Geschichte der deutschen Juden*, Berlin, 1898. *Aus der Geschichte der Juden in Rheinland — Jüd. Kult.- und Kunstdenkmäler*, ed. by Richard Klapheck, Düsseldorf, 1931.

Crusades: Selections from Jewish chronicles, *Edom: Berichte jüd. Zeugen*, etc., Berlin, 1919.

Cologne: Adolf Kober, "Die Grabsteine des alten jüd. Friedhofes," in the *Veröffentlichungen der Akademie für die Wissenschaft des Judentums*, No. 18.

Worms: Samson Rothschild, *Aus der Vergangenheit der Isr. Gemeinde Worms*, Frankfort, 1929. For synagogue and ritual bath, Kraut., 151 ff.

Speyer: F. J. Hildebrand, *Das Romanische Judenbad . . . zu Speier*, Speyer, 1920. Kraut, 145 ff.

Mayence: Sigmund Salfeld, *Bilder aus der Vergangenheit der jüd. Gemeinde Mainz*, Mayence, 1903. On cemetery, Salfeld, *Der alte jüd. Friedhof zu Mainz*, Berlin, 1898; Sali Levi, *Beiträge zu Gesch. der ältesten jüd. Grabsteine in Mainz*, Mayence, 1926. On museum, Sali Levi, *Magenza: Das Jüd. Mainz.,* Berlin-Vienna, 1927.

Frankfort: A. Freimann and F. Kracauer, *Frankfort,* Philadelphia, 1929. Heine's verse is from *Der Tannhäuser;* his description of days with Boerne is from his *Ludwig Boerne,* book i. On cemetery, M. Horovitz, *Die Inschriften der Isr. Gemeinde zu Frankfurt,* Frankfort, 1901. For museum, Erich Toeplitz, "Das Museum jüd. Altertümer in Frankfurt" in *Notizblatt der Gesell. zu Erforsch. jüd. Kunstdenkmäler,* Frankfort, 1923, No. 14; idem, "Neues von Museum" in *Notiz.* No. 15. On library, *Stadtbibliotek Frankfurt am Main—Katalog der Ständigen Ausstellung,* Frankfort, 1920; *Katalog der Judaica u. Hebraica,* Frankfort, 1932, vol. i.

Friedberg: Kraut. 187 ff.

Strasbourg: On museum, *Ost und West,* vol. xii, pp. 197 ff. On tombstones, Schwab, *Inscriptions Hebraïques de la France,* pp. 304 ff. For cathedral statues, *Legacy of Israel,* p. xii. R. E. J., 67, 188.

Alsace: Elie Scheid, *Histoire des juifs d'Alsace,* Paris, 1887. On synagogue in Rouffach, Kraut. 193 ff.

Chapter XVI.—The "Gassen" of South Germany

General: J.E., under "Germany," "Bavaria," "Württemberg," and towns and persons mentioned. Adolph Kohut, *Geschichte der deutschen Juden.*

Regensburg: Isaac Meyer, *Geschichte der Juden in Regensburg,* Berlin, 1913. For the house of the Hochmeister, Abrahams, *Jewish Life in the Middle Ages,* p. 149. On the synagogue, Kraut., 177 ff. On the tombstones, and local legends and stories for the whole region, A. Friedmann, *Bilder aus meiner Heimatgeschichte,* Ingolstadt, 1929.

Nuremberg: Kraut., 250 ff.

Fürth: Kraut., 423 ff. For the eighteenth-century prints, J. Chr. Bodenschatz, *Kirchliche Verfassung der Heutigen Juden,* Erlangen, 1748; P. Chr. Kirchner, *Jüdisches Ceremoniel,* Nuremberg, 1726.

Schnaittach, Sulzbach, Floss: Alfred Grotte, *Deutsche, böhmische u. polnische Synagogentypen,* Berlin, 1915. Kraut., 240.

Baiersdorf: For life in these south German Jewries at the end of the seventeenth century, *The Memoirs of Glückel of Hameln,* trans. with introduction by Marvin Lowenthal, New York, 1932.

Bamberg: On mediæval synagogue, Kraut., 181 ff. On the painted synagogues here and elsewhere in South Germany, Erich Toeplitz, *Die Malerei in den Synagogen* (Beiträge z. Jüd. Kulturgeschichte, Heft III), Frankfort, 1929; *Rimon-Milgroim,* Berlin, 1923, No. 2.

Heidingsfeld: Toeplitz, "Die Synagoge in Heidingsfeld," in *Notiz.* No. 16.

Offenbach: *Aus der Vergangenheit der Isr. Gemeinde zu Offenbach,* Offenbach, 1915. For illustrations of relics concerning Jacob Frank, Zalman Rubashow, *Al Tillé Bet Frank* (Hebrew), Berlin, 1922.

CHAPTER XVII.—PRUSSIA AND THE NORTH

General: J.E., under "Germany," "Hesse," "Prussia," "Silesia," and towns and persons mentioned. Kohut, *Geschichte.*

Erfurt: On synagogue, Kraut., 196 ff.

Nordhausen: Heinrich Stern, *Geschichte der Juden in Nordhausen,* Nordhausen, 1927.

Hanover and Hildesheim: *The Memoirs of Glückel of Hameln.* On cemetery in Hanover, S. Gronemann, *Genealogische Studien über die alten jüd. Familien Hannovers,* Berlin, 1913.

Hessia: Old synagogues, Fritz Epstein, "Kultusbauten u. Kultusgegenstände in der Provinz Hessen," in *Notiz.,* No. 6.

Wittenberg: On the *Judensau,* R. E. J., 20,269; Eduard Fuchs, *Die Juden in der Karikatur,* Munich, 1921, pp. 114 ff. (illustrated).

Hamburg, Altona: M. Grunwald, *Hamburgs deutsche Juden,* Hamburg, 1904; *Memoirs of Glückel.* On cemeteries, M. Grunwald, *Portugiesen Gräber auf deutscher Erde,* Hamburg, 1902 (illustrated). For Heine in Hamburg, Hugo Bieber (ed), *Heinrich Heine—Confessio Judaica.* On Moses Lump, consult Heine, *Die Bäder von Lucca,* ch. ix.

Berlin: Ludwig Geiger, *Geschichte der Juden in Berlin,* Berlin, 1870.

Breslau: M. Brann, *Geschichte der Juden in Schlesien,* Breslau,

1896 f; Erwin Hintze, *Katalog der Ausstellung—Das Judentum in der Geschichte Schlesiens*, Breslau, 1929. For *Korn-juden* medals, Fuchs, *Juden in der Karikatur*.

Brunswick: M. Grunwald in *Mitteilungen zur jüd. Volkskunde*, Hamburg, vol. iii.

CHAPTER XVIII.—BOHEMIA AND ITS BORDERS

General: J. E., under "Bohemia," "Moravia," "Prague," and other places and persons mentioned. M. H. Friedländer, *Die Juden in Böhmen*, Prague, 1900.

Prague: Teiger, *Das Prager Ghetto*, Prague, 1903 (illus. of demolished Jewry). David J. Podiebrad, *Althertümer der Prager Judenstadt*, Prague, 1870. On cemetery, L. Popper, *Die Inschriften des Alten Prager Judenfriedshofes*, Frankfort, 1893; L. Jerabek, *Der Alte Prager Judenfriedhof*, Prague, 1903 (illustrated). For legends, Wolf Pascheles, *Sippurim*, Leipzig, 1888. On museum, S. H. Lieben, *Das Jüd. Museum in Prag*, Prague (n.d.). On synagogues, Kraut, 199 ff., 234 ff.

Northwest Bohemia: Alfred Grotte, *Deutsche, böhmische u. polnische Synagogentypen*, Berlin, 1915.

Moravia: Hugo Gold, *Die Juden und die Judengemeinde Mährens*, Brünn, 1929 (illustrated).

CHAPTER XIX.—CITIES OF THE DANUBE

General: J. E., under "Austria," "Hungary," and cities and persons cited.

Vienna: Ignaz Schwarz, "Geschichte der Juden in Wien bis zum Jahre 1625," and Max Grunwald, "Geschichte der Juden in Wien von 1625-1740," both in *Geschichte der Stadt Wien*, Vienna, 1913, vol. v. Sigmund Mayer, *Die Wiener Juden 1700-1900*, Vienna, 1918. On the old cemeteries, Bernhard Wachstein, *Inschriften des Alten Judenfriedhofes*, Vienna-Leipzig, 1912-1927 (illustrated). For the Leopoldstadt settlement, Hans Rotter and Adolf Schmieger, *Das Ghetto in der Wiener Leopoldstadt*, Vienna, 1926 (illustrated).

Wiener-Neustadt: L. Moses, *Die Juden in Wiener-Neustadt*, Vienna, 1927.

Eisenstadt: Moritz Markbreiter, *Beiträge z. Geschich. der jüd. Gemeinde Eisenstadt*, Vienna, 1908. On cemetery, Wachstein, *Die Grabsteinen des Alten Judenfriedhofes in Eisenstadt*, Vienna, 1922. Budapest: Alfred Fürst, "Die Judenviertal Budapests" in *Menorah*, Vienna, 1928, vol. vi, pp. 385 ff.

CHAPTER XX.—THE FOUR LANDS OF POLAND

General: J. E., under "Russia," "Poland," "Galicia," "Lithuania," and towns and persons mentioned. S. M. Dubnow, *History of the Jews in Russia and Poland*, Philadelphia, 1916-20.

Art: On architecture, Grotte, *Deutsche, böhmische u. polnische Synagogentypen*; Mathias Bersohn, *Notes sur quelques anciennes synagogues construit en bois en Pologne*, Cracow, 1895. R. Bernstein-Wishnitzer, "Synagogentypen in ehe. Königreich Polen" in *Das Buch von den Polnischen Juden*, ed. by Agnon and Eliasberg, Berlin, 1916. For numerous illustrations of wood synagogues, *Materyely do Architektury Polskiej*, Warsaw, 1916, vol. i. On mural painting, *Rimon-Milgroim*, Berlin, 1923, Nos. 2, 3. For sculpture and painting on tombstones, Arthur Levy, *Jüd. Grabmalkunst in Osteuropa*, Berlin (n.d.); *Bericht—Kuratorie far Schitzen die Denkmeler von Yiddisher Kunst* (Yiddish), Lemberg, 1928 (both illustrated).

Lemberg: Majer Balaban, *Skizzen u. Studien zur Geschichte der Juden in Polen*, Berlin, 1911.

Lublin: Balaban, *Die Judenstadt von Lublin*, Berlin, 1919 (illustrated).

Vilna: On the Gaon, Louis Ginzberg, *The Gaon R. Elijah Wilna*, New York, 1920. For spirit of Chassidism and legends of the Baal Shem, Martin Buber, *Jewish Mysticism and the Legends of the Baalshem*, London-New York, 1931; Meyer Levin, *The Golden Mountain*, New York, 1932.

CHAPTER XXI.—THE BALKANS TO THE SEA

General: J. E., under "Rumania," "Bosnia," "Serbia," "Bulgaria," "Turkey," "Greece," and cities and persons mentioned.

Sarajevo: Moritz Levy, *Die Sephardim in Bosnien*, Sarajevo, 1911 (illustrated). On the Haggadah, David H. Müller and J.

Von Schlosser, *Die Haggadah von Sarajevo,* Vienna, 1898 (illustrated).

Salonica: R.E.J., 40, 206; 41, 98 and 250; M.G. W. J. 17, Nos. 11-12.

Delos: On antique synagogue here and in Priene and Miletus, Cohn-Wiener, 108 ff.

Chapter XXII.—Under Islam in Africa

General: Nahum Slouschz, *Travels in North Africa,* Philadelphia, 1927, invaluable for Tripoli, Tunisia, Algeria, and parts of Morocco. J. E., under countries, towns, and persons mentioned.

Morocco: J. Goulven, *Les Mellahs de Rabat-Salé,* Paris, 1927, a full account of a typical Jewry, with extensive bibliography, and replete with histories and legends of the Jewish saints. H. Ben-Shahar, "A Moroccan Note-Book" in *The Menorah Journal,* New York, 1930-31. Pascal Saisset, *Heures juives au Maroc,* Paris, 1930.

Jewish "Empire" in the Sahara. Charles de La Roncière, *La Découverte de l'Afrique au moyen-âge,* Cairo, 1924, vol. i.

Algeria: A. Garrot, *Les Juifs algériens et leurs origines,* Algiers, 1898.

Carthage: On the synagogue of Naro, Cohn-Wiener, 113 ff.; *Revue Archéologique,* vol. i (1883), pp. 160 ff.

Egypt: Description of fifteenth century Cairo and Alexandria by Jewish travellers, in Elkan N. Adler, *Jewish Travellers* (see index). For letter of Maimonides describing his daily routine, David Yellin and Israel Abrahams, *Maimonides.*

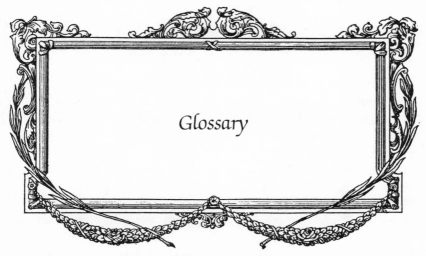

Glossary

ADONAI ECHAD. (Hebrew) The Lord is One.

ALABANZA. (Spanish) Praise.

ALJAMA. Term used by Spanish Jews for a Jewish community.

ASCAMOT. Laws governing the internal administration of an *Aljama*.

ASHKENAZIM (sing ASHKENAZI; adj. ASHKENAZIC.) North European Jews.

BARAKA. (Arabic) Blessing, or spiritual quality having magic powers.

BETH HA-MIDRASH. (Hebrew, *house of study*) Hall or academy for the exposition and study of Hebrew learning, especially the Talmud.

BETSTUBE. Prayer-room or chapel.

BIMA. Raised platform or tribune in a synagogue, from which the Torah is read, and prayers are chanted.

BLED. Countryside in Morocco.

BOCHUR. Young bachelor or Talmud student.

CABBALA. The Jewish system and literature of occult mysticism, often verging on magic.

CHASSID. Pious man, or "saint."

CHASSIDIM. Members of a mystic sect, particularly followers of the Baal Shem.

COBERTIZOS. (Spanish) Covered passageways.

ETROG. Citron.

GABBAI. Treasurer of a congregation.

GAON. Title of rank, originally given to a head of the Talmudic academies in Babylonia; in later times an honorific title.

GENIZAH. Storeroom of a synagogue, where are consigned old documents, torn or worn prayer-books, manuscripts, etc.

HAGGADAH. Prayer-book for family services on the eve of Passover.

HAHAM. Title for rabbi of a Sephardic congregation.

HALLEL. Psalm of praise.

HANUKA. Feast of Lights, celebrating the victory of the Maccabees.

HARA. Name for a Jewry in Algeria, Tunisia, Tripoli.

HAZAN. Cantor.

KADDISH. Prayer sanctifying God, also used by mourners for parents.

KARAITES. Jewish sect, originating in the eighth century C.E., which follows the Bible to the exclusion of rabbinic law and tradition.

KIDDUSH. Sanctification over wine; *kiddush-cup,* the vessel that contains the wine.

KOSHER. Clean according to ritual law.

LUACH. Calendar.

LULAB. Sheaf of palm, willow, and myrtle, used at the harvest festival, the Feast of Booths or Tabernacles.

MA'ARIV. Vesper services in synagogue.

MANHIG. A leader.

MAR. Title denoting "Master" or "Mister."

MARANOS. Spanish and Portuguese Jews who as a matter of form—or necessity—became converted to Christianity.

MEDERSA. Moslem college.

MELLAH. Moroccan term for the Jewish quarter of a city.

MENORAH. Candlestick, specifically the seven-branched candelabra; *Hanuka menorah,* candelabra with eight lights, used during the Feast of Lights.

MEZZUZA (pl. MEZZUZOT). Case of wood or metal containing Biblical passages, affixed to door-post of dwelling.

MIKVEH. Ritual bathing-pool for women.

MILCHIG and FLEISCHIG. *Milchig* food contains no meat products, *fleischig* does; the two are kept apart and eaten separately in accordance with elaborate dietary laws.

MIZRACH (Hebrew *east*). Inscribed and decorated panel, paper, or parchment set on the east wall of a synagogue or dwelling.

MUDEJAR. Moorish architectural and decorative style as carried on after the Christian conquest of Spanish provinces.

PARNAS (pl. PARNASSIM). A president of a Jewish community.

RAB. Master.

RIMONIM (sing. RIMON). Literally, pomegranates; also the metal ornaments often containing tiny bells, surmounting the wooden rollers on which are wound the scroll of the Law.

SCHALET. The classic dish for the Sabbath meal among German Jews; a baked pudding containing cinnamon, raisins, eggs, sugar, and rum.

SCUOLA. (Italian *school*). Term for synagogue used by Italian Jews.

SEPHARDIM (sing. SEPHARDI; adj. SEPHARDIC). Spanish-Portuguese Jews.

SHEHECHEYANU. Blessing on tasting fruit for first time in a season, on entering possession of a new house or piece of land, on wearing a new garment, etc.

SHEMA. First word of invocation, "Hear, O Israel, the Lord our God, the Lord is One." It is to be recited by a Jew on his death-bed.

SHOFAR. Trumpet fashioned from a ram's horn.

TALMUD TORAH. Elementary school in the traditional educational system.

TASS. Metal shield, or breastplate, hung in front of the scroll of the Law.

TORAH. Scroll of the Law, containing the five books of Moses (Genesis, Exodus, Numbers, Leviticus, Deuteronomy); likewise term for the Mosaic Law in general.

YESHIBAH. College, especially for the study of Talmudic law.

ZADDIK (pl. ZADDIKIM). A holy man; a wonder-working rabbi; a "saint."

ZEDAKAH. Alms.

Index

All places, provinces, and countries which are mentioned in the text as containing objects of Jewish interest are printed in CAPITAL letters.

Aaron, robes of, 28, 75; figure of, 81, 341.
Aaron of Lincoln 211, 212, 214-215, 290.
Aaron of York 218.
Aaron's rod, *as symbol,* 228.
Abadia, Juan de la, 178.
Abbadites 134.
Abd al-Malik, caliph, 43.
Abderrahman III 123, 176, 273.
Abd-Khiba 11, 225.
Aboab, Isaac da Fonseca, 194, 201.
Abrabanel, Isaac, 145-146, 264.
Abrabanel, Judah, 137.
Abraham 5, 6, 7, 226; figure of, 72, 95, 201.
Abraham, pseudo-messiah, 172.
Abraham ben Hasdai 250.
Abraham ben Hiya 104, 158.
Abraham of Bristol 213.
Abrahams, Israel, 21.
Abyssinia 397.
Aceca 148.
Achaia 385.
Acqui 260.
Adam, and Eve, or Eve, figure of, 227, 236, 291, 292, 365.
Addison, Launcelot, 389.
Aden 424.
Adiabene 38-39.
Adra 120.
ADRIANOPLE 383.
Ægina 387.

Aelia 44.
AFRICA, *see* North Africa.
Agadir 398.
Age of Reason 58.
Agriculture 85, 119, 213, 271.
Aguilar, Baron d', of London, 223; of Vienna, 349.
Ahel Sefrou, tribe of, 406.
Ahimaaz ben Paltiel 250.
AIX 113.
Akhenaton 11.
ALCALÁ DE HENARES 176.
Alenu prayer 77, 98.
Alexander 388; the two-horned, 5.
Alexander ben Solomon, of Frankfort, 284.
Alexander Comnenus 385.
Alexander Jannæus 28.
ALEXANDRIA 108, 123, 237, 390, 394, 411, 412.
Alfaqui, Samuel, physician, 175; sons of, jugglers, 175.
Al-Fasi, Isaac, 140.
ALGERIA 390, 407-408.
ALGIERS 407-408.
Alguadés, Meir, 168, 170.
Al-Harizi, Judah, 149.
Ali ben Rahmadan 333.
ALLERSTEIN 309.
Alliance, New and Old, *see* New and Old Faith.
Almohades 128, 134, 407.
Almovarides 134.

Alms-box 82, 151, 360, 433, 435.
Al-Muktadir 177.
Alphonse II 177.
Alphonse VI 148.
Alphonse VIII 149.
Alphonse X, the Wise, 135, 138, 160, 168, 246, 273.
Alphonsine Tables 160.
ALSACE-LORRAINE 294, 431-432.
Altar, *as symbol*, 228, 234.
Altdorfer, artist, 297.
ALTENKUNDSTADT 433.
ALTONA, *see* Hamburg.
Alva, Duke of, 190.
AMBERG 432.
Amenhotep IV *see* Akhenaton.
AMERICA 157, 201, 221.
AMIENS 52, 99.
Ammud, see Pulpit.
Amos 14, 15.
Amram ben Diwan, of Wazan, 398, 407.
AMRUS 410.
AMSTERDAM 119, 189, 191, 192-203, 222, 316, 334, 359, 367, 375, 382.
  Cemetery, German, 203
  —Portuguese, 199-202; *see* Ouderkerk
  Jewry 197
  Libraries 199
  Museums: Jan Six, 198; 'Rijks, 199; Stedelijk, 199
  Nieuwe Markt 198
  Rembrandt House 198
  Synagogues: Derde, 197; Groote, 196; modern, 197; Nieuwe, 197; Portuguese, 192-196, 228; Uilenburgwall, 297
Amulet 82, 115, 228, 317, 409, 427; case, 82.
Amurath, Sultan, 385.
Anatole France 60.
Anatoli, Jacob, 104, 246.
ANCONA 251-252.
ANDALUSIA 119-145, 178, 183, 394.
ANDERNACH 282.
Angels 5, 9, 10, 18, 92.
ANGERMÜNDE 436.
Anglo-Saxons 210, 214.
ANGOULÊME 99.

Anne, Queen, of England, 211, 222.
Ansbach 302, 307.
Antiochus Epiphanes, 29, 175.
ANTWERP 191, 208.
Apollo 12, 387.
APULIA 244, 250-251.
Aquinas, Thomas, *see* St. Thomas.
Arab, Arabic, Arabs, 23, 43, 44, 114, 121, 123, 124, 129, 140, 141, 148, 157, 161, 164, 168, 169, 246, 247, 248, 249, 250, 390, 392, 401, 404, 408, 411.
ARAGON 176-178, 183.
Arak El-Amir 35.
Arbaoua 398.
Arbués, Pedro, *see* St. Pedro Arbues.
Architects xxv, 108, 193, 197, 221, 268, 333, 342, 361, 365, 370.
ARES 174.
Arians 122.
Aristobulus 28.
Aristotle 127, 160, 165, 168, 250, 253, 361.
Ark curtain 74, 268, 275, 280, 292, 301, 309, 323, 324, 327, 328-329, 434, 438, 442.
Ark of the Covenant 10, 42, 329.
Ark of the Law 73, 108, 111, 121, 128, 156, 170, 193, 222, 248, 252, 255, 257, 259, 262-263, 265, 268, 269, 277, 292, 301, 303, 348, 324, 329, 339, 360, 362, 365, 366, 434, 438, 439, 440, 441, 443, 444, 445; *as symbol*, 42, 237.
ARLES 105, 113.
Armenians 364, 368.
Arminians 191.
Arnstein, Fanny von, 304, 323, 348, 350.
Aron Ha-Kodesh, see Ark of the Law.
Arragel, Moses, 165.
Arsuf 40.
Art, ancient Jewish, 22; Polish Jewish, 356, 358; Western Jewish, 71; Ritual, *see* Ritual art, Ritual objects.
ARTA 386.
Arts and Crafts xvii, xxvi-xxvii, 85, 119, 136, 142, 145, 148, 168, 173, 175, 177, 183, 184, 197; *see also* Metal-work.

Asher ben Yehiel xvii, 283.
Ashkelon 42.
Ashkenazim, Ashkenazic, 59, 62-64, 77, 196, 197, 198, 203, 207, 210, 222, 224, 225, 263, 265, 266, 316, 317, 383.
ASOLO 265.
Assimilation, Jewish, 36-37, 235, 254.
Assyria, Assyrians, 13, 15, 16, 368, 390.
Astarte 12, 13, 42, 43.
Astorga xi.
Astrology 152, 153, 247, 426.
Astronomy 104, 134, 138, 153, 160, 164, 172, 183, 246, 293, 333, 334, 361.
Astruc, Don, 114.
ASTURIAS 163, 174.
Athanagild, King, 147.
ATHENS 385, 387.
Atlas catalan de Charles V 84.
Atlas mts. 389, 391, 398, 402, 405, 407.
Atonement, Day of, 31, 77.
AUGSBURG 300, 432.
Augustus Caesar 116, 245.
AUSTRIA 335, 346-352.
Auto-de-fé 133, 139, 162, 166, 178, 185, 248, 252; pictures of, 165.
Avendeath 160.
Avenzoar 262.
Averroës 104, 127, 247, 262.
Avicebron, *see* Ibn Gabirol.
AVIGNON 101-106, 341, 389.
    Jewries 101, 102
    Museum, Calvet, 103
    Synagogues 102, 104
AVILA 172.
Avis, Joseph, builder, 222.
Azulai, Haim David, 60, 64.

Baal 12, 13, 26, 248, 409.
Baal Shemtob, the (Israel ben Eliezer), 360, 371, 374, 400.
Bab al-Wadi 44.
Babel, tower of, 226.
Babylon 2, 3, 5, 7, 8, 9, 10, 16, 17, 18, 29, 226, 270; hanging gardens of, 226.
Babylonia 41, 126, 287, 407.

BACHARACH 430.
Bacon, Roger, 144.
Badis, King, 143.
BAD KREUZNACH 430.
Bagdad 125, 257, 381.
BAGHAI 408.
BAIERSDORF 304, 305.
Baiersdorf, Samson, 304.
Bajazet, Sultan, 380.
Bakery, *see* Matzoth bakery.
Balak 24.
BALEARIC ISLES 121, 183-184.
BALKANS, the, 190, 200, 379-387.
Balmes, Abraham de, 262.
Balzac 66.
BAMBERG 52, 302, 305-307.
    Cathedral 305
    Synagogue, mediæval, 305
    —painted, 306-307
Banking, bankers, 52, 54, 85, 106, 113, 119, 139, 152, 173, 174, 211-214, 215, 219, 220, 223, 240, 254, 261, 269, 271, 274, 289, 302, 316, 358, 388, 402; *see also* Court Jews.
Baraka 397, 400, 403.
BARANOWICZE 440.
BARBARY STATES 183, 187, 316; *also see* Algeria, Morocco, Tripoli, Tunis.
BARCELONA 163, 179-181, 182, 383.
    Church, S. Clara, 179
    —S. Jaime 181
    Ghetto 179-180
    Montjuich 1.9
    Museum 174
Bari xvii, 286.
Bar Kochba 84, 227.
Baroque (style) 193, 202, 252, 263, 283, 304, 317, 329, 336, 349, 353, 360, 367-368, 374, 375, 434, 435, 441, 444.
Baruch, metal-worker, 445.
BASEL 177, 430.
BAVAI 208.
BAVARIA 296, 297, 344.
Bayle, Pierre, 191.
BAYONNE 59, 117, 118.
BEAUNE 92.
BECHHOFEN 300, 307-308.
Bed, ivory, 14.
Beethoven 350.

BEGORJA 442.
Behrens, Leffmann, 304.
BEILSTEIN 430.
BEJAR 172.
BELGIUM 207-208, 315.
BELGRADE 382.
Belisarius 121.
Bellaset, Jewess of Lincoln, 215.
Bells, see Rimonim.
BELMONTE, home of Marano survivors, 186.
BEMBIBRE 173.
Beni-Hezir, family of, 37.
Benjamin of Tudela 1, 115, 175.
Benveniste, Abraham, 173.
Benveniste, Sheshet, 177.
Ber ben Israel, wood-carver, 363, 445.
Berbers 122, 143, 393, 401, 404, 406, 408.
Berdichev 445.
Berechiah Ha-Nakdan 219.
Berenice (Africa) 116.
BERLIN 194, 304, 310, 320-325, 351, 374.
 Ephraimsche Haus 321-322
 Ghetto, modern, 323
 Graveyard 322
 Jewry, site, 320, 321
 Libraries: Royal, 325; Jewish, 323
 Museums: Altes, 324; Jewish, 71, 323; Kaiser Friedrich, 323-324; Neues, 324-325; Schloss, 325
 Synagogue, old, 322
BERN 430.
Berr, Cerf, 63.
Beth Din (court house) 392.
Beth ha-midrash (study-hall) 102, 103, 128, 161, 264, 339, 345, 363, 365, 369, 370, 371, 373, 396, 437.
Betrothal rings, see Rings, marriage.
BEZIERS 114.
BIALYSTOK, city, 439.
BIALYSTOK, province, 439-440.
Bible of Olivares 164-165.
Biblia Complutensis 176.
Bibliothèque Nationale, Paris, 51, 83-84, 247.
BIDACHE 117.
BIELSK 439.

Bima xix-xx, 108, 111, 193, 197, 222, 252, 257, 259, 260, 261, 262-263, 268, 277, 280, 292, 303, 307, 329, 338, 339, 345, 360, 361, 365, 366-367, 369, 373, 374, 379, 437, 438, 440, 441, 443, 444.
BINSWANGEN 432.
Bird, as symbol, 376, 377, 409, 435, 445; see also Cock, Dove, Eagle, Hawk, Peacock, Pelican, Phoenix, Storks.
Black Death 208, 272, 274, 297, 301, 305, 313, 314, 357.
Black Prince, the, 153.
Blanche de Bourbon 152.
BLOIS 98.
Blossoms, as symbol, 377.
Bodleian Bowl 219.
Bodleian Library xxvii, 49, 79, 219-220, 328, 334.
Boerne, Ludwig, 66, 68, 273, 290, 292, 293, 322.
BOHEMIA 273, 295, 303, 306, 330-345, 368.
BOLOGNE 258.
Bonacosa, translator, 262.
Bonastruc, Abraham, 180.
Bonastruc Joseph 182.
BONN 431.
Bonnet, Jew's, 52, 90, 96, 298, 306, 347, 352; rabbinical, 77.
Book of the Apple, the, 250.
Booths, Feast of, see Tabernacles.
BORDEAUX 52, 59, 116-117.
Borgoña, Juan de, painter, 165.
BORKEN 434.
BORNHEIM 294.
Bosboom, J., painter, 207.
BOSNIA 381.
Bouman, Elias, architect, 193, 194.
BOURGES 94-96.
Bowl, see Bodleian Bowl, Magic bowls.
BRABANT 209, 263.
Brahe, Tycho, 334.
BRATISLAVA 345, 353.
Brazil 191, 193, 201, 224, 257.
Breastplate, see Torah shield.
Breitner, Georges Hendrik, painter, 199.
Brescia 325.

BRESLAU 325-328, 355, 435.
  Blücherplatz 325-326
  Graveyards 325, 326
  Jewries 326-327
  Libraries 328
  Museums: Schlesisches, 326, 327;
    Jewish, 327
  Synagogues 327
BREST-LITOVSK, 440, 441.
BRINDISI 250.
Bristol 213.
British Museum 4, 16, 212, 225-227;
  Babylonian-Assyrian rooms, 226,
  423-427; Coin and Medal Room,
  227, 429; Edward VII Gallery, 227,
  428; Egyptian rooms, 226, 427; Li-
  brary, 227; Library, Kings, 428;
  Manuscript Saloon, 227, 428.
Britons 210.
BRITTANY 99.
BRODY 368, 441, 443.
Browne, Thomas, 37, 159.
BRUGES 208.
Brünn 344.
Bruno, Giordano, 144.
BRUNSWICK 328-329.
BRUSSELS 208-209.
Bubastes 412.
BUCHAU-AM-FEDERSEE xi.
Buchidan, David, of Meknes, 398.
BUCZACZ 369, 443.
BUDAPEST 353-355.
  Herzl, birthplace, 355
  Jewry, old, 353-354
  —Ludwigsgasse, 354
  Orczy mansion 355
  Synagogue 354
BÜDIGEN 434.
Bueno, Ephraim, physician, 198.
BUKOWINA 379.
BULGARIA 383.
BURGOS 174.
Burgos, Paul de, 174.
BURGSTEINFURT 436.
BURGUNDY 92-93.
BURY ST. EDMUNDS 216, 217.
Byblos 13.
Byron 322, 386.
Byzance 385.

Byzantine 23, 42, 43, 121, 250, 364,
  368, 383, 384, 408.

Cabbala 60, 240, 253, 262, 299, 333,
  361, 386.
Cabbalism 20, 116, 159.
Cabbalist 158, 168, 172, 334, 382.
Cadiz 120.
CAEN 99, 167.
Cafoussi, Hayim, 411.
Cahena, Queen, 122, 408.
CAIRO 108, 127, 220, 333, 404, 411-
  412.
  Fostat 411-412
  Graveyard 411
  Jewry 411
  Museum 79, 412
  Synagogues 411, 412
CALABRIA 244.
CALATAYUD 176.
Calatrava, Knights of, 158-159, 164-
  165.
Calendars 292.
Caligula 232.
Call, the, 179, 181.
Calmer, Liefmann, 61.
Calvin, John, 191.
Calvinists 191, 209.
CAMBERG 430.
CAMBRIDGE 220.
Camphuysen, Socinian poet, 205-206.
Canaan, Canaanite, 10, 11, 13, 23, 28,
  390, 393, 407.
Canaan, spies from, figures of, 236.
Candelabra 77, 193, 222, 228, 259,
  263, 268, 278, 280, 304, 309, 310,
  327, 328, 329, 337, 339, 365, 398,
  437, 442, 445; *see also* Hanuka can-
  delabra, Eternal Lamp, Menorah,
  Sabbath lamp.
Candia, *see* Crete.
Candle, *as symbol,* 337; *see also* Lamp.
Candlestick, seven-branched, *see* Me-
  norah.
CANEA 265.
CANNES 17, 20.
CANTERBURY 218.
Capernaum 42.
Capón, Ruy, 139, 173.
CAPUA 245.

CARCASSONNE 105, 116.
Carlyle, Thomas, 216, 217, 221.
Carmel 26.
CARMONA 140.
Caro, Joseph, 383.
Carpathians, the, 311, 353, 355.
CARPENTRAS 106-110.
  Ghetto 110
  Graveyard 110
  Matzoth bakery 109
  Mikveh 109-110
  Museum 110
  Synagogue 107-109
Carpi, Jacob da, painter, 254.
Carrière 110, 179.
Cartagena 120, 121.
Carteya 120.
CARTHAGE 13, 203, 249, 408-409, 410.
  Lavigerie museum 409
  Naro (see)
  Necropolis 408-409
Cartography 84, 183.
Carvajal, Antonio Fernandes, 224-225.
CASABLANCA 400.
CASALE MONFERRATO 260.
Casal Maggiore 260.
Casimir the Great 363.
Casimir IV, of Poland, 328.
Caspi, Joseph ben . . . Jacob, 112.
CASSEL 434.
Castellazzo, Moses da, painter, 254.
CASTELLO BRANCO 186.
CASTELLÓN DE AMPURIAS 178.
CASTILLE 126, 163, 173, 174, 183.
Catacombs 30, 233-235, 249, 250, 377, 408-409.
CATALONIA 122, 163, 176, 178-183, 382.
Cathedra 223, 325, 387.
CAUCASIA 384.
CAVAILLON 110-112
Cemeteries xxiii-xxv, Algeria, 408; Austria, 349-350, 351, 352; Bulgaria, 383; Czechoslovakia, 332-337, 345, 353, 438; Egypt, 411; England, 218, 220, 224-225; France, 61-64, 67-68, 110, 117, 118, 431, 432; Germany, 275, 282-285, 286-287, 290-292, 303, 304, 314-315, 316-318, 320, 322, 325-326, 431-436;

Greece, 386; Holland, 199-203, 207; Hungary, 353, 355; Italy, 242, 252, 257, 262, 264, 265, 267; Jugoslavia, 382; Morocco, 403-404, 405; Poland, 363, 367-368, 373, 374-378, 439-444; Portugal, 185; Rumania, 379; Spain, 171-172, 174, 178, 179, 181; Switzerland, 430; Tunisia, 408-409; Turkey, 383, 384.
Centaur 81.
CERNAUTI 379.
Cervantes 148, 176; see Sancho Panza.
Ceuta 121.
Chagall, Marc, painter, 235, 359, 367, 376.
Chair, for Bridegrooms of the Law, 195; for Elijah, see Elijah chair.
Chalchis 387.
Chalice 80.
CHALON-SUR-SAÔNE 92.
CHAM 298.
CHAMBÉRY 93.
CHAMPAGNE 86, 88, 126.
Chananiah Ha-Cohen, of Marrakesh, 398.
Chaptal, Count, 65.
Chares, Aaron de, painter, 223.
Charlemagne 47.
Charles I, of Anjou, 84, 246-247.
Charles I, of England, 220; Charles II, 225.
Charles II, of Spain, 166.
Charles IV, of Germany, 331.
Charles V, Emperor, 342.
Charles Martel 122.
Charleston, S. C., 194.
CHARTRES 94, 96.
Chassidism 20, 371, 374, 379.
CHATSWORTH 229.
Chaucer xxvi, 210, 216, 399.
Chazars 124, 357, 364, 384.
CHELM 277, 360, 441.
Chemosh 24, 25.
Cherub 81, 200, 202, 317.
Cherubim 5, 91.
CHIESCH 437.
Childebert 46.
Chilperic 45, 46.
China 41, 125, 175.
Chmielnicki 305, 306, 310, 357.

CHODOROW 369-371, 443.

Choir 223, 367.

Christendom xvi-xvii, 103, 104, 154, 160, 239, 385; *see also* Church, the.

Christians, early, 42, 120, 234, 236, 371.

Christine, Empress, of Austria, 328.

Chuetas, the, 184.

CHUFUT-KALÉ 384.

Chuppah-Stern 303, 309, 433, 434.

Church, the, xvi, xix, xxiii, xxviii-xxix, 116, 120, 122, 128, 131, 162, 178, 196, 204, 208, 211, 212, 213, 219, 238, 240, 241, 242, 252, 261, 268, 274, 297, 300, 329, 353, 364, 365, 373; *see also* Counter Reformation, *Judensau,* New and Old Faith, Papacy, Synagogue Defeated.

CHYROW 443, 444.

Cicero 231.

Cid, the, 146, 147, 148, 173, 174.

CINCINNATI, O., x.

Circumcision implements 72, 292.

Citron 28, 31, 32, 33, 154; *see also Etrog.*

City of Blood 98.

CIVIDALE 265.

Classic (style) 192, 194, 252, 268, 303, 315, 354, 368, 443.

Clemence, Queen, 55.

Cluny Museum 47, 48, 70-83, 350.

COBLENTZ 430.

Cock, *as symbol,* 371, 445.

Cohen, or priest, 291, 336.

Cohen, Judah ben Moses, 160.

Coins 28, 39, 83, 92, 120, 227, 357-358.

COLMAR 431.

COLOGNE 271, 273-275
  Cathedral 274
  Cemetery 275
  Jewry, site, 273
  Mikveh 274
  Museum, Rheinisches, 274-275

Columbus, Christopher, 104, 139-140.

Commerce, xvi-xvii, 85, 86, 103, 106, 113, 114, 117, 125, 126, 136, 148, 174, 191, 210, 223, 224, 239, 244, 252, 256, 261, 263, 265, 266, 271, 272, 296, 300, 302, 316, 326, 327, 344, 355, 358, 364, 380, 386, 391, 400, 402, 406, 408, 436.

Community offices 369, 370, 434; *see also* Town hall.

COMTAT VENAISSIN 59, 86, 104, 106-112.

CONEGLIANO 265.

Congress of Vienna 348.

Constance, Lake, 351.

CONSTANTINE 408.

Constantine, Emperor, 271.

CONSTANTINOPLE 27, 33, 257, 295, 296, 355, 380, 382, 383-384, 385.
  Graveyard 384
  National Museum 384
  Synagogues 384

CORDOVA I, 120, 122-134, 155, 176, 194, 267, 286, 331, 381, 389, 404.
  Alcázar 123
  Almodóvar gate 124-125
  Ghetto 126-128, 130-131
  Medinat az-Zahra 123-124
  Plaza Corredera 133
  Synagogue 128-130

CORFU 265, 386.

CORINTH 386-387.

Corinthian (style) 222, 268, 341, 387.

CORNWALL 210.

CORUNNA 174.

Cos 387-388.

Cosimo II, grand-duke of Tuscany, 256.

Costumes 43, 52, 60, 92, 125, 128, 136, 272, 372, 381, 385, 392, 393, 401, 406, 410, 425.

Council of the Four Lands 361, 372, 445.

Counter Reformation 241, 254.

Court Jews 35, 45, 46, 104, 119, 124, 134, 138, 139, 143, 144, 149, 152, 168, 173, 174, 177, 185, 302, 304, 321-322, 328, 333, 342, 350, 372, 380, 391.

Covenant, New and Old, *see* New and Old Faith.

CRACOW 325, 344, 345, 357, 358-363, 364, 389, 403, 442.
  Ghetto 359, 363
  Graveyard 363
  Lobzow 363

Cracow—(*Continued*)
  Synagogues: Alte, 360, 363; Isaac, 306, 361-362; Kuppah, 363; Popper, 363; Remuh, 360; Wysoka, 362-363
Creation, story of, 8, 226.
CREMONA 259.
Crescas, Hasdai, 177, 180.
Cresques, Elisha, limner, xxvii.
Cresques, Jaffuda, xxvii, 84, 183.
CRETE 253, 265, 333.
CRIMEA 296, 357, 384.
Cromwell 198, 220, 221, 224, 225.
Crown, *as symbol*, 200, 201, 329; of the Law, Kingdom, Priesthood, 75, 76, 193, 228, 378; *see also* Torah crown.
Crusaders, Crusades, xxviii, 52, 86, 89, 213, 217, 272, 274, 275, 283, 284, 286, 297, 330, 357, 385; Albigensian, 106.
CUMPTICH 208.
Cup, *see* Circumcision implements, *Kiddush* cup; *as symbol*, 36, 429.
Cymbals, *as symbol*, 376.
Cyprus 266.
Cyrenaica 116.
CYRENE 249.
CZECHOSLOVAKIA, *see* Bohemia, Moravia, Bratislava.
CZERNOWITZ, *see* Cernauti.

Dancing 164, 253, 260, 266.
Daniel 406, 407; figure of, 92, 317.
Dante 49, 144, 240.
Danube, the, 272, 295, 300, 325, 346, 351, 353, 382, 383.
DANZIG 311, 328.
Darmesteter, James, 53.
DARMSTADT 382, 431.
David 23; figure of, 48, 92, 202.
David, Alexander, 328.
David ben Zimra 411.
Davila, Eliezer, of Rabat, 398.
DEBDU 407.
DEGGENDORF 432.
Delmedigo, Elijah, 253, 262.
Delmedigo, Joseph, 333-334, 337.
DELOS 387.
Delphi 387.

Demons 19, 20.
Denmark 316.
DERBY HOUSE 229.
Descartes 191.
DESSAU 320, 323.
DEUTZ 275, 431.
Deza xi.
Dialoghi di Amore 253.
Dialoghi sull' Arte Rappresentativa 253.
Diaspora xiv.
Dibon 24.
DIGNE 109.
DIJON 91-92.
Dioscorides 124.
Dishes, *see* Gilt-glass, Passover, Platter, Purim, Sabbath.
Disraeli, Benjamin, 223, 225, 267.
DJERBA 397.
Domitian, nephew of, 231.
Don Juan 137.
Donatello 256.
Donin, Nicholas, 49.
Dönmehs, the, 386.
Doric (style) 36, 419.
Doughty, Charles, 119.
Dove 43, 234, 236, 237; *see also* Bird.
Dra'a (river) 391, 402.
Drama, dramatists, 110, 197, 253, 260.
Drawing of the Water, Feast of, 33.
DRESDEN 207.
Dreyfus, Alfred, 69.
DUBNO 369, 441.
Duero, the, 126.
Du Guesclin, Bertrand, 153.
Dulaure, J. A., 55.
Duran, Profiat, xxi, 171.
DÜRRMAUL 437.
DÜSSELDORF 275, 431.
Dutch 191, 192, 193, 198, 201, 204, 221, 229, 366; Republic 190.
DYHERRNFURTH 435.

Eagle, *as symbol*, 362, 371; Roman, 40.
East Indies 191, 316.
Ecclesiasticus, fragments of, 220, 227.
Ecuador 221.
Eden, garden of, 9, 226.
EGER 336, 338, 344, 437.

Egidio, Cardinal, 240.
EGYPT 10, 11, 24, 35, 37, 219, 226, 232, 244, 324, 390, 411-413.
Einstein, Albert, 273.
EISENSTADT 353.
El Ferrol 174.
El Greco 149, 152, 198.
Elbe, the, 311, 315.
Elbermannstadt 305.
ELCHE 121, 229.
Eleazar of Worms 284, 299, 310.
Elephantine xiv, 219, 324, 427.
Eliachim of Cologne xxi.
Elias, Samuel, "inventor of upper-cut," 223.
Elijah 108, 109, 279, 299, 335, 411, 412; figure of, 95; grotto of, 26.
Elijah chair 108, 111, 223, 280, 292, 434, 435, 436, 439, 443, 444.
Elijah, Gaon of Vilna, 360, 374, 375.
Elijah of Casablanca 398, 399, 400.
Elijah of Pesaro 266.
Elisha 14, 400.
Elizabeth, Queen, of England, 188.
ELLRICH 436.
Elte, Harry, architect, 197.
Elyas, head of English Jewry, 213-214.
Emancipation, of Jews, 62, 63, 64, 65, 68, 117, 222, 242, 270, 287, 318, 320, 327, 350.
Embroideries 82, 108, 195, 197, 228, 259, 304, 318, 327, 337, 350, 356, 434; festival, 78; see also Ark curtain, Ephod, Pulpit cover, Torah band, Torah mantle.
EMDEN 188, 197, 311, 436.
Emden, Jacob, 317.
Empire (style) 292, 436.
Encava, Ephraim, 407.
ENDIGEN 430.
Engelbert II, of Cologne, 274.
ENGHIEN 208, 209.
ENGLAND 191, 198, 210-229, 246, 272, 295, 297, 356, 391, 392.
English Bible 104.
Enns 351.
Ensisheim 284.
Ephesus 385.
Ephod 77.
Ephraim, Veitel-Heine, 321-322.

Ephraim ben Jacob 275.
Ephraim of Regensburg xxi.
Epicurus 205, 386.
EPINAL 431.
Epitaphs, see Tombs, Tombstones, Sarcophagus, Ossuary, Catacombs.
Ercole I, of Ferrara, 258.
ERFURT 312-313.
Erub, 280.
Escalana 148.
Eschol, see Grape-cluster.
Esperandeu, Juan, 178.
Espiche 185.
ESTE 264.
ESTELLA 175.
Esterka, of Poland, 363.
Esther, scroll of, 77-78, 195, 228, 229, 323, 328, 337, 350.
Eternal Lamp, see Nir Tamid.
Etrog 28, 129, 236, 237, 324, 362, 429; see also Citron.
Euclid 165.
EUPEN 208.
Eupolemos 6.
Eupolemus, son of Johanan, 230.
Euripides 387.
EVORA 185, 186.
Ewer, see Pitcher.
EXETER 225.
Expulsions 52, 106, 117, 120, 132, 145, 153, 164, 172, 173, 175, 180, 184, 208, 210, 216, 230, 248, 251, 272, 274, 286, 297, 298, 300, 301, 309, 312, 313, 314, 325, 331, 341, 347, 348, 352, 353, 356, 380, 388, 435.
Eybeschütz, Jonathan, 317.
Ezra 397, 412.

Faith, Old and New, see New and Old Faith.
FALKENSTEIN 431.
Fano 252.
Faro, Portugal, 185.
Farrachius (Farragut, Faraj ben Selim) 84, 247.
Federighi, Antonio, sculptor, 256.
FELZTYN 443.
FEODOSIA 384.
Ferdinand III, of Spain, 128, 135.

Ferdinand and Isabella 145-146, 380.
Fermosa, the "Jewess of Toledo," 149.
FERRARA 258-259, 260.
Ferrer, Vincent, see St. Vincent Ferrer.
Fesch, Cardinal, 65.
Festivals, see Atonement, Day of;
    Drawing of the Water; Hanuka;
    New Moon; New Year; Passover;
    Purim; Rejoicing of the Law; Sab-
    bath; Tabernacles, Feast of.
FEZ 127, 132, 390, 398, 402, 404-405,
    406.
    Graveyard 405
    Maimonides house 404
    Mellah 404
FIGUERAS 178.
Finance, Financiers, see Banking.
FINISTERRE, France, 99; Spain, 163.
Fire-pans 34; as symbol, 228.
Fischl, Maier, 336-337.
Fish, as symbol, 234, 409.
Flamel, Nicolas, 56, 57.
Flanders 191.
Flesh-hooks, as symbol, 228.
Flood, story of the, 8, 226.
FLORENCE 127, 252-253.
FLOSS 295, 304.
FOSTAT 411-412.
Foucault, Charles de, 399.
Fould, Achille, 68.
Fouqué, F. de la Motte, 322.
FRANCE 45-118, 56, 58, 64, 85, 106,
    157, 183, 191, 238, 244, 246, 272,
    285, 287, 356, 392, 402.
FRANCHE-COMTÉ 93.
FRANCONIA 303, 306.
FRANCONIAN SWITZERLAND 305.
Frank, Jacob, 310, 323, 331.
FRANKFORT 288-294, 310, 336, 341,
    350, 403.
    Bornheim 294
    Ghetto, site, 288
    Graveyard 290-292
    Monuments, Boerne, Heine, 293,
        294
    Museum, Jewish, 71, 292-293
    Rothschild house 288-290
    Stadtbibliotek 293
Franklin, Arthur, collection, 227.
Franks, the, 46, 271.

Franz, Ettore Roesler, painter, 242.
Frederick II, Emperor, 53, 244, 246,
    247-248, 250.
Frederick the Great 315, 320, 321.
Frederick William I 322.
French Revolution 62, 64, 117, 209,
    270, 274, 287.
Freud, Sigmund, 273.
FREUDENBURG 431.
FRIEDBERG 282, 294.
Friedländer, David, 323.
FRIESING 432.
Fuggers 272, 300.
FÜRTH 301-303, 344, 345.

GABIN 440.
GADARA 29.
GALICIA, Poland, 306, 361-371, 375,
    379, 443-445; Spain, 163, 173.
GALILEE 30, 33, 41, 194, 398.
Galileo 160, 333.
Galipapa, Hayim, "astonishing" rabbi,
    175.
Gallio, pro-consul, 387.
Gans, David, 333, 342.
Garibaldians 239.
Garonne, the, 103, 116.
GASR GARIAN 410.
Gaul, 46, 85, 208.
Geiger, Abraham, 326, 327.
GELNHAUSEN 434.
Genizah 220, 412, 428.
Genoa 324.
Geographers 172, 183, 333; see also
    Cartography.
GEORGENMÜNDE 433.
Gerard of Cremona 160.
German Jews, 236, 271-273, 360, 369,
    385; see also Ashkenazim.
GERMANY 59, 157, 191, 196, 244, 271-
    328, 356, 358, 360, 385.
Gernsheim Michael, "Jews' bishop,"
    280.
GERONA 180, 181-183, 251.
    Geronella tower 183
    Ghetto 181
    Provincial Museum 181-182
    Synagogue 181
Gerondi, Jonah ben Abraham, "the
    Saint," 182-183.

Gershom, "light of the exile," 86, 283, 286, 287, 375.
Gersonides 101, 102, 104, 140, 267; *Commentary*, 293.
Gersonides press, *see* Zemach, Mordecai.
GEX xi.
GHENT 208.
Ghetto, the, xiv-xviii, 70, 103-104, 197, 218, 238, 241, 251, 252, 259, 260, 261, 265-266, 296, 303, 320-321, 326, 332, 357, 394, 403, 405; *see also* Jewry, mention of a.
Ghetto gates, *France,* 101, 112, 113, 116; *Germany,* 276, 287, 348, 372; *Italy,* 241, 255, 261, 268, 270; *Morocco,* 394, 401; *Spain,* 125, 126, 135, 176, 184; *Poland,* 372.
Ghetto walls 179, 218, 276, 394-395.
GIBRALTAR 103, 122, 223, 224, 389, 391.
Gideon, Sampson, 223.
Gilgamesh 10.
Gilt-glass dishes 73, 83, 129, 236-238, 323, 376.
Girgenti 247.
Glass-making xxvi-xxvii, 238.
GLOGAU 435.
Glückel of Hameln 302, 304, 314, 315, 324.
GLÜCKSTADT 318.
GNIEWOSZOW 441.
Goat, *see* Ram.
God, footstool of, 7; names of, 193; throne of, 7; thunder of, 12.
Godfrey of Bouillon 89, 209, 283, 287.
Goethe 323.
Goldbaum, Samuel, wood-carver, 363, 443.
Golden Calf 10.
Golden Rose, *see* Nachmanowicz.
Goldmanaz, Samuel, wood-carver, 363, 439.
Golem, the, 334.
GORA KALWARJA 440.
GORIZIA 352.
GORODICZCZE 376, 377.
GÖRZ, *see* Gorizia.
Gothic (style) 73, 74, 129, 154, 179, 184, 186, 251, 263, 277, 279, 283,

297, 322, 339, 343, 360, 365, 374, 430, 431, 432, 434, 436, 441.
GÖTTINGEN 436.
GRANADA 134, 140-145, 154, 395, 401, 410.
  Albaicín 141, 142-145
  Alcaicería 142, 401
  Alhambra 121, 145-146
  Casa de la Lona 142
  Ferdinand and Isabella, tombs, 146
  Torquemada house 146
  Ghetto, site, 141
Grape-cluster 28, 235, 291.
GRAZ 352.
GREECE 30, 244, 383, 385-387.
Greek 33, 37, 40, 42, 43, 116, 121, 178, 234, 235, 237, 238, 250, 265, 324, 384, 385, 386, 390, 397; influence, *see* Hellenism; Jews, 384, 386, 387.
Greeks 114, 192, 205, 238, 246, 249.
Grégoire, Henri, 62, 64, 93.
Gregory of Tours 45, 46.
Grillparzer, Franz, 67, 348.
GRODNO 439.
GROJEC 440.
GRONINGEN 207.
GROSAGE 208.
Grotius 192.
GUADALAJARA 176.
Guzman, Domingo de, *see* St. Domingo.
Guzman, Luis de, 164-165.
GWODZIDZ, *see* Gwozdziec.
GWOZDZIEC 371, 444.

Habbus, King, 143.
Habdalah, cloth for, 228; *see also* Spice-box.
Habiru 11.
Hachnasat Orchim, see Hospice.
Hachuel, Solika, 404-405.
Hadad 12.
Hadrian 23.
Haek, Jan, stained-glass maker, 209.
HAGENHEIM 431.
HAGENAU 431.
Haggadah xxvii, 292, 293, 301, 380, 382, 431.

Haggai, Wadi, 406.
HAGUE, THE, 206-207.
  Cemetery 207
  Museum, Gemeente, 207
  —Mauritshuis 207
  —Mesdag 207
  Spinoza house 206
  Synagogue 207
Haifa 182, 421.
Haimhausen, Sigismund von, 344.
Hakim II 124.
HALBERSTADT 436.
Halevi, Samuel ben Meir, 152-159, 288.
Halévy, Fromental, 68.
HALICZ 371.
HALL, Swabia, 295, 308; Tyrol, 351.
Hallel 32.
Haman 78, 81.
HAMBURG 202, 257, 269, 311, 315-320, 333, 345, 375.
  Cemetery, German, 317, 318
  —Portuguese, 317-318
  Emden house 317
  Heine memorials 320
  Hospital 316
  Museum, Kunst u. Gewerbe, 318
  —Jewish 318
  Synagogues 318.
Hameln, Joseph, 314.
Hameln, Moses, 304.
HAMMAN-LIF, see Naro.
Hammurabi 3, 5.
Hands, as symbols, 291, 336, 377, 424.
HANOVER 304, 314-315.
Hanseatic League 272, 311.
Hanuka 76, 81, 290; candelabra 70, 76, 81, 228, 264, 292, 324, 352.
Hara, the, 408, 410, 411.
HARBURG (Ries) 432.
Harp, Babylonian, 17; by waters of Babylon, 362; as symbol, 228; see also David, figure of.
Harran 6.
Harun-al-Rashid 47.
Harvest fruits, as symbol, 307, 308, 329.
Harz, the, 311, 313.
Hasdai ben Joseph 177.
Hat, as symbol, 376.

Hawk, as symbol, 371.
Hayim ben Lissa, painter, 334.
Hayyun, Nehemiah, 382.
Hazael 14, 15.
Hebron, painting of, 362.
HECHINGEN 434.
Hecht 435.
Heidek, Juan Josef, 159.
HEIDINGSFELD 302, 309.
HEILBRONN 434.
HEILIGENSTADT 436.
Heine, Heimann and Simon, 315.
Heine, Heinrich, 65-68, 131, 133, 161, 225, 273, 274, 288, 290, 292, 294, 308, 316, 318-320, 322, 323, 405.
Heine, Salomon, 316.
Hekal 42.
Helena of Adiabene 38-39.
Hellenism 35, 36, 37, 121, 387.
Henri IV, of France, 200.
Henricus of Erfurt 313.
Henry II, of England, 213, 215.
Henry III, of England, 212.
Henry II, of Spain, see Henry de Trastamara.
Henry III, of Spain, 170.
Henry de Trastamara 152, 153, 174.
Herder 322.
HERFORD (Westphalia) 436.
Herod, Herodian, 28, 33, 34, 83, 227, 245, 388.
Herod Agrippa 83.
Herod Antipas 116.
Herodias 116.
Herodium 36.
Herz, Henrietta, 304, 323.
Herz, Judah Goldschmied de, architect, 333, 342.
Herzl, Theodor, 69, 273, 351, 355.
HESSIA 289, 294, 315.
Heusse des Cotes, Sire de, 59.
Hezekiah, tunnel of, 26-27, 384, 424.
HILDESHEIM 312.
Hillel Benjamin of Lask, architect, 370, 443, 445.
Hinnom 36.
Hittite 24.
HÖCHBERG 309.
Hochstraaten, dean of Cologne, 274.
HOHENEMS 351.

Hohenstauffens 246, 250.
HOLLAND 59, 157, 187, 188-207, 210, 221, 263, 368, 374.
Hollander, *see* Dutch.
Holy Alliance 351.
Horace 38, 231, 250.
Horb 306.
Horn, ram's, *see* Shofar.
Hornburg 329.
Horowitz, Aaron Meshullam, 342.
Horowitz, Jacob Isaac, "Seer of Lublin," 372.
Horowitz, Pincas, of Frankfort, 291; of Prague, 342.
Horowitz, Salman Isaiah, 332.
Hosanna 32, 33.
Hospice 103, 248.
Host 34; charge of desecrating, 54, 169-170, 208-209, 326, 432, 433.
Hound and Hare, *as symbol,* 371.
Houses, Jewish, *Austria,* 348, 351, 352; *Belgium,* 209; *Bulgaria,* 383; *England,* 214, 215, 216, 218; *France,* 110, 431; *Germany,* 276, 287, 296, 288-290, 299, 430, 431, 433, 436; *Holland,* 197, 203, 204; *Hungary,* 353; *Italy,* 268; *Jugoslavia,* 381; *Morocco,* 393, 395-396; *Poland,* 365, 372; *Sicily,* 249; *Spain,* 127, 136, 137, 141, 152, 160, 167-168, 181. *See also* Palace.
House-signs 48, 281, 283, 286, 288, 291, 292.
Huguenots 191.
Human figures, in Jewish art, xxi-xxii.
Humboldt, William von, 322.
HUNGARY 353-355, 385.
HUSIATYN 362, 369, 444, 445.
Husiel, Rabbi, xvii.
Hussites 274, 331.
Hutten, Ulrich von, 274.
Huygens 204.
Hyrcanus, *see* Tobiah ben Joseph ben Tobiah.

Ibn Attar, Mordecai, 401.
Ibn Attar, Moses, 391.
Ibn Daud, Abraham, 160.
Ibn Ezra, Abraham, 115, 128, 160, 210, 407.

Ibn Ezra, Moses, 128, 144.
Ibn Gabirol, Solomon, 119, 140, 144, 254.
Ibn Gaon, Joshua ben Abraham, limner, xxvii.
Ibn Gaon, Shemtob ben Abraham, limner, xxvii.
Ibn Hayyim, Abraham ben Judah, limner, xxvii.
Ibn Hayyim, Joseph, limner, xxvii.
Ibn Jau, Jacob, 125.
Ibn Khordadbeh 393.
Ibn Naghdela, Joseph, 144-145.
Ibn Naghdela, Samuel, 143-144.
Ibn Said, Abu Ishak, poet, 144.
Ibn Shaprut, Hasdai, 124, 126, 128, 290, 428.
Ibn Shemtob, Joseph, 167, 169.
Ibn Shoshan, Joseph, 149.
Ibn Tibbons, the, 104, 114, 392.
Ibn Verga, Solomon, xxv, 142.
Ibn Zarzal, Abraham, 152-153.
"Il Trovatore," dungeon of, 177.
ILE-DE-FRANCE 93-94.
Illuminated manuscripts, *see* Manuscripts, illuminated.
Illuminators, *see* Manuscript illuminators.
Immanuel of Rome 240.
Incunabula 247, 260, 293.
India 125, 191, 224.
Ingathering Feast, *see* Tabernacles, Feast of.
Innocent III 52, 53.
Inns, Jewish, 56, 269, 326, 355.
Innsbruck 351.
Ionic (style) 192, 193.
Inquisition 52, 89, 120, 176, 177, 186, 191, 225, 239, 248, 293, 398.
Inscriptions, *Austria,* 347, 351; *Czechoslovakia,* 339, 343, 438; *Egypt,* 411, 412; *England,* 212, 219, 223, 228, 424; *France,* 14, 18, 19, 24-27, 33, 41, 42, 43, 73, 74, 78, 79, 81, 82, 97, 103, 108, 109, 110, 116; *Germany,* 274, 275, 276, 292, 298, 299, 301, 303, 307, 308, 309, 314, 315, 317, 324, 327, 432, 436; *Greece,* 387; *Holland,* 197, 200, 204, 205, 206; *Italy,* 237, 238, 239,

242, 257, 260, 268, 269; *Jugoslavia*, 385; *Morocco*, 398; *Poland*, 358, 360; *Spain*, 121, 129-130, 135, 155-157, 159, 161, 164; *Tunisia*, 409, 410; *Turkey*, 384, 388; *see also* Catacombs, Cemeteries, Tombstones.

Inscriptions, dedicatory, for synagogues, *England*, 222; *France*, 112, 114, 115, 431, 432; *Germany*, 276, 277, 280; *Greece*, 386, 387; *Italy*, 269; *Portugal*, 185, 186; *Spain*, 130, 149, 157, 172-173, 181.

Inscriptions, funerary, *see* Catacombs, Cemeteries, Ossuary, Sarcophagus, Tombs, Tombstone.

Ir ha-dam. See City of Blood.

Isaac, figure of, 72, 95, 317, 361, 433.

Isaac ben Arama 176.

Isaac ben Eliezer 124.

Isaac ben Hayim 49.

Isaac ben Sheshet 177, 408.

Isaac ben Sid 160.

Isaac of Corbeil 49.

Isaac of Vienna (Or Zarua) 299, 347.

Isaac the Jew 47.

Isabella, Queen, of Spain, 132, 139, 393; *see also* Ferdinand and Isabella.

Isaiah, figure of, 92.

Islam 42, 103, 104, 122, 127, 129, 142, 154, 173, 204, 321, 324, 356, 385, 389, 390, 394, 400, 402-403, 404, 406.

Israels, Josef, painter, 199.

Isserles, Moses ben Israel, 360-361, 363, 373.

ISSOUDUN 96-98.

ISTEB, *see* Stobi.

ITALY 193, 230-270, 287, 295, 321, 356, 360, 366, 382, 383, 392, 407.

Itzig, Fanny, *see* Arnstein, Fanny von.

Ivanhoe 217.

Jablonow on the Pruth 306, 371.

Jachin and Boaz, 28, 340; *see also* Pillars, of Temple.

Jacob, figure of, 95, 195, 367.

Jacob ben David 276.

Jacob ben Jacob Ha-Cohen 168.

Jacob ben Yakar 286-287.

Jacob of Provins 94.

Jacobean (style) 222.

Jacobs, Joseph, 216.

Jaffa 37.

Jamaica 187, 223.

JANOW 368, 444.

Jansenists 191.

Jaroslau 444.

JASI 379.

Jason, son of Eleazar, 230.

JASSY, *see* Jasi.

JEDWABNO 439.

Jehu 16.

Jens, Zachary, 204.

Jeremiah, 412; figure of, 92.

JEREZ 140.

JERMOLINSKY 445.

JERUSALEM 23, 27, 32, 34, 36, 39, 44, 83, 171, 226, 227, 232, 241, 245, 270, 333, 382, 413; *as symbol*, 276, 307, 308, 362; vase, 28.

JESIORY 439.

JEWART 363.

Jewel-box, ivory, 43.

"Jewess of Toledo," the, 143, 348.

Jewry, mention of a, *Algeria*, 407, 408; *Austria*, 347, 348, 352; *Belgium*, 208, 209; *Czechoslovakia*, 330, 353; *Egypt*, 411; *England*, 218, 224; *France*, 47, 54, 55, 58, 59, 87, 91, 92, 93, 94, 98, 99, 101-104, 109, 110, 111, 112, 113, 116, 294, 431, 432; *Germany*, 273-274, 276, 285, 287, 288, 301, 303, 305, 309, 312, 314, 315, 320, 326-327, 328, 432, 433, 434, 436; *Greece*, 386; *Holland*, 197, 207; *Hungary*, 353, 354, 355; *Italy*, 231, 238-239, 241-242, 251, 252, 253, 255, 258, 259, 260, 261, 265-270; *Jugoslavia*, 382; *Morocco*, 393, 394, 400, 401-402, 404, 406, 407; *Poland*, 359, 366, 372-373, 375; *Portugal*, 185, 186; *Sicily*, 248, 249; *Spain*, 126-128, 130, 135-138, 140, 141, 148, 164, 167-168, 172-179, 181, 184, 185; *Tripoli*, 410; *Tunisia*, 410; *Turkey*, 383.

Jews, *see* Ashkenazim, Chuetas, Dönmehs, German Jews, Greek Jews, Karaites, Krimchak, Levantines,

Maranos, Polish Jews, Sephardim, Subbotniki.
Job, figure of, 291.
John, King, of England, 213.
Jokal, Gerson, court jester, 345.
Jonathas, of Paris, 54; of Enghien, 208.
Jopes 148.
Jopin, Jew of Lincoln, 216.
Joselowicz, Berek, 363, 367.
Joseph 226, 412.
Joseph, king of Chazars, 124.
Joseph II, Emperor, 348.
Joseph bar Ephraim, limner, xxvii.
Joseph ben Nathan Official 91.
Joseph ben Tobiah 35.
Joseph of Sidon 43.
Josephus 28, 29, 35, 40, 245.
Joshua 2, 3, 11, 28, 393, 407.
Juan II, of Castille, 173.
Judah ben Tema 371.
Judah Halevi, 66, 119, 128, 140, 160, 254, 273.
Judah he-Hasid (Judah the Pious) 279, 299, 400.
Judas Maccabaeus 29, 230.
JUDENBURG 352.
Judendorf 352.
Judensau 298, 315, 430, 432, 434, 436, 437.
Judenschmerz 66, 132.
JUGOSLAVIA 352, 380-382, 384.
Julian, Emperor, 40, 48.
Julian of Byzance, Count, 121.
JUNGBUNZLAU 438.
JUNGHOLZ 431.
JURBURG 446.
Juspa Shammes 278, 285.
Justinian 408.
Juvenal 38, 231.

Kairuwan xvii.
Kalonymus ben Kalonymus 240, 247.
Kamariné 6.
KAMENETZ-PODOLSK 369, 445.
KAMIONKA STRUMILOWA 368, 371, 444.
Karaites 196, 333, 364, 368, 371, 384, 441, 444.
KARASUBAZAR 384.
Karo, Abigdor, elegist, 333, 337, 340.

Karo, Joseph, see Caro.
Kasba, the, 394, 398.
Katzenellenbogen, Samuel Judah, 264.
Kaulan al-Yahudi 122.
Kaupert, sculptor, 293.
KAZMIERZ 441.
KEFIR BERIM 41.
KEHLHEIM 298.
KEMPEN 362, 363, 443.
Kepler 160, 334.
Ketubah, see Marriage contract.
Kiddush cup 70, 80, 81, 195, 337.
Kielce, city, 442.
KIELCE, province, 442.
Kiev 296, 357.
Kimchi, David, 104.
Kirchheim 307.
KISSINGEN 433.
KLEINPRÜFENING 298.
KLEIN-SCHÜTTÜBER 437.
Klosterneuburg 351.
Köbel, Jacob, 293.
KOBRIN 440.
Kolbe, sculptor, 293.
Kolomea 444.
KÖNIGSBERG (Bohemia) 437.
KÖNIGSWART 437.
KONSKIE 442.
Kosciusko 363.
KOSOW 444.
Kovno 446.
KOZANGRODEK 440.
Krautheimer, Richard, 342.
Krems 351.
Krimchak Jews 384.
KRUMAU 438.
KUBA 384.
KULMBACH-BAYREUTH 304.
KURNIK 362, 370, 441, 443, 444.
KUTTENPLAN 344-345, 437.

LACHWA 440.
La Guardia (Spain) 161.
LAIBACH, see Lyubjana.
Lalla Maghnia 407.
Lamb, as symbol, 317.
LAMOTHE-MONTRAVEL 116.
Lamp, Eternal, see Nir-Tamid.

Lamp, glazed, 292; terra-cotta, 28, 30, 233, 236, 249, 405, 409; *as symbol*, 201, 257, 376—*see also* Candle.
Lamps, *see* Candelabra.
LANCKORONA 445.
LANCUT 367, 444.
LANDERNAU 100.
LANGENDORF 435.
LANGUEDOC 104, 106, 113.
Lassalle, Ferdinand, 67, 273.
Lateran Council 52, 53.
Latin (chiefly inscriptions) 40, 84, 115, 121, 194, 205, 212, 234, 238, 246, 250, 299, 324, 347, 409; tongue, use of, among Jews, 121, 157, 190, 238, 245, 250, 266, 326.
Laver, *see* Pitcher.
Law, the Jewish, 73, 242, 254, 280.
Lazara, see Town hall.
Lazare, Bernard, 113.
Lazina, see Social Centre.
Leeuwenhoek 204.
LEGHORN, *see* Livorno.
LEICESTER 218.
LEIPZIG, 436.
Leiria 293.
LEMBERG xi, 303, 305, 344, 345, 362, 363, 364-368, 444, 445.
    Ghetto 366
    Graveyard 367-368
    Houses, old, 365-366
    Synagogues: Golden Rose, 345, 364-365; Städtische, 367; Vorstädtische, 366-367
LENGNAU 430.
LENINGRAD xxvii, 384.
Leo Hebraeus (Judah Abrabanel) 253, 257.
LEÓN 173.
Leonora, Queen, of Navarre, 175.
LEONTOPOLIS, *see* Tell el-Yahudiya.
Leopard, *as symbol,* 74, 371.
Leopold I, of Austria, 350.
Lessing 321, 322.
LESZNIOW 441.
Levantines 252, 266, 355.
Levi, Joseph, sculptor, 254.
Levi, Moses Uri, 189.
Levita, Elijah, 240, 267.
Levites 33, 136, 291, 336.

Lewisohn, Ludwig, 82.
Leyden 203.
Liber Continens, of Rhazes, 84.
Libraries, *see* Bibliothèque Nationale, British Museum, Bodelian, *and following cities*: Amsterdam, Berlin, Breslau, Cambridge, Darmstadt, Erfurt, Evora, Frankfort, Leningrad, London, Lublin, Madrid, Paris, Parma, Rijnsburg, Rome.
Libya 390, 412.
LICHTENSTADT 437.
Liebmann, Jost, 304.
LIENZ 351.
Lights, *see* Candelabra.
Lilith 19, 20.
Lily, *as symbol,* 36, 150, 154, 429.
LIMAY 84, 94.
LIMBURG on the Lahn 431.
Limners, *see* Manuscript Illuminators.
LINCOLN 211, 214-216, 218.
    Cathedral 214, 215
    Jews' houses 214-215.
Linz 351.
Lion, *as symbol,* 81, 154, 200, 307, 308, 335, 350, 365, 371, 379.
Lion-tamers 177.
LISBON 139, 185-186, 389.
    Carmo Museum 185
    English cemetery 185
    Ghetto 185
L'Isle-sur-Sorgue 110.
LITHUANIA 190, 333, 446.
Litta of Regensburg, poetess, 296.
LIVORNO 257-258, 410.
Lobzow, *see* Cracow.
Locke, John, 222.
Lodz 443.
Lomza 439.
LONDON 119, 188, 194, 211, 215, 217, 220-229, 269, 320, 351.
    Disraeli statue 225
    Ghetto, modern, 224
    Graveyards 224, 225
    Heine tablet 225
    Jewry, site of old, 220
    Library, Jews College, 227
    —Mocatto 227

London—(*Continued*)
  Museums, Galleries: Bridgewater House, 229; British Museum, 225-227 (*see also* British Museum); Buckingham Palace, 229; Hampton Court, 229; National Gallery, 229; Record Office, 212; South Kensington Museum, 227-229
  Synagogue, in Bevis Marks, 222-223; on Duke Street, 222, 223-224
  Westminster Abbey 211
Longhena, Baldassarre, 268.
Looz 208.
LORRAINE 93.
Louis IX, of France, *see* St.-Louis.
Louis XIV 117.
Louis XIV (style) 107.
Louis XV 58, 61.
Louis XV (style) 108, 111.
Louis XVI (style) 108.
Louvre 2-44, 225, 226, 361, 413, 414-422.
  Asiatic Department 2-44, 414-417, 422
  Egyptian — 10-11, 422
  Jewish Room 2, 22-44, 417-422
  Phoenician — 43, 422
  Picture Gallery 422
Löw, Judah ben Bezalel, 70, 334-335, 337, 342, 343, 344.
LOZÈRE 114.
LUBLIN, city, 360, 367, 372-373, 389, 441.
  Ghetto 372, 373
  Graveyard 373
  Library 373
  Synagogues: Maharam, 373; Maharshal, 373; Saul Wahl, 372
Lublin, Meir ben Gedaliah (Maharam), 373.
LUBLIN, province, 441.
LUBOML 369, 441.
Lucca 286.
LUCENA 140.
Lucera 250.
LUCK, Bohemia, 437; Poland, 367, 369, 441.
LUGO 173.

Lulab 21, 30, 31-33, 84, 121, 129, 228, 234, 236, 237, 307, 324, 362, 429.
Lump, Moses, 319-320.
LUNEL 114.
Lunel, Armand, 110.
LUNÉVILLE 93.
Luria, Solomon (Maharshal), 360, 373.
Luther, Martin, 315, 325.
LUTOMIERSK 370, 443.
Luzzatto, Simone, 267.
Lydda 37.
LYONS 96, 103, 112.
LYUBJANA 352.

MAASTRICHT 207.
Maccabees 28, 36, 81, 227, 342, 387; feast of, *see* Hanuka.
Macedonia 385.
Machiavelli 252.
Machir, Jacob, 140.
Machpelah, painting of, 362.
Machzor, see Prayer book.
MÂCON 93.
MADRID 164-166, 167, 175.
  Biblioteca Nacional 164
  Casa Alba 164
  Ghetto, site, 164
  Museums: Arqueológico, 164; Arte Moderno, 164; Prado, 165-166
  Plaza Glorietta 166
  —Mayor 166
MAGDEBURG 436.
Magic 18, 19, 20, 21, 31-33, 154, 231, 299, 317, 380, 390, 396, 404, 408, 433; *see also* Amulet; *Baraka;* Embroideries, festival.
Magic bowls 17-20, 426.
MAHALLA EL-KUBRA 411.
Maharil (Jacob ben Moses Mölln) 284.
Maimaran, court Jew, 391.
Maimaran, Ephraim, of Salé, 398.
Maimonides (Moses ben Maimon, Rambam) 87, 114, 122, 127, 160, 182, 196, 227, 254, 262, 267, 273, 284, 320, 361, 392, 404, 411-412; *Mishneh Torah,* 293, 428.
Main, the, 295, 300, 305, 309.
MAINZ, *see* Mayence.
MALAGA 120, 140, 143.

MALAUCÈNE 112.
Malfante, Antonio, 393.
MALTA 244, 249.
Manasseh ben Israel 82, 197, 198, 199, 221, 334.
Manasseh Bueno Barzillai Azevedo da Costa 223.
Manfred 250.
Manfredonia 250.
MANRESA 178.
MANS 96.
MANTES 94.
Mantineia 387.
Mantle for scrolls of the Law, see Torah mantle.
MANTUA 253, 260-261, 293.
Manuscript illuminators xxvii.
Manuscripts 164, 186, 199, 219, 220, 227, 239, 242, 287, 313, 323; see also Papyri.
Manuscripts, illuminated, xxii, xxvii, 73, 84, 164-165, 183, 227, 260, 280, 293, 324, 328, 356, 428; see also Haggadah; Marriage Contract, Ode; Pentateuch; Prayer book.
Mappa, see Torah mantle.
Maqueda 148, 165.
Marano, Maranos (New Christians), xi, 82, 99, 117, 131, 138, 139, 177, 178, 180, 184, 186, 191, 196, 197, 220, 221, 224, 252, 254, 258, 266, 316, 405.
MARAZION, or Market Jew, 210.
MARBURG 352.
March (river) 325, 345, 353.
Marco Polo 175, 183.
Marcus Aurelius 346.
Marduk 9.
María da Padilla 152.
María del Salto 171.
Maria Theresa 331.
Marienbad 344.
MARKET JEW, see Marazion.
MAROILLES 208.
MARRAKESH 389, 401-404.
  Graveyard 403-404
  Mellah 401-402
Marriage 80, 302, 303, 396; canopy, see Wedding canopy; contracts, 79, 292, 323, 327; courtyard, 302, 303;

girdle, 292; hall, see Social Centre; rings, see Rings; stone, see Chuppah-Stern.
Marseilles 103, 246.
Martial 231.
Martínez, Fernando, 136.
Marx, Karl, 67, 273.
Masada 36, 40, 217.
Mathematics 104, 143, 16c, 246, 247, 333, 334.
Matthew Paris 213.
Mattifart, Simon, 55.
Matzoth, as symbol, 228; bakery, 102, 109, 345, 437, 438.
MAYENCE 85, 88, 276, 286-288, 375, 431.
  Cemetery 286-287
  Jewry, site, 287-288
  Museum, Jewish, 287
Medals 82, 417; Korn —, 327.
Medici, Lorenzo de', 253.
Medicine 104, 114, 247, 262; see also Physicians.
Medicis, the, 254.
Medina, the, 394, 403.
Mediterranean isles 187.
Megilla, see Esther, scroll of.
MEININGEN, Saxony, 436.
Meir, Rabbi, Master of Miracles, 228, 398.
Meir ben Joel Ha-Cohen 277.
Meir of Eger 278.
Meir of Rothenburg xxi, 49, 267, 278, 279, 283-284, 309, 310, 314.
Meisel, Frommet, 333.
Meisel, Mordecai, 333, 341, 343-344.
MEKNES 398, 403.
Mekom ha-zedek 257, 258, 302, 435.
Meleager 388.
Melkart 248.
Mellah 137, 394-396, 400, 401-402, 403, 404, 406, 407.
Menahem ben Saruk 428.
MENDE 113.
Mendelssohn, Moses, 273, 291, 304, 320-321, 322, 323.
Mendesia, Gracia, 384.
Mendoza y Bovadilla, Francisco, 139.
Menephtah, pharaoh, 412, 413.
Mennonites 203.

Menorah 108, 195, 292; *as symbol*, 29-30, 41, 74, 84, 115, 121, 234, 235, 236, 237, 238, 249, 271, 308, 323, 324, 329, 405, 409, 427, 428.
Merchants, *see* Commerce.
MERIDA 121.
Merovingian 46, 357.
Mesha, king of Moab, 24, 25.
Meshullam ben Kalonymus 286.
Meshullam ben Menahem of Volterra 412.
Mesopotamia 368, 390.
Mesullamim, bankers, 269.
Metal-work, in brass, bronze, copper, gold, iron, pewter, silver, tin, xxvi, 41, 108, 111, 136, 142, 184, 197, 254, 292, 318, 327, 331, 350, 356, 361, 365, 367, 381, 383, 390, 400, 401, 402, 405, 410, 434, 441, 442; *see also under* Ritual Objects.
Metternich 348.
METZ 345, 431.
Mezzuza 80, 292, 396.
Michael the Scot 246.
MICHALPOL 445.
Michelangelo 4, 92, 231, 256.
MIDI, the, 103-106, 112.
MIEDZYBOZ 371, 445.
MIELEC 444.
Mikveh xxiii, 93, 102, 109, 114, 174, 192, 274, 281-282, 285, 294, 305, 313, 333, 434, 435, 436, 438.
Milan 245.
Milcah 6.
MILETUS 387.
Millenarians 221.
MILOSLOW 443.
MILTENBERG 434.
Milton, John, 220.
MINTRACHING 298.
Minz, Judah, 262.
Mirabeau 322.
Mirandola, Pico della, 253.
Mizrach 365.
Moabite stele 24, 25, 424; warrior, 23.
Modena 73, 74.
Modena, Leone da, 267, 269.
Mohammed 103.
MOHILEV 276, 371, 445.

Molcho, Solomon, 260, 331, 342.
MOLDAVIA 379.
MOLSHEIM 432.
Moncalvo 260.
Money-lending, *see* Banking.
Monfatil, Moslem poet, 143.
MONHEIM 433.
Monophysites 42.
MONS 208.
Monstrance 80.
MONTAGNANA 264.
Montaigne 58, 116, 241.
Montefiore, Judith, 225.
Montefiore, Moses, 258.
Montezinos, Antonio de, traveller, 221.
Montoro, Antonio de, 131-133, 308.
MONTPELLIER 114.
Moorish (style) 136.
Moors, Moorish, xxviii, 125, 126, 127, 134, 141, 142, 143, 145, 146, 147, 148, 154, 157, 160, 163, 164, 167, 169, 174, 176, 177, 183, 184, 191, 215, 254, 274, 381.
MORAVIA 310, 325, 345, 353.
Mordecai, figure of, 78, 81, 202.
More Judaico, oath, 320, 323.
MOROCCO xxiv, 41, 126, 127, 142, 175, 189, 200, 382, 389, 390, 392-407.
Mosaics xxvi, 36, 121, 231, 249, 371, 409-410.
Moscow 440.
Moses 4, 5, 24, 29, 30, 94, 398, 412; figure of, 81, 92, 95, 202, 223, 231, 256, 341, 361, 362, 428, 433.
Moses ben Enoch 126, 286.
Moses of Palermo 247.
Moslem, Moslems, *see* Islam.
Mudejar (style) 129, 136, 150, 155.
MUIDERBERG 203.
Mulay Ismail, sultan, 391.
MULHOUSE 432.
MÜNDEN 434.
MUNICH xxvii, 433.
Munk, Solomon, 68, 323.
MÜNSTER 436.
Mural painting, in synagogue, xx, 276, 303, 305, 306-308, 324, 329, 352, 356, 362, 369, 370-371, 379, 437, 439, 440, 442, 444, 445.
MURCIA 140, 407.

Murner, Thomas, 293.
Museums, *see* British Museum, Cluny, Louvre, *and following cities:* Alexandria, Algiers, Amsterdam, Arles, Asolo, Athens, Augsburg, Bamberg, Barcelona, Basel, Berlin, Bern, Beziers, Bologna, Breslau, Brindisi, Cairo, Canea, Capua, Carpentras, Carthage, Cassel, Castello Branco, Chalon-sur-Saône, Cividale, Coblentz, Colmar, Cologne, Constantinople, Corinth, Dijon, Eger, Erfurt, Evora, Feodosia, Gerona, Graz, The Hague, Hamburg, Leningrad, León, Lisbon, London, Lyubjana, Madrid, Marburg, Mulhouse, Munich, Naples, Narbonne, Nuremberg, Padua, Palencia, Palermo, Paris, Regensburg, Rome, Rothenburg (Tauber), Sarajevo, Schlestadt, Seville, Siena, Speyer, Strasbourg, Syracuse, Taranto, Tarragona, Toledo, Tortosa, Toulouse, Trèves, Treviso, Tunis, Ulm, Vienna, Volubilis, Würzburg.
Museums, or Collections, Jewish, *see* British Museum, Cluny, Louvre, *and following cities:* Amsterdam, Berlin, Breslau, Brunswick, Cincinnati, Danzig, Frankfort, Friedberg, Göttingen, Hamburg, Hechingen, Jungbunzlau, London, Mayence, New York, Odessa, Prague, Ramsgate, Rome, Strasbourg, Venice, Vienna, Warsaw, Worms.
Music 134, 260, 266, 332.
"Music" panels 362-363, 443.
MUTZIG 432.

Nachmanowicz, Isaac, 364; "Golden Rose," his daughter-in-law, 365, 368.
Nahmani, Nahmanides, 158, 182.
NANTES 99.
NAPLES 187, 245-247, 251.
Napoleon 59, 65, 270, 287, 289, 300.
NARBONNE 84, 115.
NARO 409-410.
NAROL 444.
NAROWLA 445.
Nasi, Gracia, 82.

Nasi, Joseph, duke of Naxos, 82, 380, 382, 384.
Nathan ben Yehiel 240.
NAVARRE 174-175.
Nazis, the, xxiv, 282, 313.
Near East 38, 229, 258, 361.
Nebuchadnezzar, 175, 425.
Neckar, the, 295, 308.
NEDROMA 407.
Nehemiah 220.
Nereid 195.
Nero, wife of, 231.
NETHERLANDS 295; *see also* Belgium, Holland.
NEUSTADT 435.
NEUZEDLISCH 437-438.
New and Old Faith 51-54, 92, 94-96, 99, 259.
New Christians, *see* Maranos.
New Moon, festival of, 30, 302.
New Year, festival of the, 30, 31, 77-78.
NEW YORK x, 38, 119, 187, 223, 224, 269.
    Museum, Jewish, x, 71, 72
    Cemetery 200
NEWPORT, R. I., 194.
Nice 103, 260.
Niederbreisig 431.
NIKOLSBURG 345.
NIKOPOL 383.
NÎMES 105, 113.
Nimrod 10, 226, 427.
Nineveh 16, 226, 424.
Ningal 6.
NIORT 99.
Nir Tamid 303, 362, 365, 367, 443.
Noah and ark 226, 362.
NORDHAUSEN 313-314, 436.
Norman (style) 214, 215, 216, 249.
NORMANDY 99.
Normans 210, 211, 212, 247, 250, 273.
NORTH AFRICA 20, 30, 41, 121, 122, 142, 200, 244, 258, 338, 361, 381, 389-410.
Norwich 218.
NOTO 249.
NOVOGRODEK, city, 440.
NOVOGRODEK, province, 440.

Nowy Sacz 444.
Nuñez, Maria, 188.
Nuremberg 295, 300-301, 302, 303, 382, 438.

Oberwesel 431.
Occupations 43, 59, 119, 211, 290, 320, 331-332, 338, 358, 373, 380, 383, 401-402, 410, 430; *see also* Agriculture, Arts and Crafts, Banking, Commerce, Metal-work, Physicians, Printers and Presses, Scribes.
Oder, the, 311, 325, 353.
Odessa x.
Oels 435.
Offenbach 309-310.
Offenbach, Jacques, 68.
Offenburg, Baden, 282.
Oil-jar, *as symbol,* 236.
Old Faith and New, *see* New and Old Faith.
Oliviero, architect, 361.
Olyka 441.
Omphalos 238.
Onias IV 412.
Onias the High-Priest 35.
Opatow 442.
Opoczno 442.
Oporto 185.
Oppenheimer, David, of Prague, 328, 334, 337.
Oppenheimer, David, of Worms, 280.
Oppenheimer, Samuel, 304, 349, 350, 354.
Optics 104, 204, 231.
Or Zarua, *see* Isaac of Vienna.
Oria 250.
Orla 362, 439.
Orleans 94.
Orley, Bernard van, stained-glass maker, 209.
Osiory, *see* Jeziory.
Ossuary 36-38.
Ostrog 441.
Ostrolenka 439, 440.
Ostropol 445.
Ostrowiec 442.
Otranto 250, 286.

Ouderkerk 199-202, 203, 207, 257, 258, 316.
Oudjda 407.
Oxford 49, 218-220.

Padua 261-264, 354, 438.
 Cemeteries 264
 Ghetto site 261
 Synagogues: Ashkenazic, 263-264; Italian, 262-263; Spanish, 263
Painters, painting, xxvi, 199, 223, 233, 234, 242, 254, 334, 338; *see also* Mural painting, Portraits.
Painting, on tombstones, 367, 374, 375-378; *see* Appendix C.
Palace 34, 152, 197.
Palache, Samuel, 200.
Palache, Simon, 189.
Palencia 173.
Palermo 247-248.
Palestine 21, 23, 35, 43, 50, 103, 106, 171, 182, 229, 234, 244, 287, 371, 382, 395, 397, 409, 412.
Palm, palm-leaf, *as symbol,* 36, 74, 129, 154, 237, 276, 409, 429.
Palma, Majorca, 180, 183-184.
Pampeluna 175.
Panshanger 229.
Papacy, Popes, 52, 53, 105, 106, 107, 231, 239, 243, 251, 252, 259, 342.
Pappenheim 433.
Papyri 219, 324.
Parczew 441.
Paris 1, 45-83, 85, 86, 94, 122, 175, 182, 208, 247, 323.
 Churches: Notre Dame, 49, 54; Protestant, 54; St.-Julien-le-Pauvre, 46
 Ghetto, modern, 55
 Graveyards 61-64, 67-68
 Heine landmarks 66-68
 Herzl — 69
 Jewries, sites of old, 47, 49, 54, 55, 58-61
 Libraries: Alliance Israélite, 84; Bibliothèque Nationale 51, 83-84 (*see also* Bibliothèque Nationale)

Paris—(*Continued*)
Museums: Carnavalet, 49, 84; Cluny, 47, 48, 70-83 (*see also* Cluny); Louvre, 2-44, 47, 414-422 (*see also* Louvre); St.-Germain, 84
PARMA 259-260.
Parochet, see Ark Curtain.
Parrot, *as symbol*, 371.
PARZECZEW 443.
PASSAU 351, 433.
Passover 76, 78; dishes, 70, 274, 292, 301; prayer book, *see* Haggadah.
Pastoureaux, *see* Shepherds Massacre.
Patras 387.
Paul, *see* St. Paul.
Paul IV 241.
Paul V 239.
PAUTEN 438.
Peacock, *as symbol*, 234, 409.
Pedro the Cruel 137, 152-153, 154, 158, 161.
Pegasus 234, 235, 409.
Pelican, *as symbol*, 371.
Pentateuch xxvii, 49, 81, 227, 291, 321, 428; *see also* Scrolls of the Law; Torah.
Penzance 210.
Perfume boxes 77.
Pernambuco 187, 201.
Perpignan, Salomon, 61.
Perseus, figure of, 81.
Persia, Persian, Persians, 23, 74, 226, 296, 368, 390, 425, 427.
PESARO 252, 253.
Pesaro, Guglielmo de, 253.
PESKI 445.
Petachiah of Regensburg, traveller, 296, 299.
Peter, *see* St. Peter.
Peterborough 215.
PETSCHAU 438.
Pews 193, 223, 277, 307, 339.
PEYREHORADE 117.
Phatir 46, 47.
Philip II, Augustus, of France, 96, 97, 215.
Philip IV, of Spain, 106.
PHILIPPOPOLIS 383.
Philo 232, 411, 412.

Philosophy 104, 128, 143, 144, 160, 176, 177, 182, 183, 203-206, 240, 244, 246, 247, 253, 254, 262, 266, 267, 273, 320, 321, 322, 323, 333, 334, 360.
Phoenicia, Phoenicians, 13, 26, 28, 120, 121, 141, 210, 247, 249, 390, 393, 406, 408.
Phoenix, *as symbol*, 317.
Physicians 124, 134, 138, 159, 168, 175, 182, 198, 200, 253, 312, 331, 333, 386, 404.
Physics 104, 273.
Pichon, Joseph, 174.
PIEDMONT 260.
Pilate 148.
Pilgrimage 68, 284, 291, 363, 368, 398-399, 400, 403-404, 405, 406, 407, 411, 412.
Pilgrims, the (English sect), 191.
PILICA 442.
Pillars, of Temple, *as symbol*, 28, 258, 268, 324, 338, 339, 340, 367.
Pilsen 304, 344, 437, 438.
Pimental, Manuel, 200.
Pincas family, the, 333.
PINCZOW 442.
Pine cone, *as symbol*, 150, 154.
PINSK 440, 441.
Piotrkow 442.
PISA 127, 244, 256-257.
Pisano, Niccolo, 244, 256.
Pitcher 195, 294, 324, 430, 435; *as symbol*, 228, 291, 336.
Plates, *see* Passover dishes, Purim plate, Sabbath dish.
Platter 41, 195, 292, 365, 435.
Pliny 165.
Plock 440.
Plutarch 33.
POBREBYSZCZ 445.
PODOLIA 361, 368, 379, 445.
Poets, Poetry, 66, 90, 104, 110, 119, 124, 128, 132-133, 143, 144, 149, 152, 174, 197, 201, 206, 240, 253, 267, 275, 288, 296, 308, 313, 316, 332.
Pointer for scrolls of the Law, *see* Torah pointer.

POITIERS 96, 122.

POLAND 59, 129, 190, 196, 202, 235, 272, 287, 295, 296, 302, 303, 304, 305, 311, 316, 325, 333, 336, 338, 345, 356-378, 379, 435, 438.

Poles, Polish, 190, 357, 359, 369, 435.

POLESIE 440-441.

Polish Jews 256, 305, 306, 310, 327, 356-358, 359, 379; *see also* Ashkenazim.

POLONKA 441.

Pombal, Marquis de, 187.

Pomegranate, *as symbol*, 28, 129, 228, 307; *see also Rimonim.*

Pompeii 246.

Pompey 28, 116.

Popes, *see* Papacy.

Portaleone, Leone di Sommi, 253.

Portrait, of Fanny von Arnstein, 348; Moses Arragel, 165; Ludwig Boerne, 293; Ephraim Bueno, 198; Disraeli, 225; Farrachius, 84, 247; Michael Gernsheim, 280; Heine, 294; Manasseh ben Israel, 198; Moses Mendelssohn, 322; Mayer Amschel and Gütele Rothschild, 293; Spinoza, 206, 207; unknown Jews, 198, 199, 229, 236, 324, 359, 442; unknown rabbis, 199, 229, 324; portraits, unspecified, 223, 323.

PORTSMOUTH 225.

PORTUGAL 117, 163, 185-186, 191, 194, 224, 283, 293, 316, 355, 383.

Portuguese 100, 157, 172, 188, 189, 191, 195, 201; *for Portuguese Jews, see* Sephardim.

Posen, city, 443.

POSEN, province, 361, 443.

Pottery, ancient Jewish, 27-28.

Pozzuoli 245.

PRAGUE 202, 258, 276, 277, 278, 293, 296, 304, 305, 328, 330-344, 360, 364, 372, 401, 441.

    Charles Bridge 343

    Ghetto 330

    Graveyard 332-337

    Hradčany 343

    Museum, Jewish, 71, 337-338

    Rathaus 344

Prague—(*Continued*)

    Synagogues: Altneu, 331, 334, 336, 338-341, 360, 435; Hochschul, 341; Klaus, 342; Meisel, 342-343; Pincas, 303, 331, 342; Wechsler, 343

    Town hall, Jewish, 336, 341

Prayer book 77, 280, 293, 314, 328, 428, 431.

Praying-shawl, bag for, 82.

PRESSBURG, *see* Bratislava.

PRIENE 324, 387.

Printers and Presses, Hebrew, 198, 252, 253, 258, 260, 293, 303, 325, 331, 333, 373, 380, 435.

Priscus 45-47, 92.

Prisons, Jewish, 103, 303, 341, 365.

Procopius 393.

Proselytes 38, 231-32.

Prosskurow 445.

PROVENCE 104, 113, 163, 179, 214, 240, 254.

PROVINS 91.

Pruth (river) 353, 379.

PRUZANY 376, 377, 441.

PRZEDBORZ 442.

Przemysl 443.

PRZEWORSK 367, 444.

Ptolemies 34.

Ptolemy, *Almagest*, 160.

Ptolemy Euergetes 325.

Puentedéume 174.

Pulpit 74; cover, 195, 228.

Pumbeditha 126.

Purim 77, 81, 110, 365; plate, 70, 81.

Puritans, English, 191.

PURSCHAU 438.

Pyrenees, the, 118, 163, 167.

Queen of Sheba, figure of, 195.

RABAT 400.

Rabbit, *as symbol*, 371.

Rachel, figure of, 202, 317.

Rain, prayer for, 32-33, 78.

RAKOW 443.

Ram, *as symbol*, 235, 258, 285, 445.

Rambam, *see* Maimonides.

Rameses II 226, 412.

Ramleh 42.

Ramon Berenguer IV, count, 180.
RAMSGATE 225.
Ram's horn, see Shofar.
Rashi xi, 47, 86, 87-89, 240, 276, 279-280, 283, 284, 287, 320; Commentary, 260, 280.
RATISBON, see Regensburg.
Rebecca 8; figure of, 375.
Reccared I 122.
RECHNITZ 352.
Reform Judaism 175, 318, 327, 345.
REGENSBURG xi, 295-300, 342, 351, 360, 372.
    Cathedral 298
    Jewry, site, 296
    Judenstein 299
    Historical Museum 299
    Sallern 299
    Tombstones as trophies 298
REGENSTAUF 298.
Reggio, Calabria, 260.
Rejoicing of the Law, festival of, 302.
Reliquary 38, 80.
Rembrandt 192, 198-199, 207, 229, 324, 359, 422, 434.
Renaissance (style) 81, 158, 193, 251, 263, 264, 283, 297, 306, 336, 342, 345, 349, 361, 365, 367, 376, 434, 441, 444.
Renaissance, the, xix, xxiv, xxix, 53, 144, 227, 240, 244, 252, 253-254, 255, 256, 260, 262, 266, 267, 273, 276, 291, 304, 321, 366, 417.
Renan, Ernest, 24, 68, 206, 254.
Reshef 12.
Reubeni, David, 240, 342.
Reuchlin 240.
Rhazes 84, 247.
RHEIMS 52, 99.
Rhine, the, 191, 269, 272, 275, 283, 294, 296, 311, 391.
RHINELANDS 85, 86, 126, 286.
RHODES 388; Knights of, 388.
Rhône, the, 101, 103, 106, 112.
Ribbon, infolding, as symbol, 36, 37.
Richard the Lion-heart 214-215, 217.
Richter, Jean Paul, 322.
RIES AM RHEIN 431.
Riesser, Gabriel, 318.
RIF, the, 399.

"Righteous Place" see Mekom hazedek.
Rights of Man 59.
RIJNSBURG 203-206.
Rimini 252.
Rimon, Moses, parchment maker, 183.
Rimonim 75, 184, 195, 242, 248, 257, 292, 323, 337, 435.
Rings, marriage, 79, 227, 228, 292, 323, 434; signet, 14, 82, 226, 327.
RINN 351.
Ritual art 70-83; see also Ritual objects.
Ritual Bath, see Mikveh.
Ritual murder, charge of, 89, 98, 161, 216, 297, 326, 351, 388, 430.
Ritual objects, see Alms-box; Altar; Ark curtain; Ark of the Law; Bima; Calendars; Candelabra; Cathedra; Chair for Bridegrooms of Law; Chuppah-Stern; Circumcision implements; Elijah chair; Embroideries; Esther, scroll of; Eternal Lamp; Gilt-glass dishes; Haggadah; Kiddush cup; Lamps; Lulab; Marriage contracts, girdles; Mezzuza; Passover dishes; Pews; Pitcher; Platter; Prayer book; Praying-shawl; Pulpit; Purim plate; Rimonim; Rings, marriage; Sabbath dish; Scrolls of the Law; Spice-box; Torah band, case, crown, mantle, pointer, shield; Wedding canopy.
Rizzi, Francisco, painter, 165.
Robert the Good, of Naples, 247.
Rokeach, see Eleazar of Worms.
Roman, Commendador, 132.
Roman, Romans, 31, 34, 36, 37, 39, 46, 85, 103, 114, 116, 120, 121, 140, 167, 208, 234, 236, 244, 261, 271, 273, 311, 346, 351, 390, 397, 405, 406, 408, 409, 412.
Roman Empire xiv, 30, 38, 41, 233, 239.
Romanesque (style) 102, 113, 168, 179, 276, 277, 281, 282, 285, 435, 444.
Romano, Paolo, architect, 365.

ROME 38, 129, 166, 177, 203, 230-243, 251, 252, 286, 323, 341, 408, 409.
  Catacombs, Jewish, 233-235
  Churches: S. Angelo in Pescheria, 241; S. Paolo fuori le Mura, 236; S. Pudenziana, 232
  Fountain of Acqua Paola 239
  Ghetto 238-239, 241-242
  Graveyard 242
  Jewries, sites of ancient, 231
  Libraries: Casanatense, 239; Vatican, 237
  Michelangelo's "Moses" 231
  Museums: Benito Mussolini, 242; Biblioteca della Vallicella, 237; Borgiano, 237; Conservatori, 232; Kircher, 236; Lateran, 235-236; Thermes, 237; Vatican, 237, 238
  Synagogues: on Lungo Tevere Sanzio, 242; modern, 242
RONDO 140.
RONSPERG 438.
Rosette, six petal, *as symbol*, 36.
Rossi, Europa, singer, 260.
Rossi, Solomon, composer, musician, 260.
ROTHENBURG on the Fulda 434-435.
ROTHENBURG on the Tauber xi, 295, 309.
Rothschild, Gütele, 288, 289, 290.
Rothschild, Lionel Mayer, 224.
Rothschild, Mayer Amschel, 288, 289-290.
Rothschild, in Paris, 66.
Rothschilds, the, 292, 293, 319, 320.
ROTTERDAM 194, 207.
ROUEN 96, 99, 211, 214, 220.
ROUFFACH 432.
ROVIGO 264.
Rovno 441, 442.
ROZANY 440.
ROZDOL 444.
Rudolph II, of Austria, 334, 342, 343-344.
Rudolph of Hapsburg 284.
RUMANIA 190, 262, 371, 379.
RUSSIA 272, 276, 333, 357, 371, 383, 445.

RUSSIAN VOLHYNIA 445.
Ruthenians 364.
RZESZOW 366-367, 369, 373, 444.

Sabaism 6.
Sabbatai Zevi 199, 310, 317, 380, 385.
Sabbath 38; cup, *see Kiddush* cup; dish, 292; lamp, 292.
Sachs, Hans, 300, 301.
SADAGORA 371.
Safed 333.
SAGUNTO 121, 184.
SAHARA 126, 390, 402, 406, 408.
SAINS 208.
SAINT-PAUL-TROIS-CHÂTEAUX 112.
Sala, E., painter, 164.
Saladin, sultan, 404.
SALAMANCA 172.
SALÉ 389, 398, 400.
SALLERN 299.
SALONA 265.
SALONICA 119, 229, 383, 385-386.
Salons 267, 304, 322-323, 348, 405.
Salvador, Joseph, 223.
Samaria 16; Samaritan inscription, 424; manuscript, 428; Samaritans, 196.
Samson, Abbot, of Bury, 216.
Samson, figure of, 249.
Samuel, figure of, 202.
Samuel Halevi, *see* Halevi, Samuel ben Meir.
Samuel the Nagid, *see* Ibn Naghdela, Samuel.
SAN DANIELE DEL FRIULI 265.
SAN FRANCISCO, Cal., 73.
Sanballat 34.
Sancho el Mayor 174.
Sancho Panza 146, 177.
SANDOMIR 361, 363, 442.
Sanhedrin 59, 65.
SANT' ANTIOCO 249.
Santa Pola 121.
Santangel, Luis de, 139.
SANTIAGO DE COMPOSTELLA 174.
Santob de Carrión, poet, 152.
SARAGOSSA 176-178, 180.
SARAJEVO 380-382.
  Ghetto 381
  Graveyard 382

Sarajevo—(*Continued*)
National Museum 382
Synagogue, old, 381
Sarcophagus 30, 39, 235, 236, 323, 409.
SARDINIA 244, 249.
Sargon, king of Assyria, 16, 423.
Sargon the Great 4.
Sassoon, David, collection of, xxvii, 227.
SAVOY 93.
Sayings of the Fathers xxii, 74, 371.
Schadow, Gottfried, 322.
Schalet 132, 288, 294.
Schiff, family of, 288, 289.
Schlegels, the, 322.
Schleiermacher 322, 323.
SCHLESTADT 432.
SCHLÜCHTERN 435.
SCHNAITTACH 303, 344.
SCHONER 438.
SCHÖNWALD 438.
Schools (chiefly Talmud Torahs), 102, 192, 302, 309, 369, 370, 431, 433, 434, 435, 437, 438.
Schubert, Franz, 351.
Schutz-Juden 320, 348.
SCHWABACH 434.
Schwäbisch Hall, *see* Hall, Swabia.
Schwarz, Hayim, printer, 435.
SCHWARZRHEINDORF 431.
SCHWEINFURTH 309.
Science, *see* Astrology, Astronomy, Geographers, Mathematics, Medicine, Optics, Physics, Translation.
Scribes, 77, 143, 246, 331.
Scroll of Esther, *see* Esther, scroll of.
Scrolls of the Law 73, 74, 75, 195, 248, 257, 280, 336, 361; *as symbol*, 236, 237, 324.
Sculpture, among Jews, 30, 33, 36, 39, 129, 150, 154-155, 200-202, 224, 233, 235, 236, 254, 257, 258, 283, 291, 304, 316-318, 326, 336, 338, 349, 356, 367-368, 373, 374, 433, 435; *see also* Wood-carving.
Seattle 119.
SEBASTE 36.
Sefer Chassidim 299.
SEFROU 406.

Segelmessa 126, 406, 407.
SEGOVIA 151, 167-172, 176, 208.
Cathedral 171
Cuesta de los Hoyos 171-172
Ghettos 167-168
Synagogue 168-170
Seleucids 34.
SELWA 362, 440.
Seneca 127, 387.
Senior, Abraham, 145-146, 168.
Sennacherib 16, 423, 426.
SENNERVILLE 94.
SENS 91.
Sephardim, Sephardic, 58, 59-62, 63, 119, 192, 195, 196, 198, 199, 200, 207, 210, 220, 222, 224, 229, 252, 253, 257, 258, 263, 265, 266, 267, 316, 349, 355, 369, 380, 383, 385, 386, 388, 390, 391, 406, 407, 408, 410, 433.
Serach ben Nathan 333.
Serapis 42.
Seret (river) 379.
SERETH 379.
Serpent of brass, *as symbol*, 347-348, 428.
SEVILLE 134-140, 152, 153, 381, 407.
Alcázar 152
Archaeological Museum 138
Barrio de Santa Cruz (ghetto) 135-138
Cathedral 135, 139
Golden Tower 153
La Tablada 138-139
Shakespeare 210.
Shalmaneser III 16, 226, 424.
Shamash 3.
Shapiro, Nathan, of Cracow, 363.
Shechem 391.
Sheep, *as symbol*, 376, 377.
Shekinah 30.
Shelley 386.
Shepherds Massacre 116.
SHESHAWAN 399-400.
Sheshonk III, pharaoh, 324.
Shew-bread table, *as symbol*, 238, 308, 329.
Shield for scrolls of the Law, *see* Torah shield.

Shield-of-David 129, 150, 303, 304, 317, 324, 331, 338, 392
Ship, *as symbol*, 202, 375.
Shofar 30-31, 78, 228, 234, 236, 307, 324, 362, 428.
Shulchan Aruch 383.
SICILY 244, 246, 247-249.
Sidon 120.
SIENA 255-256, 325.
Sierra de Guadarrama 167.
Sigismund III, of Poland, 372.
SILESIA 183, 325-328, 335.
Simon Maccabee 83, 230.
Simon Peter, *see* St. Peter.
Simon the Zaddik 35.
Sin, moon god, 6.
Sinai, *as symbol*, 307, 339, **371.**
Sklov, Mordecai, 327.
Slaughter house 102, 303.
Slav, Slavonic, 311, 325, 381.
SLONIM 440.
Sluter, Claus, sculptor, 92.
SNIADOWO 439.
Snuffers, *as symbol*, 236.
Social Centre xxii, 102, 218, 281.
Socinians 191.
SOFIA 383.
Sokolka 439.
Soliman II, Sultan, 354.
Solomon, figure of, 195, 246.
Solomon, M.S., collection of, 227.
Solomon Halevi bar Buya, limner, xxvii.
Soncinos, printers, 252, 260, 293, 325.
SOPOCKINIE 439.
SPAIN, Spanish, 41, 103, 104, 117, 119-185, 187, 191, 193, 194, 195, 198, 200, 214, 215, 220, 224, 225, 238, 244, 246, 254, 272, 273, 283, 321, 325, 355, 356, 380, 381, 382, 383, 394, 399, 401, 408, 411.
SPALATO 265.
SPALBECK 208.
Spanish Jews, Spanish-Portuguese Jews, *see* Sephardim.
SPEYER 274, 276, 282, 285-286.
Spice-box 70, 80-81, 195, 228, 229, 280, 292, 294, 318, 323, 337, 434, 435.

Spinoza 192, 195, 196, 197, 201, 203-206, 257.
Spira, Aaron, 334.
SPIRE, *see* Speyer.
Spitz 351.
SPOLETO 251.
St. Albans, England, 212.
St. Bernard of Clairveaux 275.
St. Bernardino of Feltre 254.
St.-Bertrand-de-Comminges 116.
St. Carlo of Borromeo 254.
ST.-DENIS, France, 96.
St. Domingo de Guzman 180.
St. Francis of Assisi 178.
St. Hugh of Lincoln, Little, 216.
St. Joan of Arc 178.
St. John the Baptist 407.
St. John, Knights of, 249.
St. Juan de Capistrano 183, 325-326.
St.-Louis 49, 174-175.
St. Paul 38, 245, 385, 386.
St. Pedro Arbues 178, 183.
St. Peter 232, 233.
St. Theresa 172.
St. Thomas Aquinas 127.
St. Vincent Ferrer 151, 183, 185.
"Staff of Jacob" 104, 140, 293.
Stag, *as symbol*, 291, 371, 376.
Stalpaert, Daniel, architect, 197.
Star, six-pointed, *see* Shield-of-David.
Star-worship 29.
STARASOL 444.
STEPAN 361, 441.
Stettin 311.
Steyr 351.
STIPLJE, *see* Stobi.
STOBI 384.
Storks, *as symbol*, 307.
STRASBOURG 52, 294.
STRAUBING 298.
STRIEGAU 435.
Strindberg, August, 347.
Study hall, *see* Beth Ha-midrash.
STYRIA 352.
Subbotniki, the, 384.
Succoth, *see* Tabernacles, Feast of.
SUCHOWOLA 439.
Sue, Eugene, 66.
Sullam, Sarah Coppio, 266, 267.
SULZ 432.

SULZBACH 303.

Sura 126.

Suson, Don Diego, 138, 139.

Susona, La, 138.

Süsskind of Trimberg 308.

Sussman, Eliezer, mural painter, 306, 307, 308.

Sweden 316, 338, 357, 369, 433.

SWITZERLAND 430.

Symbols xx-xxi, 28-33, 70-81, 200-202, 224, 228, 234-238, 291, 306-308, 317, 336, 371, 376-378; see Aaron's Rod; Altar; Ark of the Covenant; Ark of the Law; Bird; Candle; Cherub; Citron; Cock; Crown; Cup; Dove; Eagle; Etrog; Fire-pans; Fish; Flesh-hooks; Grape-cluster; Hands; Harp; Harvest fruits; Hawk; Hound and Hare; Jerusalem; Jachin and Boaz; Lamb; Lamp; Leopard; Lily; Lion; Lulab; Matzoth; Menorah; Oil-jar; Omphalos; Palm; Peacock; Pegasus; Pelican; Phoenix; Pillars, of Temple; Pine-cone; Pitcher; Pomegranate; Rabbit; Ram; Ribbon, infolding; Rosette, six petal; Serpent of brass; Shew-bread table; Shield of David; Ship; Shofar; Sinai; Snuffers; Stag; Storks; Tabernacle, the; Tablets of the Law; Temple, the; Temple veil; Trees; Twelve Tribes; Urim and Thummim; Urn; Vine; Wailing Wall; Zebra; Zodiac.

Symbols, non-religious, 291, 306-307, 308, 326, 336, 362, 375, 376, 377, 378, 379.

Synagogue, the, xviii-xxii, 30, 33, 41, 42, 59, 71, 73, 74, 75, 76, 77, 193, 276-277, 340, 396-397.

—fortified, in Poland, 360, 363, 367, 368-369; see also Appendix C

—wooden, in Poland, 362, 369-371; see also Appendix C

—mural painting in, see Mural painting

Synagogue Defeated, figure of, 51, 68, 83, 95, 96, 99, 107, 116, 285, 294, 306, 315.

Synagogues, described, Czechoslovakia, 338-341, 342-343, 344-345, 438; England, 222-224; France, 102, 107-109, 111-112; Germany, 276-279, 297, 302-303, 306-308, 309, 310, 322, 329; Greece, 387; Holland, 192-196, 197; Italy, 251-252, 255, 257, 259, 260, 262-264, 268-269; Morocco, 396-398; Poland, 360, 361-363, 364-365, 366-367, 368-371, 373, 374; Portugal, 186; Rumania, 397; Sicily, 248; Spain, 121, 128-130, 149-152, 154-159, 168-170; Tunisia, 409-410.

Synagogues, mentioned, Austria, 350, 351, 352; Algeria, 408; Bulgaria, 383; Czechoslovakia, 331, 338, 341, 344, 345, 353, 437, 438; Egypt, 411, 412; England, 211, 225; France, 60, 112, 113, 114, 431, 432; Germany, xi, 285, 286, 289, 296, 301, 303, 304, 305, 308, 309, 313, 315, 318, 320, 326-327, 430-436; Gibraltar, 391; Greece, 386; Holland, 197, 207; Hungary, 354, 355; Italy, 231, 242, 252, 256, 260, 261, 264, 265, 269, 324, 352; Jugoslavia, 381, 382, 384-385; Morocco, 393; Palestine, 29, 41; Poland, 362, 363, 367, 371, 372, 373, 374, 439-445; Russia, 371; Spain, 136, 161, 174, 178, 179, 181, 184, 324; Tunisia, 410; Turkey, 383, 384, 388.

Synagogues, or balconies, for women, xxii-xxiii; Czechoslovakia, 339, 342, 438; England, 222; France, 108, 111; Germany, 277-278, 286, 303, 305, 307, 309, 310, 322; Greece, 387; Holland, 193; Italy, 255, 257, 263, 268, 269; Morocco, 396; Poland, 361, 369, 370; Spain, 128, 150, 155, 157, 169; Tunisia, 409.

Synagogues, print or painting of, 165, 198, 207, 297, 302, 338.

Synagogues, site of former, Austria, 347, 348; Belgium, 209; England, 215, 216, 218, 220; France, 87, 93, 432; Germany, 274, 297, 301, 313, 431, 432, 433, 434, 435, 436; Hun-

gary, 353, 354; *Italy,* 251; *Portugal,* 185; *Spain,* 136, 137, 140, 141, 161, 173, 174, 176, 184.
Synods 88, 91.
SYRACUSE 249.
Syria, Syrian, 8, 36, 397.
SZYDLOW 363, 442.

Tabernacle, the, *as symbol,* 329.
Tabernacles, Feast of, 21, 31-33, 78, 289, 437.
Tablets of the Law, *as symbol,* 51, 193, 228, 285, 291.
TACHAU 304, 344, 438.
TAFILALET 402, 407.
Talith, see Praying-shawl.
Talmud, Talmudic, xxi, xxiv, 18, 20, 32, 41, 42, 50, 81, 85, 87, 121, 124, 126, 165, 182, 240, 244, 274, 286, 287, 293, 304, 308, 334, 350, 361, 369, 371, 383, 390, 393, 398, 400.
Talmud-Torah, *see* School.
Tam, rabbi, 86, 94.
TANGIER 257, 389, 392-393, 394, 404.
Tanta 411.
Tanzhaus, see Social Centre.
Taouirt 407.
TARANTO 250.
TARASCON 112.
Tarica, Eliezer, 388.
Tarif 122.
Tarifa 122.
Tarik 122, 148.
TARNOPOL 368, 369, 371, 379, 444.
TARNOW 444.
TARRAGONA 120, 121, 184.
TARREGA 178.
Tartars 274, 364, 384.
Tartary 296.
Tass, see Torah shield.
Taxes xvii, 102, 106, 127, 213, 239, 256, 297, 300, 312, 341, 385, 394.
TELAKI 439.
Tel-Aviv 40, 44.
Tell-el-Armana tablets, 11, 325.
TELL EL-YAHUDIYA 412, 421.
Telouet 399.
TEMESVAR 355.

Temple, the, 28, 29, 32, 33, 34, 39, 40, 41, 44, 232, 340, 384; *as symbol,* 228, 237, 324, 429; veil, 74.
Temples, Phoenician, 13.
Ten tribes, the lost, 210, 220, 221.
Tenth Legion 39-40.
Terah 6.
Teraphim 8.
Terbruggen, Hendrick, painter, 229.
Teshub 12.
TETUAN 393-398.
   Mellah 394
   Synagogues 396-398
THANNHAUSEN 433.
Tharsis 120.
Theodora, Empress, 383.
Theodosius II 59.
Thirty Years War, the, 191, 272, 302, 304, 314.
Tiamat 9.
TIBERIAS 182, 340, 398.
Tiberius, Emperor, 249.
TIFLIS 384.
Timbuctoo 406.
Tirado, Jacob, 190.
TIRLEMONT 208.
Titus 227, 241, 271; Arch of, 29, 338.
TLEMCEN 407.
Tobiah ben Joseph ben Tobiah 35.
TOLEDO 1, 120, 147-161, 164, 178, 182, 246, 267, 381, 403.
   Amphitheatre 162
   Calle Plata, 159; Pozo Amargo, 161
   Churches: Cathedral, 161; El Cristo de la Luz, 147; Santiago del Arrabal, 151
   Corral de Don Diego 159
   El Greco house 152, 153-154
   Ghettos 148
   Palace of Pedro 161
   Provincial Museum 149, 159
   Synagogues: Calle del Angel, 161; El Tránsito, 121, 129, 152, 153, 154-159; Santa María la Blanca, 149-152
TOMAR 186.

Tombs 34, 43, 171, 225, 335, 398, 400, 403, 405, 407, 408; of the Kings, 36, 39; of the Judges 36.

Tombstones *Austria*, 350; *Czechoslovakia*, xi, 333, 334, 338, 437; *England*, 424; *France*, 30, 48, 49, 84, 91, 93, 94, 100, 113, 115, 116, 294, 431; *Germany*, 280, 282-283, 286, 297-298, 299, 301, 309, 313, 314, 431, 433; *Greece*, 387; *Holland*, 200-202, 206; *Hungary*, 354; *Italy*, 235, 236, 242-243, 245, 250, 258, 264, 265; *Jugoslavia*, 352; *Morocco*, 405; *Portugal*, 185, 186; *Russia*, 371, 384; *Spain*, 120, 121, 135, 138, 151, 159, 173, 174, 176, 179, 180, 182, 184; *Switzerland*, 430; *see also* Catacombs, Cemeteries, Ossuary, Tombs.

Tongres 208.

Torah 3, 9, 168; *see also* Law, the Jewish; Scrolls of the Law.

Torah band 71-72, 195, 228, 259, 280-281, 293, 433; case, 75; crown, 195, 242, 248, 255, 257, 280, 292, 294, 318, 323, 367, 434, 435; mantle, 76, 195, 223, 228, 242, 255, 292, 309, 323, 328; pointer, 76, 318, 350, 435; shield, 76, 195, 292, 294, 318, 350, 435.

Torquemada, Thomas de, 145-146, 164, 172, 178.

Torres, Luis de, 139.

TORTOSA 121, 182, 184.

TOULOUSE 103, 115, 116.

Tournai 208.

TOURS 96, 98, 122.

Town hall xxii, 102, 181, 248, 302, 310, 341.

TRANI 251, 252, 253.

Translation, translations, translators, 81, 84, 104, 124, 127, 144, 160, 165, 176, 219, 246, 247, 250, 262, 291, 293, 321, 392.

TRAPANI 248-249.

Trattato dell' Arte del Ballo 253.

Travellers, Jewish, 247, 266, 296; *see also* Azulai, Hayim David; Benjamin of Tudela; Delmedigo, Joseph; Elijah of Pesaro; Meshullam ben Menahem; Antonio de Montezinos; Obadiah da Bertinoro; Petachiah of Regensburg.

Tree of life 8, 9, 74, 129, 200, 377.

Trees, *as symbols*, 200, 202, 224, 291, 307, 308, 317, 323, 326, 365, 371, 376, 377; *see also* Palm, Tree of Life.

TREMBOWLA 445.

Trent 297.

Treuenberg, Hendel Bassevi von, 334.

TRÈVES 52, 431.

TREVISO 265.

TRIER, *see* Trèves.

TRIPOLI 390, 410.

TROYES 1, 87-91.

TÜCHERSFELD 305.

TUDELA 175.

Tulln 351.

Tumilat, Wady, 412.

TUNIS 381, 409-410.
    Bardo museum 409-410
    Hara, the, 410
    Synagogue, Great, 410

TUNISIA 390, 408-410.

Turk, Turkish, 23.

TURKEY, Turkish Empire, 157, 187, 252, 263, 333, 380, 382, 383-384, 387, 388, 445.

Tuscan (style) 192.

Twelve Tribes, *as symbol*, xx; names of, 193.

Tyre 37, 120, 248, 392.

Udine 265.

UKRAINE 296.

ULM 433.

Unicorn's horn 47, 83.

UNITED STATES 64, 157, 194, 289, 338.

UNTERLIMPURG 308.

Ur 5, 6, 226.

Uracca, Queen, 173.

Uriel da Costa 196, 197.

Urim and Thummim, *as symbols*, 228.

Urn 37; *as symbol*, 36.

Usque, Samuel, 253.

Usury, *see* Banking.

UZLANY 445.

VALENCIA 163, 176, 185.
Valladares, Diego Sarmiento, 166.
VALLADOLID 173.
Vanderborght, Jacques, 209.
Vardar (river) 382.
Varnhagen, Rahel, 304, 322, 323, 405.
Vase, Jerusalem, 28; glass, 28.
Vecinho, Joseph, 139.
Veil of the Synagogue, 96, 107.
Veil of temple, see Temple veil.
VEITHÖCHSTEIN 309.
VENICE 79, 187, 245, 254, 265-270, 374.
    Ghetto 266, 267, 268, 269
    Graveyard 267
    Synagogues: Ashkenazic, 269; Canton, 269; Italian, 269; Levantine, 268-269; Luzzatto, 269; Mesullamim, 269; Spanish, 268
VENICE, Republic of, 261, 264-265.
VENOSA 245, 250.
Venus, Figure of, 195.
VERONA 254, 259, 261.
VESOUL 93.
Vespasian 113, 116, 241.
Vianen, Adam van, 195.
VICH 178.
Victoria, Queen, of England, 223.
Vidal, Abraham, limner, 183.
VIENNA 75, 295, 302, 304, 321, 323, 345, 346-351, 352, 374.
    Cathedral 347
    Ghetto, site, 347
    Graveyards 349-350, 351
    Leopoldstadt 348
    Museum, Historisches, 348; Jewish, 350
    Synagogues 350, 355
VIENNE 112.
Villars, Madame, 166.
VILNA 291, 296, 345, 373-375.
    Ghetto 374
    Graveyard 374-375
    Schulhof 374
    Synagogues 374
    Yiddish Institute 374
Vine, vine leaves, as symbol, 28, 114, 154, 339, 409, 435.
Virgil 245.

Visigothic, Visigoths, 120, 121, 122, 147.
Vistula, the, 283, 311, 325, 353, 356.
VITEBSK 376.
VITTORIO 265.
VOHLYNIA 361, 368, 441-442.
Volga, the, 357.
VOLLMERZ 435.
Voltaire 53, 58, 59, 60, 315, 317.
VOLUBILIS 405.
VOORBURG 206.

Wahl, Saul, 264, 372, 373.
Wailing Wall, as symbol, 228.
WALDESGRÜN 431.
WARSAW 363, 375-378, 439, 440.
    Graveyard 375-378
    Museum, Jewish, 375
    Nalewki, the, 375
WARSZAWA 440.
WASMES 208.
WAZAN 398-399.
Weapons, bronze, 11.
Wechsler, Isaac, 343.
Wedding canopy 72, 80.
WEISENAU 431.
Weiss, Solomon, of Luck, architect, 370.
Wellington, Duke of, 348.
WELTENBERG 298.
Wertheimer, Samson, 349, 350.
Weser, the, 311, 314.
West Indies 191, 316.
WESTHOFEN 432.
WIENER-NEUSTADT 352.
Wild ox 10.
William of Newbury 217.
William the Conqueror 47, 211, 214.
WIMPFEN 437.
WINCHESTER 218.
WITTENBERG 315.
WITZENHAUSEN 435.
WODZISLOW 442.
WOLPA 439.
WOMMERSON 208.
Wood-carving xxv, 308, 356, 362-363, 367, 379, 438, 439, 440, 441, 442, 443, 444, 445.

WORMS xi, 1, 267, 274, 275-285, 314,
345, 354, 360, 372.
Cathedral 285
Ghetto 276
Graveyard 282-285
Mikveh 281-282
Museum, Jewish, 72, 280-281
Rashi chapel 279-280
Synagogue 276-279
Wrought-iron work 303, 337, 338,
339, 342, 360, 361-362, 365, 373,
374, 379, 438, 443, 444.
WÜRZBURG 307, 308-309.
WYLKOWYSZKI 446.
WYSZOGROD 362, 440.

Ximénez, Cardinal, 176.

Yad, see Torah pointer.
Ybbs 351.
Yehiel ben Joseph, of Paris, 49-50, 68,
182, 219, 283, 400.
Yeshibah xxii, 161, 192, 279, 345,
396, 434.
YORK 216-218.
YPRES 208.

ZABLUDOW 362, 363, 371, 439.
Zacuto, Abraham, 172.

Zacuto, Moses, 197.
Zaddah, *see* Helena of Adiabene.
Zaddikim 398, 400.
Za-kir 15.
Zambrow 440.
ZAMORRA 173.
Zangwill, Israel, 62, 144.
ZANTE 386.
ZARAGOROD 369, 445.
Zarfati, Isaac, 385.
ZDOLBUNOWO 442.
Zebra, *as symbol*, 371.
Zechariah 228; figure of 92.
Zedakah, see Alms-box.
Zemach, Mordecai, 333, 337, 341.
Zenobia, Queen, 324.
Zeus, hymn to, 33.
Zichy, Countess, 354.
Zirites 142.
ZLOCZOW 445.
ZNAIM xi.
Zodiac 79, 371, 440; *see also* Star-
worship.
Zohar 377, 399.
ZOLKIEW 367, 368-369, 438.
ZÜLZ 435-436.
Zunz, Leopold, 273, 323, 328.
Zurich 430.
ZWESTEN 435.